T3-ALT-385

DP
2

F47
2016

29.95

THE

MYTH

OF THE

ANDALUSIAN PARADISE

Muslim horsemen and their black slave warriors herding Christian prisoners and their cattle: from the *Cantigas de Santa María*, thirteenth-century illuminated manuscript

THE
MYTH
OF THE
ANDALUSIAN PARADISE

Muslims, Christians, and Jews
under Islamic Rule in Medieval Spain

Darío Fernández-Morera

Colo. Christian Univ. Library
8787 W. Alameda Ave.
Lakewood, CO 80226

ISI
BOOKS

Wilmington, Delaware

Copyright © 2016 by Darío Fernández-Morera
Second printing, May 2016

All rights reserved. No part of this publication may be reproduced or transmitted in any form or by any means, electronic or mechanical, including photocopy, or any information storage and retrieval system now known or to be invented, without permission in writing from the publisher, except by a reviewer who wishes to quote brief passages in connection with a review written for inclusion in a magazine, newspaper, broadcast, or online publication.

Library of Congress Cataloging-in-Publication Data

Fernández-Morera, Darío.

The myth of the Andalusian paradise : Muslims, Christians, and Jews under Islamic rule in
    medieval Spain / Darío Fernández-Morera. Wilmington, DE : ISI Books, 2015.
Includes bibliographical references and index.
LCCN 2015042615 | ISBN 9781610170956 (hardback)
LCSH: Andalusia (Spain)—Politics and government. | Andalusia (Spain)—Ethnic
    relations—History. | Spain—History—711–1516. | Islam and politics—Spain—History. |
    Muslims—Spain—Andalusia—History. | Christians—Spain—Andalusia—History. |
    Jews—Spain—Andalusia—History. | Religious tolerance—Spain—Andalusia—History. |
    | Social control—Spain—Andalusia—History. | Myth—Political aspects—Spain—History.
    | BISAC: HISTORY / Europe / Spain & Portugal. | HISTORY / Medieval.

Published in the United States by:

ISI Books
Intercollegiate Studies Institute
3901 Centerville Road
Wilmington, DE 19807-1938
www.isibooks.org

Manufactured in the United States of America

Dedication

Dedico este libro a los Fernández-Morera y a los que ayudaron a criarme: Darío ("El Gran Dary"), mi padre, el mejor mago que ha dado Cuba; su ayudante "la bella Ester" ("Sonia"), mi querida madre; mi hijo Brent ("El Árbol"); mi prima Rosa María ("Pety"); mi tío-abuelo Gomer ("Gordo"), conocedor de Voltaire y de la poesía de Victor Hugo y de Rubén Darío, y quien tanto me ayudó en mi adolescencia; mi abuelo Oscar, el pintor de nuestra ciudad natal, Sancti-Spiritus, y el mejor pintor que ha dado Cuba; mi tía Selmira, pintora y profesora, quien siempre insistió en que me hiciera de una profesión, porque de pintor y ajedrecista "te vas a morir de hambre"; mi tío Plinio ("Cuco"), el cazador, el primero que me enseñó el uso de las armas; mi tía Flérida, lectora voraz, siempre elegante; mi tío-abuelo Higinio ("El intelectual"), periodista y editor de la revista literaria *Hero*; mi tío-abuelo el finísimo poeta y también editor de *Hero*, Anastasio ("El Poeta"); mi tío-abuelo Jacinto ("el Jacintico"), admirador de Herodes; mi bisabuelo Jacinto Gomer Fernández-Morera, fundador de *Hero*, poeta de corte clásico, maestro, y crítico valiente y lúcido; mis Padrinos Federico e Iluminada del Castillo, quienes también ayudaron a criarme; y mi querida María Rojas, gran practicante de la Santería, quien tanto me quiso y cuidó en mi niñez.

Ma, sendo l'intento mio scrivere cosa utile a chi la intende, mi è parso più conveniente andare drieto alla verità effettuale della cosa, che alla immaginazione di essa.

—*Niccolò Machiavelli,* Il Principe, *capitolo XV*

Contents

THE

MYTH

OF THE

ANDALUSIAN PARADISE

Introduction

On the intellectual level, Islam played an important role in the development of Western European civilization by passing on both the philosophy of Aristotle and its own scientific, technological, and philosophical tradition.... Religious tolerance remained a part of Islamic law, although its application varied with social, political, and economic circumstances.

—*Bert F. Breiner and Christian W. Troll, "Christianity and Islam," in* The Oxford Encyclopedia of the Modern Islamic World, *ed. John L. Esposito (New York: Oxford University Press, 2009)*

[In the Middle Ages there emerged] two Europes—one [Muslim Europe] secure in its defenses, religiously tolerant, and maturing in cultural and scientific sophistication; the other [Christian Europe] an arena of unceasing warfare in which superstition passed for religion and the flame of knowledge sputtered weakly.

—*David Levering Lewis, two-time Pulitzer Prize winner and Julius Silver Professor of History at New York University,* God's Crucible: Islam and the Making of Europe, 570–1215 *(New York: W. W. Norton, 2008), 335*

Muslim rulers of the past were far more tolerant of people of other faiths than were Christian ones. For example, al-Andalus's multi-cultural, multi-religious states ruled by Muslims gave way to a Christian regime that was grossly intolerant even of dissident Christians, and that offered

1

Jews and Muslims a choice only between being forcibly converted and being expelled (or worse).
—*"Islam and the West: Never the Twain Shall Peacefully Meet?"* The Economist, *November 15, 2001*

The standard-bearers of tolerance in the early Middle Ages were far more likely to be found in Muslim lands than in Christian ones.
—Tony Blair, *then prime minister of Great Britain, "A Battle for Global Values,"* Foreign Affairs, *January/February 2007*

THIS BOOK AIMS to demystify Islamic Spain by questioning the widespread belief that it was a wonderful place of tolerance and *convivencia* of three cultures under the benevolent supervision of enlightened Muslim rulers. As the epigraphs throughout this book illustrate, the nineteenth-century romantic vision of Islamic Spain has morphed into today's "mainstream" academic and popular writings that celebrate "al-Andalus" for its "multiculturalism," "unity of Muslims, Christians, and Jews," "diversity," and "pluralism," regardless of how close such emphasis is to the facts. Some scholars of the Spanish Middle Ages have even openly declared an interest in promoting these ideas.[1]

Demythologizing this civilization requires focusing a searching light on medieval cultural features that may seem less than savory to modern readers and that perhaps for this reason are seldom discussed. The first two chapters of this book examine how Spain was conquered and colonized by the forces of the Islamic Caliphate. Some scholars have argued that the Muslim takeover was accomplished largely through "peaceful pacts"; some even refuse to call it a "conquest," preferring to call it a "migratory wave." Other scholars argue that the conquest was carried out by force.[2] Neither side is entirely right. The Muslim conquerors used force to defeat the resistance of the Christian Visigoth kingdom, a nascent civilization. But they also granted pacts to those Visigoth lords and Christian leaders who saw it as advantageous to accept the offered "peace" and become *dhimmis* (those Christians and Jews living in subaltern status in Islamic lands) rather than face the consequences of resisting. Behind the "peaceful pacts" was always the threat of brutal force. The remaining chapters of this book examine fundamental aspects of Islamic Spain that are rarely highlighted: religious and therefore cultural repression in all areas of life and the marginalization of certain groups—all this in the service of social control by autocratic rulers and a class of religious authorities.

The proponents of a harmonious and fruitful *convivencia* sometimes adduce as proof the mutual influences among Muslims and non-Muslims and their military alliances. But this argument overlooks that mutual influences, coexistence in the same territory, cooperation, military alliances and even intermarriage, and productive and fascinating artistic results frequently obtain as a matter of course in places where different cultures have been antagonistic—from Spanish and Portuguese Latin America to British India to French Algeria to the American West to even the slaveholding American South—without this in any way diminishing the fact of conflict between cultures or the existence of some groups who dominate and others who are dominated. Of course there was *convivencia*, in this rather banal sense, between conquerors and conquered, but this cannot be considered characteristic of Islamic Spain: it is characteristic of cultural clashes between hegemonic and hegemonized groups most everywhere.[3]

This book's interpretive stance is Machiavellian, not Panglossian. Those who portray Islamic Spain as an example of peaceful coexistence frequently cite the fact that Muslim, Jewish, and Christian groups in al-Andalus sometimes lived near one another. Even when that was the case, however, such groups dwelled more often than not in their own neighborhoods. More to the point: even when individual Muslims, Jews, and Christians cooperated with one another out of convenience, necessity, mutual sympathy, or love, these three groups and their own numerous subgroups engaged for centuries in struggles for power and cultural survival, manifested in often subtle ways that should not be glossed over for the sake of modern ideals of tolerance, diversity, and *convivencia*.

A "Culture of Forgetting"

The Umayyad Caliphate collapsed in the eleventh century.... In 1085, Alfonso VI, Christian king of Leon and Castile, captured Toledo; unlike the Franks, he knew better than to impose Catholicism on the people at the point of a sword.... The spirit of tolerance that the Arabs

had created survived their departure. It took nearly four more centuries to get ... to the religious intolerance of the Spanish Inquisition.
—*Kwame Anthony Appiah, Laurance S. Rockefeller University Pro-*
fessor of Philosophy, Princeton University, "How Muslims Made
Europe," New York Review of Books, *November 6, 2008*

It is not easy to explain the existence of this "culture of forgetting" that
has allowed the fashioning of a certain kind of Islamic Spain. It can hardly
be explained by linguistic ignorance, since the primary medieval Latin,
Spanish, Arabic, and Hebrew sources required for a good general understanding of Islamic Spain have been translated into accessible Western
languages such as Spanish, French, English, and German, in some cases
more than once; and in any event, many scholars of Arabic and Islamic
studies also engage in this hagiographic fashioning.

Perhaps writers have thought that the artistic achievements of al-
Andalus cannot withstand a more realistic appraisal of its society. Perhaps it has to do with what economists call "stakeholder interests and
incentives," which affect the research of academics in the humanities no
less and perhaps even more than those in the sciences.[4] Perhaps it has to
do with what psychologists call "motivated blindness," which inhibits an
individual's ability to perceive inconvenient data.[5] Perhaps it has to do
with the "innocence of intellectuals."[6] Perhaps it is simply the result of
shoddy research by a number of university professors repeated by many
journalists. Or perhaps since the eighteenth-century Enlightenment the
critical construction of a diverse, tolerant, and happy Islamic Spain has
been part of an effort to sell a particular cultural agenda, which would
have been undermined by the recognition of a multicultural society
wracked by ethnic, religious, social, and political conflicts that eventually
contributed to its demise—a multicultural society held together only by
the ruthless power of autocrats and clerics.[7]

This ideological mission would then be the ultimate reason for the
tilting of the narrative against Catholic Spain prevalent since the Enlightenment and the writings of Voltaire and Edward Gibbon. Briskly selling,
beautifully illustrated books have contributed to this intellectual construction.[8] In the past few decades, this ideological mission has morphed into
"presentism," an academically sponsored effort to narrate the past in terms
of the present and thereby reinterpret it to serve contemporary "multi-

cultural," "diversity," and "peace" studies, which necessitate rejecting as retrograde, chauvinistic, or, worse, "conservative" any view of the past that may conflict with the progressive agenda. Thus it is stupendous to see how some academic specialists turn and twist to downplay religion as the motivating force in Muslim conquests, and even to question the invasion of Spain by Muslim Arab-led Berbers as the conquest of one culture and its religion by another. Failing to take seriously the religious factor in Islamic conquests is characteristic of a certain type of materialist Western historiography which finds it uncomfortable to accept that war and the willingness to kill and die in it can be the result of someone's religious faith—an obstacle to understanding that may reflect the role played by religious faith in the lives of many academic historians. This materialist approach has also generally prevailed in scholarly analyses of the Crusades.[9]

In Spain, the reality of al-Andalus is better known, thanks to the work of historians like Luis A. García Moreno, Francisco García Fitz, Manuel González Jiménez, Miguel Ángel Ladero Quesada, and Antonio Domínguez Ortiz; legal scholars like Ramón Peralta; Arabists like María Luisa Ávila, Soha Abboud-Haggar, Serafín Fanjul, Ana Fernández Félix, María Isabel Fierro, Mercedes García-Arenal, Teresa Garulo, Felipe Maíllo Salgado, Manuela Marín, Celia del Moral, Cristina de la Puente, Joaquín Vallvé Bermejo, and María Jesús Viguera Molins; and popularizers like César Vidal.

Nonetheless, even in Spain, rhapsodic accounts predominate, perhaps traceable to a nineteenth century Spanish historiography that did not distinguish among "Muslim," "Arab," "Berber," *muladi*," "*dhimmi*," "Slav," and other cultural and ethnic categories but fashioned instead a simple and wonderful entity called *civilización hispano-árabe*. The twentieth-century polemics between the literary scholar Américo Castro and the historian Claudio Sánchez-Albornoz on "the nature of the Spaniards" fell victim to this starry-eyed intellectual conflation. Castro did not cite Islamic legal texts from al-Andalus or anywhere else, and he made no use of archaeological materials.[10] These lacunae prompted him to repeat inherited shibboleths about tolerance and *convivencia*. Sánchez-Albornoz was better informed, but lack of familiarity with legal texts was also evident in his writing.[11] Thus, for Sánchez-Albornoz, too, Muslim women in al-Andalus enjoyed an enviable "freedom" when compared to Muslim women elsewhere.

In Germany, Italy, and France, the works of scholars such as Adel Theodor Khoury, Roberto de Mattei, Alfred Morabia, and Sylvain Gouguenheim are exceptions to the rule, but they have struggled against the resistance of experts in university departments.[12] Significantly, none of these books were published by university presses.

Gouguenheim's case is instructive. Gouguenheim argued that medieval Islamic culture remained, with the exception of science, construction techniques, and some aspects of philosophy, generally unreceptive to the spirit of Greek civilization. Among other things, it was indifferent or antagonistic to such fundamentals of that civilization as representational sculpture and painting, drama, narrative, lyric, and political theory and practice. Even in philosophy, Islam remained in part a stranger to the Greek spirit. Gouguenheim's book also reminded its readers that Greek texts had not been "lost," to be graciously "discovered" and "transmitted" by the Islamic empire, but in fact had been preserved, transmitted, and commented upon in the Christian Greek Roman Empire (usually referred to as the "Byzantine" Empire); that the translations of Greek scientific and philosophical texts into Arabic were done by Greek-speaking Christians from the conquered lands of the Christian Greek Roman Empire; that Aristotle had been translated in France at the abbey of Mont Saint-Michel before translations of Aristotle into Arabic (via the Syrian of the Christian scholars from the conquered lands of the Christian Greek Roman Empire) surfaced in Islamic Spain; and that there was a continuity between Greek and European civilization, via the Christian Greek Roman Empire, that did not require Islam's appearance on the historical scene.

Gouguenheim's book was considered so threatening to the educational establishment that "an international collective of 56 researchers in history and philosophy" found it necessary to sign an open letter, published in the Marxist newspaper *Libération*, attacking his work. His book was said to offer nothing that was not already well known to scholars. The demonization of Gouguenheim and the apparent need for acts of academic exorcism of his work continued when the Sorbonne University organized a scholarly colloquium to denounce his book, and then his own school declared publicly that it did not share his views. Among the milder scholarly epithets used to describe his book have been "ignorant" (*ignare*), "a polemic disguised as scholarship," "full of conceptual incoherence," "a diatribe," "a plundering book" (*saccageur*), "a work scientifically dishonest," "a dishonor to its publisher," "an amateurish work based on compilation and a priori assumptions," "a sad case," "a work of fear and hatred," "cultural racism," "embarrassing," "discredited," "a dereliction of historical deontology," "a product of retrograde Catholic ideology," "not qualified to go against the consensus of specialists regarding medieval Islam and Christianity," and, of course, "Islamophobic" and part of a contemporary "scholarly Islamophobia" (*islamophobie savante*).

Islamic studies professors brandished the "argument from authority" against Gouguenheim by gleefully pointing out that he was not an "Arabist" but an ideologically motivated interloper, who had no business in a scholarly field not his own—and then combed his book in a remarkably thorough search for errors, slips, or bibliographical inaccuracies. But then no Arabist or Islamic studies academic expert would have been likely to write a book questioning the claims made by Arabists and Islamic studies academic experts regarding the beneficial influence of medieval Islam on Christian Europe. A hermeneutics of suspicion would point out that such questioning would endanger the attractiveness of the field of research that provides a living for the Islamic studies experts, and that such questioning would also risk an end to travel to Muslim countries to do research, a loss of funding for the heretical scholars and their universities (not only from grant-giving institutions but also from governments such as Saudi Arabia, Qatar, the United Arab Emirates, Libya under Gaddhafi, and Turkey), ostracism as graduate students, and difficulty finding university positions (assuming the scholars were able to complete a PhD in a department of Middle East Studies). Critics have documented the way money from Islamic nations has compromised Islamic and Middle East studies in Western universities.[13]

Gouguenheim's case is redolent of that of the great Spanish Arabist Francisco Javier Simonet (1829–1897) more than a century earlier: Simonet's monumental work on the "Mozarabs" could not find a publisher during his lifetime because of the opposition of influential "liberal" Spanish Arabists who objected to Simonet's "Catholic" and "conservative" views on Islamic Spain.[14]

Doubtlessly, professional self-preservation as well as political correctness and economics has affected academic research in certain fields of study, in contrast to the fearlessness demonstrated by professors when unmasking horrors in such dangerous areas of investigation as Christian

Europe (the burning of witches! colonialism!) and Catholic Spain (the ubiquitous Spanish Inquisition!). Islamic Spain is no exception to the rule. University presses do not want to get in trouble presenting an Islamic domination of even centuries ago as anything but a positive event, and academic specialists would rather not portray negatively a subject that constitutes their bread and butter. In addition, fear of the accusation of "Islamophobia" has paralyzed many academic researchers.

The publication of a book on Muhammad cartoons by Yale University Press illustrates all these problems. Initially, the book was to be accompanied by cartoons of Muhammad published in Denmark, which many Muslims had protested by killing at least two hundred people around the world between 2005 and 2006 alone. But comments on the manuscript's material by some academic experts in history and religion prompted the Yale University administration to cancel the publication of the cartoons—as well as an illustration, by the nineteenth-century artist Gustave Doré, of a passage in the *Divina Commedia* where Dante places Muhammad in hell. So in 2009 the book on the Muhammad cartoons was published by Yale University Press—but without the Muhammad cartoons.

"What Is Real"

> God's universe, in al-Andalus, had three principal and interlocking features which are at the heart of its importance for us, and which were in its own time at the heart of that culture's extraordinarily vigorous well-being: ethnic pluralism, religious tolerance, and a variety of important forms of what we could call cultural secularism—secular poetry and philosophy—that were not understood, by those who pursued them, to be un- or anti-Islamic.
> —*María Rosa Menocal, R. Selden Rose Professor of Spanish and Portuguese and Director of the Whitney Humanities Center at Yale University, "Culture in the Time of Tolerance: Al-Andalus as a Model for Our Time," Yale Law School Occasional Papers (Year 2000, Paper 1)*

Scholars who celebrate, for example, the presumed laxity of religious and moral restraints enjoyed by the people of al-Andalus, or these people's ability to be both religious and capable of writing delightfully erotic heterosexual and homosexual poetry, may do so not simply because they operate in a particular historical, political, and educational context with its resulting ideology, fears, and taboos; their work may also reflect the more technical factor of limiting oneself to the examination of certain kinds of documents. Wide-eyed visions of a wonderful because morally loose al-Andalus extrapolate from the dissolute lives of some Muslim rulers and their court intellectuals to the everyday life of the Muslim (or Jewish, or Christian) masses. The hedonistic ways of the *taifa* monarchs of the eleventh century have been particularly entrancing to some English-speaking academics, who pay little regard to the fact that, as Spanish Arabists like Serafín Fanjul and Felipe Maíllo Salgado have pointed out, the average Muslim's life in al-Andalus was marked by clerical supervision of detailed religious observance, and often by family, tribal, and blood feuds.[15]

This selective approach is as scholarly defective as would be assessing the everyday life and moral preferences of twentieth-century American families based on a reading of the historical records left behind by Hollywood actors and American *artistes* and literati, or assessing the everyday life and moral preferences of twentieth-century Saudis based on the historical record left behind in Europe by some princes and princesses of the Saudi royal family. Such evidence, though quite fascinating and perhaps of great aesthetic value, is not indicative of how the vast majority of a population lives or what its beliefs and moral preferences are. A different approach is needed for a better understanding of a civilization. As the brilliant Muslim political thinker Ibn Zafar wrote in the twelfth century, "[Priority must be given] to what is real rather than approximation."[16]

Some recent scholars in the English-speaking world have done excellent work, but with the exception of Emmet Scott they have either concerned themselves mainly with the Jewish experience or not adopted the approach of the present book, which looks at these cultures synchronically and comparatively, examining literary, historical, legal, religious, biographical, archaeological, and other cultural materials in order to show a humanity both suffering and inflicting suffering.[17] All too often, books in English do not show a mastery of the work of Spanish scholars.[18]

This book examines certain cultural aspects of the condition of Muslims, Jews, and Christians in medieval Islamic Spain in order to throw light upon the mental structures and the collective representations of this society. It does not pass judgment on today's Muslims, Jews, or

Christians, or on their religions. It does not support a "clash" between present-day civilizations, although it does not adopt as its goal to "build bridges" either. It advises readers to be cautious and keep in mind the differences that exist between the medieval and the modern worlds of Islam, Judaism, and Christianity before trying to find reassuring or disturbing similarities between the two. And it rejects all anti-Muslim, anti-Jewish, and anti-Christian viewpoints. Or, as modern critical jargon would put it: readers should keep in mind that the texts examined are "historically situated cultural constructs."[19]

This book does not attempt to examine the possibility, entertained by many Western experts on Islam and by some modern Muslim scholars influenced by Western thought, that, for centuries, intelligent and learned *ulama* (clerics) and Muslim rulers either misunderstood the Quran or purposely distorted it in various ways, including through the invention of *ahadith* (traditional narratives of Muhammad's sayings and deeds, or *sunnah*), because of "prescriptions of gender and power," or because of their patriarchal interests, or because they were shaped by the socioeconomic forces of their time, or for some other covert reason that today's scholars somehow are not subject to and can therefore unmask and explain disinterestedly. Nor does the book attempt to examine the assumption that truth is on the side of those among today's Western expert interpreters who argue, in what has become a veritable literary subgenre, not only that the Quran does not really mean what for centuries *fuqaha* (experts on Islamic law) variously thought it meant but even that *sharia* has nothing to do with Muhammad's teachings and that Islamic texts can be reconciled with Western notions of political, religious, and sexual liberty.[20]

This particular understanding of the Quran may be true, but, to borrow Cervantes's words, "it matters little for our story." What matters much for our story is that, for the culture of medieval Islam in al-Andalus, the important texts were not so much the Quran as the religious laws as interpreted by the *ulama* of the Maliki legal school; that for the Maliki school of Islamic jurisprudence that dominated al-Andalus, as was also the case generally for other schools of law in classical Islam, the *ahadith* and their *sunnah* were as authoritative as the Quran; that, in fact, Maliki *ulama* in al-Andalus accepted the famous saying of such respected traditionists as al-Awzai (ca. 704–774) and Yahya Ibn Abi Kathir (d. 748) according to which the Quran is in greater need of the *sunnah* for its elucidation than the *sunnah* is of the Quran²¹; and that Islamic texts were not open to interpretation by just any individual believer but must be mediated by properly qualified clerics.²²

Without "questioning" or "interrogating" the "subjectivities" of the scholars of the Maliki school of jurisprudence in al-Andalus, this book takes seriously and at face value their interpretations and practices, including their belief in a divine revelation independent of changing socioeconomic or historical conditions. This understanding of Islamic law as something transcendent and not subject to innovation was shared even by the great *alim* (meaning "wise" or "learned") Ibn Hazm, not a friend of Malikism.²³ For all these traditionists and enemies of innovation, and despite their individual rivalries and differences, Islam did not need to be and must not be "adapted" to new circumstances.

This book gives special attention to primary sources (medieval Christian, Muslim, and Jewish chronicles; literary works; religious and legal texts; and biographies), and usually quotes them verbatim so that nonscholars can read these materials (which in modern publications on Islamic Spain frequently are not part of the narrative and often not even part of the notes) and decide for themselves whether the widespread hagiographic interpretations of Islamic Spain are warranted or not. Unless otherwise indicated, assertions in this book are abundantly supported by these medieval Christian, Muslim, and Jewish primary sources, which are either quoted in the text or cited in the notes.

One may disagree with and instinctively reject one, two, three, or four of these sources, whose assertions contradict comfortable beliefs, or one may raise questions about what these testimonies really mean in order defensively to undermine their authority; but after a while the sheer number of assertions from so many different sources becomes difficult to refute and their cumulative effect even harder to dispel. As far as the available documentary evidence and the limited space have allowed, this book follows the hermeneutic criterion of multiple attestations: thus, for example, the more widely distributed a particular religious or legal teaching and its accompanying practice are across sources, the greater the probability that such teaching and practice permeated everyday life; and the more in agreement antagonistic sources—say, Muslim, Jewish, and Christian—are on a particular cultural or historical proposition, the greater the truth value of that proposition.

All sorts of arguments have been made to question the validity of the Muslim sources: some Western scholars today describe them as texts embellished by legends, serving political and religious agendas, and written too many centuries after the events.[24] But dismissing Muslim chronicles presents problems. One is that the chronicles claim to use earlier materials closer to the events described, and that some of the Muslim chronicles probably date from less than two centuries after the conquest.

Another problem is that some scholars who doubt the accuracy of the Muslim sources have often employed them to make claims regarding the splendor of the civilization of Islamic Spain and also to reduce the figure of traditional Christian heroes such as El Cid to impious warriors and mere mercenaries. One cannot have it both ways.

Finally, disregarding primary sources because they may contain embellishments and legends, or serve a political and religious agenda, can leave scholars with limited working material and deprive them of a great deal that legends, fiction, embellishments, and political and religious agendas can tell about a culture, and even about historical happenings. In any event, as even the professor of Hebrew studies Norman Roth admits, "A detailed analysis of these sources results in a remarkably coherent and generally consistent account of the invasion and conquest of Spain." The scholar of Islamic and Arabic studies Tarif Khalidi's examination of the various factors that affected the writing of the medieval Muslim chronicles confirms their historical usefulness.[25]

Fortunately, even if we correctly regard parts of the Muslim chronicles as possible falsifications at the service of religion, we can check their narratives against other important primary sources. This book gives particular attention to the Christian sources and archaeological findings, among which are the earliest and possibly most accurate accounts of the Muslim conquest and its aftermath. Christian sources such as the *Chronica mozarabica* of 754 and the *Chronica Byzantia-Arabica* of 743 date from only a few decades after the conquest and can confirm or contradict the Muslim chronicles. As Luis A. García Moreno has observed, Christian sources, including Latin hymns such as *Tempore belli*, have been all too often neglected in the study of the Islamic conquest of Spain. Christian accounts offer the additional interest of having been written from the perspective of the defeated.

Another way to check the veracity or, at times, the falsity of the Muslim chronicles is through archaeology. Thus, archaeological evidence from North Africa in the region of Cyrenaica points to the destruction of churches along the route the Islamic conquerors followed in the late seventh century, and the remarkable artistic treasures buried along the routes leading to the North of Spain by fleeing Visigoths and Hispano-Romans during the early eighth century consist largely of religious and dynastic paraphernalia that the Christian inhabitants obviously wanted to protect from Muslim looting and desecration.

Most of the important primary sources have been translated from medieval Latin, Spanish, Arabic, and Hebrew into one or more Western languages. The English-speaking readers of this book, who may lament having to look at all this material in translation, can find consolation in the fact that they are no worse off than the celebrated Córdoban Muslim cleric Ibn Rushd ("Averroes"), a polymath who achieved lasting fame by commenting on the technical and difficult texts of Aristotle without knowing Greek and after reading them in twice-mediated translations. (Those translations existed thanks to Christian scholars at home in the Greek culture of the Middle East: for centuries the Philosopher's works had been kept and studied in the Christian Greek Roman Empire, and Christian scholars under Muslim rule translated them from Greek into Syrian and then from Syrian into Arabic, the language in which all learned Muslims read Greek philosophy and science.)[26]

All translations into English are mine unless otherwise specified in the sources. To facilitate the reading by nonspecialists, I have generally avoided the use of diacritical symbols: thus Quran instead of Qur'an, *taifa* instead of *ta'ifa,* and Muhammad instead of Muḥammad. The use of multiple-language sources, including translations printed in various countries in different centuries, has created occasional but I hope minor inconsistencies in the spelling of some words and personal names.

WHAT'S IN A NAME?

None of the Western coverage wondered what kind of Islam would come out of the new Granada mosque. How strict were its views on the Sharia? On the role of women? Even the most obvious question went unanswered: Would this mosque emulate the great intellectual Islam

of the Andalusian Moors, with its pan-confessional humanism...?
The Islam of Moorish culture at its height was not pure but thoroughly
evolved after eight centuries of collaboration with Jews and Christians.
In fact, one could argue that the oft-bewailed missing "reformation" of
Islam was under way there until it was aborted by the [Spanish] Inqui-
sition. At any rate, Moorish Islam was anything but fundamentalist.
    —Melik Kaylan, "Houses of Worship: Back Again After 500 Years,"
    Wall Street Journal, July 18, 2003

I use the terms *Spain, medieval Spain*, and *Islamic Spain* rather than *Iberia,
medieval Iberia*, and *Islamic Iberia*. The use of the term *medieval Iberia*,
standard in most academic specialized writing since the 1990s (before
then, all scholarly research used the term *medieval Spain*), presents a
number of factual and theoretical difficulties. *Iberia* is a pre-Roman and
therefore premedieval term. Romans, who variously dominated Spain
from approximately 215 B.C. to the disintegration of the Western (or
Latin) Roman Empire in the early fifth century A.D., called Spain *Hispania*. This is a Latin word (possibly borrowed from Carthaginian) that
evolved into the medieval word *Spannia* and eventually into *España*. Thus
the noun *Spain* resulted from a process of language evolution from "vulgar" Latin (the simpler Latin used by the Roman soldiers and merchants)
that obtains for the various peninsular Romance dialects, such as Castilian, Navarrese, and Leonese, before the Castilian Romance dialect became
the standard for the Spanish language. Such a process can be seen in other
Romance languages: the Tuscan Italian dialect gave rise to modern Italian, and the French dialect of the region of Paris (*île-de-France*) gave rise
to modern French. Phonologically, morphologically, syntactically, and
mostly lexically, modern Spanish is, like French, Italian, Catalan, Portuguese, or Romanian, an evolved form of Latin, the language of the Western
Roman Empire. Therefore it is a *Romance* language. The influence of other
languages on Spanish has been mostly lexical. Thus only about 6 percent
of the total vocabulary of Spanish is traceable to Arabic as a result of the
Muslim conquest. In contrast, about 30 percent of the vocabulary of English, which is a Germanic language, is traceable to French, a Romance
language, as a result of the Norman conquest of 1066.[27] By the time the
Romans controlled most of Spain in the first half of the third century B.C.,
the land was already called in Latin *Hispania*, not "Iberia."

Moreover, the highly Romanized Germanic Visigoths,[28] who began to take over Spain from the Romans in the fifth century A.D., also referred to the land as *Hispania*, not "Iberia." In the sixth century, the Visigoth scholar Saint Isidore, bishop of Seville, sang the beauty of *Hispania*, not "Iberia." As the Spanish dialects gradually elbowed out Latin, the word *Hispania* evolved into the medieval Latin *Spannia*, and then into the Romance language word *España*. So Spain, not "Iberia," was in the Middle Ages a universally recognized *geographical* entity.

In fact, as we will see in chapter 1, for centuries medieval Christians considered the lands conquered by Islam to be part of Spain, not part of Islam, and therefore they did not use the term *al-Andalus* and certainly not *Iberia*. The Arabist Joaquín Vallvé Bermejo has pointed out that medieval Christian chronicles always referred to the land occupied by Islam as *Spain*.[29] The inhabitants of the Christian kingdoms of northern Spain referred to the Christians remaining as *dhimmis* in Islamic Spain as "*Spani*," not "Iberians." The *Cantigas de Santa María* of King Alfonso X (1221–1284), written in a mixture of Galician and Portuguese, refer to the lands occupied by the Muslims as part of the land "d'Espanna."[30] The kingdom of Portugal (dating from the twelfth century) was, like that of Castile or León, a kingdom in Spain (not a kingdom in "Iberia"); so the use of medieval "Iberia" instead of medieval Spain to avoid offending the Portuguese (or the Catalonians) has no historical justification.[31]

Even Muslims used the word *Spain*, not *Iberia*, to refer to the land they had conquered. The earliest Muslim coins in Spain, dating from the first half of the eighth century, show on one side the name *Alandalus*, in Arabic, and on the other the abbreviation *SPAN*, for "Spannia."[32] Prominent Muslim chroniclers, including the historian al-Tabari (839–923) and the geographer al-Masudi (d. 956), referred to Spain as *Spain*.[33] Others, including the Arabic geographer al-Idrisi (d. 1165), the great Tunisian historian Ibn Khaldun (1332–1406), and the Algerian historian al-Maqqari (c. 1578–1632), used the term *Isbania* or *Ishbaniah*—that is, Hispania/España.[34] The historian Luis A. García Moreno has observed that "in a text containing Andalusian references, compiled by the encyclopedist of the Abbasid Caliphate Ibn Khurdadhbeh in the middle of the tenth century…, the inhabitants of Córdoba are surprisingly called *al-Isban*, a simple Arabic transcription of the word *Hispani*.… So it does not seem that one can doubt that the mozarab [*dhimmi*] elite of these centuries still maintained the consciousness of being part of an ethnic-geographical identity called Spain, whose unity and political expression had been the Regnum Hispaniae, founded on the epic virtues of the Goths as the axis for this ideological reality."[35]

It is true, however, that there was an effort among later Muslim historians, poets, and intellectuals in general, who were economically dependent on the Muslim rulers, to call the conquered land *al-Andalus* and praise it as an earthly paradise.[36] This tactic is a well-known colonialist maneuver; changing geographical names in an occupied territory reinforces the conqueror's authority. In fact, as chapter 1 will show, the Muslim conquerors Arabized as many ancient names in the Spanish land as they could. The toponymic results of this methodical Arabization endure in southern Spain to this day. However, the subject population in Spain, as elsewhere in the Islamic empire, often clung tenaciously to the ancient names as part of their cultural resistance against the Islamization of their land.

One reason for the use of the artificial term *Iberia* in much of today's academic writing is that it avoids offending non-Christian sensibilities. It is analogous to the ideological academic use of another artificial term, "C.E.," short for "Common Era," which many academic publications in English now demand instead of "A.D.," or "Anno Domini" ("in the year of the Lord"); the same publications also insist on "B.C.E.," or "Before the Common Era," instead of "B.C."—"Before Christ." Of course, the actual dating in such academic usage remains fixed to the birth of Christ—whose name, however, must not be spoken. In contrast, scholars of Islamic studies are, quite prudently, very respectful of the Islamic calendar and usually add to "C.E." etc. the "hegira" dating—the Islamic calendar fixed to Muhammad's journey from Mecca to Medina—or even use the hegira dating only.

Spain was part of the battle cry of the Reconquista (*¡Santiago y cierra, España!*),[37] and many Muslims (including Osama bin Laden) have claimed a right of return to and rule in *al-Andalus*, which they consider—like Palestine, the entire Middle East, and other areas of the world once conquered by Islam—an inalienable "Islamic bequest" (*Waqf*). So historians now use either *al-Andalus* (following the Muslim propagandists) or *medieval Iberia*.

Another reason for the use of these words is to "de-essentialize" the idea of "Spain," with its extremely undesirable Christian and European and Spanish "nationalistic" connotations, and make this entity open to academic reinterpretations as something "diverse," something mixed of Christian, European, Arab, Jewish, African, and other such essences. In other words, this terminological legerdemain works against privileging Christianity and Europe but not against privileging the other essences.

This discursive legerdemain even includes doubting that the followers of the banners of medieval Christian kingdoms like León, Castile, Aragon, and Portugal had a sufficient religious, political, social, cultural, and ethnic connection with the conquered Catholic Visigoth kingdom to qualify them as reconquerors of a lost Christian realm in a religious, military, and political enterprise called *La Reconquista*—but not doubting that the followers of Islam in Spain had a sufficient religious, political, social, cultural, and ethnic connection with Islam elsewhere to qualify them as part of an entity called "Islam."[38]

1

CONQUEST AND RECONQUEST

The traditional interpretation has been that the invasion was impelled by belief in the notion of *jihād* in the sense of Holy War. When writing history in certain epochs, particularly in the nineteenth century, it was natural to ascribe the growth of Islam to the ardour of the faith of the early Muslims.... The pursuit of *jihād* as Holy War is not...a motivating factor relevant to the clashes between Muslims and the people they vanquished in the first century of Islam, at least not as far as the conquest and subsequent occupation of the Iberian peninsula is concerned.
  —*Richard Hitchcock, Professor Emeritus of Arab and Islamic Studies at the University of Exeter,* Mozarabs in Medieval and Early Modern Spain: Identities and Influences *(Aldershot: Ashgate, 2008), 7–8*

We should think of the Muslims, in some way, as a migratory wave, just like the Visigoths, except two hundred [*sic*] years later.
  —*David Nirenberg, Deborah R. and Edgar D. Janotta Professor of Medieval History and Social Thought at the University of Chicago, in the PBS film* Cities of Light: The Rise and Fall of Islamic Spain *(2007)*

MUSLIM AND CHRISTIAN chronicles tell us, and archaeological evidence corroborates,[1] that, in the second half of the seventh century, the Islamic Caliphate's armies from Arabia and the Middle East swept through North African coastal areas held by the Christian Greek Roman Empire (usually referred to as the "Byzantine" Empire).[2] North Africa had been largely Christian territory since at least the early fourth century. This was the land of Tertullian (ca. 160–ca. 225) and Saint Cyprian (ca. 200–258) of Carthage, Saint Athanasius of Alexandria (ca. 296–373), and Saint Augustine of Hippo (354–430). In Egypt alone, a vast network of Christian (Greek and Coptic) monasteries, filled with ancient manuscripts and precious art, ran from Alexandria on the coast to Kharga and Luxor in the hinterland. But Islamic forces destroyed this network and eventually reduced both Greek and Coptic Christians to small and periodically harassed minorities.[3]

The Muslim warriors also defeated and converted to Islam, though not always thoroughly, a number of Berber pagan tribes in the interior of North Africa and incorporated them into the invading armies. Persecuted by Islam, the original Berber religion, culture, and language have remained marginalized until the present day.[4]

The records go on to tell us that, during the first half of the eighth century, perhaps around 711, Islamic forces crossed the narrow strait (then called by its ancient Greek name "the Pillars of Hercules," the name still used by the Christian *Chronica mozarabica* of 754)[5] separating Africa from the land that the Romans called *Hispania*—the Latin word from which evolved the late Latin term *Spannia* and the modern Spanish *España*. (The Romans did not call this region *Iberia*, which is an earlier Greek term many scholars today have adopted.)

Early accounts differ on the exact composition and number of these forces, and on the exact details and sequence of events. The invasion seems to have been preceded in 710 by a raid featuring several hundred Berber Muslim troops led by Tarif, a Berber *mawla* (plural: *mawali*—in his case, a freed slave converted to Islam who remained linked as a "client" to his former Muslim master in a relationship of allegiance and "protection") to the governor of North Africa, Musa Ibn Nusayr.[6] Musa himself was possibly the son of a Christian Syrian freed slave convert to Islam, according to the famous Muslim historian Ibn Hayyan of Córdoba (d. 1076) and to the anonymous tenth- or eleventh-century Muslim chronicle *Akhbar Majmua*.[7] Tarif came back with loot and with "female captives so beautiful as Musa and his people had never seen."[8] The results of this raid, the *Akhbar Majmua* and other sources tell us, enticed Musa to proceed with the invasion. Therefore he sent a scouting force of several thousand men to probe the defenses of the enemy, in accordance with the customary military tactics of the early Islamic conquests.[9] This force was made up largely of Muslim Berber warriors led by Tariq Ibn Zayd, another Berber *mawla* of Musa. Tariq might have found less resistance than anticipated and therefore was followed by a large army led by Musa and composed of a small Arab contingent and a large number of Berber warriors, later reinforced by troops from Syria and Yemen.[10]

What seems less debatable is that the Islamic armies took advantage of dynastic conflicts, military unpreparedness, plagues, and treason by Visigoth nobles before, after, and probably during combat to defeat the Visigoth king of Spain, Rodrigo, at the battle traditionally known as Guadalete, probably on July 26, 711. Thus ended what the Christian *Chronica mozarabica* of 754 calls the "nearly three hundred and fifty years of the Goths' rule in Spain."[11] In less than ten years, Islam controlled most Spanish territory. Hispano-Romans and Visigoths became *dhimmis*—that is, Christians living in subaltern status in Islamic lands—or converted to the hegemonic religion, or fled for their lives. Many escaped to the mountainous regions of Asturias and Galicia in the Northwest, which remained, as the Arabist and scholar of Islamic law Felipe Maíllo Salgado has shown, largely free from Muslim control.[12] Others eventually escaped to France— among them the Visigoth poet and theologian Theodulf (ca. 750–821), a connoisseur of the poetry of Ovid and Virgil, who became bishop of Orleans and one of the pillars of the Carolingian Renaissance.

After consolidating their grip on most Spanish territory, the Muslim conquerors sent a scouting force to raid southern France. This force sacked Bordeaux, burned all the churches on its way, and reached the outskirts of Poitiers in central France, where it burned the basilica This time, however, the Islamic invaders were beaten. In what has become known as the Battle of Tours (or Battle of Poitiers, October 10, 732), a Frankish army led by the Franks' Christian leader (and de facto ruler), Charles Martel, defeated the Islamic forces. As the *Chronica mozarabica* of 754 describes the battle, "these northern men of robust limbs and iron hands stood like an unmovable wall of ice and cut the Arabs to pieces."[13]

After this defeat at the hands of the Europeans—*europenses*, as the *Chronica mozarabica* of 754 calls Martel and his Frankish warriors to distinguish them from the "others," with that eighth-century chronicler demonstrating an early awareness of a geographic, cultural, and even ethnic oneness called "Europeans"—Islamic armies from Spain never again seriously threatened Europe.[14] Martel's Christian forces had effectively checked the Muslim attempt to make all of Europe submit to Islam—at least until Muslim Turks defeated the Serbians at Kosovo in 1389 and captured Constantinople on May 29, 1453 (thus completing their destruction of the Christian Greek Roman Empire and the subjection of the Christian Greeks, which would last for four hundred years), and then moved through the Balkans to defeat the Hungarians at Mohács in 1526 (fourteen thousand Hungarian soldiers were slain, and with the heads of prisoners, including those of seven bishops, the Turks built a mound as a warning to Christians who dared to resist) and finally reached the gates of Vienna in 1529 (Battle of the Siege of Vienna) and again in 1683 at the momentous Battle of the Gates of Vienna.[15]

A RELIGIOUSLY MOTIVATED INVASION

Although the lust for booty and slaves was undoubtedly part of the Muslim armies' motivation, the fundamental impulse for the movement of these armies through North Africa and then on to Europe was to carry out a religious war—*jihad*. Both Muslim and Christian sources referring to the invasion of North Africa and Spain as well as archaeological evidence attest to the importance of the religious factor in the Islamic conquest.

Before we look at these sources, it is important to examine the way the concept of *jihad* as a religiously motivated war was understood in the Muslim legal texts and in other Andalusian sources of the time. Today, many academic specialists insist that *jihad*—in Arabic, literally "effort" or "struggle"—means in Islamic law principally a spiritual inner effort or an individual struggle for self-improvement.[16] They emphasize this meaning to strengthen their claim that the Muslim invasion was motivated by something other than religion—perhaps by some harmless desire to "expand," or "migrate," or "exert" themselves in the search for perfection. For example, Richard Hitchcock, professor emeritus of Arab and Islamic studies at Britain's University of Exeter, challenges the "traditional interpretation... that the invasion was impelled by belief in the notion of *jihād* in the sense of Holy War." Hitchcock notes that "the meaning of the word *jihād* is 'striving' or 'exertion.'" He cites approvingly the comments of one famous twentieth-century translator of the Quran, Maulvi Muhammad Ali, who wrote that "it shows an utter ignorance of the Arabic language" to interpret the reference to *jihad* in *surah* (chapter) 9 of the Quran "as meaning *to fight with sword*." Ali added that "the greatest *jihād* that a Muslim can carry out is one by means of the *Qur-án*,...not with the sword."[17]

This spiritualizing academic interpretation has even made it into schoolchildren's education in the West. Houghton Mifflin's *Across the Centuries* teaches children that *jihad* is an "inner struggle" that urges the faithful to "do one's best to resist temptation and overcome evil."[18] This view of *jihad* is now taught in many schools in the United States.[19] The publicly funded and produced BBC hagiographic documentary *The Life of Muhammad* (2011), regularly broadcast by educational television stations in England and the United States, makes this claim as well. Many Western-educated Muslims today also deny that the term *jihad* has martial implications. For example, Dr. Qanta Ahmed, a British-born physician of Pakistani descent who practiced in Saudi Arabia, told a reporter, "One of the central errors westerners are constantly assaulted with is the use of this term *jihad*." She added, "The central *jihad* for all of us is to constantly improve and be the best we can be and try to adhere to some very pure ideals."[20]

Now, it is certainly possible that, for centuries, the medieval Muslim scholars who interpreted the sacred Islamic texts, as well as Muslim military leaders (including perhaps Muhammad himself when he led his armies into battle against infidels unwilling to submit), misunderstood (unlike today's experts in Islamic studies) the primarily peaceful and "defensive" meaning of "*jihad*," and that, as a result of this mistake, Muslim armies erroneously went and, always defensively, conquered half the known world. Or perhaps these conquering Muslim armies were, somehow, merely "exerting" themselves "to resist temptation and overcome evil."

Nevertheless, what the correct understanding of the term is according to today's expert academic interpreters matters little for what actually happened. That is because, as Felipe Maíllo Salgado points out, when the legal texts of the Maliki school of Islamic law prevalent in al-Andalus mention *jihad*, they do not talk of a "spiritual inner struggle," or of some kind of "self-perfecting exertion": they talk of war against infidels—a Sacred Combat, or Holy War, or Holy Struggle, or whatever other name one may choose to give this religiously mandated war against infidels.[21] (See chapter 3 on the dominance of Malikism in Islamic Spain.) Thus what many Islamic studies academics call today "little *jihad*," as opposed to "greater *jihad*" (the "spiritual" one), turns out to be the only *jihad* examined in the Maliki religious treatises and actually practiced in Islamic Spain. In the words of Soha Abboud-Haggar, professor of Islamic and Semitic studies at the Complutense University of Madrid, the objective of *jihad* thus understood is "to make war in order to outspread the Islamic religion and implement its law throughout the entire world, and its reward is Paradise."[22]

My examination of the available sources relevant to Islamic Spain leaves little doubt on these matters. Imam Malik Ibn Anas's foundational eighth-century treatise on Islamic law, *al-Muwatta* ("The Easy Path" or "The Well-Trodden Path"), in the most authoritative recension (that of the Córdoban jurist Yahya Ibn Yahya Ibn Kathir al-Andalusi) discusses *jihad* or "holy struggle" only in the martial sense (book 21, "Jihad").[23]

The passages in the *Muwatta* on the obligation of waging this religious war were doubtlessly inspiring for any Muslim warrior and go a long way toward explaining the often irresistible fighting ardor of the Islamic armies. Among many examples: "The Messenger of Allah (may the peace and blessings of Allah be upon him) said: Allah (the Exalted and Almighty) undertakes to let that who fights in his way enter Paradise.... That he returns him to his dwelling of which he went out, with what he gained of the reward and the booty" (21.1.2). The superior benefits of making Holy War are clear in this ranking of good behavior: "The Messenger of Allah...said: Shall I tell you about the best in rank among the people? A man who takes the rein of his horse to fight in the way of Allah.... Shall I tell you of the people who follow him in rank? A man who lives alone with a few sheep, performing the prayer, paying the Zakat, and worshipping Allah" (21.1.4).

Martyrdom while fighting in the way of Allah is exalted throughout Malik's writings. For example: "The Messenger of Allah...said:...I would like to fight in the way of Allah.... I would be killed, then I would be brought to life, then I would be killed, then I would be brought to life and I would be killed" (21.14.27). "The messenger of Allah...said: Had not I been concerned for my community, I would never like to stay behind a raiding party going out in the way of Allah.... I would like to fight in the way of Allah...and be killed, then brought to life so I could be killed and then brought to life so I could be killed" (21.18.40). "The Messenger of Allah...had exhorted for the Holy Struggle, and had mentioned Paradise while a man of the Ansar was eating dates in his hand. Then he said: Am I so desirous of this world that I should sit until I finish them? Then he threw out what is in his hand, and carried his sword; he fought until he was killed" (21.18.42). "The Messenger of Allah...said: ...no one who is wounded in the way of Allah (the Exalted and Almighty), and Allah knows best who is wounded in His way, but comes on the Day of Resurrection, and his blood gushes forth from his wound. The color is the color of blood, but its scent will be that of musk" (21.14.29). "The Messenger of Allah...once came to her [Umm Haram] and she fed him. And she sat to delouse his hair. Then the Messenger of Allah...slept and later he woke up smiling. She said: What makes you laugh O Messenger of Allah...? He said: People of my nation, raiding in the way of Allah.... They were riding in the middle of the sea. Kings on the thrones" (21.18.39).

Doubtlessly it was a strong incentive for a male warrior fighting in the way of Allah that he could take all the property of those enemy fighters he had killed in combat, including his women, who would not be considered "free women" and therefore could be taken as sexual slaves.[24] The willingness to die while killing the infidels, taught in the religious texts on *jihad*, gave Muslim warriors a tactical advantage over their enemies during the Islamic conquests. This willingness to die is found, for example, in the words of the Islamic Caliphate's Arab commander Khalid Ibn Walid in 633, ordering the Persians to submit to Islam, or else: "Otherwise you are bound to meet a people who love death as much as you love life."[25]

All Maliki legal treatises follow this exclusively martial understanding of *jihad*. The tenth-century *Kitab al-Tafri*, one of the Maliki manuals most widely read in Islamic Spain, discusses *jihad* only as Holy War (231–39).

Another tenth-century Maliki treatise influential in Islamic Spain, the *Risala* by the "little Malik" al-Qayrawani, discusses *jihad* only as Holy War (30.1–30.6): "[Christians and Jews] either accept Islam or pay the *jizya* [tax]; if not, they are to be fought."

Likewise, the legal manual *Suma de los principales mandamientos y devedamientos de la ley y çunna, por don Içe de Gebir, alfaquí mayor y muftí de la aljama de Segovia*, written in 1492 in *aljamiado*—Spanish written with Arabic signs used by many of the Muslims under Spanish

Christian domination—examines *jihad* (*al-chihed*) only as Holy War and as obligatory for the believer (35). The same is true of the legal manual *Leyes de moros*, written in Spanish and possibly dating from the fourteenth century (see the allusion to *jihad* in 250). The persistence of the understanding of *jihad* only as Holy War in these works is quite telling because they were written for the use of Muslims already under Christian rule (*mudéjares*).[26] The *Suma* makes clear that waging *jihad* is obligatory for all free Muslim males and that before fighting the infidels one must ask them first either to submit to Islam and pay the *jizya* or to convert to Islam (chapter 35).

The *Bidayat*, a Maliki treatise for the instructions of Muslim judges by the great twelfth-century Córdoban jurist Ibn Rushd (better known in the West as "the philosopher Averroes"), discusses *jihad* only as Holy War and confirms the tribute of *jizya* as a payment for sparing the lives of Christians and Jews while they remain unbelievers under the power of Islam (10.1.1–10.2.7.6).

Likewise, one of the greatest minds of Islamic Spain, the polymath Ibn Hazm (994–1064), spoke of *jihad* only as a Holy War against the infidel. As the French scholar of Islam Roger Arnaldez points out, "*Jihad* remains for him armed war, and he makes no attempt to 'spiritualize' the word."[27] Moreover, Ibn Hazm observed that "*jihad* is for the service of God, rather than men"—the same rigorous sense in which the great imam of the Berber Almoravids, Abd Allah b. Yasin, understood *jihad* and preached it to his irresistible warriors.[28] In his *Fisal*, Ibn Hazm in fact emphasizes that it is obligatory for a Muslim to participate in *jihad* regardless of who is the military commander at the time, even if the commander has usurped power by force and is an unjust tyrant—as long as he is carrying out the war on behalf of Islam. Ibn Hazm then cites the well-known verses from the Quran (5:3): "Kill the polytheists wherever you find them, take them as prisoners, beseech and ambush them."[29]

Al-Shafii, who for several years studied under Malik but later founded a legal school of his own, discusses *jihad* exclusively as Holy War: "God has imposed [the duty of] *jihad* as laid down in his Book and uttered by His Prophet's tongue. He stressed the calling [of men to fulfill] the *jihad* as follows: '[The believers] fight in the way of God; they kill and are killed; that is a promise binding upon God (Quran 9:112).'"[30]

Non-Maliki Sunni Muslims consider al-Bukhari's collection of traditional narratives of Muhammad's sayings and deeds (singular: *hadith*; plural: *ahadith*) to be second only to the Quran as a source of Islamic law and religion. But even al-Bukhari's *ahadith* placed *jihad*, understood as Holy War, at the top of a Muslim's obligations, right after believing in Allah and His Prophet:

> Narrated Abu Huraira: Allah's Apostle was asked, "What is the best deed?" He replied, "To believe in Allah and His Apostle (Muhammad). The questioner then asked, "What is the next (in goodness)?" He replied, "To participate in Jihad (religious fighting) in Allah's Cause." The questioner again asked, "What is the next (in goodness)?" He replied, "To perform Hajj (Pilgrimage to Mecca) 'Mubrur (which is accepted by Allah and is performed with the intention of seeking Allah's pleasure only and not to show off and without committing a sin and in accordance with the traditions of the Prophet)."
>
> Narrated Abu Huraira: The Prophet said, "The person who participates in (Holy battles) in Allah's cause and nothing compels him to do so except belief in Allah and His Apostles, will be recompensed by Allah either with a reward, or booty (if he survives) or will be admitted to Paradise (if he is killed in the battle as a martyr). Had I not found it difficult for my followers, then I would not remain behind any *sariya* [army unit] going for Jihad and I would have loved to be martyred in Allah's cause and then made alive, and then martyred and then made alive, and then again martyred in His cause."[31]

Jihad was so widely understood as Holy War in Islamic Spain that the famous work on *jihad* as Holy War by Abu Ishaq al-Fazari (d. after 802) remained popular in Spain long after it had ceased to be edited in other lands.[32]

Moreover, extant letters from Islamic Spain that use the word *jihad* display no other meaning but Holy War ("*al-jihad*").[33]

The Muslim *Anonymous Chronicle of the Taifa Kings* (twelfth century) refers to *jihad* solely as a Holy War that kings must wage against the infidel Christians to be worthy of leadership.[34]

Ibn al-Khatib's fourteenth-century *History of the Kings of the Alhambra* is replete with praise for those numerous rulers of the *taifa* kingdom of

Granada who made Holy War and the persecution of infidels, heretics, and violators of *sharia* their primary goal in life.[35]

Other authoritative non-Spanish Muslim sources similarly examine *jihad* solely as a religiously mandated war against the infidels, not as some spiritual struggle to improve oneself. Thus the famous Persian historian al-Tabari (839–923), in his famous treatise on *jihad*, talks of it only as a collective Holy War, not as trying to "be the best we can be."[36] The great Tunisian historian Ibn Khaldun (1332–1406) noted that one of the ten religious duties of the caliph was the responsibility "to wage the Holy War [*jihad*] himself and with his armies at least once a year."[37]

Ibn Khaldun also emphasized a crucial difference between the way medieval Muslims understood religion, political power, and war and the way non-Muslims did—a difference many scholars overlook when they equate Christian Crusades with Islam's *jihad*. Ibn Khaldun explained:

> In the Muslim community, the holy war is a religious duty because of the universalism of the Muslim mission and the obligation to convert everybody to Islam either by persuasion or by force. Therefore caliphate and royal authority are united in Islam, so that the person in charge can devote the available strength to both of them at the same time. The other religious groups did not have a universal mission and the holy war was not a religious duty to them, save only for purposes of defense. It has thus come about that the person in charge of religious affairs in other religious groups is not concerned with power politics at all. Among them royal authority comes to those who have it—by accident or in some way that has nothing to do with religion.[38]

In Islamic Spain, Muslim clerics regarded as particularly worthy the combination of personal virtue and a willingness to make war against the infidels—*jihad*.[39] And as Ibn Khaldun's list of the caliph's religious duties indicates, medieval experts on Islam saw *jihad* not as a "secondary" religious activity (as again many of today's academics insist) but rather as a principal one.[40] Thus the *Muwatta*, in book 21 ("Jihad"), which treats *jihad* solely as war against the infidels, says:

> Yahya related to me from Malik from Abu'z-Zinad from al-Araj from Abu Hurayra that the Messenger of Allah, may Allah bless him and

grant him peace, said, "Allah guarantees either the Garden [Paradise] or a safe return to his home with whatever he has obtained of reward or booty, for the one who does jihad in His way, if it is solely jihad and trust in his promise, that brings him out of his house."

Yahya related to me from Malik from Abu'z-Zinad from al-Araj from Abu Hurayra that the Messenger of Allah, may Allah bless him and grant him peace, said "Someone who does jihad in the way of Allah is like someone who fasts and prays constantly and who does not slacken from his prayer and fasting until he returns."

As Maíllo Salgado observes, Maliki manuals stipulate that "Holy War must be waged each year.... It is a duty of solidarity (some must contribute with their own selves, others with their possessions) imposed on every free Muslim male."[41]

Moreover, when the Maliki legal texts spoke of the *jizya*, the special tax Christians and Jews paid once they had submitted to Islam, they made clear that imposing the *jizya* meant humiliating these "People of the Book" before the newly hegemonic political and religious entity, Islam. The *Muwatta* emphasizes the important distinction between *jizya* and the tax imposed on all Muslims: "*Zakat* is imposed on the Muslims to purify them and to be given back to their poor, whereas *jizya* is imposed on the people of the Book to humble them" (17.23.46). The *Muwatta* follows the Quran (9:29): "Fight those who do not believe in Allah or in the Last Day and who do not consider unlawful what Allah and His Messenger have made unlawful and who do not adopt the religion of truth from those who were given the Scripture—[fight] until they give the jizyah willingly while they are humbled."[42]

Maliki jurisprudence advised the holy warriors to spare from destruction during *jihad* only bees, small children, women, decrepit old men, and monks and hermits who lived by themselves and posed no threat. They could be left just enough to subsist. But this mercy did not necessarily apply to priests.[43] The Maliki juridical treatise *al-Tafri* dictated that a Muslim leader on the *jihad* battlefield could kill or spare the defeated Christians at will.[44]

Although Christian women and children must not be killed during *jihad* as long as they did not present a danger, they could be captured and enslaved.[45] Of course, women or children or priests who fought could be killed.[46] And the Maliki legal texts made clear that, in *jihad* territory, the Muslim warrior faced no restrictions to having sexual intercourse with the captive women adjudicated to him as booty and therefore as slaves.[47]

In Islamic Spain, Holy War was not only for the benefit of the individual soul of the believer but also for the ultimate triumph of Islam. Holy War, wrote Ibn Hazm rather ominously, "makes the *kafir* [unbeliever] leave the darkness of *kufr* to be brought to the light of Islam."[48] In other words, so that "the darkness of infidelity be defeated, it is necessary that the light of Muslim law be extended over an ever increasing number of men, or at least that those men who resist disappear."[49] Ibn Hazm, like the other Muslim scholars we have cited, would have been aware of the well-known words of Muhammad in one of the *ahadith* cited by al-Maqqari: "I have seen before my eyes the East and the West, and every one of the regions comprised in them shall be subdued by my people."[50]

The infidel had practically no right in this struggle that took place in *dar al-Harb* (infidel lands); the Muslim had every right. Only after submission, when *dar al-Harb* had become *dar al-Islam*, could those who submitted be granted, always at the will of the victor, the status of "protected," or *dhimmi*. But for both *dhimmis* and Muslims, "rights" were defined always and only according to Islamic law.

Alfred Morabia, author of what may be the definitive study of the concept of *jihad*, argues that the idea that *jihad* is primarily a "spiritual inner struggle" may rest on a late and apocryphal *hadith*, invented or publicized by Islamic clerics (*ulama*; singular: *alim*) wanting to reinforce their control over the lives of Muslims. The *hadith* says that one must endeavor to be as strict as possible in one's life because one must fight *jihad* every day and at all times against all sorts of enemies, including oneself. Who better than the *ulama* to tell the faithful how to carry out this relentless inner struggle even when there is no actual war to fight?[51]

Morabia also suggests that the idea of *jihad* as some sort of "defensive" war may have been a relatively late development as well. After all, the early Muslim armies swept out of the Arabian Peninsula and conquered areas ranging from present-day Spain in the west to India in the east. There was nothing "defensive" about this massive "expansion." But eventually some of Islam's conquered enemies experienced a resurgence, and new enemies emerged as well. After centuries of conquest, Islam could legitimately see itself as being on the defensive, at least in some areas (including Spain).

Morabia's theory is substantiated by the new emphasis on defense found in a twelfth-century treatise on *jihad* by the Andalusian Ibn Hudhayl, written when, under pressure from the Christian *Reconquista* (Reconquest), Andalusian Muslims could barely hold on to what little territory they had left, let alone attack Christian lands.[52]

Still, the historical events of the preceding five hundred years cannot be ignored. Muhammad's wars against infidels in the Arabian Peninsula, and Islam's impressive conquests well beyond the Arabian Peninsula, including much of Spain, were made possible not by a peaceful "inner struggle" but by a bellicose outward one. Learned medieval *ulama* and Muslim military leaders associated war against infidels with a sacred duty, thereby turning war into an inseparable part of a Muslim's religious life. War sacrifice and martyrdom became part of the religious-cultural ethos of medieval Islam.[53]

In this association may reside much of the early success of Islamic imperialism: as Morabia observes, what for the pre-Muslim Arabs had been simply *razzia*, lightning raids against other Bedouin tribes, under Muhammad became Holy War; and what for nations outside Arabia had been merely "war" became for Islam under Muhammad's successors a perennial Holy War.[54]

Other religions and nations remained at a disadvantage when confronting the highly motivating Islamic religious concept of *jihad* as Holy War. As we will see shortly, Christian Spain did successfully turn its war of reconquest against Islam into a religious war of its own in the thirteenth century, a Crusade. But even a Crusade, as Ibn Khaldun observed above, never could have the same internalized degree of everyday spiritual obligation that Islam's *jihad* as Holy War achieved.

Attempts to equate *jihad* with Crusade do not withstand analysis. For devout Christians, the sacred war of a Crusade *was a unique event that only a pope could proclaim*. But as Ibn Khaldun pointed out, for devout Muslims the sacred war of *jihad* was *a permanent state of being decreed by Islamic law* that the caliph must wage at least once a year.[55]

Now we can return to examining the evidence for the religious motivation of the Muslim conquest of Spain. In downplaying religious motivations for the Islamic invasion, some Western academics make much of the fact that the earliest Christian chronicle narrating the conquest— the *Chronica mozarabica* of 754—refers to the invaders not as "Muslims" but as "Saracens" or "Arabs."[56] According to this line of thinking, if the Christians did not see the invaders as Muslims, they could not have seen the invasion as a religious confrontation. Thus the Muslim "expansion" (the word *invasion* is avoided in this sort of argument) would have been motivated by material rather than religious reasons, just like other "expansions" throughout history (presumably including such mere "expansions" or "migratory waves" or "exertions" as those of the Spaniards in the Americas, the French in Algeria, the Dutch in South Africa, the British in India, or the Belgians in the Congo).

There are several problems with this argument. First, it overlooks the fact that *Muslim* chronicles of the Muslim conquests portray *jihad* as Holy War, not as a "peaceful individual struggle or exertion for self-improvement," and that Andalusian Muslim leaders saw their wars against the Christians as Holy War as well. The chronicles usually identify the invaders as "Muslims" and the Christians as "idolaters," "polytheists," and "infidels," as well as "Rum" or Romans—as inhabitants of the Christian Greek Roman Empire. The historian Ibn al-Qutiyya (d. 977), who was of Visigoth ancestry, narrates how one of the Muslim commanders was inspired by his dreaming of Muhammad and His Companions, with their drawn swords, entering Spain. The same commander, Tariq, is portrayed haranguing his men before battle by reminding them of the religious benefits of martyrdom in *jihad*.[57]

One of the early Muslim leaders of al-Andalus, the capable governor Uqba Ibn al-Hayyay al-Saluli (d. 741), is described by the tenth-century Muslim historian al-Khushani as "a courageous champion of *jihad*, frontier warrior, intrepid and valiant, burning in his desire to hurt the polytheists [that is, Christians, who believed in a triune god—the Father, the Son, and the Holy Spirit]."[58]

The twelfth-century historian Ibn al-Kardabus highlights the religious fervor of the invaders: "The Muslims fought with bravery and they charged intrepidly, like one man, against the polytheists (*musrikun*), whom Allah had abandoned and whose legs he would make tremble."[59] Using tenth-century sources, Ibn Idhari al-Marrakushi's *Kitab al-Bayan al-Mughrib* refers to the enemy Christians as "infidels" and "polytheists" and to the conquerors as "the Muslims." Significantly, al-Kardabus tells us that the Arab leader Musa Ibn Nusayr was accompanied by *tabiun*, wise men of the second or third Muslim generation who knew at least one of the Companions of Muhammad and who were in charge of supervising the proper Islamization of a conquered land and the establishment of the first mosques—another feature of the early *jihads*.

Thus the Muslim warriors seem to have been conscious of conducting a religiously motivated war—*jihad*—against infidels, not a peaceful means of perfecting or "exerting" themselves spiritually. The devout Muhammad Ibn Abu Amir al-Mansur (c. 938–1002, known to Christians as Almanzor), probably the most brilliant military mind among the rulers of Islamic Spain, could have justified his burning of Catholic cities with Maliki Islamic teachings: *al-Tafri* and the *Mudawwana* make clear that burning the towns of infidels was allowed in *jihad*.[60] So was flooding them and "cutting their trees and their fruits, killing their animals, and destroying their buildings and all that can be broken down."[61] Motivated by his religious zeal, al-Mansur ordered all philosophy and logic books in Córdoba publicly burned.[62] These subjects, observed the Muslim historian Said al-Andalusi, remained proscribed afterward in the *taifa* kingdoms, although their rulers fostered such "common arts" as poetry and grammar.[63]

Al-Mansur was so devoted to Holy War that in a single year (981) he sent five expeditions against the Christian kingdoms. He demolished the entire city of León with the exception of a tower, which he left standing so that from the thickness of its walls later generations could realize the accomplishment involved in his victory.

It is significant that Muslim leaders punished their own if they suspected a lack of Islamic zeal. Muslim warriors could be punished with death for apostasy, which contributed to the fervor of the invaders. According to al-Qutiyya, when Musa Ibn Nusayr's son was named governor, he married the wife of King Rodrigo and began adopting Christian ways—and military leaders cut his head off in the *mihrab* of a mosque and sent his head to the caliph.[64]

A second problem is that the early use of the Greco-Roman word *Saracen* rather than *Muslim* in the *Chronica mozarabica* of 754 does not mean, as a number of historians repeat, that Christian chroniclers failed to detect religious motives behind the invasion. As far back as the eighth century, early Greek Christian religious polemics against Islam, which certainly portrayed things in religious terms, used the term *Saracen* as well.[65] For the *Chronica mozarabica*'s eighth-century historian and for his

Spanish Christian readers (or listeners), the names *Saracens* and *Arabs* meant—as they had meant for Greek Christian historians—nothing other than the followers of Muhammad: that is, Muslims.

But the most telling fact is that the *Chronica mozarabica* of 754 mentions Muhammad (*Mammet*) as the "leader" of the invaders, and at least once as "their prophet" (*propheta eorum Mammet*).[66] Surely calling Muhammad a "prophet" of the invaders indicates that the Christian author of the *Chronica mozarabica* of 754, one of the earliest and most reliable accounts of the Islamic conquest of Spain, was aware of at least some kind of religious belief informing the actions of Muhammad's followers.

In addition, the *Life of Muhammad*, written in Latin by a Christian, circulating among the Spanish *dhimmis* and former *dhimmis* (that is, Christians subject or formerly subject to Muslim domination), and dating very likely from the second half of the eighth century—just decades after the Muslim conquest—presents an insulting biography of Muhammad, which once more indicates the Spanish Christians' awareness of Islam as the motivating force behind their Muslim enemies' invasion.[67]

Also corroborating the early testimony of the *Chronica mozarabica* of 754 is the similarly early testimony of the Visigoth hymn *Tempore belli*, probably composed in the first half of the eighth century, only some decades after the conquest. This hymn laments the invasion of the land by a barbarian *non-Christian* people who has defeated the *Christians* and has inflicted cruelty upon *Christian* temples, priests, and virgins. As the medieval historian Luis A. García Moreno observes, this liturgical hymn is a contemporary testimony of the "terrible impression made upon the Christian society of the Visigoth kingdom by the total defeat of its army at the hands of an invader from overseas, who professed a faith different from that of the Christians." This hymn indicates, García Moreno continues, that "the idea of a Reconquest was born immediately after the defeat."[68]

Archaeological findings provide even more evidence: coins minted in North Africa shortly before the invasion of Spain call upon the protection of Allah for *jihad*. García Moreno observes that the documented invocations of the name of Jesus by the Christians in their struggle against the invaders were "doubtlessly a response to the Muslim invaders' invocations of God [Allah] as the motive of their actions, as demonstrated by the well-known Islamic coins preparing the conquest."[69]

Making a secular modern Western distinction between a religious and a "political" motivation on the part of the Muslim warriors, as many scholars now do, is hardly more historically astute. In medieval Islam there was simply no distinction between religious and political motivations for making war against infidels, as chapter 3 will document. Thus, while narrating the conquest of Persia, the great historian al-Tabari (839–923) has the Muslim spokesmen clarify to the Persian infidels that, unlike the pre-Islamic Arabs, "Muslims do not fight for worldly possessions or in order to improve their standard of living. Their only objective is to spread the new faith of Islam."[70] And, of course, without *Islam* there would have been no *Muslim* "expansion" ("Arab expansion" will not do, since by the early eighth century Muslims and their armies were no longer just "Arab").

My examination of the primary sources therefore confirms the assessments of French Arabists such as George Henri Bousquet (former professor of law at the University of Algiers) and Dominique Urvoy (professor of Arabic civilization and thought at the University of Toulouse), who have pointed out that the Muslim conquest of Spain was indeed motivated by the notion of *jihad*.[71]

Shock and Awe

A full assessment of Islamic rule in medieval Spain requires examining how the forces of the Islamic Caliphate gained control of this region. The ruthless tactics they often employed foreshadowed some of the measures by which later Andalusian rulers would maintain their power (see chapter 4).

Historians have often marveled at the speed of the Islamic conquest of Spain, which took less than ten years. In fact, it was not faster than other rapid victories in the history of war. The Greek warriors of Alexander the Great conquered a much stronger foe, the Persian Empire, in less time. The Mongols and Tartars of Genghis Khan and Tamerlane carried out comparable conquests, including the crushing defeat of Muslim armies in the Middle East, in an even shorter time. The relative speed of the Islamic conquest is no mystery, as military historians such as Commander José Miranda Calvo and Hans Delbrück, medieval historians such as García Moreno, and Arabists such as Felipe Maíllo Salgado have explained so convincingly.[72]

García Moreno has shown, against much "established opinion," that there was no "social decomposition" or "decadence" in Visigoth Spain and that the Islamic conquest was far from "inevitable."[73] Nonetheless, a few centuries of life in the Capua-like environment of southern Spain had weakened the military structure of the warlike Visigoths, who had once beaten back the previously undefeated Huns of Attila at the Battle of the Catalaunian Plains (451). The noblemen who led the Visigoth warrior class were now more interested in enjoying life in their large estates than in contributing militarily to a standing army. Moreover, living far apart from one another in their vast properties, these noblemen could not rapidly assemble their armed retinues for military service. In addition, the Visigoth state was politically weak because of the nonhereditary nature of its monarchy: the king was elected by the nobility from among a small number of noble families. Therefore a key factor in the relative facility of the Muslim conquest, emphasized by the military historian Miranda Calvo, was that, as a number of the primary sources indicate, a competing royal faction sided with the invaders against the Visigoth king Rodrigo and defected to the Islamic forces before, during, and after the main battles. The invaders were also helped by a Christian lord from North Africa mentioned in many of the sources as "Count Julian," but who was probably a Greco-Roman ("Byzantine") count by the name of Urbanus, as García Moreno has shown. For personal or other reasons, this Christian lord transported Muslim forces across the strait, guided them into the land, and helped them in combat with his own retinue.

By contrast, the forces of the Islamic Caliphate were unified, skilled, fierce, and well led. Their commanders were experienced, having fought and won against the Christian Greek Roman Empire and against pagan Berber tribes. The Berbers who made up the majority of their troops were particularly ferocious warriors, as even Muslim historians point out.[74] These former pagans were imbued with the religious fervor of the new convert and the hunger for loot of the marauding tribesman.

In addition, several primary Muslim sources (among them *Akhbar Majmua*, al-Qutiyya, Ibn al-Athir, al-Khatib, al-Razi, Ibn Idhari al-Marrakushi, and al-Maqqari) as well as Christian sources (among them Rodrigo Jiménez de Rada [1170–1247]) record that the Jewish community sided with the invaders and kept guard over major cities after they had fallen to Muslim armies—a collaboration not surprising in view of the Visigoths' anti-Jewish legislation.[75] This support also helps explain militarily the relative speed of the Muslim conquest: it permitted Islamic forces to move rapidly on without having to leave behind substantial contingents to protect their rear guard and lines of communication, which allowed them to show up unexpectedly at key strategic points, terrifying both civilians and enemy garrisons.

Finally, the invaders used a mixture of "shock and awe" tactics and "peaceful" treaties. In the "peaceful" treaties, the Muslim conquerors granted momentary privileges and autonomy to those Visigoth secular and religious leaders who did not resist and who paid a tribute (as shown in the treatise with the lord Theodomir),[76] allowing them to keep, at least for a time, their land, servants, and religion. This approach was necessary because the invaders were initially far less numerous than the natives.

But as both Muslim and Christian sources attest, the Islamic forces were more ruthless and knew how to demoralize an enemy better than any army since the Roman conquest. Both Muslim and Christian sources mention a story that, even if apocryphal, illustrates the knowledge of the tactical use of terror in psychological warfare. Shortly after the Islamic forces landed, the flesh of the cadavers of some Christians killed in battle were boiled in large cauldrons under the sight of terrified Christian prisoners, who became convinced that the Muslims were cannibals. The Muslims then set loose the prisoners, who, al-Kardabus says, "told every Christian they met what they had seen, so that Allah filled their hearts with panic. Afterwards came the battle against Rodrigo."[77]

The Muslim historians al-Kardabus and Abd al-Wahid al-Marrakushi write that Musa Ibn Nusayr sacked, enslaved, and spent three years waging *jihad* against the Spanish infidels.[78] Along with al-Kardabus, al-Marrakushi and al-Maqqari say that Musa spent as much time "pillaging" as "organizing" the conquered land. These sources also mention that several members of the *tabiun* (a generation of pious Muslims who were direct disciples of Muhammad's Companions) entered Spain to direct the *jihad* and the conversion of the land. The presence of these members of the *tabiun* underlines the fundamentally religious motivation of the invasion—a *jihad*.

If Christians resisted, a massacre would follow after a Muslim victory. Near Orihuela, the defeated Christians were punished with extermination.[79]

After the Muslims took Córdoba in a furious assault, the remaining Christian defenders retreated to a church to continue fighting. According to al-Maqqari, the Muslims put the building to the torch and the Christians inside died, without surrendering; according to al-Kardabus, when the Christians surrendered, the Muslim commander had them beheaded. According to the *Akhbar Majmua*, the Muslim commander then left Córdoba in the hands of the Jewish community.[80]

Toledo, the Visigoth capital, offered no resistance to the rapid advance of the Islamic forces because most warriors had marched with King Rodrigo to meet the enemy. Nonetheless, Musa executed some aged Toledan nobles for reasons that scholars do not agree on, but perhaps it was simply *pour encourager les autres*.[81] According to al-Athir, the invaders left Jews, accompanied by a certain number of Muslim warriors, in charge of Toledo and moved on to Guadalajara. The Muslims forces captured Seville after a siege, sending the Christian warriors fleeing to the North. According to al-Athir, the invaders again left the Jewish community to guard the city. In front of Merida, the Islamic forces followed a victory with a massacre of the fleeing "polytheists."[82] Back in Seville, when Christians revolted against the occupying Muslim-Jewish garrison, a reinforced Muslim army retook the city and massacred the inhabitants.[83] According to the *Akhbar Majmua* and al-Khatib, after taking Elvira (Arabic garbling of the ancient name Illiberis, eventually renamed Granada), the conquerors also left the Jewish community in charge.

Christian sources such as the *Chronica mozarabica* of 754, written not too long after the conquest, and the *History of Spain* (*Primera crónica general*) commissioned by King Alfonso X in the thirteenth century corroborate the carrot-and-stick methods described in the Muslim chronicles. These Christian accounts tell us that Musa offered peace and privileges to those Christian noblemen and church leaders who did not resist but killed those who did. Musa burned any city that resisted, "crucified the nobility and the older men," and "cut to pieces the young men and the infants (*iubenes atque lactantes*)," so that towns surrendered in terror and many inhabitants fled to the mountains.[84] Both methods, the ruthless crushing of any opposition and the granting of pacts to those lords who agreed not to fight, as well as the deception involved in the pacts (a deception, as we will see, noted by other Christian sources and by Muslim historians such as Ibn Abd al-Hakam), are recorded by the *Chronica mozarabica* of 754: "After ravaging the land as far as Toledo, the royal city, Musa conquers with deceitful peace offers the surrounding regions with the help of [Visigoth lord] Opas, son of [former king] Egica, and executes a number of senior [Visigoth] lords that had remained in the city and puts all of them to the sword with his help."[85]

The peaceful pacts' "deceitful" nature mentioned in the Christian and Muslim sources was in fact justified by the Islamic legal tradition. An Islamic law scholar quite sympathetic to Islam, Majid Khadduri, has pointed out that the abrogation of pacts in case of necessity was acceptable in medieval Islamic legal practice because

> Islam, emerging in the seventh century as a conquering nation with world domination as its ultimate aim, refused to recognize legal systems other than its own. It was willing to enter into temporary treaty relations with other states, pending consummation of its world mission. The Prophet and his successors, however, reserved the right to repudiate any treaty or arrangement which they considered as harmful to Islam.... Although the normal relationship between Islam and non-Muslim communities is a state of hostility, it is not considered inconsistent with Islam's ultimate objective if a treaty is concluded with the enemy, whether for purposes of expediency or because Islam suffered a setback.[86]

Written shortly after the Visigoth defeat, the Visigoth church hymn *Tempore belli* corroborates what other Christian and Muslim sources tell us regarding the terrifying but effective tactics used against the Christians. As the Spanish historian M. C. Díaz y Díaz put it, this liturgical Latin poem describes an "implacable enemy," "full of enthusiasm in the exercise of war" (*continuo fervida bello*), "forcing Christian troops to turn around and flee in panic," sacking Christian temples and homes, burning the cities of those who resisted, and taking their young women as sexual slaves, all creating an "indescribable terror."[87] The *Chronica mozarabica* of 754 echoes these laments about the looting of treasures and the sexual enslavement of beautiful young Christian women (57.1–5).

Alfonso X's *History of Spain* (*Primera crónica general*) also tells how the Muslim conquerors killed the men, burned cities, wasted the land, took young women as sexual slaves, and sacked church treasures, causing bishops to flee with sacred Christian relics. Another thirteenth-century history, written by Rodrigo Jiménez de Rada, speaks of how the Muslims burned towns, cut down fruit trees, destroyed churches, regarded sacred music as blasphemy, and profaned chalices. On the other hand, like Alfonso's *History*, it describes "treaties" with which the conquerors gained the acquiescence of many Christian leaders—though the Muslims broke these agreements once they had control of the land. The ninth-century Muslim historian al-Hakam also mentions such deviousness: "When the Muslims conquered Spain, they looted it and committed many frauds."[88] The *Chronicon mundi* of Lucas de Tuy, written in the early years of the thirteenth century, echoes these descriptions: "the Moors forced into submission, through iron and fire, almost all of Spain.... Only those Goths who retreated to the heights of the Pyrenees in Asturias and Galicia escaped. The Moors kept the best places, won with the vengeful knife.... And they changed the towers of ancient cities; destroyed castles...monasteries; burned the books of the sacred law, and committed many bad deeds."[89]

As these Muslim and Christian sources indicate, burning Christian churches and sacking their treasures played an important role in the conquerors' shock-and-awe tactics. This destruction helped demoralize the Christian resistance. Muhammad Ibn al-Razi (887–955), one of the earliest Muslim historians of the Islamic conquest, recounts that the founder of the Emirate of Córdoba, the Umayyad Abd al-Rahman I, consistently burned Christian churches and relics.[90]

As the Spanish Arabist Susana Calvo Capilla has pointed out, when Muslim chronicles mention churches, it is usually to gloat over their destruction or over their transformation into mosques as part of the humbling of the infidels.[91] Christian accounts corroborate the Muslim ones: thus the *Crónicas anónimas de Sahagún* (twelfth or thirteenth century) tell of the destruction of a chapel and its relics of saints near the Cea River during the *jihads*; and the *Crónica de Alfonso III* (ninth century: attributed to Alfonso III, king of Asturias, who lived c. 852–910) tells how Alfonso I of Asturias (693–757) rebuilt churches in the reconquered cities and returned Christians to their fatherland (*patria*).[92]

It could hardly be otherwise given the injunctions of medieval Islamic law. Thus a legal treatise by the influential Andalusian jurist Ibn Rushd al-Jadd (d. 1126) has Malik answer as follows a question on what to do with the crosses and sacred books of the Christians defeated in *jihad*:

> Question: What should be done with the sacred books that one finds inside the churches of the *Rum* [that is, "Romans," one of the generic names Muslims gave to Christians] in enemy land? What should be done with their golden crosses and other objects one finds?
>
> Answer: The [gold] crosses must be broken up before being distributed [as booty to the Muslim warriors] but one must not distribute them directly. As for their sacred books, one must make them disappear.[93]

In his commentary on Malik's answer, Ibn Rushd al-Jadd clarifies that he has read that the sacred books of the defeated Christians must be burned to make them "disappear"—unless one can erase their content completely so one can then sell the blank pages to make a profit. But if one cannot sell these erased pages, they must be burned.

Archaeology in Spain corroborates all this textual evidence. Thus we have magnificent Visigoth religious treasures found buried along routes leading from southern Spain to the North, confirming what written sources tell us of the Christian population's fear of and flight from the Muslim looting of the churches.[94] What the kingdom of the Visigoths had met was indeed a "lethal and uncompromising enemy."[95]

But such terror and destruction tactics were nothing new. They had been standard procedure in the conquests of the medieval Islamic Caliphate. The Muslim historian Ibn Khaldun describes how an Islamic commander devastated his enemy in Greek Christian North Africa:

> Hassan [Yemenite Muslim commander Hassan Ibn al-Numan] attacked Carthage so violently that the Greeks were forced to flee, some to Sicily and some to Spain. Hassan, having entered the place, did nothing but pillage, kill, and take slaves. He sent detachments to the surrounding areas and gave orders to demolish the city. Muslims, destroying everything that they could, learned that some Greeks and Berbers had reassembled at Satfoura and Bizerte. [The

Muslim leader] attacked them and killed large numbers.... The inhabitants of Ifriqiya were desolated.[96]

The attempted destruction of the pyramid of Giza by the Abbasid caliph al-Mamun (d. 833) illustrates another terror tactic of the Islamic Caliphate's conquests: the destruction of the enemies' monuments. This tactic was prompted not only by the religious teachings of medieval Islam—all constructions of a pre-Islamic past that may overshadow in their beauty or height Islamic buildings or that have religious representations ("idols") must be destroyed—but also by the demoralizing effect it had on the enemies of Islam, and by the need to eliminate any non-Muslim monument that might compete in greatness with a Muslim ruler's constructions. Another dramatic example is the successful demolition by Harun al-Rashid (the celebrated caliph of the *Thousand and One Nights*, the famous collection of mostly Persian and Indian tales written in Arabic) of the extraordinary palace of the Persian king Chosroes (Khosrau or Kasra, d. 579) at the once-great Persian city of Ctesiphon (where al-Madain, Iraq, stands today).[97] Several medieval Muslim historians, among them Abd al-Latif al-Baghdadi (1162–1231), and at least one medieval Christian (Coptic) historian state that the great library of Alexandria was burned with the permission or by order of the second caliph, Umar, in 642 during the Muslim conquest of Egypt. As part of a long lament over the loss of the sciences of the ancients (except the sciences of the Greeks, thanks to Caliph Marwan I and the money he spent to pay Christian translators) in connection with the Islamic conquests, Ibn Khaldun writes that the "sciences" of the Persians were destroyed by Caliph Umar's orders, and that the celebrated sultan Saladin (a Muslim Kurd) destroyed the libraries of his "heretical" Muslim enemies, the Fatimids.[98]

Other Islamic sources confirm such terror tactics during the conquest of the mostly pagan (some were Christian) Berber tribes in North Africa. They tell of battles of "extermination" against the Berber tribes, after which other Berbers, terrified at what happened to those who resisted, submitted to Musa and asked to convert to Islam and join the victorious Muslims. The abundant loot obtained, along with the huge numbers of slaves of both sexes, enticed the faithful from all over the *Umma* (the realm of Islam) to flock to North Africa to join Musa's successful armies:

Musa [Ibn Nusayr] fought with them battles of extermination; he killed myriads of them, and made a surprising number of prisoners...to say nothing of the camels, cows, sheep, horses, mules, grain, and articles of dress.... After this, Musa and his men returned with their prey to Qayrawan, all these forays taking place within the year eighty (A.D. 699–700). And when the soldiers of distant countries inhabited by the Moslems heard of the success which God had granted to Musa's arms, and the immense spoil collected by the men under his orders, they all wished to go to Western Africa, Musa's army being soon reinforced by numbers which increased it to double its original form.... [After one battle], innumerable maidens, inestimable by their beauty and accomplishments, and the daughters of the kings and chiefs, were on this occasion the prize of the victors. When the spoils gained in this battle were to be divided, Musa caused the daughters of the kings to stand before him, and having sent for his son Merwan, he said to him, "Come, O my son! Come and choose among these maids." And Merwan chose among them one that was the daughter of their late king...and who became afterwards the mother of two sons by Merwan.[99]

We also read that the number of captives taken by Musa was greater than in any previous Islamic conquest:

Musa went out against the Berbers, and pursued them far into their native deserts, leaving wherever he went traces of his passage, killing numbers of them, taking thousands of prisoners, and carrying on the work of havoc and destruction.... When the nations inhabiting the dreary plains of Africa saw what had befallen the Berbers of the coast and of the interior, they hastened to ask for peace and place themselves under the obedience of Musa, whom they solicited to enlist them in the ranks of his army.[100]

As the Spanish Arabist Pascual de Gayangos observed: "Owing to the system of warfare adopted by the Arabs, it is not improbable that the number of captives here specified fell into Musa's hands. It appears both from Christian and Arabian authorities that populous towns were not infrequently razed to the ground and their inhabitants, amounting to several thousands, led into captivity."[101] Al-Hakam relates that the Muslim leader Hassan had captured, in the words of a contemporary of Hassan, the poet Nusayb, "young female Berber slaves of unparalleled beauty, some of which were worth a thousand dinars."[102] Al-Hakam confirms that up to one hundred thousand slaves were captured by Musa and his son and nephew during the conquest of North Africa. In Tangiers, Musa enslaved all the Berber inhabitants. Near Qayrawan, Musa sacked a fortress and took with him all the children as slaves.

The *Byzantine-Arabic Chronicle* of 743, which is consistently friendly toward Islam, records similar Muslim shock-and-awe tactics in Greek Christian North Africa: "[Muslim commander Habedela] reached Tripoli and with his army he attacked Cidamo and Leptis Magna. After having destroyed many cities, he subjugated to Saracen power all these devastated provinces. Afterwards, still thirsty with blood, he moved on...and all the army of the Mauritanians fled and all the nobility of Africa with [Greek] Count Gregory at its head was completely annihilated. Then Habedela, abundantly loaded with treasure, returned to Egypt."[103]

The seventh-century chronicle of the Coptic bishop John of Nikiû, which records the Muslim conquest of the lands of Greek Christian North Africa, echoes the terror tactics mentioned in other accounts:

> And thereupon the Moslem made their entry into Nakius [*sic*], and took possession, and finding no soldiers (to offer resistance), they proceeded to put to the sword all whom they found in the streets and in the churches, men, women, and infants, and they showed mercy to none. And after they had captured (this) city, they marched against other localities and sacked them and put all they found to the sword. And they came also to the city of Sa, and there they found Esqutaws and his people in a vineyard, and the Moslem seized them and put them to the sword.[104]

In 646 Muslim armies set fire to the great Greek Christian city of Alexandria, killing its men and enslaving its women and children—as punishment for the Christians' rebelling after having signed an agreement of submission in 642 to become *dhimmis*.[105]

Other Christian Coptic sources from the late twelfth century also mention Muslim burnings of churches and convents in Egypt. On one occasion, the Christian Copts hid a column commemorating the Virgin Mary and the child Jesus to avoid its destruction by the warriors of the newly hegemonic iconoclastic religion. These sources add that the invading Muslim armies were accompanied by more than a hundred Companions of the Prophet, which scholars agree indicates that the invasion was motivated by the religious mandate to wage a religious war—*jihad*—to force the infidels to submit to Islam. (Recall that some of the Muslim chronicles of the conquest of Spain similarly mention the presence among the invading Muslim armies of wise men—the *tabiun*—who had known at least some of the Companions of Muhammad, and whose presence likewise indicates that the conquest of Spain was a *jihad*.)

These details are significant because in general the Coptic sources narrate the Muslim invasion of Egypt with relative neutrality, since the Muslim conquerors, following their standard tactic of divide and conquer, treated the Copts better than the Muslims treated the ruling Christian Greeks, who persecuted the Christian Copts and who resisted the Islamic invasion.[106]

Another Coptic source from the late tenth century tells that, following earlier instructions from their "leader" Muhammad, the Muslim conquerors spared those who submitted to Islam without resistance. (Conversion was unnecessary as long as the submission of the Christian infidels was achieved; conversion was impractical, because it would mean the end of the taxation of the *dhimmis*, off which Muslims were supposed to live indefinitely, as the second caliph, Umar, had observed.)[107] But per Muhammad's instructions, the Muslim conquerors sacked the cities that resisted and enslaved their people. Therefore they killed the resisting Greeks in Upper Egypt and their commander. The Greeks that escaped "the massacre" fled to Alexandria.

Islamic forces employed similar shock-and-awe tactics in their conquest of the Persian Empire. If Persian villages and cities capitulated peacefully, they would receive *dhimmi* status. But if they resisted, the villages were sacked, their men killed, and their women and children enslaved. The Muslim conquerors would chase down the defeated armies until they were utterly destroyed and their surviving soldiers enslaved. If Persian *dhimmis* revolted, their cities were put to the torch, and likewise their men were killed and their women and children enslaved.[108]

In the lands of the Christian Greek Roman Empire in Syria, Palestine, and Caesarea, both Islamic and Christian sources tell of similar methods. Al-Waqidi (747–823), one of the earliest and most famous historians of the Islamic conquests, tells of the strict measures taken by the great Muslim leader Umar, a Companion of Muhammad who became the second caliph in 634, only two years after Muhammad's death. Umar is said to have warned one of his men: "Whoever enters our Din [Muslim religious path] and then apostatizes will be killed by us. Beware of leaving Islam. Beware that I would hear that you have sexually approached the sister whom you have divorced, for then I will stone you to death."[109]

Al-Waqidi narrates other stories that illustrate the Islamic conquerors' methods. In one narrative, a pious Muslim leader named Khalid defeated a Christian force. He beheaded seven hundred Christians and took three hundred prisoner. He then offered peace to the surviving Christians if only they converted to Islam. But the Christians declined, requesting instead to pay ransom. Al-Waqidi describes what followed: "'We will strike your necks to terrorize Allah's enemy,' retorted Khalid, who proved true to his word."

In another narrative, pious Khalid encountered a Christian Arab who pretended to be a Muslim. But Khalid suspected the man of being, as he put it, "a cross worshipper" spying for the Christian fighters. Khalid then tested the man by asking him to recite two chosen passages from the Quran. The Christian Arab could not. At this point Khalid offered the man conversion to Islam or death (Arabs were not allowed to become *dhimmis*). The Arab man then proclaimed, "I bear witness that there is no deity besides Allah and that Muhammad is His Messenger." (This effective method of testing potential infidels has been used by Muslim fighters down to our times.) Khalid was in fact paying attention to a letter that Umar had sent to all his troops: "Invade Syria.... If they offer to surrender, then accept, otherwise fight them. Send a spy to Antioch and be on guard against the Christian Arabs."

But the conquerors could also win by using "kindness," as al-Waqidi puts it. Thus he reports that after some towns in Christian Syria had been raided, the Muslim warriors came back loaded with loot and hundreds of captives—men, women, and children. The captives pleaded for mercy from the Muslim commander, who asked them if they would be willing to pay the *jizya* and the land tax. The Christians agreed and the Muslim commander then returned to them their possessions and freedom, but of course under Islamic rule. In this manner, al-Waqidi writes, "other Romans came to [commander] Abu Ubaydah seeking safety from the Muslims upon payment of the *jizya* and the land-tax." In yet another narrative, a priest leading a Christian community asked of the Muslims warriors what they wanted. The priest was then told that he had "three options; either Islam or Jizyah or the sword."

Christian historian Michael the Syrian (1126–1199), Jacobite patriarch of Antioch, records several accounts of the Muslim devastation during the conquest of Palestine and Caesarea, which were also part of the Christian Greek Roman Empire.[110]

Ibn Khaldun pointed out how the use of terror was fundamental in the Islamic conquests from the beginning:

> One understands Muḥammad's statement: "I was helped through the terror (that befell the enemy)...." (The same fact explains) Muhammad's victory with small numbers over the polytheists during his lifetime, and the victories of the Muslims during the Muslim conquests after (Muhammad's death). God took care of His Prophet. He threw terror into the hearts of the unbelievers.... Terror in the hearts of their enemies was why there were so many routs during the Muslim conquests.[111]

No wonder that Eastern Christian religious polemics against Islam, from the seventh century on, uniformly include the argument that Muslims use violence to extend their religion, and that early Spanish religious polemics against Islam also consistently point out the use of violence by its followers.[112]

Thus the three options Musa gave to the Hispano-Visigoths were the standard ones Muslim conquerors offered Christians: (1) convert to Islam, (2) submit as *dhimmis* to Islamic supremacy and pay the tribute (*jizya*) expressly intended to humiliate infidels and remind them of their submission, or (3) be killed (in the case of men) or enslaved (in the case of nonfighting women and children).[113]

Here lies the source of the conflicting interpretations of the Muslim conquest of Spain—those who claim that the Muslim takeover was largely "peaceful," achieved by means of "pacts," and others who claim it was largely "violent."[114] The Muslim conquerors indeed offered peace to those who surrendered without fighting, though under Muslim domination and strict conditions—but they swiftly destroyed those who resisted. Those who surrendered to the Muslims' "peaceful" system did so knowing full well the consequences if they resisted. The Muslim conquest, then, mixed brutal force and peaceful pacts.[115] The second, however, were inseparable from and a consequence of the first. And, as we have seen, the Muslim forces reserved the right to abrogate "peaceful pacts" whenever it was advantageous to do so because, as the legal scholar Majid Khadduri pointed out, "the normal relationship between Muslim and non-Muslim communities is a state of hostility" until Islam achieves hegemony.

For the Christian faithful, what Musa and his Muslim forces established was a "savage kingdom" (*regnum efferum conlocant*), as the *Chronica mozarabica* of 754 puts it.[116] Alfonso X's *History of Spain* summarizes the Muslim conquest as described in the medieval Christian sources:

> The sanctuaries were destroyed; the churches were broken down.... They threw out from the churches the crosses and the altars, the holy oils and the books and the things which were honored by Christendom, all was scattered and discarded.... The enemies ravaged the land, they burned the houses, they killed the men, they burned the cities, the trees, the vineyards and anything they found green they cut. So much grew this plague that there remained in Spain no good village or city...that was not burned or brought down or taken over by the Moors; and the cities that they could not conquer they tricked them and conquered them with false treaties.[117]

A Muslim chronicle makes the point even more forcefully: according to al-Hakam, so awesome was the conquest of Spain that, when Musa wrote to his caliph, he described it as "not a conquest, but the Judgment Day."[118]

RENAMING THE CONQUERED LAND

The very name that Muslims gave to the land they had conquered—*al-Andalus*—reflects the domination strategy at work.

As noted, the name *España* (Spain) evolved from the Romans' Latin name *Hispania* (possibly derived from a Carthaginian word). It is not surprising that the Islamic conquerors renamed the land. Changing geographical names in occupied territories has been a standard colonialist move, regardless of the faith of the conquerors. Islamic armies, however, executed the maneuver with unusual thoroughness. Everywhere they went, Muslims replaced ancient names with new ones. Perhaps most famously, in the twentieth century they replaced the Christian Greek Κωνσταντινούπολις (Constantinople, or the City of Constantine) with the word *Istanbul* (itself a Turkish garbling of a Greek phrase).[119] Beyond that, the Turkish names *Iskece* and *Gumulcine* replaced the Greek Xanthi and Komotini, respectively; Armenia's Amid became *Diyarbakir*; Jerusalem became the Arabic *al-Quds*; the Hebrew Hebron transformed into *al-Khalil*; Bethshemesh (the House of the Sun) became *Ain Shams* (the Eye of the Sun); Bethhoron (the House of the Light) became *Beit 'Ur* (the House of the Blind); Bethlehem became *Beit Luhm*; and the Latin name Africa the Muslim conquerors changed to *Ifriquiya*. They renamed the river Baetis as *al-Wadi al-Kabir* (Guadalquivir). And they turned the Greek "The Pillars of Hercules" into *Gibt al-Tariq*, which led to today's Gibraltar.

Although the etymology of *al-Andalus* is uncertain, the Spanish Arabist and historian J. Vallvé Bermejo has argued that the word may be an Arabic garbling of the Greek words for "Atlantis island," Ατλαντία νησος. The term would have come to early Islam in the Middle East via the Christian Greek Roman Empire, which occupied southeastern Spain from 552 to 624. And Greek colonies had existed in Spain since at least the eighth century B.C. This origin would put *al-Andalus* in the same politico-linguistic category as *Istanbul*, also derived from Greek.[120]

In Spain, the Islamic conquerors proceeded not only to rename the land but also to Arabize as many ancient names in the region as they could. Today one can still find throughout southern Spain the toponymic results of this Arabization, which, to adapt the words of an anthropologist, served medieval Islam well in the "formation and enactment of its colonial-national historical imagination and...the substantiation of its territorial claims."[121]

The problem for the Islamic conquerors was that the Latin *Hispania/Spannia/Spania* had sufficient historical weight and political importance to endure for centuries after the conquest. It is not uncommon for conquered populations to cling to their ancient names; this tenacity was evident throughout the Islamic empire as various peoples resisted the Islamization of their lands.[122]

Medieval Christians considered the lands Islam had conquered to be part of Spain, not part of Islam, and therefore not as *al-Andalus*. Their chronicles refer to "Spannia," avoiding the Arabic term.[123] The mid-thirteenth-century *Poema de Fernán González*, which sings in medieval Spanish the deeds of a tenth-century Castilian hero, specifies that Castile is the best of the lands of *Spannia* and that Fernán González fought even against the Christian kings of *Spannia*.[124] In fact, Christians in the North of Spain initially referred to Christian *dhimmis* in Islamic Spain as *Spani*—that is, as Spaniards. "Until the twelfth century," the historian Miguel Angel Ladero Quesada writes, "Christians, especially those in the Pyrenean area, frequently called the lands of 'al-Andalus' Hispania, and so did the 'gothicists' from the kingdom of Leon, since they considered it unliberated territory."[125] Vallvé Bermejo and fellow historian Reinhart Dozy have pointed out that the Latin chronicles by Christians in the North of Spain designated as *Spania* precisely the land that Muslims had conquered.[126]

Significantly, these political references to the land as Spain occurred despite the fact that in the Middle Ages there was no single "kingdom of Spain." Nonetheless, in 1077 Alfonso VI of León and Castile called himself "*imperator totius hispaniae*" (emperor of the whole of Spain). Another chronicle calls Sancho II of León and Castile (1036–1072) "*rex totius Castelle et dominator Hispaniae*" (king of Castile and dominator of Spain). A chronicle from 883 tells that Alfonso III of Asturias will reign "in all the Spains." Christian historians as early as 754, in the *Chronica mozarabica*, were lamenting "the loss of Spain."[127] Saint Isidore (560–636), bishop of Seville, wrote a *Laus Spaniae*, a praise of Spain. Julian of Toledo (d. 690), a prelate of Jewish origin who became bishop of all Visigoth Spain, wrote a *History of King Wamba* (*Historia Wambae*), which has been considered a "nationalistic work" defending the *patria* and the people of Spain in contrast to those of such "foreign lands" as *Francia*.[128]

Muslims themselves often used the word *Spain* rather than *al-Andalus*. The Arabic geographer al-Idrisi (d. 1165) referred to the land that Muslims had conquered as *Isbania*.[129] In the fourteenth century, Ibn Khaldun (1332–1406) told of his travels to Spain, not al-Andalus.[130] The earlier sources cited by al-Maqqari referred to the land as *Ishbaniah*.[131] Other Muslim historians also spoke frequently of *Isbanians* and *Isbania*. In chronicling the Umayyad Abd al-Rahman I's violent takeover of Abbasid Islamic Spain, the historian al-Tabari referred to Spain as *Spain*.[132] Recounting the reign of the Umayyads, Córdoban historian Ibn Hayyan (987–1076) referred to *Hispania*.[133]

Archaeology confirms this Muslim usage: numismatics tells us that the earliest Muslim coins in Spain, dating from the first half of the eighth century, a few years after the conquest, show on one side the name *Alandalus* in Arabic and on the other, for proper identification, the Latin abbreviation *SPAN*—that is, Spania.[134]

At no point do these medieval documents, either Christian or Muslim, use the now academically fashionable term *Iberia*.

How, then, did the name *al-Andalus* gain currency in later centuries? One factor involved Islam's ongoing domination strategies. Later Muslim historians, poets, and other intellectuals, who were usually at the service of their rulers, undertook efforts to call the conquered Spanish territory *al-Andalus* and praise it as an earthly paradise.[135] Today, many Western historians, no friends of either Christianity or the idea of "Spain," pointedly avoid using the term *Islamic Spain*, preferring *al-Andalus*, just as they prefer *medieval Iberia* to *medieval Spain*.

THE CHRISTIAN RECONQUEST

Although Islamic forces conquered the land swiftly, they never quelled entirely the resistance in Spain's northwestern mountains. The tough native Asturian and Galician populations in this region joined with those Hispano-Visigoths who had fled the invasion. Felipe Maíllo Salgado observes that Muslim chronicles called the Asturian rulers "kings of the Goths," and he argues that these Christian leaders from early on had a "program of re-conquest," even before Christian *dhimmis* fleeing Islamic Spain began to arrive in the ninth century.[136] Over the next several hundred years these Christian groups intermittently fought against Islam (and frequently among themselves—sometimes with Muslim help). As a Muslim historian lamented in the thirteenth century, these at first seemingly insignificant and fugitive Christians increased their numbers over time, until they chased Islam away from both the Northwest and Castile.[137]

A key turning point came when the great Muslim leader Abu Amir Muhammad al-Mansur died in 1002. Keeping the child caliph as a puppet ruler, al-Mansur had established a ruthless military dictatorship, which for a while maintained the strength of the Caliphate of Córdoba. His death, however, brought infighting. The Caliphate eventually broke up into several petty and tyrannical kingdoms, or *taifas*, ruled by families of Arabs, Berbers, and freed Muslim white slaves—"Slavs" or *saqaliba*, many of whom were indeed of Slavic origin, as were the rulers of Almeria, Badajoz, Valencia, and Murcia, and also Mujahid (his name means "fighter in a *jihad*") Yusuf al-Amir al-Siqlabi, the very capable founder of the *taifa* of Denia. These little kingdoms did not have the military strength of the former Caliphate of Córdoba.

From the beginning, rulers of Islamic Spain had relied on armies of foreigners notable for their military prowess and Islamic fervor (such as Berbers), on armies of mercenaries (Berbers, but some Christians as well), on slave warriors (many black Africans but also white slave warriors, the *saqaliba*), and on "clients" (*mawla*) who often had been taken captive in war, had converted to Islam, and then had been freed from slavery, and who were therefore indistinguishable from emancipated slaves. (Tariq was a *mawla* of Musa Ibn Nusayr.) By the eleventh century, the military historians David Nicolle and Angus McBride point out, "the local elite were largely demilitarized, the army being drawn almost entirely from European slaves and 'new' Berbers from North Africa."[138] As the historian of Islam Patricia Crone has observed, the numbers of slaves the Arabs took during their conquests were "staggering."[139]

But these were not always stable alliances. As early as 741, the Berbers had revolted, unhappy with the Arab rulers' allocation of the best land to the Arabs (Arabs stood at the top of the social hierarchy, and therefore even those who were not Arab often tried to pass themselves as such). The Islamic rulers eventually ran out of new lands easy to conquer and from which to loot or otherwise extract wealth and slaves. The wealth that they formerly extracted from the *dhimmis* of Islamic Spain had largely dried up because few *dhimmis* were left. Therefore Andalusian rulers after al-Mansur lacked the resources to pay skilled mercenaries or to acquire slaves to breed for war, at least on the scale of earlier times.

But Spain's Christian armies were gaining strength. These forces were made up of hardy free peasant-soldiers and townspeople's militias from northern Spain, combined with a social class of noble knights born and bred for combat on heavy warhorses—the seemingly invincible Rodrigo Díaz de Vivar, "El Cid," was the most famous of these warriors. The Christian kingdoms' feudal structures, which had become more developed over time, helped produce these superior fighting forces animated by a strong religious faith.[140]

By 1085 this Christian *Reconquista*—a term today's multicultural historians question or deride[141]—had achieved a great triumph: Alfonso VI of León and Castile retook the ancient capital of the Visigoth Christian kingdom, Toledo. This was less than a decade after Alfonso declared himself *imperator totius hispaniae*—emperor of the whole of Spain.

The Muslim rulers of the *taifa* kingdoms continued to face challenges. They were already heavily taxing their subjects to maintain their ostentatious way of life—their harems, their palaces, their slaves, and their courts of poets and intellectuals who sang their praises. As Ibn Khaldun reminds us, this heavy taxation, combined with the tyrannical rulers' often un-Islamic behavior, had by 1088 caused the Muslim people and the *ulama* (Muslim religious scholars) of Spain, North Africa, and even Iraq to support and justify theologically first the Berber Almoravid takeover of the *taifas* (1088–1138) and later that of another Berber confederation, the Almohads (1172–1212).[142] The Almohads in particular have been demonized by admirers of Islamic Spain as fanatical Muslims who ended the wonderful Islamic tolerance of other religions prevailing in al-Andalus. As we will see, this belief does not stand up to scrutiny.[143]

By the early thirteenth century, the *Reconquista* was practically complete. In what is probably the best study of the subject, Felipe Maíllo Salgado lists the causes for the end of al-Andalus: the more cohesive social organization of the Christians, their superior fighting "efficiency," their rootedness in their ancestral land—as opposed to the Andalusian Muslims' reliance on abstractions (the *umma* or community of believers and the Muslims' genealogical links)—and al-Andalus's ethnic and religious diversity (*"abigarramiento étnico y confesional* of Arabs, Berbers, Hispanics—some Islamicized, others *dhimmis*—Slavs, African blacks, etc."), which made it socially and ideologically weaker when compared to the Christian kingdoms.[144]

On July 16, 1212, a Christian army defeated the Almohads at the important Battle of Las Navas de Tolosa. As the historian Francisco García Fitz explains in his masterful study of the battle, the Almohad army was a very large, heterogeneous force, made up of Berbers, tough black slave warriors (the "Imesebelen," who were chained together as an unbreakable guard around the Almohad caliph's tent), Arabs, Turkic mounted archers, Andalusian Muslim levies (made up of the descendants of the Hispano-Romans and Visigoths who had converted to Islam and of the descendants of the Muslim invaders), *mujahideen* (volunteer religious fighters—jihadists—from all over the Islamic world), and even Christian mercenaries and defectors. The kings of Castile, Navarre, and Aragon formed the Christian coalition army, which included Catalan warriors; noble knights; the knights of the military orders of Santiago, Calatrava, and the Temple; the free militias of the Castilian towns; and 150 volunteer noble knights from the rest of Europe—all united under the banner of the Crusade that Pope Innocent III had declared against Islamic Spain.[145] Tradition has it that, at the battle's decisive moment, when all seemed lost, the display of the standard of the Black Virgin from the sanctuary of Rocamadour, one of the stops on the Camino de Santiago, rallied the Christians and led them to victory. For a long time afterward, July 16 was celebrated in the Spanish Catholic calendar as the day of the "Triumph of the Holy Cross." Pope John XXIII abolished the festivity as part of the liturgical reforms of the Second Vatican Council.[146]

In 1248 Ferdinand III (The Saint) of Castile took the kingdom of Seville. Afterward, only the small kingdom of Granada, in southern Spain, remained in Muslim hands. Although the *Reconquista* is usually recorded as ending in 1492, when the Christian monarchs Isabella of Castile and Ferdinand of Aragon defeated the kingdom of Granada, the fall of Seville in 1248 effectively marked the end of Islamic control in Spain.

Nonetheless, for nearly five and a half centuries (although not seven or eight centuries, as is often repeated), Islam had dominated a good part of Spain. The subject Christian population (the *dhimmis*) had gradually fled (or "migrated," as some academics prefer) to the North, or converted, or been expelled to North Africa. The cultural loss was immense. By the ninth century in Merida, none of the few remaining Christian *dhimmis* could read a church inscription in Latin; the Muslim rulers took the inscription down and carried it to Córdoba as a trophy of Islamic supremacy. In the same century in Córdoba, Eulogius (a future martyr to the Umayyad ruler) lamented the preference of many young *dhimmis* for things Muslim, including the Arabic language. By 1085, few Christians were left south of Toledo. When Aragon's king, Jaime the Conqueror, annexed the Muslim kingdom of Valencia in 1238, he found no Christians there.[147] When Ferdinand and Isabella conquered Granada in 1492, no Christian *dhimmis* were found in the city.

But this process of Islamization of the existing Hispano-Roman-Visigoth Christian culture was reversed over time. As the *Reconquista* progressed, Christians from the North, as well as those Christian *dhimmis* and Jews who had once fled to the North from Islamic Spain, repopulated the land. Many Muslims escaped to North Africa. Others chose to remain and were allowed for a few centuries to practice their religion under Christian rule and were called *mudéjares* by the Christians (for whom it meant "tributary," but as Gerard Wiegers and Hans Wehr point out, the word derives from the Arabic *mudajjan*, meaning "tamed" or "domesticated," and some Maliki jurists considered *mudéjares* vile Muslims for accepting to live under Christian rule).[148]

After a number of unsuccessful *mudéjar* uprisings over the centuries, however, the Spanish authorities feared—with justification—the collusion of these Muslims with the increasingly powerful Islamic empire of the Ottoman Turks, with Muslims in North Africa (in *Don Quixote*, Cervantes has one of his characters point out that the king of Fez used *mudéjares* as his preferred warriors), and even with other enemies of the Spanish crown such as England, France, and the Protestants of Europe.[149] Therefore the Spanish authorities gave the *mudéjares* the choice of either exile or assimilation through their conversion to Christianity (centuries earlier, the Almohads had given an analogous choice to Christians and for analogous reasons: convert or be expelled from al-Andalus). Many left for North Africa, but thousands converted, many of them only to avoid deportation.

These presumably converted Muslims were called *moriscos*. But many if not most continued to practice Islam in secret, wear Muslim dress and veils, celebrate Ramadan, and speak Arabic among themselves. Several *morisco* uprisings occurred, involving the stoning, dismembering, beheading, impaling, and burning alive of Christians.[150] The Spanish army put down these uprisings with great difficulty. Finally, between

1609 and 1614, the Spanish authorities expelled the *moriscos*, most of them to North Africa (though modern research indicates that the expulsion was not carried out as thoroughly as it was once thought). The Spanish authorities reasoned that these hundreds of thousands of former Muslims, with their very high birth rates,[151] constituted a dangerous fifth column in collusion with the enemies of Spain (a reasoning analogous to that used earlier by Almoravids and Almohads in their decision to expel the Christian *dhimmis* from al-Andalus).

Those enemies posed real threats. Agents of England and France had offered cooperation to the leaders of these former Muslims for a possible general uprising. Some *moriscos* were in contact with Muslims in North Africa. Pirates from Muslim North Africa continued to raid the Mediterranean coasts of Europe in search of loot and Christian slaves. (Cervantes himself was captured at sea in 1575 by Muslim pirates; he was kept as a slave in Algiers for five years before being ransomed by the friars of the Trinitarian Order.)[152] Also, *moriscos* used envoys to communicate with the sultan of the Ottoman Empire—the new caliph of Islam. The Ottoman Turks' Islamic empire had defeated the Christian Serbs at Kosovo in 1389, conquered Greek Constantinople in 1453, subjugated the Christian Greeks (a subjugation that would last for four hundred years), and almost conquered Vienna in 1529 (Siege of Vienna). Now this Muslim empire concentrated its awesome military power against the heartland of Europe.

2

THE EFFECTS OF THE *JIHAD*

The Destruction of a Nascent Civilization

The failure of the Visigothic state...was also reflected in its technological atony, which was at the core of the elite's inability to adapt to any
ecology other than that with which it was originally familiar: the men
of the woods never strayed too far from there.

> —*Thomas F. Glick, Professor of Medieval History and Director of
> the Institute for Medieval History at Boston University,* Islamic and
> Christian Spain in the Early Middle Ages *(Princeton, NJ: Princeton
> University Press, 1979; rpt. New York: Brill, 2005), 31*

[A] great empire would replace the Romans in Spain, but it would be a
Muslim empire rather than the Visigoth dynasty.... [Muslim conquer-
ors] accomplished what Visigoths never could: they lifted Spain from
her Dark Ages gloom and depression, making her worthy of Isidore's
boast: "the pride and the ornament of the world, the most illustrious
part of the earth."

> —*Chris Lowney,* A Vanished World: Muslims, Christians, and Jews
> in Medieval Spain *(New York: Oxford University Press, 2006), 26*

European culture had, since the sack of Rome in A.D. 455, gone into a
dramatic decline known as the Dark Ages. Middle Eastern culture, by
contrast, was flowering, with the added impetus provided by the new
religion of Islam.

> —*Antony Wild,* Coffee: A Dark History *(New York: W. W. Norton,
> 2005), 30*

THE WORKS OF the Persian al-Tabari (839–923) and other Muslim historians indicate that the conquest of the Spanish Visigoth kingdom during the early years of the eighth century was part of an Islamic onslaught against Christendom. That onslaught targeted the lands of the former Latin (or Western) Roman Empire, which included *Hispania*, and the lands of the Christian Greek Roman Empire, whose capital was in Constantinople.[1] This strategic "pincer" movement ultimately failed: Muslim Spain under the Umayyads became independent from and a rival to the Abbasid Caliphate and even carried on mutually beneficial commercial and cultural exchanges with the Christian Greek Roman emperors in Constantinople. But the Muslim conquest had powerful effects on Spain.

Most important, it interrupted the process of cultural and ethnic fusion of Christian Hispano-Romans and Visigoths, and therefore the full emergence of a new Christian Hispano-Visigoth civilization. The ethnic fusion began with the laws of King Leovigild (reigned 568–586), known as *Código de Leovigildo*, or *Codex Revisus*, which allowed the intermarriage of Visigoths and Hispano-Romans. The cultural fusion began with the Third Council of Toledo (589) and the conversion, the same year, of Leovigild's son, King Recared, and his people from Arianism (a Christian heresy reflecting the teachings of the presbyter Arius) to Catholicism, which was the religion of most Hispano-Romans. Joseph Cardinal Ratzinger (later Pope Benedict XVI) praised this Third Toledan Council as a milestone in the union of Europe through the strength of the Christian spirit—the union, that is, of the Christian citizens of the former Latin (Western) Roman Empire with the northern nations that had taken it over. Indeed, French historians such as Jacques Fontaine and Christine Pellistrandi have pointed out how much medieval Europe owes to Visigoth Spain.[2]

Nevertheless, historians often gloss over Islam's destruction of Hispano-Visigoth Spain. The Islamic invasion is frequently described as bringing enlightenment to a cultural wasteland—the so-called European Dark Ages. Many historians insist on how much more cultured the indigenous Hispano-Romans were compared with the "barbaric" Visigoths.

Never mind that modern archaeology has confirmed that the "Dark Ages" were less dark than is usually proclaimed and quite enlightened when compared with Muslim culture prior to the Arabs' conquest of the Middle East and North Africa;[3] or that Spain was under Roman control and influence longer than any Western land outside of Italy and produced more Latin writers and emperors than any other Roman province; or that the Visigoths were the most Romanized of all the peoples that took over the Latin Roman Empire and that they played an important role in the making of Western civilization;[4] or that Visigoth leaders spoke Latin and had spent generations in military and political service to Rome; or that Visigoth warriors, fighting side by side with the Romans, were decisive in the Latin Roman Empire's victory over the Huns of Attila at the Battle of the Catalaunian Plains in 451; or that recent discoveries of urban archaeology have underlined the importance of Visigoth architecture in Spain, its magnificent metallurgy, its great city of Recópolis, the innovative and transformational nature of Visigoth culture, and how it provided the basis for the construction of medieval Europe;[5] or that Visigoth law was no more "brutal" than contemporary medieval Islamic or Jewish law; or that Visigoth women enjoyed a degree of autonomy in the public sphere not available to a free Muslim married woman (*muhsana*) because of the greater modesty of *muhsana* life in medieval Islam; or that the Visigoths had several female monarchs who played important political roles in the Visigoth kingdom.[6]

Overlooked, too, is that the Visigothic Code of Law was, for its time, an impressive document that combined Visigoth practices with Roman law and Christian principles, and that evidences a guiding desire to limit the power of government many centuries before Magna Carta. (The following headings in title 1 of book 2 give an idea of this concern with freedom from tyrannical rule: "II. The Royal Power, as well as the Entire Body of the People, should be Subject to the Majesty of the Law. III. It is Permitted to No One to be Ignorant of the Law.... V. How the Avarice of the King should be Restrained.")[7]

The Islamic invasion of Spain in the eighth century differed qualitatively from that of Visigoths in the fifth century. By the time Visigoth forces entered the Spain of the Latin Roman Empire in 415 to help the Romans militarily against such Germanic nations as the Sueves (or Suevi), Alans, and Vandals, they had been serving the empire for generations, were culturally Romanized, and considered themselves the rightful inheritors to the empire. Moreover, unlike Muslims, the Visigoths had not been motivated by their religious faith to conquer the land and force its inhabitants to convert, or submit and pay a particular tax (*jizya*) designed to humiliate them and remind them of their submission, or die.[8] In fact, the Visigoths did not make their faith (Arianism, a form of Christianity that orthodox Christians considered a heresy) the dominant religion of the land; they eventually converted to the existing and prevalent form of Christianity, Catholicism. The contrasts become clear with language as well: the Visigoths were linguistically close to the Hispano-Romans, since they spoke an Indo-European language, and their leaders and eventually the people at large adopted the form of spoken Latin used by the Roman soldiers and merchants ("vulgar" Latin, from which Spanish evolved); the Islamic invaders imposed their own Semitic language, Arabic, as the hegemonic language of the land. As Indo-Europeans, the Visigoths were also ethnically close to the Hispano-Romans; the Arab and Berber invaders were not.

All these factors made it easier for the Visigoths to unify Spain culturally.

"Filled with Treasures"

Despite the bubonic plague, locusts, drought, and civil wars that ravaged Spain in the years before the Muslim conquest,[9] the Catholic kingdom of the Visigoths still presented itself as a wonderland to the uncultured eighth-century Berber invaders. Medieval Muslim chronicles tell of the astonishment the Islamic warriors experienced at the splendor of Toledo, Seville, Córdoba, Mérida, and other Visigoth cities. They also tell us that the Muslim armies' sacking of Spain was stupendous. Christian chronicles corroborate these accounts, as does the archaeological evidence of the treasures Christians buried before fleeing the invaders.

A Muslim chronicle attributed to Abu Jaafar al-Kortobi recounts that the traitor Count "Ylian" (Julian, the usual name given to the Greek Roman lord Urbanus) enticed Musa Ibn Nusayr to conquer Spain by describing it as a land "filled with treasures of all kinds, whose inhabitants would make very handsome slaves, a country abounding in springs, gardens, rivers, and a land yielding every description of fruit and plants."[10] According to al-Kortobi, the Muslim leader Tariq confirmed Julian's account when he found, near the Visigoth capital of Toledo, "one and twenty copies of the Torah, the Gospels, and the Psalms, as well as a copy of the book of Abraham, and another of that of Moses [probably Deuter-onomy]." The account continues:

> He found likewise five-and-twenty royal diadems, beautifully orna-mented with jewels, one for each of the kings who had ruled over the country.... He found also...books treating of the manner of using plants, minerals, and animals, advantageously for man, besides many wonderful talismans, the work of ancient philosophers, and another work on the great art [which teaches the construction of tal-ismans], and its roots and elixirs; all these precious objects, together with an immense quantity of rubies and other coloured gems, stored in golden and silver urns of beautiful workmanship, and ornamented with large pearls, were the fruits of Tarik's conquest.[11]

Tariq and other Muslim leaders helped themselves to these "fruits" of their conquest. Al-Kortobi reports that when Musa went to Damascus to pay homage to the caliph, he brought with him "all the spoil...consisting of thirty skins full of gold and silver coin, necklaces of inestimable value, pearls, rubies, topazes, and emeralds, besides costly robes of all sorts; he was followed by eleven hundred prisoners, men, women, and children, of whom four hundred were princes of the royal blood."[12] Such looting and enslavement is reported also in the Christian *Chronica mozarabica* of 754, written only a few decades after the Islamic conquest.[13]

Many Muslim accounts confirm this rampant looting. According to the chronicler al-Hakam, the conquerors loaded themselves with booty and committed numerous "frauds."[14] One of the earliest Muslim chroni-clers of Islamic Spain, al-Razi, tells of the looting of Toledo: "There were no cities nor castles in Spain where Tariq found and took more jewels and a greater treasure than in Toledo."[15] Al-Razi observes that a Visigoth bridge over the Tagus River "was so well built that there was nothing like it in the whole of Spain"—and that a Muslim leader ordered it destroyed. According to the chronicler al-Maqqari, as late as 1145 a Muslim ruler pulled down and melted a great bronze statue the Visigoths had erected in the city of Cádiz, thinking that the statue, which Muslims considered an "idol," was made of gold.[16]

All these chronicles point not only to the rapaciousness of the Muslim conquerors but also to the splendor of the Visigoth society modern

historians dismiss as barbaric. Similarly, historian Ibn al-Qutiyya narrates that Musa's men found in a treasure hidden by fleeing Christians "a
cascade of emeralds and rubies in such abundance as no man had seen
before and were astonished. Such a quantity of precious stones were there
that they exclaimed: 'Let us send for Emir Musa so he can see the treasures with his own eyes, otherwise he will not believe us.' So they sent for
Musa, and when he came and saw the treasure he was speechless at its
size and value."[17] (Again, such written references to buried Visigoth treasures are confirmed by archaeology.) Al-Qutiyya writes that after all their
looting, Muslim warriors were so full of booty that they paid no attention
to a mere tapestry embroidered with gold, silver, pearls, and rubies. The
Akhbar Machmua narrates that in a raid on Algeciras, Musa captured
more prisoners and booty than they had ever seen before.[18]

According to the Muslim historian al-Maqqari, a Muslim chronicler
describes the former Visigoth palace in Córdoba as full of "wonderful
remains of the Greeks, Romans, and Goths." The chronicler adds, "The
interior apartments were so magnificently decorated as to dazzle with the
beauty of their ornaments the eyes of beholders."[19] The Muslim beholders were mostly Berbers from North Africa, who formed the bulk of the
invading armies and who had never before contemplated such a degree
of civilization. "This [Visigoth] palace," the chronicler continues, "the
Kalifs of the house of Merwan [meaning the Umayyad rulers of Spain,
who belonged to the Umayyad caliph Marwan's family] chose for their
residence."

A work attributed to Ibn Qutaybah al-Dinawari says that the immense
booty Musa took included not merely slaves, jewels, and precious metals
but also Christian relics. This account describes a stupendous "jeweled
table," the craftsmanship of which Muslims had never seen before, made
of "pure gold and silver mixed," ornamented "with three rows of inestimable jewels, one of large pearls, another of rubies, and a third of emeralds."[20] "Nothing," the Muslim author concludes, "could be conceived
more rich or beautiful." This "table," as the Islamic conquerors called it—
and which they carried away after their colossal sacking of Toledo—may
have been part of the altar furnishings of the city's great cathedral, and on
it would have rested the Gospels while they were not being read at Mass.[21]

The chronicler Ibn al-Faradhi reveals the fate of other Christian
monuments: "I was told by Abu Mohammed Ath-thegri [*sic*], that Kar-

kashunah [Carcassone] is a city distant five-and-twenty miles from Barcelona, and that when the Muslims conquered it, they found a magnificent church, called by the Christians Santa Maria, wherein were seven
pillars of massive silver; so beautifully wrought, that no human eye ever
saw the like of them; so huge were their dimensions, that a man could
hardly encompass one within his arms extended."[22] After the Muslim
conquest, all this disappeared.

According to Ibn Idhari al-Marrakushi, when Musa brought all this
"incalculable wealth" back home,[23] he amazed "the inhabitants of the
countries through which he passed with the immense treasures he carried, treasures the like of which no hearer ever heard of before, and no
beholder ever saw before his eyes."

Musa's own account of the Visigoths counters the simplistic depic-
tion of them as barbarians. When his lord, Suleyman, questioned him
about the nature of the "people of Ishban" (that is, Hispania/Spain: the
Muslim name al-Andalus had not yet gained common currency among
Muslims), Musa answered: "They are luxurious and dissolute lords,
but knights who do not turn their faces from the enemy.... Among the
nations just described there are men of honour and probity, there are also
traitors and knaves."

The historian Manuel Rincón Álvarez has drawn out the contrasts
between the uncultured invading Muslim armies and the peoples they
conquered:

> The North African mass [that conquered Spain] was by and large
> Berber, war-like, hungry for booty, but with no or very little capacity
> for absorbing culture and even less of interacting with the indig-
> enous population. Within that mass, there was an Eastern, Arab
> minority, with greater cultural formation, but equally impelled by
> the explosion of the Jihad, or Holy War.... But whereas among these
> Bedouins from the desert one could rarely find people who knew
> how to read and write, in the indigenous population rested the sedi-
> ment of Roman civilization and the Isidorian flowering and, even if
> we recognize that this was the culture of an elite, it had already pro-
> duced encyclopedias like the *Liber Glossarum*, and there remained
> still the fruits of the scientific schools of Seville and Toledo, among
> so many other cultural examples from that time. To underestimate

the cultural level of pre-Islamic Spain in 711 is, at the same time, to ignore what came before it, namely the fusion of the Hispano-Roman element with the Visigoth component. It should be unnecessary to remember that indigenous Iberia had reached a high level of Romanization.[24]

For years after their conquest of Spain, the invading Berbers continued to lead a primitive, nomadic life, taking along wherever they went their many wives and children. According to the chronicler Ibn al-Abbar, in 755 the Umayyad Abd al-Rahman I, emir of Córdoba, for the first time made them build villages and live a sedentary life.[25]

THE INFLUENCE OF THE CHRISTIAN GREEK ROMAN EMPIRE AND THE VISIGOTH KINGDOM ON ISLAMIC CIVILIZATION

Indeed, the years of Muslim semibarbarism in Spain are usually forgotten by those who focus on the brilliance of the Caliphate of Córdoba (929–1031). But even this brilliance was the result, on one hand, of the increasing Islamization of the more cultured Hispano-Romans and Visigoths who remained under Muslim rule and, on the other hand, of Spanish Islam's assimilation of certain aspects of Hispano-Roman, Visigoth, and Christian Greek civilization.

The great historian Ibn Khaldun underlined the low cultural level of Muslim Arabs prior to their being civilized by Greeks and Persians: "The Arabs were coarse, without education, and not very skilled in the arts of writing and mathematics; thus they used Jews, Christians, and freed foreigners [former slaves] to handle their administrative affairs. Among the Arabs there was only a very small number who knew this art; their nobility in particular was very unskilled because among them a lack of knowledge was their distinctive characteristic."[26] "The Arabs," Ibn Khaldun also writes, "barely coming out of their nomadic existence and having become spectators of the way of life in a sedentary civilization, were too busy... because of their position in the armies... even to pay attention to scientific knowledge. They made up the highest class in the state and made up the armed force that sustained the empire; they were the only depositors of authority and, what is more, they despised culture."[27] Al-Gahiz, too, observed that "it was from the Sassanides [Persians] that we borrowed the rules of governing and of a kingdom, the organization of private and public affairs, and the administration of subjects."[28]

Ibn Khaldun pointed out that the one civilization from which the uncultured Arabs had learned the sciences, after their destruction of the learning of the Persians and other civilizations, was that of the Greeks, thanks to the translations by Christian scholars of Greek texts into Syriac and then into Arabic.[29] Ibn Khaldun also records that the caliph al-Mansur requested from the emperor of the Greek Roman Empire the mathematical works of the Greeks.[30] The ancient Greeks had, of course, discovered and applied algorithms ("Euclidean Algorithm," "The Sieve of Eratosthenes") and algebra (Diophantus),[31] although it may have been from the seventh-century Indian mathematician Brahmagupta that the Persian Muslim al-Khwarizmi (ca. 780–ca. 850; he worked in Baghdad at the "House of Wisdom," where scientific and philosophical works, particularly Greek, were translated into Arabic) got the idea of the algorithm, among other things, including "Arabic" numerals. But the great mathematician Georg Cantor saw "traces of Diophantine methods" even in the "Hindu solutions of determinate equations," and the historian of mathematics Florian Cajori pointed out that "some technical [Hindu] terms betray their Greek origin."[32] Cajori shows that the Hindus also drew on Pythagoras.[33] George Sarton, professor of the history of science at Harvard University, wrote that there was nothing comparable in the history of science to Euclid's "prescience" in realizing that his fifth postulate needed proof but that proof was impossible.[34] Because of this realization, he called Euclid (ca. 300 B.C.) the "spiritual ancestor" of the non-Euclidean geometry of Nicolai Ivanovich Lobachevsky (1792–1856). Sarton also wrote that there was nothing comparable to the *mathematical* mechanics of Archimedes (ca. 287–212 B.C.) until the work of Galileo (1564–1642), eighteen centuries later. The Greek historian Theophanes the Confessor (d. 818) reports in his *Chronographia* that Caliph al-Walid I (d. 715) required that the Christian bureaucrats who served him keep all accounts "in Arabic rather than in Greek—except for some of the more complicated as exceeded the potentialities of the Arabic language."[35]

The much-vaunted Islamic "universities" of the Middle Ages were in fact *madrasas*, centers for the study of religious texts and law. Only after the Arabs came in contact with the institutions of higher learning of the Christian Greek Roman Empire during their conquests did the *madrasas* begin to teach other subjects as well—but the only degree granted remained that of expert in religious law: "There was no other 'doctorate' in any other field, no license to teach a field except that of the religious law."[36]

Dimitri Gutas and other scholars have examined the phenomenon of "Greek thought, Muslim culture." A good example is medicine. In 854 the Nestorian Christian Stephanos had translated the medical works of Dioscorides into Arabic. Muslims used this translation as their medical text for more than a century. In 948 the Christian emperor of the Greek Roman Empire, Armanius, gave Abd al-Rahman III, the Umayyad caliph of Córdoba, Dioscorides's works in the original Greek. But Muslims in Córdoba did not have anyone who knew Greek. As a result, the Roman emperor also sent a Greek monk, who instructed the Muslim ruler's slaves in Greek.[37] One does not learn of such stories in the many textbooks and other writings on Muslim Spain. Nor does one learn of the immense scientific knowledge, including Galenic medical knowledge, that fell into Muslim hands upon the military conquest of Greek Christian Alexandria in 642.[38] Muslim physicians would build upon these Greek works for their later reputation in the medical field. According to Ibn Khaldun, as late as the conquest of the Greek Roman province of Egypt in 641, Caliph Umar (who in 634, only two years after Muhammad's death, became the second caliph upon the death of Caliph Abu Bakr) still forbade Muslims to navigate the sea because "the sea was a great pool, which some inconsiderate people furrow, looking like worms on logs of wood."[39]

The Spanish Arabist Julio Samsó has shown that, even as late as the eleventh century, Muslim scholars in al-Andalus were still assimilating the science of the Greco-Roman classics as well as that of the Latin culture of the Christian *dhimmis* ("Mozarabs").[40]

The recurring assimilation of the nonrepresentational features of the art of other civilizations by Islam supports the art historian Basilio Pavón Maldonado's studies arguing that "Spanish-Muslim art...derives in large part from Roman, paleo-Christian, Byzantine, and Visigoth art."[41] Another art historian, Isidro Bango Torviso, has pointed out that the art of Islamic Spain was the result of "the inertia of a late antiquity art carried out under an Islamic hegemony."[42]

Eventually, the flowering of Islamic art in Spain took advantage of the nonrepresentational aspects of Hispano-Roman-Visigoth art. Famously, Muslims adopted the Visigoth horseshoe arch, seen in many Islamic buildings. Of course the horseshoe arch was itself of Greco-Roman origin,[43] and even before conquering Spain, Islam had imitated the architecture and construction techniques of the Christian Greek Roman Empire in the Middle East and North Africa.[44] Indeed, Ibn Khaldun pointed out that in North Africa the constructions built by the Arabs themselves did not last very long because of the Arabs' sloppiness, poor materials, and lack of knowledge of building techniques.[45] Among many other examples, Bango Torviso has pointed out that the *ventana bífora* (usually called by its Arabic-derived name, *ajimez*; it is a type of window with two openings divided vertically into two equal halves by a thin column) is in fact a Roman creation widely used in Hispano-Visigoth Spain long before the Muslim conquest.[46] Celebrated "Muslim" crafts, such as that of leather, existed before the invasion, with pre-Islamic Córdoba being an exporter to Europe.[47]

Popular lyric poetry (evident in the famous *jarchas* of Islamic Spain) was so common among the Christian Hispano-Visigoths living as *dhimmis* ("Mozarabs") under Islam as to be incorporated as a final stanza into the classic Arabic poetry of the *muwassahah* (*muwashshah*); but the *muwassahah*, too, was a poetic form invented, according to Ibn Khaldun, by a poet of *dhimmi* ("Mozarabic") and therefore Christian ancestry, Muccadam de Cabra, in the tenth century.[48]

The famous mosque of Córdoba offers a particularly good example of how Muslims incorporated Hispano-Roman-Visigoth art into their own work. In reputedly tolerant Muslim Córdoba, Abd al-Rahman I demolished the stately Christian basilica of Saint Vincent to build upon it his mosque.[49] (Perhaps with poetic justice, in 1236 King Ferdinand III turned the mosque back into a Catholic church: it is now the Cathedral of Córdoba, although tourists, tour guides, and many Spaniards and even scholars still call it, quite contrary to fact, "the mosque" of Córdoba.) The Islamic conquerors used the church of Saint Vincent's main facade for the facade of their mosque. They also cannibalized columns and other building materials from Hispano-Roman and Visigoth churches. They adopted a Roman technique (*opus vittatum mixtum*) in alternating red brick and white stone in the arches; that alternating pattern is still visible today in some Roman aqueducts of Spain, such as the *Acueducto de los Milagros* in Mérida. The mosque's horseshoe arches imitated Greek Roman arches and Visigoth arches. Finally, the mosque's mosaics were of Greek manufacture.[50]

The Muslims' penchant for incorporating elements of conquered cultures also explains the "bath culture" of southern Spain, which many scholars have regarded as a Muslim invention. In fact, the Greek-Roman culture of water and baths was part of the Hispano-Roman life of southern Spain, which has a warm, Mediterranean climate. The Visigoths inherited the bath culture, which Muslims from arid Arabia happily took over when they encountered it.

However, medieval Islam did not display interest in all aspects of Greco-Roman civilization: Islam remained inimical to classical art, drama, and narrative. Moreover, as we saw in chapter 1, during the early Muslim conquests there was a conscious destruction of the monuments of the pre-Islamic past. And in Spain, historian al-Andalusi tells us that such rulers as the Umayyad Abd Allah (888–912) and the dictator Muhammad Ibn Abu Amir al-Mansur (c. 938–1002, known to Christians as Almanzor) had precious books of ancient Greek and Latin poetry, lexicography, history, philosophy and law burned for their presumably impious content.[51]

THE INFLUENCE OF THE CHRISTIAN GREEK ROMAN EMPIRE ON THE VISIGOTH KINGDOM

In fact, a brilliant Hispano-Roman-Visigoth culture already existed in Spain when Islam was born in Arabia among Bedouins, tents, sheep, and camels (horses did not enter the culture until Arabs stole them in their raids on the Persian empire). There was a wealth of sacred music. There were learned men, such as Saint Leander (who lived in the Greek Roman Empire for a number of years and presided over the Third Toledan Council in Visigoth Spain and the religious union of Hispano-Romans and Visigoths), Bishop Eugene of Toledo (expert in mathematics and astronomy), Conantius of Palencia (expert in music), and the poet-king Sisebut (who wrote an astronomical poem in Latin). In the city of Seville a Catholic archbishop, Saint Isidore (560–636), wrote linguistic studies (*Differentiarum libri*), natural science and cosmology treatises (*De natura rerum* and *De ordine creaturarum*), biographies of biblical personages (*Sententiarum libri*), historical works, and compendia of Greco-Roman civilization (such as the *Historia gothorum* and the *Etimologiae*). Saint Isidore of Seville became the most widely cited author of the European High Middle Ages; Dante praised him in the *Divina Commedia* (*Paradiso* X, 130).[52]

The latest archaeological studies confirm the pronounced cultural influence of the Christian Greek Roman Empire on Visigoth Spain. Pedro Marfil, professor of archaeology and art at the University of Córdoba, has examined the church of Saint Vincent, which Abd al-Rahman I destroyed to build upon it the mosque of Córdoba. Marfil's work reveals the presence of Christian Greek Roman ("byzantine," "oriental") techniques and even materials in a seventh-century Christian renovation of the church.[53] Excavations in the ruins of the immense royal city of Recópolis (near Zorita de los Canes in the province of Guadalajara), built by the Visigoth king Leovigild, have shown a topographic imitation of Constantinople, the existence of an aqueduct, a palatial basilica (likely an imitation of the Greek Christian basilica of Hagia Sophia in Constantinople), commercial and residential centers, paved streets, coin manufacturing, sturdy buildings constructed with stones extracted with Roman technology from local stone quarries, and other features usually associated with thriving Greek-Roman cities.[54] Excavations in Visigoth Toledo have likewise shown that the Visigoth planning of Toledo consciously imitated the features of Greek Roman Constantinople.[55]

Similarly, the continuity of the Roman aqueduct system under the Visigoths has been shown, among others, by the archaeologist Javier Martínez Jiménez and the historian Luis A. García Moreno.[56] In the Visigoth ruins in Mérida, the presence of private commercial baths and an aqueduct to supply them with water has been pointed out by archaeologist Miguel Alba Calzado. And in Córdoba the Muslim conquerors took advantage of the existing Visigoth aqueduct, as indicated by archaeologist Rafael Hidalgo Prieto.[57]

All this architectural and technological achievement is remarkable given the relatively short period of Visigoth hegemony and especially the unsettled nature of their control over the land during the many years of unruliness and internal warfare that immediately preceded and followed the demise of Roman power in *Hispania*.

In Visigoth Spain, as was the case in the rest of Christian Europe, the classics had been part of education since the early Middle Ages (the so-called Dark Ages) in the Trivium and the Quadrivium of liberal arts instruction. Jan Ziolkowski, professor of medieval Latin at Harvard University, notes that in Visigoth Spain "monks and clerics were grounded in classical literature as part of their preparation for using biblical Latin, for chanting biblical and liturgical Latin, and for employing a half-living oral Latin that fused biblical and classical components with many others." In addition, they studied the classics in order to reconcile them with Christian doctrine.[58]

Another scholar of medieval Latin, Dag Norberg, writes: "The originality of Visigoth culture was reflected in the role of grammar and rhetoric. The ancient educational program had survived there; the learned bishops studied ancient poetry, for instance, without the repugnance felt by many other Christians studying a literature filled with pagan elements."[59] As we saw in chapter 1, a Visigoth poet and theologian, Theodulf, was very learned in the poetry of Ovid and Virgil, and after fleeing Spain he became one of the founders of the Carolingian Renaissance.

The great churches, the stupendous bridges, the colossal aqueducts— all the features of Hispano-Roman-Visigoth civilization astonished the Berbers, if not their Arab leaders, some of whom might have been exposed already to a superior civilization during their conquest of the Christian Greek Roman Middle East and North Africa. The conquerors marveled at the Roman roads that still traversed Spain in all its length.[60] They considered Visigoth Seville, where Saint Isidore had lived, "the abode of the sciences."[61] They marveled at engineering works they had never seen before, such as the Roman aqueduct of Cádiz, which (according to one Muslim chronicle) "conveyed fresh water from a spring in the district of the idols to the island of Cádiz, crossing an arm of the Ocean," and the Roman aqueduct of Tarragona, which "conveyed the water from the sea to the city by a gentle level, and in the most admirable order, and served to put in motion all the mill-stones in the town, the whole being one of the most solid, magnificent, and best contrived buildings that ever were erected."[62] They also marveled at the abundance of olive trees in the land.[63]

This was the culture that the Islamic conquerors destroyed. With its conquest of the Visigoth kingdom of Spain and with its eventual control of the Mediterranean Sea, the Muslim empire cut off Christian Spain— and indeed, Christian Europe—from its previous direct contact with the science, medicine, art, and literature of the Christian Greek Roman Empire. This was the thesis of the great French historian Henri Pirenne, which will be examined below.[64]

OBSCURING THE CHRISTIAN GRECO-ROMAN INFLUENCE

It was Muslim scholars who preserved Graeco-Roman science and philosophy throughout medieval Europe's prolonged Dark Ages—an era when, in the words of historian Philip Hitti, Arab rulers were delving into Greek and Persian technologies "while Charlemagne and his lords were dabbling in the art of writing their own names."
—*Gene W. Heck,* When Worlds Collide: Exploring the Ideological and Political Foundations of the Clash of Civilizations *(Lanham, MD: Rowman & Littlefield, 2007), 29*

The oft-repeated assertion that Islam "preserved" classical knowledge and then graciously passed it on to Europe is baseless. Ancient Greek texts and Greek culture were never "lost" to be somehow "recovered" and "transmitted" by Islamic scholars, as so many academic historians and journalists continue to write: these texts were always there, preserved and studied by the monks and lay scholars of the Greek Roman Empire and passed on to Europe and to the Islamic empire at various times.[65] As Michael Harris points out in his *History of Libraries in the Western World*:

The great writings of the classical era, particularly those of Greece... were always available to the Byzantines and to those Western peoples in cultural and diplomatic contact with the Eastern Empire.... Of the Greek classics known today, at least seventy-five percent are known through Byzantine copies.

The historian John Julius Norwich has also reminded us that "much of what we know about antiquity—especially Hellenic and Roman literature and Roman law—would have been lost forever if it weren't for the scholars and scribes of Constantinople."

The Muslim intellectuals who served as propagandists for Caliph Al-Mamun (the same caliph who started the famous Islamic Inquisition to cope with the rationalism that had begun to infiltrate Islam upon its contact with Greek knowledge),[66] such as al-Gahiz (d. 868), repeatedly asserted that Christianity had stopped the *Rum* (Romans—that is, the inhabitants of the Greek Roman Empire) from taking advantage of classical knowledge.[67] This propaganda is still repeated today by those Western historians who not only are biased against Christianity but also are often occupationally invested in the field of Islamic studies and Islamic cultural influence.[68] Lamenting the end of the study of ancient philosophy and science upon the presumed closing of the Athenian Neoplatonic Academy by Emperor Justinian I in 529 is part of this narrative.[69] Yet this propaganda does not correspond to the facts, as Speros Vryonis and others have shown, and as evidenced by the preservation and use of ancient Greek knowledge by the Christians of the empire of the Greeks.

The Christian Greeks themselves were aware of their own civilizational superiority as well as the medieval Muslim propaganda against it. Thus when in the ninth century Saint Cyril (née Constantine), the apostle to the Slavs, was sent by the Greek Roman emperor in an embassy to the Arabs, he astonished his Muslim hosts with his knowledge of philosophy and science as well as theology. The historian Maria Mavroudi recounts:

> When asked how it was possible for him to know all that he did, he [Cyril] drew an analogy between the Muslim reaction to his erudition and the pride of someone who kept sea water in a wine skin and boasted of possessing a rare liquid. He finally encountered someone from a region by the sea, who explained that only a madman would brag about the contents of the wine skin, since people from his own homeland possessed an endless abundance of sea water. The Muslims are like the man with the wine skin and the [Greeks] like the man from the sea because, according to the saint's concluding remark in his response, all learning emanated from the [Greeks].[70]

In the West several works of Aristotle were available to Roman Catholic medieval scholars in Latin translations from Greek dating back to Boethius in the sixth century and Marius Victorinus in the fourth century. By the end of the twelfth century, the *Columbia History of Western Philosophy* reminds us, "authors of the Latin West were quite familiar with the logical works (*Organon*) of Aristotle."[71] As the historian Sylvain

Gouguenheim has shown, with the translations made at the monastery of Mont Saint-Michel, medieval scholars hardly needed translations of Aristotle from Arabic into Latin.[72] Moreover, we know that Saint Thomas Aquinas read Aristotle translated directly from the Greek texts into Latin by William of Moerbeke (1215–1286), a Dominican who was Latin bishop of Corinth—that is, a Roman Catholic bishop of a city in largely Christian Orthodox Greece. William produced more than twenty-five translations of Aristotle in addition to translations of Archimedes, Proclus, Ptolemy, Galen, and many other Greek thinkers. In fact, as will be shown, it was Christian scholars who were responsible for bringing Greek knowledge to Islam, and this knowledge came to Islam only because Muslim forces had conquered areas (the Middle East and North Africa) where a rich Greek Christian civilization had developed.[73]

The direct translations from the Greek enjoyed by Western scholars contrast with the twice-removed translations used by the likes of the Córdoban Ibn Rushd ("Averroes") and the Persian Ibn Sina (Latinized "Avicenna," from the Greek Αβιτζιανος), which were Arabic translations made by Christian scholars from Syriac translations also made by Christian scholars from those classical Greek texts preserved by the Greek scholars of the Christian Greek Roman Empire.[74] This fact is not altered by alleging the influence on Europe of the Muslim "commentators" of Aristotle, who read him not in the original Greek but in translations made by Christians, from Greek to Syriac and then from Syriac to Arabic. As a short story by Jorge Luis Borges ("La busca de Averroes") illustrates, this twice-mediated reading of such technical and difficult texts by such a different culture in such a different language necessarily had to lead to misunderstandings of Aristotle.

Continuity between the Greek Roman Empire and the classical heritage needs to be emphasized because it bears on both Christian and Islamic civilizations. However, the word *Byzantine* hides this continuity. It is a word even less justifiable to designate the inhabitants of the Christian Greek Roman Empire of the Middle Ages than the word *Indian* is to designate the sixteenth-century inhabitants of the Americas or the word *Iberia* (now almost universally adopted among specialists in the English-speaking scholarly world) is to designate medieval Spain. The word *Indian* is an involuntary error resulting from an unavoidable lack of knowledge about an existing continent, but the words *Byzantine* and *Iberia* are artificial academic constructions resulting from ideology. Just as the inhabitants of medieval Spain never called themselves "Iberians" but Christians, Spaniards, or Muslims (see chapter 1), or as the inhabitants of the Americas never called themselves "Indians," so the Greek-speaking inhabitants of the Greek Roman Empire never called themselves "Byzantines"—a term that, as Clifton R. Fox and other historians have pointed out, would have been meaningless to them. They called themselves Ρωμιοι (singular Ρωμιος), as many modern Greeks have called themselves—that is, Romans.[75]

But the word *Byzantine* also would have been meaningless to the enemies of the empire, who called its people either *Rum* (that is, Romans) or Greeks, as do the Quran and the Arabic chronicles of the Muslim conquests in the Middle East and North Africa. So does the testimony of the historian Ibn Khaldun: see, for example, his narrative of the Abbasid caliph al-Mansur's request to the "king of the Greeks" to send him the Greeks' mathematical works.[76]

Likewise, it would have been meaningless to western Europeans in the Middle Ages, such as Bishop Liudprand of Cremona (920–972), who referred to the inhabitants of the empire as either Romans or Greeks, and called their empire "The Empire of the Greeks."[77] It would have been meaningless, too, to Saint Thomas Aquinas, who referred to them as Greeks (for example, in his treatise *Contra errores Graecorum*, written in 1263).

It also would have been meaningless to Greek medieval historians, such as Niketas Koniates (ca. 1155–1217) in his *History of the Empire of the Greeks*, who referred to its people as Ρωμαιοι—that is, Romans.[78] Today's Greeks are their descendants, hence the modern Greek concepts of Ρωμιοι and Ρωμηοοσυνη. Though no more overwhelmingly ethnically Greek in its periphery than the Latin Roman Empire had been overwhelmingly ethnically Roman outside of Italy (several Latin Roman emperors were born in Spain, and others like Postumus, Tetricus, and the "Illyrian emperors" were hardly of Roman ethnic origin), nonetheless this Christian Greek Roman Empire was Greek in language and culture, just as the Latin Roman Empire had been Latin in language and culture. And in the lands and islands of what is today's Greece, as well as in much of today's Anatolian peninsula, the Greek Roman Empire was ethnically Greek as well (on these issues see the work of Speros Vryonis).

The University of Vienna scholar Ioannis Stouraitis has defined the problem theoretically (italics and bold italics are in the Stouraitis text):

One could plausibly argue that the problem of decoding Byzantine identity lies in the fact that the term "Byzantine," commonly used in the present to define the state and the subjects of the Christian Roman Empire (either since the time of Constantine I or alternatively since the post-Justinianic period), is a **terminus technicus**, a retrospective construct of scholars of the Early Modernity in Western Europe. This **terminus technicus** removes the spotlight from *this society's normative self-designation, i.e. Roman*, and thus imposes upon the modern historian a latent bias, namely the bias that this society's collective identity must be called and therefore understood differently from what its name denotes.[79]

In fact, the term *Byzantine Empire* was invented in 1557 by the German scholar Hieronymus Wolf, who as a Protestant would not have been sympathetic to Eastern (or Orthodox) Christians, to indicate that these culturally Greek people of the Eastern Roman Empire were not Romans, and somehow not even Greeks. His scholarly decision may also have been influenced by the fact that the Holy Roman Empire of Charlemagne and his successors had claimed the name *Roman* for itself.

Eighteenth-century Enlightenment scholars such as Montesquieu, who despised Orthodox Christianity perhaps even more than Roman Catholicism, adopted the term, thereby emphasizing that these presumably retrograde Christian Greeks had nothing in common with those pagan Greeks admired by the Enlightenment. This artificial construction, *Byzantine*, already charged with Enlightenment-created connotations of convoluted formalism and corruption, has continued to be used by most Western historians.[80] The Roman Catholic Church also condoned using the name *Byzantines* rather than Romans for the Orthodox Greeks for these reasons: the Roman Catholic Church not only came to stand in opposition to Christian Greek Orthodoxy but also supported the Holy Roman Empire claims to be the only "Roman" empire; using the word *Romans* to designate the Orthodox Greeks would also conflict with the Roman Catholic Church and its claim to being the true "Roman."

Indeed, the most extraordinary city during the early Middle Ages—until its first political decline, a decline that, significantly, as the historian Emmet Scott has underlined, coincides with the Muslim assault upon the Christian Middle East and North Africa in the seventh century—was not

Damascus, or Baghdad, or Córdoba, or Rome, but Christian Constantinople, or "New Rome." Byzantium was merely a Greek town on the Bosphorus when the Roman emperor Constantine the Great began to create there in 330 the vast and mighty city that became the most advanced in the world in medicine, education, law, hygiene, social services, hospitals, commerce, industry, science, technology, art, music, architecture, and philosophy. This city continued to bear his name, Κωνσταντινούπολις, even after it had been conquered, sacked, and raped for three days by the Muslim Turks in 1453, until in the twentieth century the Turkish dictator Kemal Atatürk had its name changed to "Istanbul"—but even in this change the Greek heritage prevailed, as "Istanbul" is a name derived from the Greek phrase στην Πόλη, "to the Polis," that is, to the City of Constantinople.

Christian Europe, including the Christian kingdoms in Spain, could not benefit more from its commerce with the superior civilization of the Christian Greek Roman Empire because, as Henri Pirenne pointed out long ago, Islamic warriors' attacks had turned the then-Christian Mediterranean sea into a battlefield, and eventually into an Islamic lake, and had consequently short-circuited the *direct* cultural exchange between Europe and the empire of the Greeks. Therefore the Islamic empire was arguably the cause of the relative slowing down of European development in the early or "dark" Middle Ages.[81] The scholarly attacks against the Pirenne thesis have failed to invalidate its importance to illuminate what happened: of course cultural and especially commercial exchange between West and East continued to occur, and now largely via the Islamic empire, but this happened not because of the civilizational properties of medieval Islam but *because medieval Islam had interrupted the direct communication in the first place.*

Therefore the torrent of Islamocentric academic publications; television documentaries from PBS, the History Channel, and the BBC; declarations by UNESCO; and the National Geographic traveling exhibits extolling the "transmission of Greek science and technology" by Islam to the backward West overlooks that, whatever the actual degree of this transmission, the transmission not only of Greek science and technology *but also of Greek sculpture, painting, drama, narrative, and lyric*, which could not and did not take place via Islam because of religious barriers, would equally have taken place *without* Islam, *if Islam had not interrupted with its military conquests* of the seventh and eighth centuries the direct communication between the Christian West and the Christian East.

In fact, when Greek scholars began to arrive in Italy escaping from the final destruction of the Christian Greek Roman Empire by Islam in the fifteenth century (a destruction facilitated by the Christian West's weakening of the empire during the infamous Fourth Crusade that sacked Constantinople in 1204), they brought Greek drama, narrative, lyric poetry, philosophy (significantly Plato), and art to the West. They decisively contributed to (and perhaps even started, as many scholars have argued)[82] what would be the Italian Renaissance. This massive cultural transmission showed the sort of impact the Christian Greeks could have had on western Europe centuries earlier, perhaps as early as the seventh century, *without the Islamic interruption.*

Thus the Pirenne thesis continues to be valid to demystify the role of Islam in European history: medieval Islam had interposed itself between Christian Europe and the Christian Greek Roman Empire. Cultural communication continued, of course, but diminished and in a different form. Therefore, precisely because of the problem that the Islamic empire had created, this communication between Christian Europe and the Christian Greeks now had to take place often through the mediation of the Islamic empire itself, which had benefited and continued to benefit from its direct contact with the superior culture of the Greek empire. When this Greek material arrived via Islam, it did so diminished, distorted, and mediated by a faith that was fundamentally inimical to the spirit of Greek civilization.

Moreover, in Constantinople alone, we know from contemporary testimonies that the medieval Islamic conquest was responsible for the destruction of hundreds of thousands of Greek manuscripts during the capture and sacking of this Christian Greek city by the Ottoman sultan (and caliph of all Muslims) Mehmet II in 1453.[83] We will never know how much of Greek literature and art and scientific knowledge was lost with the destruction of the Christian Greek Roman Empire. To this damage caused to European civilization should be added the demographic disaster resulting from the millions of European men, women, and children captured or bought as slaves by Islam throughout the Middle Ages and beyond. The historian Robert Davis has estimated that more than a million white slaves were traded in Islamic lands between the sixteenth and the seventeenth centuries alone.[84]

A material example of the superior science and technology of this medieval Christian Greek Roman Empire was the famous "Greek Fire" (the Arabs did not call it "Byzantine Fire"), which helped keep the numerically stronger but technologically inferior Muslim navies at bay for centuries. Another material example of the superior science of the Christian Greek Empire is a wonderful mechanical sundial with mathematical gearing dating from the sixth century A.D., which "indicates that the Hellenistic tradition attested by the Antikythera machine (first century B.C.) continued to be active in the Byzantine period, and suggests that it may have influenced the Islamic tradition. Once again an artefact has shown up the inadequacy of the evidence derived from literary sources."[85] This Greek science and technology, and some philosophy (but not that of Plato, nor Greek literature, representational painting, or sculpture), in translations made by Christians, were obtained by and impacted Islamic civilization when Muslim armies invaded and conquered the lands of the Christian Greek Roman Empire in the Middle East, North Africa, and generally the Mediterranean world.[86]

ERASING THE VESTIGES OF A NASCENT CIVILIZATION IN VISIGOTH SPAIN

Over time, the Muslim conquerors' pillaging, conscious destruction of the monuments of the pre-Islamic past, and conversion or expulsion of the Christian population erased most of the cultural vestiges of this nascent civilization. We have few literary records of Visigoth Spain: "the debacle caused by the Arabic invasion carried away all official documents," according to the Spanish historian Antonio Domínguez Ortiz.[87] We have mentions of beautiful churches that have disappeared. Today, the remains of even small "Mozarabic" churches can be found only outside the former "al-Andalus," and none of them in major urban centers. Moreover, freestanding public Roman and Hispano-Roman-Visigoth decorative sculpture and painting disappeared, as was to be expected of art under a religion that forbade physical representation and considered sculpture a manifestation of idolatry.[88]

This architectural and iconographic debacle cannot be attributed to the Visigoths, since they were already highly Romanized by the time they entered Spain. They were interested not in destroying but in preserving and elaborating upon the symbols of Roman power because they considered themselves its inheritors. Thus we have records of the Visigoths' practice of sculpture and a great artistic center in Mérida, of which little remains because of the centuries of iconoclastic Islamic domination. The Spanish historian and priest José Orlandis has shown the influence of the Christian Greek Roman Empire on Visigoth art, architecture, and even church ritual and theology. But the Muslim conquest interrupted the Visigoths' assimilation and adaptation of the preexisting Roman and Hispano-Roman Christian art, especially the immensely rich art of the Christian Greek Roman Empire, as well as Christian Greek science.[89]

Islamic historians attest to the iconoclastic zeal of early Umayyad rulers, such as Abd al-Rahman I. According to the historian al-Razi, this leader was ruthless against the "polytheists," as Christians were called: "He would take all the bodies which Christians honor and call saints [probably a reference to relics], and he would burn them; and he would burn their beautiful churches; and in Spain there were many and very magnificent churches, some built by the Greeks and some by the Romans. Seeing this, the Christians, when they could, would take their sacred things, and would flee to the mountains."[90]

Changing prominent Christian churches into mosques was a standard feature of Muslim conquests. Muslims transformed many Greek basilicas in the Middle East and North Africa into mosques in the seventh and eighth centuries. They tore down many others to use their superior construction materials, including marble, gold, and silver (traditional Arabic architecture used poor construction materials such as plaster, wood, and brick, evident in Andalusian palaces such as the Alhambra, and this is one of the reasons why Ibn Khaldun claimed that the constructions of the Arabs were not solidly built and quickly fell into ruins).[91] This is how mosques including those of Damascus (the Great Umayyad Mosque), Jerusalem (al-Aqsa), and Cairo (Amran) were built—and by Christian Greek architects to boot. According to the geographer Ibn al-Faqih (d. 903), even the minarets of the Damascus mosque were originally watch towers in the Greek Basilica of St. John the Baptist—all of which accounts for the "byzantine" look of the mosque.[92] As the Arabist Maria Isabel Fierro has observed, all Umayyad mosques feature mosaics of Christian Greek origin, including the Great Mosque of Damascus (built upon the demolished Greek Basilica of St. John the Baptist), which was designed with the conscious intention to dwarf and humiliate the neighboring Christian churches.[93]

The transformation of Christian churches into mosques could be very swift if Christians did not submit without fighting. This was the case with Hagia Sophia in Constantinople, the most extraordinary building of the early Middle Ages. During the three-day sack of Constantinople in 1453, the Muslim Turks defaced or painted over murals and paintings depicting holy figures (icons), removed crosses from inside and outside the building, and transformed the Greek Orthodox basilica into a mosque. Muslim rulers eventually constructed four flanking minarets, which stand to this day. Hagia Sophia was converted into a museum by the Turkish dictator Kemal Atatürk in the twentieth century. But the signs of desecration and of the supremacy of Islam are still present in this "museum": a large *mihrab* (a prayer niche pointing toward Mecca and the focal point of all mosques) stands where the altar used to be; and on either side of the *mihrab* and around the nave hang eight huge black medallions (at least twenty-five-feet wide) with yellow Arabic script proclaiming "Muhammad, Peace Be Upon Him," "Allah," the names of the first four caliphs, and the names of Muhammad's two grandsons—to remind all visitors to the "secularized building" that this is a Muslim, not a Christian site. Other extraordinary Greek Orthodox churches in Constantinople suffered a similar fate, such as the Church of the Holy Savior in Chora: it was converted into a mosque, all its icons were covered with plaster, and all crosses were removed even from the inside walls. It is now a museum.[94] In Spain, as late as 1195 Muslims on the offensive were still turning Catholic churches into mosques—as a sign, Muslim chroniclers proudly note, of Christian defeat and submission.[95] (For the medieval Islamic hegemonic tactic of destroying churches, see also chapter 1.)

Significantly, no churches built prior to the Catholic Reconquest can be found today in southern Spain. As the historian Jacques Fontaine observed, the destruction of the Hispano-Roman-Visigoth Christian heritage may have been the result not only of the religious teachings of Islam but also of a conscious policy of systematically erasing all Christian "power signs" from "al-Andalus."[96] As we saw in chapter 1, this policy of erasing during a *jihad* the signs of pre-Islamic grandeur had been part of the hegemonic tactics of the Islamic conquests.[97]

The few examples that we have of Visigoth artistic craftsmanship have survived largely in treasures kept hidden from the conquerors' pillaging. These buried treasures give only a faint idea of the exquisiteness of this art, and they make the Arabic accounts of the Visigoth king Rodrigo's riding into battle in bejeweled armor more plausible.[98]

A FEEBLE ECHO

Under the Visigoths, Toledo was an artistic center, as the archaeological remains of exquisite marble fragments indicate.[99] But under Islam, the art of the Visigoth capital decayed, as the conquerors wiped out the traces of Christian grandeur while focusing their artistic interests on their new southern capital, Córdoba. Toledo, however, continued to be a focus of cultural and political resistance—or "unruliness," as a Muslim historian put it. It sided with the Fhiries against the Umayyads in 761; in 797 a Christian convert to Islam, the poet Garbib, led a revolt; in 829 another Christian convert, Hashim, led a revolt as well; and in 852 the Christian *dhimmis* and Christian converts to Islam revolted in response to the Umayyad emir Muhammad's oppression and sought the support of the Christians in the North.[100]

As the French historian of Muslim and Spanish art Henri Terrasse observed, the Visigoth Spain of the sixth and seventh centuries produced a Renaissance of European art and civilization in which the Visigoth monarchy and the Catholic Church were fundamental.[101]

Unfortunately, the splendor of the Christian Visigoth royal court in Toledo, which archaeological excavations have shown tried to imitate the splendor of the Christian Greek Roman Empire in Constantinople, has reached us only as a feeble echo in the Muslim chronicles and the material evidence of buried treasures and excavated archaeological sites.[102] Since the Renaissance, and especially during the Enlightenment, anachronistic condemnations of the Visigoth kingdom as "socially unjust" have accompanied the dismissal of Visigoth art and culture, as the art and culture of Muslim Spain have been correspondingly exalted.[103]

Why is this the case? How can Hispano-Roman-Visigoth Spain be portrayed as a land of "Dark Ages gloom and depression" while Islamic Spain is hailed as "the pride and the ornament of the world, the most illustrious part of the earth"?[104] Why has the history of both Islamic Spain and its Hispano-Roman-Visigoth predecessor been so distorted?

One factor may be that scholars are simply unaware of the reality. Consider that the best monographic studies of Hispano-Roman-Visigoth art and culture are available only in Spanish and French.[105] Those Islamic studies scholars who write on Islamic Spain may not understand how the achievements they ascribe to Islam in Spain actually reflect Islam's assimilation of elements of other cultures.

In some cases, however, the unfavorable portrayal of Visigoths in Spain could be the result of bad faith on the part of academic historians and their antipathy to anything connected to Christian Spain. Thomas F. Glick, professor of medieval history at Boston University, writes: "The economic regressiveness of Visigoth Spain is well illustrated by the failure of the Goths to carry on the vast mining enterprise begun by the Romans." But as the historian Emmet Scott has observed: "The only evidence Glick has that mining declined under the Visigoths is the 'meager details supplied by Isidore of Seville and the fact that the most important Roman-age mines of Spain are now known by Arabic names.' This hardly constitutes convincing evidence upon which to make such a sweeping statement." Scott concludes: "The impression of bad faith on the part of the author is reinforced by his pronouncements on almost every topic [related to the Visigoths]."[106] Indeed, Glick (who calls the Visigoths "men of the woods [who] never strayed too far from there") seems to have no idea about such cities as Visigoth Recópolis, the magnificent treasures of wrought gold and jewelry that the Visigoths buried to protect them from the rapaciousness of the Islamic invaders, or any of the other achievements of the Hispano-Roman-Visigoth culture.

Professor Glick is not alone. Too many of those scholars who make pronouncements on Islamic Spain display an ignorance of—or perhaps even a blatant disregard for—what the primary sources and archaeological findings show.

3

THE DAILY REALITIES OF AL-ANDALUS

The Andalusian experience is also recognized for its tolerance and cultural syncretism among members of the Muslim, Christian, and Jewish faiths over a period of eight centuries (A.D. 711–1492).

—*John W. Fox, Nada Mourtada-Sabbah, and Sulayman N. Khalaf,* "Ethnography and the Culture of Tolerance in al-Andalus," *Harvard Middle Eastern and Islamic Review (2006), 146–71*

The flexibility of Islamic legal concepts and categories...accommodated intercommunal interaction and integration into the Muslim community.

—*Janina M. Safran, Associate Professor of History and Director of the Middle Eastern Studies Minor at Pennsylvania State University, on her department website (http://history.psu.edu/directory/jxs57)*

At the beginning of the eighth century, the Arabs brought one of history's greatest revolutions in power, religion, culture, and wealth to Dark Ages Europe. The Arabs were to stay there until the end of the fifteenth century, and for much of that time—until roughly the beginning of the twelfth century—Islam in *al-Andalus* (Muslim Spain) was generally religiously tolerant.

—*David Levering Lewis, two-time Pulitzer Prize winner and Julius Silver Professor of History at New York University, in* God's Crucible: Islam and the Making of Europe, 570–1215 *(New York: W. W. Norton, 2008), xxii–xxiii*

THE SPANISH PHILOSOPHER José Ortega y Gasset pointed out that the "Arabic society of al-Andalus was different from and other than the society or societies not Arabic that inhabited Spain at the time."[1] Ortega's observation was anticipated by the brilliant cleric Ibn Hazm of Córdoba (994–1064), whose ancestry was Christian, and who explained to fellow Muslims the cultural and theological distance separating Muslims from Christians.[2] Yet a tide of publications glosses over the otherness of Muslim life in Islamic Spain. Both scholars and popular writers present al-Andalus as an exemplary land of harmonious diversity and tolerance, and they dismiss contrary assessments as mere Western "Orientalism."

Thus, in the introduction to his *Convivencia: Jews, Muslims, and Christians in Medieval Spain*, Thomas Glick, professor of medieval Spanish history and director of the Institute of Medieval Studies at Boston University, writes, "Historians' views of cultural contact frequently conceal two ideological modes or sets of preconceptions: one that emphasizes conflict and one that, while recognizing the reality of conflict, stresses cultural congruence and creative interaction." Dismissing the former, he suggests that the twentieth-century literary scholar Américo Castro was basically right when he put forward the idea of *convivencia* in Islamic Spain. Glick says that to Castro's concept we must add "the admission that cultural interaction inevitably reflects a concrete and very complex social dynamic," though he stresses that we must retain "the understanding that acculturation implies a process of internalization of the 'other' that is the mechanism by which we make foreign cultural traits our own."[3] *Creative interaction, internalization of the other, complex social dynamic*: here is the grounding for the normative, academic, ideological project of "diversity," and a "plural" and multicultural society.

Many contemporary scholars and other intellectuals join Glick in this ideological enterprise, as the epigraphs at the beginning of sections in this chapter demonstrate. Their views, however, do not conform with what the primary sources tell us of the system of cultural practices in Islamic Spain. The daily realities of al-Andalus bear little relation to the fashionable mythology.

A HIEROCRATIC SOCIETY

> In arts and agriculture, learning and tolerance, Al Andulus [sic] was
> a beacon of enlightenment to the rest of Europe.... Among its finest
> achievements was its tolerance. Jews and Christians were welcomed,
> if not as equals, then as full-fledged citizens. They were permitted to
> practice their faith and their rituals without interference. This toler-
> ance was in keeping with the principles of the Koran, which taught
> that Jews and Christians were to be respected as "peoples of the Book"
> or believers in the word of God. Jews and Christians were assimilated
> into Islamic culture, and occasionally, Moorish leaders helped to build
> Christian houses of worship.
>   —James Reston Jr., Dogs of God: Columbus, the Inquisition, and
>   the Defeat of the Moors (New York: Anchor Books, 2006), 7–8

Perhaps the most fundamental fact in the life of Muslims in al-Andalus is
that no distinction existed between civil and religious law. Put otherwise,
throughout the history of Islamic Spain, from the conquest in 711, to its
reduction to the small kingdom of Granada after 1248, to its final demise
in 1492, religion was the law, and therefore Islam was the law. As the Spanish Arabist José Aguilera Pleguezuelo observes: "Western concepts such
as Public Law, Private Law, and distinctions among religious, juridical,
or moral norms make no sense in Islamic Law.... Juridical norms have at
the same time a religious and moral sense. Western laicism in juridical
matters has no reality in Islamic Law."[4] As the scholar of Islamic studies Soha Abboud-Haggar points out, in Islamic Spain *sharia* pervaded
every aspect of life, from the private and familiar to the social and public
sphere.[5] In this sense, Muslims in al-Andalus lived under a theocracy.
As we will see, however, a more accurate name would be a hierocracy—a
government of clerics.

In Umayyad Córdoba, the tenth-century chronicler al-Khushani
explicitly referred to the indivisibility of the religious and the secular
spheres at the highest levels of power and emphasized that the political
ruler was also a "born" religious authority.[6] The great historian Ibn Khaldun pointed out the supremacy of religious law over all aspects of human
behavior and the unity of the religious and the secular in the person of
the ruler. He listed ten *religious* duties of the caliph, among them the duty

"to wage the Holy War [*jihad*] himself and with his armies at least once a year."[7] Muhammad and his successors, the early caliphs, held both religious and political power.[8]

In this "Golden Age of Islam," Muslims lived under the sway of *sharia*, which strictly speaking means not the Islamic legal system but a religiously inspired view of the world, a path of right conduct that Allah has given to men through his messengers and especially through The Messenger, the Prophet Muhammad: *sharia* was divine law.[9] *Sharia* applied, therefore, to all human life. It was a religiously oriented view of things that permeated the everyday behavior of the believer as well as the laws under which he lived.[10]

These laws, which Islamic clerics called *fiqh* ("wisdom" or "understanding"), developed over years of applying *sharia* to everyday, national, and international matters. In al-Andalus *fiqh* regulated Muslims' family life, sexual life, the penal code, public law, war and peace, relations with non-Muslims, and all other aspects of individual, social, and political life, as well as what Western thought would call "religious" life proper. (The idea of a separate religious sphere was foreign to medieval Islamic thought.)

The religious and, therefore, also civil authorities in everyday life were a class of people in charge of developing and interpreting *fiqh*: the *ulama* (singular: *alim*, meaning "wise" or "learned"), or Islamic clerics. From among the *ulama* were drawn the legal experts proper, the *fuqaha* (singular: *faqih*). The *ulama* were men, and only men,[11] learned in, among other things, the eternal Holy Book (the Quran), which presumably Allah dictated to Muhammad through the Angel Gabriel, and the variously authoritative traditional narratives (singular: *hadith*; plural: *ahadith*) of Muhammad's sayings and deeds (*sunnah*). Strictly speaking, then, Muslims in al-Andalus lived under a hierocracy.

At times the *ulama* would conflict with a ruler over political and therefore religious matters. Sometimes strong monarchs would prevail; other times the *ulama* would have the upper hand. Thus, the Umayyad emir al-Haqam I gave in to an adverse ruling by the Córdoba *qadi* (judge) al-Mosad ibn Imran; on the other hand, this same al-Haqam I sent his soldiers against the seditious Córdoba *ulama*, who were unhappy with the Umayyad ruler's despotic and violent ways, and destroyed their houses and mosques in an entire neighborhood of the city, crucified seventy-two *ulama*, and exiled many to the island of Crete.[12]

But no ruler or dynasty could long survive without the *ulama*'s support. In the eleventh century, Andalusian *ulama* unhappy with the lukewarm religiosity of the rulers of the *taifas* (the small kingdoms that resulted from the collapse of the Umayyad Caliphate of Córdoba after 1009)[13] supported the traditionist Berber Almoravids in their takeover of the weak *taifas*.[14] No wonder that the Umayyad ruler Abd al-Rahman II (reigned 822–852) considered it prudent to accept a penance of sixty days of fasting that the *faqih* Yahya b. Yahya al-Layti had imposed because the monarch had intercourse with a sexual slave ("concubine") in daytime during Ramadan.[15] *Ulama* in Morocco and other parts of Africa have continued to hold enormous prestige and power, and their *fatwas* have sometimes led sultans to be deposed.[16]

The Islamic clerics' functions explicitly included making sure that Muslims behaved in a religiously proper manner, which meant a manner always in accord with Islamic teachings and exacting daily ritualistic details as interpreted by the clerics. Thus the public spaces of the cities of this Golden Age of Islam were patrolled by a religious functionary drawn from the *ulama* class, the *muhtasib*, who had the powers of a judge to enforce *sharia* in the people's personal, social, and commercial behavior.[17]

In this regard, the words of one of the Islamic governors of al-Andalus, Uqba ibn al-Hayyay al-Saluli (d. 741), to his judge are instructive. Al-Khushani described this governor as a "courageous champion of Holy War [*jihad*], frontier warrior, intrepid and valiant, burning in his desire to hurt the polytheists [that is, Christians, who believed in a triune God—the Father, the Son, and the Holy Spirit]. His religious zeal was such that, when a war prisoner fell in his hands, he would not kill him without giving him some time during which he would invite the prisoner to embrace Islam, inspiring in him the desire to convert, telling him of the excellencies of the new religion, while showing him the existing doubts regarding his false religion. It is said that because of [this great warrior] two thousand people converted to Islam."[18] This pious warrior of Allah wrote a long letter to the *alim* Mahdi ibn Muslim upon naming him judge of the city of Córdoba. Al-Khushani describes Uqba al-Saluli's letter:

> He prescribed to him the fear of [Allah]; that he should place all his efforts in obeying [Allah]; that he should carry out those works that were most pleasing to [Allah], privately as well as in public.... He

ordered him to take the Book of [Allah] [the Quran] and the *sunnah* of the Prophet Muhammad as guides whose light would lead him on the right path, as a goal toward which to walk, as a lamp to light the way; for with both [texts] one attains the right direction and avoids losing one's way.... He ordered him to keep in mind that he had not been chosen to act upon purely mundane or political issues, since the investiture of a judge, whose power [Allah] praised and mentioned honorably (as in Qur'an 5: 46: "[Allah] loves those who judge equitably"), was ennobled precisely because upon it [the investiture of judge] was conferred the noble virtue of deciding upon and solving, on [Allah's] side, those issues that relate intimately *with the life of religion, the noble mission of making Muslims practice their religious duties, making those who have the duty to follow the divine precepts obey those precepts* [emphasis added].... [The governor] ordered him that his ministers, his counselors and helpers, be in agreement with the temporal and spiritual mission that has been entrusted to him, that is, men wise in the divine law, who know morality and law, religious men with the complete trust of the person who will accept their advice.... For the men...whom he must use to fulfill judicial functions, ought to be honest and continent people [who abstain from what is illicit], completely unmixed with society's low lives.[19]

The Islamic faith of Andalusian judges fostered some paragons of probity who resisted the temptations of power and lived frugal lives dedicated to the study of divine law.[20] This was the case with the judge Masrur. Al-Khushani told one of many anecdotes related to his exemplary life:

Once upon a time there was a judge known as Masrur: he was an ascetic man. One day he asked permission of the litigants in the audience to get up and go do something personal. Those present granted him permission. Our man got up and left carrying in his hand a loaf of bread that was still unbaked and started walking to a bakery to have it baked. One of those present offered him to take the bread to the bakery for him; but the judge said: "When I am deposed as judge, will I be asking you every time I need it so you can help me with this? No: the one who carried my bread before I became judge must still carry this bread now."[21]

THE RULE OF THE ISLAMIC CLERGY

Had 'Abd al-Rahman's men prevailed that October day [at the Battle of Tours or Poitiers, 732], the post-Roman Occident would probably have been incorporated into a cosmopolitan, Muslim *regnum* unobstructed by borders…one devoid of a priestly caste, animated by the dogma of equality of the faithful, and respectful of all religious faiths.
—*David Levering Lewis,* God's Crucible, *173*

The *ulama* constituted a social class of religious intellectuals who ruled over the daily life of the Muslim population. These clerics issued judgments about details of an individual's existence that in a different religious context would be considered insignificant, such as whether donkey's milk should be drunk, or whether objects or water touched by Christians could be used for ritual purposes, or whether a Muslim was allowed to wipe his hands on his socks after an ablution, or whether one could enter a mosque after eating garlic, or what hand should be used for eating and drinking, or what the correct punishment should be for having intercourse with one's wife during Ramadan, or the proper blood cost of a cut-off penis or testicle, or whether children should be allowed to enter a mosque (they should not).[22]

Legal treatises and manuals from Islamic Spain indicate that such close attention to ritualistic practices originated for the most part in a conception of the deity—Allah, an absolutely unipersonal God, not the triune God of the Roman Catholic, Orthodox, and other Christian churches—as so pure an entity that to honor and pray to Him, the faithful must keep not only moral but also physical purity.[23] Being pure in Islamic Spain necessitated being free of pollutants, which included everything the body ejects, such as excrement, urine, sperm, blood, menses, and saliva. Bodily purity also required the faithful to keep away from the objects, people (such as Christians),[24] and animals (such as dogs,[25] but not cats) that might carry traces of these effluvia and to clean the body properly after it had been polluted. After each bodily ejection the faithful must clean their sexual parts and other parts of the body with large amounts of water or, if water was not available, with sand, earth, or even stones (prescribed alternatives that betrayed the origin of the religion in the arid lands of Arabia).[26] Menstruation and childbirth discharges created a state of contamination requiring purification before praying; sexual inter-course, or the mere touching of the circumcised male and circumcised female sexual organs, required purification of both husband and wife before praying; and a husband who kissed or fondled his wife must also purify himself (but the wife need not) before praying.[27]

Before each of the five daily prayers, the faithful must carry out detailed ablutions of the hands, mouth, nose (inside and out by aspira-tion and expiration), face, hands up to the elbows, and the two feet up to the ankles.[28] During menstruation, a woman was an impure being;[29] she was not allowed to prostrate herself and therefore could not partici-pate in mosque services;[30] nor could she attend mosque at Mecca during the required pilgrimage if she was menstruating; and after menstruation she needed to perform supplemental ablutions to purify herself.[31] A man must not have sexual intercourse with his wives while they were men-struating; a man could still get some satisfaction by fondling the woman above the waist while she remained covered from the waist down, but he must purify himself afterward before praying.[32] Women must perform their ablutions separately from men.[33] Attending weekly services at the mosque was not required of Muslim women (whereas Christian women were supposed to attend weekly Mass); if Muslim women attended ser-vice, it would be at a different time from men, because, among other rea-sons, the sight of women repeatedly elevating the posterior part of their bodies while prostrating themselves could prove distracting to the other sex; but women were not forbidden to go to mosque.[34] Women must pray covered from the top of the head down to the top of their feet, but with their faces uncovered.[35]

In other words, so that praying might be agreeable to Allah, in Islamic Spain purity of the body went hand in hand with purity of the soul, and both must be as perfect as possible within one's circumstances.[36] The Islamic concept of purity contributed to making nonsensical the Christian idea of an all-powerful God who nevertheless allowed Himself to be bloodied and then crucified. Such was the importance of bodily purity that Muhammad reportedly said: "If a man does *wudu* [ablution], and makes sure he does it correctly, and then does the prayer, he will be forgiven everything that he does between then and the time when he prays the next prayer."[37]

All life was organized around these and other exacting religious prac-tices, which made the Muslim neighborhoods of the cities of al-Andalus more hygienic than Christian neighborhoods. These strict practices also contributed to a daily discipline that braced the spiritual teachings of Islam and strengthened the piety and cohesiveness of the faithful.

The *ulama* who oversaw the definition and application of these practices in Islamic Spain formed a clergy, a complex network of religious men of superior but varying authority and functions, among them *fuqaha* (jurists or lawyers), *muftis* (promulgators of *fatwa*, or religious-legal decrees), *qadis* (judges), and *muhtasibs* (judges of the public spaces).

As several Spanish and French scholars have pointed out, in no other place within the Islamic empire was the influence of Islamic clerics on daily life as strong as in al-Andalus.[38] The occupation of *ulama* ran within families, sometimes through many generations.

These clerics were supposed to think always in religious terms about the nature and application of the *fiqh*. Their functions and actions reflected the inseparability of the religious and secular spheres in the life of Muslims in al-Andalus. The *ulama* were legal scholars and therefore also religious practitioners, theologians, religious leaders, and moralists.

Just as in Christian Spain members of non-Christian (usually Jewish) families who had converted to Roman Catholicism (called in Spanish *conversos*) could achieve positions of authority within and without the Catholic Church (among many: Julian, archbishop of Toledo and primate of all of Visigoth Spain; Petrus Alphonsi; Abner of Burgos; Francisco, archbishop of Soria; Pablo de Santa María, archbishop of Cartagena; Luis de Santangel, treasurer of King Ferdinand of Aragon), so in Islamic Spain did some influential *ulama* belong to families who had converted from Christianity to Islam. The descendants of these converts were called in Spanish *muladis*, from the Arabic *muwalladun*, meaning "hybrid" or "mixed"—a word derived from cattle breeding and historically used by Muslim writers to refer to converts as well as to children of Muslim fathers with non-Muslim women (in contrast, non-Muslim men could not marry or have intercourse with free Muslim women).[39]

Ulama appointed as judges officiated in mosques, led regular Friday prayers, and delivered the homily (*khutba*).[40] One of their essential qualifications was that they had to be well-known experts in the fundamental texts of Islam: the sacred Quran and the *ahadith*.[41] These clerics frequently held court inside the mosque.[42] They saw themselves as preachers and missionaries to all Muslims.[43]

Extant primary sources on Islamic Spain confirm the theoretical requirement of deep religious knowledge and piety as a prerequisite to becoming a judge. It reoccurs throughout the biographies in al-Khushani's *History of the Judges of Córdoba.*[44] The opening lines of the widely used Maliki legal treatise *Tuhfat al-Hukkam*, by the Andalusian jurist Abu Bakr Ibn Asim (1359–1427), also make it clear: "On the office of the judge and what relates to it: The person who executes judgment deputises for the Muslim ruler.... [He] should be courageous in giving judgement, and should also satisfy the condition of being responsible and a man of integrity. He should also be a free man and free from loss of sight, hearing and speech. It is also required that he should be a man of learning and piety. He must know the principles of Islamic jurisprudence."[45] Modern countries that have instituted Islamization programs, such as Pakistan in the 1970s and Iran in the 1980s, understand the fundamental importance of this issue and have therefore replaced judges having a secular training with those having a religious education—*ulama.*[46]

THE CONTRASTS WITH CHRISTIAN EUROPE

[Conic decoration] derives... from the high level of tolerance exercised by the first Muslim rulers.
—*Jerrilynn D. Dodds, Professor of Art History at Sarah Lawrence College, in* Convivencia: Jews, Muslims, and Christians in Medieval Spain, *ed. Vivian B. Mann, Adjunct Professor of Jewish Art and Visual Culture at the Jewish Theological Seminary; Thomas F. Glick, Professor of Medieval History and Director of the Institute for Medieval History at Boston University; and Jerrilyn D. Dodds (New York: G. Braziller in association with the Jewish Museum, 1992), 118*

One can only imagine an equivalent type of judge in medieval Catholic Europe: a man who, to be chosen as an interpreter and dispenser of the law, must also be an expert on the New Testament and know how to officiate, lead prayer, and deliver the homily at Sunday Mass. In other words, such a judge would have to be a priest.

This, of course, was not the case. The Roman Catholic Church had its own system of law by which it ruled itself and to which priests were subject:

canon law. The lay population, however, was ruled by civil law. Although ultimately inspired and certainly influenced by the Christian principles on which the post-Roman medieval societies were partly based, this European civil law was nonetheless an organic artifact that variously incorporated secular autochthonous practices, secular Roman law, and the equally secular laws of the Germanic and Baltic invaders of the Roman Empire who created the modern European nations.[47] This civil law, in Catholic Spain as in the rest of Christian Europe, was administered by laypeople, not priests.[48]

These legal issues are overlooked in all the more or less subtly "subversive" or "demystifying" arguments insisting on the intermingling of the religious and the political in western Europe and on the lack of any real difference between Christian Europe and Islam regarding the separation of religion and the state.[49] These arguments cannot see the forests because they are looking at the patterns in the bark of trees.

Medieval Islam did not have anything comparable to the political separation between spiritual power and secular power in medieval Europe. But the point is not so much the political separation of the spiritual power (the Church) and the secular power (the state), or the presence of Christian principles and even influence in political decision making and the crafting of laws, or the way religion and the Church legitimized monarchs, or the lordships the king granted to some bishops over certain villages, or the involvement of priests in administering sacraments like marriage and baptism, or the efforts of popes to acquire secular power to the point of resorting to subterfuges such as the "Donation of Constantine," or the profound ways in which Christianity influenced the development and administration of civil law.[50] Rather, the point is the distinction between Church law and civil law, which reflects a different ethos that influences the dynamics between the spiritual power (the Church) and the secular power (the state), and, perhaps more important, the dynamics between an individual's religious well-being and his responsibilities and freedoms before the law.[51]

In some Christian lands the differences between Church law and civil law became very sharp. In England, common law derived from the decisions of local judges in concrete cases, decisions that were based on local customs and that effectively created legal precedents.[52] As the legal scholar Richard Posner has pointed out, if these judges guided themselves by one set of principles, it would be economic efficiency, not religion.[53]

Some scholars have even argued that, because common law developed independently of royal power, it had a politically "liberating" effect. Regardless of the actual effectiveness of this "independence" from royal power, what seems incontestable is that no priests and no Church were involved in the application and rise of English common law.

In Castile—from the beginning involved in intermittent war with, and serving as a buffer to, the Muslim invaders, and therefore in a centuries-long "frontier society" condition—a similar development took place: there a judge was "a legislating judge, creator of the law, of a law that arises from the idea of justice proper to the Castilian peoples," in the words of the Spanish law professor Ramón Peralta, who concludes, "We are in the presence of the law as a social product."[54] The Spanish historian Miguel Angel Ladero Quesada observes that judges based decisions in part on "a traditional law rooted in the population, and the knowledge of which law was guaranteed by its oral transmission."[55] Eventually this tradition-based but evolving law was written down in the *fueros*, or towns' rights, confirmed by the crown in royal charters. The *fueros* included both rights and obligations in the form of "a set of liberties and privileges regarding due process, tributes and the economy."[56]

Another characteristic of this Spanish Christian frontier society was, Ladero Quesada says, the "administrative and functional autonomy of town councils," especially after the second quarter of the twelfth century.[57] Important in the administration of the law were the popularly elected local mayors or *alcaldes* (a name derived from the Arabic *qadi*, though this Muslim functionary was not elected by the people but imposed by Muslim rulers).[58] And the limited but still substantial secular feudal power of a medieval monarch was part of this complex Castilian legal mixture.

But again, no priests and no Church created or administered the law.[59] All this was conceptually and existentially remote from the condition of Muslims in al-Andalus, with its religious/legal and administrative monopoly by a class of religious intellectuals.

THE MALIKI SCHOOL OF ISLAMIC JURISPRUDENCE

Muslim rulers of the past were far more tolerant of people of other faiths than were Christian ones. For example, al-Andalus's multi-cultural, multi-religious states ruled by Muslims gave way to a Christian regime that was grossly intolerant even of dissident Christians, and that offered Jews and Muslims a choice only between being forcibly converted and being expelled (or worse).

   —*"Islam and the West: Never the Twain Shall Peacefully Meet?"* The Economist, *November 15, 2001*

One should not assume that legal systems indicate how the law is applied or obeyed. Anyone can find examples in his own time and place where the written law does not reflect what some individuals do, or rulers choose to enforce, or judges decide.[60] Working within the same legal system, judges may disagree in their interpretations of the law.[61] In Islamic Spain people of course violated the commands of their religion and the mores of their society, and they might or might not have been punished for it. Moreover, bribery, which exists in every culture, probably played a role in the application of Islamic law in al-Andalus as it has everywhere else.

Islamic Spain was not unique in failing to enforce the law, or in the law's being "flexible and contested in everyday practice."[62] Similar examples can be found as much in seventh- or sixteenth-century Christian Spain as in the twenty-first-century United States. But they do not lessen the importance of taking into account the legal system of a given culture in order to understand its customs, ethics, and beliefs. As Edward Gibbon wrote, "The laws of a nation form the most instructive portion of its history."[63] If, as is the case with Islamic Spain, we also have many examples of actual legal cases, biographies of judges, historical or quasi-historical narratives, legal decrees, and treatises on jurisprudence, we can form a fairly accurate picture of the everyday life of those subject to the laws and regulations that were supposed to guide their society.

Among the many extant legal treatises, collections of cases, and related writings, one of the most widely read was the *Kitab al-Tafri*, written under Umayyad rule by the *faqih* Ibn al-Gallab (d. 988). This manual, which cites the great imam Malik Ibn Anas as its first legal authority, was so widely used that it remained in circulation even after the Muslims' final defeat in Spain in 1492: we have copies of it in Aljamiado, the Spanish dialect written in Arabic characters used by the *mudéjares* (Muslims in reconquered Catholic lands) and later among the Moriscos (Muslims supposedly converted to Catholicism who remained in Spain after 1526).[64] Even more influential were the ninth-century North African Maliki treatise *al-Mudawwana*,[65] the complementary *Utbiyya*,[66] the tenth-century *Risala* by the "little Malik" Ibn Zayd al-Qayrawani, and the twelfth-century treatise *Madhahib al-Hukkam*.[67] Also informative is the law manual *Tuhfat al-Hukkam*, by the famous Granada *faqih* Muhammad Ibn Asim al-Andalusi (1359–1427), still used today in the *sharia* courts of appeal of Nigeria and West Africa.[68] The great book of instruction for judges written by the celebrated Córdoban *alim* Ibn Rushd (1126–1198)—known in the West as "the philosopher Averroes"—the *Bidayat al-Mujtahid wa Nihayat al-Muqtasid*, illuminates the Maliki legal frame under which Muslims and their subject *dhimmis* lived.[69] Ultimately, a student of the Maliki legal system in al-Andalus must go to the great collection of religious and therefore legal materials, *al-Muwatta* ("The Easy Path" or "The Well-Trodden Path"), by the founder of the Maliki school of Islamic law, Imam Malik Ibn Anas (711–795), as narrated by his Andalusian disciple Yahya b. Yahya b. Kathir al-Laith al-Andalusi. As the Spanish Arabist J. M. Forneas has observed, in al-Andalus the impact of the *Muwatta* was immense on "great problems and attitudes, as well as the most insignificant details of daily existence."[70] But the most interesting piece of extant writing may be al-Khushani's *History of the Judges of Córdoba*, which gives biographies of judges and examples of their deliberations and decisions.[71]

These and many other documents indicate that the hegemonic legal system in Islamic Spain for most of its history, including that of the kingdom of Granada, was the Maliki school (*madhhab*), one of the four principal schools of Sunni jurisprudence.

Malikism is one of the more conservative schools, though not the most conservative—an honor that corresponds to the Hanbali school, predominant in the Arabian Peninsula. The Hanafi school is probably the least conservative (though it calls for stoning in cases of fornication and adultery—provisions included even in the Pakistani Constitution of 1979).[72] The Shafii school occupies an intermediate position between the Maliki and the Hanafi.[73]

Various Umayyad rulers, beginning with Hisham I (reigned 788–796) and including Abd al-Rahman III and al-Hakam II, declared Malikism "official." As the Spanish Arabist Miguel Asín Palacios pointed out, in al-Andalus the *fuqaha* relied on the Maliki manuals for their juridical decisions.[74] Writing in the tenth century, al-Muqaddasi, a geographer of the

Muslim world, noticed that *ulama* in Umayyad Spain followed only the teachings of Malik and claimed as authorities only the Quran and Malik's *Muwatta*.[75] Andalusian *ulama* adhered most closely to Malikism in matters of family, personal behavior, and relations between the sexes.[76] The great traditionist *alim* Ibn Hazm, not a follower of Malikism, observed that there were not many Islamic sects in al-Andalus. In fact, the followers of Malik burned Ibn Hazm's books and even forced him into exile.[77]

The historian al-Maqqari records a testimony from Umayyad Córdoba that illustrates the social control the Maliki religious authorities exerted during this Golden Age of Islam: "On the outskirts of Córdoba there are 3000 *alquerias* [villas where various kinds of business were transacted] and in each one of them...a faqih to whom one goes as an interpreter of norms and of sharia. Among them only those who have memorized the *Muwatta* can utter fatwas, or one who knows 10,000 prophetic ahadith and the *Mudawwana*. These fuqaha who live around Córdoba come to the city on Fridays to do the communal prayer with the Caliph, to say hello to him, and keep him informed of what is going on in the neighboring towns."[78] Thus the Maliki clerics played a central role in the inquisitorial system of surveillance perfected by the "tolerant" Umayyad ruler Abd al-Rahman III (see chapter 4).

During Almohad rule in Spain (ca. 1163–ca. 1236), Malikism was temporarily in official disfavor.[79] And there were always *fuqaha* who disagreed with other *fuqaha* over this or that legal issue—as judges everywhere disagree while operating within the same legal system.[80] Moreover, these clerics frequently and sometimes ruthlessly clashed over who knew the religious texts best, who had learned the most in his recent trip to the Orient, who was the most orthodox, or who was the most brilliant among them.[81] In the *taifa* kingdoms during the tenth and eleventh centuries, less-than-pious rulers allowed individual Jews and Christians an influence that weakened the *ulama* and not by chance coincided with the nadir of Islamic power in medieval Spain. Many of today's scholars consider that Jewish and Christian influence to be a wonderful example of *convivencia* and tolerance—never mind that the king of one of those supposedly enlightened *taifas*, the Sevillian al-Mutamid, following the advice of the Maliki *ulama*, burned Ibn Hazm's books.

Even after Umayyad rule, Malikism continued to function in a profitable symbiosis with Andalusian rulers. The judge al-Malaqui (d. 1105) memorized the *Mudawwana* and the *Muwatta*.[82] According to the thirteenth-century Andalusian writer al-Saqundi, the inhabitants of Córdoba were the most zealous observants of "authentic" Maliki rulings, so that no one would be named judge unless it was clear he would not depart from Malik's school.[83] Under the Almoravids, the Maliki *ulama*'s influence remained as strong as or even stronger than it had been under the Umayyads.[84]

The proud knowledge of Maliki texts was not limited to Andalusian jurists: it included poets and other litterateurs as well as people considered particularly worthy because of both their personal virtue and their skill in making Holy War against the infidels (*jihad*).[85]

THE GOLDEN AGE OF ISLAM: PUNISHMENTS FOR BLASPHEMY, APOSTASY, HERESY, WITCHCRAFT, SODOMY, THEFT, AND ADULTERY

> More astonishing than [Islamic] Spain's wide-ranging accomplishments, however, was the simple fact that until the destruction of the last Muslim Kingdom by King Ferdinand and Queen Isabella in 1492, Spain's Muslims, Christians, and Jews often managed to bestow tolerance and freedom of worship on the minorities in their midst.
> —*Publisher's blurb for the book* A Vanished World: Muslims, Christians, and Jews in Medieval Spain *(New York: Oxford University Press, 2006) by Chris Lowney*

As the historian of Islamic jurisprudence Abdel Magid Turki has emphasized, Malikism in al-Andalus was notoriously intolerant of other Muslim viewpoints.[86] Some scholars today have attempted to diminish the importance of this fact by insisting on the lack of "immutability" of Islamic juridical schools or on the "flexibility" of Malikism, or by repeating that Malikism was not "monolithic."[87] But the evidence from Andalusian juridical treatises and from contemporary comparative accounts overwhelmingly points to the intolerance of Andalusian Malikism pointed out by Turki and other historians of Islamic jurisprudence.

The widely used juridical manual *al-Tafri*, which Muslims continued to use even after the Christian conquest of Granada, prescribed death for unrepentant Mutazili heretics.[88] *Al-Tafri* also forbade marrying, socializing with, or even saluting someone who followed any of the other three main Sunni schools of law. Even Ibn Hazm, not a member of the Maliki school, agreed that Arab apostates must be killed without receiving the opportunity to repent.[89]

The geographer al-Muqaddasi observed this intolerance in al-Andalus. In addition to noting the *ulama*'s reliance on Malikism, he recorded that if they got hold of a Hanafi or a Shafii, they expelled him, and that if they got hold of a Mutazili or a Shiite, they might kill him.[90] The Andalusian Maliki-Ashari Abu Bakr b. Al-Arabi (d. 1148) tells us: "Imitation became their [the Malikis'] religion and emulation their conviction. Whenever someone came from the East with [new] knowledge, they prevented him from spreading it and humiliated him, unless he went into hiding among them, acting as a Maliki and putting his knowledge in a position of subordination."[91] In the early fourteenth century, the Andalusian *alim* al-Fakhkhar (d. 1323) confirmed that in his time heretical sects had been rare and short-lived, and that when heretics appeared, they could be killed.[92] The Maliki treatises used in al-Andalus repeatedly warn Muslims against "innovation" in religious matters.

Heretics were also persecuted in the *taifa* kingdoms, sometimes touted by historians as particularly tolerant. The king of Granada Muhammad Ibn Nasr (murdered in 1350) was praised by the historian Ibn al-Khatib because he "was rigorous against heretics and those who do not fulfill their religious obligations." Al-Khatib explained: "One day in his presence there was a discussion about religion and he said, 'the foundations of religion are two as far as I am concerned: say "He is the only God" and this,' and pointed to his sword."[93] Al-Khatib reported that in the *taifa* kingdom of Granada there were simply "no heresies or sects."[94]

Malikism in Spain represented well the Sunni tradition of the Islamic West, which historically has been more rigid than the Sunni tradition of the Islamic Middle East. Citing several medieval Muslim sources, the great Hungarian Arabist Ignaz Goldziher confirmed that, contrary to popular opinion, the practice of Islam in Spain was much more rigorous than in the East.[95] If anything, the presence of large Catholic populations to the north and in their midst, along with the conversion to Islam of many of the earlier inhabitants, seems to have exacerbated the Andalusian clerics' zeal in adhering to Maliki teachings. In other words, far from being conducive to tolerance, living close to Christians exacerbated Islamism in al-Andalus.[96]

Malik's *Muwatta* exemplified the "permeation of the whole legal life by religious and moral ideas," as the great scholar of Islamic law Joseph Schacht noted.[97] As is the case in many legal systems, Islamic or not, Maliki practice at times had sufficient flexibility to adapt to circumstances, or to an interpreter's whims, provided he was crafty enough to read and argue the law in a particular way. A good example involved the maneuvers jurists employed to face a natural disaster like the plague in such a way as not to violate *sharia* while taking effective sanitary measures.[98] Another example can be found in the legal acrobatics clerics used to circumvent the Islamic prohibition against usury in the face of economic necessity or plain greed.[99] Sometimes a ruler would fire a particular judge, thereby sabotaging the entire legal process.[100] In other words, the Maliki clerics' legal opinions, like those of judges everywhere, could be affected by their piety, situation, and preferences, and by external factors, including a ruler's enmity or favoritism.[101] Nonetheless, such notions as "toleration," "freedom of conscience," and "adapting to changing conditions" were essentially foreign to Malikism. Ibn Hazm, too, admonished the Muslim faithful to reject innovations, for all innovations were heretical and would be condemned to the flames.[102]

Under the Maliki school of jurisprudence, a Muslim who practiced another religion while pretending to be a Muslim was the worst kind of apostate and must be executed even if he repented. (Ironically, after 1492 many Muslims and Jews who had converted to Catholicism under Catholic rule would practice their religion in secret, an act of apostasy that made them targets of the Spanish Inquisition.) Following *Muwatta* 36.18.15–16, the Maliki juridical treatise *al-Tafri* prescribes that "one who pretends to be a Muslim, but secretly practices an unbeliever's faith, must be killed, and the possibility of repentance must not be given to him."[103] Likewise the *Risala*: "A freethinker (*zindiq*) must be put to death and his repentance is rejected. A freethinker is one who conceals his unbelief and pretends to follow Islam."[104] Only open apostates were given the opportunity to come back to Islam, but if they refused, they should be killed; and if after returning to Islam they again fell into open apostasy, they must be killed.[105] According to the Córdoban Maliki jurist Ibn Rushd (known in his time as a great *faqih*, judge, and adviser to the ruthless Almohad caliph, though some scholars today ignore those roles and deal with him as the great and enlightened philosopher Averroes), apostates received capital punishment, without distinction between men and women: both must be killed.[106]

Witches, too, must be killed, as *al-Tafri*, *Risala*, and *Leyes de Moros* instruct.[107] The persecution of witches in premodern Islam is still waiting for a sociological study of the kind regularly bestowed on the persecution of witches in Europe and the Americas, although the more expeditious punishments meted out in al-Andalus may have acted as a stronger deterrent than the more protracted and spectacular Western witch trials.[108]

For blasphemy against Muhammad or Allah, *al-Tafri* prescribed death without possibility of repentance: "Whoever blasphemes against Allah or his Messenger, be he a Muslim or an unbeliever, must be killed, and the opportunity to repent must not be given to him."[109] The *Risala* was similarly decisive: "Whoever abuses the Messenger of God—peace and blessing of God be upon him—is to be executed, and his repentance is not accepted."[110] In Umayyad Córdoba, Maliki authority Uthman ibn Kinana (d. 802) asserted that a ruler could choose what kind of punishment to administer for blasphemy, either beheading or crucifixion.[111] The few documents that have reached us confirm the application of these penalties. The *qadi* (judge) Said ibn Sulayman al-Balluti agreed that death must be dealt to a blasphemer.[112] In Umayyad Córdoba between 961 and 976, the *ulama* condemned to death a man, Abu al-Hayr, for insulting the Companions of the Prophet publicly and saying that one should be allowed to drink wine (something expressly prohibited, as we will see).[113] Earlier, in 919, a Córdoban *qadi* prescribed death for a Christian female *dhimmi* guilty of saying publicly that Jesus was God and Muhammad a false prophet.[114] In 1064, in Muslim-ruled Toledo, a Muslim man was crucified for blasphemy at the entrance to the city's main bridge.[115]

In the *History of the Judges of Córdoba*, al-Khushani gives another instructive example under Umayyad ruler Abd al-Rahman II in the mid-ninth century. Abd al-Rahman removed a judge for prescribing a punishment less strict than death against a Muslim man accused of uttering words offensive to Allah—blasphemy. The ruler then named a new judge, who had the impious man suffer the death prescribed by Maliki jurisprudence: crucifixion.[116] While being placed on the cross, the blasphemer shouted that he was innocent and that he did believe after all that there was no other God but Allah and that Muhammad was indeed His Prophet, but this repentance did not stop his crucifixion.[117] An extant account of the punishment of an *alim* accused of blasphemy under Abd al-Rahman II indicates that in Islamic Spain a blasphemer could be both crucified and stabbed on the cross, a curious combination that was in fact proper according to Maliki doctrine.[118]

To be sure, as in Catholic Spain, the authorities could finesse what constituted blasphemy in view of their interests of the moment, and a blasphemer might be given the opportunity to recant and be guided back to the straight path. A blasphemer's life, however, remained always at serious risk in al-Andalus.

Heresy also was punishable with death, though circumstances, or a ruler's intervention, could save the occasional *alim* suspected of heresy. Al-Khushani records that a favorite of the Umayyad ruler Muhammad I (reigned 852–886) was accused of holding heretical views. The Córdoban *fuqaha* decided that this heretic deserved death "to extirpate the bad effects that his ideas would cause." The only way Muhammad I found to save his favorite was to remove the judge before whom the case was being argued, thereby nullifying the judicial process, which then died out through legal inertia.[119]

Islamic law treatises used even by Muslims under Christian domination prescribed death for a Muslim who, after three days in jail, still did not repent from his heresy; after he was killed, his property went to the community. In these treatises, apostasy and blasphemy were even worse than heresy: if a Muslim practiced another religion in secret, he must be killed and no attention must be given to his denials or his vows of repentance; a Muslim who offended Allah must be killed; whoever insulted the Prophet Muhammad must be killed and no repentance was acceptable.[120]

The punishment for apostasy extended beyond the grave. Abd al-Rahman III (reigned 929–961), founder of the presumably tolerant Umayyad Caliphate of Córdoba, had the rebel Umar Ibn Hafsun disinterred and exposed to public desecration; Umar came from a *muladi* family of Christian converts to Islam and was accused of having died as a Christian.[121]

In al-Khushani's *History of the Judges of Córdoba*, a Muslim proved to have died as an apostate to Christianity had his property pass to the public treasure (de facto the ruler's treasure).[122] The Maliki *Risala* dictates that whenever an apostate was executed, his property would pass to the Muslim community.[123] *Al-Tafri* says that a Muslim who gave up Islam openly could be given the opportunity to reconsider; if he repented, and reconverted, he would be accepted back, but if he refused, he must be beheaded, and his relatives would not inherit any of his possessions.[124] The *Mudawwana* stipulates that if after repenting a Muslim again fell into apostasy, all the Quranic punishments for apostasy, except mutilation, would be inflicted on him before he was killed.[125] The *Utbiyya* echoes its basis, the *Mudawwana*, clarifying that if the apostate attacked and took booty from Muslims, he must be killed without being given a chance to repent. By contrast, if a Muslim in a state of apostasy robbed or even killed Christians, such factors posed no obstacle to giving him a chance to repent. And if he went back to Islam, he could not be punished, since the talion law applied among Muslims but not to a Muslim, even an apostate, who hurt or killed a Christian.[126] Apostasy by either the husband or the wife broke up the marriage automatically.[127]

Al-Tafri stipulates that women and Muslim captives who turned away from Islam and did not repent must be killed if they fell back into Muslim hands: "And if a woman turns to another religion and does not repent, kill her; and the same for the captive: kill him if he turns to another religion."[128]

High office might not protect someone suspected of apostasy. As seen in chapter 1, the son of Musa Ibn Nusayr, who had succeeded his father as Abbasid governor of Islamic Spain, was beheaded by his officers while praying in a mosque after he took as one of his wives the widow of Visigoth king Rodrigo and began displaying Christian inclinations.[129]

Malik's *Muwatta* prescribed stoning for a sodomite, even if he was not married.[130] Stoning the sodomite was still the prescribed punishment hundreds of years later in the treatises used by Muslims under Christian domination, with the caveat that, if one of the sodomites is underage, the underage one must be freed but the adult must be stoned.[131]

A thief would have his hand cut off for stealing a quarter of a dinar and upwards. No hand was cut off, however, if the thief stole "fruit hanging from a tree or...sheep kept in the mountains."[132] Ibn Rushd (Averroes) approvingly observed that Malik and al-Shafii agreed on the appropriateness of amputating the right hand of the thief, then the left foot in case of reincidence, then the left hand if the thief stole for a third time, and then his right foot if he stole yet again.[133]

As will be seen in chapter 5, in al-Andalus the punishment for adultery against a free, married Muslim female (*muhsana*) was stoning, and female circumcision was considered "honorable." Most Arabists and other academic experts on Islamic studies, as well as popularizing writers, have studiously overlooked these and other such topics in their encomiastic accounts of this Golden Age of Islam. As Ibn Hazm explained, an adulteress, even one who was otherwise an exemplary Muslim, must be killed, even if she repented.[134]

DRINKING WINE AND EATING

> Because of the strict prohibition on any form of intoxication, coffee was a genuinely sticky issue which required a ruling. Kahir Bey was the first man to attempt to provide it. He quickly assembled a team of learned men, doctors, clerics.... The inherent moderating influences of Islam demanded that it not be banned on the basis of an exaggerated sense of piety, yet perhaps coffee was harmful to the body?
> —*Antony Wilde,* Coffee: A Dark History *(New York: W. W. Norton, 2005), 49–50*

Emphasizing the self-discipline and control that were central to medieval Islam, Andalusian legal treatises laid out concrete rules governing virtually all aspects of an individual's daily life. For example, the rules instructed males not to adorn themselves with jewels, or wear gold and silver rings or other such ornaments, or wear clothes made of silk, or deform with tattoos God's given body, or drink in vessels of gold or silver, or have luxury objects made of gold and silver in their house, or play dice or chess, which is "even more weakening than dice."[135] Thus the *Risala* reminds Muslims that "it is not permissible to play backgammon or chess" (45.03).

Injunctions against drinking wine were in tune with other rules that imparted sobriety and strength to believers. But they took on special importance in Islamic Spain given the large wine-drinking Christian populations in al-Andalus and in the neighboring Christian kingdoms, whose presence probably "contaminated" Muslims and doubtlessly undermined many a good Muslim's strict adherence to the wine-drinking prohibitions of *sharia*. Documents from tenth-century Umayyad Córdoba record double punishment against someone for both making and selling wine.[136] Al-Khushani laments that some judges administered "excessively benign" punishment to drunkards and even turned their eyes away from displays of drunkenness.[137]

Even the often dissolute rulers of the *taifa* kingdoms could be ruthless in their punishments of violators. Granada's Muhammad Ibn Nasr was praised by the historian al-Khatib because he "was rigorous against... those who do not fulfill their religious obligations" and "very zealous in his application of legal punishments and in the punishment of those who drank alcoholic beverages."[138]

As late as the sixteenth century, legal treatises used by Muslims under Christian domination prescribed eighty lashes for someone who drank wine, even if it was mixed with water. The transgressor must receive the lashing after he was sober. If he relapsed in his drinking, after his fourth relapse he must be killed.[139]

Of course, as in every society, the law would be violated by the powerful, the wealthy, and the drunkards. Ibn Hazm lists one Umayyad caliph in al-Andalus and a few other rulers in the *umma* rumored to have drunk wine.[140]

Yet Maliki understanding of *sharia* leaves no doubt on the matter. The Maliki jurist Ibn Rushd (Averroes) declares: "Filth is of two kinds. First is that about the prohibition of whose sale the Muslims are all agreed. Of these is wine (*khamr*)."[141] The judges who supervised correct behavior in the public spaces of al-Andalus, the *muhtasibs*, could enter a house if they heard the sounds of drunkenness and arrest the drunkards.[142] *Al-Tafri* asserts that even a slave who drank wine or any other alcoholic beverage must be punished and that whoever made wine drunk by Muslims must be not only punished but also have his wine-making operation destroyed.[143] Ibn Rushd points out that the consensus among jurists was to rely on Caliph Umar's views, according to whom the punishment for drunkenness was eighty lashes.[144] Indeed, *al-Tafri* prescribes eighty lashes for someone who drank an alcoholic beverage, whether or not the person got drunk.[145] The *Muwatta* (books 41–42) stipulates that a free Muslim who even had alcohol on his breath must receive at least eighty lashes (the punishment was half that number for a slave).

Drinking wine could and did have dire political consequences. It could ruin a caliph's career: according to the thirteenth-century historian

Abd al-Wahid al-Marrakushi, a fondness for wine was the main factor in stopping the eldest son of Almohad caliph Abd al-Mumim (d. 1163) from succeeding his father.[146] Arabic historians blamed the destruction of the corrupt *taifa* kingdoms on the dissolute life of the rulers: "because of the lack of care of their kings, because of their abandonment of ruling, because of their abandonment of war, because they delegated power, and because of their indolence and their liking for good living, since the only preoccupation of each one of them was the wine they drank, the female singers they listened to and the amusements in which they spent their days."[147]

Even in today's Algiers, where Malikism is prevalent, wine is so unacceptable socially that the sale of wine is confined "to dark storerooms, expensive tourist restaurants, or illicit wine-cellars," writes Peter Scholliers, an expert in the history of food. "That the French consume [wine] in such large quantities is seen by many Muslims as a sign of the French lack of sobriety, self-control and virtuousness."[148]

The consumption of pork, common among Christians, was seen as particularly disgusting in al-Andalus.[149] But other prohibited foods presented similar problems to "*convivencia*" as well. Garlic, for example, was rejected by Malikism: "Yahya related to me from Malik from Ibn Shihab from Said ibn al-Musayyab that the Messenger of Allah, may Allah bless him and grant him peace, said, 'Anyone who eats this plant should not come near our mosques. The smell of the garlic will offend us.' "[150] Scholliers observes, "The consumption of certain foods was thus integral to the way Muslims distinguished themselves, or were distinguished, from Christian and Jewish groups."[151] Malikism also forbade eating the flesh of animals with "upper front teeth" and domestically raised donkeys and horses, as the *Risala* indicates (40.24).

Malik's *Muwatta* offers *ahadith* illustrating the low regard that devout Andalusian Muslims would have had for the infidels' excesses in eating and drinking. In these narratives Muhammad is said to have pointed out that whereas the good Muslim eats in only one intestine, the infidel eats in seven, and that whereas the good Muslim drinks in only one intestine, the infidel drinks in seven.[152]

Had medieval Islam prevailed in Spain and Europe, it is likely that the Western "cultures of wine and beer," which Christian practices not only allowed but even furthered, would have disappeared.[153]

MUSIC AND SINGING

> According to [the seventeenth-century French man of letters] De Fon-
> tenelle, "The Moors of Granada, a small black people, burned by the
> sun, full of wit and fire, always in love, writing verse, fond of music,
> arranging festivals, dances, and tournaments every day."
>
> —*John G. Jackson, "The Empire of the Moors," in* Golden Age of the
> Moor, *ed. Ivan van Sertima, Professor of Africana Studies at Rutgers
> University (New Brunswick, NJ: Transaction Publishers, 1991), 86*

Some scholars today claim that Islam can, after all, accept music, in
spite of the laws and practices that severely limit music in today's strictly
Islamic societies, like those of the Arabian Peninsula and Iran. These
learned scholars may well be right in their understanding of how Islamic
teachings approach music, whereas the learned *ulama* in those Islamic
societies may be wrong. But such debates, while interesting, are not ultimately relevant to what actually happened in history.

The fact is that, in al-Andalus, the Maliki school of Islamic law forbade
musical instruments and singing. *Muhtasibs* had the power to enter a house
if they heard string and wind instruments being played and break them
up.[154] Al-Khushani records that under the presumably tolerant Umayyad
ruler Abd al-Rahman III, highly respected judges ordered people's musical instruments confiscated and destroyed.[155] Some were even percussion
instruments, which Malikism sometimes treated more leniently.[156]

These Andalusian judges were just diligently following Muslim religious teachings. Al-Qayrawani's *Risala* explains the Maliki school's position on music (bracketed comments are the translator's):

40.27. Things one should not listen to:
     It is not lawful for you to deliberately listen to all of a falsehood
nor to take pleasure in listening to the words of a woman who is not
lawful for you nor to listen to musicians and singers.

40.28. *Qur'an* recitation:
     It is not permitted to recite the *Qur'an* with quavering melodies
as in the quavering used in singing. The Mighty Book of Allah must
be respected and recited with calm and gravity in a way which is

certain to please Allah and bring one near to Him with attention and understanding of that. [Nor should one listen to it with musical tunes. It must be respected and recited with stillness....]

42.4 Going to a wedding feast:
    If you are invited to a wedding feast, you must go unless there is well-known or objectionable entertainment there. It is up to you whether you eat. Malik stated that it is allowed not to go if it is too crowded. [It is said that this is a recommendation and it is said that it is an obligation. It is obliged to accept the invitation when one is specifically invited. He adds more preconditions: that there are not forbidden musical instruments there and disliked things like men and women mixing and silk couches.]

The philosopher al-Ghazali confirmed the Maliki school's views on music: "And as for Malik (May God have mercy on him!), he has forbidden singing. He said, 'When a man buys a slave-girl and finds that she is a singer, then it is his duty to send her back.'"[157] The great historian al-Tabari, too, confirms Malikism's injunctions against music and singing.[158] Maliki jurisprudence warned women not to listen to musical instruments. The Arabist Pascual de Gayangos observed, "Music being a science almost unknown to the Arabs before their conquests, they necessarily borrowed from the subdued nations their knowledge of it, as well as the names of almost all their instruments."[159] According to the scholar Irfan Shahid, extant sources point to the foreign influence of the Christian Greek Roman Empire and Persia in the development of music in Arabia.[160]

    Even today, if ever one hears music in Maliki mosques, it is limited to the sound of tambourines—an instrument not very conducive to the writing of great musical scores.

    Of course, the restrictions on musical instruments and singing did not stop some rulers and other prominent or rich people in al-Andalus from violating law and mores. Al-Maqqari, writing in the seventeenth century but using much earlier materials, reports poems being set to music and gives the names of prominent musicians.[161] Abd al-Rahman II protected and enjoyed the music of Ziryab, a ninth-century Persian virtuoso singer and instrumentalist who is said to have introduced music

to al-Andalus, but to be played at court by slaves. Abd al-Rahman's treasurers, however, refused on religious grounds to pay the musician with
the state's money; the emir then paid him out of his own pocket.[162] Less
prominent people would also try to and surely did get away with playing
and listening to music and singing.

But violating legal prohibitions happens in any society, Muslim or
not: the powerful and wealthy believe they can get away with anything,
and they often do. Of course music was played in Islamic Spain; records
even attest to the building of percussion and string instruments in Seville
and other cities.

The point, however, is that music and singing existed in spite of
the Andalusian Islamic teachings, not because of them. Overlooking
this simple fact has led to much unnecessary academic work debating
whether or how much music was allowed in al-Andalus.[163] The Maliki
school clearly laid out prohibitions on music and singing. For that reason,
singers and musicians were most often slaves (as we will see in chapter 5);
devout males and especially female *muhsana* would not go around singing and playing music.

Al-Khushani records an anecdote that illustrates this pious disregard
for music as well as the potential for powerful people to violate the teaching (though in this case the violator is unsuccessful). Occurring during
the reign of Umayyad ruler al-Hakam I (796–822), the story involves
the famous judges Yahya b. Yahya al-Layti and Muhammad b. Bashir
["Baxir"]. It is told from the perspective of Yahya b. Yahya:

> We had ridden along in the war expedition against Narbonne [in
> present-day France].... When we Muslims took booty and a great
> deal of it was piled up in our hands, we would distribute it according
> to our [Islamic] advice.... Upon returning from the expedition to
> Narbonne, [the military leader Abd-al-Melik] told me, "...I would
> like to give you a sample of my esteem: I would like to honor you
> and your companion [Muhammad b. Baxir]." "How? With what,"
> I asked. "By having you listen," he told me, "to a good concert of
> good music." "Alas!," I said, "You do not want to honor us: you want
> to offend us." "Don't think that way," said Abd-al-Melik, "there are
> many people of your station in life who do not feel one honors them
> properly until one presents them with good music." "In that case,"

I said, "Allah will not reward that behavior, not them, and not you either: how can this be an honorable thing if it offends Allah and His Prophet?" Upon hearing my words, he became ashamed of himself and did not insist any more.[164]

This sober attitude toward music among sincere, practicing Muslims in Spain lasted into the sixteenth century. Around 1567 the nobleman Francisco Núñez Muley defended his fellow Moriscos (Muslims who had converted to Catholicism) against the Spanish crown's prohibitions of presumably unseemly Islamic practices. He argued that good Muslims in Spain had never engaged in disorderly festivities; that in fact whenever gypsies started their *zambras* (a gypsy, not Muslim, dance that some relate to *flamenco*), the *fuqaha* would leave the place; and that even the Muslim kings of Granada forbade the impious playing of instruments whenever the king and his court marched through the city.[165]

No great music can develop within a culture whose all-encompassing religion does not incorporate music into its ritual and even rejects music as something undesirable. Had medieval Islam prevailed in Spain and Europe—had there been no Battle of Tours, no *Reconquista*, no Battle of Las Navas de Tolosa, and no Battle of the Gates of Vienna—the musical development of the West could have mirrored that of Islamic lands. Western music could have consisted of mostly simple, mostly orally transmitted, and mostly percussion folk pieces—or could have been prohibited outright. In other words, for better or worse, there might be no Gregorian chant; no polyphony; no organs (which developed as part of Roman Catholic church music); no vocal and instrumental masses of Victoria, Bach, Mozart, and Beethoven; no symphonies; no operas; no great composers; and no jazz.[166]

PRACTICAL OBSTACLES TO *CONVIVENCIA*

The most valuable lessons of the era [of the Islamic conquests] are not about tyranny and intolerance but how Islam can effectively navigate a pluralistic world.

    —*Christian C. Sahner, "The Crescent and the Scimitar," First Things, May 2008, 55*

Ritual purity was of special importance to the Andalusian clerics because of the Muslims' proximity to masses of infidels. Christians were a particularly worrisome source of potential defilement.

Whereas Malik did not object to a Muslim's using water left over by a menstruating woman or by a Muslim in a state of impurity, he forbade using the water left over by a Christian, or using for ablutions anything that a Christian had touched, or eating food left over by a Christian.[167] "This opinion establishes a sharp distinction between a Muslim—even in a state of impurity—and a Christian, creating a barrier to interaction," in the words of the historian Janina Safran.[168] It was not advisable to eat even what a Christian had hunted.[169]

Eating at a Christian's house would present major problems, if nothing else because of the concerns regarding purity. Christian meals might contain forbidden foods, such as garlic or pork. Then there was the barrier presented by the Christians' consumption of wine (which in other Christian societies found an equivalent in the drinking of beer, consumed at breakfast even by Reformation Puritans).[170] Dishes, if not properly purified according to Islamic rules, might remain contaminated by such Christian foods and drinks. Indeed, even instruments used to prepare *haraam* (forbidden) meals (usually Christian meals) should not be used to prepare *halal* (approved) meals.

In Umayyad al-Andalus, the ninth-century Maliki cleric Ibn Habib warned against performing ablutions with whatever a Christian had touched or used.[171] Safran cautiously observes that this warning could have "implied" that Muslims should also, for example, keep away from bathhouses used or owned by Christians. In fact, all Maliki manuals of jurisprudence contain many injunctions regarding the problems posed by water, garments, and food touched by Christians.

Maliki scholar Yahya ibn Umar al-Kinani (d. 901), who grew up in Umayyad Córdoba before traveling to pursue his divine studies in Egypt, Baghdad, and Hejaz, warned Muslims against Jews or Christians who in the marketplace might try to blend with Muslims by not wearing the distinguishing piece of cloth or belt that was required of both.[172] If Muslims lived among "People of the Book," they must use their own utensils for eating and drinking. Only if they had no other choice could they use the utensils of the infidels, and then only after washing them carefully.[173]

The legal opinions in the ninth-century *Utbiyya* affirm that places touched by the naked feet of Christians became impure and must be avoided. This was part of the reason why a Muslim should avoid entering a Christian church, since Christians were thought to step with naked feet on the church floor.[174] The *Utbiyya* confirms that Malik taught that Christians should not be allowed to build new churches, and that if the churches had been built, they should be destroyed. Muslims were forbidden to help even in the renovation of existing churches.[175]

Dogs, a common presence in Christian homes and traditionally regarded in Western civilization as close friends of humans as far back as the ancient Greeks (see Odysseus's moving encounter with Argos in the *Odyssey*), constituted another obstacle, in addition to pigs (animals kept by Christian farmers), to the interaction between Andalusian Muslims and Christians. The *Risala* exemplifies this Islamic viewpoint: it describes dogs as religiously unclean beasts that must be kept outside the home, as mere working or hunting accessories (44.05). And of course, Christian food was *haram* (forbidden) because Christians did not follow *dhabiha*, or Islamic ritual slaughter of animals for eating: *dhabiha* involves bleeding an animal to death with a cut to the throat that severs the trachea, the esophagus, and the jugular veins but does not separate the head from the body.[176]

Explicit distinctions between Muslims and non-Muslims produced all sorts of consequences for the Christian *dhimmis*. In Maliki jurisprudence, the "blood money" (the compensation for injury and some kinds of death) of a killed Christian was half that of a free Muslim. If a free Muslim killed a Christian, he must not be punished with death, unless the killing had been treacherous, whereas the murder of a free Muslim could be punished with death. Injuries to Christians caused by Muslim slaves were also treated differently.[177] The testimony of a Christian (or a Jew) was not valid in disputes between Muslims.[178] Malik observed, "I think *that Christians should be compelled to wear belts, and that used to be required of them of old. I think that they should be compelled to be humble. Umar wrote that they should be mounted sideways on donkeys* [emphasis added]." Umar (ruled 634–644) succeeded Abu Bakr (ruled 632–634) as the second caliph after Muhammad's death and is the alleged author of the Pact (or Covenant) of Umar, a Muslim document that allowed Christians to practice their religion indoors and under severe restrictions, in exchange for submission to Muslims and the payment of a "protection" tax, the *jizya*.[179]

Coincidentally, some centuries after Malik, Greek Christians were forced to ride only on donkeys, and sideways, during the *Tourkokratia*, the Muslim Turks' four-hundred-year domination of Greece. As with Islamic Spain, some scholars today argue that the Muslim domination of the Christian Greeks was not too bad after all.[180]

The *Utbiyya* confirms that if the children of a Muslim father and a Christian mother wanted to become Christians, they must be forced to remain Muslims or be killed; children born of an apostate while the apostate was still a Muslim must be forced to be Muslims even if they did not wish to do so; and children born of an apostate while the apostate was no longer a Muslim (and had survived to have children) must be forced to become Muslims if they had not yet reached puberty.[181]

Even in 1100, centuries after the Muslim conquest of Spain, the Andalusian clerics' obsessive preoccupation with the contaminating potential of the infidels was echoed in the regulations issued in Seville by the *faqih* Ibn Abdun:

A Muslim must not massage a Jew or a Christian nor throw away his refuse nor clean his latrines. The Jew and the Christian are better fitted for such trades, since they are the trades of those who are vile. A Muslim should not attend to the animal of a Jew or of a Christian, nor serve him as a muleteer [neither Catholics nor Jews could ride horses; only Muslims could], nor hold his stirrup. If any Muslim is known to do this, he should be denounced.... No... [unconverted] Jew or Christian must be allowed to dress in the costume of people of position, of a jurist, or of a worthy man [this provision echoes the Pact of Umar]. They must on the contrary be abhorred and shunned and should not be greeted with the formula, "Peace be with you," for the devil has gained mastery over them and has made them forget the name of God. They are the devil's party, "and indeed the devil's party are the losers" (Qur'an 57:22). *They must have a distinguishing sign by which they are recognized to their shame* [emphasis added].[182]

A court document from tenth-century Umayyad Córdoba confirms that Christians were forbidden from even walking across Muslim cemeteries (*maqabir*) because their walking by the Muslim tombs would pollute them.[183]

Today's scholars devoted to an imaginary *convivencia* and diversity overlook that the polluting potential of Christians, along with Islam's numerous praying rules, its complicated purification rituals, and its injunctions against drinking and eating during daytime in Ramadan, presented all sorts of obstacles to the everyday integration of Muslims, Jews, and Christians.[184] In view of these and other issues, the Islamic cities' de facto division into Muslim, Jewish, and Christian semiautonomous neighborhoods helped the rulers' efforts not only to maintain Muslim hegemony but also to keep the peace among the multicultural population of Islamic Spain.

Some scholars point out as an example of *convivencia* that Muslims in thirteenth-century Córdoba "shared" in Christmas celebrations. They overlook the fact that Catholics had reconquered Córdoba in 1236. It was not a Muslim city. It is misleading to seize on what some Muslims did *in Christian-controlled cities* as evidence of religious tolerance and harmony in Islamic Spain. *In Muslim-controlled cities*, Christians were forbidden to celebrate their religion *in public*, even in their own neighborhoods (crosses could not be displayed even on the outside of church walls or on top, and bells could not be wrung), so of course Muslims could not participate in public festivities that did not exist. In any case, a Muslim's "having fun" unlawfully during Christian festivities in various ways would not have been the same as truly *sharing* in the celebration, which entails accepting the birth of the Son of God—a "Son of God" being a blasphemous concept from the Muslim viewpoint.[185]

A collection of Islamic legal documents from the fourteenth century shows a ruling by a Maliki jurist in ninth-century Umayyad Córdoba that is quite clear on the subject of Muslims' accepting presents from Christians during Christmas (brackets are the translator's):[186]

Abu'l-Asbagh Isa b. Muhammad al-Tamili was asked... "Do you think (may God be generous to you!) that it is a forbidden innovation, which a Muslim cannot be permitted to follow, and that he should not agree to [accept]...? Is it disapproved of, without being unambiguously forbidden? Or is it absolutely [forbidden]? There are traditions handed down from the Prophet of God (may God bless him and grant him salvation!) concerning those of his community who imitated the Christians in their [celebration] of Nauruz and Mihrajan, to the effect that they would be mustered with the Christians on the Day of Judgment. It is also reported that he said, 'Whoever imitates a people, is one of them.' So explain to us—may God be generous to you—what you consider correct in this matter, if God wills."

He answered: I have read this letter of yours and have understood what you are asking about. It is forbidden to do everything that you have mentioned in your letter, according to the *ulama*. I have cited the traditions that you mentioned to emphasize that, and I have also cited Yahya b. Yahya al-Laithi, who said, [Receiving] presents at Christmas from a Christian or from a Muslim is not allowed, neither is accepting invitations on that day, nor is making preparations for it. It should be regarded as the same as any other day. He produced a *hadith* on this subject going back to the Prophet (may God bless him and grant him salvation), who one day said to his Companions, "You will become settled among the non-Arabs; whoever imitates them in their [celebration] of Nauruz and Mihrajan will be mustered with them." Yahya also said, I asked Ibn Kimana about that, and informed him about the situation in our country, and he disapproved and denounced it. He said, Our firm opinion about that, is that it is *makruh* (repugnant). Similarly, I have heard Malik say, In the words of the Prophet, may God bless him and grant him salvation, "Whoever imitates a people, will be mustered with them."

This ruling indicates the sort of temptations that living in a multicultural environment near the polluting Christians might pose for pious Muslims—an environment that actually made Islam in al-Andalus even more rigid because it forced the *ulama* to come up with ways to counter the temptations.

Maliki jurisprudence in al-Andalus forbade socializing even with Muslims of a different school of law, let alone "sharing" with Christians or Jews.[187] As we have seen, even a non-Maliki cleric like Ibn Hazm agreed on the need to keep away from Christians. Muslim clerics correctly realized that participating even in the more superficial aspects of an alien religion's festivity could gradually erode beliefs. In some cases the *ulama* took no measures to prevent this "sharing," but that was during times of Christian supremacy, as in thirteenth-century reconquered Córdoba.

Even then, however, the *ulama* countered the more insidious of these festivities, Christmas, with festivities celebrating the birth of Muhammad.[188]

In short, Islamic Spain enjoyed no harmonious *convivencia*; rather, Muslims, Christians, and Jews had a precarious coexistence. Members of the three communities had to come into contact now and then. Sometimes they did business, or collaborated with one another, or dwelled near one another. As everywhere on earth, the kinder members of the population might help "the others" in case of need, in spite of their religious differences, while the less pious might more or less furtively even adopt some of the more enjoyable practices of "the others." The scholar and priest Rafael Jiménez Pedrajas has recorded a number of examples of kindness between Muslims and Christians, bright points in his book on the long history of religious oppression of Christians by Muslims in al-Andalus.[189] As happens wherever one culture is hegemonic over another, words from one language were picked up here and there in the other languages. The subject peoples gradually adopted the hegemonic religion's dress and language—Arabic—or a combination of Arabic and their own language. Some leaders of the subject Christian and Jewish communities, the *dhimmis*, did serve the Muslim rulers, sometimes even in positions of authority over Muslims, and therefore contrary to Islamic law. Many Christian communities eventually ceased to exist as distinct cultural entities because members converted to improve their condition and because of simple demographics helped by Muslims' taking Christian wives and having children who must be raised as Muslims. But the masses stayed by and large in their own neighborhoods, where their families and coreligionists spent most of their lives and where they could practice their religion, gladly oblivious to "the others."

Some academics today have tried to argue, rather desperately, and against earlier research (fashionably dismissed as "Orientalist"), that Muslims, Jews, and Christians in Muslim-controlled cities did not separate into neighborhoods.

This position does not withstand scrutiny. Different communities developed naturally, even without official sanction or force, around mosques, synagogues, and churches. The Muslim documents of the medieval era contain numerous references to Muslim, Jewish, and Catholic *neighborhoods*. For example, under the Umayyads, Maliki jurists Ibn al-Qadim (d. 806) and Ibn al-Majishun (d. 829) ruled that Catholics in a non-Muslim territory could, if they submitted to Islam and paid tribute, build new churches—as long as they did not build them in *Muslim neighborhoods*.[190] Instructive, too, is a Maliki *fatwa* from al-Suyuri (d. 1067) regarding the problems created by a Jew who bought a house on a *Muslim street*: "He has settled there and bothers his neighbors by drinking wine and doing other reprehensible things. With his bucket, his rope, and his pitcher, he extracts water, like the Muslims, from a nearby well, and therefore the Muslim neighbors refuse to use the well." Unless the Jew changed his behavior, the *fatwa* ruled, his house would be taken away.[191]

The presence of distinct Muslim neighborhoods is also obvious in all versions of the famous Pact of Umar, of which Malik spoke approvingly. That pact forbade Christians from even repairing churches in *Muslim neighborhoods*, having houses that looked on *Muslim houses*, gathering in churches that had existed in *Muslim neighborhoods*, and showing wine or pork or crosses in *Muslim neighborhoods*.[192]

The rebel Ibn Hafsun's ability to stand up to the power of the Umayyads for so many years was the result not only of his military ability but also of the support he received from *neighborhoods and villages* inhabited by *muladis* and Christian *dhimmis*.

Archaeological research by Basilio Pavón Maldonado, Leopoldo Torres Balbás, and Antonio Almagro has shown customary divisions into Muslim, Jewish, and Christian quarters in several Muslim cities in Spain.

A number of Muslim cities even had gates specifically designated as "Jewish Gates" (*Bab al-Yahud*).[193]

The division extended to the grave: there were Muslim, Jewish, and Christian cemeteries.

Military logic suggests that Muslim rulers would favor keeping the division of the three main ethnic and religious groups within the larger cities. Such divisions would not only minimize frictions but also facilitate control in case of civil disturbances or war.

On the whole, the evidence indicates that Muslim religious leaders' justified fear of the "other" as a source of influence and possible conversion, the three religions' marked differences in worship and purification practices, and the religious laws' exclusionary dictates and warnings against socializing with other groups made living even in the same block difficult at best.[194]

The Muslim clerics' fear of contamination only increased as Christians reconquered the land. The Spanish reconquest was almost complete as of 1248, after the capture of Seville. Only a diminished kingdom of Granada remained under Islamic rule. In the reconquered territories, Catholics allowed Muslims, the so-called *mudéjares*, to practice their religion but deprived them of military and political power and forbade them from displaying Islamic rituals publicly—much the same sort of restrictions Muslims had once imposed on the Christian *dhimmis* under the Islamic system of "protection." Fearing a weakening of the faith among the conquered, many *ulama* issued *fatwas* urging Muslims in the reconquered lands—*ahl aldajn*, or "the people of submission"—to leave infidel lands, *dar al-Harb*, and move to Islamic territory, *dar al-Islam*.[195] In the surrender treaty of 1492, the last Muslim king of Granada inserted a clause stipulating that no Jews would be allowed to have authority over Muslims or collect any taxes from them.[196]

4

THE MYTH OF UMAYYAD TOLERANCE

Inquisitions, Beheadings, Impalings, and Crucifixions

Muslim Spain...experienced a golden age beginning in the latter half of the eighth century under the enlightened rule of the Umayyad dynasty based in Córdoba.
— *Mark Tessler, Samuel J. Eldersveld Professor of Political Science at the University of Michigan,* A History of the Israeli-Palestinian Conflict *(Bloomington: Indiana University Press, 1994), 22*

When al-Andalus was invaded by the conservative North African dynasties, the Almoravids and Almohads,...the traditional policy of toleration was undercut.
— *Jerrilynn D. Dodds, Professor of Art History at Sarah Lawrence College, in* Convivencia: Jews, Muslims, and Christians in Medieval Spain, *ed. Vivian B. Mann, Adjunct Professor of Jewish Art and Visual Culture at the Jewish Theological Seminary; Thomas F. Glick, Professor of Medieval History and Director of the Institute for Medieval History at Boston University; and Jerrilynn D. Dodds (New York: G. Braziller in association with the Jewish Museum, 1992), 119*

LIKE MOST THINGS concerning Islamic Spain, the rule of the Umayyads is praised enthusiastically by many of today's admiring academics, Islamic studies experts or not, as an inspiring example of tolerance and *convivencia* of the three faiths (Islam, Judaism, and Christianity).

In fact, as Ibn Hazm gleefully put it, of all the dynasties of Islamic Spain, the Umayyads were "the most afflicting to the enemies of God."[1]

The celebrated Umayyads actually elevated religious and political persecutions, inquisitions, beheadings, impalings, and crucifixions to heights unequaled by any other set of rulers before or after in Spain.

THE "TOLERANCE" SHOWN TOWARD CHRISTIANS

> [The Almoravids and the Almohads] were very different from their Arab predecessors; they were driven by an intolerant orthodoxy that made it impossible to sustain the centuries-old intellectual openness that had made Umayyad Spain a place of scientific and philosophical learning.
> —*Kwame Anthony Appiah, Laurance S. Rockefeller University Professor of Philosophy at Princeton University, "How Muslims Made Europe,"* New York Review of Books, *November 6, 2008*

The founder of the Umayyad dynasty, Abd al-Rahman I—an "intrepid young man," as an admiring Yale university professor has called him[2]—set the tone for what was to follow under Umayyad rule. The Muslim historian al-Maqqari records that Abd al-Rahman I, a pious man, demolished the ancient basilica of Saint Vincent, which had been the spiritual center of the city's Catholics. The Muslim ruler then used the materials from the demolished church, as well as from other Roman and Visigoth buildings, to build the famous mosque of Córdoba on Saint Vincent's ruins. In a way that is typical of the academic approach to Muslim Spain, the University of Córdoba website carefully avoids mentioning Abd al-Rahman's destruction of the Catholic church: "Caliph [*sic*; he was in fact an emir; the Caliphate was implemented by Abd al-Rahman III] Abd ar-Rahman I ordered the Mosque to be built in A.D. 785 *on the site of* the former Visigoth basilica of San Vicente [emphasis added]."[3] And that is all the university site has to say about it. The myth of Umayyad tolerance remains conveniently untouched.

Al-Razi, one of the earlier historians of Islamic Spain, tells us that Saint Vincent had been the only place left where Christians could worship in Córdoba. Muslims had taken the city years before and had destroyed all the other churches in and around Córdoba, using the materials to build mosques. With the money that Abd al-Rahman I had given them to surrender Saint Vincent in an offer that they could not refuse, Christians erected another church, but outside the walls of the city, the only place Christians were allowed to build it.

According to al-Razi, what Abd al-Rahman I did to the church of Saint Vincent was part of the Umayyad ruler's policy of destroying the temples and saintly relics of "the polytheists": "He [Abd al-Rahman] would take all the bodies which Christians honor and call saints, and he would burn them; and he would burn their beautiful churches; and in Spain there were many and very magnificent churches, some built by the Greeks and some by the Romans. Seeing this, the Christians, when they could, would take their sacred things, and would flee to the mountains."[4] Al-Maqqari confirms that, after the conquest, all other churches in and out of Córdoba "were immediately pulled down."[5]

As examined in chapter 1, and as al-Maqqari also reminds us, Abd al-Rahman I was following a pattern established in earlier Islamic conquests and continued by later Islamic conquerors.[6] In the Christian Middle East and North Africa, Muslims routinely took over for prayers a building within a site belonging to the most important Christian temple in a city that had peacefully surrendered. (In cities that resisted, the Islamic victors would immediately demolish the Christian temples and turn them into mosques.) Eventually the Muslim population increased and the Christian population decreased, almost inevitably, because of several reasons: Christians would convert to escape the condition of dhimmitude, or flee; Islam's marriage laws allowed Muslim men to marry Christian women but required the children to be raised as Muslims, and punished Christian men with death if they fornicated with or married a Muslim woman; and polygyny fostered the creation of large families. When the Muslim population was large enough and therefore conveniently "needed more space for worship," Muslims would take over the entire Christian site, demolish the Christian temple, cannibalize it, and build a mosque.

Such a fate befell many Christian buildings. In the early eighth century in Damascus, the Umayyad caliph al-Walid demolished the great Greek basilica of Saint John the Baptist to build upon it the "Great Mosque of Damascus" (or "Umayyad Mosque"). The magnificent Greek basilica of Hagia Sophia in Constantinople (today's Istanbul) is probably the best-known example of a Christian temple that, though not demolished, was turned into a mosque: the Ottoman Turkish sultan and caliph of Islam Mehmet II ordered the conversion of Hagia Sophia as soon as the city was conquered in 1453. The Muslim conquerors painted over or destroyed all offending Christian icons, removed al crosses from within and without the basilica, and surrounded Hagia Sophia with four minarets that still stand today. The Cathedral of Saint John at Ephesus, reputed to have the tomb of the Apostle John, was converted directly into a mosque by the tolerant Muslim Turks in 1330. After the bloody Islamic conquest of Cyprus by the Turks in 1571, Famagusta's fourteenth-century Gothic-style Cathedral of Saint Nicholas, where the Lusignan kings of Cyprus were crowned as kings of Jerusalem, was turned into a mosque. In today's Cyprus, Christian churches continue to be vandalized, looted, and torn down in the part of the Greek island forcefully occupied by Turkey in 1974.[7] In the seventh century the Islamic conquerors of Greek Christian North Africa demolished many churches to build mosques.

An admiring professor of Arabic at the London Middle East Institute of the University of London calls these actions not hegemonic maneuvers but examples of "tolerance," since at least for a while Muslims were willing to share religious sites with Christians (as we will see, this is a myth repeated by historians) and to use building materials from the demolished churches. He gives as a further instance of this tolerance the transformation of part of the Persian royal palace of Ctesiphon into a mosque.[8] Enthusiastically reviewing this scholar's book, another academic expert on medieval and Islamic history observes, "The most valuable lessons of the era [of the Islamic conquests] are not about tyranny and intolerance but how Islam can effectively navigate a pluralistic world."[9] Many scholars in the English-speaking world, including specialists in medieval Spain such as Kenneth B. Wolf, repeat that Muslims initially "shared" the church of Saint Vincent as well as other Christian temples.

But as the archaeologist Pedro Marfil and other Spanish scholars have pointed out, archaeological research provides no evidence of "sharing." Indeed, it is unlikely that Muslims would have shared the churches of the Christians prior to converting them into mosques, simply because of the differences between the two religions.[10] Strict Muslims would not pray in the midst of icons and sculptures, which they considered idols, or in front of the cross, which they considered blasphemous. More likely, Muslims took over a sacristy or a nearby building, or built an adjacent mud construction, prior to demolishing the church and building a mosque. But this would not constitute a sharing.

UMAYYAD BRUTALITY

> The Israelis and Palestinians, even if they could achieve a workable peace, would still be surrounded by a Muslim world very remote from the Andalusia of Abd al-Rahman and his descendants. It is salutary to be reminded of what Cordoba and Granada once were, and yet it is also disquieting.
> —*Harold Bloom, Sterling Professor of Humanities at Yale University, from his foreword to María Rosa Menocal,* The Ornament of the World: How Muslims, Jews, and Christians Created a Culture of Tolerance in Medieval Spain *(New York: Little, Brown and Company, 2002), xv*

A less enthusiastic Spanish Arabist, Maribel Fierro, explains:

> The rulers of al-Andalus, most especially the Umayyads, carried out indiscriminate beheading of prisoners of war, and took great pains to transport the severed heads to the capital, as symbols of the extension of their power and of the submission of their enemies. The source that recorded the Almohads engaging in the same practice took care to signal the similarity of this practice with that followed in the time of the Umayyad caliphs. That the decapitation of defeated enemies after battle was a military practice well ingrained in Andalusi and, more generally, in Islamic military conduct of war is clearly shown in narratives found in different literary genres, apart from chronicles and manuals on the conduct of war.[11]

Thus when Ismail, son of the ruler of Seville, was defeated, as a matter of course "he was immediately beheaded, and his head carried to Malaga, to be presented to Idris Ibn Ali."[12]

Barely a year after Abd al-Rahman I had overthrown the Islamic governor in 756, he faced a rebellion from al-Fihri, the Muslim lord of Toledo, the former capital of the Visigoth kingdom. This would be one of many uprisings the Umayyad monarch would encounter during his rule. Abd al-Rahman besieged rebellious Toledo but was unable to overcome its defenses. Before lifting the siege, he beheaded al-Fihri's son and catapulted the head over the wall as a warning to the father.

Having enlarged his army with many African slave-warriors, Abd al-Rahman returned a year later, and this time he invested the city so effectively that the famished inhabitants betrayed al-Fihri and delivered him and his closest followers to Abd al-Rahman. The Umayyad ruler had the prisoners' heads and beards shaved, dressed the prisoners in wool rags, paraded them on donkeys through the city, and then crucified them publicly.

After defeating an uprising by the former Islamic governor, Yusuf, in 758, Abd al-Rahman I ordered Yusuf's head displayed in Córdoba, "nailed under the central arch of the bridge," al-Maqqari tells us. Then he had Yusuf's son beheaded, too, and ordered that the heads be "placed on two spears under the gate of the royal palace." Another of Yusuf's sons was put in a dungeon and later strangled.

In 763 Abd al-Rahman faced an Abbasid invasion from North Africa. Al-Maqqari tells us that the Umayyad ruler defeated the invaders and had the heads of all the prisoners cut off, taken to Cairo and Mecca, and "cast at night into the squares and principal streets of those two cities together with the black banners of the Abbasids."

According to al-Maqqari, when the defeated Abbasid general and his officers were brought before Abd al-Rahman, the Umayyad ruler had the men's hands cut off, then their feet, and finally their heads. Then "Abd al-Rahman caused labels, inscribed with the names of the deceased, to be suspended from their ears; their heads were then stored in sealed bags, together with the black banners of the house of Abbas, and the whole given to a trusty merchant, who was directed to convey his cargo to Mecca, and deposit it in public places at a certain time."

Social turmoil in Islamic Spain included chronic struggles between the ruler du jour and the Arab nobility. As an Umayyad refugee in an Islamic-conquered land, Abd al-Rahman could not entirely trust the Arab nobility and military. He brought in specially trained troops who had no tribal or family ties and therefore were loyal only to the Muslim ruler: non-Arab slave-warriors and Berber mercenaries. In this use of armies of slaves and mercenaries loyal only to him, he was following a common practice of rulers in the Islamic empire. "In this manner," writes the eleventh-century Arab historian Ibn Hayyan, "Abd al-Rahman collected an army of slaves and Berbers, amounting to upwards of forty thousand men, by means of whom he always remained victorious in every contest with the Arabian tribes of Andalus."[13] Still, dynastic conflict was such that Abd al-Rahman I could never rest: between 779 and 783 he executed a number of people, including some nephews, suspected of conspiracy.

The Umayyads imposed brutal punishments on the *dhimmis* who dared to openly proclaim their religious beliefs. In the ninth century, *alim* Ibn al-Qasim asserted that if a Christian said, "Our religion is better than yours, for truly yours is the religion of the Ass," he must be punished.[14] Al-Qasim cited imam Malik's view that when an infidel insulted the Prophet, he must be killed. In the same century, *alim* Muhammad explained that just as Islam did not allow a *dhimmi* to kill or steal from a Muslim, so it did not allow a *dhimmi* to insult the Prophet, because by doing so, the infidel blasphemer violated the covenant of "protection" granted to *dhimmis*.

In 919 the head judge of tolerant Umayyad Córdoba invoked the punishment that contemporary *sharia* law prescribed against a Christian woman accused and found guilty of having said publicly that Jesus was God and that Muhammad was a liar who pretended to be a prophet: "whoever deprecates Allah, praised be Allah, or deprecates his Messenger, peace be upon him, be he a Muslim or an infidel, he must be killed and must not be allowed to repent."[15]

The tenth-century ruler Abd al-Rahman III (the name means "Servant of the Merciful"), the first Andalusian Umayyad to proclaim himself caliph, has earned particular admiration among Western scholars, as in this rhapsodic description: "Under this energetic and dazzlingly successful monarch...the territorial expansion and cultural achievement of Spanish Islam reached its zenith."[16]

In fact, Abd al-Rahman III's political success was inseparable from and dependent on his inquisitorial network of spies and his large-scale beheadings and crucifixions of Muslim heretics, Christian prisoners, and political enemies. As a Spanish scholar puts it, "The enhanced beheading activity under Abd al-Rahman III was notorious."[17] Moreover, his "cultural achievement" rested on the wealth collected through the various taxes (including the *jizya*) imposed on Christian and Jewish *dhimmis*, and on the loot he obtained in his periodic incursions into Christian kingdoms.

The Muslim historian Ibn Hayyan praised Abd al-Rahman III as enthusiastically as have twentieth- and twenty-first-century Western scholars, but not always for the same reasons. Ibn Hayyan praised the Umayyad ruler for, among other things, his ruthless Córdoban Inquisition against heretics:

> Religion, after the Prophet, continued firm and straight under the aegis of the Perfect Caliphs [successors of Muhammad including the Umayyads; n. of M. J. Viguera] ... who kept the norms of the *Sunnah*, safeguarding the religion, putting out the fires of sedition, destroying the schismatic sects, expelling the *rafidis* [those who reject the right path of Islam, such as the Shiites], humbling the rebels and making them submit, struggling [doing *jihad*] and defending God with the sword of God.... [The good Caliphs] fought all innovators [cf. Malik's dictum, "no innovation must be accepted"; n. M. J. Viguera], and they did not allow innovation to enter the nation. But then came the rule of the twisted and deviationist faction of the Abbasids, and innovations proliferated.... [But] God protected the people of al-Andalus, preserving their religion from calamities thanks to ... the Prince of the Believers [Abd al-Rahman III; n. M. J. Viguera] ... whom [God] wanted as a Caliph ... who followed in the steps of his ancestors, adhering closely to Scripture and proclaiming the *Sunnah* ... so that no devilish heresy would arise that he would not destroy, no flag of perdition was raised that he did not humble, so that with him God kept the community of Islam together, obedient, peaceful ... with him science flourished, people prospered.... He expelled innovation and gathered in his capital [Córdoba] the most perfect culture of the times, as never before existed ... and he attended to matters of religion, investigating the behavior of the Muslims [authorities had the duty to keep an eye on people's customs; n. M. J. Viguera], and their gatherings in their mosques by means of spies whom he ordered to penetrate the most intimate secrets of the people, so that he could know every action, every thought of good and bad people, and ... the explicit and hidden views of the different groups of the population.... God showered gifts upon him ... because of his keeping of the law and his subjugating of men, so they sang his praise and his defense of the people's

hearts against heresy... following the true and witnessed traditions [ahadith] attributed to the greatest of all Imams, Malik Ibn
Anas, Imam of the people of Medina.... [These traditions] are the
ones that have benefited this country, and purified the people from
those tendencies which [Abd al-Rahman III] punished in those who
held them, and he ordered his zalmedina [Muslim judge in charge
of patrolling the public spaces to enforce sharia] Abdallah b. Badr,
his mawla, to interrogate the accused and carry out an Inquisition
against them... terrifying them and punishing them severely.[18]

With his Inquisition, the Umayyad ruler Abd al-Rahman III echoed the
ruthless methods of the Middle East Abbasid caliph al-Mamun (786–
833), who had developed an Islamic Inquisition as a way to cope with the
Greek philosophy that Islam had encountered.[19]

But apostasy and its accompanying capital punishment struck within
Abd al-Rahman III's own family: he had his relative Ibrahim b. Ahmad b.
Abd al-Aziz killed for secretly practicing Christianity.[20] Against a charismatic "prophet" named Hamim and his numerous followers (whose
heresy was probably influenced by Christianity), Abd al-Rahman sent an
army that destroyed the forces of the apostate and brought his head back
to Córdoba to be publicly exhibited.[21]

According to Ibn Hayyan, Caliph Abd al-Rahman III carried out
Inquisitions against masarri heretics (followers of the gnostic cleric Ibn
Masarra) at various times (952, 956, 957), ordering the ulama to read the
following proclamation in all the mosques of al-Andalus:

The Caliph has decided to include in his decision all his lands, sending it to the countryside and to the cities, and asking you and the
other qadis and governors to carry out its enforcement, so that it is
read in the pulpits of the Muslims [so that everyone benefits from]
the purification and liquidation of this filth and of the protection
of all Muslims against all doubt and motive for sedition because
nations are lost, works are erased, people deserve extermination and
God destroys nations for things like what this evil group of people
has brought about, who adulterate tradition, and attack the great
Quran and the ahadith of the loyal Prophet.... Persecute them by all
means available, send them your spies, make an effort to know their

secrets and when it is clear that someone belongs to them write to the Caliph a list with their names, location, names of the witnesses against them and their accusations so that one may order to have them brought to the gate of al-Sudda and punished in their capital.[22]

This "Gate of al-Sudda" or "Gate of the Threshold" was one of the arched entrances to Abd al-Rahman III's renowned palace of Medinat al-Zahra. Modern admiring scholarly accounts of this palace omit the fact that on this ornamented gate the "Servant of the Merciful" routinely exposed to the elements and to the awed Córdoban populace the crucified bodies and severed heads of his enemies.

In suppressing dissent, Abd al-Rahman III persecuted any Muslims who followed a legal school other than the Maliki, so that Malikism could remain dominant.[23] This may have been the reason for Abd al-Rahman III's murder of his own son, Abd Allah, who had shown a preference for Shafiism.[24]

In fact, all Umayyad rulers were careful to allow, promote, and protect only those works and authors considered orthodox by the Andalusian Maliki clerics. According to Ibn Hayyan, it was the duty of the Islamic chain of executive authority, from the caliph to the *qadis*, to enforce *sharia* and therefore correct Islamic behavior on the population.[25] As the scholar Abdel Magid Turki and others have pointed out, in this chain of authority Maliki orthodoxy played an official ideological role in the Umayyad dynasty.[26]

Ibn Hayyan gives a good example of Abd al-Rahman III's treatment of Christian prisoners:

Muhammad [one of the officers of Abd al-Rahman III] chose the 100 most important barbarians [that is, Christians] and sent them to the alcazar of Córdoba, where they arrived Friday, 7 of the *yumada* I (March 2, 939), but since an-Nasir [Abd al-Rahman III] was vacationing in the orchard of an-Naura [La Noria], they were taken there, their marching coinciding with the people's exiting from the aljama mosque of Córdoba, upon the conclusion of the Friday prayer, so that many gathered and followed to see what end the prisoners would have, and it turned out that an-Nasir was installed on the upper balcony over the orchard facing the river...to watch the execution. All the prisoners, one by one, were decapitated in his presence and under his eyes, in plain sight of the people, whose feelings against the infidels Allah alleviated, and they showered their blessings on the Caliph. The death of these barbarians was celebrated in a poem by Ubaydallah b. Yahya b. Idris [one of the many sycophantic intellectuals in the pay of the Umayyads who relentlessly praised their greatness], saying,

> Defeated the prisoners arrived,
> Carried and shackled by *Allah*,
> Like an angry lion you looked at them,
> Surrounded by wild lions and dragons,
> And in plain sight of everyone your sword annihilated them,
> Among blessings and praises to *Allah*.[27]

But "The Servant of the Merciful" ingeniously varied his methods of killing. Spectacular crucifixions instead of simple beheadings were particularly effective when his soldiers failed in their duty. Ibn Hayyan describes one of these ceremonies upon the crushing defeat Christian forces inflicted on Abd al-Rahman at Alhandega in Castile-León (939) (after which the "dazzlingly successful" caliph prudently decided never to lead another *jihad* in person). The historian relates how the Umayyad ruler returned home and ordered an attic to be built on the top floor of one wing of the palace:

He put almenas [turrets] and ten door-like openings in it.... Having prepared ten high crosses, each one placed in front of each door of the attic, an arrangement that awed the people, who did not know his purpose, and therefore more people came to watch than ever before. When the army arrived, he ordered the zalmedina to arrest 10 of the principal officers of the army, the first ones to break rank the day of Alhandega, who were there in the ranks, whom he named and ordered to be placed on the crosses, which was done by the executioners right away, leaving them crucified, among their supplications for mercy and pardon, which only increased his anger and insults, while letting them know that they had let him down.[28]

Ibn Hayyan describes a witness's horror at this mass crucifixion, a reaction which was undoubtedly Abd al-Rahman's intention to provoke: "I was caught in the midst of the crowd.... I turned away my eyes, almost fainting with horror at the sight...and such was my state, that a thief stole my pack [without my noticing it].... It was a terrible day that scared people for a long time afterwards."

Crucifixion was also useful against Muslim challengers to the Servant of the Merciful's rule. Early in his reign, in 913, Abd al-Rahman III ordered the rebel Muhammad b. Yusuf al-Yayyani crucified on the door of the royal palace in Córdoba.[29] This was, writes Ibn Hayyan, the first of several crucifixions during the Umayyad caliph's reign.

Death might not save an enemy from crucifixion. After the death of Ibn Hafsun, a rebel and apostate to Christianity, Abd al-Rahman III had his cadaver disinterred, crucified, and exposed as a Christian. This sort of crucifixion-after-death did not stop when the reign of the "tolerant" Umayyads ended. The Almoravids followed this Umayyad practice. They disinterred the cadaver of Malaga judge al-Husyan, crucified it, and took his head to the Almoravid capital of Marrakesh for exhibition. Similarly, the Almohads disinterred, crucified, and exposed the cadaver of the rebel Ibn Hamdin.[30]

Ibn Hazm laments that Abd al-Rahman III was one of a number of depraved caliphs who gave themselves up "in body and soul to pleasure."[31] A poem by the Catholic nun Hrotsvitha von Gandersheim (935–ca. 1001) tells the story of the Umayyad caliph's homosexual passion for a thirteen-year-old male Catholic hostage, Pelayo (later Saint Pelayo); Abd al-Rahman ordered Pelayo beheaded after repeated tortures because the boy had turned him down.[32]

Ibn Hayyan tells several interesting stories regarding Abd al-Rahman III's other personal inclinations. One tells of his burning the face of a beautiful female sexual slave who had dared reject his advances:

I must say that I have heard from ulama, generationally close to that dynasty [the Umayyads], about the brutality of an-Nasir li-din towards the women that were under his protection and discretion, similar to what he showed in public towards men, according to the words of the principal ones among his most intimate servants— eunuchs who lived in his house and witnessed his personal life: a female slave who was one of his most highly regarded favorites, but whose haughty personality did not bend easily to his vanity, having remained with him alone in one of his leisure days to drink in the garden of az-Zahra [a palace that Abd al-Rahman III had built for his favorite sexual slave and that contained 300 baths, 400 horses, 15,000 eunuchs and servants, and a harem of 6,300 women], sitting by his side until drinking had an effect on him, and he threw himself upon her face to kiss and bite her, and she got disgusted by this and turned her face away, raining on his parade; this so provoked his anger that he ordered the eunuchs to seize her and put a candle to her face, burning and destroying her beauty...until they destroyed her face, burning her badly and finishing with her—one of his worst actions.

Another story concerns the brutal execution of a sexual slave who had offended the caliph:

His executioner, Abu Imran [Yahya], whom he always had at the ready with his "instruments," said that one night he called him to his room in the palace of an-Naura, where Yahya had slept with his sword and leather floor mat. [Yahya] then entered the room where [Abd al-Rahman III] was drinking and found him squatting, like a lion sitting on his paws, in the company of a girl, beautiful like an oryx, who was being held by his eunuchs in a corner of the room, who was asking him for mercy, while he answered her in the grossest manner. He then told [Yahya] "Take that whore, Abu Imran, and cut her neck." [Yahya] said, "I procrastinated, asking him again, as was my custom, but he told me: 'Cut it, so may *Allah* cut your hand, or if not, put down you own [neck].' And a servant brought her close to me, gathering up her braids, so that with one blow I made her head fly; but the strike of the blade made an abnormal noise, although I had not seen it hit anything else [but the neck]. Afterwards they took away the body of the girl, I cleaned my sword on my leather mat, I rolled up the mat, and I left; but when I entered my own room and I unfolded the mat, there appeared in it pearls big and shiny, mixed with jacinths and topazes that shone like red-hot coals, all of which I gathered in my hands and I hurried to take it to an-Nasir; he rejected it immediately and told me, 'We knew they were there, but we wanted to give them to you as a gift: take it and may *Allah* bless it to you.' And with it I bought this house." So says the one who transmits this story.

Ibn Hayyan tells also of the Servant of the Merciful's use of lions to terrorize the Córdoban population:

I must also mention a horror with which an-Nasir terrorized people, which was by means of lions to make their punishment even more terrible, an action more proper of the tyrannical kinds of the Orient, in which he imitated them, having the lions brought to him by the little kings on the North African coast, since they are not animals proper to al-Andalus.[33]

Ibn Hazm describes in similarly unflattering terms other episodes of Abd al-Rahman III's life, including the presumably humorous use of black children hanged as counterweights from a well:

Abd al-Rahman an-Nasir was not far from his great grandfather al-Hakam b. Hisam in the way he threw himself into sin and committed doubtful acts, abusing his subjects, giving himself cynically to pleasure, punishing with cruelty and caring little for the effusion of blood. He was the one who hanged the sons of the blacks from the well of his palace as a sort of counterweight to draw water, making them die; and he had his impudent buffoon Rasis in a cortege, with sword and helmet, when in fact she was a shameless old woman, not to mention other hideous hidden things, that *Allah* knows better.[34]

"BY RUIN AND DESTRUCTION"

The Umayyads preferred to be religiously tolerant and accepting of other religions.
    —Timothy C. Hall, The Complete Idiot's Guide to World History
    (New York: Alpha, an imprint of the Penguin Group, 2008), 80

Among the Umayyad predecessors of Abd al-Rahman III, al-Haqam I deserves mention for his effective brutality, facilitated by an enormous army of slaves and mercenaries (his personal body guard was made up of Christian warriors on his pay) loyal only to him rather than to other leaders or to the *ulama* class. According to the historian Ibn al-Qutiyya, al-Haqam successfully eradicated a heretical Islamic sect in Algeciras by knifing the city's inhabitants.[35] In 805 this illustrious Umayyad ruler, who was very pious (he aggrandized the mosque of Córdoba and dutifully made *jihad*—as Holy War, not as an effort to improve himself—against the Christian infidels) and who loved poetry and the arts, had seventy-two *ulama* crucified for conspiring against him.

Previously, in 797, the Umayyad ruler had carried out the famous beheadings of the "Foso," during which he wiped out the elite of Toledo's unruly Christian converts to Islam. Ibn Hayyan describes the emir's ingenious ruse:

> [Al-Haqam I] organized a banquet in which he would honor the notable people of Toledo.... He ordered that the guests entered through one door and exited through another, presumably to avoid bottle necks at the banquet. And he put in practice his plan against them, for he had already placed men inside the Alcazar with their drawn swords, so that as soon as one of the Toledans entered and crossed the door he would be taken to the brink of a deep pit that the ruler had prepared and then his head would be cut off.... And their bodies were thrown into the pit, but the Toledans, who were arriving in large numbers, did not realize what was happening and thought that they were exiting through a door, until many of them were exterminated. Finally... [they] realized what was happening...and fled. And the massacred reached 700 men. And [the people of the city] were impressed by a catastrophe that humiliated them for a long time.[36]

Between 851 and 859, the Umayyad rulers Abd al-Rahman II and Muhammad I killed nearly fifty Christians ("The Martyrs of Córdoba"). Some of these martyrs were *dhimmis*. Many others had been born in Muslim families that had once been Christian (*muladi* families); now, however, these *muladis* had converted back to Catholicism and proclaimed the divinity of Jesus and the falseness of Muhammad as a prophet. Although beheading was his preferred method of execution, Muhammad I used other methods as well: the nun Laura, thrown into a cauldron of molten lead (a variation of the Roman emperor Domitian's attempted killing of Saint John in a cauldron of boiling oil); the old monk Jeremiah, lashed to death; and the young soldier Sancho, impaled.

Although most scholars today do not dispute the primary-source evidence of the Umayyads' brutal killings of these Christians, they point out the "extremism" of the *martyrs*, not of the presumably tolerant Umayyad rulers who ordered their slaughter. They have called these executed Christians "fanatics," "troublemakers," and "self-immolators." As that last term suggests, scholars have argued, in essence, that the Catholics "asked for it" by openly doing things clearly punishable by Islam. Thus the Martyrs of Córdoba episode has been turned into a scholarly version of "blaming the victim." For example, one professor of medieval European history claims, "To the extent that Muslims in Córdoba did actively persecute Christians, they did so after the martyrdoms began, not before, so that the martyrs' movement was more likely the cause of ill-treatment than a response to it."[37] Another professor points out that our "modern sensibilities" and "greater objectivity" precludes any admiration for the Christians and revulsion at their Muslim killers.

As Abd al-Rahman III's handling of apostates demonstrated, Umayyad repression was especially harsh against Muslim transgressors. As part of the Umayyads' effective system of social control, the powerful religious functionary known as the *muhtasib* policed the cities of Islamic Spain, enforcing *sharia* in everyday activities, including the marketplace. A central element of the job involved informing the Umayyad rulers of any potential subversion on the part of the masses. The Muslim historian al-Khushani tells us that Muhammad I had instructed his *muhtasib* to be ruthless, resorting if necessary to amputations and crucifixions, without needing to request authorization to carry out these penalties. Thus whenever those accused of a crime were brought before Córdoban *muhtasib* Ibrahim b. Husayn b. Asim, he would tell the accused, "Prepare your will."[38]

Among the successors of the Umayyads, the bloodiest, but also the most successful, was the able leader Muhammad Ibn Abu Amir, known to Muslims as al-Mansur ("The Victorious") and to Catholics as Almanzor.[39] In the late tenth century he positioned himself as regent for the child Caliph Hisham al-Muayyad, the last of the Umayyads. The usurper hired more Berber mercenaries from Africa and implemented a ferocious military dictatorship backed by a huge army.

A pious Muslim, "The Victorious" carried out nearly sixty successful *jihads* and ordered that the dust on his clothes be collected after each expedition against the hated Christians so that he could be buried under that glorious dust when he died. In addition to building more palaces and further subsidizing the arts in Córdoba with the wealth of Jews and Christians, al-Mansur burned heretical books and terrorized Christians by sacking and burning Zaragoza, Osma, Zamora, León, Astorga, Coimbra, and Santiago de Compostela, among other places. In 985 he burned down Barcelona, enslaving all those he did not kill.

Al-Mansur built an enormous addition to the Córdoba mosque with demolished churches, whose remains he ordered carried to Córdoba on the heads of Catholic captives.[40] He ordered the Christian slaves to carry the great bells of the Cathedral of Santiago de Compostela to Córdoba, where the bells were melted and turned into lamps for the mosque. Admiring chronicler al-Maqqari tells us that al-Mansur had the famous addition to the Córdoba mosque built by Christian slaves from Castile and "other infidel countries working in chains at the building instead of the Moslems, thus exalting the true religion and trampling down polytheism."[41]

Al-Mansur followed the example of the Umayyad ruler Abd al-Rahman III in his religious zeal. During his reign he carried out virulent persecutions and book burnings against theological deviations and the Greek philosophy that might contribute to them. As part of his coup d'état against child caliph Hisham al-Muayyad, he allied himself with the Andalusian Maliki *ulama* and proceeded to upstage them in their enmity toward heresy. According to the chronicler Said al-Andalusi (1029–1070), al-Mansur once again proved his religious piety by ordering the *ulama* to do a public burning of all philosophical works in the caliphate's library.[42] Al-Andalusi explains: "Whoever had studied those sciences [philosophy] became regarded as prone to heterodoxy and suspected of heresy. Most of those who until then had studied philosophy now lost their interest in it, became terrified and kept secret the fact that they knew the subject. The more talented men of the times, until the collapse of the Umayyad dynasty in Spain...cultivated only those sciences which were allowed to be studied, such as arithmetic...medicine and similar disciplines."

"The Victorious" died in 1002 in the course of a *jihad* against one of the spiritual sites of Spanish Catholicism, the monastery of San Millán de la Cogolla. An anonymous Muslim historian tells us that, at the time of his death, al-Mansur lamented not having done more to thwart the Christian Reconquest: "God Almighty inspired me more than once with the means of salvation; but I constantly disregarded the admonition. Had I laid waste all the territories subdued by my arms, had I by ruin and destruction made a desert of at least ten days' march between our extreme frontier and that of the Christians, we might then have averted the approaching tempest."[43]

BEHEADING AND CRUCIFIXION IN ISLAMIC SPAIN AND IN THE WEST

> The apogee of Umayyad rule came with the dazzlingly successful reign of Abd al-Rahman III.... Despite occasional persecution, the Christian and Jewish minorities were allowed to play their full part in a tolerant, multi-confessional society.
> —Grove Encyclopedia of Islamic Art and Architecture, *ed. Jonathan M. Bloom and Sheila S. Blair (Oxford: Oxford University Press, 2009), 372*

Spanish Christians did not crucify their enemies. Beheading the defeated had been frequent among the Normans and Celts, and occasional among some other nations,[44] but in western Europe crucifixion stopped being used as a form of capital punishment with the Christianization of the land. As we have seen, however, in Islamic Spain both crucifixions and beheadings reached unheard-of proportions.

As the Arabist Maribel Fierro and historians Francisco García Fitz, José Manuel Rodriguez García, and others have shown, Andalusian Muslim accounts of beheading do not present it as a characteristically Christian practice; on the other hand, Spanish Christian accounts present beheading as a characteristically Muslim practice.[45] In other words, neither Catholic nor Muslim sources associate beheading with the culture of the Catholic kingdoms, whereas Catholic sources associate it with the culture of Islamic Spain. "[Beheading] Muslim enemies," Fierro and Fitz write, "was not the general type of behavior among Castilian and Leones rulers, nor does it indicate a will to exterminate violently the Muslim population."

These differences may originate in the absence of Christian religious texts that justified beheading as a form of killing. Beheadings of Muslims were carried out by some Christian military commanders in medieval Spain against Muslims, but beheading the enemies of Christianity was not a teaching of the Christian New Testament. By contrast, as the Arabist Fierro points out, Islamic culture had a long religious textual tradition that was seen as justifying beheading against dangerous enemies of the true faith.[46]

Of course, it is entirely possible that, as many professors of Islamic and Middle East studies insist today, these texts urging the beheading of the defeated enemies of the faith are actually "metaphorical." But the relevant fact is that, throughout the history of Islamic Spain, both *ulama* and rulers interpreted these Muslim religious texts not metaphorically but literally, and acted accordingly.

As Fierro points out, "The main representatives of Arab ethnicity in al-Andalus, namely the Umayyads and the Abbadids [an Arab family who ruled parts of al-Andalus after the fall of the Caliphate of Córdoba], appear to have been great head hunters. They cut off the heads of the most dangerous rebels and exhibited them publicly, an act that both Almoravids and Almohads performed in equal measure, and that eventually found some legal support in the [Islamic religious] material dealing with rebellion, according to those jurists who advocated a harsh policy toward rebels, such as the Hanafi al-Sarakhsi (d. ca. 1096)."[47]

Some Spanish Christian leaders decapitated Muslims in the course of war but were outdone by Muslim rulers, who used decapitation against their fellow Muslims even more than against Christians.[48] This last difference may be attributable to the submissive condition of Christians as *dhimmis* in Islamic Spain, which lessened the number and danger of their revolts.[49]

Nevertheless, in favor of the Andalusian rulers' mass use of beheading, crucifixion, impaling, and other such rather harsh methods of killing, one could use historical contextualization: multicultural and pluralistic al-Andalus was plagued with religious, racial, political, and social con-flicts, so that the most successful rulers must apply brutal and terrifying force to keep the place from disintegrating, as in fact it ultimately did.

Therefore, Muslim leaders would have been encouraged in their par-ticularly intensive practice of beheading and crucifixion by their need to keep under control the boiling cauldron that was "multiethnic" and "multireligious" al-Andalus. Failing to do so might have, among other things, cost them their own heads. After all, massive terror can be an effective political tool, and in al-Andalus it worked for the most success-ful rulers.[50] In contrast, the relatively more ethnically and religiously uni-fied Catholic kingdoms did not present the same problems for their rulers and therefore did not encourage the same drastic solutions.[51]

5

WOMEN IN ISLAMIC SPAIN

Female Circumcision, Stoning,
Veils, and Sexual Slavery

For nearly a century, scholars have debated how the roles of Muslim women in al-Andalus became markedly more relaxed than those found in much of the Arab world.

> —*John W. Fox, Nada Mourtada-Sabbah, and Sulayman N. Khalaf,*
> *"Ethnography and the Culture of Tolerance in al-Andalus,"* Harvard
> Middle Eastern and Islamic Review *(2006), 146*

In Christian Europe ninety-nine percent of the people were illiterate, and even kings could neither read nor write. [Meanwhile, in Islamic Spain] you had Moorish women who were doctors and lawyers and professors.

> —*John G. Jackson, "The Empire of the Moors," in* Golden Age of the
> Moor, *ed. Ivan van Sertima, Professor of Africana Studies at Rutgers*
> *University (New Brunswick, NJ: Transaction Publishers, 1991), 86*

IN DEPICTING ISLAMIC Spain as a model of tolerance and multiculturalism, scholars have attempted to show that Muslim women in al-Andalus enjoyed a surprising degree of freedom, especially compared with women in Christian lands at the same time. But like so much else about Islamic Spain, this claim does not hold up to scrutiny.

The concern of the present chapter is not to discuss whether "true" Muslim teachings include a proper Muslim woman's wearing of a veil and other forms of face or hair covering, or a proper Muslim woman's limiting her public activities, or stoning to death adulterous free married women and circumcising females. Rather, this chapter examines the actual Islamic teachings and practices in medieval Spain according to the Maliki school of Islamic jurisprudence that dominated this Muslim realm for most of its history.

FEMALE CIRCUMCISION (*KHIFAD*)

> Islam has a proud tradition of tolerance. We see it in the history of Andalusia and Córdoba during the Inquisition [*sic*].... Likewise, it is important for Western countries to avoid impeding Muslim citizens from practicing religion as they see fit—for instance, by dictating what clothes a Muslim woman should wear. We can't disguise hostility towards any religion behind the pretence of liberalism.
> —*President Barack Obama, speech at Cairo University, June 4, 2009*

The Muslim female's circumcision (*khifad*, or "lessening") was legal, taken for granted, and praiseworthy in al-Andalus. Curiously, this cultural practice has not been pointed out in the general scholarly histories on the Islam of al-Andalus. Even the best scholars have prudently tiptoed around it.[1] Yet several examples easily found in contemporary legal documents make the presence of female circumcision rather clear.

While discussing the need for a full ablution before praying after sexual contact, Malik's foundational legal treatise, *Muwatta*, collects several examples that make religious cleansing obligatory after one "circumcised part" has touched or passed through the other "circumcised part."[2]

> Yahya related to me from Malik from Abu'n Nadr, the mawla of Umar ibn Abdullah that Abu Salamaibn Abdar-Rahman ibn Awf related that he had asked A'isha, the wife of the Prophet, may Allah bless him and grant him peace, what made ghusl obligatory. She said, "Do you know what you are like, Abu Salama? You are like a chick when it hears the cocks crowing and so crows with them. When the circumcised part passes the circumcised part, ghusl is obligatory." (2.19.74)
>
> Malik said, about a man who had intercourse with his wife during hajj after he had come down from Arafa but before he had stoned the Jamra, "He must sacrifice an animal and do hajj again in

another year. If, however, he had intercourse with his wife after he stoned the Jamra, he only has to do an umra and sacrifice an animal and he does not have to do another hajj." Malik said, "What spoils a hajj or an umra and makes sacrificing an animal and repeating the hajj necessary is the meeting of the two circumcised parts, even if there is no emission." (20.46.161)

One can notice how the *Muwatta* considers the circumcision of the female so normal, so taken for granted in this medieval Islamic culture, that it merely *mentions* "circumcised" sexual parts in the course of talking about *something else*. Would most Muslim women in al-Andalus have been circumcised? Probably: how many fathers (or mothers) do not want their little girl to grow up to be an honorable woman in a society where female circumcision is considered "honorable"? And how many little girls would have the physical strength or conviction to refuse circumcision in a society where every little girl goes through this rite of passage? Probably the only females who might try to resist would be adult non-Muslim sexual slaves, likely from Christian lands, where the practice was abhorred.[3] As we will see, Malik ruled that even female sexual slaves that a Muslim master wanted to keep could be circumcised.

Since Malik's authoritative *Muwatta* and other Maliki treatises took female circumcision for granted and recommended it as honorable, Maliki *fuqaha* in al-Andalus would have followed this teaching, as indeed do all the Andalusian Islamic legal manuals, even those widely used among *mudéjares* (Muslims under Christian domination who until the sixteenth century were allowed by Christian rulers to keep their religion) and *moriscos* (Muslims under Christian domination who in the sixteenth century had been given the choice of converting to Christianity or leaving Spain, many of whom continued to practice Islam secretly).

Thus, the Maliki juridical manual *al-Tafri*, widely used in al-Andalus, and even as late as the seventeenth century translated into *aljamiado* by the *moriscos*, ruled that circumcision was "sunnah" (obligatory) for men and "honorable for women."[4] Moreover, following Malik's *Muwatta*, *al-Tafri* took female circumcision for granted when prescribing purification before praying if the two "circumcised organs" (*hatenados*) have touched.[5]

The influential treatise *Risala* by Maliki authority al-Qayrawani also considered female circumcision *makruma* or praiseworthy (bracketed text is part of the citation): "Female circumcision (*khifad*) is praiseworthy (*makruma*). [To remove what the woman has of excess. It is recommended.... It is worthy because it brightens the complexion and makes intercourse pleasurable.]."[6] Al-Qayrawani's *Risala* emphasizes the desirability of female circumcision also in the section on personal upkeeping rules (*fitra*): "Circumcision for men is a sunna [*sic*] of the Prophet (P.B.U.H.), while for ladies it is a mark of honor" (41.01).

According to al-Qayrawani's legal manual *Kitab al-jami* ("Comprehensive Book"), Malik in fact makes the Muslim master responsible for the circumcision of sexual slave women that he wants to keep: "He [Malik] said, 'Whoever buys a female slave may have her circumcised if he wishes to keep her. If she is for resale then that is not his responsibility.'"[7] Al-Qayrawani also wrote that, according to Malik, only women must perform circumcision on girls.

For the *Risala* of great legal authority al-Shafii, who belonged to the same tribe as Muhammad (the Quraysh), and who had studied under Malik before moving on to found his own school of Islamic law, female circumcision was compulsory.[8] The non-Maliki *Sahih Muslim* collection also took female circumcision for granted.[9]

In Abu Dawud's authoritative collection of sunnah, the Prophet is said to have advised for the female only "moderate" cutting, which would make sex more pleasurable.[10] Women would circumcise women, since men were forbidden to see the genital parts of females not their wives or sexual slaves.[11]

It must be pointed out that a modern translator of Islamic religious texts observes: "The traditional circumcision of the Muslims must not be confused with that practiced today, widespread in parts of Sudan and Africa, known as Pharaonic circumcision. The former is a very minor operation involving no damage to the woman, when carried out by suitably qualified practitioners. The latter is a particularly abhorrent mutilation."[12]

A renowned Maliki scholar from Córdoba, al-Qurtubi (thirteenth century), affirmed that, "for our fellow malikis," and always following the Messenger of Allah, circumcision was a *sunnah* for males and acceptable for women. Al-Qurtubi also echoes Abu Dawud's telling of a woman in Medina who circumcised women, to whom the Prophet had said that female circumcision should not be total but partial. Al-Qurtubi mentions another version of this hadith, according to which a partial circumcision is better because it makes the complexion clearer and it also benefits men.[13]

The fourteenth-century anonymous legal treatise *Leyes de Moros*, written in Spanish for the use of the *mudéjares*, also follows these Maliki teachings: "Circumcision is the law for men and honorable for women" (CCCIV). Thus even in Christian territories, Muslim law continued to make female circumcision "honorable." Commenting on this fourteenth-century treatise, the Arabist Soha Abboud-Haggar praises the "wise tolerance" of the Christian rulers who gave the Muslims under Christian domination "the right to rule themselves by their own laws."[14]

As in other schools of medieval Islamic jurisprudence, in Malikism the circumcision of the male was a sunnah; and during a certain period in the history of al-Andalus, Muslim authorities decreed the forced circumcision of male Christians as well.[15]

Seemingly unaware of these texts we have examined, the Arabist Manuela Marín cites several different texts from al-Andalus showing that female circumcision was taken for granted. For example, in the biography of the legal scholar Ibn al-Yabbad (d. 934), Ibn al-Yabbad is asked whether one should perform an ablution after "the meeting of two circumcisions without ejaculation," a situation also treated, as we have seen, in several texts from the Maliki school of law.

Today's discussions on whether or not the practice of female circumcision is actually prescribed "by Islam," or whether it was a pre-Islamic practice that Islam kept, or whether it was a practice that Muhammad did not condone but that later clerics implemented, are irrelevant to the fact of its approval in Maliki law and therefore to the logic of its practice in lands ruled by the Maliki law right down to the twenty-first century.

STONING (*RAJM*)

> The truth is at the time of the great caliphates the center of the Muslim world was highly tolerant.
> —*Carly Fiorina, former Hewlett-Packard CEO and 2016 GOP presidential candidate, on HBO's* Real Time with Bill Maher, *January 9, 2015*[16]

As in the case of female circumcision, the scholarly histories of Islamic Spain have not talked about the cultural practice of stoning a female *muhsan* (a free Muslim of sane mind who has married properly and has had sexual intercourse with a spouse in a proper way).[17] Free married Andalusian Muslim women were supposed to enjoy sex fully, but within the confines of the marriage structure. And Muslim men were supposed to enjoy sex only with their wives or their sexual slaves (*Risala*, 40.19).

Therefore, according to Maliki legal texts and manuals, sexual intercourse of a Muslim woman (or, theoretically at least, of a man) outside marriage constituted fornication and was punishable with public stoning to death (*rajm*) if the woman was a *muhsan*, or a minimum of eighty publicly administered lashes, plus exile for a year, if she was not.[18] Thus we read in Malik's *Muwatta* that an adulterous *muhsan* woman must be stoned, although this legal treatise thoughtfully takes into account the possibility that the woman may be pregnant, in which case her stoning must wait until her baby has been weaned:

> Malik related to me from Yaqub ibn Zayd ibn Talha from his father Zayd ibn Talha that Abdullah ibn Abi Mulayka informed him that a woman came to the Messenger of Allah, may Allah bless him and grant him peace, and informed him that she had committed adultery and was pregnant. The Messenger of Allah, may Allah bless him and grant him peace, said to her, "Go away until you give birth." When she had given birth, she came to him. The Messenger of Allah, may Allah bless him and grant him peace, said to her, "Go away until you have suckled and weaned the baby." When she had weaned the baby, she came to him. He said, "Go and entrust the baby to someone." She entrusted the baby to someone and then came to him. He gave the order and she was stoned.[19]

Malik's *Muwatta* prudently insists that, according to the Messenger of Allah's teachings, a pregnant woman must not be stoned until she has given birth and suckled the baby sufficiently:

> Malik related to me that he had heard that Uthman ibn Affan was brought a woman who had given birth after six months and he ordered her to be stoned. Ali ibn Abi Talib said to him, "She does

not deserve that. Allah, the Blessed, the Exalted, says in His Book, 'Their carrying and weaning is thirty months,' (Sura 46 ayat 15) and he said, 'Mothers suckle their children for two full years for whoever wishes to complete the suckling.' (Sura 2 ayat 233) Pregnancy can then be six months, so she does not deserve to be stoned." Uthman ibn Affan sent for her and found that she had already been stoned.[20]

Al-Qayrawani's Maliki *Risala* confirms the Islamic teaching and explains the term *muhsan* (all bracketed comments are part of the citation):

37.21 ILLICIT INTERCOURSE (ZINA) BY THE MARITALLY RESTRICTED: If a freeborn Muslim who has been married (muhsan) commits adultery or fornication, he [or she] is to be stoned to death. What is meant by 'muhsan' is a man who has married a woman properly and has had sexual intercourse with her in a proper way [or a woman who has married a man properly and has had sexual intercourse with him in a proper way].

37.22 ILLICIT INTERCOURSE BY THE NON-MARITALLY RESTRICTED: But if he [or she] has not been a muhsan, he [or she] is beaten one hundred lashes and then banished to another town where he [or she] should be imprisoned for a year. A slave who commits adultery or fornication is to be beaten fifty lashes. A slave woman is to be treated likewise, even if [she is] married. Besides, [male slaves who fornicate] are not exiled nor is a [slave] woman exiled.

However, the Maliki manual *al-Tafri*, widely used in Islamic Spain, stipulates that not only a *muhsan* woman who fornicated must be stoned, but also married female slaves who fornicated should be stoned.[21]

The twelfth-century expert on the Maliki school of Islamic jurisprudence in Spain, the Córdoban Ibn Rushd (known by Western scholars usually only as "the great philosopher Averroes"), confirms that the punishment for adultery in the case of a *muhsan* woman must be stoning; and that no pit need be dug for the punishment (whereas, according to al-Shafii, a pit must be dug to stone a woman, but not a man).[22]

The fourteenth-century *Leyes de Moros*, written for the benefit of the Muslims under Christian domination, also followed the Maliki teachings on the stoning of adulterers: "If two married Muslims are found to have fornicated, they must be stoned until they die" (CLXVIII).

But conviction for illegal intercourse must follow certain rules to avoid a possible injustice, as al-Qayrawani's *Risala* indicates:

> 37.23 CONVICTION FOR ILLICIT INTERCOURSE: The person who committed adultery does not receive the hadd punishment except through confession, or through pregnancy which becomes evident, or through the testimony of four freeborn adult men of integrity who witnessed the action like a mirwad in a mukhulah. (A 'mirwad' is the little stick for applying kohl or antimony to the eyelids. 'Mukhulah' is the container for kohl or antimony.) The witnesses must see the action at the same time. And if one of them failed to complete the description, the three should receive hadd punishment for qadhf (or false accusation of fornication).

Since Quran 24:2 specified that a fornicator and a fornicatress must be scourged, al-Shafii's *Risala* explained that this injunction remained true only in the case of unmarried adult free Muslims; in the case of married ones (*muhsan*), the *hadith* according to which Muhammad ordered an adulterous man and woman stoned abrogated mere scourging and banishment for adulterers and replaced such punishment with stoning (*rajm*).[23]

Legal treatises used by Muslims under Christian domination prescribed that, when a married Muslim fornicates with another married Muslim and there are four Muslim witnesses who saw it happen, the married fornicating Muslims must be stoned; and if neither Muslim is married, they must be given one hundred lashes and the male must be exiled for a year and kept in jail while he is exiled; and the male must be lashed sitting and naked, whereas the woman must be lashed sitting but covered, but not so much that she does not feel the lashing.[24] An unmarried pregnant woman who says she was forced to have intercourse must be tortured if she cannot prove what she claims; a man who commits sodomy with a woman must be tortured, and if she was married he must be killed; but a woman must not be punished if she shouts that she is being raped or if she was sleeping or if she is out of her mind or younger than twelve years of age; nor will a woman be punished who has sex with a male not yet of age (*Suma*, LIV).

THE VEILING OF MUSLIM WOMEN IN AL-ANDALUS

Research by Spanish Arabists such as María Luisa Ávila indicates that the activities of *slave* women, unknowingly or knowingly used by scholars of Islamic studies and by medievalist historians who talk enthusiastically about the relative "freedom" or "relaxed role" of women in al-Andalus compared to the rest of the Islamic world, are not representative because the slave women's "legal status and social situation were wholly different from those of the *hurra*, the free woman," and their "activity in society cannot therefore be considered typical of the Andalusi woman in any way—a point many commentators have missed."[25]

The Spanish Arabist Manuela Marín cites a case in tenth-century Umayyad Córdoba taken from the biography of famous jurist (*faqih*) al-Tuyibi (940–1018), which illustrates the prescribed use of the face-covering veil for a *muhsana* (a free Muslim woman of sound mind in a properly consummated marriage) in Spain under Islamic law (*muhsan* was the normal status for a free Muslim woman of sound mind and marriageable age in Islamic Spain, because a free Muslim woman—a *hurra*—was usually married as soon as she reached puberty, and even before, although consummation could not take place until she had reached puberty).[26]

The legal case has as protagonists a woman and three males, one of them a legal counselor or jurist (*faqih*). This jurist was highly regarded as a legal counselor, we read in the documents, by "the *veiled women who stayed in their houses* [emphasis added] and belonged to families of good birth."

This sentence indicates the proper practice for a respectable Muslim woman: *staying in her house and being veiled when going out in public*. As the narrative continues, an *alim* (Muslim scholar, and therefore a religious scholar—pl. *ulama*) brings his wife and son to this famous *faqih*. The *alim* tells the story: "I went to see him [the famous *faqih*] to ask for a certified testimony regarding my wife and my son." Once the *alim* has been seated, the *faqih* asks the son, still a child, to sit down as well. But he does not ask the woman to sit. Then the *faqih* turns to the son and, pointing to the standing woman, asks, "Who is that one?" The child answers, "That is my mother." The *faqih* then proceeds to write down the certified testimony. The episode ends with the *alim* expressing satisfaction with the way the *faqih* had handled the case.

This episode illuminates the condition of a female *muhsan* in al-Andalus. Although she could have title to property, inherit it, and receive it as dowry, she needed a man as an agent, in this case the husband, in order to engage in legal transactions—as Maliki Islamic law prescribed. Moreover, *the woman was not asked to sit in the presence of men: she remained standing, unlike the men. The woman could not speak for herself and needed a male, even if he was a child, to speak for her. And there was need for testimony from her male child to ascertain that "that" was his mother—a woman who, because she wore a face veil, was unrecognizable.*

According to the Maliki legal manual *al-Tafri* by *faqih* Ibn al-Gallad (tenth century), so widely used in medieval Spain that it was even secretly adhered to among the *mudéjares*, a *hurra* or a *muhsan* woman must not walk in the company of a man, except one she would be legally forbidden to marry (such as a very close relative); and she must not walk alone, but only in the company of other women.[27]

The widely used *Risala* of al-Qayrawani equally confined *hurras* and *muhsan* women to the house and underlined the prescribed modesty: "A woman must not come out in the public unless moved by necessity, such as attending the funeral ceremonies of her parents or near relatives, or occasions of similar nature, which are lawful to her. She must not attend a funeral ceremony at which professional mourners scream. Nor is it lawful for her to attend ceremonies where clarinets and lutes or similar musical instruments are played. However, she is permitted to attend weddings where tambourines are played" (41.07); "It is incumbent upon Muslims to avoid looking at women who are strangers to them" (40.6).

The Spanish Arabist Cristina de la Puente shows that other Maliki legal texts from al-Andalus prescribe that a *hurra* or a *muhsan* woman must be veiled whenever she leaves her house and that she can leave her house only with the husband's permission and only for absolutely urgent reasons.[28]

Manuela Marín provides examples from different centuries and social levels that illustrate the sheltered status of Muslim free women (*hurras*) in al-Andalus. One example from the Umayyad court in Córdoba records a ninth-century conversation between a *visir* (minister), Muhammad b. Mubassir, and a literary scholar, Abu l-Hakam. To a grammatical question from the literary scholar regarding the proper feminine form of an Arabic verb in the imperative if it were used hypothetically to order a woman to attack, *visir* Muhammad b. Mubassir answers: "Oh Abu l-Hakam! I have never heard a question more detestable than the one you pose! Allah orders woman to stay in her house and you want to know how to order her to go to war!"[29] This example shows how keeping Muslim women away from public places was part of the ethos of the Umayyad court and considered to have a religious sanction.

Illustrations in *El libro de ajedrez* of Alfonso X (reigned 1252–1284) show thirteenth-century Muslim women with veils covering their faces from the eyes down, their heads also covered, and their bodies wrapped in ample robes—in stark contrast to Christian women in the court of the same Alfonso X, who are depicted with faces uncovered and bodies unwrapped.[30]

Women who might dare go about with loose hair and rich garments and jewels were *sexual slave girls*; the *hurra* or *muhsana* would wear the proper head and body dress.[31] Many documents attest to that. In Islamic Spain, wearing elegant attire and golden jewelry in public was something that, though still not proper, slave girls might do, but not *hurras* or *muhsanas*.[32]

Even slave girls, however, could be punished for not being properly veiled: according to the *Risala*, "He [Malik] strongly rejected the behavior of . . . slave-girls in going out uncovered. . . . He said, 'Beat slave girls if they do that.' He said, 'There is not harm in it if she wraps her clothes around her.'"[33]

Following Malik, *al-Tafri* even forbade women to loosen their hair when cleaning it during ablution: it was sufficient to throw water on the hair and rub the water into the scalp with the hands.[34] In fact, Spanish Maliki jurisprudence advised proper Muslim women to keep their hair short, as indicated in the *Risala* of al-Qayrawani:

> The sunna for women is to shorten the hair. [It is disliked for her to shave and it is said that it is haram because it is mutilation. She shortens her hair. The basis for that is what Abu Dawud related that the Prophet said, "Women do not have to shave. Women shorten their hair."] (28.14b)[35]

Andalusian Muslim women could not play around in a swimming pool, even fully dressed, as some imaginative Western academics fancy today. *Al-Tafri* made clear that women could not go to the public baths, no matter how fully dressed, except in case of a bleeding illness or other dire necessity.[36] As we have seen, al-Qayrawani's Maliki *Risala* likewise insisted that women must not go out in public except in exceptional circumstances.

The legal manual *Suma de los principales mandamientos y deve-damientos de la ley y çunna, por don Içe de Gebir, Alfaquí Mayor de la aljama de Segovia*, written in 1492, prescribes similar restrictions: "A Muslim wife can be allowed to see those relatives whom she could not have married [if she were single] and to go to the mosque during the day and to places which are beyond suspicion and to have fun with other women with whom there are no men—but only during the day and only once a week."[37] It is significant that these laws were used by Muslims in territory already reconquered by the Christians, where Christian women had much easier access to the public sphere.

The highly respected collection of *ahadith* by al-Bukhari has Malik refer to the face veil covering even the *huries* in Paradise who will receive a man killed while engaging in *jihad*:

> Narrated Anas: Um (the mother of) Haritha came to Allah's Apostle after Haritha had been martyred on the Day (of the battle) of Badr by an arrow thrown by an unknown person.... The Prophet said..., "There are many Paradises, and he is in the highest Paradise of Firdaus." The Prophet added, "A forenoon journey or an afternoon journey in Allah's Cause is better than the whole world and whatever is in it...and if one of the women of Paradise looked at the earth, she would fill the whole space between them (the earth and the heaven) with light, and would fill whatever is in between them, with perfume, and *the veil of her face* [emphasis added] is better than the whole world and whatever is in it."[38]

Malik praised Muhammad's youngest wife, Aisha, for veiling herself even for blind men: "He [Malik] said, 'Aishah, may Allah be pleased with her, veiled herself in the presence of a blind man.' Someone said, '*He can't see you*' [emphasis added]. She said, 'But I can see him.'"[39]

Relevant sunnah can be found also in the *Sunan Abu Dawud*, much cited in the *Risala* and other Maliki manuals: "Narrated Abdullah ibn Amr ibn al'As: The Prophet (peace-be-upon-him) said: 'After some time the lands of the non-Arabs will be conquered for you, and there you will find houses called hammamat (hot baths) [Arabs found baths for the first time in the Christian Greek Roman Empire ('Byzantine')], so men should not enter them (to wash) except in lower garments, and forbid the women to enter them except a sick or one who is in a childbed.' "[40]

In some *taifa* kingdoms, *muhsanas* might go to the baths on days prescribed to women, but only in order to carry out the ablutions necessary for their praying, or in case of illness, and even then they could legally be forbidden to go by their husbands.[41]

But the laxity of religious observance among some rulers of the *taifa* kingdoms, much liked by many scholars as proof of the enlightenment of al-Andalus, was not a virtue in the eyes of the *ulama* or the population at large. This laxity among the rulers affected the custom of wearing the face veil among women in the royal courts. Chronicling the eleventh-century rule of Idris Ibn Yahya (al-Ali) in the *taifa* kingdom of Malaga, the historian Abu Abdillah Mohammed Ibn Abi al-Homaydi of Córdoba laments that, among other weaknesses that made Idris unfit to rule and eventually landed him in a dungeon, was his indifference to his wives' appearing unveiled in the presence of his guests.[42]

As Marín has observed, the question of the seclusion of Muslim women in al-Andalus is counterintuitive. In medieval Maliki Islamic law and practice, higher socioeconomic status actually conferred less autonomy and power in the public arena (what Western scholars generally regard as "freedom"). Conversely, the lower the social esteem and class of a woman, the less strict was her seclusion and segregation from society at large.[43] A Muslim woman's status depended on the status of her husband or father—or master, in the case of a female sexual slave ("concubine").

The veiling of women's faces, or even the tight wrapping of cloth over the head, around the face and neck and under the chin, historically characteristic of the proper Muslim woman, cannot be ascribed, as it has been by some Western scholars, to the influence of the Christian Greek Roman Empire ("Byzantine") after Islam's military conquest of the Christian Middle East in the seventh century A.D. Rather, veiling derived from the interpretation, right or wrong, of Quranic verses, and perhaps also from Bedouin customs.

The evidence from paintings and documents indicates that the Muslim veiling of all adult women outside their home or in the presence of men not their immediate relatives could not have been an imitation of practices in the Christian Greek Roman Empire, because in the empire Greek women did not normally cover their faces with a veil or anything else. Art works reveal that Greek Christian empresses, some of whom ruled the empire on their own, showed their abundant hair under their crowns.[44] Moreover, Harvard professor of Byzantine art Harvard Ioli Kalavrezou points out, "Many elite women...delighted in luxurious display, wearing 'long dresses bright with purple and rustling with gold.'...They also wore their hair uncovered and piled high, 'structured and castellated with layers of ropes and interwoven locks.'"[45] Older, widowed, or married women might wear a veil over their heads in public, but not in their houses even in the presence of men other than their husbands; even when such women were veiled on the street, they covered only the head, not the face; and younger, unmarried, fashionable, well-to-do, and educated women would wear elaborate hairdos to match their luxurious clothes and expensive jewelry.[46]

A medieval Greek manuscript illustration from the twelfth century depicts a Greek Orthodox marriage ceremony with a royal woman sitting and displaying her hair down to the neck with only a diadem around her temples.[47] And in the court of the Greek Roman Empire, upper-class women would participate in "mixed receptions of both men and women."[48] Kalavrezou writes: "The empress Irene Doukaina followed her husband, Alexios I, on campaigns. Other imperial wives or daughters ruled various cities in the fourteenth century. Aristocratic ladies held literary salons and freely consorted with men, in the eleventh century as in the twelfth and the fourteenth: Anna Komnene, with her circle of intellectuals who discussed philosophy, is a prime example."[49] Many other examples could be added.

This Greek Christian culture emphasized the enjoyment of bathing, and in the early Christian Greek Roman Empire there were coed baths.[50] In Constantinople alone there were 9 large public baths and 153 private baths in the fifth century A.D. The early church's acceptance of baths as a natural part of life continued to inform the empire, and there were even monastic baths in the later empire. Men and women would go to the baths on separate days.[51]

It was also a society where, given the right circumstances, a woman could be well educated and even learned. Aristocratic ladies would receive a good education. We have an extant treatise on midwifery authored by someone with a Greek female name, Metrodoras.[52] The learned Greek

Anna Komnene (b. 1083 Constantinople, d. 1153 Kecharitomene) authored a still extant great poetic work of history, the *Alexiad*, where the influence of Greek epic poems such as the *Iliad* is evident.[53] (Non-Greek medieval Europe, however, would eventually have the likes of nun Hildegard von Bingen, and of Marie de France and Christine de Pisan.) In short, the Christian Greek Roman Empire was not a "veiled society."[54]

One may contrast this relative openness to women's public roles in Greek Christian culture with Malik's allowing a man to see the hair of a woman other than his wife (or his slave girl) only under very precise circumstances: "Malik said, 'There is no harm in a man's looking at the hair of his son's wife or the hair of his wife's mother.' "[55] According to the *Mudawwana*, if even part of the hair of the woman comes out from under her veil during prayer, she must restart the prayer.[56] Asked whether a Muslim man could look at the hair of a non-Muslim woman serving as wet nurse of a Muslim child (something undesirable in itself), Malik dryly answered: "It does not please me."[57]

The Muslim face veil might be a response to the unique conditions of life in Arabia, which were different from those in the Christian Greek Roman Empire. Bedouins would raid one another for women; therefore, hiding the form and face of women might help protect them from abduction.[58] The custom of veiling might also respond to the need to hide what was considered the most erotic part of a woman—namely, the mouth. In many places of the Arabian Peninsula even today, the anthropologist Lois Grant Beck writes, "Veiling and seclusion of women are seen as 'a loving protection,' developed in the past as an adaptation to life in the desert when tribal raids were a threat to the women who embodied the honor and purity of the family and tribe. In few ways do women's lives seem degraded by these 'restrictions,' and in fact the higher a woman's social status the more carefully she is concealed and protected."[59]

THE NONEXISTENT FREEDOM OF MUSLIM WOMEN IN THE PUBLIC REALM OF AL-ANDALUS

We have already seen the many restrictions that Andalusian Islamic law placed on women—beginning with its detailed injunctions on ritual purity. In judicial matters, their testimony was unacceptable in matters of spilled blood, and in other cases it had only half the value of the testimony of a Muslim man.[60] Yet belief in the "freedom" of Muslim women in al-Andalus continues to be a commonplace among many scholars.

In fact, most of the "learned" women mentioned in the Muslim sources were slave girls. This is especially the case in the "profane" arts, such as literature, medicine, singing, and crafts. But as the Arabist María Luisa Ávila points out, the slave girls engaged in these activities not out of their free will but as a reflection of their condition as slaves and as a result of the "specialized training to which they submitted."[61] "But," Ávila continues,

> free women were not really free either when it came to learning one or another science. With very few isolated instances, by far most of the time the cultural formation of a *hurra* [a free Muslim woman] was nothing else but the residuals left in her by her family environment. Behind these educated women we always find a father who had intellectual prestige: the *fuqaha* [experts in religious law] were daughters of *qadis* [Muslim judges] or of famous jurists; the traditionists [who memorized *hadith*] were daughters of some experts in *hadith*; the only medic we know about belonged to the celebrated family of the Avenzoar. We must avoid allowing ourselves to be impressed by these one hundred and sixteen "learned" women.... Many are mentioned only because of the family connections; others for having written some smart verses; there are a number of copyists; others are mentioned because they were part of some anecdote about male personages.

Ávila concludes: "Because of this evidence, to pretend that Hispano-Arabic women enjoyed freedom is out of place. On the contrary, it is logical to deduce from the evidence that in the social realm in which these 'learned' women moved, aside from the slave girls, their lives were spent solely within the family circle and their relationships were circumscribed to their parents and to other women."

Elsewhere Ávila observes, "In spite of the existence of sporadic instances of women whose activities seem to indicate a certain independence and freedom—the most famous example being that of the well-born poetess Wallada—all indications are that freedom of activity for Andalusi [free] women was limited to the domestic sphere."[62] Wallada was the daughter of a sexual slave of foreign origin, from whom she may have inherited her mores, and she was never married, so she never became a *muhsan*.

Yet even many seasoned medievalist scholars seem unaware of the distinction between Muslim sexual slaves and *muhsana* and *hurra*, and make statements on the "freedom" of women in al-Andalus that don't hold up to scrutiny.[63]

We have texts indicating that some women achieved reputations as "transmitters" of *ahadith*.[64] For example, Shuhda "the writer" appears to have spoken on the *ahadith* of al-Bukhari. But listening to what she had to say must not have been accepted by the Andalusian *ulama*, because, as Ignaz Goldziher points out, those who attended her talks (which would have taken place behind a curtain) lied about having done so.[65]

As Ávila again observes, some of these learned female "transmitters" of *ahadith* talked behind curtains to the men present in the room to avoid violating Islamic strictures against mixing with or being seen by men. Some of the other women did not have to hide behind curtains because "their masters were their fathers and brothers and their only disciples their own sons."[66] Obviously a resourceful free Muslim woman in al-Andalus, under certain conditions, might have been able to overcome some of the limitations on her public activities imposed by her society's religious views— but this would be true of any restrictive society.

The Spanish Arabist Teresa Garulo corrects further the widespread belief in the social freedom of Muslim female poets in al-Andalus:

> Certain data in the biographies of Wallada, Nazhun and Hafsa ar-Rakuniyya have led some to think that women poets enjoyed great freedom to socialize with male poets, but although a number of historians have echoed the theories of H. Pérès, who sustains that in al-Andalus, and because of Christian influence, the Islamic norms that tend to keep women inside the house would have become relaxed, and that therefore the Hispano-Arabic woman, as shown in the concrete case of the princess Wallada, enjoyed a freedom unknown to Oriental Muslims, it seems instead that...as M. Marín points out..."from the conquest to the end of the Córdoba Caliphate, at

least in the social circles we study, a woman could not freely socialize with men who were not part of her family." More concretely: given the data offered by the biographies of women poets in al-Andalus, who belonged mostly to the upper classes, we do not see that there were such free contacts and instead we see many indications to the contrary. We only find Hafsa ar-Rakuniyya, Nazhun, Wallada, and Ibnat Ibn as-Sakkan, and she was very old.... [in some sources] one hears, besides the use of the veil, that these women, upon the arrival of men not part of their families, would withdraw behind a curtain, or would receive men while hiding behind a curtain, like Rayhana, who follows in this fashion the classes of the famous litterateur Abu Amr ad-Dani.[67]

Since poetic activity can take place in seclusion, and the artistic use of words has been a traditionally acceptable art form in Islam, writing poems did not in principle conflict with religion. Therefore some free Muslim women wrote poetry in their houses, always in separation from men who were not their immediate relatives.[68]

Given the restrictions imposed by Islamic jurisprudence and society on women's public activities, these women poets would have rarely moved outside the domestic sphere, solely for very specific purposes, and only properly veiled.[69] For the same reasons, unless these women were sexual slaves, they would not have been able to meet men poets to discuss literature. Some, however, did correspond with men poets.

In favor of the women's presumed freedom, some Western scholars have quoted Ibn Hazm, who wrote that "women taught me the Quran, they recited to me much poetry, they trained me in calligraphy."[70] But again, such women as Ibn Hazm talks about would be not *muhsan* but skilled sexual slave girls in the caliph's harem, with whom children brought up at court, like Ibn Hazm, were allowed to play.

The words of the great Maliki jurist Ibn Rushd ("Averroes") summarize the condition of Muslim women and again contradict today's widespread perception that women enjoyed great "freedom" in al-Andalus:

These societies of ours overlook the skills of women because women are only used for procreation, being therefore destined to the service of their husbands and relegated to the cares of procreation, upbringing and education [of the children]. But this underutilizes their other possible activities. Since in these communities women do not prepare for any of the human virtues, it happens that many times they resemble plants in these societies, turning into a burden for men, which is one of the reasons for the poverty of these communities, where they are twice as numerous as males, while at the same time and in so far as they lack any preparation they do not contribute to necessary activities, except in very few, like spinning and knitting, which they do mostly when they need money to subsist.[71]

In fact, in Maliki jurisprudence modesty in the case of the *hurra* (a free Muslim woman) was so important that a man could see his future wife only if she had not yet reached puberty. Muhammad had set the precedent by marrying a girl, Aisha, when she was only six years old.[72] So we read in al-Bukhari's collection of *ahadith*:

Volume 7, Book 62, Number 64: Narrated 'Aisha: that the Prophet married her when she was six years old and he consummated his marriage when she was nine years old, and then she remained with him for nine years (i.e., till his death).

Volume 7, Book 62, Number 65: Narrated 'Aisha: that the Prophet married her when she was six years old and he consummated his marriage when she was nine years old. Hisham said: I have been informed that 'Aisha remained with the Prophet for nine years (i.e. till his death).

Volume 7, Book 62, Number 88: Narrated 'Ursa: The Prophet wrote the (marriage contract) with 'Aisha while she was six years old and consummated his marriage with her while she was nine years old and she remained with him for nine years (i.e. till his death).

Volume 7, Book 62, Number 118: Narrated 'Ursa: Aisha said, "While the Ethiopians were playing with their small spears, Allah's Apostle screened me behind him and I watched (that display) and kept on watching till I left on my own." So you may estimate of what age a little girl may listen to amusement.[73]

From the above it is evident that although a man could marry a pre-pubescent girl, the marriage could not be consummated until the girl had reached puberty: again Muhammad gave the precedent by marrying Aisha, as Bukhari indicates, when she was six years old but not consummating the marriage until she was nine and presumably had reached puberty.[74]

FEMALE SEXUAL SLAVERY IN AL-ANDALUS

Universalism, longtime-defended by the prophets since Noah, Abraham, and Moses, reaffirmed by Christ in the name of the new covenant, and realized in Islam, *in the Andalusian model of Spain*, is a permanent virtue in a Palestinian model [that would supersede Israel] in which Jews, Christians, and Muslims can live again and under its protection [emphasis added].
     —*Hassan Hanafi, Chairman of the Department of Philosophy at Cairo University, cited as "a leading exponent in contemporary Islam of the reconciliation between faith and reason" in Arthur Herzberg,* Jewish Polemics *(New York: Columbia University Press, 1992), 224*

In Maliki jurisprudence, a slave girl, either bought at the marketplace or captured in war, with whom her master had sex, became his sexual slave or *jariya* (or *djariya*, a "concubine").[75]

Under the Umayyads, al-Andalus became a center for the trade and distribution of slaves: young female sexual slaves, sometimes as young as eleven years old; male children castrated to become eunuchs in the harems; male children brought up in barracks to be slave warriors; male children used as the sexual playthings of the powerful and wealthy (as in the case of Abd al-Rahman III's "love" for the Christian boy Pelayo);[76] men used as servants or workers—for every conceivable use human beings of all ages and races were bought and sold.

The price of a slave depended on his or her race, sex, age, and abilities.[77] White slaves, especially blond ones, often captured in raids of Christian lands, were the most prized. In the year 912, during the Islamic Golden Age of the Umayyad Caliphate of Córdoba, the price for a male black slave was 200 dirhems [coins] of silver. A black girl from Nubia went for 300 dinars of gold. A white girl without education cost 1,000 dinars of gold. A white girl with singing abilities cost 14,000 dinars. In Abd al-Rahman III's court there were 3,750 slaves, his harem had 6,300 women, and his army included 13,750 slave warriors. A document from the twelfth century tells of the tricks used by sellers of slaves in the Muslim slave markets: merchants would put ointments on slave girls of a darker complexion to whiten their faces; brunettes were placed for four hours in a solution to make them blond ("golden"); ointments were placed on the face and body of black slaves to make them "prettier." "The merchant tells the slave girls to act in a coquettish manner with the old men and with the timid men among the potential buyers to make them crazy with desire. The merchant paints red the tips of the fingers of a white slave; he paints in gold those of a black slave; and he dresses them all in transparent clothes, the white female slaves in pink and the black ones in yellow and red."

A thirteenth-century epistle by the *faqih* Abu Bakr al-Bardai shows how a respectable Muslim man in al-Andalus would regard a sexual slave girl as a source of "love."[78] The poetry of the twelfth-century writer al-Saraqusti Ibn al-Astarkuwi is a good example of this "delightful Andalusian love poetry" that so many Western scholars have praised, oblivious to its sordid cultural context: that it is about sexual slave girls, not about the secluded *hurras* or *muhsanas* of al-Andalus, who went about covered from head to toe.[79]

In the Islamic world, harems (not a Christian institution, for contrary to what is sometimes written, there were no harems in the Christian Greek Roman Empire)[80] swarmed with female captives from foreign lands: white women from Persia, Kurdistan, the Christian Greek Roman Empire, Christian Spain and Armenia; darker ones from Ethiopia, Sudan, and India. Harun al-Rashid had a thousand sexual slaves; Al-Mutawakkil had four thousand; Abd al-Rahman III had more than six thousand; al-Mutamid of Seville, overthrown by the Almoravids, left behind a harem of eight hundred women, counting wives, sexual slaves, and female domestic servants. The Moroccan writer Fatima Mernissi recounts:

The harems became places of the greatest luxury where the most beautiful women of the world played their cultural differences and mastery of diverse skills and knowledge like winning cards for seducing caliphs and viziers. In order to seduce these men, it was not enough just to bat one's eyelashes. One had to dazzle them in the fields that fascinated them, astrology, mathematics, fiqh, and history. On top of these came poetry and song. Pretty girls who got lost in serious conversations had no chance to be noticed, and even less chance to last; and the favorites, who knew this very well, surrounded themselves with competent teachers.[81]

Ibn Hazm commented on these women's total dedication to sexual conquest as the underlying reason for their various skills: "As for the reason why this instinct [this preoccupation with sexual matters] is so deeply rooted in women, I see no other explanation than that they have nothing else to fill their minds, except loving union and what brings it about, flirting and how it is done, intimacy and the various ways of achieving it. This is their sole occupation, and they were created for nothing else."[82] If these sexually skilled girls succeeded in becoming favorites of their masters, they could themselves have women servants.

Some ingenious academic specialists have argued that by permitting slave girls to learn skills that increased their sexual attractiveness in the eyes of their masters and granting them relatively greater freedom in the public sphere, sexual slavery under Islam actually promoted women's liberation.[83] An article published in the *New York Times* has likened the sexual slaves' conniving for power in the harem to the struggles of Western women in the corporate world.[84]

Other efforts to downplay the phenomenon of massive slavery in the Islamic empires have been similar marvels of academic ingenuity.[85] Thus, defending slavery in the Islamic Mamluk empire, a medieval studies scholar offers the official view among specialists:

It is important to understand that medieval Islamic civilization had a different attitude towards slavery than that seen in western Europe. Slaves were much better treated and their status was quite honourable. Furthermore, the career opportunities [!] open to a skillful *mamluk*, and the higher standards of living available in the Islamic Middle East, meant that there was often little resistance to being taken as a *mamluk* among the peoples of Central Asia and south-eastern Europe. Many young Kipchaq Turkish women, slaves and free, also arrived in the wake of *mamluk* recruits, bringing with them some of Central Asia's traditions of sexual equality.[86]

One can certainly imagine the throngs of girls and boys in Greece, Serbia, and Central Asia clamoring to be taken away from their families to be circumcised, to become sexual slaves, or to be castrated to guard harems as eunuchs, or, in other cases, to be raised in barracks with the sole purpose of becoming fearless slave-soldiers. Or one can imagine among Egyptian youth the same interest in a "career" as a slave, which would have made it unnecessary for Mamluk rulers in Egypt to raid foreign lands to obtain replacement slaves or to buy them at the slave markets. But aside from the basic human problem involved in all this, the professor overlooks that in fact, as Bernard Lewis and Daniel Pipes have pointed out, in Islam there existed two fundamental categories of people: slaves and nonslaves. That is why enslaving Muslims was soon discouraged in early Islam and eventually prohibited.[87] Against this distinction (being enslaved or selling oneself into slavery was *not* honorable, and that is why it did not accord with being a Muslim), the rest are mere academic discussions about how the various Islamic empires (or the various Western empires and cultures) handled this "peculiar institution": "more humanely" or "less humanely"; "with more sophistication" or "with less sophistication"; "with greater possibility of well being" or "with less possibility of well-being"; "with the possibility of having children who would become rulers"; "being a slave soldier, which had greater prestige," etc. There was nothing "better" about slavery under medieval Islam: it was a system based on the looting of humans and their degradation in the slave markets.

The existence of female slaves—often Christians captured in war or bought at the market—as poets, singers, dancers, litterateurs, "physicians" and other occupations was common throughout the Islamic world and not just al-Andalus. They were as common as male slaves, frequently of Christian origin, who were used as soldiers.[88] Both male and female slaves—military, sexual, and other kinds—and freed slaves (*wala*) dramatically shaped the history of Islam, culturally, socioeconomically, militarily, and genetically.[89]

Ibn Hazm, himself of European (Spanish) Christian origin, wrote that most Abbasid rulers in the Middle East and all Umayyad rulers in al-Andalus had sexual slave mothers.[90] Many of these mothers were of Caucasian origin. The Arab chronicler Ibn al-Qutiyya, himself of European (Visigoth) Christian descent, affirmed that the descendants of Sarah "The

Goth," a Christian sexual slave, were more illustrious and prestigious within the Andalusian Islamic community than the children her Muslim husband had with other women (in Islamic law, children of Muslim men and non-Muslim women must be brought up as Muslims).[91]

As Arabist Celia del Moral observes, the Umayyads particularly valued blond or red-haired Franc and Galician women as sexual slaves.[92] Indeed, the physical appearance of several Spanish Muslim princes betrayed their descent from Caucasian slave mothers. The Middle East–born founder of the Umayyad dynasty in Spain, Abd al-Rahman I (reigned 755–788), was blond; Hisham I (reigned 788–796) had very white skin and reddish hair; Muhammad I (reigned 852–886) had a pink face; Abd Allah b. Muhammad (reigned 888–912) had white skin, a pink face, blue eyes, and blond hair; Caliph Abd al-Rahman III (reigned 912–961) had white skin, a pink face, and blue eyes, and he tinted his blond hair black to appear more "Arabic" to his subjects; Caliph Hakam al-Mostancir II (reigned 961–976) had reddish hair; and Caliph Hisham II (reigned since 976 variously as a puppet until his assassination in 1013), the last Umayyad ruler, and the son of a Basque sexual slave, a "skilled singer [who] exerted over [his father] great influence," was blond, with blue eyes and a reddish beard.[93] Abd al-Rahman V al-Mustazhir (assassinated in Córdoba in 1024), who reigned briefly after the death of Almanzor, was blond, and the son of a sexual slave.[94] The founder of the presumably "Arab" dynasty of the Nasrids of Granada, Muhammad b. Nasr (d. 1273), was called "The Red One" (al-Hamar) because of his red beard. Initially, the invaders of al-Andalus were mostly men. Therefore, as Arabic sources indicate, the practice of having children with Spanish Christian women probably began when the son of Musa took as one of his several wives Queen Egilo (or Egilona), widow of the Visigoth king Rodrigo.[95] The European presence in the lineage of Muslim rulers did not stop with the arrival of the Berber Almohads: the Almohad caliph Abu Yusuf Yaqub b. Yaqub b. Abd al-Mumin b. Ali (d. 1198) was the son of a Christian sexual slave girl.[96] Similarly, we know that one of the kings of the *taifa* kingdom of Granada, Muhammad Ibn Yusuf Nasr (d. 1310) took as one of his wives the captured female Christian ruler of the city of Bedmar, María Jiménez, and had from her several children.[97]

The Spanish Arabist Julián Ribera calculated that, as a result of this sexual intercourse with Caucasian Christian girls, each generation of

Umayyad rulers saw its genetic "Arab" component reduced by half, so that the last Umayyad, Hisham II (976–1013), would have had approximately 0.09 percent of "Arabic" genetic makeup. Ribera concluded that already by their second generation Umayyad rulers in al-Andalus had far more European than "Arab" genes; that a similar process of geometrically increased mating between Muslims and native Spanish Christian women or their eventually Muslim female descendants must have diluted dramatically the non-European genetic makeup of the general population of al-Andalus; and that this European Christian factor, with its presumably greater love of individual liberty and regard for the individual human being as opposed to the group, contributed to the again presumably greater "freedom" women enjoyed in Islamic Spain as opposed to other regions of the *umma*.[98] Whatever one may think of Ribera's imaginative last conclusion in view of what we now know about the actual condition of Muslim women in Islamic Spain, it is not unlikely that the process he describes would have influenced al-Andalus culturally and socially. Writing in the fourteenth century, the historian Ibn al-Khatib described the inhabitants of Granada as "white skinned."[99] The Arabist Felipe Maíllo Salgado has pointed out that modern genetic studies show that the genetic presence of populations from the Middle East and Berber North Africa in the present-day Spanish population is minimal.[100]

Such was the cultural impact on the Islamic Middle Ages of Caucasian sexual slaves from Christian lands that the Turkish word *kiz*, meaning "girl," "slave girl," and "sexual slave girl" (or "concubine") came to mean also "Christian woman" in Islamic usage.[101]

Analogously, the Arabic word *sakaliba* (probably derived from the Greek Σλάβος or "Slav"), referring to blond or red-haired peoples, came to designate the child or adult slaves from the eastern and northern European lands, who played a key role in the armies and politics of Muslim states.[102] The tenth-century historian and geographer Ibn Hawqal wrote that in Spain the name *sakaliba*, as well as "Slavs," was given to all the white slaves of foreign origin, not only from northern and eastern Europe but also from Christian Galicia and northern Spain, Lombardy, the land of the Franks, and Calabria, who populated the palaces, harems, and the armies, especially the body guards, of the Andalusian rulers.[103] As Mohammed Meouak, professor of Islamic civilizations at the University of Cadiz, points out, in Umayyad Córdoba these Islamized white slaves made up most of the administrative personnel in the Umayyad palaces and courts.[104] As freedmen, some of these "Slavs" seized power and became kings of *taifa* kingdoms after the disintegration of the Caliphate of Córdoba.

The impact of Caucasian sexual slave women on the Muslim rulers of the Middle East was equally significant. As Ibn Hazm noted, in the Middle East the mothers of most Abbasid caliphs were Caucasian sexual slaves, often of Greek, Balkan, or Persian origin. In Egypt, slaves of Turkish, Mongol, Caucasian (Circassians, Georgians, Greeks or *Rum*, Frankish), and other origins constituted a dynasty, the Mamluks, that lasted for several generations.[105] With the eventual takeover of the Mamluk leadership by the Circassians, the word *mamluk* ("owned" in Arabic) came to designate *any male white slave.*[106] In the Ottoman Empire, the most decisive and influential branch of the army, the *janizaries*, was made up of European children taken from Christian Greek and Balkan lands and brought up as fearless Muslim warriors.

The massive trade in captured or bought black and white slaves was a cultural feature of Islamic Spain, as it was of the Muslim world in general. The Arab trade in African black slaves reached vast proportions with the growth of the Islamic empire and led to several revolts. The Persian al-Tabari dedicates one his historical treatises to one of these black slave revolts: between 869 and 883, hundreds of thousands of Bantu (Zanj) slaves went on a rampage through southern Iraq, and their rioting was put down with great difficulty by the army of the Abbasid caliph.[107] Muslim paintings in the Topkapi museum depict Muhammad (his face left blank to comply with Muslim law) with black slaves.[108]

In fact, Islamic warriors pioneered the slavery of African blacks.[109] Although the Quran does not proclaim the superiority of any racial group, both Muslim Arabs and Muslim North African Berbers considered themselves different from and superior to blacks, whom they enslaved.[110] In Islamic lands, the trade in black slaves from Africa, sometimes of predominantly young men, sometimes of predominantly young females, was immense.[111] The *Kitab al-Bayan al-Mughrib* mentions that Musa, when back in Africa loaded with treasure looted from Spain in the first half of the eighth century, was able to give to each one of his victorious Muslim warriors both a black male and a black female slave.[112]

In the course of his examination of various human groups' contributions to civilization, the Andalusian *qadi* from Toledo Said al-Andalusi (d. 1070) illustrates what were not-uncommon views about African blacks:

> For those peoples on the other hand who live near and beyond the equinoctial line to the limit of the inhabited world in the south, the long presence of the sun at the zenith makes the air hot and the atmosphere thin. Because of this their temperaments become hot and their humors fiery, their color black and their hair woolly. Thus they lack self-control and steadiness of mind and are overcome by fickleness, foolishness, and ignorance. Such are the blacks, who live at the extremity of the land of Ethiopia, the Nubians, the Zanj and the like.[113]

Such views of black Africans in the medieval Islamic empire were not confined to al-Andalus. The early-tenth-century writer Ibn al-Faqih wrote that Arabs in Iraq were superior to the Slavs and to the blacks because the sun cooked them just right: the Slavs were undercooked and therefore had a color between "blond, buff, blanched, and leprous," while the blacks were overcooked by the sun and therefore "overdone in the womb until they are burned, so that the child comes out something between black, murky, malodorous, stinking, and crinkly-haired, with uneven limbs, deficient minds and depraved passions, such as the Zanj, the Ethiopians, and other blacks who resemble them. The Iraqis are neither half-baked dough nor burned crust but between them."[114] An Arab proverb states that "the black, when hungry, steals; sated, he fornicates."[115]

The most famous literary work produced by the Islamic Caliphate, the *One Thousand and One Nights*, also known as the *Arabian Nights* (although most of the tales are of Persian, Indian, and even Greek origin), evidences a similar cultural fear of the black male. The charming narrative that frames the tales centers on the discovery by two rulers that their wives are having sex with black slaves. Both black slaves are described in very unflattering terms, one of them depicted climbing down a tree to have sex with the queen. The younger ruler slays his wife and her black lover. His elder brother, a sultan, kills his wife, her black lover, and everyone else in his harem. To punish women in general, he proceeds to have sex every night with a different young virgin taken from the helpless population; after the night of love he orders her beheaded in the morning.

This goes on for three years, until he has almost depleted the virgin population of his realm. Then one of the hundreds of virgins he has sex with—the elder daughter of his vizier (minister)—charms him with her tales and wit, is pardoned, and all ends well.[116]

The trade in white slaves was not far behind that of black slaves: from the 1530s to the 1780s, it is estimated that in Islamic lands between 1 million and 1.25 million white slaves were traded, taken from the Mediterranean coasts, Greece, the Balkans, Armenia, Persia, and Slavic lands, among other places.[117]

The tenth-century geographer Ibn Hawqal observed that one of the main exports of al-Andalus was slaves: "A well-known article of exportation consists of slaves: boys and girls taken from France and Gallicia, as well as Slav eunuchs. All the Slav eunuchs that one finds on the face of the earth come from Spain [sic]. One forces them to undergo castration in this country: the surgery is done by Jewish merchants."[118]

In Umayyad al-Andalus and after, a class of older slave women was part of the slave trade, participating as trainers, buyers, and sellers of the sexual slave women fantasized about in Ibn Hazm's celebrated treatise on "love" (El collar de la paloma, as it is famously known in Spanish), and later in the writings of wide-eyed Western scholars seemingly unaware of the rather sordid reality behind this much admired book on "love."[119]

Nothing remotely comparable in quantity and quality to these phenomenal permutations of human servitude occurred within Christian Europe in medieval times. There were slaves in Christian Europe as well, but nothing close to their numbers in Islamic lands. Attempts to use medieval serfdom as an equivalent to the slavery of the Muslim world does not work at several levels, including the serfs' limited role in the armies and in the noble and warrior classes of Europe. Moreover, serfs, who were peasants, could not be bought or sold. In addition, in places like Castile there were no serfs at all: as the legal scholar Ramón Peralta has observed, in medieval times Castile was basically a land of free property-owning peasants and hidalgos in search of adventure in the wild southern frontier.[120] And of course harems full of sexual slaves guarded by slave black and white eunuchs were not part of the social fabric of Christian Spain or Europe.

Some Western scholars mention women copyists in al-Andalus, or women acting as "physicians."[121] But as María Luisa Ávila has observed, such women would be mostly slave girls—and usually Christian slave girls at that—since female *muhsan* would not be allowed by their husbands to leave the house to engage in such activities; Manuela Marín has pointed out that well-off women were not supposed to work even at home, where daily work would be performed by slaves.[122] It is logical to assume, however, that some Muslim women would have known at least how to perform the surgery needed for female circumcision, since men were forbidden to look at the genital parts of women who were not their wives or sexual slaves.

There are many records in al-Andalus of the sexual slaves' intellectual skills. In the eleventh century, for example, the ruler Hudayl had 150 slave girls trained in singing and dancing, but a number of them became famous as well for their scientific and literary knowledge.[123] A properly trained female sexual slave in an Andalusian ruler's court could have more "operational room" than the *muhsan*, especially if the court was particularly "artistic," "intellectual" or otherwise "sophisticated." Or the slave of a pedagogically inclined *alim* might benefit from his master's proclivities and status. In addition, a lower-class and lower-income Muslim woman would by necessity do some kind of work outside the house, such as spinning or knitting, as Averroes noticed, or as a saleswoman at the local market, all of which would give her an opportunity to widen her sphere of activity—though always within the confines of contemporary Islamic practice. But none of these women would be a proper *muhsan*, who would willingly segregate herself into her home and veil herself in front of anyone not her husband, fellow family women, or very close family men.[124]

Market regulations in twelfth-century Seville provide further information on the condition of women in general. These regulations would not apply to a proper *hurra* or *muhsan* woman, who would be made to stay home, unless her family or husband were willing to lose honor or worse:

Women should not sit by the river bank in the summer if men appear there.

No barber may remain alone with a woman in his booth. He should work in the open market in a place where he can be seen and observed.

Each [person] should keep to his own trade and not claim any skill of which he is not an acknowledged master—especially with women, since ignorance and error are greater among them.

Only good and trustworthy men, known as such among people, may be allowed to have dealings with women in buying and in selling. The tradespeople must watch over this carefully. The women who weave brocades must be banned from the market for they are nothing but harlots.

On festival days men and women shall not walk on the same path when they go to cross the river.

The contractor of the bathhouse should not sit there with the women, for this is the occasion for license and fornication. The contractor of hostelries for traders and travelers should not be a woman, for this is indeed fornication. The broker of houses shall not be a young man, but a chaste old man of known good character.

Prostitutes [always slave girls] must be forbidden to stand bareheaded outside the houses. They must be stopped from coquetry and party making among themselves, even if they have been permitted to do this [by their masters].... Dancing girls [always slave girls] must be forbidden to bare their heads.[125]

The not unlikely violations of Islamic mores by an indeterminate number of *hurras* or *muhsana* in Islamic Spain would be more frequent during regimes of weak religious zeal and therefore weak political control, as in the *taifa* kingdoms, which are often praised today,[126] but *which from a political and religious viewpoint marked the nadir of Islamic rule in Spain*—as *ulama* then pointed out and *ulama* today still do. These times of weaker Islamic devotion in fact prompted Andalusian *ulama* to welcome invasions by fundamentalist dynasties like the Almoravids and the Almohads.

In short, the vision of scores of bejewelled free Muslim women walking about al-Andalus with long flowing hair and elegant silk dresses, displaying their undulating and voluptuous bodies while freely enjoying life in public places and working as poets, lecturers, teachers, librarians, copyists, physicians, and so forth under the tolerant and enraptured eyes of Muslim men is a wishful Western academic fantasy at best, and a shoddy professional reading of the historical evidence at worst.

THE CONDITION OF MUSLIM WOMEN IN MEDIEVAL SPAIN COMPARED TO THE CONDITION OF CHRISTIAN WOMEN

> As an anthropologist who has spent decades doing research on and with women in different communities in the Middle East, I have found myself increasingly troubled by our obsession with Muslim women.... Representing Muslim women as abused makes us forget the violence and oppression in our own midst. Our stereotyping of Muslim women also distracts us from the thornier problem that our own policies and actions in the world help create the (sometimes harsh) conditions in which distant others live. Ultimately, saving Muslim women allows us to ignore the complex entanglements in which we are all implicated and creates a polarization that places feminism only on the side of the West.
>
> —Lila Abu-Lughod, Professor of Anthropology and Women and Gender Studies at Columbia University, and author of Do Muslim Women Need Saving? (Cambridge, MA: Harvard University Press, 2013), "Do Muslim Women Need Saving?" Time, November 1, 2013

Differences between Muslim women in Islamic Spain and Christian women in Christian Spain in their respective access to the public arena can be noticed at the higher levels of authority as well as at the lower levels of everyday life.

If one starts at the top, no Muslim woman in al-Andalus ever became or could become a female emir, or a female caliph. Efforts to find Andalusian Muslim women in positions of political authority have unearthed only mothers, wives, or sexual slaves who may have variously influenced the behavior of important sons, husbands, or masters.[127] This sort of influence can of course occur, and does, in any society, Islamic or not. Moreover, Muslim historians blamed the influence of women for the decline of dynasties, and Muslim thinkers warned against it.[128]

In contrast, as the historian Henry Kamen points out, "[Catholic] Spain was one of the areas in Europe where the political and property rights of women were most guaranteed to give them a political role, so that there was absolutely no prejudice against female rulers, nor against female succession to noble titles."[129] In a reversal of the situation in Islamic Spain, in the Christian kingdoms women at the higher levels of society could enjoy greater power in the public arena, given the right conditions.

Even earlier, in Visigoth Spain, what we know of the Visigoth queens indicates their "considerable dynamism and relevance."[130]

Some Spanish Catholic queens became sole rulers of their land. Even when not ruling alone, but in conjunction with a husband, and probably more than in other western European countries, Spanish Catholic queens functioned with the king in "a complementary dynamic...that was fundamentally contractual."[131]

The best known of all female Catholic rulers was Isabella I ("La Católica), queen of Castile and León (1451–1504), who had to overcome the opposition of the followers of yet another female candidate to the monarchy, Juana *la Beltraneja*, and who eventually became a ruler as powerful as her husband. As the Spanish saying put it, "*Tanto monta, monta tanto, Isabel como Fernando*" (as much matters, matters as much, Isabella as does Ferdinand). There were others before Isabella. Toda Aznárez (b. ca. 895) ruled Navarra with her husband, Sancho Garcés El Grande, and after his death governed jointly with her son, plotted, made and unmade alliances, and reputedly traveled to Córdoba to talk to Abd al-Rahman III.[132] Mayor Sánchez (d. 1066), last countess of Castile, survived the ambush that killed her husband, Sancho Garcés III, ordered the avenging of his death, and built a number of public works. Urraca of Castile (ruled alone 1109–1126) fought against many enemies, took her armies personally to war, reputedly had numerous lovers, and is remembered as a strong if not widely beloved queen. Queen Petronila of Aragon (1136–1173) ruled with her husband until his death, when she abdicated in favor of her son.

Among Aragonese rulers, Maria de Luna (1357–1406) showed that she could handle court politics, invasions, uprisings and financial problems and even protect "her" Jews. Jaime I of Aragon avowed that he relied on the counsel and help of his queen, Violant (1235–1251). Costanza of Castile's daughter, Catalina of Lancaster (1374–1418), governed as queen of Castile and León for ten years after losing her husband and during the minority of her son, and is reputed to have eaten food and drunk wine as heartily as any of her courtiers. One of her trusted advisors was Leonor López de Córdoba (1352–ca. 1427), daughter of Martín López de Córdoba, the courtier and soldier of Peter I the Cruel of Castile, who wrote a fascinating though incomplete memoir of her life. In the kingdom of Aragon, queens ruled with or in the absence of their kings. Likewise, Maria of

Castile (reigned 1421–1423 and 1432–1453) and Juana Enríquez (reigned 1461–1477) were effective queens in the absence of their husbands.

As for women from a lower social level than that of queens, the extant records of reconquered frontier towns in the Catholic kingdoms indicate an analogous freedom of action. These Catholic women's access to and power in the public sphere cannot be found replicated or even approximated by *free*, married Muslim women in any Muslim town during the Middle Ages.[133]

Such Christian women, many from Castile, profited from the greater freedom accorded to both men and women by the unique judicial system of this Catholic kingdom, a system that grew out of and reflected a population made up largely of fiercely independent and self-reliant peasant-soldiers and hidalgos in the perpetual combat readiness of a frontier territory.[134] This legal system of Castile, with its dynamic political, linguistic, and social accompaniment, may find its only analogy in Europe in the development of the English common law.

A Catholic woman from the aristocracy who inherited the lordship of a town would be royally appointed *Señora de villa* (Mistress of the Town). Such a woman would be an absentee ruler who could name her local bureaucrats and military officers to administer the town and collect revenues.[135]

A Catholic woman property owner could and did participate in the politics of the local assemblies. According to Heath Dillard: "She may sometimes have voiced her opinions in weekly meetings of the assembly of property owners where matters of general community concern were discussed and important announcements made. A few tenth- and eleventh-century notices of women who took an active part in defending the privileges of their communities against outsiders have survived. The small Navarrese settlement of La Novenera fined women for assaulting other women both outside and during the assembly."[136]

Married Catholic women worked at all sorts of town businesses, such as bakeries, where the wife of the baker, the *fornera* (*hornera*), was supposed to deal with the female customers.[137] Dillard writes: "Ovens and bakeries, like a river or spring, were daily destinations for all sorts of women in a town, but dependable property owners' wives and daughters were frequently the only informants the court would heed about deceptive sales practices, pushing and shoving, or any other disturbance that arose at the place."[138] Married women could work as *taverneras* at their husband's *taverna*, though the occupation of barmaid was regarded as lower than that of a woman working at a bakery, an *hornera*.[139] They could work as shopkeepers and as marketplace sellers of various kinds of goods.[140] They could also work in the fields:

> Townswomen managed their own properties and supervised the raising of crops and flocks outside the walls in the alfoz. Others found employment in agricultural pursuits or, as in urban trades and crafts, they complemented the occupations of their husbands. Although some of these farm workers may have lived in town, many were village women who came to the walled municipal centre of their community on diverse errands: for safety in time of danger, on legal business at court, to celebrate a fiesta or attend church when there was none in the village, or perhaps to conclude a day of selling produce with a stop at the baths. Some village women were rural tenants of town dwellers for whom they evidently did routine farm chores. Paid agricultural labour, however, was commonplace in towns, and at Cuenca a salaried ploughman, whose services were those of a farm manager for grain crops, was assisted at harvest by his wife and another woman whom he hired for gleaning.[141]

One of the great literary works of the Spanish Middle Ages, the *Libro de buen amor* by Juan Ruiz, Archpriest of Hita (ca. 1283–1350), describes village Christian women working in the sierras of Spain and earning a living by transporting men across rivers.

Women could own farmland and work as cowherds as well as farmers. Again, Dillard:

> The fundamentally agrarian character of many towns' economic base meant that townswomen were often involved in agricultural pursuits but frequently as managers of property they owned, leased to others or cultivated themselves. Women of thirteenth-century Toledo owned not only vineyards, gardens, cropland and an occasional olive grove but also cottages, mills, corrals, salt works and other productive assets in the immense territory of the city. Women here were engaged in diverse rural occupations, earning their liv-

ings from rural enterprises although they lived inside Toledo.... Numerous women worked in partnership with their husbands at trapping rabbits, milling and gardening but especially at planting and harvesting grapes and other crops. Here many married towns-women and widows, like those to whom towns frequently guaranteed small subsistence holdings out of matrimonial assets, were engaged in agricultural work, not as labourers or entrepreneurs but as producers of foodstuffs to supply their own cellars and municipal customers.... Women participated in the livestock industry more as owners than as caretakers of animals, at least of the large commercially valuable flocks and herds which pastured primarily on the town commons and in the mountains of the alfoz. Women as well as men contracted with shepherds and cowhands in agreements by which the latter often received shares of hides, cheese or wool as wages.... The village women of a municipality, in particular, performed agricultural work, and many must have grown up with the rough ways of Juan Ruiz's mountain girls who were herders of cows and mares.[142]

Christian women are recorded working as cowgirls in the lyrics of a famous *serranilla* by another great poet of the Spanish Middle Ages, Íñigo López de Mendoza, Marquis of Santillana (1398–1458) (*"Moza mas fermosa no vi en la frontera / que aquesta vaquera de la Finojosa"*).

This sort of life was inconceivable for a *hurra* or *muhsana* because of her higher level of modesty in everyday life. Catholic women could be present at their parish church after Saturday vespers or Sunday mass to witness "the arraignment of a neighbour, announcements of land for sale, notification of changes in a marriage agreement, and other matters of local importance that required publicity."[143]

Catholic townswomen dominated some public sectors: "Townswomen congregated at sites which served as focal points of much of a woman's work, social life and feminine exchange. Here any man who presented himself would find himself more or less off-limits, sometimes definitely out of bounds, and doubtless more than a bit ill-at-ease. Together they comprised female 'space' or 'turf' within a medieval municipality. These meeting places for townswomen are identifiable in customs which set forth the contexts in which women were expected to serve as witnesses to disputes that came before the municipal courts of late twelfth- and thirteenth-century communities."[144]

Their testimony was not legally half that of men, as was the case in Maliki jurisprudence, but equal, though some towns had local regulations that made their testimony less weighty. Moreover, in commercial and territorial matters that required feminine competence, such as disputes involving springs, bakeries, spinning, and other such places and occupations, women's testimony was preferred. And the evidence suggests, as Dillard says, that "the word of a reliable woman would be preferred in any case to that of some shifty, feckless and untrustworthy man."[145]

As in the case of Muslim towns, certain days were allotted to Catholic women to go to public baths, as days were allotted too for Jews and Muslims.[146] But Catholic women did not have religious caveats against being polluted by non-Catholics and against leaving the house to go to the baths and could therefore in principle share the baths with whatever Jewish or Muslim women might dare to attend the facilities.

The first recorded lyric poems in a dialect of medieval Spanish, the *jarchas*, were probably created by Spanish *dhimmi* women under Islamic rule—"Mozarabs"—and are likely a manifestation of the popular Spanish lyrics known as *villancicos*.[147] The *jarchas* are short pieces that often express love for a male beloved. The *jarchas* are composed in Andalusian Arabic, in classical Arabic, and in Mozarabic Romance—these last written down with Arabic or Hebrew characters.[148] They always appear at the end of a type of poem composed and written in Arabic, the *muwassaha*. To create a particular aesthetic effect, authors of *muwassaha* incorporated these popular medieval lyrics, the *jarchas*, into their Arabic *muwassahas*, much as many Western poets (such as Ezra Pound and T. S. Eliot) have incorporated foreign language verses into their poems. It is possible, however, that even the *muwassaha* itself is not of Arabic origin but patterned after the Spanish *villancico* as well and therefore ultimately also of Christian origin. In fact, according to the great historian Ibn Khaldun, the creator of the *muwassaha* (and possibly the creator of the Arabic type of poem called *zejel*) was Muccadam de Cabra, a tenth-century poet of *dhimmi* ("Mozarabic") origin.[149]

Finally, it should be remembered that in the convents of Christian lands, many women, such as the Greek Saint Kassia (805/810–ca. 865), the German Hildegard von Bingen (1098–1179), and the Spanish Saint

Teresa of Ávila (1515–1582), attained high levels of creativity.[150] In music, Christian Spain had no known equivalent of the Greek nun Kassia or the German nun Hildegard von Bingen, great medieval composers. We know, however, that in Spain women abbesses, like Hildegard in Germany, or Kassia in Greece, were elected by the community of nuns, knew canon law, and functioned as today's CEOs—as executives in charge of the operations of congregations of nuns. Abbesses of the larger medieval abbeys in Spain, as well as in other lands in Christian Europe, were women of distinction, having as much power and influence within and without the Church as abbots did, some of these women even appearing at medieval church councils.[151]

One may conclude this examination of women's access to the public sphere in medieval Spain with another comparative assessment. An interesting aspect of official political power among Catholic female rulers in the Spanish kingdoms was that, as Theresa Earenfight has noticed, generally females with supreme political authority did not seem to their Christian contemporaries an extraordinary thing: María of Castile, queen of the crown of Aragon, "governed Catalunya as official *Lloctinent general* (lieutenant general) for over two decades—from 1420 to 1423 and again from 1432 to 1453—while her husband, Alfonso V, king of the Crown of Aragon (1416–1458), conquered and governed the kingdom of Naples. Her career may seem anomalous to us, but she was in fact quite unexceptional to her contemporaries."[152] Joseph F. O'Callaghan has pointed out that for the Castilian king Alfonso X, monarchy was a collaborative function between king and queen in his legal code *Las Siete Partidas* and other Castilian treatises.[153] This political role of female monarchs in Christian Spain, as we have seen, already had a precedent among Visigoth queens.[154]

The historical acceptance of a greater public role for women in Christian Spain may be ultimately traceable to Visigothic culture and law and to the relative greater public importance of women in medieval Christianity—not only in the Christian West, with its numerous queens, but also in the lands of the Greek and Russian Christians, with their many empresses and tsarinas.[155]

6

THE TRUTH ABOUT THE
JEWISH COMMUNITY'S
"GOLDEN AGE"

The era of Muslim rule in Spain (8th–11th century) was considered the
"Golden Age" for Spanish Jewry. Jewish intellectual and spiritual life
flourished and many Jews served in Spanish courts. Jewish economic
expansion was unparalleled.

—*Rebecca Weiner, "Sephardim,"* Jewish Virtual Library

AS THE EPIGRAPHS throughout this chapter indicate, it is widely
believed that Islam granted to Spain's Jewish community, composed
largely of Sephardic Jews, a substantial degree of liberty and tolerance.[1]
According to this view, the idyllic life for Spain's Jews was interrupted
by the invasion of the "fanatical" Almoravids and Almohads, and later
by the "intolerant" Christian kingdoms during the Spanish Reconquista.
However, the fact of the matter is that the life enjoyed by the Sephardim,
within and without their communities, was full of limitations long before
the invasion of the Almoravids and the Almohads, and that the Catholic
kingdoms eventually became a place of refuge for Jewish families. As the
historian of Islam Bernard Lewis has pointed out, "The Golden Age of
Equal Rights was a myth, and belief in it was a result rather than a cause
of Jewish sympathy for Islam."[2]

Jews had suffered much under the laws of the Visigoth kingdom.[3] It
is therefore not surprising that, as both Muslim and Christian medieval
sources tell us, the Jewish community supported the Muslim invaders
and even guarded major Catholic cities conquered by the Islamic warriors, thus facilitating the rapid advance of the Muslim forces.[4] The Jewish

community continued to collaborate with the Muslim rulers, functioning as a counterpoise to the majority subject Catholic population. Such an alliance of convenience had a precedent in the earliest Muslim conquests of the Christian lands of the Greek Roman Empire in the Middle East and North Africa.[5] An even earlier precedent had been established in the wars between Persia and the Christian Greek Roman Empire.[6]

Variations on this type of alliance, which has nothing to do with the fundamental beliefs held by the parties to it, can be found among many marginalized groups, from ancient times to the present. In the sixteenth century, the Spanish Conquistador Hernán Cortés favored his Indian allies, mainly the Tlaxcalans, in his struggle against the Mexica (often referred to as the Aztecs). In the twentieth century, colonial Belgian authorities in the Congo favored the minority Tutsis against other groups; in Algiers the colonizing French gave Algerian Jews a "superior status" to counterbalance the Muslim majority; and the United States worked with the Montagnard Hmong against the Marxist-Leninists in Southeast Asia.[7] More recently, with the 2003 war in Iraq, the U.S. and coalition forces initially favored the majority Shiites against the Sunni and al-Qaeda, the Kurds against both, and then for a while the Sunni militias against the Shiite militias.

This simple political explanation has been overlooked by even seasoned scholars who marvel at the "tolerance" the Islamic conquerors displayed toward Jews compared to the treatment Jews experienced under Christianity.[8] The Muslims did not treat Jews as allies, because doing so would have contradicted Islamic teachings (Quran 5:51: "Oh you who believe, do not take the Jews and the Christians as allies. They are allies to each other. Whoever takes them as allies, he becomes one of them"). Indeed, Islamic scripture held Christians in higher esteem than Jews, as expressed in a notoriously anti-Jewish part of the Quran (5:82): "Strongest among men in enmity / To the Believers wilt thou / Find the Jews and Pagans; and nearest among them in love / To the Believers wilt thou / Find those who say, / 'We are Christians': / Because among these are / Men devoted to learning /And men who have renounced / The world, and they / Are not arrogant." To avoid contradicting such Islamic teachings, Muslim rulers labeled Jews a "servant" group.

It is true, then, that the Jewish community experienced better living conditions under Spain's Muslim conquerors than under the Catholic

Visigoths. It is also true that, as a result, for some centuries Andalusian Jewry thrived, producing a brilliant cultural output.[9]

But none of this meant that Islamic Spain represented a beacon of tolerance. Fernando Díaz Esteban, professor of Hebrew language and literature at the Complutense University of Madrid, has observed that the Muslim masses resented the Jewish community's influence and visible material success, particularly given that this largely urban minority was relatively well educated and prosperous when compared with the poor and illiterate non-Jewish peasant masses.[10] This resentment contributed to several anti-Jewish riots, pogroms, assassinations, and expulsions, and eventually to a precipitous decline in status during the Almohad rule. Bernard Lewis points out that by the fourteenth and fifteenth centuries the Jewish population in Spain had shifted from Islamic lands to the Catholic kingdoms in search of a better life, following a general migration pattern through which those living in Christian lands became a majority of the Jewish world community.[11]

THE PEOPLE OF "PROTECTION"

> The years between 900 and 1200 in Spain and North Africa are known as the Hebrew "golden age," a sort of Jewish Renaissance that arose from the fusion of the Arab and Jewish intellectual worlds. Jews watched their Arab counterparts closely and learned to be astronomers, philosophers, scientists, and poets. At its peak about one thousand years ago, the Muslim world made a remarkable contribution to science, notably mathematics and medicine. Baghdad in its heyday and southern Spain built universities to which thousands flocked. Rulers surrounded themselves with scientists and artists. A spirit of freedom allowed Jews, Christians, and Muslim to work side by side.
> —Francis Ghiles, "What Is Wrong with Muslim Science," Nature, March 1983

The Maliki school of Islamic jurisprudence, the dominant school of Islamic law in medieval Spain, prescribed that Jews must pay to the Muslim rulers the *jizya*, the yearly poll tax intended not only as the price of their being *dhimmis* but also as a sign of their humiliation before Islam.[12]

As *dhimmis*, Jews were under the supervision of an Islamic function-ary from the *Kitabatu-dh-dhimam*, or "office of protection."[13] Jews were allowed to practice their religion and rule themselves according to their religious laws, but only within their communities. To prevent the expan-sion of Judaism, building new synagogues was seldom permitted. Jew-ish buildings must be lower than Muslim buildings. Jews must not carry weapons. They must not ride horses. They must show deference to Mus-lims. They must not give court evidence against a Muslim. No Muslim life must be taken for a Jewish life (but a Jewish life could be taken for a Muslim life). Jews must not criticize Islam, Muhammad, or the Quran. They must not proselytize. They must not have sexual relations with or marry a Muslim woman (although a Muslim man could marry a Jewish woman but their children must be brought up as Muslims). Jews must not dress as Muslim chiefs, scholars, or nobility. They must not dress in such an ostentatious manner as to offend poorer Muslims. They must not hold Muslims as slaves or servants. They must wear a distinctive sign on their clothes, usually a yellow band, badge, or cap, so that they could not "pass" as Muslims. Eating implements used by Jews must not be used by Muslims. A Muslim must not salute first a Jew or a Christian. The sum of these and other conditions, under which Jews in Islamic Spain were allowed to live and prosper, was part of the Muslim *dhimma*, or "writ of protection."

These legal restrictions both reflected and shaped the attitudes of the Muslim masses toward Jewry. Islamic scholars were unanimous in the assertion that *dhimmis* must not be placed in positions of authority over Muslims. These laws were intended to keep the infidels in their place and aware of their subordinate status.

As in other societies, in Islamic Spain legal restrictions against minorities were not always enforced, and sometimes were completely dis-regarded by the Muslim rulers. Already under Caliph Abd al-Rahman III, a physician and Jewish law scholar, Hasdai (Abu Yusuf ben Yizhak ben Ezra) ibn Shaprut (d. ca. 970), attained a position of influence as de facto foreign minister to the caliph and was active as a benefactor and protec-tor to the Jewish community.[14] But again, pointing out that the law was not always enforced is hardly an argument, because the same can be said of any judicial system, including those with the harshest prohibitions or penalties.[15]

Islamic rulers had a number of reasons for sometimes ignoring the religious injunctions, but none of those reasons had anything to do with the "tolerance" of Spanish Islam. The considerations were entirely political and practical. We have already examined the need to use the Jewish community as an ally ("servant") against the initially more numerous conquered Christians. Another important consideration was that in an Islamic realm beset by ethnic, class, religious, and political rivalries, functionaries chosen from among the Jewish leadership offered to Muslim rulers not only administrative skills and financial support but also a loyalty and dependence on the goodwill of the rulers undivided by allegiance to the *ulama* or to other Muslim families. Muslim rulers continued to favor the Jewish community as long as it was politically and economically helpful.

The Muslim rulers' disregard for religious law increased as Islam's energy and power declined. Legal barriers against Jewish ascendancy sometimes went unobserved, especially after the disintegration of the Caliphate of Córdoba in the early eleventh century. During the rise of the *taifa* kingdoms, the Sephardic community in general, and its leaders in particular, achieved positions of power unheard of before in Islamic Spain—although the Spanish Arabist Felipe Maíllo Salgado has observed that the role of Jewish viziers (high-ranking officials who served the Muslim ruler), such as that of Samuel Ibn Naghrela ("The Prince"), has been unduly inflated by scholars anxious to promote a "Golden Age" of Jewish life.[16] Periods of weak Islamic faith and power did coincide with periods of Jewish flourishing. Even then, however, circumstances could adversely affect the Jewish condition, always insecure because ultimately dependent solely on a given Muslim ruler's favor.[17]

Even in the *taifa* kingdoms not every Muslim ruler was fond of the Jewish community. King of Granada Muhammad Ibn Nasr (murdered in 1350) was praised by historian al-Khatib because he "imposed upon the Jewish *dhimmis* the obligation to carry a sign that would make them recognizable and separate so that they should pay their tax [*jizya*] of social *convivencia*."[18]

Several expulsions and pogroms further demonstrated the insecurity of Jewish life. Jews were expelled from Córdoba in 1013 and their wealth was confiscated as punishment for taking the side of a defeated Muslim leader in one of the frequent internecine struggles of the *taifa* kingdoms.

The Córdoban Sephardic community—which included the young rabbi Samuel Ibn Naghrela (993–1055), who would become the most powerful of Jewish leaders, eventually known by the Jewish title HaNagid ("The Prince")—fled to Granada, Toledo, Zaragoza, and Catholic lands.[19] In 1039 in the *taifa* kingdom of Zaragoza, a Muslim mob raided the palace of the Jewish vizier and killed him after the assassination of the ruler, al-Mondhir.[20] In 1066, only a few years after the death of the Prince, the rioting Muslim populace of Granada killed his son, the vizier Rabbi Joseph Ibn Naghrela, in a pogrom that destroyed the city's Sephardic community.[21] Muslim sources tell of other anti-Jewish Muslim riots in *taifa* kingdoms, including in Córdoba again in 1135.[22]

What could happen in al-Andalus to individual Jewish bureaucrats, no matter how highly positioned, is further illustrated by the fate of a Jewish vizier of al-Mutasim Ibn Sumadih, king of the *taifa* kingdom of Almeria (1051–1091). The *faqih* (Muslim cleric expert on Islamic jurisprudence) Abd Allah Ibn Sahl Ibn Yusuf saw the vizier in a bath frolicking in the company of a Muslim boy. The *faqih*, scandalized at what he saw, hit the vizier on the head with a stone, killing him. The *faqih* then walked away and was not punished for his action.[23]

The Muslim masses resented and the Muslim courtiers envied Jewish prosperity and influence. Such views were not uncommon in Islamic Spain. Even Rabbi Samuel Ibn Naghrela was regularly insulted by a Muslim merchant whenever the powerful Jewish vizier rode through the gates of the city of Granada.[24] In his lifetime, Ibn Naghrela also fended off at least two courtly conspiracies against him.[25]

The *alim* Abu Ibn Ishaq (d. 1067) criticized the ruler of Granada for favoring the Jewish community. His satiric poem, which brings up both religious and political issues, reflects Andalusian popular views regarding the "power of the Jews":

> He has chosen an infidel as his secretary / when he could, had he wished, have chosen a Believer. / Through him, the Jews have become great and proud / and arrogant—they, who were among the most abject. / And have gained their desires and attained the utmost / and this happened suddenly, before they even realized it. / And how many a worthy Muslim humbly obeys / the vilest ape among these miscreants. / And this did not happen through their

own efforts / but through one of our own people who rose as their accomplice. / Oh why did he not deal with them, following / the example set by worthy and pious leaders? / Put them back where they belong / and reduce them to the lowest of the low, / Roaming among us, with their little bags, / with contempt, degradation and scorn as their lot, / Scrabbling in the dunghills for colored rags / to shroud their dead for burial.../ Those low-born people would not be seated in society / or paraded along with the intimates of the ruler.... / God has vouchsafed in His revelations / a warning against the society of the wicked. / Do not choose a servant from among them / but leave them to the curse of the accurst! / For the earth cries out against their wickedness / and is about to heave and swallow all. / Turn your eyes to other countries / and you will find the Jews are outcast dogs. / Why should you alone be different and bring them near / when in all the land they are kept afar?.... / I came to live in Granada / and I saw them frolicking there. / They divided up the city and the provinces / with one of their accursed men everywhere. / They collect all the revenues, / they munch and they crunch. / They dress in the finest clothes / while you wear the meanest. / They are the trustees of your secrets, / yet how can traitors be trusted? / Others eat a dirham's worth, afar, / while they are near and dine well.... / Their chief ape has marbled his house / and led the finest spring water to it. / Our affairs are now in his hands / and we stand at his door. / He laughs at our God and our religion.... / Hasten to slaughter him as an offering, / sacrifice him, for he is a fat ram! / And do not spare his people / for they have amassed every precious thing.... / Do not consider it a breach of faith to kill them, / the breach of faith would be to let them carry on. / They have violated our covenant with them.... / God watches His own people / and the people of God will prevail.[26]

The great polymath Ibn Hazm referred to "the Jews" as corrupters of religion. This pronouncement came in the context of his lamenting the disintegration of the Caliphate of Córdoba and the rise of the *taifa* kingdoms.[27] Arabists Emilio García Gómez and Ignaz Goldziher have pointed out that Ibn Hazm was part of literary circles where these anti-Jewish polemics were not unheard of, and that he probably drew on the anti-rabbinical and therefore anti-Talmud writings of the Jewish Karaites. In other words, Ibn Hazm's views on the Jewish community not only had a theological basis in Islam but also reflected political conditions in Islamic Spain.[28]

Ibn Abbas, the Arab vizier of the ruler of the *taifa* kingdom of Almeria, hated Berbers and despised Jews.[29] Arab poets in the *taifa* kingdom of Seville accused the Granadan rulers of "believing in Judaism even though they called themselves Berbers."[30] The last king of Granada from the Berber Zirid dynasty, Abd Allah Ibn Buluggin (reigned 1073–1090), virulently attacked in his memoirs Rabbi Joseph Ibn Naghrela, insisting on the vizier's Jewish treacherousness and favoritism toward coreligionists, all of which presumably justified the vizier's murder in the pogrom of 1066.[31] All Muslim sources that mention this pogrom agree with Abd Allah's assessment of "the Jews."[32]

Jewish documents from Islamic lands in the Middle Ages show the existence of a word not found in the Torah but coined to designate such Jew-haters: *sone* ("a hater").[33] Muslim narratives and traditions fueled medieval Islamic anti-Judaism. According to the historian al-Masudi (d. 956), one tradition had it that Jews poisoned the first successor of Muhammad, Abu Bakr.[34]

In spite of such generalized anti-Jewish attitudes, the Sephardic community prospered as long as *taifa* rulers continued using capable Jewish functionaries, bankers, and tax collectors. For example, after escaping the Granada pogrom of 1066, Rabbi Isaac Ibn Albalia served as astrologer to the ruler of Seville, al-Mutamid, and became leader and protector of all the kingdom's Jewish communities. But al-Mutamid was an equal opportunity employer in every way: he crucified a Jewish ambassador sent to him by King Alfonso VI of Castile and León because of the demands the man carried.[35]

Like the Umayyads before them, the *taifa* kings may have used Jewish functionaries because these functionaries would be more loyal to the kings than to the *ulama*, or even to Islam itself, and also because they did not pose a threat to the Muslim rulers, who were always looking over their shoulder for potential enemies. In Granada, the quick action of Rabbi Samuel Ibn Naghrela stopped a rebellion against the ruler Badis from the ranks of his Berbers.[36] *Taifa* kings also brought in gifted Jewish leaders as they subsidized intellectuals, poets, and artists of all creeds to compensate for their political and military weakness and "enhance the prestige of their courts."[37]

The *taifa* rulers' generally favorable treatment of Jewry continued to elicit critiques from the *ulama*. One anonymous document from the eleventh century complains that the "princes of the Believers" were giving themselves up to pleasure while handing over their power to "the Jews."[38] A twelfth-century Muslim anthologist, Ibn Bassam, complained that someone had told him of having seen the ruler Badis with his Jewish vizier, Rabbi Joseph Ibn Naghrela, and been unable to tell who was the ruler and who was the subject.[39]

Arabic sources insistently lament the Jewish community's hegemonic status in the administrative echelons of the *taifa* kingdoms. They offer this perceived Jewish control as the explanation for the various anti-Jewish riots and even for the political decline of Islam.[40] The historian Ibn al-Kardabus, complaining of the Sephardic influence in Seville, connected this presumed "Jewish power" to the increasing danger of the Christian Reconquest: "The affairs of the Muslims were given to the Jews; then they caused in these affairs the destruction of lions, as they became chamberlains, viziers, and secretaries. Meanwhile Christians every year went around al-Andalus, pillaging, burning, destroying, and taking away prisoners."[41] As late as 1492, when King Boabdil of Granada capitulated to the Catholic monarchs, he included in the treatise of surrender a clause stipulating that "Your Highnesses will not allow Jews to have any authority over Muslims nor collect any kind of taxes from them."[42] These Muslim perceptions do not seem different from those that some scholars, concentrating solely on medieval Catholic Europe, have identified as among the root causes of modern anti-Jewish prejudice and persecution.[43]

In 1086 the devout Muslim Berber warriors the Almoravids (*al-murabitun*, "those dwelling in frontier garrisons")[44] invaded Spain from Africa. The invasion initially threatened the well-being of the Jewish community. The *ulama* class and the Muslim masses generally supported the Almoravid invasion, in part because of their unhappiness with the *taifa* monarchs' favoritism toward Jewish leaders. Many Jews fled to the Catholic kingdoms. Jewish contingents fought on the side of the Catholics under Alfonso VI of Castile at the Battle of Zalaca; others, on the side of the victorious Berbers.

These developments provide still more evidence that there was nothing unique about the "tolerance" of Islamic Spain: the Jewish community found similar arrangements under Catholic monarchs. In the Catholic kingdoms, Jewish notables occupied important positions in the royal courts, and the Sephardic population at large benefited from the rulers' favor.[45] Catholic monarchs such as Alfonso VI made use of and protected the Jewish community. At Alfonso's death in 1109, there were riots against Jewish neighborhoods, as the masses' pent-up resentment against Jewish prosperity and influence exploded.[46]

The Jewish community survived the Almoravid invasion, in part because of the skillful maneuvering of Jewish leaders and the lavish contributions they made to the coffers of the Almoravid emir Yusuf Ibn Tashufin (whom only El Cid, among Catholic warriors, was able to defeat). In time the Almoravids would use Jewish functionaries as well, despite the anti-Jewish enmity of the *ulama*. After the death of Ibn Tashufin, his son Ali Ibn Yusuf (reigned 1106–1143) began to rely on Jewish functionaries as administrators, bankers, and tax collectors.[47]

Less fortunate were the Christian *dhimmis*, who were already a minority, and who under the Almoravids suffered persecutions and mass expulsions to Africa. In 1099 the Almoravids sacked the great church of the city of Granada. In 1101 Christians fled from the city of Valencia to the Catholic kingdoms. In 1106 the Almoravids deported Christians from Malaga to Africa. In 1126, after a failed Christian rebellion in Granada, the Almoravids expelled the city's entire Christian population to Africa. And in 1138, Ibn Tashufin took masses of Christians with him to Africa.[48]

Judaism was endangered again in the mid-twelfth century, when even more devout Berber Muslim warriors, the Almohads (*al-Muwahhidun*, or "Those who assert the unity of God"), swept into Spain under the military leadership of their formidable caliph Abu Yaqub Yusuf (reigned 1163–1184). Yusuf captured Seville from its Almoravid rulers in 1147, and soon the entire Almoravid empire fell to these new Berber invaders.

To try to unify their quarrelsome multicultural domains, the Almohads gave both the Jewish and the Catholic communities the choice of either conversion to Islam or expulsion to Africa—as the Catholic monarchs Ferdinand and Isabella would do with the Jewish community in 1492. Also as would happen in 1492, many Sephardim chose false conversions in order to stay in Spain, as the great Andalusian rabbi Moses Maimonides had advised and as he may have done himself (while living in Egypt as a Jew he was accused by Andalusian *faqih* Ibn Maisha of being an apostate from the Muslim faith).[49] But some might not have given up without resistance: the Muslim historian Ibn Sahibi-s-Salat accused the Sephardic community of Granada, led by Rabbi Sahr Ben Ruiz Ibn Dahri, of having opened the doors of the then Almohad-controlled city to the Andalusian chieftain Ibn Humushk (said to be of Christian extraction) around 1161.[50]

As for the Catholic *dhimmis*, whatever was left of their population in Granada was exterminated in the aftermath of a revolt against the Almohads in 1164. Yusuf boasted that he had left no church or synagogue standing in al-Andalus.

Those Sephardim who refused to convert escaped to the Catholic kingdoms, Africa, and the Middle East, while the remaining Catholic *dhimmis* fled to the Christian kingdoms in a movement that ended Christian *dhimmi* life in al-Andalus for all practical purposes.[51] Many of these *dhimmis* would return, however, during the rapid advance of the Reconquest, following the defeat of the Almohads at the Battle of Las Navas de Tolosa (July 16, 1212) by the combined armies of the Catholic kings of Castile, Navarre, and Aragon.

CONVIVENCIA AND TOLERANCE

> Jews lived happily and productively in Spain for hundreds of years before the Inquisition and the Expulsion of 1492.
> —*Harold S. Kushner,* To Life! A Celebration of Jewish Being and Thinking *(Boston: Warner Books, 1993), 273, a high school textbook*

The splendor of the Jewish culture of medieval Spain ("Sepharad," in Hebrew) would be hard to exaggerate. In a symbiotic relationship with Muslim and then Christian rulers, Jews enjoyed from the eighth through the tenth centuries (in al-Ándalus) and from the eleventh through the fourteenth centuries (in Christian Spain) as much stability and legal protection as they had ever had. They prospered economically and demographically, and made up a larger proportion of the population than in any other European country. During some periods Jews

considered Spain a historically Jewish country, and their new homeland. Jewish intellectual life and the Hebrew language were reborn in
Spain. There was the greatest flowering of Hebrew poetry since Biblical
times, and Hebrew was used for the first time for secular poetry.
    —*"Jews, Sephardic,"* Encyclopedia of Homosexuality, *ed. Wayne
Dynes (New York: Garland, 1990)*

In Islamic Spain, there was no more *"convivencia"* and "tolerance" *within*
the Jewish community than *outside* it.

Even in the best of times, Judaism in medieval Spain was surrounded
by two powerful religions that constituted a potential source of heretical
ideas, apostasy, and infiltration by alien practices. As Edward Kessler and
Neil Wenborn have observed in *A Dictionary of Jewish–Christian Relations*, throughout history Jewish religious laws have helped a perennially
imperiled community preserve its identity by creating practical obstacles
to assimilation with majority non-Jewish religions.[52] In medieval Spain
these laws made *convivencia* with Muslims and Catholics problematic at
best.

By preventing Sephardim from converting to Islam and Christianity,
religious laws preserved Jewish identity in the face of difficult odds. The
Jewish masses used the Arabic language and Arabic names, as did many
of the most brilliant scholars and leaders. As the Christian Reconquest
gained strength, they adopted the language and names of the Catholic
culture. The religious laws enabled sincerely practicing Sephardim to
become devoted to worship, family, community, and fellowship, and they
led to spiritual and physical discipline as well as cleanliness.[53]

Scholars devoted to the myth of *convivencia* have typically glossed
over or ignored these barriers to everyday social intercourse with members of other faiths and therefore to *convivencia*. They overlook the
behavior of the masses of Islamic Spain in favor of more or less charming
examples of Muslim, Jewish, or Christian intellectuals, poets, and leaders,
or of segments of the general population, who adopted or "learned" from
this or that feature of the other's culture, such as dress, language, material
techniques, or poetic forms. But as far as the critical mass of the Jewish
population was concerned, the religious laws achieved their purpose of at
least slowing down conversions to Islam and, later, to Christianity.

Whereas the Sephardic elites might interact with their peers of other religions whenever necessary, the Sephardic masses carried out their legal and business transactions as much as possible within their community.[54] That separation was not unique to Islamic Spain. The historian E. Mary Smallwood has observed that in ancient times Jewish dietary laws and the prohibitions of the Sabbath prevented Roman attempts at Jewish integration into the foreign contingents of the legions.[55] According to another historian, David Stone Potter, Emperor Constantine failed in his later attempts to make Jewish authorities take up civic duties even if they conflicted with Jewish customs; eventually a law exempted these authorities from any civic business involving manual labor.[56]

Jewish exclusionary laws against non-Jews mirrored Muslim and Christian exclusionary laws against Jews as well as against each other. But one should also note the asymmetry in the demographic, political, and general social power of the three communities during the Middle Ages. That is to say, anti-Jewish conditions prevailed under both Islamic and Christian hegemony, but nowhere did the Jewish community exercise hegemony. Suspicion on the part of the Jewish community was not entirely "irrational," as why-can't-we-all-get-along scholars usually label such fears.[57] The famous episode in the twelfth-century Spanish *Poem of the Cid* in which the hero brazenly deceives the honest Jewish money lenders captures the prevailing attitude of the time in Spain. The coexistence of the "three cultures" sabotaged rather than helped *convivencia* in Islamic Spain.[58]

Of course, Jewish religious laws were not always followed, just as Muslim and Christian laws were sometimes skirted in the Muslim and Christian communities of Spain. Conversions to and infiltrations by other religions and cultures inevitably occurred, and a number of individuals would have paid only lip service to the religious laws. Scholars desperate to find proof of *convivencia* point to cases of Jews in Islamic Spain disobeying religious laws. For example, they cite an eleventh-century *fatwa* recording the case of a Jewish merchant who entered Muslim houses to sell his goods, another eleventh-century *fatwa* approving a wealthy Jewish man's decision to have his charity apply to poor Muslims as well, and a fifteenth-century *fatwa* pointing out that Jews dispensed sweets at Passover (the *fatwa* ruled that Muslims must not accept the sweets). But this "evidence" is notable precisely because it marks exceptions in the context of the religious laws.

Medieval Muslim historians corroborated the general practice of Jewish religious laws. In the twelfth century, Ibn Bassam mentioned a Jewish carpenter who refused to use tools previously handled by a Muslim worker, and al-Idrisi pointed out that the central part of the city of Lucena was occupied by a very wealthy Jewish neighborhood where "Muslims never entered."[59] Also instructive is the Maliki *fatwa* from al-Suyuri (d. 1067) noted in chapter 3. The *fatwa* involves a Jew who bought a house in a *Muslim street*: "He has settled there and bothers his neighbors by drinking wine and doing other reprehensible things. With his bucket, his rope, and his pitcher, he extracts water, like the Muslims, from a nearby well, and therefore the Muslim neighbors refuse to use the well." Unless the Jew changes his behavior, the *fatwa* rules, his house will be taken away.[60]

As we have seen, a number of cities in Islamic Spain had gates designated as "Jewish Gates" (*Bab al-Yahud*).[61] The historian S. D. Goitein pointed out that in medieval Islamic cities the bulk of the Jewish population was concentrated in a few neighborhoods, even though Jewish houses could border on non-Jewish houses and some Jewish houses could be found in non-Jewish areas. As Islamic rule consolidated in Spain, the Sephardic community continued to live by and large in identifiable neighborhoods within Muslim cities. From the point of view of the Islamic authorities, such segregation facilitated Muslim control and minimized friction among Muslims, Jews, and Catholics. From the point of view of the Jewish community, this distribution reflected the convenience of having synagogues in the vicinity of Jewish dwellings and made it easier to practice Jewish law unobstructed.[62] Muslims did not want Jews to live in Muslim neighborhoods, and many if not most Jews would not have wanted to live there anyway. As Goitein noted, because of this segregation the Sephardic masses under medieval Islam did not see or experience the spiritual life of other religious communities.[63]

The Spanish medieval Jewish community lived an autonomous existence in their *aljamas* (self-ruling Jewish communities) under the rule of its religious law (*Halakhah*). The Jewish community lived also under the authority of the transmitters and interpreters of that law—the rabbis, from whose ranks came the magistrates and leaders of the community.[64] Life revolved around the synagogue, and there was no distinction between civil law and religious law. As in Islam (but not Christianity), all law was religious. It applied to even the most mundane of personal as well as interpersonal and communal relations, to everyday individual and public activities, to sexual relations, and to contact with non-Jewish groups—and the rabbis were the arbiters and dispensers of that law. In other words, the Sephardim in Spain lived in a hierocracy.

Medieval historian Luis A. García Moreno has underlined the lack of separation between politics and religion in the Jewish communities of Spain. Moreover, as he observes of the *aljamas* under the Visigoths, "in their functioning, the Sephardic communities would be democratic in appearance and oligarchical in reality." García Moreno writes that, at the very top of a hierarchy made up of a "Council of Elders," of the small ruling group within that council, and of the leader of that ruling group, there existed yet another leader who directed the affairs of the entire community. This personage would have a preeminent position within and without the synagogue. Of great wealth and power, he would function as the lifelong protector and leader of the community, and his position would not infrequently be inherited. The historian Yitzhak Baer called attention to this rabbinical elite of medieval Spain made up of "the rich and powerful men in control of the aljamas."[65] In Islamic Spain, this type of Jewish leader described by Baer and García Moreno would be exemplified by Rabbi Samuel Ibn Naghrela (and later by his son Rabbi Joseph) in the *taifa* kingdom of Granada, by Rabbi Isaac Ibn Albalia in the *taifa* kingdom of Seville, or by physician and "Jewish law scholar" Hasdai Ibn Shaprut, who served under Abd al-Rahman III in Córdoba. In Christian Spain, an example would be the brilliant Rabbi Isaac Abravanel, who served as treasurer under Alfonso V of Portugal and later Ferdinand II of Aragon, and who tried unsuccessfully to dissuade Ferdinand from carrying out the expulsion from Spain of the Jewish community in 1492.[66]

The law in the Jewish community was demanding, and the rabbis were exacting in their rulings. As professor of Jewish studies Sacha Stern has observed, in medieval Spain rabbis showed little tolerance toward violators of the law, toward heretics, and especially toward apostates.[67] The brilliant Sephardic leader Rabbi Samuel Ibn Naghrela boasted that Andalusian Jews "were free of heresy, except for a few towns near Christian kingdoms, where one suspects that some heretics live in secret. Our predecessors have lashed a part of those who deserved to be lashed, and they have died from lashing."[68] When Ibn Naghrela mentioned "some heretics," he referred to the Karaites, who rejected the "Oral Law" and therefore the authority and the institution of the rabbis.

As we have seen in the case of Spanish Islam when compared to Islam in the East, Spanish Judaism was much more rigid than elsewhere, including northern Europe. Daniel Jeremy Silver, a professor of Jewish studies, has noted: "In matters of liturgy, the Sephardim were insistent on prescribed forms and formulas. The Spanish schools were heirs to a tradition which opposed, rather consistently, any flexibility in the formulas of the liturgy. Maimonides mirrored this attitude when he legislated."[69]

As the historian Yitzhak Baer pointed out, the Spanish rabbis in al-Andalus as well as in the Christian kingdoms persecuted the Karaites as heretics: "Under Muslim rule, the Karaites had been forced [by Orthodox Jews] to withdraw to the border regions adjoining the Christian territories and eventually to seek refuge in the fortress towns of Castile. The relentless persecution by three generations of [Orthodox] Jewish courtiers in the service of [Catholic kings] Alfonso VI, Alfonso VII, and Alfonso VIII, overtook them there and succeeded in destroying the sect with the aid of the governing powers."[70] (Historians have generally neglected the story of the destruction of the Karaite Jewish community, a topic that will be explored later in this chapter.)

The religious hatred against apostates was compounded by the justified fear that from their ranks came the "informers"—the snitches who, with their knowledge of Judaism put at the service of non-Jewish authorities, had historically constituted a set of dangerous enemies. The scholar Israel Abrahams pointed out: "For the informer the medieval Jews had no pity; he was outside the pale of humanity. Death was his penalty, and executions of this kind were far from rare. The greatest rabbis of the Middle Ages fearlessly sentenced informers to death, and cases of this severity occurred in all parts of the Jewish world."[71]

The great rabbi and philosopher Moses Maimonides, who lived under Islamic rule, asserted in his compilation and interpretation of Jewish law that a Jew who turns "informer" (*moser*) need not be brought to trial and may be killed by any member of the community.[72] In his formidable summary of religious law, *Mishneh Torah* (or *Yad Hahazakah*, "The Strong Hand"), Maimonides explained the need to police people's behavior: "The Jewish court is obligated to appoint officers who will circulate [among the people] on the festivals and check the gardens, orchards, and river banks to see that men and women do not gather there to eat or to drink, lest they [conduct themselves immodestly and come to] sin."[73]

Extant rabbinical *responsa* (rulings on religious-legal cases or practices where rabbis were consulted) from Catholic kingdoms indicate the demanding nature of religious law in medieval Spain's Jewish communities. As late as the fourteenth century in Castile, rabbis had the power to mete out death sentences on informers and on those found guilty of murder and adultery.[74] Rabbinical sentences could include "graduated punishments" in the form of the severing of appendages in accordance with the gravity of the offenses (first one hand, then the other, then a foot, and so on). In one *responsum*, the widely respected Rabbi Asher b. Yehiel agreed that a certain Jewish woman who had had sexual relations with a Christian man must have her nose cut off. In another case, he recommended that the tongue of a blasphemer be "drawn out of his mouth and partly cut off." Rabbi Asher praised the judges in the Seville *kahal* (Jewish governing council) who had imposed the death penalty on a Jewish man because he had carried "information to the Gentiles about the Jews and about the Jewish community." In a letter to the Spanish *aljamas*, Barcelonan rabbis Judah and Abraham b. Hisdai stated that the tongues of Jewish informers who had denounced Maimonides's *Moreh* to Christian authorities had been cut off.[75]

In a 1281 letter, Barcelona rabbi Solomon Ibn Adret urged a rabbi in Toledo "to proceed from gentle to severe measures, to begin with soft speech; but, should that not avail, to end by 'tearing, pulling, and by clubbing the skull.'" A case submitted to Rabbi Adret illustrates this expedient approach to the law. Resentful against the communal authorities, a Jewish man had shouted in the streets, "in the presence of Christians, that Jews exact a higher rate of interest than is allowed them by royal ordinance." Consulted, Ibn Adret concluded that the man was to be considered an informer, therefore deserving the penalty of death.

In a 1310 *responsum*, Rabbi Yom-Tob b. Abraham Asbili of the town of Bejar approved of a judge's decision to cut off a hand and the tongue of an informer. A judge, the rabbi said, was the "father of the community" and therefore did not have to follow proper procedures when he "must take care of the reform of the social order, extirpate wickedness from the land, and make a fence round the Torah."

Only by the early fifteenth century did rabbis in the Christian kingdoms begin to show in their *responsa* growing leniency toward the *anusim*, a term for those considered to have apostatized under duress. By that point Christians had reconquered most of Spain, and the increasing number of converts to Catholicism probably prompted or made necessary the rabbis' leniency.

The medieval historian Enrique Cantera Montenegro has corroborated the evidence contained in the rabbinical *responsa* and in such compilations of religious law as that of Moses Maimonides. Montenegro has documented the harshness of punishments handed out in Jewish communities of medieval Spain.[76] Rabbi Samuel Ibn Naghrela, writing in al-Andalus in the first half of the eleventh century, repeatedly argues in one of his poems that a domineering wife must be beaten up by her husband if necessary in order to make her accept his authority, and that the best wife is submissive and obedient.[77]

Despite all this evidence, some scholars have been reluctant to acknowledge that, during this "Golden Age" of Jewish culture, Jewish authorities would punish transgressors with beatings, mutilation, and even death—just as the other two religions did. Scholars who deny this evidence frequently argue that the death penalty had ceased to be applied in post-Talmudic times. This claim overlooks the fact that, as Montenegro, Abrahams, and others have pointed out, until at least 1379 Jewish authorities could, if it was justified to defend the social health of the community, inflict the death penalty, usually without interference from the outside world.[78] It also overlooks earlier evidence that Jewish communities had inflicted severe punishments on apostates: in the *Lex Romana Visigothorum* (506), Visigoth rulers had gathered edicts forbidding the Jewish persecution of apostates to Christianity; and in the fourth century, Emperor Constantine had forbidden the Jewish stoning of apostates.[79]

As Rabbi Emanuel Quint has noted, as late as the sixteenth century the great Spanish rabbi Joseph Ben Ephraim Caro (1488–1575) stated in his influential legal compendium *Shulchan Aruch* that in cases of necessity Jewish courts, including those with "non-ordained" judges, could inflict the death penalty, and did not require conclusive evidence to do so.[80] Caro listed a number of cases in which those who are "zealous for the Torah laws" (the "zealots") may kill guilty Jews, including those apostates who are "sinful" and "persistently do evil."[81] In Maimonides's *Mishneh Torah*, devout Jews (zealots) were allowed as a group, without the need

(continued from front flap)

of Christians and other groups—all this in the service of social control by autocratic rulers and a class of religious authorities.

The Myth of the Andalusian Paradise provides a desperately needed reassessment of medieval Spain. As professors, politicians, and pundits continue to celebrate Islamic Spain for its "multiculturalism" and "diversity," Fernández-Morera sets the record straight—showing that a politically useful myth is a myth nonetheless.

"Fernández-Morera takes on the long-overdue topic of assessing medieval Muslim Spain's reputation for ethnic pluralism, religious tolerance, and cultural secularism. Finding this view based on a 'culture of forgetting,' he documents the reign of strict *sharia* in Andalusia, with its attendant discrimination against non-Muslims and subjugation of women. **So much for the charming fantasy of open-mindedness and mutual respect.**"

—**DANIEL PIPES**, historian of Islam and publisher of the *Middle East Quarterly*

DARÍO FERNÁNDEZ-MORERA is Associate Professor in the Department of Spanish and Portuguese at Northwestern University. A former member of the National Council on the Humanities, he holds a BA from Stanford University, an MA from the University of Pennsylvania, and a PhD from Harvard University. He has published several books and many articles on cultural, literary, historical, and methodological issues in Spain, Latin America, and the United States.

Jacket design: Nadia McDannels

Cover image: Muslim horsemen and their black slave warriors herding Christian prisoners and their cattle, from the *Cantigas de Santa María,* thirteenth-century illuminated manuscript for judges, to destroy a Jew who blasphemed the Holy Name in the name of a false god ("idol").[82] A Jew who worshiped idols without being forced to do so must be stoned, even when the worshiper recanted, as long as he had been warned once before and his idolatry had been witnessed; otherwise he was merely punished with a "cut off" (karet), which meant being exiled from the Jewish community.[83] A Jew who created images even for the sake of art or beauty must be lashed—a prohibition that made blasphemous all representational painting or sculpture.[84]

In Islamic lands inhabited by Christians, such "idols" would include paintings and statues of Jesus Christ, the Virgin Mary, and the Christian saints. Maimonides wrote that Christianity, like Islam, could have a "positive" role to play in the world (both religions could lead people into the general concept of One God, which might open the way to their accepting the Messiah's coming).[85] Nonetheless, he considered Christians idolaters, since they were Trinitarians, believed in the divinity of a mere man (Jesus), and venerated statues and paintings of saints and the Virgin Mary. Moreover, he regarded Christianity as a heresy.[86] Rabbi Eliyahu Touger observes that, in the censored and therefore more available editions of the Mishneh Torah, "The term 'Canaanite' is the censor's alteration: the original texts of the Mishneh Torah state 'Romans' [that is, the Rum, or Christians of the Greek Roman Empire] or 'Christians.'" Rabbi Touger also notes that Maimonides's Sefer HaMitzvot (Positive Commandment 187) "states that the Canaanites no longer exist." He adds that the uncensored text of Maimonides's Commentary on the Mishneh (Avodat Zarah 1:3) "explicitly describes the Christians as idolaters and forbids doing business with them."[87] Similarly, the professor of Hebrew studies Norman Roth points out that in the uncensored Mishneh Torah Maimonides considers Christians idolaters and explicitly rejects such doctrines as the Trinity.[88]

But of course Christians in either Islamic or Catholic Spain could not be subject to medieval Jewish law and its harsh punishments against idolaters because they were not Jewish idolaters—a point overlooked by anti-Jewish polemicists and assorted anti-Semites through the ages.[89] The key point in all this is that Jews living in Catholic lands had to be careful in not voicing that they regarded as idolaters the Christian majority surrounding the Jewish communities. This would explain the statement of medieval Ashkenazi authority Rabbi Tam, who, living in a Catholic land, declared that Christians were not idolaters. In Islamic-dominated lands, this precaution would not be necessary.

Gerald Blidstein, an expert on Maimonides and Jewish law, has observed that for Maimonides one of the dangers of Karaism was precisely that it might lead a Jew to the "true heresy," Christianity.[90] Maimonides included Jesus of Nazareth and his Jewish followers, the early Christians, among the Jewish heretics (*minnim*) and apostates who must be killed.[91] He also referred to Jesus as a false prophet correctly executed: "Jesus of Nazareth who aspired to be the Messiah and was executed by the court."[92] (In a note, Rabbi Touger corrects Maimonides: "The Jews did not actually carry out the execution, for crucifixion is not one of the Torah's methods of execution. Rather, after condemning him to death, the Sanhedrin handed him over to the Roman authorities who executed him as a rebel against Roman rule.")[93] Norman Roth has noticed that Jewish polemical treatises and poetry in medieval Islamic Spain attacked not so much Islam, within which the Sephardic community lived, but mostly Christianity, although not many Sephardim lived in Catholic Spain at the time.[94]

Maimonides's dislike of Christianity is explicit in his *Mishneh Torah*: "Can there be a greater stumbling block than Christianity? All the Prophets spoke of the Messiah as the redeemer of Israel and its savior, who would gather the dispersed and strengthen their observance of the Mitzvot. By contrast, Christianity caused the Jews to be slain by the sword, their remnants to be scattered and humbled, the Torah to be altered, and the majority of the world to err and serve a god other than the Lord."[95]

But Maimonides's dislike of Muslim Arabs may have been greater than his dislike of Christians. In his *Epistle to Yemen* he called Muhammad "the maniac" and reminded Jews that "on account of the vast number of our sins, God has hurled us into the midst of this people, the Arabs, who have persecuted us severely, and passed baneful and discriminatory legislation against us, as God has forewarned us: 'Our enemies themselves shall judge us' [Deuteronomy 32:31]. Never did a nation molest, degrade, debase, and hate us as much as they."[96]

To be sure, Maimonides is a complicated and often controversial figure. In his own time, some rabbis condemned his *Mishneh Torah* for simplifying complex legal issues to make them accessible to the unlearned and even to the hostile, and for a lack of references disclosing his sources.[97] In the first half of the thirteenth century, rabbis in Northern France opposed to Maimonides's approaches to the sacred Jewish texts and to his making Jewish law more widely accessible to those uninstructed in rabbinical knowledge banned Jews from reading Maimonides's *Moreh Nebuchim (Guide for the Perplexed)*; this ban was answered with a counter-ban by rabbis from some Spanish cities (such as Zaragoza) against those who might have spoken against Maimonides.[98] As a possible result of this "Maimonidean Controversy," Christian authorities in Montpellier burned Maimonides's *Moreh Nebuchim*, allegedly at the instigation of such rabbis as Solomon b. Abraham and Jonah b. Abraham Gerundi of Montpellier.[99] Modern Jewish authorities consider the *Mishneh Torah* (along with Caro's original *Shulchan Aruch*) to reflect an exclusionary understanding of Jewish law, an understanding historically conditioned by a medieval setting in which Judaism was frequently fighting for its very survival.[100]

But the essential point is that Maimonides's legal views, whatever their merits or shortcomings, carried considerable weight in the Sephardic community of medieval Spain under Islam and under Christianity.[101] In the *Mishneh Torah* he presented in a compressed manner what he believed to be Jewish law as it had been traditionally interpreted and applied in Spain.[102] These religious laws, as Maimonides interpreted and codified them, made everyday interaction with non-Jews difficult.

This fact alone could dispose of the myth of *convivencia*. Maimonides explicitly ruled against eating and drinking with non-Jews.[103] Practicing Jews must not drink milk produced by a non-Jew, though cheese might be acceptable if dictated by necessity.[104] One must not eat crab, lobster, oysters, squid, octopus, pork, or blood products, among other things—prohibitions that again made eating with non-Jews religiously risky and therefore inadvisable. Blidstein notes that, for Maimonides, mixing meat with milk was representative of the sort of "infidel" thinking that deserved to be punished with death.[105] Utensils bought from non-Jews must be thoroughly cleansed from Gentile handling before they could be used.[106] Entering a non-Jewish shop was sinful if a kosher shop was available.[107] Goitein showed that letters and legal documents from Sephardic merchants in Islamic lands in the Middle Ages reflect how such laws affected even commercial transactions by making them more difficult.[108] Stern and Herbert Alan Davidson point out that the obligation (*mitzvo*) to eat food, including bread, prepared only according to kosher procedures dictated that Sephardim must avoid eating and drinking with non-Jews; as Maimonides put it, "through the prohibited sexual relations and food restrictions, God made us holy and separated us from the gentiles."[109]

Maimonides's teachings also forbade Jews to marry non-Jews.[110] Collective anxiety about sexual interaction with the "other" dictated a number of legally sanctioned customs and prohibitions. In fact, Maimonides ruled against eating and drinking with non-Jews partly because doing so could lead to intermarriage.[111] The injunction against intermarriage—part of a large body of detailed laws involving marriage, family, and sex—seems to have been quite effective: the massive collection of medieval Jewish documents known as *Cairo Genizah* shows no instance of intermarriage in a Mediterranean Sephardic community in a large city under Islamic rule.[112] This religious law helped fend off the threat of assimilation and religious conversion by preserving lineage and internal cohesion—always in danger for any minority group within a society.[113] But the injunctions also acted as a barrier between the Jewish community and the other communities, in spite of the occasional violations of both Jewish and Christian law in the Christian kingdoms.[114] In Muslim lands, a *Cairo Genizah* document from around 1065 shows how a Sephardic woman got in serious trouble from *both* Muslim and Jewish authorities for having sexual relations with a Christian physician.[115] Stern points out that a Jewish woman was forbidden to meet with a non-Jewish man even if his wife was present, the assumption being that a non-Jewish man would be willing to fornicate despite the presence of his wife.[116]

Other rabbinical *responsa* from Christian Spain confirm the centrality of Maimonides's teachings. Rabbi Yehuda ben Asher of Toledo (1269–ca. 1343) ruled that one should denounce to the Jewish authorities any Jewish man who had intercourse with an idolater woman, and that the transgressor should be hounded by zealots and banished from the community.[117] The rabbi also wrote that the "seed" of the Jewish people was so holy that it must not be sullied by contact with Gentiles, meaning that Jewish prostitutes, though still "a source of sin," were preferable to Gentile ones.[118]

In general, non-Jews were considered to have much worse morals. Thus, for Maimonides, "all Israel must constantly keep in mind that cruelty and impudence are qualities of the 'uncircumcised gentiles' and not of 'the seed of Abraham, our father.'"[119] This teaching imposed an obligation to set an example for the "others" and consequently made greater demands on the morals of the Jewish community.[120]

The exclusionary injunctions of Maimonides's *Mishneh Torah* were generally confirmed by Spanish rabbi Joseph Caro's *Shulchan Aruch* (1565), which claimed to follow "majority opinion" rather than one single authority. According to the *Shulchan Aruch*, being a guest of someone who might not keep dietary laws was not advisable, unless refusing could create animosity; utensils should not be left in a non-Jewish home, for fear that they might be used; even if a utensil were given to a non-Jew for repair, fear of contamination required consulting with a rabbi on the matter; it was forbidden to purchase wine or food from sources that did not comply with Jewish laws; it was forbidden to drink wine (made from grapes) that had been touched by a non-Jew; and cooking in a pot near the pot of a non-Jew was risky because food from the other pot could contaminate the Jewish pot, making the food there inedible.[121]

Other exclusionary laws in Caro's *Shulchan Aruch* were similarly motivated by fear of the "others." It was forbidden to draw or keep in the house a picture of a human being, or even an angel, or keep in the house the image of any face, unless it was disfigured or incomplete, as in a profile. It was forbidden to stare at "idols" even for their beauty. One must keep a distance of at least four cubits from the temples of non-Jews and from their false gods ("idols"), and one must not have dealings with non-Jews at their temples. One must not pronounce with respect the names of non-Jews' holidays named after an "idol." It was forbidden to lend money with interest (usury) to other Jews, although it was allowed to do so to non-Jews.[122] Children must not be educated by non-Jews or nursed in their houses.[123]

As we will see in the next chapter, the laws under which the Catholic *dhimmis* ruled themselves had a number of similarly exclusionary laws, also motivated by a fear of the "others."

THE DESTRUCTION OF THE KARAITE COMMUNITY

At its best, the culture gave Jews greater religious, social, economic, and intellectual freedom than they knew in any other medieval (non-Muslim) society.... Its limitations notwithstanding, convivencia has been described as the defining issue in the history of al-Andalus, and it resulted in a major renaissance of Arabic and Hebrew literature and learning, and in an early flowering of Spanish culture.

—*Poet Peter Cole, The Dream of the Poem: Hebrew Poetry from Muslim and Christian Spain, 950–1492 (Princeton, NJ: Princeton University Press, 2007), winner of the R. R. Hawkins Award from the Association of American Publishers, and praised by the literary critic Harold Bloom for giving "the best account of convivencia I have encountered" ("The Lost Jewish Culture,"* New York Review of Books, *June 28, 2007)*

The story of the Karaite Jewish community has been neglected in the general histories of medieval Spain, and, when mentioned, its disappearance is usually explained as the natural self-dissolution of an unimportant sect. The available documentation tells otherwise.

The Sephardic community in medieval Spain was not monolithic. As Yitzhak Baer observed, various internal conflicts beset Spanish Judaism. Kabbalists struggled with anti-Kabbalists, and the rabbinical elite, composed of the "rich and powerful men in control of the aljamas," who might develop worldly and secularizing inclinations, faced criticism from rabbis more loyal to Jewish tradition.[124] But such conflicts did not affect the fundamental structure of religious life. Karaism (called a "sect," or at best a "heresy," by its medieval Orthodox enemies, who were referred to as "rabbanites" since the tenth century) represented the gravest internal threat to the unity of medieval Spanish Judaism.[125]

This Jewish religious movement had started in the Middle East and from there it had spread to other lands. Possibly founded around 760 by Anan Ben David, it claimed to be a return to the true form of Judaism.[126] The word *Karaite* derived from the Hebrew *Karaim*, meaning "Disciple of Scripture." Karaites accepted no intermediaries in their understanding of the written law (basically the Pentateuch, or what Christians called the Old Testament). According to Orthodox Judaism, Moses handed down the Oral Law to selected sages at the time he handed down to the Jewish people the written law of the Pentateuch; the Oral Law complemented the written law. But Karaites rejected the authority of the Oral Law, which rabbis had written down between the third and the sixth centuries.[127] Karaites disagreed with several other aspects of medieval Orthodox Jewish religious beliefs and practice. For example, the treatise *Eshkol ha-Kofer*, by the twelfth-century Karaite thinker Judah ben Elijah Hadassi, writing in Christian Constantinople, rejected the Talmud and considered Jesus a bona fide prophet.[128] Karaites also kept a different religious calendar, forbade the marriage of a widower to his deceased wife's sister or to his brother's wife, and, unlike Orthodox Jews, rejected sex between married couples during the Sabbath as a desecration.[129]

As Nathan Schur and other non-Karaite historians observe, by the early twelfth century Karaism had become "quite influential in Spain."[130] Daniel J. Lasker, professor of Jewish thought at the Ben Gurion University, confirms that by the twelfth century in Spain "there was a substantial Karaite community living side by side with the [Orthodox Jewish] population."[131] Karaism won an increasing number of Jewish converts under the leadership of Said Ibn al-Taras (Cid Ibn Altaras) and, upon his death, of his wife al-Mualima (which means "The Teacher"; Karaite women were not barred from serving in religious offices, in contrast to medieval rabbinical Judaism).

Therefore, in the eyes of the leaders of medieval Orthodox Judaism, Karaism had become dangerous. Rabbis such as Judah Halevi (d. 1141), Abraham Ibn Ezra (d. 1167), Judah Ibn Balaam (late eleventh century), Judah ben Barzillai al-Bargeloni (or Barceloni, early twelfth century), Moses Ibn Ezra (early twelfth century), Joseph Ibn Zaddiq (d. 1149), Zerahiah Halevi (late twelfth century), and Judah al-Harizi (d. 1235) saw it necessary to write against Karaism. Maimonides also wrote against Karaism and contributed to its demise from Egypt. He was willing to accept back into the Orthodox Jewish fold repentant Karaites, but for the unrepentant he urged their physical elimination, and recommended to Yemenite Jews to follow the example of the Spanish rabbis in dealing with Karaism.[132]

"Karaism," Daniel J. Lasker writes, "came to be perceived as a persistent, viable threat to [Orthodox Judaism] at that time."[133] Since rabbinical anti-Karaite polemical writings had failed to convince the recalcitrant heretics, Orthodox leaders took more decisive action. As Rabbi Samuel Ibn Naghrela boasted, rabbis in al-Andalus successfully extirpated Karaism from Muslim lands. Karaism then took refuge in the frontier lands of the Catholic kingdoms. During the reign of Alfonso VI of Castile and León (1072–1109), Orthodox Jewish courtiers, among them Joseph

Cidellius, physician to the king, used their influence on the Spanish monarchy to obtain edicts expelling the Karaites from Castilian towns.[134]

Many Karaites went underground, remaining in Castile as crypto-Karaites. Undeterred, Orthodox leaders obtained new edicts against the Karaites from Alfonso VII (reigned 1126–1157) and Alfonso VIII (reigned 1158–1214). When Alfonso VII reconquered Calatrava, he put in charge of the city one of his tax collectors, Rabbi Judah ben Joseph b. Ezra of Toledo, who convinced the Catholic king to persecute the Karaites. According to chronicler Abraham Ibn Daud (ca. 1110–1180), Rabbi Ezra "asked the king not to let the [Jewish] heretics open their mouths in the whole land of Castile and the king complied with the request and the heretics were subdued and did not continue to lift their heads."[135] Under Alfonso VIII, Rabbi Joseph Ibn al-Fakhahr (also known as Joseph Farissol, or Ferrizuel, and perhaps also as Cidellius) and Rabbi Todros Abulafia (Todros Halevi) and his son Joseph used their influence to suppress the heretics.[136] Afterward, Rabbi Joseph boasted: "My father and master of blessed memory went in the footsteps of my grandparents in his zeal to remove from our provinces the abominations of the heretics until he succeeded in destroying their fortresses and pulled down to earth their glory and there was not on the day of God's wrath a remnant when he executed judgment upon them and upon their books."[137] In the thirteenth century, the celebrated rabbi and poet Judah ben Solomon al-Harizi (1165 Toledo–1225 Aleppo) referred to the Karaites as "moral insects," "schismatics," "malformed," "miscreated," "thieves," and a "sickly sect," in contrast to the Orthodox, whom he described as "Believers" and "Faithful."[138]

By then Karaism in Spain was practically finished. However, during the second half of the thirteenth century the celebrated Kabbalist rabbi Moses de León (1250–1305) wrote a letter asking for the persecution of a few Karaites who somehow managed to survive in Catholic Burgos.[139] Small groups of Karaites may have continued to live a precarious existence in Christian Catalonia until the fifteenth century.[140] But the destruction of the Spanish Karaite community was so thorough that none of its writings survives, and the complete name of only one of its thinkers, Said Ibn al-Taras (or Altaras), has been preserved. All that is known about Spanish Karaism comes from the dismissive writings of medieval rabbis or from scattered references in Muslim and Christian texts.[141] As Baer observed, after the defeat of Karaism in the twelfth century, internal religious Jewish disagreements, no matter how bitter, never again involved questioning the principle of rabbinic tradition.[142] Today, Karaism constitutes only a very minor part of Judaism. Its anti-rabbinical arguments, however, are echoed in Messianic Judaism.[143]

It is easy today to condemn traditional medieval Judaism's elimination of the Spanish Karaites. It was achieved at a human cost. But Karaism had targeted the hierarchy and a fundamental doctrine of Orthodoxy: the rabbinate and the Oral Law. Moreover, as Maimonides realized, Karaism could open the way for good Jews to fall into the arms of an even worse Jewish heresy: Christianity. From the point of view of traditional medieval Judaism, then, the true religion was threatened in its essence, and after the failure to convince the heretics to give up their erroneous beliefs and rejoin the traditional Jewish community, only force could neutralize their threat. Thus—again from the point of view of Orthodoxy at the time—the destruction of Karaism in Spain saved the future of traditional Judaism.

7

THE CHRISTIAN CONDITION

From *Dhimmis* to Extinction

Under the normal course of events, Christian practices [under the Umayyads] were allowed a wide degree of tolerance. Public and ostentatious displays of faith like processions and ringing of bells were discouraged, at least in the capital, but neither churches nor monasteries were directly threatened.

> —*Hugh Kennedy, Professor of History in the Department of Languages and Cultures of the Near Middle East of the University of London,* Muslim Spain and Portugal: A Political History of al-Andalus *(London: Routledge, 1996), 48*

[Under Abd al-Rahman III] Muslim tolerance of the so-called People of the Book was high, and social intercourse at the upper levels was easy and constant.

> —*Jane I. Smith, Associate Dean for Faculty and Academic Affairs at Harvard Divinity School, "Islam and Christendom," in* The Oxford History of Islam, *ed. John L. Esposito, University Professor as well as Professor of Religion and International Affairs and of Islamic Studies at Georgetown University (Oxford: Oxford University Press, 1999), 318*

Once upon a time in the mid-eighth century, an intrepid young man named Abd al-Rahman abandoned his home in Damascus, the Near Eastern Heartland of Islam, and set out across the North African desert in search of a place of refuge.... This was a chapter in Europe's culture when Jews, Christians, and Muslims lived side by side and, despite their intractable differences and enduring hostilities, nourished a complex culture of tolerance.... The new Islamic polity not only allowed Jews and Christians to survive but, following Quranic mandate, by and large protected them.

> —*María Rosa Menocal, R. Selden Rose Professor of Spanish and Portuguese and Director of Special Programs in the Humanities at Yale University,* The Ornament of the World: How Muslims, Jews, and Christians Created a Culture of Tolerance in Medieval Spain *(New York: Little, Brown, 2002), 5, 11*

MUSLIMS HAD MANY names for the Christian Hispano-Visigoths who, after the Islamic conquest, remained as Christians subject to Islamic hegemony rather than fleeing to the North: *Nazarenes* ("*nasrani*"), *rumies* (Romans, a reference to the inhabitants of the Christian Greek Roman Empire), *al-hamra* ("reddish ones," because of their white and rosy skin), *mushriks* (polytheists), *elches* (infidels), *kafirs* (infidels), *isawis* (followers of Jesus), *agemies* (barbarians, as in *ayami*, barbarian), *kuties* (Goths), *aduw* (*aduw Allah*, enemies of God), *abid al-asnam/al-sulban/al-awtan* (worshippers of the idols-crosses-icons), *muahid* (one under a subjugation agreement), and, more generally, *dhimmis* ("beneficiaries of the contract [of protection]").[1] An insulting name used in popular speech for a Christian was *pig* (*khanzir*), as Almoravid emir Yusuf Ibn Tashfin (d. 1106) calls King Alfonso VI of Castile and León (1040–1109) twice according to Muslim historian Abd al-Wahid al-Marrakushi (1185–1230); in his treatise on *hadith*, the great Persian scholar Ibn Qutaybah (d. 889), well-known in al-Andalus, mentions humorously the word *pigs* as applied to Christians.[2] One name the Muslims of al-Andalus did not use for Christians was "Mozarabs."[3] Nor did Christians from the North call the Christian *dhimmis* in the South "Mozarabs." As the historian Miguel Ángel Ladero Quesada has pointed out, they called them *Spani*— that is, Spaniards.[4]

The name *Mozarab* did not exist until after 850, when Christian *dhimmis* began to escape (or "migrate," as some Islamic studies scholars tactfully prefer) from their presumably good life under the Umayyads to the northern Christian kingdoms. These former *dhimmis* had kept rich and ancient Christian practices and rituals that predated the Muslim conquest. To the Christians of the North, these former *dhimmis* sounded and looked strange. The refugees spoke an archaic Romance dialect that had not changed much since 711. In addition, they knew Arabic, and many had Arabic-sounding names. They showed other signs of having lived subject to Muslim rule for generations. Northern Christians, perhaps following the lead of these former *dhimmis* themselves, began to call these refugees "muztarabes," "muzarabes," "almozarabes," or "mozarabes"— all probably derived from the Arabic *mustarib*, or "Arabicized." Eventually scholars adopted the word *Mozarab* to designate not only the Christian *dhimmis* who fled to the North but also the Christian *dhimmis* who remained under Islamic rule.[5]

Despite the name, the "Mozarabs" were not Arabs in any shape or form. They had, in fact, tried to keep their religion, language, and customs—in other words, their culture—for several centuries and under exceedingly difficult political, social, and religious circumstances. As late as the ninth century, Eulogius of Córdoba had a large library where he produced a copy of Saint Isidore's *De natura rerum*. As they watched the decay and sometimes the destruction of their churches and monasteries, *dhimmis* preserved the memory of their lost Christian kingdom. Thus the *Chronica mozarabica* of 754 still makes reference to those happy times when Visigoth Toledo was *a royal city* ("When the pious Bishop Eugenio was at the royal city of Toledo...").[6]

Inevitably, however, *dhimmis* yielded to the hegemonic culture and adopted the language and many customs of the dominant Muslims. The only option for the conquered Hispano-Romans and Visigoths, if they did not become *dhimmis* and pay a special tax (*jizya*) or flee for their lives, was to convert to Islam. Many Christians did convert, of course.

In al-Andalus, Muslims referred to the converts to Islam as *musalima* or *asalima* and to the descendants of these converts as *muwalladun* (singular *muwallad*; Spanish: *muladi*)—a word derived from the language of cattle breeders and meaning "cross breed" or "mixed ones."[7] In other words, a descendant of a convert was seen as a "cross breed," a "mixed one," different from "pure" Arabic Muslims. The Islamic law scholar Felipe Maíllo Salgado has pointed out that in the Middle East the social inequality of the *mawali* (pl. of *mawla*: a non-Arab convert to Islam, often a former slave, who remains linked as a "client" to his Arab Muslim "protector" in a relationship of allegiance and "protection") gave rise to a movement that brought about the fall of the Umayyad dynasty in Damascus and the rise of the Abbasid dynasty, which was supported by Persian *mawali*.[8] As we will see, the social inequality of the *muladis*, the descendants of the former Christians in al-Andalus, would cause analogous problems for the Umayyad dynasty in Córdoba.

By the end of the twelfth century, as a result of flight (or "migration") to Christian lands, expulsions to North Africa, executions, and conversions, the Christian *dhimmi* population had largely disappeared from al-Andalus.[9] When Christians entered Granada in 1492, there were no Christian *dhimmis* in the city.

As we will see, however, the Christian *dhimmi* culture influenced the dominant Muslim culture, and the culture of the Christian *dhimmis* who fled to northern Spain ("Mozarabs") shaped the culture of northern Spain's Catholic kingdoms.

THE PEOPLE OF SUBMISSION

> The limited but real tolerance enjoyed by Christians benefiting from Córdoba's prosperity may explain why the movement [of martyrs] never roused wider public support. Simply put, Eulogius's Christian coreligionists liked things as they were. Isaac, Argimirus, and Sanctius were not the only Christians prospering in Muslim Córdoba. And those who were doing well hardly wanted their prospects threatened by the fanatic Christian fringe.
> —*Chris Lowney,* A Vanished World: Muslims, Christians, and Jews in Medieval Spain *(New York: Oxford University Press, 2006), 61–62*

Muslims in medieval Spain considered Islam the final and most perfect form of divine revelation. They also believed that the "People of the Book"—Christians and Jews—had strayed from the teachings of their Bible in various ways that rendered them religiously inferior to Muslims, who had kept the true faith. Given this conviction of superiority, Islam in medieval Spain could hardly be said to be "tolerant" of other religions. To prevent other faiths from contesting the religious and therefore political, social, and cultural supremacy of Islam, rulers and clerics endeavored to keep every type of hegemony over the "People of the Book."

Of course, in some circumstances Christian *dhimmis* assumed positions of varying authority even while remaining outsiders. The Muslim regime sometimes enlisted skilled Christians to serve as bureaucrats or soldiers for the same reason it enlisted skilled Jewish functionaries: they would be loyal to the Muslim ruler and to nobody else because they had no allegiance to potential Muslim rivals and in fact owed only to the ruler their improved condition; and a given ruler who lacked strong religious convictions might also turn to a Christian for whom he had personal sympathy. This "success" is often presented as evidence that Christian life under Islam was favorable. But as was the case with Jews who assumed positions of authority under Muslim rulers, such "success" involved only elites and did not extend to the masses. Moreover, it occurred in spite of—and in direct opposition to—Islamic injunctions, and it created resentment among the *ulama* and the Muslim population.

Those Islamic injunctions, and the assumption of Islamic superiority from which they followed, are the crucial matters to understand when considering the condition of Christians in Islamic Spain. To be sure, Islamic law was not enforced everywhere, every time; as in any other legal system, expediency, necessity, favoritism, bribery, inefficiency, politics, and other factors could alter an outcome. But the plain fact is that Islamic law in medieval Spain imposed humiliating conditions on Christian *dhimmis* to ensure that absolute power remained in the proper hands. Those restrictions were quite successful in their purpose, at least for several centuries.

Under the Islamic institution of the *dhimma* (writ or contract of "protection"), the Christian *dhimmis* of al-Andalus must pay a special tax, the *jizya*, for a "protection" intended, as Maliki legal texts make clear, to remind them of their submission. Malik's *Muwatta* declares, "Zakat is imposed on the Muslims to purify them and to be given back to their poor, whereas *jizya* is imposed on the people of the Book to humble them."[10] Therefore the *jizya* ought to be paid in a humiliating manner:

> The *dhimmi*, standing, would present the money to the Muslim collector who would be sitting higher up on a sort of throne; this Muslim bureaucrat would hold the *dhimmi* by the throat telling him "Oh *dhimmi*, enemy of Allah, pay the *jizya* that you owe us for the protection and tolerance we grant you"; the other Muslims present

would imitate the collector, pushing around the *dhimmi* and whoever other *dhimmi*s accompanied him. To this amusing spectacle
should be admitted any Muslim who wanted to enjoy it.[11]

As part of the *dhimma* system, a Muslim "officer of protection" regulated
all affairs related to Christians.

The *dhimma* system, then, was a gangster-like "protection racket"
(pay "protection" or else) that was quite profitable for the Muslim rulers. Muhammad's father-in-law, companion, and second caliph, Umar (a
caliph so just and pious that he was known as al-Farooq, "one who distin-
guishes between right and wrong"), made clear that this was a profitable
system of extortion: *dhimmi*s were even more productive for Muslims
than slaves and therefore should be kept "protected" as *dhimmi*s rather
than parceled out as slaves precisely because Muslims could live off them
much better. After citing the verses from Quran 9:29 ("Fight against those
who do not believe in God nor in the Last Day, who do not hold forbidden
what God and His Apostle have forbidden, who do not practice the religion of truth but are of those to whom a Book has been given, until they
pay the poll tax from their hand, they being humbled"), Umar admonished his followers (bracketed material is the translator's):

> Have you considered, if we take them [as slaves] and share them
> out, what will be left for Muslims who come after us? By God, the
> Muslims would not find a man to talk to and profit from his labors.
> The Muslims of our day will eat [from the work of] these people as
> long as they live, and when we and they die, our sons will eat their
> sons forever, as long as they remain, for they are slaves to the people
> of the religion of Islam as long as the religion of Islam shall prevail.[12]

It was a brilliant and pioneering triumph of medieval Islamic rhetoric
that the word *dhimmi*, meaning "beneficiary of the contract of protection"[13] (*dhimma*)—that is, a "protected" individual or "beneficiary"—was
chosen to designate the helpless victim of a religiously based extortion
system.

Besides the *dhimma*, the conquerors used other strategies, drawn
from Islamic law, to ensure Islamic hegemony. Consider some injunctions from the legal manuals used in Islamic Spain. A Muslim who raped

a free Christian woman must be lashed; a Christian who raped a free Muslim woman must be killed.[14] Whoever calumniated a Muslim must be flogged, but whoever calumniated a Christian (or a slave, a small boy, one possessed by the devil, one whose penis had been cut off, or one who had been castrated) was not flogged.[15] A Muslim was entitled to full "blood money" (compensation for injury and perhaps death), but a Christian was entitled to only half.[16] Whereas a Christian was allowed to convert to Islam, a Muslim was forbidden, under punishment of death, to convert to a different faith.[17] A Muslim must not be executed for the death of a Christian, unless the killing was treacherous,[18] but a Christian could be executed for the death of a Muslim, even if the killing was not treacherous. The testimony of Christian men or women was not acceptable in any legal matter involving only Muslims.[19] A Muslim could have a Christian slave, but a Christian could not have a Muslim slave; a Muslim could have sex with a Christian sexual slave, but a Christian could not have sex with a Muslim sexual slave.[20] A Muslim could use for ablution the water previously used by a Muslim man in a state of impurity, or even by a menstruating Muslim woman, but not water previously used by a Christian, for that water would be polluted.[21] A Christian woman was not recommended as wet nurse because she was polluted with pork and wine.[22]

Plenty of other examples can be recited. A Muslim must not initiate the greeting when meeting a Christian.[23] A Muslim judge must not hire a Christian as secretary.[24] A Muslim must feed a poor Muslim, but he must not feed a poor Christian.[25] A Muslim had an obligation to free, at some point, Muslim slaves, but not an obligation to free Christian slaves.[26] A Muslim man could marry a free Christian woman, although this was not advisable, but a Christian man could not marry or fornicate with a Muslim woman, free or not, under penalty of death. The children of Muslim men and Christian women had to be raised as Muslims—a not-too-subtle instrument to further the decline of the Christian population and the growth of the Muslim one.[27] The Muslim master of a Christian slave man could marry him to a Christian slave woman owned by the Muslim master, but if the woman converted to Islam, the Christian slave man was forbidden to have sex with the now-Muslim slave woman.[28] A Muslim man could not marry Christian slave women but could marry Muslim slave women.[29]

Muslims celebrated their religion publicly, but Christians could not hold processions on the streets and must discreetly celebrate their religion within their churches and neighborhoods.[30] In Umayyad Córdoba, Christians must not walk through Muslim cemeteries because their presence would pollute the Muslim tombs. Water, food, garments, and utensils touched by a Christian became polluted. As late as the fifteenth century in Christian-held territory, Muslim law told the *mudéjares* (Muslims under Christian domination): "water touched by an infidel, a wine-drinker, a cat, or a dog cannot be used for ablution; do not adopt ways of speaking, manners or customs of the Christians, nor their clothing, nor those of sinners."[31] New mosques could be freely built and old ones repaired, but Christians could rarely build new churches or even repair old ones, and never without the Muslims' authorization. Mosques could stand proudly in Islamic cities, but Christian churches must not challenge the mosques by opening to main thoroughfares. Mosques and other Muslim buildings could be as high as architecturally feasible, but no Catholic church or other Christian buildings could tower above Muslim buildings. Mosques could not be converted into churches, but churches could be, and often were, converted into mosques. Muslims could have the muezzin loudly proclaim the call to prayer, but Christians could not ring their church bells. Muslims could proselytize, but Christians could not. Christians could be placed under Muslim law if they wished, but Muslims were forbidden to do the opposite. Christians could not display crosses on themselves. Christians could not display crosses on the outside or on top of their churches. Christians could not display figurative art on the outside walls of their churches. Christians could not wear Muslim-like clothes. Christians must wear distinctive signs. Christians must stand up in the presence of Muslims.

Christians could not exercise political sovereignty in any form. They must not carry weapons. They must not ride horses in Muslim areas—a notable prohibition repeated by Muslim Turks during their occupation of Greece, when the Greek Orthodox *raya* (flock) could not ride horses, only donkeys, and had to ride sideways so they could readily dismount and genuflect before Muslims.[32] Imam Malik, agreeing with the second caliph, Umar, observed: "I think that Christians should be compelled to wear belts, and that used to be required of them of old. I think that they should be compelled to be humble. Umar wrote that they should be mounted sideways [like women] on donkeys."[33] During a certain period of Umayyad rule in Spain, Muslim authorities even decreed the forced circumcision of male Christians.[34]

To these ways of oppressing and *intentionally* humiliating the *dhimmi* population, one must add the taxes that Muslim rulers could at any time arbitrarily pile up on top of the *jizya*, prompted by the rulers' perennial need for cash to maintain their ostentatious lifestyle, poets, intellectuals, slaves, palaces, harems, and city-embellishment programs.[35] Even Spanish Arabists sympathetic to Islamic Spain recognize that the harsh measures listed by jurist Ibn Abdun in eleventh- and twelfth-century Seville agreed with the teachings of medieval Maliki jurisprudence regarding the proper way to keep the *dhimmis* in a "condition of humiliation and subservience (*sigar*) or tolerated discrimination."[36]

In short, contrary to what is commonly believed, the institution of the *dhimma* in Islamic Spain did not generously grant religious autonomy to Christians. It actually limited their religious practices in numerous ways, and it left the subject Christians without any possibility of attaining political power. Eventually reduced to minority status, Christian *dhimmis* saw their numbers slowly decline as a result of conversions that promised an escape from Islamic law's humbling limitations and special taxation and also as a result of Islamic laws that, for example, forced the children of a Muslim man and a Christian woman to be raised as Muslims, and allowed a Muslim man to have children with up to four wives and as many sexual slaves as he could keep.[37]

The situation of Christians under Muslim rule in Spain was similar to the presumably "benign" condition of the Greek Orthodox *raya* under Turkish Muslim rule: in the words of the historians John S. Koliopoulos and Thanos M. Veremis, Greek Orthodox Christians "were tolerated as long as they accepted the inferior status of the *raya* (flock) and were prepared to obey the ruler who had imposed that inferior status on them."[38]

The much-praised "tolerance" of al-Andalus was thus part of Islam's imperialist system of separation from and subordination of Christians. Christians could practice their religion, but only on Islam's terms. Islamic clerics and rulers remained effectively in control in matters of religion, and because religion informed everything, they remained effectively in control of everything.

The system of "protection," then, was in reality a system of exploitation and subjugation. All the onerous details of everyday practical differentiation and subordination followed from—and reinforced—general assumptions of Islam's religious and therefore political hegemony.

Medieval Islamic conquests quite methodically began this process of submission. After Muslim forces had invaded a place, overcome the locals militarily, and chosen a capital, they would pause in their forward advance to subjugate the defeated.[39] All the various forms of differentiation and superiority, including the proliferation of mosques and the limitations on churches and Christian public worship, fostered conversion and Islamization—without any need to resort to "forced" conversion— while at the same time reinforcing the conquerors' power.

Islamic colonization had another ally in the compelling need to use Arabic. Arabic was the language of the Muslim sacred texts and the accompanying rituals. Converts, therefore, must learn Arabic, which reinforced their acculturation. But Arabic also gradually supplanted the language of the conquered *dhimmis* who remained Christians, because these *dhimmis* found it necessary to speak, read, and write Arabic in their commercial, social, and political transactions. In fact, to make their own lives easier in a Muslim-dominated society, Christian *dhimmis* adopted Arabic-sounding names and even dressed like Muslims when they could.

As noted in chapter 1, the Muslim conquerors also adopted the common colonialist tactic of renaming villages, towns, cities, and geographical landmarks, giving them new, Arabic-sounding names. In Spain, they even changed the name of the land, *España*—derived from the Latin *Hispania* and the late Latin *Spania*—to al-Andalus, a word that is probably a garbling of the Greek words for "Atlantis island," Ατλαντίσ νησος.[40] Consequently, the history of Islamic conquests shows a rapid decline in the languages of the subject populations. In the sixteenth century, after the Reconquest, a Morisco—a Muslim who had presumably converted to Christianity—boasted, "Egyptians, Syrians, Maltese, and other Christian peoples, speak, write, and read in Arabic."[41] In the Middle East, pre-Islamic languages, with the exception of Farsi, effectively vanished. In North Africa, Berber languages and cultures were quickly marginalized. In Islamic Spain, Jews spoke and wrote Arabic in preference to Hebrew. Over time Christian *dhimmis*, despite their efforts to maintain their culture, became "Arabicized," adopting the Arabic language and, when allowed, Arabic clothes.

An even more effective hegemonic strategy consisted of transforming the most significant cultural materials of the conquered: their houses of worship. Turning Christian temples into mosques was a standard demor-alizing and hegemonic feature of Muslim conquests. The strategy had been used in the seventh and eighth centuries in North Africa and the Middle East, lands that for centuries had been largely Christian under the rule of the Greek Roman Empire.[42] Since Islam would not allow any Christian temple to tower over a mosque, the magnificent Greek basili-cas in the cities of the Christian Middle East and North Africa were turned into mosques. The best example is the Umayyad Grand Mosque of Damascus, built on the site of the Greek Basilica of Saint John the Bap-tist, which was demolished and cannibalized in the early eighth century.

As it happened, the splendidly constructed Damascus mosque was built and decorated by workers and architects from the Christian Greek Roman Empire. Even its minarets, according to the Persian geographer Ibn al-Faqih (903), were originally watchtowers in the Greek Basilica of Saint John the Baptist. All these influences account for the "Byzantine" look of the mosque.[43] Greek architects also built the mosque of Caliph Umar in Jerusalem (the al-Aqsa mosque), in 688, and the earlier mosque of Amran in Cairo.[44] In the early centuries of Islam, Muslim rulers endeavored to copy in their mosques the exterior architectural features of Christian churches with the explicit purpose of dwarfing them.[45]

If a Christian city offered armed resistance, the conversion of Chris-tian temples into mosques occurred soon after the conquest of the city. The ninth-century Muslim chronicler al-Waqidi records that during the conquest of Egypt, the Islamic forces immediately turned a Coptic church into a mosque in a city where Greek troops had resisted.[46] Shortly after Muslim forces disembarked in Spain, they occupied the ancient city of Carteya, a Visigoth stronghold, and demolished its church; on that spot they built their first mosque. Under Islamic occupation, Carteya disap-peared from history.[47] The Muslim conquerors carried out the same strat-egy throughout Spain.

This domination strategy is best illustrated by the Umayyad mosque of Córdoba, which since the thirteenth century has been the Cathedral of Córdoba. As we have seen, this celebrated mosque was built in the eighth century after the Umayyad emir Abd al-Rahman I destroyed the ancient church of Saint Vincent, the main basilica of Córdoba. Left without a church, Christians were allowed to build a smaller one, but only out-side the city walls. Recent investigations by archaeologists such as Pedro Marfil confirm that the mosque of Córdoba was constructed with col-umns, capitals, and other superior materials cannibalized from Christian and Roman buildings, including Saint Vincent.[48]

The process did not stop with Abd al-Rahman I. Whenever Muslim chronicles make reference to Christian churches in Spain, it is to boast of their transformation into mosques or their outright destruction as sym-bols of Islamic dominance over the *mushriks* ("polytheists")—as Chris-tians were called because they prayed and genuflected in front of icons and statues of the Virgin Mary, Jesus Christ, the saints, and the angels, as well as the cross.[49] Churches were destroyed as part of the persecution of Christians under the Umayyad ruler Muhammad I (reigned 852–886).[50] In the late tenth century, al-Mansur was a notorious burner of Christian churches during his military campaigns, and his additions to the mosque of Córdoba, we learn from al-Maqqari, were "built with the materials of demolished churches brought to Cordova on the heads of Christian captives."[51] As late as 1195, Muslims on the offensive were still turning Christian churches of conquered Spanish territory into mosques as a sign of Christian defeat and submission.[52] Muslim historians emphasize that, like the *jizya*, the destruction of Christian churches, statues, and relics was intended to humiliate the "People of the Book" and affirm Islamic hegemony.[53] The suppliant Christians might be allowed to repair their crumbling church buildings, but only when it suited the Muslim rulers. As a result, granting the humbled *dhimmis* permission to repair their temples was equally effective at reminding Christians that they remained always at the mercy of their conqueror.

As several Muslim chroniclers attest, the *tabiun* accompanied the Islamic armies that conquered Spain to oversee the Islamization of the land.[54] The *tabiun* were holy men who enjoyed great prestige because they had been trained under the first generation of Companions of the Prophet. They were in charge of supervising the religious aspect of every Islamic conquest, such as the founding of mosques and their proper orientation, as well as the distribution of booty and lands according to Islamic principles. These men, only a couple of generations removed from Muhammad and his personal teachings, would have overseen the early process by which Islam displaced Christian culture from power in Spain.

After a Muslim victory over infidels, whether the defeated Christians lived or died was entirely up to the Muslim leader. Recall, from chapter 4, Ibn Hayyan's account of how an officer of Abd al-Rahman III beheaded one hundred Christian prisoners in Córdoba in full view of Muslims exiting the mosque after the Friday prayer: "All the prisoners, one by one, were beheaded...in plain sight of the people, whose feelings against the infidels Allah alleviated, and they showered their blessings on the Caliph."[55]

Slavery was the other normal alternative for Christians captured in battle. Although women and children should not be killed, they could be legally enslaved.

TOLERANCE AMONG THE CHRISTIAN *DHIMMIS*

> Both Jews and Christians, who were "People of the Book," were treated well, aside from taxes, and allowed to worship freely, with a few restrictions—the Christians were not to ring their church bells. Muslims, Christians, and Jews all dressed similarly, and the Muslims often attended Christian celebrations. These Christians who lived in many ways like the Muslims were known as Mozarabs, from the Arabic word *musta'rib*, meaning *Arabizer*.
> —*"A Brief History of al-Andalus," at the high-traffic website http:// home.earthlink.net/~lilinah/Library/HistoryAndalus.html*

There was no more a culture of tolerance in what remained of the Christian community in Islamic Spain than there was in the Muslim or Jewish communities.[56] Like the Sephardic Jewish community, the Christian *dhimmis* ruled themselves through exclusionary laws motivated by a fear of the "others." Those laws endured from the time of Visigoth rule in Spain.

After King Recared converted to Catholicism (a conversion made official when he convened a great third church Council in Toledo in 589), Visigoth law added provisions against the only heresy known in the kingdom before the Muslim invasion: Arianism, the teachings of the Christian presbyter Arius. (Recared had converted from Arianism.) The Visigoth law prohibited the use of the Arian creed in churches and forbade Arians from occupying public office. The Visigoth regime also punished with exile the former Arian bishops who, in collusion with Visigoth nobles, had militarily rebelled against the crown: some bishops were exiled internally (such as to a monastery), and some were sent to Africa.[57] It is notable that the death penalty was not part of the Visigoth law's punishment of the Arian heretics.

Visigoth law also included many rules against the Jewish community, intended to make it disappear eventually. These provisions placed Jews on an unequal footing with respect to Catholics.[58] Upon Recared's conversion, the Third Council of Toledo (589) and the later councils produced a number of canons that restated ancient laws regarding Jews and even created new ones. The fact that, under Muslim rule, Christian *dhimmis* could no longer enforce all the earlier anti-Jewish Visigoth legislation did not contribute to harmonious *convivencia*; the best that could be expected was some kind of grudging coexistence.

Here again, as in all legal systems, these laws would not have been enforced every time in the Visigoth kingdom, everywhere. Repeatedly one finds Catholic councils addressing issues that the canons of previous councils were supposed to have resolved, such as Christians violating the laws against the Jews.[59] The medieval historian Luis A. García Moreno has argued that the violations indicate that there was no generalized anti-Semitism among the Christian population, since Christians of all social conditions were willing to protect the Jews in spite of the laws; he has also pointed out that many of the laws existed under Visigoth Arianism, before Recared's conversion to Catholicism.[60] When Muslims invaded Spain in the early eighth century, they found a Jewish community still sufficiently strong, in spite of all the laws trying to force them to convert, to become an ally in their conquest of the Christian realm. Therefore the Visigoths' numerous anti-Jewish laws must have been suspended at times, or not well enforced, or applied in a "flexible" manner, or not applied because of bribery,[61] or otherwise not completely effective.

Nonetheless, it is important to understand these laws because they indicate the unfavorable legal frame within which Jews lived in Visigoth Spain. Moreover, they give an idea of how the Christian community in Islamic Spain, which followed Visigoth law, must have generally viewed Jews, especially after witnessing the Jewish community side with the invaders and enjoy, for a time at least, a position of superiority. The "Psalter of Hafs the Goth" (a product of Mozarabic literature in Arabic dating from the ninth or tenth century) exemplifies the lingering animosity of some Christian *dhimmis* toward the Jewish community.[62]

The legal code by which Christian *dhimmis* ruled themselves in Islamic Spain was gathered in manuals including *Lex visogothorum* (506) and *Liber iudiciorum* (694). The Visigoth laws included injunctions against apostasy from Christianity to Judaism; against the marriage of Jews and Christians; against protecting Jews; and against eating with, living in the same house with, or bathing in the same baths as Jews. Laws also forbade Jews from proselytizing; occupying public office; owning, buying, and selling Christian slaves; performing circumcision; publicly observing Jewish holidays; keeping Jewish books thought to deprecate Christianity (including the Talmud); practicing dietary laws; building new synagogues; and persecuting Jewish converts (apostates) to Christianity.[63] The Visigoths imposed special taxes on Jews as well. Often, the penalty for violating these laws was death.

Children born of the marriage of a Christian and a Jew must be baptized. This law indicates that this forbidden intermarriage or concubinage did happen, even if rarely, *before* the Muslim invasion, in spite of the legal prohibitions against it. Moreover, canons of various councils stipulated that the daughters of Christians must not marry or be mistresses of unrepentant heretics, Jews, and schismatics: for example, the Sixty-Fourth Canon of the Third Council of Toledo (589) and the Sixty-Third Canon of the Fourth Council of Toledo (633).

One can notice certain parallels among Muslim, Christian, and Jewish exclusionary practices. For example, the Visigoth law against mixed marriages was no different from medieval Jewish law, for both rejected *all* mixed marriages. Muslim law, however, carved out an exception: it allowed a Muslim man to marry a free Christian woman. The Visigoth law stipulating corporal punishment against *judaizantes* (those who practiced or promoted Judaism but were or had become Christians) was no different in intent from Islamic and Jewish laws against apostasy and proselytism, which prescribed equally harsh or even harsher physical punishments, including death. The law prescribing a special tax on Jews had an equivalent in Islam's *jizya*; it had no equivalent, however, in Jewish law. The Visigoth law against allowing Jews to occupy public office was similar to the Muslim law that forbade non-Muslims from having positions of authority over Muslims. It was also similar to the Jewish law forbidding non-Jews from occupying public office in a Jewish kingdom. Finally, the Visigoth law forbidding Jews to own Christian slaves was no different from Islamic laws forbidding non-Muslims to own Muslim slaves and Jewish laws forbidding non-Jews to own Jewish slaves.

Significantly, though, those last two Jewish laws (and others) were unenforceable, because Jews did not have a kingdom of their own. As we have seen, the anti-Jewish conditions that prevailed under Islamic and Christian hegemony necessarily had no equivalent in the Jewish community, which never exercised an analogous hegemony over the other two religious communities.

Scholars have differed in trying to explain the reasons for the Visigoth anti-Jewish legislation.[64] A few of the laws could be traced back to the Roman Empire, especially after Emperor Theodosius (not Constantine, as is usually repeated) declared Christianity the official religion in 380. Some scholars have argued that the legislation reflected Christian fear of the religious attractiveness of Judaism for Christians or for Jewish converts to Christianity who might be tempted or forced to relapse. A related viewpoint explains the laws as reflecting old popular views of the Jews as killers of Christ (and persecutors of the early Christians), who must, however, be allowed to exist as examples of the unhappy life that befalls a people who reject Jesus. Related to this may have been knowledge during the reign of Visigoth king Sisebuth (612–621) of the Jewish alliance with the Persians against the Christian Greek Roman Empire and the possible role of the Jews in the massacre of Christians in Jerusalem after the city fell to the Persians in 614 (see chapters 1 and 6).[65]

Other scholars have argued that legislation got worse only after the Visigoth king Egica (reigned 687–702) accused Jews of conspiring with their coreligionists in Africa to have Muslims invade the kingdom: Egica decreed the enslavement of all Jews who could not prove they were Christians. Again, Egica was probably aware of the alliance between Jews and Muslims in the Islamic conquest of the Christian Middle East (Patriarch Sophronius asked for protection against the Jews as a condition of the surrender of Jerusalem to the Muslim commander). Egica's anxieties may have derived in part from the writings and ideas of an ardent enemy of crypto-Judaism, Bishop Julian of Toledo (who himself came from a family of sincere Jewish converts to Christianity and became primate of the Catholic Church over the entire Visigoth kingdom from 680 to 690).[66]

Other scholars have given an economic explanation: that the superior economic condition of Jews (who, simply by virtue of being principally urban dwellers, enjoyed a higher standard of living than did the mostly peasant Christian population) elicited rather un-Christian envy. Others have argued a related hypothesis: the Christian masses resented the political and social influence over the monarchy and the nobility that some Jews achieved. According to still other scholars, the Visigoths were intent on addressing the political and social fragmentation of the realm, and thus, after the conversion of Recared, the monarchy together with the Church tried to create difficult conditions that would push Jews into becoming Christians in order to bolster the unity and social cohesion of the realm.

But other scholars have argued that, for its era, Visigoth Spain sometimes displayed a relative respect for other religious confessions. They point out that under Saint Isidore's advice, the Third Council of Toledo (589) made clear that heretics were not to be killed and that Jews were not to be forced to convert (though both heretics and Jewish apostates from Christianity were anathematized).[67] Similarly, bishops were generally opposed to forced conversion; some Jewish leaders were even given opportunities to accuse a bishop of using force and deceit to have Jews convert to Catholicism. Scholars have also pointed to a presumed *convivencia* between Jews and Christians in Merida, depicted in the *Vidas de los santos padres emeritenses*. Even King Egica in 693, as part of the Sixteenth Council of Toledo, had granted all Jews who converted unusual Christian privileges of *nobles* (noble) and *honrados* (honorables), exempting them from taxation, to make of them an example to recalcitrant Jews of the advantages of becoming sincere Christians. García Moreno writes:

> Simply by acknowledging publicly that they were Christians and by participating openly in Christian celebrations, these *marranos* [Jewish converts to Christianity suspected of practicing Judaism in secret] would be considered equal to Christians in everything and could thereby engage freely in business activities, including the profitable overseas commerce. Penalties were reserved for those who relapsed [into Judaism] and also for those who refused to show such outward manifestations of their Christian Faith. The first group was punished with the confiscation of all their property. The second group was excluded from any profitable activity which implied

dealing with Christians, and they had to pay special taxes; in addition, they would lose all the property that they might have acquired during the time they were supposed to have been Christians, presumably to be given to whomever the king wished. Those who transgressed these laws would become slaves of the government. Those Christians who participated in or protected such transgressions would be punished severely; if a nobleman, he would have to pay a heavy fine of three pounds of gold, or three times the value of the illegal commercial transaction; if the Christian was of humble extraction, he would receive a hundred lashes and the confiscation of his property as determined by the king.[68]

By the following year, however, Egica's approach to the conversion of the Jews had hardened: determined to destroy the cohesion of the *aljamas* (self-governing Jewish communities), he decreed the "dispersion and slavery of all *marranos* of dubious [Christian] Faith, and the breakup of their families." Some scholars believe that his son Witiza (d. 510, succeeded by Rodrigo, the last king of the Visigoths) may have reversed Egica's edict against the Jews.[69] The *Chronica mozarabica* of 754 certainly speaks of Witiza's granting pardons to people exiled by Egica, accepting them back as vassals and returning to them their confiscated property.[70]

Nevertheless, whatever the reason for Visigoth anti-Jewish laws and for their ultimate failure to convert the Jews to Christianity or break up the Jewish communities, the indisputable fact is that the legislation created animosity against the Visigoth kingdom. It led to many false conversions among Jews who wanted to remain in Spain but escape the laws and still practice Judaism (secretly). And the resentment eventually helped make the Jewish community side with the Islamic invaders.

As for the Christian population, the legislation both fostered and possibly reflected negative attitudes toward the Jewish community. Such attitudes likely persisted under Islamic rule, even if the Visigoth anti-Jewish legislation could no longer be enforced. After all, Christian *dhimmis* continued to rule themselves according to Visigoth laws, and they certainly remembered the support the Jewish community gave to the Muslim invaders and the resulting favor some Jewish leaders enjoyed (if only for a time). None of this contributed to tolerance and *convivencia* between Christian and Jewish *dhimmis* in Islamic Spain.

THE CHRISTIAN CULTURAL INFLUENCE

> During [Abd-al-Rahman III's] reign there emerged a brand of Islamic culture open to multiple currents of influence, integrating and nourishing them under what might be called, following Marshall G. Hodgson, an "islamicate" culture.
>
> —The Edinburgh Companion to the Arab Novel in English: The Politics of Anglo Arab and Arab American Literature and Culture, ed. Nouri Gana (Edinburgh: Edinburgh University Press, 2013), 208

The *dhimmis* who fled to the northern Christian kingdoms frequently encountered the same Visigoth law by which they had ruled themselves under Islam. This Visigoth law continued to inform Spanish law for centuries. Recall that the *Fuero juzgo* (ca. 1241) was essentially a translation of Visigoth legal manuals of the sixth and seventh centuries. Moreover, Alfonso X's monumental *Siete partidas* (finished in 1256), though intended to replace the *Fuero juzgo*, includes Visigoth legislation in addition to Aristotelian ideas, Roman law, the Bible, Saint Augustine's writings, and elements from the *fueros* (laws and rights granted by a Spanish monarch to certain areas of the kingdom).[71] Thus many of the Christian inhabitants of Spain were unified by their legal system as well as by their religion.

In the northern Christian kingdoms, these former *dhimmis* built churches and monasteries, and brought with them valuable books from former Visigoth Spain. Some of these books may have served as models for several jewels of medieval art: the extraordinary illuminations that accompany the biblical commentaries, written in Latin but in Visigoth script, by the monks Beato de Liébana (ninth century) and Beato of San Miguel de Escalada (tenth century). As the scholar of Islam and Christianity Marie-Thérèse Urvoy has shown, these "Mozarabs" preserved the tradition of Visigoth spirituality and influenced and were influenced by the culture of the northern Christians; and they added to the earlier cultural contributions that Hispano-Visigoths who had fled the initial Muslim invasion made to northern Spain and Europe.[72] Some art historians argue that they influenced the great art of the Spanish Romanesque.[73]

Meanwhile, the culture of the Christian *dhimmis* made an impact on Muslim Spain even as that culture gradually disappeared. Muslim rulers and their intelligentsia owed much culturally, ethnically, and otherwise to the heritage of the Christian kingdom of the Visigoths.[74] Astonished by the more advanced civilization they had encountered, the invaders cannibalized and imitated Hispano-Visigoth architecture. That was certainly the case with the mosque of Córdoba, which, as we have seen, was constructed with materials taken from Christian and Roman buildings, and included arches and other architectural features that imitated Visigoth design. Furthermore, one still finds Muslim coinage dated as late as 730 that copies the Latin inscriptions and busts of the Visigoth monarchs; Arabic texts translated and glossed Saint Isidore's *Laudes Hispaniae*; and as late as the eleventh century the geographer Ubayd al-Bakri still used Isidorian texts.[75] According to Ibn Khaldun, the famous classic Arabic poetic form called *muwassaha* was invented around the ninth century by a poet of Christian *dhimmi* ancestry, Muccadam de Cabra.[76] And the popular poetry of the Christian *dhimmis*, in Mozarabic Romance (the ancient dialect of Spanish used by the Christian *dhimmis* of al-Andalus, which shows the lexical impact of Arabic), became part of this *muwassaha* in the so-called *jarchas* (verses found at the end of the *muwassahas*). Some of these *jarchas* are in Mozarabic Romance, written in Arabic (and sometimes Hebrew) script, and showing the persistence of a spoken Spanish Romance among Christian *dhimmis*.[77]

The Hispano-Visigoth influence on Islamic Spain extended beyond art and architectures. Ethnically, the Umayyads can hardly be called "Arabic," because their mothers were frequently Balkan and Slavic slave girls or Visigoth and Hispano-Roman women, as noted in chapters 4 and 5. Many Umayyads had rosy skin and reddish hair.[78] A number of famous Muslim intellectuals were also descendants of Christians, such as the historian Ibn al-Qutiya, the son of a Goth woman, and the polymath *alim* Ibn Hazm, grandson of a Christian convert to Islam. At least one Muslim heresy in al-Andalus, ruthlessly persecuted by Abd al-Rahman III, was influenced by the Catholicism of the *dhimmis*.[79] And we already examined, in chapter 1, the mediating role of Christian *dhimmis* between the more primitive society of the Islamic invaders and the superior civilization of the Christian Greek Roman Empire, not only in Spain but also, earlier, in the Middle East and North Africa.[80]

The Christian culture of pre-Islamic Spain endures in some forms to this day. As the Reconquest progressed, Christians who had fled to the

North settled in the newly reconquered lands. They eventually assimilated into the Christian population and were forced to adopt the Gregorian rite of the Catholic Church. Today, a couple of thousand Christians, most of them in Toledo, still practice a version of the ancient Christian rite of pre-Islamic Spain: the "Mozarabic" rite.[81]

A CULTURE OF RESISTANCE

> Within a common cultural framework which might be termed Arab-Andalusi, there long subsisted—perhaps through the whole period under review—Christian and Jewish minorities. Like the harmonious process of conversion to Islam and consolidation of the majority group..., this is an indication of the spirit of tolerance which characterizes the history of al-Andalus.
> —Rafael Valencia, "Islamic Seville: Its Political, Social, and Cultural History," in The Legacy of Muslim Spain, ed. Salma Khadra Jayyusi (Leiden: Brill, 1992), 138

Although the Christian *dhimmi* population had almost disappeared from Islamic Spain by the completion of the Reconquest, Christians did not go down without a fight. The eleventh-century chronicler Ibn Hayyan writes that the ancient city of Elvira (a garbling of the Hispano-Roman name *Illiberis*), part of the area occupied by today's Granada, was once peopled largely by Christian *dhimmis* and *muladis* and was hostile to Islam.[82] Under the Almoravids, some *dhimmi* leaders in Elvira collaborated with the Christian warriors of the Reconquest, and as a result Muslim mobs sacked the neighborhood's church, obeying the *fatwas* of the *ulama*. Records from as late as the eleventh century show Christian towns that Muslim authorities in the *taifa* kingdom of Granada considered potentially subversive. The Almoravids deported many Christians en masse to North Africa to punish them or prevent their collaboration with Christian warriors of the Reconquest. As for the Almohads, they concluded that only forced conversion could take care of the multicultural problem that these suspect Christian communities posed. Some Christian churches survived in Huesca until Christian forces retook the city in 1096. Until the eleventh century a few churches and monasteries remained in the rural villages of Islamic Spain. All these details indicate a Christian culture that indeed was declining under Islamic hegemony but that nonetheless refused to die.[83]

Some scholars have questioned whether to consider it a Catholic culture. In his unsympathetic treatment of Spanish Catholicism, Norman Roth, a professor of Hebrew and Semitic studies, writes that "Mozarabic Christianity was generally heretical."[84] It is true that some *dhimmis* gave themselves to heretical forms of Christianity, as did Egilanus, bishop of Elvira, and Elipandus of Toledo, both in the eighth century. Roth cites as evidence of widespread heresy the fact that in 1192 Pope Celestinus III ordered the archbishop of Toledo to send priests "learned in Latin and Arabic" to North Africa, Seville, and "other Muslim cities." But this order may simply reflect an effort to combat the decline in the number of Christians under Muslim rule as well as to continue asserting and extending the Gregorian Reform, which was concerned with shoring up the clergy's independence and moral integrity (the reform had started more than a century earlier but faced implementation difficulties in the outlying areas of Western Christianity).[85] This reform is an important episode in the history of the Catholic Church of which Roth seems unaware.

The truth is that most Christian *dhimmis* were orthodox, as the recent work of the historian of Islam in the West Cyrille Aillet has confirmed and as Christian chronicles from the North attest.[86] In some cases Christian *dhimmis* suffered martyrdom for their beliefs. Sometimes they revolted against Muslim hegemony. Sometimes they formed alliances with rebel *muladis* or helped the Christians of the Reconquista (provoking expulsions, such as those under Almoravids and Almohads).

Indeed, there was a long history of *muladi* insurrection in Islamic Spain. Although the inferior social status of the *muladis* was probably the main cause of their discontent, some of the unrest among the *muladi* population probably stemmed from the fact that at least some conversions to Islam would have been insincere. When the only options were exile, forced submission, or conversion, some Christians surely pretended to convert but continued to practice Christianity in secret as crypto-Catholics. As we will see shortly, in the ninth century the rebel Umar Ibn Hafsun was supported by both *muladis* and Christian *dhimmis* in his decades-long resistance to Umayyad rule, and he seems to have died as a Christian. And in a bloody episode in the mid-ninth century, the "martyrs of Córdoba" included *muladis* who publicly renounced Islam or confessed that they had been crypto-Catholics all along.

Even sincere conversion did not ensure equality for *muladis*. Arabs were at the top of the social scale, with Berbers in the middle, followed by freed white Muslim slaves who had become *mawali*; the *muladis*, further divided into first-generation converts and the rest, occupied a lower echelon, above only that of *dhimmis* and slaves. Naturally, *muladis* were not happy with their condition as third- or fourth-class Muslims. Not surprisingly, the *muladis*—"mixed ones"—earned another Arabic label: *al-adhall*, or "vile rabble."[87]

Economic factors contributed further to the instability in the supposedly harmonious, prosperous, and "Golden Age" al-Andalus of the Umayyads. The historian Roberto Marín-Guzmán observes that under Abd al-Rahman III and his Umayyad predecessors, "many people in al-Andalus had only minimum food, clothing, and shelter, and they hardly made it month after month, especially if some taxes, extraordinary contributions, fines, and some impositions by the ruler were demanded every month."[88]

Given the contempt *muladis* faced from Arab Muslims and the difficult religious, political, and economic conditions in which they lived, it is no surprise that they defended their worth against the Arabs in writing (the *shuubiya* movement) or that they occasionally rose up against the Muslim authorities. Revolts of *muladis* occurred not just in Spain but in other parts of the vast Islamic empire as well, such as Iran.[89]

Even a small sampling of *muladi* revolts in "Golden Age" al-Andalus conveys the degree of unrest among the descendants of former Christians. Ibn Hayyan relates how the ninth-century Umayyad ruler al-Hakam I frequently faced insurrections from the *muladis*—and each time responded with ruthless force. In 805 al-Hakam had seventy-two Córdoban *muladi* leaders crucified along the left bank of the Guadalquivir River.[90] The following year he crushed another rebellion in the city and had the *muladis'* leader crucified upside down. In Merida the emir had to put down a rebellion of the "barbarians" (a name normally given to Christians but here possibly applied to Berbers) that lasted between 805 and 813.

In Toledo in 807, *muladi* unrest led al-Hakam to set up a trap in which five thousand people belonging to leading *muladi* families were beheaded and then displayed crucified along the banks of the Guadalquivir River—the famous Massacre of the Ditch (*masacre de La Hoya* or *masacre del Foso*), still commemorated in Toledo. In 814 (or 818) al-Hakam used the soldiers of his personal guard to put down a *muladi* uprising in the *arrabal* (suburb) of Córdoba,[91] and then he crucified three hundred rebellion leaders and expelled twenty thousand Córdoban families to North Africa.

Al-Hakam I was not alone in facing *muladi* insurrections. His son Abd al-Rahman II confronted similar issues during his reign. Other Umayyad rulers who faced *muladi* revolts included Muhammad I, Abd Allah, al-Mundhir, and Abd al-Rahman III. In many cases, the Umayyads took on the native rebels using troops made up of mercenaries (some of them Christian) and black slaves from African regions—not an unusual method for Muslim rulers who could not count on their subjects' loyalty.[92]

No wonder that an Arab poet of the ninth century, who benefited of course from Umayyad patronage, gleefully celebrated some of the massacres of *muladis* in Umayyad Spain:

> With sword in hand,
> This day we have massacred all these sons of slaves,
> [The dead bodies of] twenty thousand of them have littered
> the road,
> The waters of the river have taken many others,
> They had as relatives only slaves and sons of slaves,
> Their number was immense,
> We have made it very small.[93]

Muladi rebels did encounter a fierce and often brutal response from Muslim rulers in this Golden Age of Islam, but they persisted. Umar Ibn Hafsun, the grandson of a Christian convert, embodied this persistence. Ibn Hafsun took to the mountains, where the Muslim authorities regarded him as a bandit while both *muladis* and Christian *dhimmis* saw him as a charismatic rebel. From his mountain fortress in Bobastro in the province of Malaga he waged war for several decades against Umayyad power. According to the historian Ibn Idhari, the Umayyads proclaimed *jihad* against Ibn Hafsun, who did not surrender until 916. His presumed daughter, or perhaps granddaughter, Argentea, suffered martyrdom for her Christian beliefs at the hands of the Umayyads in Córdoba in 931 and was beatified in the tenth century by the Catholic Church as Saint Argentea.[94]

Most *muladi* rebels, even if they allied themselves with Christian *dhimmis* and with the Catholic northern kingdoms, remained Muslims, at least nominally. Ibn Hafsun was an exception: he went back to Catholicism. Archaeologists have found the remains of a Mozarabic church in Bobastro, his mountain fortress for forty years. After Ibn Hafsun's death, Umayyad ruler Abd al-Rahman III had his cadaver disinterred and confirmed that Ibn Hafsun had been buried in the Christian fashion. For this apostasy, and as a warning to potential apostate rebels, the Muslim ruler ordered the cadaver taken to Córdoba and crucified publicly between those of Ibn Hafsun's two sons. It was not the first time Abd al-Rahman III, "The Servant of the Merciful," had tried to terrify Ibn Hafsun's followers: at the gates of Córdoba he routinely displayed the impaled heads of killed or captured rebels.[95]

Some scholars have downplayed Ibn Hafsun's Christianity, which, obviously, undermines the idea that Christians were perfectly happy as converts or practicing Christians under Islamic rule.[96] But unless one can prove that the Muslim chronicles lied, that Abd al-Rahman III lied, that the Catholic church remains in Bobastro are not Catholic church remains, and that Christian *dhimmi* villages and neighborhoods did not support Ibn Hafsun, all that is left against this famous rebel's Christianity is opinion. In any event, by the time of the fall of the Umayyad Caliphate of Córdoba in the early eleventh century, the ruthless punishment of *muladi* revolts and the broader political fragmentation of the Arabic, Berber, and Caucasian slave *taifas* had largely erased whatever group consciousness the *muladis* once had as descendants of Christian converts.

Christian *dhimmis* presented a different problem. Cowed into submission by Islam, they were more likely to give military intelligence and material help to the approaching armies of the Reconquest or to the *muladis* than to engage in open rebellion. Other Christian *dhimmis* tried to improve their condition by serving the Muslim rulers as bureaucrats and even mercenaries. (Islamic law forbade the use of non-Muslim armies, but Muslim rulers found ways to justify their use of infidel soldiers by considering them "servants.")

Some Christian *dhimmis* did, however, openly defy Islam, even in the early centuries of Muslim domination. The Muslim historian Ibn Idhari

mentions a rebellion in Beja before 753, led by Orwa b. al-Welid, supported by "those who paid tribute," a likely allusion to Christian *dhimmis*. The governor, Yusuf, crushed the revolt and massacred the rebels.[97]
In Merida between 828 and 834, Christian *dhimmis* may have participated in one of the many *muladi* rebellions in that famously ungovern-
able region of Extremadura.[98] Ibn Idhari recounts that a large number of
Christians from Granada fled to help King Alfonso VI repopulate Toledo,
the ancient capital of the Visigoth kingdom.[99] According to Ibn Hayyan,
Toledo was the most rebellious of all cities in "Hispania" (here the Muslim chronicler forgets to use the name "al-Andalus").[100] Among other
insurrections against the Umayyads, in 852 there was a revolt in Toledo
caused by the oppression of the Christians; Umayyad forces eventually
crushed the rebellion.[101]

THE MARTYRS OF CÓRDOBA

[The] historical importance [of the killing of the Martyrs of Córdoba]
is difficult to determine and...probably tells us little about the condition and attitudes of the bulk of the Mozarab population, though
[the incident] does show the tolerance and essential reasonableness of
the Muslim authorities, but it raises interesting moral and theological
points about self-inflicted martyrdom.
    —*Hugh Kennedy, Professor of History in the Department of Lan-
    guages and Cultures of the Near Middle East of the University of
    London,* Muslim Spain and Portugal: A Political History of al-
    Andalus *(London: Routledge, 1996), 48*

But the most extraordinary instance of Christian *dhimmi* resistance was
the episode of the martyrs of Córdoba.[102] Between 850 and 860, under
the reign of Umayyad Abd al-Rahman II, men and women, some of them
belonging to Christian families who had converted to Islam (*muladis*),
defied the authorities by publicly affirming their Christian faith and ridi-
culing or insulting Muhammad. The story has come down to us in the
writings of the last of the martyrs, the monk Saint Eulogius, and in the
writings of his friend Alvarus, a monk who lived through the events.
    The first one to die as a martyr was a well-educated monk named

Perfectus. In 850, having traveled from his nearby monastery to the city of Córdoba on some errand or other, this Christian *dhimmi* encountered some Muslims he knew, who asked him to explain what Christians thought of Christ and the Prophet Muhammad. He told them that they might not like the answer. When they insisted, Perfectus made them promise not to tell his answer to anyone. He proceeded to cite a passage from the gospel in which Christ declares that "many false prophets will come in my name," and Perfectus added that Christians believed Muhammad to be one of those false prophets. Perfectus then went on his way. Some days later, the same Muslims saw him in the city, pointed him out to the crowds, and accused him of having insulted the Prophet. The monk was arrested and locked in prison, although during interrogation he denied having said any insulting words. The outline of this case to this point corresponds to the pattern of cases of Christians punished for alleged blasphemy in Islamic countries even in our day.[103] While in prison, however, Perfectus recanted his earlier denial. He openly proclaimed Christ's divinity and the imposture of Muhammad. Perfectus was publicly beheaded.

According to the extant accounts of the monk Alvarus, a year later a Christian *dhimmi* named Juan was denounced by some Muslim merchants for trying to increase his sales by swearing on Muhammad. Alvarus tells us that Muslims used to laugh at Christianity and insult Christians, and that Muslim envy was the reason to accuse Juan. When several Muslims testified against Juan, the *dhimmi* was found guilty, publicly lashed, paraded through the city, and sent to prison.

But the decisive event seems to have been the case of Isaac. At twenty-four years of age, this Christian *dhimmi* abandoned a lucrative position in the city of Córdoba to enter the monastic life. Three years later, in 851, he made the momentous decision to go to Córdoba and in front of the *qadi* (judge) declare Muhammad a false prophet and Islam a false religion, knowing that he would be executed for these blasphemies. He was beheaded publicly, and his cadaver was hung upside down at one of Córdoba's city gates.

All these events had an effect on a number of *dhimmis* and *muladis* who adopted what today would be called a policy of nonviolent resistance against the dominant culture: they defied the Muslim blasphemy laws by publicly proclaiming the divinity of Jesus Christ and the falsehood of

Muhammad as a prophet, and they refused to recant. Nearly fifty men and women were publicly executed—some beheaded, some boiled to death. Their cadavers were hung upside down at the city gates to deter future martyrs. But these exhibits appeared to stimulate rather than deter Christian *dhimmis* and crypto-Catholic *muladis*. Each day new Christians volunteered for martyrdom. The Muslim authorities then turned to a different procedure: instead of exhibiting the cadavers of the Christians, they burned them and threw their ashes in the Guadalquivir. A number of these martyrs were *muladis* who openly renounced their Islamic faith or proclaimed that they had been crypto-Catholics—the worst kind of apostasy, according to medieval Islamic law.

In response to this Christian martyrdom, Abd al-Rahman II, following the advice of the *ulama*, imprisoned Catholic priests, confiscated Christians' property, and instituted a series of measures to make life more difficult for all Christians. Those measures were similar to the drastic actions the invading Muslims had taken to subjugate recalcitrant Christians, as documented in the *Chronica mozarabica* of 754 and other Christian and Muslim sources (see chapter 1). Then, threatening escalated measures against Christian *dhimmis*, Abd al-Rahman pressured Catholic bishops to convene a church council in Córdoba to address the growing problem of Christian martyrdom.[104] Under this pressure, the council of bishops ordered Catholics not to follow the martyrs' example. Eventually, the voluntary martyrdom stopped.

With their public displays of Christian faith and their open affirmation that Muhammad was not a prophet and that Jesus Christ was the Son of God (both blasphemies in Muslim eyes), the martyrs of Córdoba led a metaphorical assault against the dominant Islamic religion and culture. This public defiance released years of pent-up Christian anger and frustration at religious, social, and political subjugation. It also represented a desperate, and ultimately ineffective, effort to stem the growing tide of Islamic acculturation that was eroding Christian culture in Spain.

But scholars do not usually describe the Christian defiance in the above terms—as understandable and courageous instances of passive, nonviolent cultural resistance by members of a disempowered and marginalized group, as academics would probably characterize similar acts by any subject group but Christians. As far back as Reinhart Dozy in the nineteenth century and Emanuel Lévi-Provençal in the early twentieth, and continuing to the present, scholars have typically described the actions of the martyrs of Córdoba as the foolish decisions of religious fanatics, of recalcitrant and ignorant monks and their unthinking followers. In one representative statement, a scholar called the Christian *dhimmi* resistance the work of "an intransigent minority, not at all willing to live in peaceful *convivencia* and respect towards Islam."[105] The views of these modern scholars were already present among collaborationist Church authorities in Córdoba: the testimonies of the monks Eulogius and Alvarus were partly motivated by the need to defend the martyrs against ecclesiastical leaders who preferred to continue their lives of submission under Muslim rule in the interest of peace. Such unsympathetic views of the martyrs of Córdoba are echoed today in the relative scholarly neglect of the Christian sources on the Islamic conquest as testimonies of the Christians' loss—a neglect of the *visión de los vencidos* ("the views or testimony of the defeated") not present, for example, in studies of the Spanish conquest of the Americas.

The implication is clear: these people should have been grateful to the tolerant Muslim authorities for so graciously allowing them to practice their religion. Never mind the lowly status Christian *dhimmis* and even *muladis* occupied in Islamic society; the harsh restrictions they lived under; the extortion and humiliation they suffered through their special "taxes" (the *jizya*); the destruction of their ancient churches, as recorded by the monks Eulogius and Alvarus (testimonies either ignored by scholars or dismissed as the exaggerations of fanatics);[106] or the even harsher punishments Christians faced for violating Islamic laws. Those punishments included drastic measures such as ethnic cleansing: Christian *dhimmis* were expelled to North Africa repeatedly—from Malaga in 1106, Granada in 1126, and various parts of Islamic Spain in 1138 and 1170.[107] The punishments also included, as we have seen repeatedly, executions of the most painful and public forms.

Such was the spirit of Islamic Spain's "*convivencia*," which Norman Roth hails as "one of the many things that made Spain great, and which the rest of Europe could have learned from it to its profit."[108]

Epilogue

Modern historians seem to agree that the invasion was not particularly cruel, or destructive, and it is certain that Muslims—already familiar with both religions in the Middle East—were taught to respect Christians and Jews as "People of the Book"; moreover, a large Christian population lived on for centuries in al-Andalus with legal rights and relative freedom of worship.

> —*Colin Smith, Professor of Medieval Spanish Literature at Cambridge University, President of the Modern Humanities Research Association, Editor of the* Modern Language Review, *and Commander in the Order of Isabel La Católica,* Christians and Moors in Spain *(Warminster: Aris & Phillips, 1988), 1:10*

Islam and the West have common roots and share much of their history. Their confrontation today arises not from essential differences, but from a long and willful determination to deny their kinship.

> —*Richard W. Bulliet, Professor of Islamic History and Society at Columbia University,* The Case for Islamo-Christian Civilization *(New York: Columbia University Press, 2004), vii*

THIS BOOK HAS shown seldom-glimpsed cultural features of Islamic Spain. It has "problematized," "unveiled," and "uncovered" al-Andalus, and exposed its inescapable otherness—an otherness pointed out by José Ortega y Gasset and by Ibn Hazm (himself from a family of Christian origin), who thought Islam was characterized precisely by its anti-Christian nature.[1] In Islamic Spain there was no tolerant *convivencia*, but a *precaria coexistencia*. The book has also shown that the legal frames in which the Muslim, Jewish, and Catholic masses existed both reflected and shaped not only their attitudes toward one another but also their way of life within their own communities.

A Machiavellian analysis can apply to the Muslim invasion of *Spannia* Edward Said's shrewd observation: "thinking about cultural exchange involves thinking about domination and forcible appropriation: someone loses, someone gains."[2] The book has therefore argued that, in cultural terms alone, the invasion, conquest, and colonization of Christian Spain during the first half of the eighth century by Islamic warriors was a disaster for the Christian population because a nascent, post-Roman, Christian civilization was nipped in the bud.

The pre-Islamic Hispano-Roman-Visigoth population was in no need of being "civilized" by a hegemonic Islamic empire. As shown in chapter 2, at the beginning of the eighth century its level of civilization was far higher than that of the Muslim warriors, mostly uncultured North African Berbers, who invaded the land, led by some Arabs who had benefited or would benefit from such superior civilizations as the Christian Greek Roman Empire ("Byzantine"), Zoroastrian Persia (which had also long been influenced by Greek knowledge), and Hindu India—civilizations that, as in the cases of Zoroastrian Persia and Hindu-Buddhist Sind, the Muslim invaders had already destroyed.[3]

The Muslim Arab conquerors of Persia (today's Iran) had been ignorant Bedouins from the desert with a level of civilization well below that of the Zoroastrian Persian Empire. They had been as astonished by the cultural level of the Zoroastrian Persians as they had been by that of the Christian Greeks. As the great Tunisian historian Ibn Khaldun (1332–1406) noticed, "Where are the sciences of the Persians which Umar ordered to be wiped out at the time of the conquest?... The sciences of only one nation, the Greeks, have come down to us, because they were translated through [Caliph] Al-Mamun's efforts. He was successful in this direction because he had many translators at his disposal and spent much money in this connection." These translators were Christians from the former Christian Greek Roman Empire.

Ibn Khaldun also remarked that the majority of Muslim scholars were non-Arabs from the conquered nations, and that most of them were

Persian.[4] Speaking of the Muslim presence in North Africa, Ibn Khaldun marveled at the fact that "the buildings and constructions in Islam are comparatively few as compared to the dynasties preceding" Islam, especially "considering Islam's power." He observed that the "buildings erected by Arabs, with very few exceptions, quickly fall into ruins." The reason for this, he wrote, is the Arab Bedouin's "attitude and unfamiliarity with the crafts." "Therefore," he continued, "the buildings [of the Arabs] are not solidly built."[5]

The scholar of Islam Dominique Urvoy has pointed out that even the Arabic script may have been invented by Christian missionaries from the Christianized Arab city of Hira in ancient Iraq.[6] The art historian Oleg Grabar has explained the impact that the Christian Roman Empire of the Greeks had on the ignorant early Muslims:

> Byzantine art provided the new culture with a vocabulary and the rudiments of a grammar.... The Muslims turned again and again to the wellspring of Byzantium.... At one time he [Mu'awiyah, then governor of Syria—he would become the future first Umayyad caliph (ruled 661–680)] was upbraided by Caliph Umar for having adopted the pagan ways of the Caesars.... Mu'awiyah answered that Damascus was full of Greeks and that none of them would believe in his power if he did not behave and look like an emperor.... The early Muslims never fully understood Byzantine art, but circumstances having forced it on them, they could not but be impressed by its existence.[7]

As Robert M. Haddad, Aptin Khanbaghi, Louis Milliot, and other scholars have noticed, the Christian *dhimmis* served as an intermediary between the more primitive society of the Islamic invaders and the superior civilizations of the Christian Greek Roman Empire and the Zoroastrian Persian Empire.[8] The Persian Muslim chronicler Ibn al-Nadim (d. 990) testified that "in tenth-century Iran, the majority of philosophers were still Christian."

Similarly, the Christian Hispano-Roman civilization in the early eighth century was superior to that of the North African Berber invaders: as we have seen in chapter 2, these invaders, too, were astonished by the cultural level of the Christian Hispano-Visigoths, as much as the Arab invaders had been astonished earlier by that of the Christian Greeks in North Africa and the Middle East. Of course, there is rarely a "deserved" conquest in human history. This Christian Hispano-Roman-Visigoth population "deserved" to be conquered and enlightened by Islamic rulers no more than the population of the Americas deserved to be conquered and enlightened by the Christian Europeans in the sixteenth and seventeenth centuries, or than the population of India deserved to be conquered and enlightened by the Christian British in the eighteenth. Yet in the case of the Mexica, the Inca, the Maya, or India, the "deserving" and "enlightening" arguments are now rarely made by "mainstream" scholars, whereas in the case of Spain in A.D. 711, these arguments continue to hold a grip on both academic publications and the popular press (see the epigraphs throughout this book).

Instead, one should take a broader cultural perspective of the Islamic invasion. The Visigoths had been in *Spannia* for only a few centuries when the process of assimilation between them and the previous Hispano-Roman inhabitants—and especially the laborious process of developing a new culture out of the Christian Hispano-Roman and the Christian Greek-Roman ("Byzantine") legacy—was brutally interrupted. Yet in those brief, turbulent, and formative years, the Visigoth kingdom managed to produce, for its time and place, a remarkable cultural output. It must be remembered that it took some centuries for the newly created Islamic entity—even with the benefit of a preexisting Hispano-Roman-Visigoth culture in Christian Spain to draw upon, plus all that medieval Islam had already gained from the civilizations of the Christian Greek Roman Empire, Persia, and India—to develop the tyrannical splendor of the Caliphate of Córdoba. For its first hundred years, Islamic culture in Spain was hardly remarkable. One can only imagine what Christian Spain would have evolved into with another hundred or two hundred years of time, and especially with commerce with the immense civilization of the Christian Greek Roman Empire uninterrupted and unthreatened. As we have seen, the Visigoth kingdom had functioned as a preserver of classical culture in the difficult centuries after the disintegration of the Western (Latin) Christian Roman Empire, and was in the process of creating a new Visigoth-Hispano-Roman civilization of its own, in part by drawing upon the classical legacy of the Roman Empire preserved in the Christian Greek Roman Empire.

Few periods in history have been more misrepresented than that of

Islamic Spain. The proclaimed tolerance exhibited by Umayyad rulers is part of this narrative, and scholars continue to repeat that "the description of the Mozarabic Christians and the Jews as having been subjugated minorities quietly chafing under the restraint of Muslim laws is simply wrong."[9] We have seen that this interpretation does not hold up under scrutiny—though it is explicable when the interpreter is influenced by a selective concentration on the remains of elite culture, or by the relative and always precarious politically dictated favoritism enjoyed by the Jewish community, if only for a few centuries.

But a basic fact is lost in discussions and arguments about the details of the life of the Christian *dhimmis* of Spain, the so-called Mozarabs, and about how much or how little they benefited from Islamic "toleration"— namely, that *they were by definition a subaltern group, a fourth- or fifth-class marginalized people in a hierarchical society,* and that they were the victims of *an extortion system, the* dhimma, *that gave them the choice that gangsters give to their victims: pay to be protected, or else.* Therefore, saying that the Christians might be "content" with their status in Spain, Greece, or elsewhere under medieval Islamic rule is even more preposterous than saying that American blacks might be "content" with their second-class citizenship under the tolerant white hegemony in certain areas of the United States prior to the twentieth-century civil rights movement, or perhaps even with their treatment by slave owners in the American South before the War of Secession, who often "made them part of the family."[10] In fact, as the nomenclature described by the historian Ibn Hayyan of Córdoba indicated, Christians were at the bottom of a stratified Islamic world, where Arabs occupied the top, followed by Berbers, then by freed Muslim white slaves, and finally by *muladis* (converts), who were further divided into first-generation converts and the rest.[11] And of course Christians, again by definition, were not part of the Islamic *umma* but were merely tolerated and "protected" (a word with ominous meaning for anyone familiar with "protection" rackets) as long as they humbly kept their place and paid for said "protection"—in a hegemonic tactic also used by the Muslim Turks during their four-hundred-year subjugation of Christian Greece.

Given the religious laws of medieval Islam, this subaltern status was inevitable everywhere within the Islamic empire. As Robert M. Haddad has observed in the case of the Syrian Christians in the twentieth century, they were under an "Islamic order which, if true to its own canons, could only affirm for Christians that marginal status which had been theirs for over a thousand years."[12]

The present book has examined who were the winners and who were the losers in the new hierarchy of Islamic Spain. Without the Christian resistance and eventual Reconquest, first against the Umayyad Caliphate of Córdoba and then against the Berber Almoravid and Almohad empires, Spain today could well be an extension of the cultures of North Africa and the Middle East. As the medievalist historian José Enrique Ruiz-Domènec has commented: "The frontier between Spain and Morocco is the world frontier where there is the most visible difference between the two worlds. If the battle of Navas de Tolosa had been lost, that frontier would be on the Pyrenees. One…would not be able to eat ham or drink beer. One's name would be Hussein, Jamal or Benazir, and perhaps one would not be able to go on the street without wearing a veil."[13]

After the Muslim occupation in the eighth century, it took many years for Christian Spain to develop the greatness of its own medieval Christian culture, with its rich lyric and narrative poetry, and its powerful Romanesque and Gothic architecture and sculpture. The process continued through the Renaissance and the Catholic Counter-Reformation, and culminated in the "Spanish Golden Age," with such literary figures as Garcilaso de la Vega, Saint John of the Cross, Saint Teresa of Ávila, Fray Luis de León, Miguel de Cervantes, Lope de Vega, Tirso de Molina, Luis de Góngora, Francisco de Quevedo, and Calderón de la Barca; such a pioneer of international law as the Dominican priest Francisco de Vitoria; such thinkers on liberty and conquest as the Dominican bishop Bartolomé de Las Casas and his learned adversary the classical humanist Juan Ginés de Sepúlveda; such economic, political, and philosophical thinkers as the Dominican priests Domingo de Soto, Martín de Azpilcueta, and Tomás de Mercado and the Jesuit priests Luis de Molina and Francisco Suárez; such composers as Juan del Encina, Antonio de Cabezón, Gaspar Sanz, Francisco Guerrero, Cristóbal de Morales, and the priest Tomás Luis de Victoria; and such formidable painters as Diego Velázquez and Doménikos Theotokópoulos, "El Greco"—this last one an artist from that Christian Greek diaspora which had barely survived the centuries-long but relentless destruction of their civilization by the iconoclastic Islamic warriors.[14]

Notes

1   Scholarship has thus been placed at the service of a cultural mission. The historian of the Spanish Middle Ages Colin Smith asked H. Salvador Martínez in the 1980s whether there was any text in which "se definiese y se promoviese el concepto de convivencia entre los varios grupos étnico-religiosos que poblaban la España medieval" ("in which the concept of *convivencia* among the various ethnic-religious groups that populated medieval Spain was defined and promoted"). Salvador Martínez thought there was none, so he proceeded to write one on a period particularly suited to promoting *convivencia*. Smith's request is cited in H. Salvador Martínez, *La Convivencia en la España del siglo XIII: Perspectivas alfonsíes* (Madrid: Ediciones Polifemo, 2006), 12. An insightful account of the "romantic" vision of Islamic Spain can be found in an article by Pedro Marfil, professor of archaeology at the University of Córdoba, "La visión romántica de la Córdoba Omeya," *Ruta del Califato: Un recorrido histórico-monumental de Córdoba a Granada*, ed. Julia Saiz-Pardo de Benito (Granada: Fundación El Legado Andalusí, 2005), 205–12.

2   For the "peaceful pacts" approach, see Alejandro García Sanjuán, *La conquista islámica de la península ibérica y la tergiversación del pasado: Del catastrofismo al negacionismo* (Madrid: Pons, 2013), where he attacks the "catastrophism" of scholars like Luis A. García Moreno and Serafín Fanjul as well as the "negationism" of Ignacio Olagüe and Emilio González Ferrín. García Sanjuán accepts the idea of conquest, though says it was "largely peaceful." The peaceful approach was earlier taken to its logical conclusion by Olagüe in his *Les arabes n'ont jamais envahi l'Espagne* (Paris: Flammarion, 1969), where he argued that there was no conquest but rather a cultural domination of one form of religion (Christian Trinitarianism) by another (Christian Unitarianism). The peaceful approach has been given a different version by the Marxist Arabist Emilio González Ferrín, who argues that there was no conquest but a steady "migration" of Muslims from North Africa, which finally became hegemonic. See his *Historia general de Al-Andalus* (Córdoba: Almuzara, 2006). Ferrín's thesis ("negationism," in the words of García Sanjuán) has been very successful in both Spain and the English-speaking academic world, where denying the idea that there was a conquest facilitates denying the abhorrent idea of a Christian Reconquest. For what García Sanjuán called the "catastrophism" approach, see Serafín Fanjul, *Al-Andalus contra España: La forja del mito* (Madrid: Siglo XXI, 2000). The more sensible approach is that of the Arabist Felipe Maíllo Salgado, *Acerca de la conquista árabe de España: imprecisiones, equívocos y patrañas* (Guijón: TREA, 2011).

3   This point is overlooked even by good scholars who nonetheless lack a worldwide perspective, such as the Arabist Joaquín Vallvé Bermejo, *Al Andalus: sociedad e instituciones* (Madrid: Real Academia de la Historia, 1999), 60–62. In many other conquests (such as that of India by the British, or Algeria by the French, or the Hispano-Romans by the Visigoths) the population was indeed used to seeing ruling groups come and go. But Vallvé Bermejo overlooks the fact that with the Muslim invasion the change was far more noticeable because it entailed placing an all-encompassing religion and therefore a way of life—Islam—in a hegemonic position over the alternatives. Of course Muslims and non-Muslims influenced one another, but the same can be said of many other civilizational conflicts. In the United States, and especially in the American South, whites were shaped by the culture of the eventually liberated slaves, and these, in turn, adopted most of the ways of the former masters, including their language and religion. In the Americas, Spaniards and Amerindians influenced one another profoundly: there was widespread intermarriage, and Amerindian and mestizo artists, writers, and politicians contributed, along with Spaniards, to the creation of a new civilization. Even in India, and despite their efforts to remain unaffected, the British were influenced by Indian civilization, while the natives, who were allowed to keep their religion and culture, nonetheless adopted many of the practices of the conquerors, including their parliamentary system. In all these cases, there were culturally interesting and even attractive consequences. None of this, however, can erase the fact that the cultures in play were different and that some of them were hegemonic whereas others were hegemonized.

4   See John P. A. Ioannidis (director of Stanford University's Meta-Research Innovation Center), "Why Most Published Research Findings Are False," *PLoSMed*, October 30, 2005, at http://www.plosmedicine.org/article/info%3Adoi%2F10.1371%2Fjournal.pmed.0020124, and "How to Make More Published Research True," *PLoSMed*, October 21, 2014, at http://www. plosmedicine.org/article/info%3Adoi%2F10.1371%2Fjournal.pmed.1001747. See also Alex B. Berezov, "How to Make Scientists Publish the Truth," *Real Clear Science*, October 21, 2014, at http://www.realclearscience.com/blog/2014/10/how_to_make_sure_scientists_publish_the_ truth.html. Ioannidis has shown that most published scientific research findings are wrong, in part because of "stakeholder interests and incentives." Metaresearch continues to show the problem. See, for example, Benedict Carey, "Many Psychology Findings Not as Strong as Claimed," *New York Times*, August 27, 2015. Anyone familiar with the humanities will realize that the situation there is likely to be much worse and that, in fact, a great deal of research in the humanities today is based on the belief that there is no "true" research to begin with. The improvements that Ioannidis has proposed for scientific research might be of help in the humanities as well.

5   Max Bazerman, "Making Organizations Moral," *Harvard Magazine*, November–December 2014, 11–12.

6   The expression originated with the widely cited Marxist literary critic Fredric Jameson, who seemed to excuse himself from this weakness. See Reed Way Rasenbrock, "Fredric Jameson's *Fables of Aggression*," *International Fiction Review* 8, no. 1 (1981): 78.

7   In his masterful study of the causes of the fall of Islamic Spain, the Spanish Arabist Felipe Maíllo Salgado includes as important although insufficient reasons "its ethnic and religious diversity [*abigarramiento* étnico *y confesional*] (Arabs, berbers, *hispanos*—some Islamicized, others Mozarabs—Slavs, black Africans, etc.; Muslims, Jews, and Christians)." See Felipe Maíllo Salgado, *De la desaparición de Al-Andalus* (Madrid: Abada, 2011), 11.

8   This joyful vision of Islamic Spain has become part of a phenomenon that one might call Occidentalism, a pervasive negative interpretation of the West that often culminates in a denial of its very existence (in this approach, the West is always placed in quotation marks as an essentialist construction, unlike Islam, capitalism, etc., which presumably do exist and are not essentialist constructions). For a wide-ranging critique of this scholarly position, see Ricardo Duchesne, *The Uniqueness of Western Civilization* (Leiden: Brill, 2011). For a succinct history, see Ian Buruma and Avishai Margalit, *Occidentalism: The West in the Eyes of Its Enemies*

(New York: Penguin, 2004). I thank Daniel Pipes for reminding me of Martin Kramer and Bernard Lewis's critical examination of the role played by a number of Jewish Arabists in disseminating an enthusiastic image of Islamic Spain: Martin Kramer, ed., *The Jewish Discovery of Islam: Studies in Honor of Bernard Lewis* (Tel Aviv: The Moshe Dayan Center for Middle Eastern and African Studies, 1999). The best attempt to examine the origins of this amazing intellectual construction is probably Rosa María Rodríguez Magda, *Inexistente Al-Ándalus: de cómo los intelectuales reinventan el Islam* (Oviedo: Ediciones Nobel, 2008). A hermeneutics of suspicion would list Christianophobia, the academic historians' widespread contempt for Christianity, among the reasons behind this construction.

9   Representative of this widespread materialist view of the Islamic conquest is Richard Hitchcock, *Mozarabs in Medieval and Early Modern Spain: Identities and Influences* (Hampshire: Ashgate, 2008): "What contemporary documentation that [*sic*] is available does not appear to support the general contention that the clash of Muslims with the Visigoths in the Iberian peninsula in the early eighth century was perceived as a religious confrontation. In other words, it was not a question of Muslim armies opposing and defeating Christian forces. Rather, the invasion and conquest can be seen as one among many episodes of Muslim expansion in the extraordinary first century after the death of Muhammad in 632 A.D." (7). It does not seem to occur to this historian that the very word he is using, *Muslim*, to qualify the word *expansion*, exists because of a religion called Islam, which was the cause of that "Muslim" expansion; and that if "no Islam," then no "Muslim," and certainly no "Muslim expansion." What follows in this historian's account of things is equally instructive because it relies on readings of the sacred Quran and of the word *jihad* by some specialists today: these scholars may be more or less knowledgeable of the true meaning of Islam than learned medieval Muslim scholars, who were closer to Islam and its origins, but this possibility of an erroneous interpretation by the medieval Muslim scholars does not change those medieval interpretations of *jihad* as the religious obligation to force the infidels to convert or die, or in the case of Christians and Jews, to convert, pay a special tax, or die—as evidenced in countless medieval documents that in various forms praise and justify war against the infidel for the sake of the true religion. And thus the historian concludes: "The pursuit of *jihād* as Holy War is not, therefore, a motivating factor relevant to the clashes between Muslims and the people [*sic*; notice here the avoidance of the word *Christians* in the case of Christians] they vanquished in the first century of Islam, at least not as far as the conquest and subsequent occupation of the Iberian peninsula is concerned" (8). For a critique of this materialist approach, see G. H. Bousquet, "Observations on the Nature and Causes of the Arab Conquest," in Fred M. Donner, ed., *The Expansion of the Early Islamic State* (London: Ashgate, 2008), 23–35. For a succinct critique of the materialist interpretation of the Crusades, see Paul Crawford, "Four Myths about the Crusades," *Intercollegiate Review* 46, no. 1 (Fall 2011): 13–22.

10   Representative is Castro's *España en su historia* (Princeton, NJ: Princeton University Press, 1954), more recently translated as *The Spaniards: An Introduction to Their History*, trans. Willard F. King (Berkeley: University of California Press, 1971), from which I cite. Castro cites no medieval Islamic legal treatises, no Islamic legal scholars from Spain or anywhere else in the medieval world, and even no modern scholars on Islamic law, either Western (such as Joseph Schacht or even Ignaz Goldziher) or Islamic. He never mentions the founder of Malikism, Imam Malik Ibn Anas. The "Malikite School" is mentioned once and only within a quotation of words by another scholar (230). He calls the Quran a "monument of tolerance" (499). He seems unaware of the legal term *dhimmi*. Even his use of Muslim historians is very sparse. He mentions Maimonides a few times but does not analyze any of Maimonides's legal texts and seems unaware of the fundamental *Mishneh Torah* (the only work by Maimonides he mentions is the customarily cited *Guide to the Perplexed*).

11   Claudio Sánchez-Albornoz, *De la andalucía islámica a la de hoy* (Barcelona: Rialp, 1983); *Viejos y nuevos estudios sobre las instituciones medievales españolas* (Buenos Aires: Espasa Calpe, 1980), 3 vols.; *La España musulmana: Según los autores islamitas y cristianos medievales*

(Buenos Aires: Espasa Calpe, 1973), 2 vols.; *Spain: A Historical Enigma* (Madrid: Fundación universitaria española, 1975); *España y el Islam* (Buenos Aires: Editorial sudamericana, 1943).

12   Adel Theodor Khoury, *Toleranz im Islam* (Munich: Kaiser, 1980); Alfred Morabia, *Le jihad dans l'Islam médiéval: Le "combat sacré" des origines au XIIe siècle*, préface de Roger Arnaldez (Paris: Albin Michel, 1993); Sylvane Gouguenheim, *Aristote au mont SaintMichel: Les racines grecques de l'Europe chrétienne* (Paris: Seuil, 2008); Roberto de Mattei, *Guerra santa, guerra giusta: Islam e cristianesimo in guerra* (Milan: Piemme, 2002); translated as *Holy War, Just War: Islam and Christendom at War* (Rockford, IL: The Rockford Institute, 2007).

13   For the massive academic attack against Gouguenheim, see Paul-François Paoli, "L'historien à abattre," *Le Figaro*, July 15, 2008, http://www.lefigaro.fr/actualite-france/2008/07/08/01016-20080708ARTFIG00553-l-historien-a-abattre-.php, and "Fatwa contre Sylvain Gouguenheim," Newsgroup Archive, http://fr.soc.histoire.narkive.com/AonPwRCN/fatwa-contre-sylvain-gouguenheim. For a succinct account of the enormous amounts of money poured by wealthy Muslim countries into Islamic, Middle Eastern, and Arabic studies at Western universities, see Giulio Meotti, "Islam Buys Out Western Academia," *Arutz Sheva: Israel National News*, June 23, 2012. A more detailed study of the results of this influence on academic research and teaching is Martin Kramer, *Ivory Towers of Sand: The Failure of Middle Eastern Studies in America* (Washington, DC: Washington Institute for Near East Policy, 2001). The following examples illustrate the phenomenon: the Harvard University Islamic Studies Program bears the name of Saudi prince Alwaleed Bin Talal Bin Abdulaziz Alsaud, the result of the huge amounts of money given to it by the prince. The Center for Islamic Studies at the University of Cambridge also bears the name of the prince, for similar reasons. At the University of Edinburgh, the Center for the Study of Islam in the Contemporary World has also been funded by the prince. At the University of London, Professor Charles Burnett, the Chair of History of Islamic Influences in Europe at the Warburg Institute, is "a key associate of FSTC," the Foundation for Science, Technology, and Civilization. This FSTC is "a United Kingdom based educational entity which was formed to popularize, disseminate and promote an accurate account of Muslim Heritage and its contribution to present day science, technology and civilization. FSTC and Khalifa University [will] create interactive Science Heritage Center in UAE [United Arab Emirates]." See http://muslimheritage.com/topics/default.cfm?ArticleID=1083#sec3, accessed August 1, 2012. To the list of universities that are now grateful to this disinterested association with Islamic nations, one can add Yale, which on the anniversary of September 11 announced in 2015 that it has received $10 million from Saudi businessman Abdallah Kamel "to establish what university officials hope will become the country's top center for the study of Islamic law…. Yale officials said the center will reflect a growing interest at Yale and other institutions in Islamic law, history and culture." (See "Islamic Law at Yale: $10M," *Chicago Tribune*, September 11, 2015.) Smaller institutions have also benefited from this generosity. Thus the Lampeter campus of the University of Wales Trinity Saint Davis, founded in the nineteenth century by Anglican bishop David Burgess, now features a nice mosque. "The mosque signals the presence of many Muslim students, who are attracted by the renowned department of theology, religious studies and Islamic studies. It is also a sign that Bishop David has been followed as a benefactor of the university by Sheikh Khalifa of Abu Dhabi and the rulers of Bahrain and Qatar. Their £1.8m endowment helps fund Islamic studies in the heart of rural Wales." See "Disappearing Worlds," *The Guardian*, November 13, 2000. One may doubt that all these Islamic studies centers will undertake the sort of critical examination of their subject to which professors in other fields have subjected, say, Jesus, the New Testament, or early Christianity. Such unlikely research could include: "How, historically, did Muhammad come to be seen as 'a Prophet'?"; or "Through what complex factors or events did the Quran come to be composed and regarded as the word of God?" These are favorite questions routinely asked by inquisitive university scholars about Jesus and the New Testament. But Islamic studies experts would rather investigate how Islam made possible the computer and flying machines. Arabists and Islamic and Middle East experts

now "own" and "control" all "credentialed" knowledge of the interaction between Islam and other civilizations. For the general professional phenomenon, see Charles Derber, William A. Schwartz, and Yale Magrass, *Power in the Highest Degree: Professionals and the Rise of a New Mandarin Order* (New York: Oxford University Press, 1990). A similar fear of losing travel privileges to the country of their research and teaching, and not just sympathy for real socialism, may have accounted, too, for the paucity of frontal critiques of the Soviet Union in the writings of university professors who used to specialize in "Soviet studies." Such prudence can be found today among Anglo-American university specialists on Cuba (specialists of Cuban origin are sometimes a different breed), whose writings seem oblivious to politics—a remarkable abstention considering the role that political criticism plays in today's academic writing on matters concerning the United States and the West in general.

14   Francisco Javier Simonet, *Historia de los mozárabes de España: Deducida de los mejores y más auténticos testimonios de los escritores cristianos y árabes* (Madrid: Viuda é hijos de M. Tello, 1897–1903; re-ed. Amsterdam: Oriental Press, 1967; Madrid: Turner, 1983). For the Simonet case, see Cyrille Aillet, *Les mozárabes: Christianisme, islamisation et arabisation en péninsule ibérique (IXe–XIIe siècle)* (Madrid: Casa de Velazquez, 2010), 11.

15   Serafín Fanjul, *La quimera de al-Andalus* (Madrid: Siglo XXI, 2004); Salgado, *De la desaparición de Al-Andalus*. Curiously, neither of these scholars has examined or even mentioned in these works any of the texts that I examine in this book, such as Malik's *Muwatta*, the *al-Tafri*, the *Mudawwana*, the *Leyes de moros*, Ibn Rushd's *Bidayat*, etc.

16   Ibn Zafar, *Sulwan al-Muta fi Udwan al-Atba* (Consolation for the Ruler during the Hostility of Subjects), translated by R. Hrair Dekmejian and Adel Fathy Thabit in "Machiavelli's Arab Precursor: Ibn Zafar al-Siqilli," *British Journal of Middle Eastern Studies* 27, no. 2 (November 2000): 131. This Muslim thinker was a Machiavellian avant la lettre.

17   Among these excellent books are Emmet Scott, *Mohammed and Charlemagne Revisited: The History of a Controversy* (Nashville, TN: New English Review Press, 2012); Mark Cohen, *Under Crescent and Cross: The Jews in the Middle Ages* (Princeton, NJ: Princeton University Press, 1994; rept. with a new introduction, 2008). Another good book, but concerned with violence inflicted on the Jewish community, not with that inflicted on the Christian community or with religious laws, is David Nirenberg, *Communities of Violence: Persecution of Minorities in the Middle Ages* (Princeton, NJ: Princeton University Press, 1996). Janina Safran's well-researched book, *Defining Boundaries in al-Andalus* (Ithaca: Cornell University Press, 2013), makes no mention of stoning, female circumcision, crucifixion, beheadings, or sexual slavery. Richard Fletcher's *Moorish Spain* (New York: Henry Holt, 1992) is a good general history, but it makes scant use of legal materials from the Muslim, Jewish, and Christian sources, does not delve into the conditions within those communities, and shows little sympathy for the plight of the Catholic *dhimmis*. An earlier book, Thomas F. Glick's *Islamic and Christian Spain in the Early Middle Ages* (Princeton, NJ: Princeton University Press, 1979), applied intelligently the latest historiographical techniques but was oblivious to the exclusionary religious laws of the Jewish community, did not engage Muslim religious law, did not take into account the importance of the Christian Greek Roman Empire in medieval history, and, following what one might call the phenomenon of academic Christianophobia, was quite unsympathetic to the plight of Christian *dhimmis* under Muslim rule.

18   A perusal of the bibliographical materials in the books of some English-speaking scholars reveals a paucity of references to publications written in Spanish in Spanish scholarly journals and even in Spanish editorial houses of all kinds. The "dismissal" effect is similar to that created by, say, a German scholar who specialized in Shakespeare (a field where Germans have done very good work) but who did not rely much on the research of English-speaking Shakespearean critics. A good example of the phenomenon is Richard Fletcher's *The Quest for the Cid* (New York: Alfred A. Knopf, 1990), which makes scant reference to Spanish scholars with the exception of Ramón Menéndez Pidal, whom he largely uses as a foil for the book. Apparently unknown to Fletcher, his own "demystifying" approach to the Cid falls within a

long pattern of scholarly cidophobia that Menéndez Pidal examined in the early pages of his *La España del Cid* (Madrid: Espasa-Calpe, 1947), 1:14–45.

19 Readers should in particular avoid the above-mentioned "presentism," which vitiates much academic teaching and research today, and against which Nietzsche warned the historians of his time. For today's abuse of history, see Gordon S. Wood, *The Purpose of the Past: Reflections on the Uses of History* (New York: Penguin, 2008), 6: "Many of [today's historians] have an instrumentalist view of history and see themselves essentially as cultural critics who wish to manipulate the past for the sake of the present." Wood cites (6) Friedrich Nietzsche, *The Use and Abuse of History* (1873; New York: Cosimo, 2010), 10: "Their vision of the past turns them toward the future, encourages them to persevere with life, and kindles the hope that justice will yet come and happiness is behind the mountain they are climbing.... They do not know how unhistorical their thoughts and actions are in spite of all their history."

20 This reinterpreting literature is already vast and continues to grow. Even the Vatican has contributed to it: see Abderrazak Sayadi, "La sorgente feconda della razionalità musulmana," *L'Osservatore romano (Edizione quotidiana)*, March 13, 2009, which argues that *sharia* is "an aberration" without any religious foundation in Islam. The reader interested in the subject may start with three books which argue that, for centuries, the male *fuqaha* (the only kind of *fuqaha*) got it all wrong: Fatima Mernissi, *Le harem politique* (Paris: Albin Michel, 1987) (translated as *The Veil and the Male Elite: A Feminist Interpretation of Women's Rights in Islam*, trans. Mary Jo Lakeland [Reading: Addison-Wesley, 1991]); Barbara Freyer Stowasser, *Women in the Qur'an, Traditions, and Interpretation* (Oxford: Oxford University Press, 1994); and Asthma Barlas, "*Believing Women" in Islam: Unreading Patriarchal Interpretations of the Qur'an* (Austin: University of Texas Press, 2002). Abdullahi Ahmed An-Naim, *Islam and the Secular State* (Cambridge, MA: Harvard University Press, 2008), argues, too, that Islam is not incompatible with freedom, democracy, and so forth. None of these books mentions Malik. In an earlier book, Mernissi had argued that women indeed have power in Islam, even more than men, because of their very sexuality, and that traditional Islamic law basically tries to control that sexuality so that men are protected: see Fatima Mernissi, *Beyond the Veil* (New York: John Wiley & Sons, 1975). For doubts about Islam's being compatible with modern democracy, see Italian sociologist and political scientist Giovanni Sartori, *Pluralismo, multiculturalismo e stranei: Saggio sulla societá multietnica* (Milan: Rizzoli, 2000), and orthodox Islamic works such as *The Doubts regarding the Ruling of Democracy in Islam* (At-Tibyan Publications, 1425 H.), http://www.kalamullah.com/manhaj. html, and Abu Muhammad Aasim al-Maqdisi's *Democracy—A Religion*, trans. Abu Muhammad al-Maleki, http://www.kalamullah.com/Books/DemocracyReligion.pdf.

21 *Le Traité des divergences du hadit d'Ibn Qutayba (mort en 276/889)*, trans. Gérard Lecomte (Damascus: Institut Français de Damas, 1962), 216b (p. 222). See also the affirmation of A. J. Wensinck, "Not the *Quran*, but the sunnah, is the highest normative example" (xxiii, n5).

22 It is theoretically possible that scholars today who mediate the Quran differently from the way the earlier *ulama* mediated it do understand it better, and that, unlike earlier *ulama*, they do not distort the Quran through their publications to serve their own desire for power, political interests, or some other need, and therefore are not subject in their interpretations to the shaping influence of their own socioeconomic, ethnic, gender, and other conditions.

23 R. Arnaldez, "La guerre sainte selon Ibn Hazm de Cordoue," *Études d'Orientalisme dédiées a la mémoire de Lévi-Provençal* (Paris: Maisonneuve, 1962), 2:445.

24 For a discussion of the reliability of the Muslim sources, see Maíllo Salgado, *De la desaparición de Al-Andalus*; García Moreno, *España 702–719: La conquista musulmana* (Seville: University of Seville, 2013); and García Sanjuán, *La conquista*.

25 Norman Roth, "The Jews and the Muslim Conquest of Spain," *Jewish Social Studies* 38, no. 2 (Spring 1976): 151; Tarif Khalidi, *Arabic Historical Thought in the Classic Period* (Cambridge: Cambridge University Press, 1994). Arguing about who actually wrote a chronicle or how much one chronicle owes to another can be of great philological interest but yields diminishing returns when one is trying to get a general idea of the course of events.

26 Thomas Aquinas, in contrast, studies Aristotle in direct translations from the Greek that he commissioned from the Roman Catholic bishop of Corinth, William of Moerbeke. It must be said that the dense philosophical content of Aristotle's texts, very difficult even in the original Greek, sometimes presented specialized problems in their doubly mediated reception, which led to errors on the part of Averroes: see Jorge Luis Borges's superb short story "*La busca de Averroes*." But one can always justify error academically: after a lecture of mine on the subject, a professor of Spanish and comparative literature pointed out during the question and answer period that Averroes's erroneous interpretations are praiseworthy because "very creative."

27 Rafael Cano Aguilar, *El Español a través de los tiempos* (Madrid: Arco, 1999), 52–54. A good example of the politically correct term that now prevails in academia is Olivia Remie Constable, ed., *Medieval Iberia: Readings from Christian, Muslim, and Jewish Sources* (Philadelphia: University of Pennsylvania Press, 1997).

28 The standard view of the Visigoths is that they were a Germanic people. See, among many works, Peter Heather, ed., *The Visigoths: An Ethnographic Perspective: From the Migration Period to the Seventh Century* (Woodbridge: Boydell Press, 1999). The most readable and complete account of the history of the Visigoths in Spain is probably *Hispania tardoantigua y visigoda*, ed. Pablo C. Díaz Martínez, Clelia Martínez Maza, and Francisco Javier Sanz Huesa (Madrid: Istmo, 2007). For the possible Baltic rather than Germanic origin of the Visigoths, see Jurate Rosales, *Los Godos* (Madrid: Ariel, 2004); "El idioma que hablaron los godos," *La Torre del Virrey*, n3, Serie 6 (February 2010), Valencia, Spain, 1–12; "Las cuatro mentiras sobre los godos," Preprint of Universidad de Los Andes, Facultad de Letras y Educación, Mérida, Venezuela (July 2, 2008), 1–26. The Visigoths had served as soldiers for the Roman Empire for centuries. Their language was Indo-European, like Latin. Their chiefs spoke Latin. Eventually the Visigoths became Christians, like the Romans, adopting a heretical form of Christianity, Arianism.

29 Joaquín Vallvé Bermejo, "El nombre de al-Andalus," *Al-Qantara* 4, nos. 1/2 (1983): 301.

30 Mercedes García Arenal, "Los moros en las *Cantigas* de Alfonso X El Sabio," *Al-Qantara* 6, nos. 1/2 (1985): 148.

31 The historian Joseph Perez has observed that, until recently, even the Catalans considered themselves Spaniards. He writes that in the eighteenth century, the Catalans were proud of what was taking place in "Spain"; that in the sixteenth century Catalan and Valencian writers like Camões and Guillén de Castro wrote spontaneously in Spanish; and that there was a long tradition of compatibility with the regional cultures. He concludes that the abandonment of this tradition constitutes a cultural and probably political step backward. Cit. by Felipe Maíllo Salgado, *Acerca de la conquista árabe de Hispania: Imprecisiones, equívocos y patrañas* (Guijón: Trea, 2011) 13, n4. Maíllo Salgado concurs that today's regionalistic antagonisms are unhistorical (*ahistóricos*).

32 See the work by the University of Malaga archaeologists Salvador Peña Martín and Miguel Vega Martín, "Alandalús, es decir, España," *El Trujamán*, December 15, 2000; Rafael Frochoso Sánchez, "Las acuñaciones andalucíes del s. VIII," in Luis A. García Moreno and Esther Sánchez Medina, eds., *Del Nilo al Guadalquivir II: Estudios sobre las fuentes de la conquista islámica* (Madrid: Real Academia de la Historia, 2013), 178.

33 *The History of al-Tabari (Tarikh al-rusul wal-muluk)* vol. 28, *Abbasid Authority Affirmed*, translated and annotated by Jane Dammen McAuliffe (New York: State University of New York Press, 1995), 55; Masudi, *Les Prairies d'Or*, trans. Charles Pellat (Paris: Societé Asiatique, 1965), 2:263.

34 Vallvé Bermejo, *Al-Andalus*, 14; Ibn Khaldoun, *Les Prolegoménes*, first part, introduction, book 1, and first section, trans. William Mac Guckin de Slane (Paris: Geuthner, 1934); al-Maqqari's *The History of the Mohammedan Dynasties in Spain*, 1:24.

35 Luis A. García Moreno, "Spanish Gothic Consciousness," in Alberto Ferreiro, ed., *The Visigoths: Studies in Culture and Society* (London: Brill, 1999), 313.

36 For the propagandistic medieval Muslim praise of the land, see Francisco Prado-Vilar, "Circular Visions of Fertility and Punishment: Caliphal Ivory Caskets from al-Andalus," *Muqarnas* 14 (1997): 19–41.

37   For the symbolic and practical use of the expression, see José Javier Esparza, *¡Santiago y Cierra, España! El nacimiento de una nación* (Madrid: La esfera de los libros, 2013). In the early years of the seventeenth century, in Cervantes's *Don Quixote*, pt. 2, chap. 39, Don Quixote explains to Sancho the meaning of the expression as a battle cry against the enemies of Spain, especially Islam, which allows Cervantes (via Sancho) to make a joke about it. Of course, many academics today use the joke to explain that Cervantes, a slave of the Muslims in North Africa for five years and a hero at the Battle of Lepanto against the Muslim Turks, was in fact against the use of the expression as a battle cry against the enemies of Spain, especially Islam.

38   The legerdemain overlooks, too, that "Islamic" civilization was the result of the confluence of many other civilizations, among them Greek, Persian, Indian, Turkish, Mongol, and even Chinese; that, from a strictly historical point of view, the religion that gives Islamic civilization its name arises from two previously existing religions, Christianity and Judaism; and that therefore there are probably more reasons to doubt the existence of an "Islamic" civilization than there are to doubt the existence of a Western one. A similar privileging occurs in the case of Spanish Jewish civilization, which, unlike that of the Spanish Catholic kingdoms vis-à-vis Catholic Visigoth Spain, is seen as tightly connected vis-à-vis earlier Jewish culture.

CHAPTER 1: CONQUEST AND RECONQUEST

1   As the Spanish medieval historian Luis A. García Moreno has observed, modern Islamic studies historians of the Muslim conquest have often neglected the Christian sources. Yet these sources offer the earliest and, in the case of the *Chronica mozarabica* of 754, probably the most reliable account of the conquest. See García Moreno, *España 702–719: La conquista musulmana* (Seville: University of Seville, 2013), 191. García Moreno seconds the views of the English medieval historian Roger Collins. The Christian sources are also valuable because they serve to "check" the narratives in the Muslim chronicles, sometimes written to serve Islamic religion and tradition, as acknowledged by Jorge Aguadé in *Kitab al-Tarij*, 78, and F. Rosenthal, *A History of Muslim Historiography* (Leiden: Brill, 1968), 42ff. (Reading historical writings about Islamic Spain by some of today's scholars, as shown in the epigraphs of the present book, one cannot help but feel that, regarding the shaping of historical writing by ideology, *plus ça change, plus c'est la même chose*.) Unless otherwise pointed out in the notes, the main primary sources consulted in this chapter: *Chronica mozarabica* of 754, in José Eduardo López Pereira, *Crónica mozárabe de 754: Edición crítica y traducción* (Zaragoza: Universidad de Zaragoza, 1980); *Chronica Byzantia-Arabica* of 743, ed. Juan Gil, *Corpus scriptorum muzarabicorum* (Madrid: Instituto Antonio de Nebrija, 1973), 1:7–14; *Hymnodia Gothica (Analecta Hymnica Medii Aevi, XXVII)*, ed. Clemens Blume (Leipzig: Fues, 1897; Augsburg: Rauner, 2004); John, Bishop of Nikiû, *Chronicle*, trans. R. H. Charles (Oxford: Oxford University Press, 1916); *La Crónica Albeldense* (883), *La Crónica Rotense* (888), and *La Crónica Profética* (883), ed. Manuel Gómez-Moreno, in "Las primeras crónicas de la Reconquista: El ciclo de Alfonso III," *Boletín de la Academia de la Historia* tomo C (Madrid: Archivos, 1932): 600–23; Jan Prelog, ed., *Die Chronik Alfons' III: Untersuchung und kritische Edition der vier Redaktionen* (Frankfurt am Main: Peter Lang, 1980); Alfonso X, *Primera crónica general de España que mandó componer Alfonso el Sabio y se continuaba bajo Sancho IV en 1289*, edition and study of Ramón Menéndez Pidal with the collaboration of Antonio G. Solalinde, Manuel Muñoz Cortés, and José Gómez Pérez (Madrid: Gredos, 1955), 2 vols.; *Rodrigo Jiménez de Rada: Historia de los hechos de España*, trans. Juan Fernández Valverde (Madrid: Alianza, 1989); Ibn Abd al-Hakam (d. ca. 870) in *Ibn Abd al-Hakam, Conquista de África del Norte y de España*, trans. Eliseo Vidal Beltrán (Valencia: Anubar, 1966); Muhammad Ibn al-Razi (889–995) in *Crónica del moro Rasis*, ed. Diego Catalán and trans. María Soledad de Andrés (Madrid: Gredos, 1975); Ibn Hawkal (ninth century) in *Configuration de la Terre (Kitab Surat al-Ard)*, trans. J. H. Kramers and G. Wiet (Paris: Maisonneuve, 1964), vol. 1, 107–16; Said al-

Andalusi (ninth century), in *Kitab Tabakat al-Umam (Livre des Catégories des Nations)*, trans. Régis Blachère (Paris: La Rose, 1935); Abd al-Malik Ibn Habib (d. 853), the fragment on Spain (possibly completed by disciples in the eleventh century, according to Jorge Aguadé), in *Abd al-Malik Ibn Habib: Kitab al-Tarij*, ed. and study by Jorge Aguadé (Madrid: Consejo Superior de Investigaciones Científicas, 1991), 15–108; the anonymous *Akhbar Majmua* (either tenth or eleventh century) in *Ajbar Machmuá*, trans. Emilio Lafuente y Alcántara (1867; rpt. Madrid: Bibliófilo, 1984); Ibn al-Tabari (d. 923), *The History of al-Tabari*, trans. R. Stephen Humphreys (New York: State University of New York Press, 1990), 38 vols.; Ibn al-Qutiyya (probably late tenth or early eleventh century) in *Historia de la conquista de España de Abenalcotía el cordobés*, trans. Julián Ribera (Madrid: Revista de Archivos, 1926), 2 vols.; Ibn Hayyan (987–1075) in *Ibn Hayyan: Al-Muqtabis* 2.1, in J. Vallvé and F. Ruiz Girela, *La primera década del reinado de Al-Hakam I, según el Muqtabis II, l de Ben Hayyan de Córdoba (m. 469 h./1076 J.C.)* (Madrid: Real Academia de la Historia, 2003); Ibn al-Kardabus (mid-twelfth to early thirteenth century) in *Ibn al-Kardabus, Historia de al-Andalus (Kitab al-Iktifa)*, trans. Felipe Maíllo Salgado (Madrid: Akal, 1986); Ibn Idhari al-Marrakushi (late thirteenth century) in *Histoire de l'Afrique et de l'Espagne: Intitulée Al-Bayano 'l-Mogrib*, trans. by E. Fagnan (Algiers: Imprimérie orientale, 1904), 2 vols.; Abd al-Wahid al-Marrakushi (1185–ca. 1230), *Histoire des almohades*, trans. E. Fagnan (Algiers: Adolphe Jourdan, 1883); Ibn al-Athir (1313–1374) in *Ibn al-Athir: Annales du Maghreb et de l'Espagne*, trans. E. Fagnan (Algiers: Adolphe Jourdan, 1898); Ibn Khaldun (fourteenth century) in *The Muqaddimah: An Introduction to History*, trans. Franz Rosenthal (1958; rpt. Princeton, NJ: Princeton University Press, 2004), 183; Ibn Khaldoun, *Les Prolégomènes d'Ibn Khaldoun*, trans. M. de Slane (Paris: Librairie orientaliste Paul Geuthner, 1934); *Ibn Khaldoun: Histoire des Berbères*, trans. M. de Slane (Paris: Librairie Orientaliste, 1925); al-Maqqari (seventeenth century) in *The History of the Mohammedan Dynasties in Spain by Ahmed Ibn Mohammed al-Makkari*, trans. Pascual de Gayangos (1840; rpt. New York: Johnson Reprint, 1964); *Dos tratados de legislación musulmana. 1. Leyes de moros del siglo XIV 2. Suma de los principales mandamientos y devedamientos de la ley y çunna, por don Içe de Gebir, Alfaquí Mayor de la aljama de Segovia. Año de 1492*, ed. Pascual de Gayangos (Madrid: Academia de la Historia. Memorial histórico español, 1853), vol. 5. For the archaeological sources, see notes below.

2   The *Chronica mozarabica* of 754 always refers to it as the *Roman* Empire. By the fifth century, if not earlier, this Roman Empire with its capital in Constantinople (also called "The New Rome") was culturally both Greek and Christian. Its Muslim and Persian enemies as well as the Europeans referred to it as the Empire of the Greeks and to its inhabitants as "Greeks" (though ethnically not all its inhabitants were Greek, any more than all the inhabitants or emperors of the Western or Latin Roman Empire had been "Roman") or "Romans" ("Rum," as even the Quran refers to them). Nobody referred to this Roman Empire as "Byzantine," which is the successful invention of a German Protestant scholar in the sixteenth century. For this issue, see, among others, Fergus Miller, *A Greek Roman Empire* (Berkeley: University of California Press, 2007); Ioannis Stouraitis, "Roman Identity in Byzantium: A Critical Approach," *Byzantinische Zeitschrift* 107, no. 1 (2014): 175; and Clifton R. Fox, "What If Anything Is a Byzantine," http://www.romanity.org/htm/fox.01.en.what_if_anything_is_a_byzantine.01.htm.

3   Kristina Krüger, *Monasteries and Monastic Orders: 2000 Years of Christian Art and Culture* (Könnigswinter: H. F. Ullmann, 2008). For the de-Christianization of North Africa, see Youssef Courbage and Philippe Fargues, *Christians and Jews under Islam*, trans. Judy Mabro (London: I. B. Tauris, 1997). For the reduction and marginalization of the Copts, see Harald Suermann, "Copts and the Islam of the Seventh Century," in Emmanouela Grypeou, Mark Swanson, and David Thomas, eds., *The Encounter of Eastern Christianity with Early Islam* (Leiden: Brill, 2006), 109; A. J. Butler, *The Ancient Coptic Churches of Egypt* (1884; rpt. London: Clarendon Press 1970). One remaining example of what this vast network once contained of irreplaceable art and manuscripts is the extraordinary Greek Orthodox monastery of Saint Katherine of Mount Sinai (built from 548 to 565), declared by UNESCO a

World Heritage Site. In the tenth century, a mosque was built inside its walls, probably to placate the Muslim rulers. Since the mosque does not face Mecca, however, it has escaped use. Many Berbers had converted to Christianity, as Muslim sources attest: see, among others, al-Hakam, 37.

4   Muslim sources mention a great female Berber leader known as Kahina, possibly Jewish or even Christian (some Berber tribes had converted to Christianity), who resisted the Islamic armies until she was defeated by Musa Ibn Nusayr. See, among others, al-Athir, 29ff. According to the historian Muhammad Ibn Abd al-Raini al-Kayrawani, Kahina was beheaded, but her sons converted to Islam and led many of the Berber units "sent against the West [Spain] to make war (jihad) in the name of God." See *Histoire de l'Afrique de Mohammed-ben-Abi-el-Raini-el-Kairouani*, trans. E. Pellisier (Paris: Imprimerie Royale, 1845), 55. El-Raini, too, points out that the mountains of "Nefouça" (six days walk from Tripoli) were peopled with Christians (36). Nevertheless, the cultural, ethnic, and political phenomenon of "Berberism" shows that Berber culture is far from dead and that it continues to struggle against both Arabization (Berber is an Afro-Asiatic, not Semitic language) and Islam.

5   *Chronica mozarabica* of 754, 54.5. The entrance to this strait from the Mediterranean Sea had been known since ancient times by its Greek name, the Pillars of Hercules (Ηρακλειοι Στηλαι), after the two promontories that flank the entrance. After Muslims conquered Spain, they renamed the promontory at which Tariq had presumably landed as *Gibt al-Tariq* (rock or promontory of Tariq), from which the present name Gibraltar (*el peñón de Gibraltar,* or Rock of Gibraltar) derives. The Pillars of Hercules have been part of the Spanish coat of arms for many centuries.

6   "The vast majority of *mawali* were freedmen and descendants of freedmen": *Brill Encyclopaedia of Islam, Second Edition*, "mawlā," II. c. For Tarif and Tariq as *mawali* via former slavery, see such Muslim sources as *Ajbar Machmuá*, 20ff., and also Daniel Pipes, *Slave Soldiers and Islam: The Genesis of a Military System* (New Haven, CT: Yale University Press, 1981), 125–27, and "Mawlas: Freed Slaves and Converts in Early Islam," in *Muslims and Others in Early Islamic Society*, ed. Robert Hoyland (Farnham: Ashgate, 2004), 277–322. The *Brill Encyclopedia of Islam, Second Edition*, "mawlā," explains further: "The client recognized in early law was a non-Arab freedman, convert or other newcomer in Muslim society. Since non-Arabs could only enter this society as clients, *mawlā* came to be synonymous with 'non-Arab Muslim,' and the secondary literature usually employs the word in this sense." The Arabist and scholar of Islamic law Felipe Maíllo Salgado explains the nonfreed slave meaning and its lower social status: "Initially it meant anyone who was a 'neo-convert' to Islam, since in principle non-Arabs could only enter Islam as 'clients' of Arabs. Thus *mawla* came to be synonymous with 'non-Arab Muslim.' Also freed slaves would become, as well as their descendants, 'clients' of the former owner.... Though in theory they were not to be considered inferior, in practice the *mawali* were early on considered lowly people, and the life of a client was worth less than that of an Arab. This inequality caused a movement [in the Middle East] that brought about the fall of the Umayyad dynasty and the rise of the Abbasids, who were supported by the Persian *mawali*." *Diccionario de derecho islámico* (Guijón: Trea, 2005), 225–26. Much effort has been spent by a number of Islamic scholars (mentioned by Pipes) arguing either that slaves under Islam were wonderfully treated (an argument one has also heard from some scholars of the American slave system in the South) or that the very idea of slave soldiers is unacceptable.

7   *Ajbar Machmuá*, 20ff.; Ibn Hayyan cit. al-Maqqari, 1:251. Other sources claim his family was Yemeni. See also García Moreno, *España 702–719*, 228–379.

8   According to Soha Abboud-Haggar, professor of Islamic studies at the Universidad Complutense de Madrid, in her "Guadalete: La batalla del destino," *La aventura de la historia* 13, 147 (2011): 62, citing (I give the name as exactly spelled by Abboud-Haggar) chronicler al-Haza'ini. See also García Moreno, *España 702–719*, and the *Ajbar Machmuá*, 20.

9   Sending a scouting force to be followed by a larger army was a standard practice in the Muslim conquests, as pointed out in David Nicolle and Angus McBride, *Armies of the Muslim Con-*

quest (London: Osprey, 1993), a work that, as is the case with other sources of strictly military history, has not been used by historians of the conquest of Spain.

10 García Moreno, *España 702–719*, 228–379.

11 *Chronica mozarabica* of 754, 51.11–12.

12 Felipe Maíllo Salgado, *Acerca de la conquista árabe de Hispania: Imprecisiones, equívocos y patrañas* (Guijón: TREA, 2011).

13 *Chronica mozarabica* of 754, 80.12–14.

14 Charles Emmanuel Dufourcq, *La vie quotidienne dans l'Europe médiévale sous la domination arabe* (Paris: Hachette, 1978), 18; *Crónica mozárabe de 754*, ed. and trans. José Eduardo López Pereira (Zaragoza: Facsimil, 1980), 80. Since then, Muslim scholars and some Western ones have tried to play down this defeat, as they have tried to do also with Lepanto and even Navas de Tolosa. Sour grapes, no doubt.

15 In 1526 (Siege of Vienna), the Catholic forces, largely consisting of Spanish and German soldiers, held until the arrival of a German relief army. In 1683 (Battle of Vienna), the Catholic defenders were close to defeat when the arrival of the Polish army led by King Jan Sobiesky III and his Winged Hussars (fighting under the banner of the blessed Virgin Mary—Our Lady of Częstochowa) decisively defeated the Turks on September 11–12. This marked the beginning of the gradual expulsion of the Muslim armies from central and southeastern Europe.

16 One of the best scholarly treatments on the subject in English remains Majid Khadduri, *War and Peace in the Law of Islam* (Baltimore: Johns Hopkins Press, 1955). The most influential work today is that of Professor Juan Cole, whose eloquent works are listed at his website, www.juancole.com/about. Arabists sympathetic to Muslim Spain, such as Emilio González Ferrín (who also affirms that Marxism should be rescued from its *desprestigio* because of the "vampiresque Soviet usurpation" and that "the economic superstructure [*sic*]" is what "really tenses the historical nerve"), insist that the word *jihad* in the Quran applies only to "spiritual struggle." See Ferrín, *Historia general de al-Andalus* (Córdoba: Almuzara, 2003), 153. A more realistic and balanced appraisal of *jihad* is found in Michael Bonner, *Jihad in Islamic History: Doctrines and Practice* (Princeton, NJ: Princeton University Press, 2008), where he tries to show that the spiritual meaning is also important. But the best modern scholarly work on *jihad* as Holy War or Sacred Combat may be Alfred Morabia, *Le gihad dans l'Islam médiéval: Le "combat sacré" des origines au XIIe siécle* (Paris: Alban Michel, 1993). Those who insist on the primary spiritual meaning as "greater *jihad*" against the less important martial meaning as "lesser *jihad*" may be echoing the work of the eighteenth-century Egyptian interpreter of Islamic law Az-Zurqani (d. 1710) (who in my opinion could have been influenced by the ideas of the eighteenth-century European Enlightenment and the very small branch of Islam, the Sufis, who make this distinction): see Abboud-Haggar, "Gihad según el manuscrito aljamiado de al-Tafri de Ibn al-Gallab," *Sharq al-Andalus* 12 (1995): n6. The best short survey of the notion of *jihad* is probably E. Tyan, "Jihad," *Encyclopaedia of Islam, Second Edition* (Brill, 2012), *BrillOnline*, Northwestern University Library, accessed August 7, 2012, www.encislam. brill.nl.turing.library.northwestern.edu/subscriber/entry?entry=islam_COM-0189.

17 Richard Hitchcock, *Mozarabs in Medieval and Early Modern Spain: Identities and Influences* (Hampshire: Ashgate, 2008), 7–8.

18 *Across the Centuries* (New York: Houghton Mifflin Company, 1994). Other recent efforts can be found in Gene W. Heck, *When Worlds Collide: Exploring the Ideological and Political Foundations of the Clash of Civilizations* (Lanham, MD: Rowman & Littlefield Publishers, 2007).

19 See www.islaminourschools.com. In contrast, historian Tom Holland's documentary *Islam: The Untold Story* (produced by England's Channel 4), which is somewhat skeptical of a number of fundamental Islamic beliefs, has not found a comparable diffusion.

20 Quoted in Bruce Smith, "Woman Doctor Shares Journey into Heart of Islam," Associated Press, August 22, 2008.

21 Felipe Maíllo Salgado, *Diccionario de derecho islámico* (Gijón: TREA, 2006), "Guerra Santa (*yihad*)."

22 "Al-Gihad según el manuscrito aljamiado de *al-Tafri* de Ibn Gallab," *Sharq al-Andalus* 12 (1995): 2. In Spanish, the most readable account of the notion of *jihad* is that of historian José Javier Esparza, *Historia de la Yihad* (Madrid: La esfera de los libros, 2015).

23 The following citations according to *The Muwatta of Imam Malik Narrated by Yahya b. Yahya b. Katyir al-Laith al-Andalusi*, trans. F. Amira Zrien Matrah (Karachi: Darul Ishaat, 2005).

24 In other words, rape of females captured in *jihad* territory was religiously justified because they were considered slave women: see the influential Maliki text *Mudawwana*, tome 4, vol. 2, no. 655. The *Mudawwana* has been summarized by tome, book, and number by G. H. Bousquet in "La Moudawwana," *Annales de l'Institut d'Études Orientales* 16 (1958), 17 (1959), and 20 (1962), and *Revue algérienne, tunisienne et marocaine de législation et de jurisprudence* 74 (1958), 75 (1959), and 77 (1961). All my references to the *Moudawwana* are taken from this work, unless otherwise noted. *Muwatta*, 21.10.18; 21.9.17 explains how all the possessions of the dead enemy become the property of his Muslim killer during *jihad*. See also *Muwatta*, 40.1; Ibn Rushd, *Bidayat*, The Book of Tadbir, 54.2.2–54.2.3; and Cristina de la Puente, "Límites legales del concubinato: Normas y tabúes en la esclavitud sexual según la bidya de Ibn Rushd," *Al-Qantara* 28, no. 2 (Julio–Diciembre 2007): 409–33.

25 Cit. Abu Ubayd al-Qasim Ibn Salam (774–837) in his *The Book of Revenue (Kitab al-Anwal)*, trans. Imran Ahsan Khan Nyazee (London: Center for Muslim Contributions to Civilization, 2005), 32. Abu Ubayd confirms that, according to the Messenger of Allah, those who do not participate in *jihad* have no right to any part of the resulting booty and spoils (212). Professor Ahsan Kahn observes: "This opinion it is obligatory to follow, because it conforms with the tradition, and it is not permitted to turn away from it due to the opinion of someone even if it be that of Umar" (213n9).

26 *Dos tratados de legislación musulmana. 1. Leyes de moros del siglo XIV 2. Suma de los principales mandamientos y devedamientos de la ley y çunna, por don Içe de Gebir, Alfaquí Mayor de la aljama de Segovia. Año de 1492*, ed. Pascual de Gayangos (Madrid: Academia de la Historia, Memorial histórico español, 1853), vol. 5.

27 R. Arnaldez, "La guerre sainte selon Ibn Hazm," in *Études d'Orientalisme Dediées à la Mémoire de Lévi-Provençal* (Paris: Maisonneuve, 1962), 2:446.

28 Vincent Lagardère, *Les almoravides jusqu'au règne de Yusuf B. Tasfin (1039–1106)* (Paris: Editions L'Harmattan, 1989), 182. Many others among the greatest scholars of Islam may also have misunderstood the concept of *jihad*: see muwahhidmedia.files.wordpress.com/2013/09/al-jihad-linguistically-and-legally.pdf and www.islamicawakening.com/viewarticle.php?articleID=685.

29 Cit. Miguel Asín Palacios, *Abenházam de Córdoba y su historia crítica de las ideas religiosas* (Madrid: Archivos, Bibliotecas y Museos, 1932), 5:47–48. Asín Palacios comments: "As we can see, this [Quranic] verse has a general meaning applicable to all times and places" (48).

30 *Islamic Jurisprudence: Shafii's Risala*, trans. Majid Khadduri (Baltimore: Johns Hopkins University Press, 1961), 82–85.

31 *Sahih Al-Bukhari*, trans. Dr. Muhammad Muhsin Khan of Medina Islamic University (Chicago: Kazi Publications, 1976), 3 vols.; *Bukhari*, vol. 1, bk. 2, no. 26.

32 Michael Bonner, "Some Observations concerning the Early Development of Jihad on the Arab-Byzantine Frontier," *Studia Islamica* 75 (1992): 19.

33 Aisha Mubarak Esamil, "Cinco cartas inéditas del *katib* Abd al-Haqq b. al-Yannan procedentes del ms. 15 de la Biblioteca General de Rabat (Marruecos)," in *Homenaje al Prof. Jacinto Bosch Vilá* (Granada: Universidad de Granada, 1991), 98–107.

34 *Crónica anónima de los reyes de Taifas*, trans. Felipe Maíllo Salgado (Madrid: Akal, 1991). The name of one of the Muslim leaders of Valencia, the Slav Mujahid, means "champion of Holy War."

35 King of Granada Muhammad Ibn Nasr (murdered in 1350) is a typical example given by Ibn Khatib. One day in his presence there was a discussion about religion and he said, "the foundations of religion are two as far as I am concerned: say 'He is the only God' and this,' and pointed to his sword." Ibn al-Jatib, *Historia de los Reyes de la Alhambra*, trans. José María Casciaro Ramírez (Granada: University of Granda, 2010), 187–88.

36 Yasir S. Ibrahim, *Al-Tabari's Book of Jihad: A Translation from the Original Arabic* (Lewiston: Edwin Mellen Press, 2007).

37 "The Religious Powers of the Caliph," in *A Reader in Classical Islam*, ed. F. E. Peters (Princeton, NJ: Princeton University Press, 1994), 149.

38 Ibn Khaldun, *The Muqaddimah*, 183.

39 J. M. Forneas, "Datos para un estudio de la *mudawwana* de Sahnun in al-Andalus," in *Actas del IV Coloquio Hispano-Tunecino* (Madrid: Instituto Hispano-Arabe de Cultura, 1983), 108 and 112n33.

40 Morabia, *Le gihad dans l'Islam médiéval*; Salgado, "Guerra Santa (*yihad*)." See also chapter 3 of this book. For another clarifying work that examines some of the earliest *jihads* of Islam, see Michael Bonner, *Aristocratic Violence and Holy War: Studies in the Jihad and the Arab-Byzantine Frontier* (New Haven, CT: American Oriental Society, 1996). In a more recent work, published this time by a university press, Bonner waffles in his treatment of *jihad* and tries to show its nice side: Michael Bonner, *Jihad in Islamic History* (Princeton, NJ: Princeton University Press, 2006). See also Mathias von Bredow, *Der heilige Krieg (Gihad) aus der Sicht der malikitischen Rechtsschule (Ibn Abi Zayd al-Qayrawani)* (Stuttgart: Franz Steiner, 1994).

41 Felipe Maíllo Salgado, "La guerra santa según el derecho malikí," *Studia Historica* 1, no. 2 (1983): 3. A good example that I have found is al-Qayrawani's *Risala* (30.1–2).

42 Quran 9:29, Saheeh International translation.

43 *Muwatta*, bk. 21.

44 *Al-Tufi i*, 2.35–37.

45 *Bukhari*, vol. 8, bk. 74, no. 278.

46 *Risala*, 30.2.

47 *Moudawwana*, tome 4, vol. 2, 655; cf. *Bukhari*, vol. 8, bk. 74, no. 278.

48 For this and the following, see Arnaldez, "La guerre sainte selon Ibn Hazm," 453–54.

49 Arnaldez, "La guerre sainte selon Ibn Hazm," 454.

50 *Al-Makkari*, 1:250.

51 For this and much of what follows, see Morabia, *Le gihad dans l'Islam médiéval*, 291–342.

52 Ibn Hudhayl, *Tuhfat al-Anfus wa Shiar Sukkan al-Andalus*, ed. Louis Mercier (Paris, 1936), 8–10, cit. Majid Khadduri, *War and Peace in the Law of Islam* (Baltimore: Johns Hopkins Press, 1955), 81. Of course, a hermeneutics of suspicion might also consider the possibility that the idea of *jihad* as a peaceful inner struggle has been supported by contemporary professors of Middle Eastern studies, Arabic experts, and Islamic moderates, because it helps them present their field of expertise and/or their religion in a more palatable way to modern audiences, who might not be able to look at *jihad* from a strictly historical point of view and therefore accept it as learned *ulama* and Muslim rulers understood it to be for centuries—namely, as Holy War against infidels.

53 Bonner, "Some Observations concerning the Early Development of Jihad on the Arab-Byzantine Frontier," *Studia Islamica* 75 (1992): 8, who cites and agrees with Albrecht Noth, *Heiliger Krieg und Heiliger Kampf im Islam und Christentum* (Bonn: Rohrscheid, 1966). In a recent book published by a university press, Bonner endeavors to show that the "spiritual" meaning of *jihad* is also important, but he does not mention a number of the texts and authors we have examined that were fundamental in al-Andalus (*Tafri*, *Risala*, *Moudawana*, Ibn Hazm, the chronicles, etc.). He does mention *Muwatta* and al-Tabari but does not point out that they talk of *jihad* exclusively as Holy War.

54 Morabia, *Le gihad dans l'Islam médiéval*, 73, 90.

55 See also Roberto de Mattei, *Holy War, Just War: Islam and Christendom at War* (Rockford, IL: Rockford Institute, 2007), 61–74.

56 Kenneth Baxter Wolf, "Christian Views of Islam in Early Medieval Spain," in John Victor Tolan, ed., *Medieval Christian Perceptions of Islam: A Book of Essays* (New York: Garland, 1996), 85–89; Richard Hitchcock, *Mozarabs in Medieval and Early Modern Spain: Identities and Influences* (Hampshire: Ashgate, 2008). For a good refutation of the claim that religion

did not motivate the Muslim conquests, see Bousquet, "Some Critical and Sociological Remarks on the Arab Conquest and the Theories Proposed on This," in Fred M. Donner, ed., *The Expansion of the Early Islamic State* (Burlington: Ashgate, 2008), 21; "Observations on the Nature and Causes of the Arab Conquest," in Donner, ed., *The Expansion of the Early Islamic State*, 23–33.

57 *The History of the Mohammedan Dynasties in Spain by Ahmed Ibn Mohammed al-Makkari*, vol. 1, app. E, lxx.

58 *Kitab al-qudat bi-Qurtuba*, trans. Julián Ribera as *Al-Joxani, Historia de los jueces de Córdoba* (Madrid: Iberica, 1914), 55.

59 For this and the following, see *Ibn al-Kardabus*, 63; al-Qutiyya, 6; Ibn Idhari al-Marrakushi, *Al-Bayano 'l-Mogrib*, 2:7, 11, 13.

60 Soha Abboud-Haggar, *El Tratado Jurídico de Al-Tafri de Ibn Al-Gallab: Manuscrito Aljami-ado De Almonacid De La Sierra (Zaragoza): Edición, Estudio, Glosario y Confrontación Con El Original Árabe* (Zaragoza: Institución "Fernando el Católico," 1999), 2:231; *Mudawwana*, tome 3, vol. 2 (Book of Holy War), no. 446.

61 *Al-Tafri*, 231.

62 According to the following Muslim historians: Ibn Abi Usaibia (1203–1270), in al-Maqqari, *The History of the Mohammedan Dynasties in Spain by Ahmed Ibn Mohammed al-Makkari*, vol. 1, app. A, x; *Said al-Andalusi: Kitab Talakat al-Umam (Livre des Categories des Nations)*, trans. Regis Blachére (Paris: La Rose Editeurs, 1935), 126–27.

63 *Al-Makkari*, vol. 1, app. C, xli.

64 According to Ibn al-Qutiyya's *Conquest of al-Andalus*, trans. María Jesús Viguera Molins, "Lectura de Ibn al-Qutiyya: sobre la conquista de al-Andalus," *Del Nilo al Guadalquivir II Estudios sobre las fuentes de la conquista islámica*, ed. Luis A. García Moreno and Esther Sánchez Medina (Madrid: Real Academia de la Historia, 2013), 122.

65 See, among many, the "Polemic Between a Saracen and a Christian," attributed to John Damascene (676–749): Adel Theodor Khoury, *Les théologiens byzantins et l'Islam: Textes et auteurs (VIIIe–XIIIe s.)* (Louvain: Nauwlaerts, 1969), 68–82.

66 *Chronica mozarabica* of 754, 8.1–5; 11.1–10.

67 For the chronology, see Luis A. García Moreno, "Elementos de tradición bizantina en dos Vidas de Mahoma mozárabes," in *Bizancio y la península ibérica: De la antigüedad tardía a la edad moderna*, ed. Inmaculada Pérez Martín and Pedro Bádenas de la Peña (Madrid: Consejo Superior de Investigaciones Científicas, 2004), 247–71. García Moreno shows that it was likely written by an Andalusian "mozarab" (either a *dhimmi* or a former *dhimmi*) in the second half of the eighth century and owes much to the Eastern Church polemics against Islam. The manuscript, missing from Córdoba, was found in a northern monastery by Eulogio of Córdoba. See also the seventh-century polemic between Timothy I, patriarch of the East Syrian Church, and Caliph al-Mahdi, religious and temporal head of Islam, dating from the seventh century, where the word *Muslim* is used: "Timothy's Apology for Christianity," trans. A. Mingana, *Bulletin of the John Rylands Library* 2 (1928): v–vii and 1–15.

68 "Fuentes no Islámicas de la invasión y conquista de España por el imperio Árabe-islámico," in *Del Nilo al Ebro: Estudio sobre las fuentes de la conquista islámica*, ed. Luis A. García Moreno and María Jesús Viguera Molins (Alcalá de Henares: Universidad de Alcalá, 2009), 182. Not surprisingly, the historian Alejandro García Sanjuán, a defender of the "peaceful treatises conquest" approach, dismisses this moving hymn as "not adding any significant data about the conquest." See his *La conquista islámica de la península ibérica y la tergiversación del pasado: Del catastrofismo al negacionismo* (Madrid: Marcial Pons, 2013), 180.

69 García Moreno, "Fuentes no islámicas de la invasion y conquista de España por el imperio árabe-islámico," 186.

70 Yohanan Friedmann in *The History of al-Tabari*, translated and annotated by Yohanan Friedmann (New York: State University of New York Press, 1985), 12:xvi.

71 G. H. Bousquet, "Some Critical and Sociological Remarks on the Arab Conquest and the

Theories Proposed on This," in Donner, ed., *The Expansion of the Early Islamic State*, 21; "Observations on the Nature and Causes of the Arab Conquest," in Donner, ed., *The Expansion of the Early Islamic State*, 23–33; Dominique Urvoy, "Sur l'évolution de la notion de Gihad dans l'Espagne musulmane," in *Mélanges de la Casa de Velázquez* 9 (1973): 335–71, especially 338: "Sans exclure donc les autres raisons invoquées, il est probable que l'attaque de l'Espagne correspondait mieux aux besoins de la guerre sainte." See also Urvoy's *Histoire de la pensée árabe et islamique* (Paris: Seuil, 2006).

72   José Miranda Calvo, *Consideraciones militares sobre la conquista arábiga: del Guadalete a Toledo* (Madrid: Patronato José María Quadrado del Consejo Superior de Investigaciones Científicas, 1973). Commander Miranda Calvo's formidable study has not been cited in any of the standard English books on the conquest, perhaps because he was a military analyst, a soldier, and a professor at a Spanish army military academy rather than a university historian. Hans Delbrück, *The Barbarian Invasions*, trans. Walter J. Renfroe Jr. (1900–1920; rpt. Lincoln: University of Nebraska Press, 1980), 417–26, has also been neglected by contemporary historians; Maíllo Salgado, *Acerca de la conquista árabe de España*; García Moreno, *España 702–719*. See also María R. Valverde Castro, *Ideología, simbolismo y ejercicio del poder real en la monarquía visigoda: un proceso de cambio* (Salamanca: Universidad de Salamanca, 2000), 277. Christian chronicles repeatedly refer to the "softness" and "vices" prevailing among the Visigoth leadership, and a Muslim chronicle depicts it as courageous but living a decadent life. See also the colorful accounts in the Muslim and Christian chronicles on the betrayal of Count Julian because of King Rodrigo's rape of the count's daughter: the sexual details may or may not be fanciful, but they reinforce the fact of treason by parts of the nobility.

73   García Moreno, *España 702–719*, 26–28.

74   *Abu Muhammad Abd al-Wahid al-Marrakusi: Lo admirable en el resumen de las noticias del Magrib (Kitab al-Muyib Fi Taljis Ajbar al-Magrib)*, trans. Ambrosio Huici Miranda (Tetuán: Editora Marroquí, Instituto General Franco de Estudios e Investigación Hispano-Árabe, 1955), 149 and n1; Ana Serrano, María Jesús Viguera, et al., *Ibn Khaldun: The Mediterranean in the Fourteenth Century: Rise and Fall of Empires* (Seville: Legado Andalusí, 2006), 196.

75   See chapter 7 of this book for the Visigoths' anti-Jewish legislation. Both Muslim and Christian chronicles narrate what appears to have been a not-infrequent alliance between Muslims and Jews against Christian rule, even in the Middle East and North Africa; there is no reason why the Muslim chronicles would lie about this matter. In North Africa and the Middle East, Muslims soon realized that they could use the Jewish community, unhappy with its treatment in the Christian Greek Roman Empire, to help keep the Christians under control. A. S. Tritton cites several Muslim sources on the matter: *The Caliphs and Their Non-Muslim Subjects: A Critical Study of the Covenant of Umar* (London: Frank Cass & Co., 1930; rpt. 1970), 94–95. For primary sources on Spain that register this collaboration, see *Ajbar Machmuá*, 25, 27, 29; al-Maqqari in *The History of the Mohammedan Dynasties in Spain*, 1:280–82; Ibn Idhari al-Marrakusi, *Historia de al-Andalus*, 17–42; al-Qutiyya, 8; Ibn al-Athir in *Ibn al-Athir: Annales du Maghreb et de l'Espagne*, trans. E. Fagnan (Algiers: Adolphe Jourdan, 1898), 46–47; al-Khatib in *Ibn al-Jatib: Historia de los Reyes de la Alhambra (Al-Lamha al-badriyya): Resplandor de la luna llena acerca de la dinastía nazarí*, trans. José María Casciaro Ramírez and Emilio Molina López (Granada: Universidad de Granada, 2010), 106; al-Razi in Pascual de Gayangos, "Memoria sobre la autenticidad de la Crónica denominada del moro Rasis," *Memorias de la Real Academia de la Historia* 8 (1852): app. 2, 72; Ibn Idhari al-Marrakushi, *Al-Bayano 'l-Mogrib* (Algiers: Imprimerie Orientale Pierre Fontana, 1904), 2:18; *Rodrigo Jiménez de Rada (1170–1247)*, 3, chs. 22–23. According to the great scholar of Jewish history Salo Baron, Spanish mistrust of Jewry and *conversos* in the Middle Ages and beyond was perhaps based on the Sephardim's having been a "fifth column" for the Muslim invasion of Spain: *A Social and Religious History of the Jews* (New York: Columbia University Press, 1958), 5:135–36. Francisco Cantera Burgos states that Jews constituted a "fifth column" before the invasion: see his "Christian Spain," in Cecil Roth, ed., *The Dark Ages: Jews in Christian*

Europe, 711–1096 (Tel Aviv: Jewish History Publications, 1966), 357, 450n1. Gayangos argues that Jews invited Muslims to invade the Visigothic realm and afterward "everywhere made common cause with them" (*The History of the Mohammedan Dynasties in Spain*, 1:531n18). According to Alan Harris Cutler, "The Christians of Franco-Germany also saw the Jews as a potential Islamic 'fifth column' and at times persecuted the Jews very severely for this precise reason": see *The Jew as Ally of the Muslim: Medieval Roots of Anti-Semitism* (Notre Dame, IN: University of Notre Dame Press, 1986), 395n17. The Israeli historian Elyahu Ashtor points out that Jews supported Muslims against Christian rebels (such as Umar ibn Hafsun and Saint Eulogius) and against Christians in the North (such as King Alfonso III of Asturias c. 866–910) who attacked Muslims in the South and that Jews sat with Muslims in the Christian Council of Córdoba (863) to make sure the council did not encourage Christian rebelliousness: *The Jews of Moslem Spain* (Philadelphia: Jewish Publication Society, 1973; trans. Jenny Maklowitz Klein of *Korot ha-Yehudim bi-Sefarad ha-Muslemit*), 1:68–69, 92–93, 98–99. According to Arthur J. Zuckerman, professor of medieval Jewish civilization at the Reconstructionist Rabbinical College in Philadelphia, there was a Judeo-Islamic conspiracy to seize Christian Barcelona in 852: see his *Jewish Princedom in Feudal France, 768–900 (Study in Jewish History)* (New York: Columbia University Press, 1972), 316–18. This may be a reference to what the eleventh-century Christian *Anales bertinianorum* claim happened: "The saracens, thanks to the treason of the Jews, took Barcelona and, after devastating the city and killing most of its inhabitants, returned without difficulties": cit. Jordi Casanovas Miró, "Aspectos cotidianos de las relación entre judíos y cristianos," in *Del pasado judío en los reinos medievales hispánicos*, ed. Yolanda Moreno Koch (Cuenca: Ediciones de la Universidad de Castilla-La Mancha, 2005), 100. According to Amador de los Ríos, a contingent of Jewish troops from Africa under the command of Kaula-al-Yehudi was part of the Muslim army that defeated the Visigoths at Guadalete (Jerez), and the Muslim conquerors favored Jewish immigration from many lands as part of their political design against the Spanish Christians: *Historia social, política y religiosa de los judíos de España y Portugal* (Madrid: Fontanet, 1875), 1:116–17n1–2, 118–19. Alan Harris Cutler and Helen Elmquist cite Christian primary sources attributing the persecutions of Jews in Europe in 1010 and the 1060s to the widespread belief that Jews colluded with Islam; the authors argue that the "association of Jew with Muslim was the crucial factor in the persecution of 1096" as well: *The Jew as Ally of the Muslim*, 400–402. News of the alleged joint attack by Jews and Muslims against the Church of the Holy Sepulchre in 966, and of the Muslim Fatimids' actual destruction of the same church in 1010, had reached Europe and fostered animosity against Jews; it was a likely motivation for the eventual massacre of Jews during the conquest of Jerusalem in 1099 during the First Crusade (*The Jew as Ally of the Muslim*, 403–5). The Christian Greeks had long accused Jews of being in collusion with Muslims, and when Jerusalem capitulated to Islam in 638, the Orthodox patriarch of Jerusalem, Sophronios, requested and obtained Muslim protection against Jews to avoid a repetition of the massacres of Greek Christians that had taken place in the city in 614: see Joshua Starr, *Jews in the Byzantine Empire (Research and Source Works Series, No. 386)* (Farnborough: Gregg, 1969), 109. Without adducing any proof or taking into account any of the Muslim primary sources, David J. Wasserstein, professor of Jewish studies at Vanderbilt University, dismisses the Jewish collaboration as "stories," products of Christian paranoia, and "at least largely later inventions": "The Muslims and the Golden Age of the Jews in al-Andalus," *Dhimmis and Others: Jews and Christians and the World of Classical Islam (Israel Oriental Studies CVII)*, ed. Uri Rubin and David J. Wasserstein (Tel Aviv: Tel Aviv University, 1997), 179–80. Similarly, without even mentioning such Muslim sources as Ibn Idhari al-Marrakushi and the *Kitab al-Bayan al-Mughrib*, the scholar of Jewish history Norman Roth argues that Jewry was not an important factor in the Islamic invasion of Spain: "The Jews and the Muslim Conquest of Spain," *Jewish Social Studies* 38, no. 72 (1976): 145–58. University of Salamanca Arabist Felipe Maíllo Salgado observes that he has not found in all his research any Muslim source that contradicts the early Muslim chronicles' narratives of the collaboration of the Jewish community with the Islamic forces: "Los judíos enlas fuentes magrebíes y andalucíes: los visires," *Del pasado judío en los reinos medievales hispánicos: afinidad y distanciamiento,* ed. Yolanda Moreno Koch and Ricardo Izauierdo Benito (Cuenca: Universidad de Castilla-La Mancha, 2005), 126n20.

76   "[Theodomir's] subjects will not be killed or taken captive nor will they be separated from their children or women...and their churches will not be burned down.... So long as he acts in good faith and fulfills the conditions that we have imposed upon him. He has agreed to surrender terms covering seven towns.... [He has also agreed] that he will not give refuge to any of our runaway slaves, nor shelter any of our enemies, nor make anyone afraid who is safe with us; that he will not conceal information that he has acquired about [our] enemy; and that it is up to him and his people to pay one dinar every year and four *mudd* (bushels) of wheat, four *mudd* of barley, four *qist* (measures) of thickened grape juice, four *qist* of vinegar, two *qist* of honey and two *qist* of oil. Slaves pay half that. Witnessed by Uthman b. Abi Abda al-Qurashi, Habib b. Abi Ubaida, Ibn Maisara al-Fahmi and Abu Qaim al Hudhali. Written in Rajab in the year 94 of the hijra (April 713*).*" *Christians and Moors in Spain: Volume III Arabic Sources,* ed. and trans. Charles Melville and Ahmad Ubaydl (Warmsminster: Aris & Phillips, 1992), 11–13.

77   See, among other sources, Ibn Abd al-Hakam, *Conquista del Norte de África y de España,* 43; al-Qutiyya, 6; *The Book of Sufficiency on the History of Khalifs, by Abú Ja'far Ibn Abdi-l-hakk Al-khazráji Al-kortobí,* trans. Pascual de Gayangos, in *The History of the Mohammedan Dynasties in Spain,* vol. 1, app. D, xliii–1; the quotation is from *Ibn al-Kardabus,* 61–65; *Rodrigo Jiménez de Rada,* vol. 2, chap. 23.

78   For this and the following, see *Ibn al-Kardabus,* 68, 66; Abd al-Wahid al-Marrakushi, *Histoire des almohades,* 9–14.

79   For this and the following, see *Ajbar Machmuá,* 23–30; al-Qutiyya, 8; al-Maqqari in *The History of the Mohammedan Dynasties in Spain,* 1:277–87, 531n18, 2:1–2; Ibn Idhari al-Marrakusi, *Historia de al-Andalus,* 17–42; *Crónica mozárabe de 754,* 71, 79.

80   *Ajbar Machmuá,* 14–27. Like Muslims later, Persians in the early seventh century had taken advantage of Jewish-Christian enmity: Elliott Horowitz, "'The Vengeance of the Jews Was Stronger Than Their Avarice': Modern Historians and the Persian Conquest of Jerusalem in 614," *Jewish Social Studies* 4, no. 2 (Winter 1998): 1–25; *Reckless Rites: Purim and the Legacy of Jewish Violence* (Princeton, NJ: Princeton University Press, 2004), 229. A number of primary sources claim Jewish retaliatory killings of Christians upon the Persian conquest of Jerusalem: Theophanes the Confessor (d. 818) in *The Chronicle of Theophanes Confessor: Byzantine and Near Eastern History* A.D. *284–813,* ed. Cyril Mango and Roger Scott, with the assistance of Geoffrey Greatrex (Oxford: Clarendon Press, 1997), 431; Antiochus Strategos of Mar Saba in "Antiochus Strategos, The Capture of Jerusalem by the Persians in A.D. 614," trans. F. C. Coneybeare, *English Historical Review* 25 (1910): 502–17; the Armenian bishop Sebeos, in *The Armenian History Attributed to Sebeos,* trans. R. W. Thomson (Liverpool: Liverpool University Press, 1999), part 1, 68–69. See also Heinrich Graetz, *History of the Jews* (Philadelphia: Jewish Publication Society of America, 1894), 3:18–22. The *Jewish Encyclopedia* states that the story of Jews buying Christians and then massacring them at the Mamilla Pool in Jerusalem is fiction (see www.jewishencyclopedia.com/articles/4356-chosroes-khosru-ii-parwiz). Recent Israeli archaeological excavations in Jerusalem have discovered thousands of remains of men, women, and children, with a majority of them women (likely nuns), in the site of the Mamilla Pool, dating back to the times of the Persian conquest of the city. See Yossi Nagar, "Human Skeletal Remains from the Mamilla Cave, Jerusalem," www.antiquities.org (website of the Israel Antiquities Authority), who attributes the massacre to the Persians, www.antiquities. org.il/article_Item_eng.asp?sec_id=17&sub_subj_id=179. Israeli archaeologist Ronny Reich does not attribute the killing to the Persians and estimates the total dead at sixty thousand before the Persian army stopped the carnage: see Gil Zohar, "Massacre at Mamilla," *Jerusalem Post,* March 2, 2006.

81 *Chronica mozarabica* of 754, 54; al-Athir, 46; *Ajbar Machmuá*, 27.

82 *Ibn al-Kardabus*, 63.

83 *Ajbar Machmuá*, 30; Ibn Idhari al-Marrakushi, *Al-Bayano 'l-Mogrib*, 18, 23.

84 *Crónica mozárabe de 754*, sections 54–55; *Primera Crónica General de España*, ed. Ramón Menéndez Pidal (Madrid: Gredos, 1955), 559.

85 *Chronica mozarabica* of 754, 54.8–12.

86 Majid Khadduri, *War and Peace in the Law of Islam* (Baltimore: Johns Hopkins University Press, 1955), vii, 202.

87 M. C. Díaz y Díaz, "Noticias históricas en dos himnos litúrgicos visigóticos," in *Los visigodos: Historia y civilización: Antigüedad y Cristianismo* (Murcia) 3 (1986): 443–56. See also García Moreno, *España 702–719*, 190. One is tempted to compare these terror tactics and their quick results with the ruthless tactics and similarly swift conquests of the Islamic State in Iraq and Syria during the twenty-first century.

88 *Primera Crónica General de España*, chap. 559; *Rodrigo Jiménez de Rada*, vol. 3, chap. 22; al-Hakam, *Conquista de África del Norte y de España*, 47.

89 *Crónica de España, por Lucas, Obispo de Tuy*, trans. Julio Puyol (Madrid: Revista de Archivos, Bibliotecas y Museos, 1926), 269–71.

90 *Crónica del moro Rasis*, 281–82. Some historians have questioned attributing to al-Razi the sections on ancient pre-Islamic history. But modern research has confirmed the authenticity of the text even for the pre-Islamic period: see the introduction by Diego Catalán as well as the historian Claudio Sánchez Albornoz's *Adiciones al estudio de la crónica del moro Rasis* (Madrid: Moneda y Crédito, S.A., 1978). Other texts, of course, corroborate the destruction of churches during the Islamic period (see, for example, Susana Calvo Capilla's research).

91 Susana Calvo Capilla, "Las primeras mezquitas de al-Andalus a través de las fuentes árabes (92/711–170/785)," *Al-Qantara* 27, no. 1 (Enero–Julio 2007): 143–79.

92 *Crónicas anónimas de Sahagún*, ed. Antonio Ubieto Arteta (Zaragoza: Pedro Garcés de Cariñena, 1987), 9–10; *Crónica de Alfonso III* in Jan Prelog, *Die Chronik Alfons' III*, 34–36: *cristianos secum ad patriam duxit.... Basilicas construxit et instauravit.*

93 Cit. Cyrille Aillet, *Les mozárabes: christianisme, islamisation, et arabisation en péninsule ibérique (IXe–XIIe siècle)* (Madrid: Casa de Velázquez, 2010), 122–23. Bracketed material is mine.

94 Alicia Perea, *El tesoro Visigodo de Guarrazar* (Madrid: Consejo Superior de Investigaciones Científicas, 2001); *El tesoro Visigodo de Torredonjimeno* (Madrid: Consejo Superior de Investigaciones Científicas, 2009). Curiously, no work on the conquest has pointed out this archaeological evidence.

95 Lord Dannat, former chief of the British general staff, referring to the swift conquests of the Islamic State in Iraq and Syria, whose success and methods echo those of the early Muslim conquests: "ISIS Slaughters 400 in Ancient Syria City of Palmyra Where Hundreds of Bodies Line the Street," *Daily Mail*, May 24, 2015.

96 *Ibn Khaldoun: Histoire des Berbères*, 1:339.

97 For the destructive zeal of al-Mamun and al-Rashid, see Ibn Khaldun, *Les prolégomenes*, 2:246–47. The point is restated by one of the most respected clerics of the Salafi school of Islam, Muhammad al-Munajjid, at http://islamqa.info/en/20894. The late Hans Jansen, professor of Islamic thought at the University of Utrecht, also pointed out this procedure of the Islamic conquests: https://www.youtube.com/watch?v=6G0a06zMs-o.

98 *Relation de l'Egypte par Abd Allatif*, trans. Silvestre de Sacy (Paris: Imprimerie Impériale, 1810), 183. Ibn Khaldun, *Les prolégomènes*, 1:78. Other Muslim historians who mention the burning of the Alexandria library are al-Qifti (1172–1248) and al-Maqrizi (1364–1442). The Coptic historian Bar Hebreus (1226–1286), known in Arabic as Ibn al-Ibri, tells the story in his *Chronicum Syriacum*: A former Coptic priest, John the Grammarian, asked the Muslim commander, Amr Ibn al-As, to allow him to save the "books of wisdom" in the library. "'You have examined the whole city, and have set your seal on every kind of valuable: I make no claim for aught that is useful to you, but things that are not useful to you may be of service to

us.' 'What are you thinking of?' said Amr. 'The books of wisdom,' said John, 'which are in the imperial libraries.' 'That,' replied Amr, 'is a matter concerning which I can give no order without the authority of the Caliph [Umar].' A letter accordingly was written, putting the question to Omar, who answered, 'Touching the books you mention, if what is written in them agrees with the Book of God, they are not required. If it disagrees, they are not desired. Destroy them therefore.' On receipt of this judgment, Amr accordingly ordered the books to be distributed among the baths of Alexandria and used as fuel for heating. It took six months to consume them." For this account, see Alfred J. Butler, *The Arab Conquest of Egypt and the Last Thirty Years of the Roman Dominion* (1902; rev. rpt. Oxford: Oxford University Press, 1978), 402. Western historians sympathetic to Islam have largely dismissed these Muslim and Christian sources, alleging that they were written too long after the events. But why Muslim historians, including Ibn Khaldun, who could not be accused of being Islamophobic, would make these stories up remains unexplained. They are corroborated by medieval religious experts who cite Malik, as we have seen in the case of Ibn Rushd al-Jadd. Seemingly unaware of this religious text, the historian Bernard Lewis claims that the story of the burning of the library by Umar is invented, since Ibn Khaldun speaks of a similar event in Persia, presumably "demonstrating its folkloric character." Lewis argues that the story was promoted by Saladin to justify his own destruction of the "heretical" libraries of the Fatimid Caliphate (the Fatimids followed the Shia branch of Islam). But why all these destructions do not actually reveal a pattern of behavior and thus reinforce each other's plausibility remains unexplained as well. See Lewis, "The Vanished Library," *New York Review of Books*, September 27, 1990.

99   According to the Muslim historian Ibn Koteybah Ad-dinawari (ninth century), in *al-Makkari*, vol. 1, app. E, lxi–lxii, lxiii.
100 According to the historian As-sadfi in *al-Makkari*, 1:252–53.
101 *Al-Makkari*, 1:510n10.
102 Al-Hakam, 38–42.
103 *Chronica Byzantia-Arabiga*, 1:24.
104 John, Bishop of Nikiû, *Chronicle*, chap. 118.
105 Butler, *The Arab Conquest of Egypt and the Last Thirty Years of the Roman Dominion*, 475, 484–85. Butler argues against the common charge that it was Coptic treason against the Greek Orthodox that caused the fall of Egypt (vi–vii, 480). For a summary of the destruction the Muslim conquest wrought on the Middle East, see Emmet Scott, *Muhammad and Charlemagne Revisited: The History of a Controversy* (London: New English Review Press, 2012).
106 Soha Abboud-Haggar, "La conquista musulmana en las fuentes coptas en lengua árabe (II)," in *Del Nilo al Guadalquivir II: Estudios sobre las fuentes de la conquista islámica*, ed. Luis A. García Moreno and Esther Sánchez Medina (Madrid: Real Academia de la Historia, 2013), 349, 359–60. Abboud-Haggar attributes to "non-Muslim" Arabs the burning of Coptic churches, overlooking that by the time covered in the Coptic text she comments on—the reign of Heraclius—Muhammad had already unified the Arabs under the aegis of Islam. For the account below of the massacre of Greeks, see Abboud-Haggar, "La conquista musulmana en las fuentes coptas en lengua árabe (III)," 382.
107 Turning *dhimmis* from productive people into mere slaves would also end the profitable *jizya* system, off which Muslims were supposed to live till the end of time. As Caliph Umar is reported to have written, "God made this clear to you and to us when He said in His book, 'Fight against those who do not believe in God nor in the last Day, who do not hold forbidden what God and his apostles have forbidden, who do not practice the religion of truth but are of those to whom a Book has been given, until they pay the poll tax from their hand, they being humbled' [Quran 4:29].... Have you considered if we take them [as slaves] and share them out, what will be left for the Muslims who come after us? By God the Muslims would not find a man to talk to and profit from his labors. The Muslims of our day will eat [from the work of] these people as long as they live, and when we and they die, our sons will eat their sons forever, as long as they remain, for they are slaves to the people of the religion of Islam as long

as the religion of Islam shall prevail." Abu Yusuf, *Kitab al-Kharaj*, trans. and ed. by Bernard Lewis, *Islam from the Prophet Muhammad to the Capture of Constantinople* (Oxford: Oxford University Press, 1987), 2:224. One must not kill the goose that lays the golden eggs.

108 Mohsen Azizi, *La domination arabe et l'épanouissement du sentiment national en Iran* (Paris: Les Presses Modernes, 1938), 34, 55, 301–2.

109 For this and the following, see al-Waqidi, 391, 329–30, 181, 184, 380.

110 *Chronique de Michel le Syrien*, 2:430–31. Michael the Syrian writes that when Jerusalem surrendered after a siege, Muslims sacked the city and imposed the *jizya* on the Christians. In Cilicia, Muslims put many of the inhabitants to the sword, tortured the leaders so they would tell where they had hid their treasures, and committed many "impurities" in the churches. The survivors were enslaved. Michael claims that "Amrou, son of Said," forbade having crosses outside churches on the exterior walls, and that Jews convinced the Arab leaders that turning all crosses upside down would help them build mosques better wherever a church had stood. For a study of the process of how Christians have become an insignificant presence in a once-Christian land, see Islamic and Asian studies scholar Raphael Israeli, *Green Crescent Over Nazareth: The Displacement of Christians by Muslims in the Holy Land* (Oxford: Routledge, 2014).

111 Ibn Khaldun, *The Muqaddimah*, 2:35.

112 In a document dating back probably to the tenth century but of course expressing views commonly held since the eighth century. See Luis A. García Moreno, "Literatura antimusulmana de tradición bizantina entre los mozárabes," *Hispania Sacre* 57 (2005): 11.

113 The *Chronica mozarabica* of 754 mentions the taxation Islam imposed on Christians as one of the conditions for allowing them to practice their religion, but under Muslim terms—a probable reference to the Islamic *jizya*. Moreover, the Maliki school of Islamic law, which was prevalent in Islamic Spain, underscores this meaning and purpose of the *jizya*.

114 For a discussion of these two interpretations of the conquest of Spain, see Maribel Fierro and Francisco García Fitz, eds., *El cuerpo derrotado: Cómo trataban musulmanes y cristianos a los enemigos vencidos (Península Ibérica, ss. VIII–XIII)* (Madrid: Consejo Superior de Investigaciones Científicas, 2008), 23–25. A number of Gothic lords, among them the followers of the Witiza faction, which had allied itself with the invaders, willingly accepted their dhimmitude, which allowed them to continue as Christian lords of their vast estates. Eventually, as sources both Muslim (al-Hakam) and Christian (Lucas de Tuy, Alfonso X's *Primera crónica general*) observe, these lords and their successors fell prey to the conquerors' "frauds" as the Muslim state became stronger and able to violate the terms of the submission. As the historian Jesús Lorenzo Jiménez from the Universidad Autonoma of Barcelona caustically observes: "Whoever pacts does it because he is forced to agree to a pact. No one gives up things because he wants. It is imposed on you." (Cit. Santiago Belistigoitía, "El cambio histórico de 711," *El País*, February 20, 2011.)

115 This is the soundest statement of the matter, as in Maíllo Salgado, *Acerca de la conquista árabe de Hispania*, 30. Representative of the pacts was the one through which the Visigoth lord Teodomiro ("Tudmir") submitted to Tariq. But the "peaceful pact" included the obligation of Teodomiro to pay or else (brackets are the translators'): "[Teodomiro] has agreed [surrender] terms covering seven towns.... [He has also agreed] that he will not give refuge to any of our runaway slaves, nor shelter any of our enemies, nor make anyone afraid who is safe with us, that he will not conceal information that he has acquired about [our] enemy; and that it is up to him and his people to pay one dinar every year and four *mudd* (bushels) of wheat, four *mudd* of barley, four *qist* (measures) of thickened grape juice, four *qist* of vinegar, two *qist* of honey and two *qist* of oil. Slaves pay half that." (*Christians and Moors in Spain: Volume III Arabic Sources (711–1501)*, ed. and trans. Charles Melville and Ahmad Ubaydli [Warminster: Aris & Phillips, 1992], 12–13.) In 2013 the city of Orihuela (in Murcia) *celebrated* the pact in an official commemoration: see Alejandro García Sanjuán, *La conquista islámica de la penin- sula ibérica y la tergiversación del pasado: Del catastrofismo al negacionsimo* (Madrid: Marcial

Pons Historia, 2013), 19. García Sanjuán is an advocate of the "peaceful pacts" school and he attacks the "catastrophism" of Arabists like Serafín Fanjul and historians like García Moreno (García Sanjuán, *La conquista*, 49–50). See also his "Formas de sumisión del territorio y tratamiento de los vencidos en el derecho islámico clásico," in Maribel Fierro and Francisco García Fitz eds., *El cuerpo derrotado: Cómo trataban musulmanes y cristianos a los enemigos vencidos* (Península Ibérica, Ss. VIII–XIII) (Madrid: 2008), 61–111.

116 *Chronica mozarabica* of 754, 54.

117 *Primera chrónica general*, 554.

118 John Harris Jones, ed. and trans., *Ibn Abd el-Hakem's History of the Conquest of Spain* (London: Williams & Morgate, 1858), 23; al-Hakam, 47, where Vidal Beltrán translates it with the equally awesome term "Resurrection." Al-Hakam also cites Malik as saying that during the conquest of Spain the Muslims looted the place and did many "fraudulent" things (al-Hakam, 47). The seventeenth-century historian Mohammed Ibn al-Raini al-Qayrawani quotes the phrase "End of the World" as used by Musa to describe the conquest in the translation by E. Pellisier: *Histoire de l'Afrique de Mohammed-ben-Abi-el-Raini-el-Kairouani*, trans. E. Pellisier (Paris: Imprimérie Royale, 1845), 59.

119 Ironically, the word *Istanbul*, used to eliminate the memory of the politically and religiously charged Constantinople, arises from the conquerors' mispronunciation of the Greek phrase εἰς τήν πόλι, "eesteen Pohlee," or "to the Polis!"—that is, "to *the* City!" or "to Constantinople!"

120 For the possible Greek origin of the name al-Andalus, see Joaquín Vallvé Bermejo, "El nombre de al-Andalus," *Al-Qantara* 4, no. 2 (1983): 353–55. For the origin of the name Istanbul, see previous note.

121 Nadia Abu El Haj, *Facts on the Ground: Archaeological Practice and Territorial Self-Fashioning in Israeli Society* (Chicago: University of Chicago Press, 2001), 2. Professor El Haj refers to Israeli, not Islamic, imperialism.

122 For this and the previous list of names changed by the Muslim conquerors, see Y. Aharoni, *The Land of the Bible: A Historical Geography* (London: Burns & Oates, 1979); Bat Ye'or, *The Decline of Eastern Christianity under Islam: From Jihad to Dhimmitude* (Madison: Farleigh-Dickinson University Press, 1996), 240. More than five hundred years after the Muslim conquest of their Christian city, Greeks still today refuse to call Constantinople *Istanbul*.

123 Vallvé Bermejo, "El nombre de al-Andalus," 301.

124 *Poema de Fernán González*, ed. Alonso Zamora-Vicente (Madrid: Espasa-Calpe, 1946), stanzas 146 and 176.

125 Miguel Ángel Ladero Quesada, *La formación medieval de España: Territorios, Regiones, Reinos* (Madrid: Alianza, 2004), 16.

126 Joaquín Vallvé Bermejo (citing and agreeing with Dozy), *Al-Andalus: Sociedad e instituciones* (Madrid: Real Academia de la Historia, 1999), 14n2.

127 Thus the Latin *Crónica mozárabe de 754*, especially 103, but the historian uses the name *Spania* all over the place (cf. pp. 54, 58, 68, 72, 88, and 92). The deepest treatment of the concept of "Spain" in the Spanish Middle Ages is probably José Antonio Maravall, *El concepto de España en la Edad Media* (Madrid: Instituto de Estudios Políticos, 1964), but see also Vicente A. Álvarez Palenzuela and Luis Suárez Fernández, *Historia de España: La España musulmana y los inicios de los reinos cristianos (711–1157)* (Madrid: Gredos, 1991).

128 According to the medievalist scholar Isabel Velázquez, Julian of Toledo's *Historia Wambae* is a "passionate hymn... most of all to the motherland herself, *Hispania*, as opposed to the *gentes externae, Francia*, even *Gallia*... which, though part of the *regnum*, is here denigrated and insulted by the author." "Pro patriae gentisque Gothorum stato," in H. W. Goetz, J. Jarnut, and W. Pohl, eds., *Regna and Gentes: The Relationship between Late Antique and Early Medieval Peoples and Kingdoms in the Transformation of the Roman World* (Leiden: Brill, 2003), 212.

129 Vallvé Bermejo, *Al-Andalus*, 14.

130 *Ibn Khaldoun: Les Prolegoménes d'Ibn Khaldoun*, trans. M. de Slane (Paris: Librairie orientaliste Paul Geuthner, 1934), part 1, vi–lxxxiii.

131 Al-Maqqari, in *The History of the Mohammedan Dynasties in Spain*, 1:24.

132 *The History of al-Tabari*, vol. 28, translated and annotated by Jane Dammen, 55.

133 Ibn Hayyan, *Al-Muqtabis*, 2:1, in J. Vallvé and F. Ruiz Girela, *La primera década del reinado de Al-Hakam I, según el Muqtabis II, l de Ben Hayyan de Córdoba (m. 469 h./1076 J.C.)* (Madrid: Real Academia de la Historia, 2003), 117.

134 For this and the following, see Manuel Rincón Álvarez, *Mozárabes y mozarabías* (Salamanca: Universidad de Salamanca, 2003), 195, and University of Málaga archaeologists Salvador Peña Martín and Miguel Vega Martín, "Alandalús, es decir, España," *El trujamán*, December 15, 2000, at cvc.cervantes.es/trujaman/anteriores/diciembre_00/15122000.htm.

135 For the propagandistic medieval Muslim praise of al-Andalus as a paradise, echoed by many of today's writers on Islamic Spain, see Francisco Prado-Vilar, "Circular Visions of Fertility and Punishment: Caliphal Ivory Caskets from al-Andalus," *Muqarnas* 14 (1997): 19–41.

136 Felipe Maíllo Salgado, "De los musulmanes en Asturias en el alto Medievo: Inciertos pactos, efímera presencia," in Juan Ignacio Ruiz de la Peña and Jorge Camino Mayor, eds., *La Carisa y La Mesa, Causas políticas y militares del origen del Reino de Asturias* (Oviedo: Asociación de Amigos de La Carisa: 2010), 187. See also his *Acerca de la conquista árabe de Hispania*, where he argues that Muslims never conquered the Spanish Northwest.

137 Ibn Idhari al-Marrakushi, *Al-Bayano 'l-Mogrib*, 19–20.

138 *El Cid and the Reconquista: 1050–1492* (London: Osprey, 1988), 4. But the practice of slave warriors had started and been perfected by the Umayyads. See the classic by the historian of Islam Daniel Pipes, *Slave Soldiers and Islam: The Genesis of a Military* System (New Haven, CT: Yale University Press, 1981).

139 See Patricia Crone, *Slaves on Horses: The Evolution of the Islamic Polity* (Cambridge: Cambridge University Press, 1980), 50; see also Pipes, *Slave Soldiers and Islam*.

140 For this and the following, see *El Cid and the Reconquista* as well as Felipe Maíllo Salgado, *De la desaparición de al-Andalus* (Madrid: Abada, 2011); Pierre Guichard, *Al-Andalus frente a la conquista cristiana: Los musulmanes de Valencia, siglos XI al XIII* (Valencia: Universidad de Valencia, 2001), 43, 60, 135, 328, 381, 391, 533, 596. Another excellent up-to-date examination of the concept of *Reconquista* is Francisco García Fitz, "La Reconquista: un estado de la cuestión," *Clio y Crimen*, no. 6 (2009): 142–215, available online at https://www.durango-udala.net/portalDurango/RecursosWeb/DOCUMENTOS/1/2_1945_6.pdf.

141 An excellent summary and analysis of the debate over the use of the word *Reconquista* and also of this word's connection with the Christian medieval concept of just war is given by historian Francisco García Fitz, *Las Navas de Tolosa* (Madrid: Ariel, 2008), 393–403. His conclusion seems eminently valid: "In our judgment, independently of the posture one adopts in this debate, what seems incontestable is that in the Christian kingdoms of the peninsula, from very early on, was elaborated an ideological construction, to which, because of its content, it does not seem outlandish to call *Reconquista*, and which was configured as a system of mental representations and moral, religious, political, and juridical values at the service of such an expansion [*Reconquista*]" (p. 398, my translation).

142 *Ibn Khaldūn: Histoire des Berbères*, 2:79–80. Among the *ulama* who supported the takeover was the great philosopher al-Ghazali. The *taifa* rulers, much liked by today's Western historians, taxed their subjects relentlessly and frequently did not keep other Islamic teachings, which included not drinking wine and not allying oneself with infidels.

143 Amira K. Bennison and María Ángeles Gallego, "Religious Minorities under the Almohads: An Introduction," *Journal of Medieval Iberian Studies* 2, no. 2 (2010): 151.

144 Felipe Maíllo Salgado, *De la desaparición de al-Andalus* (Madrid: Abada, 2011).

145 The best work on this battle is Fitz, *Las Navas de Tolosa*. Most of the Christian volunteers from the rest of Europe, initially numbering in the thousands, abandoned the crusade before the battle, mistrusting the intentions of Alfonso VIII (who appeared to them more interested in gaining territory without losing fighters than in killing Muslims) and suffering under the intense summer heat and the scarcity of supplies. Contrary to what some English scholars

seem to believe, the king of León did not participate in the battle on the side of the Almohads or anyone else for that matter. No Muslim troops are recorded as having fought on the side of the Christians.

146 This approach has also been adopted by the Spanish Church: in May 2004, the Church authorities at the Cathedral of Santiago de Compostela decided to remove the statue of Santiago Matamoros (Saint James the Moor-Slayer) from its place in the cathedral, send it to the cathedral's museum, and replace it with a statue of Santiago as a pilgrim. The reason was to make Santiago's image fit "the teachings of Christ" and avoid offending "the sensitivities of other ethnic groups." See "Church to Remove Moor-Slayer Saint," BBC News, May 3, 2004. The announcement was welcomed by members of the Muslim community as "a step towards peace," in the words of Houssam El Mahmudi, president of the Association of Moroccan Students in Santiago. But the announcement provoked an outcry from Spanish Catholics. As a result, the Church backtracked and decided to keep the statue in its place for the "foreseeable future." See "Public Outcry Forces Church to Keep Moor Slayer's Statue," Telegraph, July 22, 2004.

147 R. Burns, "Muslims in the Thirteenth-Century Realms of Aragon: Interaction and Reaction," in J. Powell, ed., Muslims under Latin Rule, 1100–1300 (Princeton, NJ: Princeton University Press, 1990), 77.

148 The word mudéjar did not appear in written Spanish until the second half of the fifteenth century. According to Isidoro de las Cagigas, mudéjar meant simply "tributary" for the Spaniards of the time. But it derives from the Arabic dadjin, said of an animal that is "domesticated" or "submissive." In fact, Muslims referred to those Muslims who had willingly accepted the domination of the Unbelievers as al-dadjn, and mudajjan—that is, "domesticated." Thus mudéjar, derived from mudajjan, means "tamed" or "domesticated." For all this, see Gerard Wiegers, Islamic Literature in Spanish and Aljamiado: Yva of Segovia (fl.1450), His Antecedents and Successors (Leiden: Brill, 1994), 3, and Hans Wehr, A Dictionary of Modern Written Arabic (Wiesbaden: Harrasowitz, 1979), 314. Indeed, some Maliki jurists considered mudéjares vile for their willingness to remain under Unbeliever rule: Kathryn A. Miller, "Muslim Minorities and the Obligation to Emigrate to Islamic Territory: Two Fatwas from Fifteenth-Century Granada," Islamic Law and Society 7, no. 2 (2000): 258. For P. Chalmeta, mudéjar also means simply "tributary": "Mudéjar," Encyclopaedia of Islam, Second Edition, ed. P. Bearman (Brill, 2012), BrillOnline, Northwestern University Library, accessed July 18, 2012, www.encislam. brill.nl.turing.library.northwestern.edu/subscriber/entry?entry=islam_COM-0772. None of these scholars mention that the sixteenth-century Suma de los principales mandamientos y devedamientos de la ley y çunna, por don Içe de Gebir, Alfaquí Mayor de la aljama de Sego via: Año de 1492, also tells Muslims not to live in the land of infidels: Dos tratados de legislación musulmana. 1: Leyes de moros del siglo XIV 2: Suma de los principales mandamientos y devedamientos de la ley y çunna, por don Içe de Gebir, Alfaquí Mayor de la aljama de Segovia: Año de 1492, ed. Pascual de Gayangos (Madrid: Academia de la Historia, Memorial histórico español, 1853), 5:251.

149 An academic historian generally sympathetic to mudéjares and moriscos admits that "many mudejars harbored sentiments of allegiance to the wider Islamic world.... Ottoman victories in the East raised a faint glimmer of hope that Granada might be saved and Islamic rule reestablished.... Thus they offered the Turks their support in the unlikely event of an invasion of Spain." And there were "mudejar extremists" who offered their support to the North African Muslim pirates. See Mark D. Meyerson, The Muslims of Valencia in the Age of Fernando and Isabel (Berkeley: University of California Press, 1990), 81–82.

150 See the contemporary documents included by the Arabist Serafín Fanjul in his Al-Andalus contra España: La forja del mito (Madrid: Siglo XXI, 2005), 263–66.

151 Cervantes has one of his characters mention this fear of their high birth rate in his novel El coloquio de los perros. In 1612 the scholar Pedro Aznar de Cardona wrote, "[The moriscos] married their children at a tender age, it seeming to them perfectly fine for the female to be eleven years

of age and the male twelve to get married. They did not care much about having a dowry before getting married for (except the rich among them) they were content with a bed of clothes and ten pounds of money. Their intention was to grow and multiply like weeds, and truly they had managed it so well that they overflowed their neighborhoods and towns and expanded everywhere and contaminated everything, very anxious to see fulfilled those words in a song of theirs that I have heard sing, in which they ask Muhammad to favor their growth.... And they indeed grew because no one stayed single or became a [celibate] priest, or friar, or nun.... All got married, the poor and the rich, the healthy and the lame, not like the Old Christians, who if they have five or six children, they are happy to marry the eldest son or daughter, and have the others become priests, or nuns, or soldiers." Fanjul, *Al-Andalus contra España*, 285. One of Cervantes's characters in his novel *El coloquio de los perros* also criticizes the *moriscos*' high birth rate and the danger they posed for the integrity of Spain. Today's debates on the subject, such as the possibility of a Eurabia, echo these seventeenth-century fears. But even some conservative authors dismiss them, such as Fox News commentator and "strategic consultant" Ralph Peters, former U.S. Army lieutenant colonel: see Peters, "The Eurabia Myth: Muslims Take Over Europe? Sorry, No Chance," *New York Post*, November 26, 2006.

152 For Cervantes's views on Islam, see Darío Fernández-Morera, "Cervantes and Islam: A Contemporary Analogy," in Robert Lauer and Kurt Reichenberger, ed., *Cervantes y su Mundo 3* (Kassell: Reichenberger, 2005), 126–66, at http://books.google.com/books?id=NQz5W94fbys C&pg=PA123&lpg=PA137&ots=WAirwAnr1G&dq=christians+enslaved+cantigas&ie=ISO8 8591&output=html.

CHAPTER 2: THE EFFECTS OF THE *JIHAD*

1   According to al-Tabari, Caliph Uthman (ca. 579–656) declared: "Only through Spain can Constantinople be conquered. If then you conquer [Spain], you will share the reward of those who conquer Constantinople"; see *The History of al-Tabari*, translated and annotated by R. Stephen Humphreys (New York: State University of New York Press, 1990), 15:22. Al-Tabari also recounts this statement by Kab al-Ahbar, a Jewish convert to Islam who served as counselor to Caliph Uthman: "They [who cross the sea to conquer Spain] will be known by their radiance on the Day of Resurrection." The belief that the conquest of Constantinople would happen via al-Andalus was common among Arabic historians: see Sais al-Andalusi in *Kitab al-Tarij*, ed. Jorge Aguadé (Madrid: CSIC, 1991), 92n56. Unaware of these texts, Manuela Marín cites other Muslim historians who echo this connection between the conquest of Spain and that of Constantinople: "Constantinopla en los geógrafos árabes," *Erytheia* 9, no. 1 (1988): 53 and n27.

2   Joseph Cardinal Ratzinger, "Perspectivas y tareas del catolicismo en la actualidad y de cara al futuro," A.A. V.V. eds., *El Concilio III de Toledo: XIV Centenario 589–1989* (Toledo: Arzobispado de Toledo, 1991), 107. On the importance of the Visigoth tradition for the spirit of the Reconquest, see J. I. Ruiz de la Peña, "La monarquía asturiana (718–918)," in *El reino de León en la Alta Edad Media. III: La monarquía asturleonesa. De Pelayo a Alfonso VI. 718–1109* (León: Centro de Estudios e Investigación, San Isidoro, 1995), 120–27. For the concept *Spain* originating in Visigoth Spain, see among many José Antonio Maravall, *El concepto de España en la Edad Media* (1954; rpt. Madrid: Centro de Estudios Constitucionales, 1997), 299–337; Adeline Rucquoi, "Les Wisigoths fondement de la nation Espagne," *L'Europe Héritière de l'Espagne Wisigothique*, ed. Jacques Fontaine and Christine Pellistrandi (Madrid: Rencontres de la Casa de Velázquez, 1992), 341–52.

3   Peter S. Wells, *Barbarians to Angels* (New York: W. W. Norton, 2008). The technical innovations of the "Dark Ages" are no less impressive than its preservation of a great deal of the classical heritage by the monks in their monasteries. See also James Hannam, *The Genesis of Science: How the Christian Middle Ages Launched the Scientific Revolution* (Washington, DC: Regnery Publishing Inc., 2011).

4   Among many works on the role the Goths played in building Western civilization, see Chris-
     topher Dawson, *The Making of Europe: An Introduction to the History of European Unity* (1932;
     rpt. Washington, DC: The Catholic University of America Press, 2003), and *Religion and the
     Rise of Western Culture* (New York: Sheed &Ward, 1950); Jacques Fontaine and Christine Pel-
     listrandi, eds., *L'Europe héritière de l'espagne wisigothique: Colloque international du C.N.R.S.*
     (Madrid: Rencontres de la Case de Velazquez, 1992). Traditionally the Visigoths have been
     regarded as a Germanic people though not part of the history of what today are called "the
     Germans." The view of the Visigoths as a Germanic people (but again not part of the history
     of what today are called "Germans") with many other ethnic Indo-European elements in it
     ("polyethnic") is formulated by Herwig Wolfram, *Geschichte der Goten* (Munich: Beck, 1979),
     translated as *History of the Goths* (Berkeley: University of California Press, 1988), and *Die
     Goten: Von den Anfängen bis zur Mitte des 6. Jahrhunderts. Versuch einer historischen Eth-
     nographie*, 3rd ed. (Munich: Beck, 1990). See also Peter Heather, ed., *The Visigoths: From the
     Migration Period to the Seventh Century, an Ethnographic Perspective* (Woodbridge: Boydell
     Press, 1999). For the possibly Baltic (but not Scandinavian) rather than Germanic origin of
     the Visigoths, see Jurate Rosales, *Los Godos* (Barcelona: Ariel, 2004), trans. *Goths and Balts*
     (Chicago: Vydino Fondas, 2004); "El idioma que hablaron los godos," *La Torre del Virrey* n3,
     Serie 6 (February 2010), Valencia, Spain: 1–12; "Las cuatro mentiras sobre los godos," Preprint
     of Universidad de Los Andes, Facultad de Letras y Educación, Mérida, Venezuela (July 2,
     2000), 1 26. For the Spanish historian Pío Moa, the Visigoths may have come from Scandi-
     navia before wandering in eastern and central Europe: "¿Qué debe España a los Visigodos?"
     Libertad Digital, October 14, 2009.
5   Gisela Ripoll and Eduardo Carrera, "Art wisigoth en *Hispania*: en quête d'une révision néces-
     saire," *Perspective* 2 (June 2009): 256, 267.
6   Amancio Isla Frez, "Reinas de los Godos," *Hispania* 44/2, no. 217 (2014): 409–33.
7   *The Visigothic Code (Forum Iudicum)*, ed. and trans. S. P. Scott (The Library of Iberian Resources
     Online, accessed January 8, 2015). I have not seen any work on the Visigoths that quotes these
     important words from the Visigoth Code. All the laws of the Visigoths through the centuries can
     be found in *Leges visigothorum* (In *Monumenta Germaniae Historica* LL nat. Germ. I, 1), ed. Karl
     Zeumer (Hannover/Leipzig: 1902). The antipathy to government power among the ancient Ger-
     manic nations was noticed by Roman historian Tacitus ca. A.D. 98 in his *De origine et situ germa-
     norum* (chapters 7, 11, and 13). Ironically, Tacitus's work (commonly known as *De Germania*) was
     used by the National Socialists in their propaganda, overlooking not only that "Germanic" was
     not exactly the equivalent of today's "Germans" but also the contradiction between the ancient
     Germans' love of freedom and the totalitarian control of the citizenry by the National Socialist
     system. For a critique of the National Socialists' use of Tacitus, see, among others, Kristopher B.
     Krebs, *A Most Dangerous Book: Tacitus' Germania from the Roman Empire to the Third Reich* (New
     York: W. W. Norton, 2012). The Visigoths' love of freedom was also their weakness. The Visigoth
     monarchy was not hereditary but elective. Like the barons who imposed the Magna Carta on
     King John in England many centuries later, the Visigoth nobles were suspicious of royal power
     and contributed to the instability of the monarchy. But they went beyond the English barons, to
     the point of supporting not only usurpers but also foreign invaders (in which unruliness some
     ecclesiastics participated, such as Oppas and Elipando). Among the best English-language stud-
     ies of the subject, see Roger Collins's *Visigothic Spain, 409–711* (Oxford: Blackwell, 2004), which
     exemplifies the tendency of English historiography to downplay Hispano-Roman-Visigoth cul-
     ture and to overlook making a comparison, which would be favorable to Visigoth Spain, with the
     level of culture of other parts of the world at the time, such as Muslim Arabia. The Visigothic Code
     forbade abortion under severe penalty: Hispano-Romans and Visigoths would have been horri-
     fied at a culture that declares it a "constitutional" right for a pregnant woman to have her unborn
     child killed and to donate the body parts of the little cadaver for medical research, and that allows
     commercial films making abortion a praiseworthy act (cf. the Hollywood movie *Grandma*). The
     best books on life in Visigoth Spain are José Orlandis, *La vida en España en tiempo de los godos*

(Madrid: Rialp, 1991), and his *Historia del reino visigodo español* (Madrid: Rialp, 2003). For the Visigoths' effort to present themselves as inheritors and defenders of the Roman Empire, see Federico-Mario Beltrán Torreira, "El concepto de barbarie en la hispania visigoda," *Antigüedad y cristianismo* 3 (1986): 56–57; Salvador Caramunt, *Historia de la Edad Media* (Barcelona: Ariel, 1995), 19; Maria R. Valverde Castro, *Ideología, simbolismo y ejercicio del poder real en la monarquía visigoda* (Salamanca: Universidad de Salamanca, 2000), 155–56. Visigoth monarchs even adopted the purple vestments and the crown of the Roman emperors, and as late as 578, coins issued by King Leovigild had on one side the king's name and on the other the name of the emperor of the Greek Roman Empire in Constantinople (the only surviving Roman empire): Jesús Vico and María Cruz Cors, "La moneda visigoda," *Gaceta numismática*, no. 169 (June 2008): 25–26.

8   *The Muwatta of Imam Malik narrated by Yahya B. Yahya B. Kathir al-Laith al-Andalusi*, trans. F. Amira Zrien Matraji, corrected and revised by Dr. Mahmood Matraji (Karachi: Darul Ishaat, 2005), bk. 17, 24.46; Malik appears to be following Quran 9:29. I use the version of the *Muwatta* compiled by Malik's student from Córdoba, Yahya al-Laithi.

9   Isidro G. Bango Torviso, *Alta Edad Media: de la tradición hispanogoda al románico* (Madrid: Silex, 1989), 52.

10   According to *al-Makkari*, vol. 1, app. D, xlv. Both Muslim and Catholic chronicles attribute Count Julian's treason to his desire for revenge after King Rodrigo violated his daughter. Today's historians usually dismiss this reason as legend, overlooking the importance of family honor in those long-gone times.

11   Ibid., xlviii–xlix.

12   Ibid., li.

13   *Chronica mozarabica*, chap. 2, 56.

14   *Ibn Abd al-Hakam, Conquista de África del Norte y de España*, trans. Eliseo Vidal Beltrán (Valencia: Anubar, 1966), 47.

15   *Crónica del moro Rasis*, ed. Diego Catalán y María Soledad de Andrés (Madrid: Gredos, 1975), 354–57; for what follows, see 64.

16   Al-Maqqari in *The History of the Mohammedan Dynasties in Spain by Ahmed Ibn Mohammed al-Makkari*, trans. Pascual de Gayangos (1840; rpt. New York: Johnson Reprint Corporation, 1964), 1:79.

17   *Historia de la conquista de España de Abenalcotía el cordobés*, trans. Julián Ribera (Madrid: Archivos, 1926), 114–15.

18   *Ajbar Machmua*, trans. Emilio Lafuente y Alcántara (1867; rpt. Madrid: Bibliófilo, 1984), 20. The enormous looting and enslavement is echoed in all the Muslim histories. Thus, for example, the seventeenth-century history by al-Raini al-Qayrawani, which uses much earlier sources: *Histoire de l'Afrique de Mohammed-ben-Abi-el-Raini-el-Kairouani*, trans. E. Pellisier (Paris: Imprimerie Royale, 1845), 59–60.

19   *Al-Makkari*, 1:207.

20   Ibn Koteybah Ad-dinawari, *Traditional Stories of Relating to Supreme Commanders and Wise Rulers*, in *al-Makkari*, vol. 1, app. E, lxxviii–lxxix.

21   Jaime Cobreros, *Guía del prerrománico en España: Visigodo; Asturiano; Mozárabe* (Madrid: Anaya, 2005), 39. This "table" is part of the legend according to which the Table of Solomon ended up in Spain after the destruction of the Jewish Temple.

22   *Al-Makkari*, 2:6.

23   For this and the following, see Ibn Idhari in *Al-Bayano 'l-Mogrib*, translated and annotated by Edmond Fagnan (Algiers: Imprimérie Orientale Pierre Fonatana, 1904), 25.

24   Manuel Rincón Álvarez, *Mozárabes y mozarabías* (Salamanca: Universidad de Salamanca, 2003), 192–93. Leandro, Julian, Braulio, Isidoro, and Ildefonso are some of the best-known representatives of this culture. If around 100,000 warriors entered Spain, and if one postulates four relatives to each warrior, we have nearly half a million Visigoths entering Spain in the fifth and sixth centuries (when the entire population moved to Spain after the Visigoths were defeated by the Franks), not the 200,000 that historians often mention.

25 *Al-Makkari*, 2:413, n18. Here and elsewhere I give Gayangos's transcription of the names cited in *al-Makkari*.

26 *Les Prolégomènes d'Ibn Khaldoun*, trans. M. De Slane (Paris: Librairie Orientaliste Paul Geuthner, 1938), 2:6.

27 *Les Prolégomènes d'Ibn Khaldoun*, 3:300.

28 Antoine Fattal, *Le Statu légal des non-musulmans en pays d'Islam* (Beyrut: Imprimérie Catholique, 1958), 240.

29 *Muqaddimah*, abridged trans. Franz Rosenthal (Princeton, NJ: Princeton University Press, 1967), 2:39, 429–30.

30 *Les Prolégomènes d'Ibn Khaldoun*, 3:126.

31 Carl B. Boyer and Uta C. Merzbach, *A History of Mathematics, Second Edition* (New York: John Wiley and Sons, 1991), 178ff.

32 *The Growth of Mathematics: From Counting to Calculus*, ed. Robert W. Marks (New York: Batamb Books, 1964), 104.

33 Marks, *The Growth of Mathematics*, 94–96.

34 For Sarton's statements, see his "Archimedes and Apollonius" in Marks, *The Growth of Mathematics*, 112, 124.

35 Cit. Saint John of Damascus, *Writings: The Fount of Knowledge*, trans. Frederick H. Chase (Washington, DC: The Catholic University of America Press, 1958), ix–x. "Al-Walid was not so lenient with his Christian subjects as his predecessors had been and in particular he imposed restrictions upon the Christian officials. The harsh policy of al-Walid towards the Christians may have been the determining factor in [St. John Damascene's] decision to embrace the monastic life" (xii). Caliph Al-Walid II (d. 744) ordered that the tongue of Peter, Metropolitan of Damascus, be cut out because he had preached against iconoclasm and therefore Islam.

36 George Makdisi, "Scholasticism and Humanism in Classical Islam and the Christian West," *Journal of the American Oriental Society* 109, no. 2 (1982): 176. See also Makdisi, "Madrasa and University in the Middle Ages," *Studia Islamica* 32 (1970): 255–54. In the fifth century the best centers of learning were in the academies of the Christian Greek Roman Empire, especially in Constantinople and Alexandria. As the scholar Robert Browning points out, after the Arabs conquered Alexandria in the seventh century, the focus of learning in the empire was in Constantinople. But the structure of the medieval Greek "universities" was not like that of the Latin universities of the West. "The medieval Greek world knew no autonomous...institutions of higher education comparable to the Latin universities of the later Middle Ages in Western Europe. But higher education, both general and professional, was provided by private teachers, by members of professional groups, and by officially appointed teachers paid by the state." See Robert Browning, "Universities, Byzantine," *Dictionary of the Middle Ages* (New York: Scribner, 1989), 12:300. This system was also copied by the Arabs as the similar structure of the *madrasas* indicates: see André Godard, "L'origine de la madrasa, de la mosquée et du caravainsérail à quatre iwans," *Ars Islamica* 15/16 (1951): 1–9. Al-Azhar, the famous university in Cairo, was initially a *madrasa* and evolved into a university only in the nineteenth century under European influence. See Jakob Skovgaard-Petersen, "Al-Azhar, Modern Period," *Encyclopaedia of Islam* (Leiden: Brill, 2010). George Makdisi is clear on the matter: "The university as a form of organisation owes nothing to Islam. Indeed, Islam could have nothing to do with the university as a corporation. Based on the [Western] concept of juristic personality, the corporation is an abstraction endowed with legal rights and responsibilities. Islamic law recognizes the physical person alone as endowed with legal personality. The university was a new product, completely separate from the Greek academies of Athens and Alexandria, and from the Christian cathedral and monastic schools; and it was utterly foreign to the Islamic experience." *The Rise of Colleges: Institutions of Learning in Islam and the West* (Edinburgh: Edinburgh University Press, 1981), 224–25. The first true university in the world was in Bologna, founded in 1088.

37 *Al-Makkari* vol. 1, app. A, xxiv–xxv. For the general phenomenon of Greek scientific knowledge passing from the Christian Greeks to the Muslims, see Dimitri Gutas, *Greek Thought*,

Arabic Culture: The Graeco-Arabic Translation Movement in Baghdad and Early 'Abbasid Society (2nd–4th/8th–10th centuries) (London: Routledge, 1998); De Lacy O'Leary, *How Greek Science Passed to the Arabs* (London: Routledge, 1949); F. Rosenthal, *The Classical Heritage in Islam* (London: Routledge, 1975). For the transmission of Aristotelian logic from Greek Christians in the Middle East to Muslims, see "History of Logic," *Encyclopedia Britannica Online*, March 17, 2011, at http://www.britannica.com/EBchecked/topic/346217/historyoflogic.

38 For a characteristic example—the Greek Christian commentaries, summaries, and compendia on the classical Greek works of Galen—see Judith T. Irvine, "Who Was Akilaos? A Problem in Medical Historiography," *Bulletin of the History of Medicine* 77, no. 1 (Spring 2003): 12–24. Greek scholarship learned by Muslims in the Middle East extended to linguistic matters: see the influence of Greek thought on Arabic linguistic writings in C. H. M. Verstecgh, *Greek Elements in Arabic Linguistic Thinking* (Leiden: Brill, 1977). The texts of philosophers from the Greek Roman Empire, such as John Philoponus (490–570), also fell into Muslim hands. An author, completely disgusted by Christian medieval Europe and enchanted by the greatness of Muslim civilization, observes, "The fourth Umayyad Caliph, Marwan I, ordered the translation…of the famous medical treatise of Aaron of Alexandria. The translation of medical literature was in fact a principal aspect of the scientific progress that distinguished the rule of the Umayyads." Gene W. Heck, *When Worlds Collide: Exploring the Ideological Foundations of the Clash of Civilizations* (Lanham, MD: Rowman & Littlefield, 2007), 28. According to a 2007 National Center for Policy Analysis site, Mr. Heck has a PhD from the University of Michigan and "served as a U.S. Army Military Intelligence Officer for many years, with U.S. Army reserve tours in Ethiopia, Turkey and Jordan. Due to his skill in mastering the Arabic language, he spent a good deal of his time in the Middle East, where he still resides today. Throughout his career, Dr. Heck has won several national awards for the design of state and local economic development programs. Currently he is a senior business development economist operating in Saudi Arabia and throughout the Middle East. He also serves as adjunct professor of government and history with the University of Maryland."

39 *Al-Makkari*, vol. 1, app. B, xxxiv.

40 Julio Samsó, *Las ciencias de los antiguos en al-Andalus* (Almería: Fundación Ibn Tufayl de Estudios Árabes, 2011), 128–29. Samsó argues that the relative rupture with the culture of the East that takes place after the collapse of the Caliphate of Córdoba accounts for the scientific decay of al-Andalus after the eleventh century (123). Many Andalusian Muslim scientists, such as the physician Arib Ibn Said, came from formerly Christian families or were outright converts, as Reinhardt Dozy observed: cit. Ann Christys, *Christians in al-Andalus* (Oxford: Routledge, 2002), 124. The astrolabe, often attributed to al-Andalus, is a Greek invention (αστρολαβος), and the mariner's astrolabe was invented by the Christian friar, philosopher, and inventor Ramon Lull in 1295.

41 Basilio Pavón Maldonado, "Influjos occidentales en el califato de Córdoba," *Al-Andalus* 33, no. 1 (1968): 206. This is the pioneering article on this curiously neglected subject. See also Sylvain Gouguenheim, *Aristote au Mont Saint-Michel*.

42 Isidro Bango Torviso, *Alta Edad Media: De la tradición hispanogoda al románico* (Editorial Silex, 1989), 12. In the mosque of Córdoba (on the site of the former Catholic church of Saint Vincent, torn down to build the mosque), one can still see in the southern part Greek-made mosaics, among other things. As early as 687 the famous Dome of the Rock in Jerusalem replicated Greek and Roman techniques.

43 I thought I had been the first to point this out, in an earlier version of this chapter, but then Horgel Michiels e-mailed me saying that it had already been noticed, as indeed it was, by Ernest T. Dewald, "The Appearance of the Horseshoe Arch in Western Europe," *American Journal of Archaeology* 26, no. 3 (July–September 1922): 316–37.

44 That the Muslim conquerors adopted the Visigoth horseshoe arch is common knowledge among Spanish art historians, though Arabists and historians of Islamic art regularly ignore

it. For remaining examples of the Visigoth horseshoe arch, see among others the church of San Juan de Baños. These horseshoe arches have a peralte of one half of the radius of the circumference, as does the "Muslim" arch—or, put otherwise, the stones that form the arch go over the 180 degrees of the imaginary circumference of the arch. No Catholic churches were left in southern Spain after the Muslim tide retreated.

45 Ibn Khaldun, *The Muqaddimah: An Introduction to History*, trans. Franz Rosenthal (New York: Pantheon, 1958), 2:267, 269.

46 Isidro Bango Torviso, "711/842. Siglo y medio de la cultura material de la España cristiana desde la invasión. Musulmanes y cristianos determinantes de una mistificación 'históricocultural' que no cesa," *Anales de la Historia del Arte* 22, num. especial 2 (2012): 65.

47 Claudio Sánchez Albornoz, "Espagne pré-islamique et Espagne musulmane," *Revue Historique* 237 (1967): 316.

48 According to Ibn Said, following Ibn Khaldun, in Manuel Gómez Moreno, "El Kitab al-Muqtataf Min Azahir al-Turaf de Ibn Said," *Al-Andalus* 13, no. 1 (1948): 28–31. Even what was noticeable in Spain of "Muslim music" (theoretically an oxymoron, given the medieval Maliki school of Islamic law's prohibition of music) may have owed much of its existence to the conquered civilizations. Malik Ibn Anas, founder of Malikism, forbade music and singing. The *Historia de los jueces de Córdoba* by al-Khushani (d. 971?) shows the attitude under the Umayyads of the most respected Córdoban Maliki *ulama* toward music: *Historia de los jueces de Córdoba por Alxojaní*, trans. Julián Ribera (1914; rpt. Madrid: Renacimiento, 2005), 89. For Malik's opposition to music, see also the testimony of al-Ghazali in Duncan B. Macdonald, "Emotional Religion in Islam as Affected by Music and Singing: Being a Translation of a Book of the Ihya Ulum al-Din of al-Ghazali with Analisis, Annotation, and Appendices," *Journal of the Royal Asiatic Society* (1901): 201 and n2. It was a musician from a conquered civilization, the Persian Ziryab (d. 857), who is said to have brought music to the Umayyad court, but to be played by slaves. Even earlier in Arabia, music may have developed upon the onset of Islam because of the Arabs' conquests; extant sources point to foreign influence, from the Christian Greek Roman Empire to Persia: see Irfan Shahid, *Byzantium and the Arabs in the Sixth Century* (Washington, DC: Dumbarton Oaks Research Library and collection, 1995), vol. 2, pt. 2, p. 184. "Music being a science almost unknown to the Arabs before their conquests, they necessarily borrowed from the subdued nations their knowledge of it, as well as the names of almost all their instruments": Pascual de Gayangos, in his translation of al-Maqqari's *History of the Muhammedan Dynasties in Spain*, 1:365n17 (see 58–59).

49 For this and what follows, see *al-Makkari*, 1:217–18. Catholics had to give up the church after receiving an offer from Abd al-Rahman that they could not refuse and then had to build a new church on the outskirts of the city. As Pedro Marfil and others have pointed out, the idea that the Muslims initially "shared" the church with the Christians is a myth. No churches remained within the city that could challenge the mosque of Córdoba. Interestingly, the University of Córdoba website avoids mentioning that Abd al-Rahman I took over and destroyed the ancient Catholic church of Saint Vincent to build his mosque: "Abd al-Rahman I (756–788) began construction on the Mosque on the site of the former Visigothic Basilica of San Vicente (Saint Vincent) dating c. 584." And that is all the university site has to say about it. The myth of Islamic tolerance remains untouched. See http://www.uco.es/internacionalcoopera/ ori/english/walkCórdoba.html.

50 Manuel Gómez Moreno, *Iglesias mozárabes: Arte español de los siglos IX a XI* (Madrid: Junta para ampliación de estudios. Centro de estudios históricos, 1919), 6; Pedro Marfil, "La basílica de San Vicente: En la Catedral de Córdoba," *Arte, arqueología e historia* (2007): 185–96, n14; "Córdoba de Teodosio a Abd al-Rahman III," *Anejos de AespA XXIII* (2000), 127–29; Patrice Cressier, "Les chapiteaux de la Grande Mosquée de Cordoue," *Madrider Mitteilungen* 25 (1994): 257–313. Almanzor further expanded the mosque using Catholic slaves and materials captured in his raids of Catholic territory.

51 Al-Andalusi, *Kitab*, 125–26.

52 Manuel C. Díaz y Díaz, "Les arts libéraux d'après les écrivains espagnols et insulaires au VIIe et VIIIe siécles," *Arts Libéraux et Philosophie au Moyen Âge: Actes du Quatrième Congrés International de Philosophie Médievale* (Montreal: Institut D'Études Médiévales, 1969), 37–46; "Noticias históricas en dos himnos litúrgicos visigóticos," *Antigüedad y cristianismo,* no. 3 (1986): 443–56; Jacques Fontaine, *Isidore de Séville et la culture classique dans l'Espagne wisigothique* (Paris: Études agustiniennes, 1959); "Grammaire sacrée et grammaire profane: Isidore de Seville devant l'exégèse biblique," *Antigüedad y cristianismo,* no. 3 (1986): 311–29; Fontaine and Pellistrandi, *L'Europe héritière de l'espagne wisigothique.* Scholars today who call Isidore "naive," "ignorant," and even "stupid" lack historical perspective.

53 Pedro Marfil, "La sede episcopal de San Vicente en la Santa Iglesia Catedral de Córdoba," *Al-Mulk: Anuario de estudios arabistas,* no. 6 (2006): 35–58. Tour guides, tourists, and many Spaniards, even scholars, continue to refer, contrary to fact, to the Cathedral of Córdoba as a "mosque."

54 See "Recópolis" at the site of the Amigos del Arte Altomedieval Español: http://www.turismo-prerromanico.com/es/visigodo/monumento/recpolis-20130212105615/, and Luis A. García Moreno, *Leovigildo: Unidad y diversidad de un reinado* (Madrid: Real Academia de la Historia, 2008), 83–84. Recópolis is the only known Visigoth-founded city that uses the Greek word *polis* (city) as a suffix: I suspect this is part of the conscious imitation of the capital of the Greek Roman Empire, Constantinopolis (Κωνσταντινουπολις).

55 See Jesús Carrobles Santos, Rafael Barroso Cabrera, Jorge Morín de Pablos, and Fernando Valdés Fernández, *Regia Sedes Toletana: La topografía de la ciudad de Toledo en la antigüedad tardía y alta edad media* (Toledo: Real Fundación de Toledo, 2007), 217.

56 García Moreno, *Leovigildo*; Javier Martínez Jiménez, "The Continuity of Roman Water Supply Systems in Post-Roman Spain: The Case of Valentia, a Reliable Example?" *ArkeoGazte,* no. 1 (2011): 125–44; Javier Martínez Jiménez, "De formis urbium gothorum. Los acueductos en el período tardorromano y visigodo: continuidad e impacto en el urbanismo," *Jornadas de Investigadores Predoctorales en Ciencias de la Antigüedad y de la Edad Media* (Barcelona: Universidad Autónoma de Barcelona, October 29, 2010), at http://www.academia.edu/1007534/The_continuity_of_Roman_water_supply_systems_in_post-Roman_Spain_the_case_of_Valentia_a_reliable_example.

57 Miguel Alba Calzado, "La vivienda en Emérita durante la antigüedad tardía: propuesta de un modelo para *Hispania,*" *VI Reunió d'arqueologia cristiana hispánica. Les ciutats tardoantigues d'Hispania. Cristianizació e topografía* (Barcelona: University of Barcelona, 2005), 139; Rafael Hidalgo Prieto, "Algunas cuestiones sobre la *Corduba* de la antigüedad tardía," *VI Reunió d'arqueologia cristiana hispánica,* 404. See also Pedro Mateos Cruz "El paisaje urbano de Mérida en torno al año 711," at http://www.academia.edu/3532436/El_paisaje_urbano_de_M%C3%A9rida_en_torno_al_a%C3%B1o_711.

58 Jan M. Ziolkowski, *Nota Bene: Reading Classics and Writing Melodies in the Early Middle Ages* (Turnhout: Brepols, 2007), 199; *Columbia History of Western Philosophy,* ed. Richard Henry Popkin (New York: Columbia University Press, 1999), 230–44. For the continuing reception of Greek texts in Europe, independently of their mediation through Arabic, see the important Sylvain Gougenheim, *Aristote au mont Saint-Michel: Les racines grecques de l'Europe chrétienne* (Paris: Seuil, 2008). I believe that the "Mozarabic" Catholic ritual, which was nothing but the surviving Hispanic rite used in Visigoth Spain, echoed the ritual of the Greek Orthodox Church, which was its contemporary before the Gregorian reform of the rite made the Latin ritual noticeably different from the Greek. Therefore the sounds of the Mozarabic rite that some people associate with Arabic music are actually redolent of those of Greek Orthodox Church rituals.

59 Dag Norberg, *Manuel pratique de latin médiéval* (Paris: Picard, 1968), trans. R. H. Johnson, http://homepages.wmich.edu/~johnsorh/MedievalLatin/Norberg/spain.html.

60 *Al-Makkari,* 1:77. The cultural superiority of Catholic Spain over a North Africa sacked by the Islamic conquests, and the pull that Spain doubtlessly exerted over the Berbers, would

actually help the otherwise loony theory of University of Seville professor of Arabic studies Emilio González Ferrín, who claims that there was no Muslim conquest but only some sort of peaceful immigration from North Africa. He follows the teachings of Ignacio Olagüe, *Les arabes n'ont jamais envahi l'Espagne* (Paris: Flammarion, 1960), whose writings had earlier been refuted by Charles-Emanuel Dufourcq, *La vie cotidienne dans l'Europe médièvale sous la domination arabe* (Biarritz: Cino del Luca, 1981).

61 *Al-Makkari*, 1:6. Historian Ibn Idhari writes in *Al-Bayano 'l-Mogrib*: "[Seville] remained, among all the cities of Spain, the largest, the most important, the best built, and the richest in ancient monuments.... The Visigoth kings had chosen Toledo as their capital, but Seville had remained the site of the Hispano-Roman followers of the sacred and profane sciences, and it is there that dwelled the Hispano-Roman nobility" (21).

62 *Al-Makkari*, 1:77. The aqueduct of Tarragona, which the Romans built probably in the first century, is said to have been "repaired" by Abd al-Rahman III, and this is usually taken to mean that it had been in ruins before the Muslim conquest. But a long time passed between the Muslim conquest of Spain (711) and the elevation of Abd al-Rahman III (891); the aqueduct could have deteriorated after the Muslim conquest. There is no indication that it was not working under the Visigoths.

63 Ibid., 81.

64 Henri Pirenne, *Mohammed and Charlemagne* (1935; rpt. New York: Barnes and Noble, 1956).

65 For this immense work of preservation, assimilation, and transmission in the Greek Orthodox Roman Empire, even in the face of constant assaults by its enemies, Islamic and otherwise, see among others: Michael H. Harris, *History of Libraries in the Western World* (Metuchen, NJ, and London: Scarecrow Press, 1995), 75–77; John Julius Norwich, *A Short History of Byzantium* (New York: Vintage, 1999), xli. See also: Anthony Kaldellis, *The Christian Parthenon: Classicism and Pilgrimage in Byzantine Athens* (Cambridge: Cambridge University Press, 2009); "Classical Scholarship in Twelfth-Century Byzantium," in C. Barber and D. Jenkins, eds., *Medieval Greek Commentary on the "Nicomachean Ethics"* (Leiden and Boston: Brill, 2008); and *Hellenism in Byzantium: The Transformation of Greek Identity and the Reception of the Classical Tradition* (Cambridge University Press, 2007); Demetrios Constantelos, *Christian Hellenism: Essays and Studies in Continuity and Change* (New Rochelle, NY, and Athens: Aristide D. Caratzas, 1999), summarized in his "The Formation of the Hellenic Christian Mind," at http://www.myriobiblos.gr/texts/english/Constantelos_1.html#2_bottom; Helene Ahrweiler, "The Hellenic Europe: Problems in Greek Continuity" (2000), at http://www.myriobiblos.gr/texts/english/1821_problems_of_greek.html; Constantine Cavarnos, *Cultural and Educational Continuity of Greece from Antiquity to the Present* (Belmont: Institute for Byzantine and Modern Greek Studies, 1995); J. C. Lawson, *Modern Greek Folklore and Ancient Greek Religion: A Study in Survivals* (Cambridge University Press, 1910); S. F. Johnson, *The Life and Miracles of Thekla: A Literary Study* (Washington, DC: Center for Hellenic Studies, 2006). For a corrective on seeing every Greek Christian manifestation as an adaptation of Greek paganism, see Gerald V. Lalonde, "Pagan Cult to Christian Ritual: The Case of Agia Marina Theseiou," *Greek, Roman, and Byzantine Studies* 45 (2005): 91–125. For the immense trade between Europe and the Greek Orthodox Roman Empire, see Marlia Mundell Mango, ed., *Byzantine Trade, 4th–12th Centuries: The Archaeology of Local, Regional and International Exchange. Papers of the Thirty-Eighth Spring Symposium of Byzantine...for the Promotion of Byzantine Studies* (London: Ashgate, 2009). Paper, which the Arabs got from the Chinese in the eighth century, was being used in the Greek Roman Empire by the ninth century, when western Europe was still using only parchment. We know of very large private libraries, and monasteries possessed huge libraries with hundreds of books that were lent to people in each monastery's region. Thus were preserved the works of classical antiquity. See Nicolas Oikonomides, "Writing Materials, Documents and Books," *The Economic History of Byzantium: From the Seventh Through the Fifteenth Century*, ed. Angeliki E. Laiou (Washington, DC: Dumbarton Oaks, Trustees for Harvard University, 2002). See also the illuminating Speros Vryonis, *Byzantium and Europe* (New York: Harcourt, Brace, and World,

1967). Vryonis's works are an extraordinary scholarly source for understanding the course from classical to medieval to modern Greek civilization. For my "existential" understanding of the Greek vision of continuity from classical times through the Greek Roman Empire to modern times, I thank τήν γυναίκα μου, Ιωάννα. As Wordsworth put it after staying in Greece: "The stream of paganism was thus taught to glide into a Christian channel with a soft and easy current.... There was generally some analogy, which regulated the transforming process, between the character transformed and that with which it was invested after the transformation," in *Athens and Attica: Journal of a Residence There (Originally published in 1836, a companion to the classical topography of Athens and Attica)*, ed. G. Brisch (Oxford: 3rd Guides, 2004), 153. For the Greek concept of Ρωμηοσύνη (*romiosini*), see http://greekodyssey.typepad.com/my_greek_odyssey/2007/10/romiosini2.htmlset and for some aspects of it set to music, hear Mikis Theodorakis, for example, at http://www.youtube.com/watch?v=g8F43rPkdI0&feature=related.

66   George Makdisi, "Scholasticism and Humanism in Classical Islam and the Christian West," 176: "The [Islamic] Inquisition was set afoot under al-Ma'mun, the great patron of the translation movement from Greek to Arabic. The Inquisition turned on the theological question of whether the Koran was the created or the uncreated Word of God. Under pain of punishment, in certain cases leading to death, the juridical theologicans were forced to answer that the Koran was not God's coeternal Word. After fifteen years, during which the philosophical theologians persecuted the juridical theologians, the Inquisition failed, and a new Traditionist leader emerged, Ibn Hanbal, hero of the passive resistance that broke the back of the Inquisition. Soon afterwards, Shafii and Ibn Hanbal were chosen as the 'patron saints,' so to speak, for two of the newly organized professional guilds of law." The Inquisition had been a way to cope with the rationalistic challenge posed by the Greek philosophy that Islam had come into contact with upon its conquest of the lands of the Christian Greek Roman Empire in the Middle East.

67   Gutas, *Greek Thought, Arabic Culture*, 85.

68   See, for example, "Mont Saint-Michel or Toledo: Greek and Arabic Sources for Medieval European Culture?" by Professor Charles Burnett, holder of the Chair of History of Islamic Influences in Europe at the Warburg Institute, University of London, and "a key associate of FSTC": "The Foundation for Science, Technology and Civilization (FSTC) is a United Kingdom based educational entity which was formed to popularize, disseminate and promote an accurate account of Muslim Heritage and its contribution to present day science, technology and civilization." "FSTC and Khalifa University [will] create interactive Science Heritage Center in UAE [United Arab Emirates]." At http://muslimheritage.com/topics/default. cfm?ArticleID=1083#sec3, accessed August 1, 2012.

69   The historians' lament may have begun with Edward Gibbon and has continued unabated ever since. Yet the closing of the Athenian Neoplatonic academy by Justinian (an extraordinary ruler responsible for the writing of one of the great documents in the history of law—the Code of Justinian), if it occurred, did not stop the preservation and study of classical philosophy and science in the Greek Roman Empire (see our text including the statements by scholars on the history of libraries like Michael Harris and John Julius Norwich, as well as the role of the Greek scholars in bringing Plato to the West). The closing, if it occurred, would have been part of Justinian's general policy of undermining pagan cults, to which the post-Plato Athenian academy was devoted (for it did not simply teach Neoplatonism), rather than a policy against classical philosophy and science. In Alexandria, the openly pagan philosopher Olympiadorus continued to teach three decades after the presumed closing of the Athenian academy (Cameron, 9). The "Seven Hellenic (pagan)" philosophers who are said to have left the academy for Persia were back a year later. The closing, if it occurred, could also have been part of Justinian's desire to centralize higher education in Constantinople, not to destroy classical philosophy and science (Hallström, 157–160, who points out that John Malalas does not mention any religious motive or the closing of any particular school). But there may have been no closing of this particular institution, contrary to what many historians have gath-

ered from John Malalas's rather generic statement in his sixth century chronicle: no other source, Greek or Syrian, even suggests a closing of the "academy." See Alan Cameron, "The Last Days of the Academy of Athens," *Proceedings of the Cambridge Philological Society* 195, no. 15 (1969): 7–29; Gunnar Hallström, "The Closing of the Neoplatonic School in A.D. 529: An Additional Aspect," in Paavo Castren, ed., *Post-Herulian Athens: Aspects of Life and Culture in Athens A.D. 267–529* (Helsinki: Suomen Ateenan-Instituutin, 1994), 157–160. For the doubts about the actual closing of the academy, see Rainer Thiel, *Simplikios und das Ende der neoplatonischen Schule in Athen* (Stuttgart: Franz Steiner, 1999), reviewed by Gerald Bechtle, *Bryn Mawr Classical Review* 4 (2000): 19. See a well-reasoned examination in Arthur P. Urbano, *The Philosophical Life: Biography and the Crafting of Intellectual Identity in Late Antiquity* (Washington, DC: The Catholic University of America Press, 2013), 315–16, who observes that saying "that the 'Academy' was closed in A.D. 529 is to presume that the institution founded by Plato continued to function as an institution for nine hundred years, or that the school founded by Plutarch in the fifth century A.D. was somehow a 'reopening' of Plato's academy. In fact the ancient sources do not mention the academy or the closing of a specific school." It is very telling that a sixth-century Christian historian like Malalas quotes Euripides as if his readers were very familiar with such a classic tragedian: Paolo Carrara, "A Line from Euripides Quoted in John Malalas' Chronographia," *Zeitschrift für Papyrologie unde Epigraphik* 69 (1987): 20–24.

70 Maria Mavroudi, "Translations from Greek into Latin and Arabic during the Middle Ages: Searching for the Classical Tradition," *Speculum* 90, no. 1 (January 2015): 41.

71 *Columbia History of Western Philosophy*, ed. Richard Henry Popkin (New York: Columbia University Press, 1999), 230–31.

72 Sylvain Gouguenheim, *Aristote au Mont Saint-Michel* (Paris: Seuil, 2008).

73 Among primary sources mentioning the work of Christians transmitting knowledge to the Arabs, see Said al-Andalusi, *Kitab*, 79–80. See also Harris, *History of Libraries in the Western World*, 75–77; Norwich, *A Short History of Byzantium*, xli; and Vryonis, *Byzantium and Europe*. For this immense work of preservation, assimilation, and transmission in the Christian Greek Roman Empire, see, among others, Kaldellis, *The Christian Parthenon*; "Classical Scholarship in Twelfth-Century Byzantium," in Barber and Jenkins, *Medieval Greek Commentary on the "Nicomachean Ethics"*; Kaldellis, *Hellenism in Byzantium*; Constantelos, *Christian Hellenism*, summarized in his "The Formation of the Hellenic Christian Mind," at http://www.myriobiblos.gr/texts/english/Constantelos_1.html#2_bottom; Ahrweiler, "The Hellenic Europe"; Cavarnos, *Cultural and Educational Continuity of Greece from Antiquity to the Present*; Lawson, *Modern Greek Folklore and Ancient Greek Religion*; Johnson, *The Life and Miracles of Thekla*; and Evanghélos Moutsopoulos, "Arts libéraux et philosophie à byzance," in *Arts Libéraux et Philosophie au Moyen Âge: Actes du Quatrième Congrés International de Philosophie Médiévale* (Montreal: Institut D'Études Médiévales, 1969), 79–88. The Greek Roman Empire may have influenced even some aspects of the legal thought of Islam: Louis Milliot, *Introduction à l'Étude du Droit Musulman* (Paris: Recueil Sirey, 1953), 772. For a corrective on seeing every Greek Christian manifestation as an adaptation of Greek paganism, see Lalonde, "Pagan Cult to Christian Ritual," 91–125. For the immense trade between Europe and the Christian Greek Roman Empire, see Mundell Mango, ed., *Byzantine Trade, 4th–12th Centuries*.

74 See Richard Henry Popkin, ed., *Columbia History of Western Philosophy* (New York: Columbia University Press, 1999), 230–44. Avicenna was Persian, and Persia had been under centuries of Greek influence in language and culture since the occupation of Persepolis by Alexander the Great in 330 B.C. In any event, Avicenna's "acquaintance with [Greek] was not direct but mediated through interpreters": Mostafa Younesi, "Avicenna's Method for Translating Greek Philosophical Terms into Persian," in William Sweet, ed., *The Dialogue of Cultural Traditions: Global Perspective* (Washington, DC: Council for Research in Values and Philosophy, 2008), chap. 35, p. 462, online at http://www.crvp.org/book/Series01/I39/chapter35.htm.

For the presence of translations and commentaries in the Christian Greek Roman Empire of the Middle East, see Cristina d'Ancona, "Greek Sources in Arabic and Islamic Philosophy," in *Stanford Encyclopedia of Philosophy*, February 23, 2009, online at http://plato.stanford. edu/entries/arabicislamicgreek/index.html#SyrBac. See also Gouguenheim, *Aristote au mont Saint-Michel*.

75 See the excellent Clifton R. Fox, "What, if Anything, Is a Byzantine," *Celator* 10, no. 3 (March 1996), http://www.romanity.org/htm/fox.01.en.what_if_anything_is_a_byzantine.01.htm.

76 Quran 30 (*ar-Rum*, "The Romans"); *Ibn Khaldoun: Les Prolégomènes d'Ibn Khaldoun*, trans. M. de Slane (Paris: Librairie orientaliste Paul Geuthner, 1934), 3:126.

77 *The Complete Works of Liudprand of Cremona*, trans. Paolo Squatriti (Washington, DC: The Catholic University of America Press, 2007), 94, 197.

78 Hieronimo Wolfio, ed., *Nicetae Acominati Choniatae, Imperi Graeci Historia* (1593), 25, 42.

79 Ioannis Stouraitis, "Roman Identity in Byzantium: A Critical Approach," *Byzantinische Zeitschrift* 107, no. 1 (2014): 175.

80 My personal experience illustrates the ideological bias. Not too long ago I asked a well-known professor of Classics whether his department offered any courses on the Christian Greek Roman Empire. "Ah," he answered with a half-smile, "the degenerate Empire! No, we don't offer classes on that." Indeed, the study of this empire, which endured for more than a thousand years, is relegated to those universities that offer "Byzantine" courses in departments or programs of "Middle East Studies," or "Asian Studies," or even "Turkish" studies.

81 Of which slowing down the more difficult reception of Greek knowledge was a component. See Pirenne, *Mohammed and Charlemagne*. Recently examined archaeological evidence supports Pirenne, as it points to a decrease even in commerce in the East Mediterranean during the early Islamic conquests: "The incessant flow of produce that had survived the political disruptions of Goths, Vandals and Slavs stopped abruptly.... Contrary to current interpretive trends identifying continuity in classical trade during the early Islamic period, shipwreck discoveries dry up in the Eastern Mediterranean by A.D. 650. Umayyad pottery is nonexistent among the shipwreck database": Sean Kingsley, "Mapping Trade by Shipwrecks," in Mundell Mango, ed., *Byzantine Trade, 4th–12th Centuries*, 33, 35. For refinements of Pirenne's thesis, see R. S. Lopez, "Mohammed and Charlemagne: A Revision," *Speculum* 18 (1943): 1438; even a scholar who questioned Pirenne's assertion that Islam slowed *economic* development within the West accepted the role of Islam as an interrupter in the *cultural* flow from the Greek Roman Empire to the entire West: "Thus the most essential influence of the Islamic expansion on the cultural development of the Occident is probably to be found in the fact that the weakening of Byzantium forced this empire to withdraw and leave the Occident at peace to pursue its own independent development" (Anne Riising, "The Fate of Henri Pirenne's Theses on the Consequence of the Islamic Invasion," in *Problems in European Civilization: The Pirenne Thesis: Analysis, Criticism, and Revision*, ed. Alfred F. Havighurst [Boston: D.C. Heath and Company, 1958], 105). Probably the least affected was the republic of Venice, which was in closest contact with the empire of the Greeks. Of course neither Islam nor Christianity prohibited trade with each other. But such exchange by means of trading colonies was limited by the fact that medieval Islam would not allow (and even today still does not allow) the building of a new church in Muslim land any more than medieval (as opposed to today's) Christians would allow mosques in Christian land. (Arguing that Islam graciously allowed Christian worship in previously built churches in the lands conquered by Islam overlooks that there is an asymmetry in the comparison: Muslims entered lands formerly Christian and saw it prudent to allow the continuation of Christian worship, whereas Christians entering Islamic lands would not be entering lands formerly Muslim, but rather formerly Christian.) The entire corpus of Greek philosophy was available to and read by scholars in the Christian Greek Roman Empire, but the interruption of relations between Europe and the empire because of the Islamic advances interrupted also the easy diffusion of this Greek philosophy in Europe. And Islam's views on representational art were likely an influence in the near

destruction of one of the world's most exquisite forms of art when some Greek Roman Empire rulers tried to abolish religious images (icons) in Greek Orthodox churches during the so-called "iconoclastic controversy" in the eighth and early ninth centuries. Islam did eventually destroy this art in some of the greatest churches of the Greek Roman Empire, such as Hagia Sophia in Constantinople (today's "Istanbul"): today it is a museum, but four minarets still flank the former church, in religious and aesthetic desecration. I thank the Liberty Fund colloquium on "Medieval Cities," Tucson, Arizona, January 10–13, 2010, for making me aware of Pirenne's thesis by including his writings in the readings for the colloquium. Pirenne's thesis has been attacked by Philip Grierson, "Commerce in the Dark Ages: A Critique of the Evidence," *Transactions of the Royal Historical Society* 5th series, 9 (1959): 123–40; Denys Hay, *Europe: The Emergence of an Idea* (New York: Harper and Row, 1966); Archibald R. Lewis, *Naval Power and Trade in the Mediterranean*, A.D. *500–1100* (Princeton, NJ: Princeton University Press, 1951); and Andrew M. Watson, "Back to Gold and Silver," *Economic History Review* 2nd series, 20 (1967): 1–34. The most recent vindication of Pirenne's thesis is Emmet Scott's excellent *Mohammed and Charlemagne Revisited*, which uses the latest archaeological evidence. I believe Pirenne's thesis stands at least from the cultural if not also the economic point of view.

82   Deno John Geanakoplos, *Constantinople and the West: Essays on the Late Byzantine (Paleologan) and Italian Renaissances and the Byzantine and Roman Churches* (Madison: University of Wisconsin Press, 1989), offers a balanced account arguing that if the Greek scholars did not give origin to the Italian Renaissance (as Renaissance scholars have generally held from the seventeenth century until the 1980s), they certainly were responsible for much of its reputed glory. For example, Plato's dialogues were brought to the attention of the West by Greek scholars at the council of Florence (variously 1438–1445), which had been convened to solve the Christian schism between the Roman Catholic West and the Orthodox East (the Orthodox Church also calls itself Catholic, *Katholikos*—that is, universal) as a prelude to the West's helping the Greek Roman Empire in its losing struggle against the Muslim empire of the Turks. The number of influential Greek scholars is too long to be listed here, but among them were Manuel Chrysoloras (who taught Leonardo Bruni how to translate from Greek into Latin), Marcus Musurus (who was the main editor of the famous Aldine press—the editorial house central to the Italian Renaissance—and who was also professor of Greek at the University of Padua and editor of the complete works of Aristophanes and Plato), John Argyropoulos (who taught Lorenzo de Medici and Angelo Poliziano), Nicholas Sigeros (ambassador to the papal court, who gave Petrarch a copy of Homer), Aristotle Gaza (who pointed out the distortions of Aristotle by the Averroists and the Roman Catholic scholastics), Gemistos Pletho (influential lecturer on the works of Plato), Demetrios Chalcondyles (who brought to the attention of the Italian scholars the work of the Church Father Saint Basil the Great, whose "Discourse on Christian Youth" became a favorite of the humanists), George of Trebyzond, Demetrios Dukas, and Michael Apostolis. The Italo-Greek monk Barlaam of Calabria (sent to Avignon in the fourteenth century by the Greek emperor Andronicus III to plead the union of the two churches in a common defense against Islam) and also the Italo-Greek Leontius Pilatus taught Greek to Petrarch and Boccaccio (Pilatus also translated Homer into Latin).

83   A. Pertusi, *La caduta di Costantinopli: Le testimonianze dei contemporanei*, vol. 1 (Verona: Mondadori, 1976), 78, 381n25; Michael Ducas (or Georgius Pachymeres, St. Nicephoros Gregoras, et alia), *Historia byzantina* (1680; rpt. Bonn: Weber, 1834 ed.), 312.

84   Robert Davis, *Christian Slaves, Muslim Masters: White Slavery in the Mediterranean, the Barbary Coast and Italy, 1500–1800* (New York: MacMillan, 2004).

85   J. V. Field and M. T. Wright, "Gears from the Byzantines: A Portable Sundial with Calendrical Gearing," *Annals of Science* 42, no. 2 (1985): 87–138. This mechanism was copied by such Arabs as al-Biruni.

86   See my endnotes and my chapter 2 with the example of the Mosque of Córdoba, the Visigoth horseshoe arch, and other borrowings. See also De Lacy O'Leary, *How Greek Science Passed*

to the Arabs (London: Routledge & Kegan Paul, 1949), which demonstrates how Christianity was a Hellenizing force throughout the Mediterranean. R. Walzer, "L'éveil de la philosophie islamique," *Revue des Études Islamiques* 38, nos. 1–2 (1970): 7–42, 207–42; F. Rosenthal, *The Classical Heritage in Islam* (London: Routledge & Kegan Paul, 1975); Dimitri Gutas, *Greek Thought, Arabic Culture: The Graeco-Arabic Translation Movement in Baghdad and Early 'Abbasid Society (2nd–4th/8th–10th centuries)* (London: Routledge, 1998). Before the works on logic by al-Kindi (805–873), al-Farabi (873–950), and the Persian Ibn Sina (980–1037, known in Europe as "Avicenna"), in the eighth century Christians in the Middle East under the Christian Greek Roman Empire had written commentaries on Aristotelian logic. Those commentaries have disappeared since the Muslim conquest: see "History of Logic," *Encyclopedia Britannica Online*, September 25, 2009, at http://www.britannica.com/EBchecked/topic/346217/history-of-logic.

87 Antonio Domínguez Ortiz, *España: Tres Milenios de Historia* (Madrid: Marcial Pons, 2007), 40. Some inscriptions are left, as are church documents that were of sufficient importance to have copies abroad, such as those of most, though not all, of the church councils.

88 For what remains of pre-Islamic sculpture, largely confined to fragments of bas-reliefs on walls in churches, towers, and bridges, see Luis Caballero Zoreda and Pedro Mateos Cruz, eds., *Escultura decorativa tardorromana y altomedieval en la Península Ibérica* (Madrid: Consejo Superior de Investigaciones Científicas, 2007); Luis Caballero Zoreda, ed., *El siglo VII frente al siglo VII: Arquitectura* (Madrid: Consejo Superior de Investigaciones Científicas, 2009); José Orlandis, *Historia del reino visigodo español* (Madrid: Rialp, 2003), 243.

89 José Orlandis points out the influence of the Christian Greek Roman Empire's theology and church ritual along with art and architecture: *Historia del reino visigodo español*, 243, 244, 249–50. For Islam's interruption of the direct communication between the Christian Greek Roman Empire and most of western Europe, see especially Pirenne, *Mohammed and Charlemagne*.

90 Diego Catalán and Maria Soledad de Andrés, eds., *Crónica del moro Rasis* (Madrid: Gredos, 1975), 281–82. See also Susana Calvo Capilla, "Las primeras mezquitas de al-Andalus a través de las fuentes árabes (92/711–170/785)," *Al-Qantara* 27, no. 1 (Enero–Julio 2007): 143–79.

91 This is an architectural approach based largely on "smoke and mirrors." Even the *Grove Encyclopedia of Islamic Art and Architecture*, very partial to Islamic culture, tells us that "[in Nasrid architecture] palaces and civic buildings were...decorated with simulated arches of colored plaster to give the illusion of dynamism and ethereality. Gravity is apparently absent from Nasrid architecture, but in reality structures are static and primitive in composition, for thick walls counterbalance the thrust of the light wooden roofs, below which hang decorative ceilings of wood or occasionally plaster": Jonathan M. Bloom and Sheila S. Blair, eds., *Grove Encyclopedia of Islamic Art and Architecture* (Oxford: Oxford University Press, 2009), 157. This is why Ibn Khaldun observed that the buildings of the Arabs in North Africa quickly fell into ruins because their buildings were "not solidly built": Ibn Khaldun, *The Muqaddimah*, 2:267, 269.

92 Huseyin Abiva and Noura Durkee, *A History of Muslim Civilization* (Skokie: IQRA International Foundation, 2003), 66; Robert Hillenbrand, *Islamic Architecture: Form, Function, and Meaning* (New York: Columbia University Press, 1994), 136; W.N. Lockington, ed., *The Iconographic Encyclopaedia of the Arts and Sciences: Architecture* (Philadelphia: Iconographic Publishing 1888), 4:125, 126; Eugène-Emmanuel Viollet-le-Duc, *Discourses on Architecture* (Boston: James R. Osgood, 1875), 452; Philip Khuri Hitti, *History of Syria: Including Lebanon and Palestine* (New York: Macmillan, 1951), 511; Ali Wigdan, *The Arab Contribution to Islamic Art: From the Seventh to the Fifteenth Centuries* (Cairo: Cairo American University in Cairo Press, 1999), 21; John Onians, ed., *Atlas of World Art* (London: Laurence King, 2004), 128; James Hastings et al., eds., *Encyclopedia of Religion and Ethics* (Whitefish: Kessinger Publishing, 2003), pt. 2, p. 757; Frederick Jones Bliss, *The Religions of Modern Syria and Palestine* (New York: C. Scribner's Sons, 1917; rpt. General Books LCC, 2009), 207; J. Petersen et al., "Masjid,"

Encyclopaedia of Islam, Second Edition, ed. P. Bearman et al. (Brill, 2012; Brill Online, Northwestern University Library, June 27, 2012), http://www.encislam.brill.nl.turing.library.northwestern.edu/subscriber/uid=1705/entry?entry=islam_COM-0694. Upon the Muslim defeat of the Crusader kingdom in Palestine, the procedure was repeated: Daniella Talman-Heller, *Islamic Piety in Medieval Syria: Mosques, Cemeteries, and Sermons under the Zangids and Ayyubids (1146-1260)* (Leiden: Brill, 2007), 36. In the early centuries of Islam, Muslim rulers endeavored to copy in their mosques the exterior architectural features of Christian churches with the explicit purpose of dwarfing them, according to Eutichyus of Alexandria, cit. Rafi Grasman and Myriam Rosen-Ayalon, "The Two Great Syrian Umayyad Mosques: Jerusalem and Damascus," *Muqarnas: An Annual of the Visual Culture of the Islamic World* 16 (1999): 11.

93   "En torno a la decoración con mosaicos de las mezquitas omeyas," *Homenaje al prof. Jacinto Bosch Vilá* (no ed.) (Granada: Universidad de Granada, 1991), 131–44.

94   In an otherwise good article, Mary Elizabeth Poodles, "A Thousand Words," *Touchstone: A Journal of Mere Christianity* (July/August 2015), 54–55, writes, "The church remains much as it was then; it had been taken over as a mosque but is now a museum." How can a church remain much "as it was" when it is no longer a church but a museum? The Turks even call it today Kariye Camii, the Chora Mosque, or Kariye Müzesi, the Chora Museum. Thanks to the work of the Dumbarton Oaks Center for Byzantine Studies at Harvard University and the Byzantine Institute of America, the plaster has been removed and much of the iconography is now visible.

95   Thus the church of Calatrava in 1195: al-Marrakusi in *Kitab al-muyib fi talljis ajbar al-magrib by Abu Muhammad Abd Al-Wahid Al-Marrakusi*, trans. Ambrosio Huici Miranda (Tetuán: Instituto General Franco de Estudios e Investigación Hispano-Arabe, 1955), 236.

96   Jacques Fontaine, *El mozárabe* (Madrid: Encuentro, 1978), 61–80.

97   These methods have been standard in all Muslim conquests. For example, upon taking over the northern part of Cyprus in the late twentieth century, the Muslim Turks proceeded to destroy the Greek Orthodox churches and their art: Judith Miller and Stephen Kinzer, "Greek Orthodox Icons Ravaged in the Turkish Part of Cyprus," *New York Times*, April 1, 1998. In the twenty-first century, the actions of the Taliban and the Islamic State follow the pattern.

98   For representative monographs on the splendor of Visigoth art shown by what remains in these treasures, see Alicia Perea, *El tesoro Visigodo de Guarrazar* (Madrid: Consejo Superior de Investigaciones Científicas, 2001), esp. 83, and by the same author, *El tesoro Visigodo de Torredonjimeno* (Madrid: Consejo Superior de Investigaciones Científicas, 2009).

99   Manuel Gómez Moreno, *Iglesias mozárabes* 1:9.

100   Ibid., 10–11. For Toledo's unruliness and the poet Garbib, see Ibn al-Qutiyya in *Historia de la conquista de España de Abenalcotía el cordobés* (Madrid: Archivos, 1926), 36–37.

101   Henri Terrasse, *L'Espagne du Moyen Age: Civilizations et Arts* (Paris: Fayard, 1966), 19. Terrasse pointed out that the industrial art of Visigoth Spain reached its apogee in the production of the votive crowns of the Visigoth kings and that this practice was an imitation of Greek Roman ("Byzantine") practice (17–19). "It seems," Terrasse wrote, "that these crowns were the product of official workshops in contact with the Byzantine world."

102   For the splendor of the Visigoth court, see José Orlandis, *La vida en España en tiempo de los godos*, 93–97; for the size of Toledo and the Visigoths' effort to emulate Rome and Constantinople, see Jesús Carrobles Santos, Rafael Barroso Cabrera, Jorge Morín de Pablos, and Fernando Valdés Fernández, *Regia Sedes Toletana*, 217.

103   Montesquieu's unhistorical and anachronistic judgment of Visigoth culture is characteristic: in *De l'esprit des lois* he wrote that Visigothic laws were "puerile and idiotic" (Orlandis, *Historia del reino visigodo español*, 152).

104   Chris Lowney, *A Vanished World: Muslims, Christians, and Jews in Medieval Spain* (New York: Oxford University Press, 2006), 27.

105   Among them are Bango Torviso, *Alta Edad Media: De la tradición hispanogoda al románico*; Pavón Maldonado, "Influjos occidentales en el califato de Córdoba"; José Orlandis, *Historia*

del reino visigodo español and *La vida en España en tiempo de los* godos; Jaime Cobreros, *Guía del prerrománico: Visigodo; Asturiano; Mozárabe* (Madrid: Anaya, 2005); Luis Caballero Zoreda, ed., *El siglo vii frente al siglo vii: Arquitectura* (Madrid: Consejo Superior de Investigaciones Científicas, 2009); Luis Caballero Zoreda, ed., *Escultura decorativa tardorromana y altomedieval en la peninsula ibérica* (Madrid: Consejo Superior de Investigaciones Científicas, 2007); Alicia Perea, *El tesoro visigodo de Guarrazar* (Madrid: Consejo Superior de Investigaciones Científicas, 2001) and *El tesoro visigodo de Torredonjimeno* (Madrid: Consejo Superior de Investigaciones Científicas, 2009); María de los Angeles Utrero Agudo, *Iglesias tardoantiguas y altomedievales en la peninsula ibérica: Análisis arqueológico y sistemas de abovedamiento* (Madrid: Consejo Superior de Investigaciones Científicas, 2007); and Javier Sainz Saiz, *Arte prerrománico en Castilla y León* (León: Lancia, 1997). An exception is Jurate Rosales, *Los godos* (Barcelona: Ariel, 2004), which has been translated as *Goths and Balts: The Missing Link of European History* (Lemont: Vydunas Youth Fund, 2004). For an example of the French research, see Jacques Fontaine and Christine Pellistrandi, eds., *L'Europe Héritière de l'Espagne Wisigothique* (Madrid: Rencontres de la Casa de Velázquez, 1992).

106 Scott, *Mohammed and Charlemagne Revisited*, 122–23, commenting on Thomas F. Glick, professor of medieval history and director of the Institute for Medieval History at Boston University and author of *Islamic and Christian Spain in the Early Middle Ages* (Princeton, NJ: Princeton University Press, 1979; rpt. New York: Brill, 2005), 29. See further evidence of Glick's animosity in one of the epigraphs to the present chapter.

CHAPTER 3: THE DAILY REALITIES OF AL-ANDALUS

1 "Prólogo to *El collar de la paloma* de Ibn Hazm," in José Ortega y Gasset, *Obras completas* (Madrid: Revista de Occidente, 1950), 7:42.

2 And therefore the need to avoid socializing with them to prevent contamination. Ibn Hazm cited Quran 4:139 and 144. See his *Fisal*, Third Treatise, translated by Miguel Asín Palacios, *Abenházam de Córdoba y su historia crítica de las ideas religiosas*, 5 vols. (Madrid: Turner, 1984), 4:106. See also Theodore Pulcini, *Exegesis of Polemical Discourse: Ibn Hazm on Jewish and Christian Scriptures* (Oxford: Oxford University Press, 1998), 139, 149, 167, 181. The Arabist Felipe Maíllo Salgado has shown how even educated Muslims in al-Andalus had cultural reference points "totally different from those of their Christian Western contemporaries": *De la desaparición de al-Andalus* (Madrid: Abada, 2011), 24–25.

3 Thomas F. Glick, "*Convivencia*: An Introductory Note," in Vivian B. Mann, Thomas F. Glick, and Jerrilynn D. Dodds, *Convivencia: Jews, Muslims, and Christians in Medieval Spain* (New York: G. Braziller in association with the Jewish Museum, 1992), 7.

4 José Aguilera Pleguezuelo, "El derecho malikí aplicado en al-Andalus. Teoría y práctica jurídicas," in *Actas de las II Jornadas de Cultura Árabe e Islámica* (Madrid: Instituto Hispano-Árabe de Cultura, 1980), 17.

5 Soha Abboud-Haggar, "Las raíces de la violencia en los textos religiosos islámicos: El Corán y al-Hadiz," in *Raíces profundas: La violencia contra las mujeres (Antigüedad y Edad Media)*, ed. María Jesús Fuente and Remedios Morán (Madrid: Polifemo, 2011), 66.

6 In *Kitab al-qudat bi-Qurtuba*, ed. and trans. Julián Ribera as *Al-Joxani: Historia de los jueces de Córdoba* (Madrid: Ibérica, 1914), 6, xxiii.

7 *Les Prolégomènes d'Ibn Khaldoun*, trans. M. De Slane (Paris: Librairie Orientaliste Paul Geuthner, 1936), 2:3; "The Religious Powers of the Caliph," in *A Reader in Classical Islam*, ed. F. E. Peters (Princeton, NJ: Princeton University Press, 1994), 149.

8 For the traditionally dual power of the caliphs in Islam, see, among others, Francisco Marcos Marín, "Notas sobre el concepto de *malik*," in *Áctas del IV Coloquio Hispano-Tunecino* (Madrid: Instituto Hispano-Árabe de Cultura, 1983), 176, who points out that *caliph* means "replacer" or "successor," and that the caliph was the first among imams or directors of prayer

as well as the highest political position; and Patricia Crone and Martin Hinds, *God's Caliph: Religious Authority in the First Centuries of Islam* (Cambridge: Cambridge University Press, 1986). Early Sunni caliphs were in theory chosen through consultation among the leaders of the various Arabic tribes. In fact, most caliphs obtained power through either inheritance or military force. Among the Shia, no consultation to choose a ruler would be necessary, since they claim that only a family descendant of Muhammad should be the supreme "imam." In Shiite Islam, therefore, a division between the two forms of authority is even less logical. It is true that classical Islamic teaching asserts that religious authority lies with the *ulama*—the intellectual religious class—whereas political authority lies with the caliph (see María Isabel Fierro, "Crone, P. y M. Hinds, *God's Caliph: Religious authority in the first centuries of Islam*" [book review], *Al-Qantara* 7, nos. 1/2 [1986]: 481–82). But one may suspect that this "classical" Islamic teaching—taught, of course, by the *ulama* themselves—is the result of the centuries-long rivalry for supreme authority between the *ulama* and the Islamic rulers. Since Islam is an organic religion and as such cannot have any division between the religious and the secular realms, the *ulama*'s purported monopoly of religious authority, if justified, would naturally give ultimate total power to the *ulama* class.

9   Christian Mueller, *Gerichtspraxis im Stadtstaat Cordoba: Zum Recht der Gesellschaft in einer malikitisch-islamischen Rechtstradition des 5./11 Jahrhunderts* (Leiden: Brill, 1999), 388; Nayer Honarvar, "Behind the Veil: Women's Rights in Islamic Societies," *Journal of Law and Religion* 6, no. 2 (1988): 361.

10   Ritual and family law in medieval Islam, despite "occasional deviations based on custom, adhered most closely to the *sharia*": Abraham L. Udovitch, "Theory and Practice of Islamic Law: Some Evidence from the Geniza," *Studia Islamica*, no. 32 (1970): 19–29; Joseph Schacht, *Esquisse d'une histoire du droit musulman* (Paris: Librairie orientale et americaine, 1953), 19.

11   No Muslim woman in al-Andalus achieved a status comparable to that of Santa Teresa of Ávila, whose writings became quite influential upon her proclamation as a saint forty years after her death in 1582, and who was named a doctor of the Catholic Church in 1969. Efforts have been made to identify women like Shaikha Shuhda, who achieved prestige in the Muslim world as "transmitters" of *hadith*. For a critique of these efforts, see chapter 5 of this book.

12   *Al-Joxani*, 55–60. For the conflict between the *ulama* and al-Haqam I (whose mother was a Christian sexual slave), see *Kitab al-muyib fi taljis ajbar al-magrib por Ab Muhammad Abd al-Wahid al-Marrakusi*, ed. and trans. Ambrosio Huici Miranda, in *Colección de Crónicas Arabes de la Reconquista* (Tetuán: Instituto General Franco de Estudios e Investigación Hispano-Arabe, 1955), 4:15–16, and Ibn Hayyan, in J. Vallvé and F. Ruiz Girela, *La primera década del reinado de Al-Hakam I, según el Muqtabis II, l de Ben Hayyan de Córdoba (m. 469 h./1076 J.C.)* (Madrid: Real Academia de la Historia, 2003), 140–50. María Calero Secall has argued that during the Nasri *taifa* rule in Granada, the power of the *ulama* diminished compared with that of the power of the palace; see "Rulers and Qadis: Their Relationship during the Nasrid Kingdom," *Islamic Law and Society* 7, no. 2, 255, and "El derecho islámico y su aplicación en al-Andalus (siglo XIII–XV)," in Fátima Roldán Castro and Isabel Hervás Jóvega, eds., *El saber en Al-Andalus: Textos y Estudios, III* (Sevilla: Universidad de Sevilla y Fundación El Monte, 2001). This weakening of the religious authorities and laws in the *taifa* kingdoms might help explain the power in the Granada court of a non-Muslim like Rabbi Ibn Naghrela, "The Prince." Eventually, however, a popular riot with *ulama* encouragement toppled his son, the equally powerful Rabbi Joseph Ibn Naghrela, and destroyed the entire Jewish community.

13   From the Arabic *taifah*, a faction or party. At one point there were twenty-three rulers before the arrival of the Almoravids, who conquered them all by 1091. Al-Marrakushi explains pejoratively: "[After the collapse of the Umayyad dynasty, the Caliphate] was divided into factions and each region was controlled by those who had local power and they shared the Caliphal titles, and one was called al-Mutadid and another al-Mamum and others were called al-Mustain and

al-Muqtadir and al-Mutasin and al-Mutamid and al-Muaffaq and al-Mutawakkil land other such Caliphal titles" (*Kitab*, ed. and trans. Ambrosio Hici Miranda, 65).

14   Lagardère, *Les almoravides jusqu'au règne de Yusuf B. Tasfin*, 207. The Almoravids were a confederation of Berber tribes from the northwestern Saharan desert who built an empire in northwestern Africa and southern Spain in the eleventh and twelfth centuries. These ferocious warriors wore black veils that showed only their eyes. They were deeply religious and ascetic followers of the Maliki school. The name is derived from the Arabic *al-Murabitun*, those who are like fortresses (singular *ribat*). Their motto was "To propagate The Truth, repress injustice, and abolish illegal taxes." For the decisive role of the *ulama* in the Almoravid takeover of al-Andalus after the decadent *taifa* rulers had called on the Berbers to help against the resurgent Catholic kingdoms, see *Kitab*, ed. and trans. Ambrosio Huici Miranda, 108–9 and n2. The Almoravids halted the Catholic advance but never took back reconquered Toledo. The Muslim masses were unhappy with the *taifa* rulers for a variety of reasons: their bickering, their taxes, their impious way of life, and their alliances with the Catholic kingdoms (see al-Marrakushi, 118).

15   Abdel Magid Turki, "La venération pour Malik et la physionomie du malikisme andalou," *Studia Islamica* 33 (1971): 62.

16   Abderrazak Moulay Rachid, *La condition de la femme au Maroc* (Rabat: Editions de la faculté des Sciences Juridiques, Economiques et Sociales de Rabat, 1985), 50–51.

17   C.L. Caen et al., "Hisba," *Encyclopaedia of Islam, Second Edition*, ed. P. Bearman et al. (Brill, 2011), www.encislam.brill.nl.turing.library.northwestern.edu/subscriber/uid=1705/entry?entry=islam_COM0293; Roy Mottahedeh and Kristen Stilt, "Public and Private as Viewed through the Work of the *Muhtasib*," *Social Research: An International Quarterly* 70, no. 3 (Fall 2003): 735–48; Pedro Chalmeta Gendrón, *El señor del zoco en España* (Madrid: Instituto Hispano-Árabe de Cultura, 1973), 408. In Umayyad al-Andalus, the first treatise on the obligation to keep and enforce morals in the public spaces (*hisba*), attributed to the *muhtasib* Ahmad Ibn al-Rauf, dates from the second half of the ninth century, but the office was a feature of the Abbasid empire and therefore of the Abbasid Spain taken over by Umayyad ruler Abd al-Rahman I: see Ahmad Ghabin, *Hisba, Arts and Craft in Islam* (Wiesbaden: Otto Harrassowitz, 2009), 83. Under the Middle East Umayyads, the title was *amil al-suk*: see Joseph Schacht, *An Introduction to Islamic Law* (Oxford: Clarendon Press, 1964), 55.

18   *Al-Joxani*, 23.

19   Ibid., 24–28.

20   For the origins and functions of the *qadi* in Islam in general, see Louis Milliot, *Introduction à l'étude du droit musulman* (Paris: Recueil Sirey, 1953), 695–703; for al-Andalus, see Alfonso Carmona, "Le Malékisme et le conditions requises pour l'exercise de la judicature," *Islamic Law and Society* 7, no. 2, 122–58.

21   *Al-Joxani*, 97. *Qadi* Said ibn Suleiman was not only honorable and virtuous but also modest and humble (137). The asceticism of the Sevillian Yahia ibn Maamar was proverbial (104).

22   *Al-Joxani*, 81. See the legal manual *al-Tafri* in Soha Abboud-Haggar, *El Tratado Jurídico de Al-Tafri de Ibn Al-Gallab: Manuscrito Aljamiado De Almonacid De La Sierra (Zaragoza). Edición, Estudio, Glosario y Confrontación Con El Original Árabe* (Zaragoza: Institución "Fernando el Católico," 1999), 2:44–45 (I cite by page); *Mudawwana*, tome 1, bk. 1, no. 12, in "La Moudawwana (Recension de Sahnoun): Analyse par G.H. Bousquet," *Annales de l'Institut d'Études Orientales* 16 (1958), 17 (1959), and 20 (1962), and *Revue algérienne, tunisienne et marocaine de législation et de jurisprudence* 74 (1958), 75 (1959), and 77 (1961); all my references to the *Mudawwana* are taken from this work, unless otherwise noted. See also Maliki *faqih* Ibn Habib according to Janina M. Safran, "Identity and Differentiation in Ninth-Century al-Andalus," *Speculum* 76, no. 3 (July 2001): 582. The problem of wiping or not wiping one's hands on one's socks arises from a passage in Quran 5:6. For the command to use only the right hand for eating and drinking unless incapacitated, see *al-Tafri*, 586. The fine points of violating prohibitions against sex during Ramadan are treated by Imam Malik in his *Muwatta* 18.9.22 in *The Muwatta of Imam Malik by Imam Malik b. Anas 95–179 (A.H.). Narrated by*

Yahya b. Yahya b. Kathir al-Laith al-Andalusi, trans. F. Amira Zrien Matraji, corrected and revised by Dr. Mahmood Matraji (Karachi: Darul Ishaat, 2005), from which all my citations are taken unless otherwise specified. For the blood cost of a severed penis or testicle, see *Muwatta*, 43.8.6a. The case against entering a mosque after eating garlic is made in *Muwatta*, 1.8. Children were not allowed to enter a mosque, according to a tenth-century Muslim judicial document cited by Christine Mazzoli-Guintard, *Vivre à Cordue au Moyen Age: Solidarité citadines en terre d'Islam aux Xe–Xie siècles* (Rennes: Presses Universitaires de Rennes, 2003), 224.

23 For this and the following, see, among others, *al-Tafri*, 21–49; *Mudawwana*, 16 (1958); *Muwatta*, 2.2; Octave Pesle, *La Femme Musulmane Dans le Droit, la Réligion et les Moeurs* (Rabat: Les éditions La Porte, 1946).

24 *Al-Tafri*, 44–45; the *Mudawwana* permits using for ablution water that a menstruating woman has left over, but not water left over by a Christian (tome 1, bk. 1, no. 12 in *Mudawwana* 16 [1958], 182); Maliki *fiqh* Ibn Habib according to Safran, "Identity and Differentiation in Ninth-Century al-Andalus," 582.

25 *Muwatta*, 54.5.12: according to Malik, a *hadith* claims that Muhammad ordered dogs killed. *Muwatta*, 31.29.68: dogs must not be kept in houses or as mere companions, but if at all outside with livestock. See also Ibn Rushd, *Bidayat* vol. 2, 24.2.1 (the *Bidayat* is translated as *The Distinguished Jurist's Primer* by Imran Ahsan Kahan Nyazee [Reading: Garnet Publishing Limited, 1994], 2 vols., and all my citations refer to this edition); *The Risala of 'Abdullah ibn Abi Zayd al-Qayrawani (310/922–386/996): A Treatise on Maliki Fiqh*, trans. Aisha Bewley with her clarifying comments in brackets, 44.05, Aisha Bewley's Islamic Home Page, accessed June 5, 2010, bewley.virtualave.net/Risalatitl.html. All my citations of the *Risala* are from this translation, checked against Abu Muhammad Abd Allah Ibn Abi Zayd al-Qayrawani, *Risala ou traité agrégé de droit Malékite et moral musulmane*, trans. Edmond Fagnan (Paris: Geuthner, 1914), at http://gallica.bnf.fr/ark:/12148/bpt6k5813421p, unless otherwise specified. Among other relevant works involving Maliki *fiqh* by Aisha Bewley are *Al-Muwatta of Imam Malik Ibn Anas: The First Formulation of Islamic Law* (London: Kegan Paul International, 1989), and *Muawiya: Restorer of the Muslim Faith* (London: Dar al-Taqwa, 2002).

26 *Al-Tafri*, 32, 41–42; *Muwatta*, the entire book 2.

27 *Al-Tafri*, 1; *Muwatta*, 2.17.66; 2.18.

28 *Al-Tafri*, 1. All this is of much complexity; one ritual, namely washing of the hands, is already very complicated in view of the numerous opinions on the matter. See María Isabel Fierro, "La polémique a propos de raf' al-yadayn fi 'lsalat dans al-Andalus," *Studia Islamica* 65 (1987): 69–90.

29 She was in a state of "major ritual impurity": *Muwatta* 2.23.88; 2.28.101. Al-Bukhari also cites Muhammad on the subject. *Sahih Al-Bukhari*, trans. Dr. Muhammad Muhsin Khan (Chicago: Kazi Publications, 1979), tome 1, bk. 6, no. 301: "Narrated Abu Said Al-Khudri: Once Allah's Apostle went out to the Musalla (to offer the prayer) o 'Id al-Adha or Al-Fitr prayer. Then he passed by the women and said, 'O women! Give alms, as I have seen that the majority of the dwellers of Hellfire were you (women).' They asked, 'Why is it so, O Allah's Apostle?' He replied, 'You curse frequently and are ungrateful to your husbands. I have not seen anyone more deficient in intelligence and religion than you. A cautious sensible man could be led astray by some of you.' The women asked, 'O Allah's Apostle! What is deficient in our intelligence and religion?' He said, 'Is not the evidence of two women equal to the witness of one man?' They replied in the affirmative. He said, 'This is the deficiency in her intelligence. Isn't it true that a woman can neither pray nor fast during her menses?' The women replied in the affirmative. He said, 'This is the deficiency in her religion.'" Muhammad, however, allowed a man to sleep in the same bed with a menstruating woman: *Bukhari*, vol. 1, bk. 6, no. 320.

30 *Muwatta*, 19.4.8.

31 Ibid., 2.2; 15.5.16; 20.14.55.

32 Ibid., 2.27.95: "Yahya related to me from Malik from Zayd ibn Aslam that a man questioned the Messenger of Allah, may Allah bless him and grant him peace, saying, 'What is permitted

me from my wife when she is menstruating?' The Messenger of Allah, may Allah bless him and grant him peace, said, 'Let her wrap her waistwrapper round herself tightly, and then what is above that is your concern.'" 2.27.97: "Yahya related to me from Malik from Nafi that Ubaydullah ibn Abdullah ibn Umar sent a question to A'isha asking her, 'May a man fondle his wife when she is menstruating?' She replied, 'Let her wrap her waistwrapper around her lower part and then he may fondle her if he wishes.'"

33   Malik points out that in the time of Muhammad men and women did their ablutions together but that this togetherness is no longer the accepted practice: *Muwatta*, 2.3.15.

34   *Muwatta*, 14.5.12; 14.5.14. For this generalized Islamic practice, see also Pesle, *La Femme Musulmane Dans le Droit, la Réligion et les Moeurs*, 193.

35   *Muwatta*, 8.10.

36   For example, accidentally vomiting while praying at the mosque may require only a rinsing of the mouth before continuing prayer, and *wudu* before praying might be skipped after eating cooked food. See *Muwatta*, 2.5. If no water is available, sand or rocks may be used: *Muwatta*, 2.2.

37   Ibid., 2.6.30. Things are actually more complicated because a fuller ablution is called *ghusl*.

38   Manuela Marín, "Una familia de ulama cordobeses: los Banu Abiisa," *Al-Qantara* 6, nos. 1/2 (1985): 291–320. For a general work on the fundamental role of the *ulama* in Islamic Spain, see Hussain Mones, "Le rôle des hommes de religion dans l'histoire de l'Espagne musulmane jusqu'à la fin du Califat," *Studia Islamica* 20 (1964): 47–88; Emile Tyan, *Histoire de l'Organisation Judiciaire en Pays d'Islam* (Paris: Librairie du Recueil Sirey, 1938), 339–40. For the *ulama* in general in the Muslim world, see Milliot, *Introduction à l'étude du droit musulman*, 703–12. The word *imam* is normally used to designate someone who leads the Friday prayer. But the title *imam* was also a permanent honorary and highly respectful title given by consensus to an *alim* of great knowledge and therefore authority, such as Malik Ibn Anas or Bukhari. In Shia Islam this title carried even more authority, since it entailed access to revelation.

39   Rather than *muwalladun* ("mixed" or "hybrid"), today converts are more correctly politically called *muallaf*—that is, "reconciled" to the true faith. Córdoban *qadi* Mahdi b. Muslim was a convert. The rise of converts within Islamic ranks took place not always without some lingering suspicion among their enemies regarding their orthodoxy: *Al-Joxani*, 23. In the Catholic Church, among the more famous examples of men and women of formerly Jewish families who rose to important offices are Bishop Pablo de Santa María, Inquisitor General Tomás de Torquemada, and religious reformer and (posthumously) doctor of the Church Saint Teresa of Ávila, all of *converso* families—that is, with Jewish ancestors who at one point had converted to Catholicism. In late fifteenth-century Castile, Isabella's treasurer was a *converso* and a factor in Columbus's first voyage; at the time, the treasurer of the kingdom of Aragon was also a *converso*. The pejorative word *marrano* (possibly derived from the Arabic *muharram* or *mahrram*—"ritually forbidden") applied to converts to Catholicism (*conversos*) who secretly continued to practice their previous religion. Some sources link the American English term *mulatto* to *muladi*, a link plausible in view of the central role played by Arabs in the slave trade.

40   *Al-Joxani*, 19, 33, 42, 43, 57, 195, etc.

41   Ibid., passim. In later times, under Almoravids, the *ulama*'s power if anything increased. A good study of the *ulama* under the Almoravids is Rachid El Hour, "The Andalusian *Qadi* in the Almoravid Period: Political and Judicial Authority," *Studia Islamica* 90 (2000): 67–83.

42   *Al-Joxani*, 148.

43   Ibid., 158.

44   Ibid., passim. See also Christian Muller, "Judging with God's Law on Earth: Judicial Powers of the *Qadi al-Jamaa* of Cordoba in the Fifth/Eleventh Century," *Islamic Law and Society* 7, no. 2 (2000): 159–86.

45   *Tuhfat al-Hukkam or Gift for the Judges*, trans. Alhaji Bello Muhammad (Zaria, Nigeria: Ahmadu Bello University, 1989), 3.

46   Ann Elizabeth Mayer, updated by Joseph A. Kechichian, "Law. Modern Legal Reforms. Islamization Programs," *Oxford Encyclopedia of the Islamic World: Oxford Islamic Studies Online*, www.

oxfordislamicstudies.com.turing.library.northwestern.edu/article/opr/t236/e0473#e0473s0005 (accessed August 11, 2011).

47 The organic quality of civil law was the rule in Europe at least until the Enlightenment, which was forced on Europe by the French Revolution and by Napoleon, and which introduced a constructivist, *more geometrico* approach to the law. The Catholic Church taught (see, among many others, Saint Augustine and Saint Thomas Aquinas) that Christian principles must inspire society and therefore also a society's laws to make both just. But this Christian inspiration did not mean that the law was to be the same for both Church and state. In fact, in Catholic Europe the first codifier of the concrete distinctions between canon law and civil law is probably the monk (either Benedictine or Camaldolese) Johannes Gratian with his *Decretum* (after 1139). That is to say, the Catholic Church itself was distinguishing itself from the state. The differentiation, though presented in a general way, can be traced back to Jesus, and in Catholic thought therefore to God himself, who admonishes His listeners to give to Caesar what is Caesar's and to God what is God's (Luke 20:20–26). In the Quran, Allah communicates no equivalent distinction between the two realms. For canon law statements formalizing the separation of the Church from the secular courts, see *The Summa decretorum*, which Rufinus wrote between 1157 and 1159 as an addition to the also separatist *Decretum Gratiani*. For canon law in England, see Alain Boureau, "How Law Came to the Monks: The Use of Law in English Society at the Beginning of the Thirteenth Century," *Past and Present* 167 (2000): 29–74.

48 For example, Castile chose *comtes* as judges, as Ramón Peralta, professor of constitutional law at the Universidad Complutense of Madrid, pointed out in his *Teoría de Castilla* (Madrid: Actas, 2005).

49 For example, professor of Islamic studies Richard W. Bulliet overlooks these issues during his arguments in favor of multiculturalism in *The Case for Islamo-Christian Civilization* (New York: Columbia University Press, 2004).

50 The "Donation of Constantine" was a document stating that Emperor Constantine had bequeathed to the pope political authority over the Western or Latin Roman Empire. The document is "without doubt a forgery," as the *Catholic Encyclopedia* declares flatly. It was forged "somewhere between the years 750 and 850. As early as the fifteenth century its falsity was known and demonstrated. Cardinal Nicholas of Cusa (*De Concordantia Catholicâ*, III, ii, in the Basle ed. of his *Opera*, 1565, I) spoke of it as a *dictamen apocryphum*. Some years later (1440) Lorenzo Valla (*De falso credita et ementita Constantini donatione declamatio*, Mainz, 1518) proved the forgery with certainty. Independently of both his predecessors, Reginald Pecocke, Bishop of Chichester (1450–57), reached a similar conclusion in his work 'The Repressor of over much Blaming of the Clergy,' Rolls Series, II, 351–366. Its genuinity was yet occasionally defended, and the document still further used as authentic, until Baronius in his 'Annales Ecclesiastici' (ad an. 324) admitted that the 'Donatio' was a forgery, whereafter it was soon universally admitted to be such." See "Donation of Constantine," in *Catholic Encyclopedia*, ed. Charles G. Herbermann et al., available at www.newadvent.org/cathen/05118a.htm.

51 The Church variously influenced legislation, especially the law of wills. Marriage took place according to Church procedures, and family rules were directly inspired by Roman Catholicism and the Roman Catholic Church. See Michael M. Sheehan, *Marriage, Family, and Law in Medieval Europe: Collected Studies*, ed. James K. Farge (Toronto: University of Toronto Press, 1996), esp. 24. For a general introduction on the profound impact of Christianity on law in Europe, see John Witte Jr. and Frank S. Alexander, eds., *Christianity and Law: An Introduction* (Cambridge: Cambridge University Press, 2008).

52 John Hudson, *The Formation of the English Common Law: Law and Society in England from the Norman Conquest to Magna Carta* (London: Longman, 1996).

53 Richard Posner at home.uchicago.edu/~rposner/biography.

54 Peralta, *Teoría de Castilla*, 50. Even the king was subject to the law, which he did not create. Royal power, however, finally triumphed over local autonomies in the sixteenth century.

55   Miguel Angel Ladero Quesada, *La formación medieval de España* (Madrid: Alianza, 2004), 175.

56   Ladero Quesada, *La formación medieval de España*, 176.

57   Ibid., *La formación medieval de España*, 176–80.

58   The Arabic *al-qaid*, "the judge." Some of the characteristics of this elected office have been captured in Pedro Calderón de la Barca's famous seventeenth-century play *El alcalde de Zalamea*. No priest is visible anywhere in this play.

59   Except, again, in the "properly Church" business of marrying people and in family affairs like baptism and the other religious sacraments.

60   The United States is a telling example. In cities with high levels of homicides, such as Chicago or New York, the mayors refuse to call for the enforcement of mandatory federal government penalties for armed criminals. Simple possession of a firearm by a "violent" felon should get such a felon an automatic ten-year prison sentence according to federal law, but judges in such cities do not enforce the law. Similarly, anyone who transports a firearm or ammunition across state lines with the intention to commit or aid a felony should get a minimum ten-year sentence. But judges disregard the law. Federal immigration laws are routinely not enforced by the executive branch of government, and most notoriously by cities that have declared themselves "Sanctuary Cities" and that openly defy federal laws. Bicyclists routinely go through red lights and stop signs without being ticketed. And so on.

61   Complications in Islamic law are added by the possible distinctions among *amal* (práctica jurídica), *urf* (local use of the law), and *ada* (custom). See Andrés Botero Bernal, "Al-Andalus: Una experiencia ius-histórica de convivencia entre diferentes," www.urbeetius.org/newsletters/22/news22_boterobernal.pdf. But again, this was not unique to Islamic Spain: it happens in every society.

62   This quoted phrase is from Janina M. Safran, Professor of History and Director of the Middle Eastern Studies Minor at Pennsylvania State University, as part of her effort to counter an examination of Maliki jurisprudence that can lead us to regard unfavorably the way of life of al-Andalus: see her *Defining Boundaries in al-Andalus: Muslims, Christians and Jews in Islamic Iberia* (Ithaca: Cornell University Press, 2013), 211. This well-researched book does not mention female circumcision, stoning for adultery, crucifixions, cutting of noses or tongues, and so forth. In her description of the book in her department site at http://history.psu.edu/directory/jxs57, accessed May 21, 2015, Safran follows up with a claim made by many Arabists regarding not only Islamic Spain but even Islamic law as a whole: that "the flexibility of Islamic legal concepts and categories accommodated intercommunal interaction and integration into the Muslim community."

63   *The Decline and Fall of the Roman Empire*, chap. 44.

64   See *al-Tafri*, where Malik's name is invoked at the beginning of the first chapter, which deals with purification rituals. This edition is an admirable work of scholarship by Professor Abboud-Haggar. After a number of generations under Catholic rule, many *mudéjares* and Moriscos communicated in a form of Spanish (Aljamiado, which was written in Arabic characters) rather than in Arabic, just as many Catholics under Muslim rule lost their Spanish and communicated in Arabic. The Aragon government, needing to assimilate large foreign populations that could collude with powerful Islamic realms outside Spain and that, in fact, engaged in a tremendous revolt in the early sixteenth century, adopted the Conversion Decree in 1525, forbidding the presumably former Muslims (Moriscos) from keeping Islamic texts. Thus the Aljamiado version of the treatise of Ibn al-Gallab was found hidden inside a wall in 1884 in Almonacid de la Sierra in the province of Zaragoza.

65   Instructive comparisons are made between the classic *Mudawwana* in its transcription by Sahnun and its early twentieth-century modifications in André Colomer, *Droit Musulman: Les Personnes. La famille* (Rabat: La Porte, 1962). G.H. Bousquet summarized the *Mudawwana* in "La Moudawwana," *Annales de l'Institut d'Études Orientales* 16 (1958), 17 (1959), and 20 (1962), and *Revue algérienne, tunisienne et marocaine de législation et de jurisprudence* 74 (1958), 75 (1959), and 77 (1961). For the transmission of the *Mudawwana*, see Miklos Muranyi,

Die Rechtsbuecher des Qairawaners Sahnun b. Sa'id: Entstehungsgeschichte und Werkueber-lieferung (Stuttgart: Steiner, 1999), which emphasizes the "fluidity" of the extant text in the various manuscripts. Muranyi reinforces the generally accepted timetable of Islamic writings and convincingly rejects the effort to present the *Mudawwana* as prior to the *Muwatta*, as in Norman Calder, *Studies in Early Muslim Jurisprudence* (Oxford: Clarendon Press, 1993). For the impact of the treatise in Islamic Spain, see J. M. Forneas, "Datos para un estudio de la *mudawwana* de Sahnun en al-Andalus," in *Actas del IV Coloquio Hispano-Tunecino* (Madrid: Instituto Hispano-Arabe de Cutlura, 1983), 93–118.

66 Ana Fernández Félix, *Cuestiones legales del islam temprano: la Utbiyya y el proceso de for-mación de la sociedad islámica andalusí* (Madrid: Consejo Superior de Investigaciones Cientí-ficas, 2003), especially 494–95.

67 Delfina Ferrano, "Legal Practice in an Andalusi-Maghribi Source from the Twelfth Century C.E.: The Madhahib al-Hukkam fi nawazil al-ahkam," *Islamic Law and Society* 7, no. 2, *Islamic Law in Al-Andalus* (2000): 187–234.

68 *Tuhfat al-Hukkam or Gift for the Judges*, trans. Alhaji Bello Muhammad (Zaria, Nigeria: Ahmadu Bello University, 1989). My reading of this manual, not cited, as far as I know, by María Isabel Fierro and other Spanish scholars, indicates that some presumed differences between Andalusian Malikism and non-Andalusian Malikism may be more complicated than it has appeared up to now. The treatise makes clear that only one male witness is needed to inform a judge about some case, but that every right-thinking jurist regards two men as preferable to one—and that if the witnesses are women, two are *required* (13). Written by an Andalusian jurist, this manual is still used today in, among other places, sub-Saharan Africa.

69 For the hegemony of Malikism in Islamic Spain, see *Bidayat*, vol. 2, 56.7.

70 *The Muwatta of Imam Malik by Imam Malik b. Anas 95–179 (A.H.). Narrated by Yahya b. Yahya b. Kathir al-Laith al-Andalusi*, trans. F. Amira Zrien Matraji, corrected and revised by Dr. Mahmood Matraji (Karachi: Darul Ishaat, 2005); J. M. Forneas, "Para un estudio del Kitab al-Muwatta en al-Andalus," in *Actas del Coloquio Hispano-Marroquí de Ciencias Históricas: Historia, Ciencia y Sociedad* (Madrid: M.A.E., 1992), 197–216. In *Studies in Early Muslim Jurisprudence*, Norman Calder argues that the *Muwatta* could have been actually written down first in Córdoba. Malikism was founded by Imam Malik Ibn Anas (d. 795) in Medina, the city where Muhammad migrated from Mecca in 622, thereby marking the beginning of the Islamic calendar. In the version by Malik's Andalusian disciple Yahya b. Yahya al-Andalusi, Malik's *Muwatta* held immense authority not only in Muslim Spain but through much of the rest of the Islamic world as well. Considered by its followers the first compendium of *fiqh* and *ahadith*, the oldest Islamic book after the Quran, and the carrier of the earliest Islamic traditions of the sacred city of Medina, the *Muwatta* came to be widely regarded as second only to the Quran as a fountain of Islamic knowledge. "We have in the practice of the people of Madinah, in their ordinary transactions as well as their acts of wor-ship, a clear model sanctioned by revelation, since the people of Madinah of the generation of the Companions lived their every moment with the intense knowledge that at any moment an ayah or a surah might be revealed on matters displeasing to Allah or in confirmation of matters pleasing to him" (from the introduction by Mahmood Matraji). See also Mik-los Muranyi, *Materialien zur malikitischen Relchtsliteratur* (Weisbaden: Otto Harrassowitz, 1984), 78.

71 *Al-Joxani*. The more established scholarly opinion on this book is that the first three biogra-phies are probably legendary but the rest are not. But even the possibly legendary biographies help a reader "visualize" the social milieu and system of values in which Islamic *ulama* oper-ated and the population at large lived.

72 This least conservative school of law rules over Pakistan, and the Pakistani constitution of 1979 includes stoning (*rajm*) for proven cases of fornication and adultery among *muhsan* (Muslim married women or men). See Ordinance VII, which includes a definition of *muhsan*, online at www.pakistani.org/pakistan/legislation/zia_po_1979/ord7_1979.html.

73 Abdur Rahim, *The Principles of Muhammedan Jurisprudence according to the Hanafi, Maliki, Shafi'i, and Hanbali School* (London and Madras: Luzac & Co., 1911). For the development of laws against apostasy, see pages 249–54.

74 Asín Palacios, 1:22. The Maliki jurisprudence materials are numerous. For a listing and genealogical examination of the available documents, see Muranyi, *Materialen zur Malikitischen Rechtsliteratur*. For its rule in the kingdom of Granada, see Rachel Arié, *Études sur la civilisation de l'Espagne musulmane* (Leiden: Brill, 1990), 68–69.

75 María Isabel Fierro, "Heresy in al-Andalus," in Salma Khadra Jayyusi, ed., *The Legacy of Muslim Spain* (Leiden: Brill, 1994), 2:895.

76 María Isabel Fierro, "Los malikíes de al-Andalus y los dos árbitros (al-hakaman)," *Al-Qantara* 6, nos. 1/2 (1985): 79. Fierro lists the following divergences in other areas of the law: they did not admit one single witness as proof; they accepted payment for the renting of land by means of part of the product of the land; they did not admit property associations when the intention of the associations was to pay alms; and they allowed trees to be planted around mosques. There were also controversies on the proper rules for washing hands. María Isabel Fierro, "La polémique a propos de *raf al-yadayn fi l-salat*," *Studia Islamica* 65 (1987): 69–90. *Al-Joxani* (79–80) indicates that early Muslim fashions for men differed in at least one way from that of other Islamic lands: although men shunned silk dress, as Islamic tradition requires, they did not as a rule wear a turban until the eleventh century, as was the Islamic custom elsewhere (though in some *ahadith* Muhammad is said to have commanded that no turban be worn during *ihram*, the required condition before the pilgrimage to Mecca, or *Hajj*). The miniatures of Alfonso X's (1282–1284) *Cantigas de Santa María* already portray Muslims wearing turbans.

77 Fierro, "Heresy in al-Andalus," 895. That Ibn Hazm referred to the existence of various undesirable sects and that in a different work he attacks heretics like the Murjis and the Sufis does not show Maliki tolerance; it shows the opposite, since even he attacked deviating sects.

78 Forneas, "Datos para un estudio de la *mudawwana* de Sahnun en al-Andalus," 94.

79 With a consequent rise in preexisting heterodoxies like Sufism. But Malikism remained the dominant religious school.

80 Cf., for example, Robert Brunschvig, "Polémiques Médiévales Autour du Rite de Malik," *Al-Andalus* 15, no. 2 (1950): 388, on whether one should pay more attention to Malik the compiler of *ahadith* transmitting Muhammad's *sunnah* or to Malik the originator of legal opinions.

81 Hussain Monés, "Le Rôle des Hommes de Religion dans l'Histoire de l'Espagne musulmane: jusqu'à la fin du Califat," *Studia Islamica*, no. 20 (1964): 47–88.

82 Forneas, "Datos para un estudio de la *mudawwana* de Sahnun en al-Andalus," 117n140.

83 Emilio García Gómez, *Andalucía contra berbería* (Barcelona: University of Barcelona, 1976), 127. Al-Saqundi was the author of *Elogio del Islam español (Risala fi fadl alandalus)*, trad. Emilio Garcia Gomez (Madrid: Maestre, 1934).

84 Lagardère, *Les almoravides jusqu'au règne de Yusuf B. Tasfin*, 149.

85 Forneas, "Datos para un estudio de la *mudawwana* de Sahnun en al-Andalus," 108 and 112, n33.

86 Abdel Magid Turki, "La vénération pour Malik et la physionomie du makilisme andalou," *Studia Islamica*, no. 33 (1971): 48—"La premiére caracteristique de ce malikisme andalou, c'est le fait qu'il a eté quasiment exclusif de toute autre école juridique."

87 Jorge Aguade, "Some Remarks about Sectarian Movements in al-Andalus," *Studia Islamica*, no. 64 (1986): 56–57; Maribel Fierro, "Prácticas y creencias religiosas en al-Andalus," *Al-Qantara* 13, no. 2 (1992): 470; Fierro, "Heresy in al-Andalus," 895–908. In this last article Fierro basically argues that the existence of Muslim heresies shows the flexibility and variety of Andalusian Islam. But the fact that these heresies were persecuted argues for the existence of Maliki intolerance, not its opposite. Fierro insists forcefully that there were heterodox thinkers and groups in al-Andalus. Of course there always were; some outright heretics could be found here and there too, just as there were periods when Malikism was not hegemonic. None of this erases the fact that Malikism ruled Islamic Spain for most of its history or that those who diverged from orthodoxy, especially heretics and blasphemers, spoke at their own peril.

88   *Al-Tafri*, 572.
89   See *Al-Tafri*, 585; Ibn Hazm, *Fisal*, 4:40.
90   Fierro, "Heresy in al-Andalus," 895.
91   Ibid., 903.
92   Ibid., 895.
93   Ibn al-Jatib, *Historia de los Reyes de la Alhambra (Al-Lamha al-badriyya): Resplandor de la luna llena acerca de la dinastía nazarí*, trans. José María Casciaro Ramírez (Granada: University of Granda, 2010), 187–88.
94   Ibn al-Jatib, *Historia delos Reyes de la Alhambra*, 126.
95   "Los árabes españoles y el Islam," in *Actas del Primer Congreso de Estudios Árabes e Islámicos. Córdoba, 1962*, ed. F. M. Pareja (Madrid: Comité permanente del Congreso de Estudios Árabes a Islámicos, 1964), 17, a translation of Goldziher's text published by the Academy of Sciences of Hungary in 1876.
96   Ana Fernández Félix has grasped how contact with Christians and Jews exacerbated Islamism. See Fernández Félix, *Cuestiones legales del Islam temprano*, 499.
97   Joseph Schacht, "Malik Ibn Anas," *E. J. Brill's First Encyclopaedia of Islam, 1913–1936* (Leiden: Brill, 1913–1938), 5:208; *Muwatta*, 14. The treatise's origin in Medina allowed it to claim orthodox authority: Safran, "Identity and Differentiation in Ninth-Century al-Andalus," 577–78.
98   Justin Stearns, "Contagion and Law: Ethical Considerations in the Writings of Two Fourteenth-Century Scholars of Nasrid Granada," *Islamic Law and Society* 14, no. 1 (2007): 109–29. This article covers a *taifa* kingdom, however, and *taifa* rulers were not usually celebrated for their devoted adherence to strict Islamic teachings.
99   María Isabel Fierro, "El principio malikí 'sadd al-dara'i' en el *Kitab al-hawadit wa-l-bida'* de al-Turtusi," *Al-Qantara* 2, nos. 1/2 (1981): 69.
100 *Al-Joxani*, 154, 174.
101 Abd al-Rahman I, founder of Umayyad al-Andalus, played favoritism games with his judges: see *Historia de los jueces de Córdoba*, 53. During the reigns of Abd al-Rahman II and Muhammad I, *ulama* accused of disguised apostasy and hypocrisy were exonerated because of the rulers' pressure on the courts. See Safran, "Identity and Differentiation in Ninth-Century al-Andalus," 592.
102 Ibn Hazm, *Fisal*, 5:143.
103 *Al-Tafri*, 572.
104 *Risala*, 37.19.
105 *Muwatta*, "Judgements," 36.18.15–16.
106 According to Ibn Rushd, a Muslim who had abandoned Islam openly was given the opportunity to repent before being killed: *Bidayat*, 2.552; Adel Theodor Khoury, *Toleranz im Islam* (Munich: Kaiser, 1980), 112. For Ibn Rushd's service as adviser to the Almohads, see al-Maqqari, *The History of the Mohammedan Dynasties in Spain by Ahmed Ibn Mohammed al-Makkari*, trans. Pascual de Gayangos (1843; rpt. New York: Johnson Reprint Corporation, 1964), vol. 1, app. A, xv.
107 *Al-Tafri*, 572; *Risala*, 37.19; *Leyes de Moros*, CLXXX.
108 The burning of witches in Christian Europe presumably purified and therefore saved their souls. No such preoccupation with the witches' souls bothered the Islamic clerics. A new book on the subject of the persecution of witches in Europe and the Americas comes out every few years. A recent one is John Demos, *The Enemy Within: Two Thousand Years of Witch Hunting in the Western World* (New York: Viking, 2008). One may expect, however, that these yet-to-be-written studies will attribute the persecution of witches in Muslim lands to Western influence, going back either to Muhammad or to the rise of the patriarchal and therefore intolerant *ulama* class. Thereby it will be explained away as having nothing to do with medieval Islam or Arabic culture.
109 *Al-Tafri*, 572.
110 *Risala*, 37.19.
111 Safran, "Identity and Differentiation in Ninth-Century al-Andalus," 596.

112 Ibid., 593.

113 Mazzoli-Guintard, *Vivre à Cordue au Moyen Age*, 204.

114 Soha Abboud-Haggar, "Difusión del tratado jurídico *Al-Trafi* de Ibn Al-Gallab en el Occidente Musulmán," *Aragón en la Edad Media* 1, nos. 14–15 (1999): 1–18. Such drastic actions do not square with the popular image of Islamic Spain as a land of "tolerance." They hardly seem more "tolerant" than actions witnessed in the twenty-first century, such as the widespread riots and killing of non-Muslims in response to Danish cartoons that depicted Muhammad, thereby violating injunctions against pictorial representation of his human form, or the murder of the Japanese translator of Salman Rushdie's *Satanic Verses*, the stabbing of the Italian translator, and the *fatwa* ordering the killing of Rushdie, or the actions of the Islamic State in Iraq and Syria.

115 Mazzoli-Guintard, *Vivre à Cordue au Moyen Age*, 205.

116 There were precedents in the Quran prescribing crucifixion for those who "corrupt the land." See Quran 5:33. I cite from *The Qur'an: Text, Translation, and Commentary* by Abdullah Yusuf Ali (New York: Tahrike Tarsile Qur'an, 2001). For the account below of an *alim* both stabbed and crucified, see Maribel Fierro, "Andalusian 'Fatwa' on Blasphemy," *Annales islamologiques* 25 (1990): 103–17. Other religious texts echoed the Quranic demand for the crucifixion of those "who wage war against Allah and His Apostle." See *Sunan Abu Dawud*, made available online by the University of Southern California Compendium of Muslim texts in the translation by Ahmad Hasan at www.usc.edu/dept/MSA/fundamentals/hadithsunnah/abudawud/: bk. 38, nos. 4357 and 4359. Crucifixion was never used in Catholic Spain, and punishing unrepentant heretics by burning was not practiced there until the twelfth century.

117 *Al-Joxani*, 127–29.

118 We have very few documents on these matters, of course. For one thing, time and the vicissitudes of history have erased most records. For another, the opacity of the details of the application of *sharia* law (still apparent today in Islamic countries that apply medieval *sharia*, such as Saudi Arabia) contributes to the scarcity of the documentation. That we still have even a few records from al-Andalus indicates the widespread use of these punishments. For the present-day practice of beheading and crucifixion and the opaque nature of the documentation of *sharia* in a country such as Saudi Arabia, which is a bona fide member of the United Nations, see Raziye Akkoc, "Hackers Target Saudi Websites as Teenager Ali Mohammed al-Nimr Awaits Execution," *Telegraph* (UK), September 28, 2015.

119 *Al-Joxani*, 154.

120 Pascual de Gayangos, ed., *Dos tratados de legislación musulmana. 1. Leyes de moros del siglo XIV 2. Suma de los principales mandamientos y devedamientos de la ley y çunna, por don Içe de Gebir, Alfaquí Mayor de la aljama de Segovia. Año de 1492* (Madrid: Academia de la Historia. Memorial histórico español, 1853), 5:*Suma* chap. 51.

121 The social conditions in al-Andalus were not rosy, contrary to what is normally taught. See Roberto Marín Guzmán, "The Causes of the Revolt of Umar ibn Hafsun in al-Andalus (880928): A Study in Medieval Islamic Social History," *Arabica* 42, no. 2 (June 1995): 180–221.

122 *Al-Joxani*, 161.

123 *Risala*, 37.19.

124 *Al-Tafri*, 571.

125 *Mudawwana*, tome 4, bk., 2, no. 659.

126 Fernández Félix, *Cuestiones legales del Islam temprano*, 459–67, which suggests the more usual time given for repentance: three days.

127 *Mudawwana*, tome 4, bk. 51, no. 658.

128 *Al-Tafri*, 572. The situation has not changed in some Islamic countries and even in certain Muslim families living in the West: see Sabatina James (a pseudonym), *Del Islam al Cristianismo: Mi Historia* (Madrid: Palabra, 2006).

129 See *Ajbar machmua*, ed. and trans. Emilio Lafuente y Alcántara (Madrid: Rivadeneyra, 1867), 31–32.

130 *Muwatta*, "The Mudabbar": 41.1.12 (41.1.11 in the University of Southern California website)

131 *Suma*, LIV.

132 *Muwatta*, 41.7.

133 *Bidayat*, vol. 2, 58.8.2

134 Ibn Hazm, *Fisal*, 4:40.

135 Maliki treatises are clear on such Islamic teachings. See, for example, *al-Tafri*, passim and 586, 587. Significantly, a sword could be adorned with gold and silver. Malik did not like games, including chess: *Muwatta* 52.2.7: "Yahya related to me from Malik from Nafi from Abdullah ibn Umar that when he found one of his family playing dice he beat him and destroyed the dice. Yahya said that he heard Malik say, 'There is no good in chess, and he disapproved of it.' Yahya said, 'I heard him disapprove of playing it and other worthless games. He recited this ayat, "What is there after the truth except going the wrong way."' (Sura 10 *ayat* 32)."

136 Mazzoli-Guintard, *Vivre à Cordue au Moyen Age*, 210.

137 *Al-Joxani*, 125–27.

138 Ibn al-Jatib, *Historia de los Reyes de la Alhambra*, trans. José María Casciaro Ramírez (Granada: University of Granda, 2010), 187–88.

139 *Suma*, LV.

140 Ibn Hazm, *Naqt-al-Arus*, trans. Luis Seco de Lucena (Valencia: Alemal y Vives, 1974), 98.

141 *Bidayat*, vol. 2, 24.2.1.

142 Roy Mottahedeh and Kristen Stilt, "Public and Private as Viewed through the Work of the *Muhtasib*," *Social Research: An International Quarterly* 70, no. 3 (Fall 2003): 735–48.

143 *Al-Tafri*, 275–77, 565.

144 *Bidayat*, vol. 2, 56.7.1.

145 *Al-Tafri*, 566.

146 This son, Muhammad, was a dissipated fellow whose behavior "was not advantageous to the Caliphate." After his father's death he lasted in power only forty-five days. He was deposed by his two brothers, one of whom, Abu Yaqub Yusuf b. Abd al-Mumin, became caliph. But Yusuf had to overcome the opposition of three other brothers, two of whom died in "mysterious" circumstances before Yusuf consolidated his power: *Colección de Crónicas Arabes de la Reconquista volumen iv: Kitab al-muyib fi taljis ajbar al-Magrib by Abu Muhammad Abd al-Wahid al-Marrakusi*, trans. Ambrosio Huici Miranda (Tetuán: Instituto General Franco de Estudios e Investigación Hispano-Arabe, 1955), 189 and note and 190 and note. The same Muslim history tells that this Yusuf was learned and a protector of writers. He invaded al-Andalus successfully but was defeated and killed by the Catholics (211–12). His son and successor, Caliph Abu Yusuf Yaqub b. Yusuf b. Abd al-Mumin, was the son of a Catholic sexual slave girl (215).

147 Abd al-Wahid al-Marrakushi, 118. Many of today's Islamic scholars also use this impious behavior by Muslim rulers to explain the fall of al-Andalus.

148 Peter Scholliers, *Food, Drink, and Identity: Cooking, Eating, and Drinking in Europe since the Middle Ages* (Brussels: Berg, 2001), 207.

149 Ibid., 207.

150 *Muwatta*, 1.8.30.

151 Scholliers, *Food, Drink, and Identity*, 208.

152 *Muwatta*, 49.6.

153 Peter Scholliers notes "the religious feeling that bread, especially in combination with wine, may evoke among Christians": *Food, Drink, and Identity*, 195. Bread and the sale of flour for it was forbidden by al-Shafii and some Malikis but permitted in the *Muwatta*: Ibn Rushd, *Bidayat*, vol. 1, 24.2.2.4.3.

154 Mottahedeh and Stilt, "Public and Private as Viewed through the Work of the *Muhtasib*."

155 *Al-Joxani*, 207, 255.

156 *Risala*, 41.0.

157 Al-Ghazali, *On Music and Ecstasy*, chap. 1, trans. Duncan Black Macdonald, in *Journal of the Royal Asiatic Society of Great Britain and Ireland* (Part I, 1901), 201.

158 *Al-Tabari*, 25:76; 36:24, 82; 39:147.

159 Pascual de Gayangos, in his translation of al-Maqqari's *History of the Mohammedan Dynasties in Spain*, 1:365n17 (see 58–59).

160 Irfan Shahid, *Byzantium and the Arabs in the Sixth Century* (Washington, DC: Dumbarton Oaks Research Library and collection, 1995), vol. 2, pt. 2, p. 184.

161 Al-Maqqari, *The History of the Mohammedan Dynasties in Spain*, 1:197–98. One cannot discard that al-Maqqari, writing at a time of rising European dominance, made every effort to aggrandize the cultural achievements of Islam.

162 Jesús Greus, *Ziryab: La prodigiosa historia del Sultán Andaluz y el cantor de Bagdad* (Madrid: Swan, 1987). For the treasurers' refusal to pay the musician, see *Historia de la conquista de España de Abenalcotía el cordobés*, trans. Julián Ribera (Madrid: Revista de Archivos, 1926), 2:54–55.

163 According to Pascual de Gayangos, "Music being a science almost unknown to the Arabs before their conquests, they necessarily borrowed from the subdued nations their knowledge of it, as well as the names of almost all their instruments." Gayangos in his translation of al-Maqqari, *The History of the Mohammedan Dynasties in Spain*, 1:58–59n17, 365. This would apply to the lute as well, which some scholars enthusiastically repeat that Islam "gave" to Spain: the lute was acquired by Arabs during their contact with the more advanced civilization of the Christian Greek Roman Empire, whose direct cultural contact with Europe Islam had interrupted in the first place.

164 *Al-Joxani*, 87–88. In the Spanish text the name of one of the judges is transliterated as "Baxir."

165 Luis del Mármol Carvajal, *Historia de la rebelión y castigo de los moriscos del reino de Granada* (Madrid: BAE, 1946), 2:x, 164, cit. Serafín Fanjul, *Al-Andalus contra España* (Madrid: Siglo XXI, 2002), 17.

166 Medieval Sunnis and Shiites shared these views, which are still prevalent today among sincerely practicing Muslims: in an interview in Iran in the 1970s, the Shiite imam Ayatollah Khomeini said that he had never heard of Bach, Mozart, Beethoven, or Verdi. See "Khomeini Unveiled: The Ayatollah speaks out on executions, political freedom, the crimes of the shah and the morals of youth and women. An interview by Oriana Fallaci," *Washington Post*, October 14, 1979. Those who argue that some Western composers wrote great religious music without their being themselves religious overlook the essential point that these presumably atheistic composers could not have conceived, least of all produced, their religious music without a religious culture.

167 As we learn from Maliki manuals: cf., for example, the Andalusian treatise *al-Tafri*, ii, 24–25, 44, 45, and the influential *Mudawwana*, tome 1, bk. 1, no. 12. In today's Pakistan, and under the less strict Hanafi Islamic school of law, a Christian woman has been condemned to death for drinking at a well reserved for Muslims: "Christian Woman Sentenced to Death for Drinking from Muslim Water Cup May Not Live to Face Execution After five Years Imprisonment Has Left Her with Instestinal Bleeding," *Daily Mail*, June 20, 2015.

168 Safran, "Identity and Differentiation in Ninth-Century al-Andalus," 582, referring to the treatise *Al-Mudawwana al-kubra l-il-imam Malik*.

169 *Al-Tafri*, 265.

170 For the problems with garlic, see, among others, *Sahih Al-Bukhari*, vol. 1, bk. 12, nos. 812–15. For the consumption of beer by Puritans, see Bill Bryson, *Shakespeare: The World as Stage* (New York: HarperCollins, 2007).

171 Safran, "Identity and Differentiation in Ninth-Century al-Andalus," 582.

172 Ibid.

173 *Sahih Muslim*, bk. 21, no. 4743, trans. Abdul Hamid Siddiqui, University of Southern California Center for Muslim-Jewish Engagement, www.cmje.org/religioustexts/hadith/muslim/ (accessed July 10, 2010).

174 Fernández Félix, *Cuestiones legales del Islam temprano*, 481–82. Malik allowed Muslims to sell merchandise to Christians around the churches during Christian feasts (482).

175 Ibid., 486–87. Some scholars today have made strenuous efforts to argue that some new churches were built. These efforts include pointing to Syrian "influences" on churches that

were previously thought to have been constructed prior to the Islamic conquest. All this is hypothetical, since a renovation, not a new construction, might indeed include such influences, if they do exist. In any case, a church here and there built under, say, Abd al-Rahman III would be only an exception to what was the religious teaching in Islamic Spain. As Fernández Félix points out, the word *bana* can refer to either a reconstruction or a reparation. Any such reconstruction would be carried out without Muslim help, as indicated by Maliki law.

176 *Encyclopaedia of Islam, Second Edition* (Brill): "dhabiha." See also for the Maliki school *Islamic Law in Theory and Practice*, ed. Robert Gleave and Eugenia Kermeli (London: Tauris, 2001), 58–59: the "two jugular veins" must be cut, otherwise the animal's meat cannot be eaten.

177 *Al-Tafri*, 556; *Muwatta*, 44.2.2; 43.3.3; 43.15.8b; 43.21; 43.14.

178 *Al-Tafri*, 486.

179 See Tritton, *The Caliphs and Their Non-Muslim Subjects*.

180 For Malik's pronouncement on Christians riding donkeys, see *A Madinan View of the Sunna, Courtesy, Wisdom, Battles, and History* by Abu Muhammad Abdullah Ibn Abi Zayd al-Qayrawani *(d. 386 AH)*, trans. Abdassamad Clarke (London: Ta-Ha Publishers, 1999), 113; for this Islamic injuction applied to the Greeks, see C. M. Woodhouse, *Modern Greece: A Short History* (London: Faber & Faber, 1977), 101. I thank Joanna Spilioti, την Ιωαννα, την γυναικα μου, for this knowledge. In contrast with their kind views on Muslim rule over Christians, many academics were outraged when economist Robert W. Fogel, later a Nobel Prize winner, demonstrated that the average black slave in the American South was generally treated well and in fact lived longer and had a higher caloric intake than the average northern white city dweller. It was also disturbing that Fogel, who was not Christian, had concluded that Christianity (the various Protestant and especially Puritan churches) had been a key factor in the antislavery movement and the War between the States. See Robert W. Fogel and Stanley L. Engermann, *Time on the Cross: The Economics of American Slavery* (1974; rpt. New York: W. W. Norton, 2013).

181 Fernández Félix, *Cuestiones legales del Islam temprano*, 478–79.

182 *Islam from the Prophet Muhammad to the Capture of Constantinople*, ed. and trans. Bernard Lewis (Oxford: Oxford University Press, 1974), 2:158–65.

183 Mazzoli-Guintard, *Vivre à Cordue au Moyen Age*, 207.

184 As recently as 2008, in the very different context of the United States, conflict with non-Muslim factory rules caused pious Somali-born Muslim workers to walk off their jobs at a meat-packing plant: www.foxnews.com/story/2008/09/12/somali-meatpacking-workers-fight-with-colorado-plant-over-ramadan-prayer-breaks/. The offensiveness of doing forbidden things and the obstacles this presents to *convivencia* cannot be overestimated.

185 Answering a question lamenting why *ulama* had not forbidden Muslims from sharing in Christian festivities in thirteenth-century Catholic Córdoba, the king of Ceuta, al-Azafi (reigned 1249–1278), explained that Muslims in Córdoba already had to obey so many religious prohibitions that this one on top of everything else would not have worked. Al-Azafi then proposed a defense method frequently used by non-Christians: pick or invent a festivity of one's own, no matter how minor, and elevate its importance, so that it can offer believers a fun alternative to the temptation of Christmas—in this case, the birth of Muhammad, which Sunni Muslims normally did not celebrate, to avoid imitating the idolatrous practices of the infidels and the heretic Shiites. See Fernando de la Granja, "Fiestas cristianas en al-Andalus. (Materiales para su estudio): *Al-Durr al-munazzam* de al-Azafi," *Al-Andalus* 34, no. 1 (1969): 7ff.

186 *Christians and Moors in Spain: Volume III Arabic Sources (711–1501)*, ed. and trans. Charles Melville and Ahmad Ubaydli (Warminster, England: Aris & Phillips, 1992), 29–31. Not surprisingly, the editors use this quotation actually to claim that Muslims happily participated in Christian festivities in Islamic Spain under the Umayyads. An eleventh century Muslim jurist, Ibn Abi Randaqa al-Turtushi, who spent most of his life in Egypt, complained that by his time Muslims in al-Andalus were falling into such "innovations" as buying nougat

(*turrón*, a typical Spanish Christian food during the Christmas season) during night 27 of Ramadan and fruit like the Christians during New Year's Eve, as well as other unlawful practices (see *Christians and Moors in Spain*, 121). Such violations of Islamic law (likely in lands now controlled by Christians but formerly part of al-Andalus and therefore still regarded as part of Islamic territory according to Muslim law) doubtlessly contributed to the *ulama*'s support for the Almoravid invasion, an invasion that began the final decline of the Christian population in al-Andalus completed under the almohads.

187   *Al-Tafri*, 585.

188   De la Granja, "Fiestas cristianas en al-Andalus," 1–53. Analogous efforts to match Christian Christmas can be seen today among practicing atheists who celebrate the "Solstice," an ancient pagan festivity, and by practicing Jews who have given increasing prominence to Hanukkah, in fact a relatively minor festivity in the Jewish calendar.

189   *Historia de los mozárabes en al-Andalus* (Córdoba: Almuzara, 2013), 157–159.

190   François Clément, "Les rélations interreligieuses en Andalus (Espagne musulmane) du IXe au XIIe siècle," in *Le buissonnement monothéiste* (Strasbourg: Presses Universitaires, 2010), 365. This is an inadvertent admission by the author, who like other scholars today tries to argue that the three groups did not live in separate neighborhoods.

191   H. I. Idris, *La Berbérie orientale sous les Zirides* (Paris: 1962), 2:766n437. Rather desperately, a scholar today (Mazzoli-Guintard) cites this case as an example of *convivencia*, since, after all, the Muslims and the Jew were sharing a well: Mazzoli-Guintard, *Vivre à Cordue au Moyen Age*, 89.

192   Antoine Fattal, *Le Statut légal des non-musulmans en pays d'Islam* (Beyrut: Imprimérie Catholique, 1958), 62–63.

193   Basilio Pavón Maldonado, *Ciudades Hispano-Musulmanas* (Madrid: MAPFRE, 1992), 72–77; Leopoldo Torres Balbás, *Ciudades hispanomusulmanas* (Madrid: Ministerio de asuntos exteriores, 1977), 1:197, 209–215; 2:650; Antonio Almagro, "Planimetría de las ciudades hispanomusulmanas," *Al-Qantara* 8, nos. 1–2 (1987): 424.

194   Adel Theodor Khoury observes that the Quran dictates that it "is not advisable to establish full community with Jews and Christians": *Toleranz im Islam* (Munich: Kaiser, 1980), 217. Muslim, Jewish, and Christian neighborhoods developed naturally around mosques, synagogues, and churches (such ethnic and religious clustering happens naturally in the cities of even relatively open societies such as the United States). Almagro, "Planimetría de las ciudades hispanomusulmanas," points out the presence of Christian and Jewish neighborhoods in the Muslim cities of al-Andalus; so does Évariste Lévi-Provencal, cit. Basilio Pavón Maldonado, *Tratado de Arquitectura Hispanomusulmana* (Madrid: España, 2009), 4:4, 410. For a positive assessment of the practical advantages of the standard division into Muslim, Jewish, and Christian quarters in Muslim cities, see André Raymond, "The Spatial Organization of the City," in *The City in the Islamic World*, ed. S. K. Jayyusi et al. (Leyden: Brill, 2008), 63–64. See also Leopoldo Torres Balbás, *Ciudades hispanomusulmanas* (Madrid: Instituto Hispano-Árabe de cultura, 1985). Muslim men could marry free Catholic and Jewish women (but no Catholic or Jewish men could marry Muslim women), who could continue the practice of their religion, but the offspring must be raised Muslim. Undoubtedly in such family settings coexistence presented problems that human ingenuity can sometimes resolve, but by the second generation Islamization would have taken care of them. To avoid such problems, Malik wisely recommended that Muslims not marry non-Muslims. For an example of the recent politically correct effort to counter the view of the earlier Arabists (dismissed as "Orientalists") regarding the division into Muslim, Christian, and Jewish neighborhoods, see Clément, "Les rélations interreligieuses en Andalus," and the expert Arabist Christine Mazzoli-Guintard's defense of an imaginary "solidarity" in the Spain among the three religions in *Vivre à Cordue au Moyen Age*, 85–88. Mazzoli-Guintard's final position is that the three groups indeed dwelled in "preferential but not exclusive" areas (88 and n18). While downplaying segregation, the author cannot avoid using the expressions "quartiers confessionnels" and "quartiers préferentiels"—that is, "religious neighborhoods" and "preferential neighborhoods"—and repeatedly mentions "Muslim neighborhoods" and

fatwas on limiting socialization, even when inevitable. Even in the twenty-first-century United States, not to mention Europe, and without detailed religious exclusionary laws reinforcing segregation, ethnic and religious groups in cities tend to self-segregate into identifiable areas where the majority of the population is black, Hispanic, "white," Polish, Jewish, Italian, "Middle Eastern," and so forth, with varying degrees of interaction with the other communities. One does not need much imagination to conceive of the much greater segregation that would exist in the cities of Islamic Spain, reinforced as it was by a religion that penetrated every aspect of a person's life. It is unlikely that Muslim rulers would dislike this situation, among other things because it allowed them both to control and to tax the *dhimmis* more easily.

195   For the pejorative meaning of *ahl al-dajn* as "people of the submission" and its derivation *muddajan* among Muslims, see Kathryn A. Miller, "Muslim Minorities and the Obligation to Emigrate to Islamic Territory: Two Fatwas from Fifteenth-Century Granada," *Islamic Law and Society* 7, no. 2, *Islamic Law in Al-Andalus* (2000): 257–58; also Gerard Wiegers below. Miller shows, however, that some *ulama* regarded the continuing presence of Muslims in Catholic lands as forgivable and even necessary to keep a presence in what was once and perhaps could again be part of the *umma*. Muslims in Islamic lands called Muslims who remained in Catholic lands *muddajan* (domesticated), and so Catholics came to call them *mudéjares*, although for the Catholics it meant simply "tributary": Gerard Wiegers, *Islamic Literature in Spanish and Aljamiado: Yva of Segovia (fl.1450), His Antecedents and Successors* (Leiden: Brill, 1994), 3. Muslims in *dar al-Islam*, the living *umma*, also referred to them as *ahl al-dajn*, or "the people of submission."

196   Serafín Fanjul, *Al-Andalus contra España* (Madrid: Siglo XXI, 2005), 248.

CHAPTER 4: THE MYTH OF UMAYYAD TOLERANCE

1   For this and the following, see *The History of the Mohammedan Dynasties of Spain by Ahmed Ibn Mohammed al-Makkari*, trans. Pascual de Gayangos (1843; rpt. New York: Johnson Reprint Corporation, 1964), 2:74, 79ff.; Maribel Fierro, *De muerte violenta: Política, Religión y Violencia en Al-Andalus* (Madrid: Consejo Superior de Investigaciones Científicas, 2004).

2   "Once upon a time in the mid-eighth century, an intrepid young man named Abd al-Rahman abandoned his home in Damascus, the Near Eastern heartland of Islam, and set out across the North African desert in search of a place of refuge". María Ilosa Menocal (Sterling Professor of Humanities at Yale University), *The Ornament of the World: How Muslims, Jews, and Christians Created a Culture of Tolerance in Medieval Spain* (New York: Little, Brown and Company, 2002), 1.

3   Al-Maqqari in *The History of the Mohammedan Dynasties in Spain*, 1:217–18. See the University of Córdoba site on the "mosque of Córdoba" (actually, a Catholic cathedral since the thirteenth century): http://www.uco.es/internacional/extranjeros/conocelauco/conocecordoba/cordobapatrimonio_en.html.

4   *Crónica del moro Rasis*, ed. Diego Catalan and Maria Soledad de Andrés (Madrid: Gredos, 1975), 281–82. See also Susana Calvo Capilla, "Las primeras mezquitas de al-Andalus a través de las fuentes árabes (92/711–170/785)," *Al-Qantara* 28, no. 1 (Enero–Julio 2007), 143–79.

5   Al-Maqqari's *The History of the Mohammedan Dynasties in Spain*, 1:218.

6   Ibid., 1:217.

7   "Cyprus: Destruction of Cultural Property in the Northern Part of Cyprus and Violations of International Law," Library of Congress, April 2009. See also "Destruction of Cultural Heritage" Ministry of Foreign Affairs of the Republic of Cyprus, June 2014, http://www.mfa.gov.cy/mfa/mfa2006.nsf/cyprus07_en/cyprus07_en?OpenDocument.

8   Hugh Kennedy, *The Great Arab Conquests: How the Spread of Islam Changed the World* (New York: DaCapo, 2008).

9   Christian C. Sahner, "The Crescent and the Scimitar," *First Things*, May 2008, 55. Sahner was then a Rhodes Scholar at the University of Oxford studying Islamic and medieval history. In

Spain today, some Muslim groups have asked to be able to share with Catholics the use of the Cathedral of Córdoba because the building was once a mosque, and once a given site has been part of Islam it remains part of Islam. The Mosque of Córdoba was turned into a Christian temple after the reconquest of the city in the thirteenth century, though not destroyed, as had been the fate of the earlier church of Saint Vincent.

10   M. Ocaña Jiménez, "La basílica de San Vicente y la gran mezquita de Córdoba," *Al-Andalus* 6 (1942): 349–51; Capilla, "Las primeras mezquitas de al-Andalus a través de las fuentes árabes," 160; Pedro Marfil, "Arqueología. La Basílica de San Vicente: En la Catedral de Córdoba," *Arte, Arqueología e Historia*, no. 14 (2007): 185–96; "Arqueología en la Mezquita de Córdoba," *Arte, Arqueología e Historia*, no. 6 (1999): 94–100. A more specialized synthesis is "Córdoba de Teodosio a Abd-al-Rahman III," *Anejos del Archivo Español de Arqueología* 23 (2000): 117–41. See a list of Marfil's works at http://dialnet.unirioja.es/servlet/autor?codigo=281455. Archaeologist Pedro Marfil has confirmed in personal e-mail to me that it is unlikely that the church of Saint Vincent was shared because of the difference in the religious beliefs. See Kenneth B. Wolf, *Christian Martyrs in Muslim Spain* (Cambridge: Cambridge University Press, 1988) for the typical English scholars' viewpoint.

11   Maribel Fierro, "Decapitation of Christians and Muslims in the Medieval Iberian Peninsula: Narratives, Images, Contemporary Perceptions," *Comparative Literature Studies* 45, no. 2 (2008): 158–59.

12   *Al-Makkari*, vol. 1, app. B, no. xviii.

13   For this and the following (here al-Makkari cites Ibn Hayyan), see *al-Makkari*, 2:85.

14   For this and the following, see Khallaf, *Documentos*, 1034–35, cit. Janina M. Safran,"Identity and Differentiation in Ninth-Century al-Andalus," *Speculum* 76, no. 3 (July 2001): 589.

15   Soha Abboud-Haggar, "Difusión del tratado jurídico *Al-Trafi* de Ibn Al-Gallab en el Occidente Musulmán," *Aragón en la Edad Media* 1, nos. 14–15 (1999): 1–18.

16   Robert Hillenbrand, "The Ornament of the World," in *The Legacy of Muslim Spain*, ed. Salma Khadra Jayyusi (Leiden: Brill, 1992), 17. In fact, Catholic forces defeated Abd al-Rahman III's forces more than once; and at the Battle of Alhandega, in Caracena (Soria), Abd al-Rahman himself was defeated, after which he never led a *jihad* in person again. See Ibn Hayyan de Córdoba, *Cronica del Califa Abdarrahman III An-Nasir entre los anos 912 y 942 (al-Muqtabis V)*, trans. María Jesús Viguera and Federico Corriente (Zaragoza: Anubar, 1981), 323–24. This work will be cited as *Muqtabis V*.

17   Fierro, "Decapitation of Christians and Muslims," 152.

18   Ibn Hayyan, *Muqtabis V*, 28–30. Bracketed material not attributed to M. J. Viguera is mine. Given what we know of Abd al-Rahman III, Ibn Hayyan's encomium reminds one of the Greek Sophists' rhetorical exercise consisting of a panegyric on characters proverbial for depravity.

19   For al-Mamun's Inquisition, see George Makdisi, "Scholasticism and Humanism in Classical Islam and the Christian West," *Journal of the American Oriental Society* 109, no. 2 (April–June 1989), 176. Not surprisingly, the article on al-Mamun by Dominique Sourdel in the *Encyclopedia Britannica* online mentions al-Mamun's interest in Greek knowledge but omits to mention that he used an Inquisition in his attempt to impose rationalism upon the Islamic traditionists, who, led by Shafii and Ibn Hanbal, nonetheless eventually prevailed in Islamic thought.

20   Fierro, *De muerte violenta*, 70. Al-Aziz might have had a Catholic mother—one of the thousands of sexual slaves of European or Balkan and Greek origin in Abd al-Rahman III's harem—which would lend force to Malik's wise warning against Muslim men marrying infidels because the women might lead them and especially their children astray.

21   Ibid., 70–71.

22   Ibn Hayyan, *Muqtabis V*, 34–35.

23   Fierro, *De muerte violenta*, 72.

24   Ibid.

25   Ibn Hayyan, *Muqtabis V*, 29n17.

26 Abdel Magid Turki, "La vénération pour Malik et la physionomie du malikisme andalou," *Studia Islamica*, no. 33 (1971): 41–65.

27 Ibn Hayyan, *Muqtabis V*, 322–23.

28 Ibid., 334–35.

29 Ibid., 53–54.

30 Rachid El Hour, "La transición entre las épocas almorávide y almohade vista a través de las familias de ulemas," in *Estudios onomástico-biográficos de Al-andalus IX* (Madrid: Consejo Superior de Investigaciones Científicas, 1999), 264, 269.

31 Ibn Hazm, *Naqt al-Arus*, trans. Luis Seco de Lucena (Valencia: Alemal y Vives, 1974), 102.

32 Enrico Cerulli, "Le Calife 'Abd Ar-Rahman III de Cordoue et le martyr Pélage dans un poème de Hrotsvitha," *Studia Islamica*, no. 32 (1970): 69–76. The youngster, Pelayo, became a Catholic martyr and saint.

33 Ibn Hayyan, *Muqtabis V*, 40–41. Maribel Fierro writes that in the episode of the girl and the jewels, the executioner's blade struck a bejeweled necklace (see Fierro, *De muerte violenta*, 74). But the jewels could not have been in a necklace around her neck, because the executioner would have seen them, especially since they were so bright; and the executioner is explicit in saying that he did not see jewels before finding them inside his mat after beheading the woman. I believe Fierro is underestimating Abd al-Rahman's exquisite cruelty and ingenuity in torturing people. My interpretation of the episode is that, before the arrival of his personal executioner, Abd al-Rahman had forced the girl to swallow the jewels, which came up her throat as she was forced to bend down for the beheading and which were struck by the blade as it cut through the flesh.

34 Cited by Ibn Hayyan, *Muqtabis V*, 40.

35 *Historia de la conquista de España de Abenalcotía el Cordobés*, trans. Julián Ribera (Madrid: Archivos, 1926), 39.

36 J. Vallvé and F. Ruiz Girela, eds. and trans., *La primera década del reinado de Al-Hakam I, segun el Muqtabis II, 1de Ben Hayyan de Córdoba (m. 469 h./1076 J.C.)* (Madrid: Real Academia de la Historia, 2003), 113–14.

37 Jessica Coope, *The Martyrs of Córdoba* (Lincoln: University of Nebraska Press, 1995), x–xi. The primary sources for the Catholic martyrs in pre-Islamic and Islamic Spain can be found in the monumental *España Sagrada*, ed. E. Florez (Madrid: 1754) in 17 volumes. The most detailed scholarly account is still Francisco Xavier Simonet's formidable *Historia de los mozarabes de España* (1897–1903; rpt. Madrid: Turner, 1983), 4 vols. Naturally, Simonet is dismissed today for his "anti-Islamic bias." Among many other secondary works that cast an unfavorable light on Catholic martyrs: Ann Christys, *Christians in al-Andalus, 711–1000* (Richmond, Surrey: Curzon Press, 2002), 28–51; Coope, *The Martyrs of Córdoba*. Kenneth B. Wolf, *Christian Martyrs in Muslim Spain* (Cambridge: Cambridge University Press, 1988), now online, is the most widely cited study; it includes such statements as: "The proliferation of legal restrictions on Christian activity did not necessarily mean that the actual situation of Christians living under Islam deteriorated to any appreciable degree. For the same inexorable movement towards physical integration that occupied Muslim legal minds [!] inevitably proved stronger than the laws they created." For our "greater objectivity" and "modern sensibility," which preclude sympathy toward the Christians, see María Isabel Fierro's review of Dominique Millet-Gérard, *Chrétiens mozarabes et culture islamique dans l'Espagne des viiie–ixe siécles* (Paris: Études Augustiniennes, 1984), in *Al-Qantara* 6, nos. 1–2 (1985): 560–61. Millet-Gérard characterizes these Christian martyrs as partisan fanatics inexplicably wanting total separation from the Muslim community (78 and 94n67).

38 Cit. Eduardo Escartín González, *Estudio económico sobre el tratado de Ibn Abdun* (Seville: Fundación El Monte, 2006), 270–71. The *muhtasib* was also known as the *sahib al-suq*, or the lord of the public sites. Other functionaries had similarly repressive responsibilities: the *sahib al madina* (Spanish "zalmedin," the extremely powerful head of state security in the city), the *sahib al-surta*, or head of the police force (273–75).

39   For this and the following, see Abd al-Wahid al-Marrakushi, *Histoire des almohades*, trans. E. Fagnan (Algiers: Adolphe Jourdan, 1883), 30–32. For al-Mansur's brilliant campaigns against the Christians, the most up-to-date secondary source is Juan Castellanos Gómez, *Geoestrategia en la España musulmana: las campañas militares de Almanzor* (Madrid: Ministerio de Defensa, 2003).

40   *Al-Makkari*, 1:41.

41   Ibid., 1:228.

42   This and the following according to *Said al-Andalusi. Kitab Talakat al-Umam (Livre des Categories des Nations)*, trans. Regis Blachére (Paris: La Rose Editeurs, 1935), 126–27.

43   In *The Book of Sufficiency on the History of the Khalifs*, excerpted in *Al-Makkari*, vol. 1, app. C, no. xxiv.

44   Fierro, "Decapitation of Christians and Muslims," 156–58. Spanish warriors may have learned the practice of decapitation from their Muslim enemies and eventually used it against them.

45   Maribel Fierro and Francisco García Fitz, eds., *El cuerpo derrotado: Cómo trataban musulmanes y cristianos a los enemigos vencidos (Península Ibérica, ss. VIII–XIII)* (Madrid: Consejo Superior de Investigaciones Científicas, 2008), 25. José Rodríguez García observes: "the Christian sources show that beheading, though common to both Muslims and Christians, was more common in the Islamic world than in the Peninsula Christian one" (*El cuerpo derrotado*, 394). Fierro writes: "Whereas Andalusi Muslim sources are by no means reticent in their descriptions of the decapitation of Christians by Muslims, they are considerably more limited in their references to Christian beheadings of Muslims.... On the other hand, Christian sources, which openly discuss Christians beheading Muslims, also record Muslims beheading Christians and tend to portray the beheading of enemies as a Muslim custom first and foremost, a view whose opposite is not conveyed in Muslim sources" (Fierro, "Decapitation of Christians and Muslims, 159). The academic editor of this issue of *Comparative Literature Studies* put a politically correct spin on what Fierro is saying: "While some medieval Christian sources associate beheading with a specific feature of Islamic culture and practice, Fierro argues that decapitation had its origins in antiquity and was common among various world cultures, including medieval Muslims and Christians." In fact, Fierro is quite clear on the point that *both* Catholic and Muslim sources show decapitation to be far more widespread in al-Andalus than in Catholic Spain, and that whereas Catholic sources present decapitation as characteristic of Muslim practice, Muslim sources do not present it as characteristic of Catholic practice.

46   Maribel Fierro believes that the intensity of decapitation in al-Andalus was partly the result of religious beliefs: "The practice of beheading defeated enemies, with a long tradition in pre-Islamic times, was legitimized in Islamic terms and perhaps reinforced by some interpretations of the Koranic verse 8:67 regarding the treatment of prisoners, and by the Prophetic precedent of Badr that was adduced by al-Zarqawi" (Fierro, "Decapitation of Christians and Muslims," 159). Fierro refers to Quran 8:67: "It is not fitting/for an Apostle/That he should have/Prisoners of war until/He hath thoroughly subdued/The land." (All translations are from *The Qur'an: Text, Translation, and Commentary* by Abdullah Yusuf Ali [Elmhurst: Tahrike Tarsile Qur'an, 2001], 418, 432.) But Arabist Fierro curiously overlooks other and more relevant Islamic texts, such as Quran 8:12: "Remember thy Lord inspired/The angels (with the message):/...I will instill terror/Into the hearts of the Unbelievers:/*Smite ye above their necks* [emphasis added]/And smite all their/Finger-tips off them"; *Bukhari*, vol. 9, bk. 93, no. 512: "Narrated Al-Mughira: Sa'd bin 'Ubada said, 'If I saw a man with my wife, I would strike him (behead him) with the blade of my sword.' This news reached Allah's Apostle who then said, 'You people are astonished at Sa'd's Ghira. By Allah, I have more Ghira than he, and Allah has more Ghira than I, and because of Allah's Ghira, He has made unlawful Shameful deeds and sins (illegal sexual intercourse etc.) done in open and in secret. And there is none who likes that the people should repent to Him and beg His pardon than Allah, and for this reason He sent the warners and the givers of good news. And there is none who likes to be praised more than Allah does, and for this reason, Allah promised to Grant Paradise (to the

doers of good).' 'Abdul Malik said, 'No person has more Ghira than Allah'; *Bukhari*, vol. 1, bk. 3, no. 121: "Narrated by Abu Huraira: I have memorized two kinds of knowledge from Allah's Apostle. I have propagated one of them to you and if I propagated the second, then my pharynx (throat) would be cut (i.e., killed)." The justification for beheading is found also in al-Sarakhsi (d. ca. 1096), according to Khaled Abou El Fadl, *Rebellion and Violence in Islamic Law* (Cambridge: Cambridge University Press, 2001), 197–98. The closest thing in the Christian New Testament are Jesus's metaphorical words, "I came not to send peace but a sword" (Matthew 10:34). Of course, the Islamic texts may be asking for beheadings in a "methaphorical" way; however, they have been interpreted not metaphorically but literally by very learned *ulama* and by very intelligent rulers through the history of Islam.

47 Fierro, "Decapitation of Christians and Muslims," 158.

48 Ibid., 150.

49 For an example of a serious uprising, apparently by Muslims, against the Almohads in Mallorca, see Ambrosio Huici Miranda, ed. and trans., *Kitab al-Muyib Fi Talijis Ajbar al-Maghrib by Abu Muhhamad Abd al-Wahid al-Marrakusi* (Tetuán: Instituto General Franco de Estudios e Investigación Hispano-Arabe, 1955), 223n1. Beheading as a characteristically Islamic way of killing continues to be taken for granted by some Muslims. Gilles Kepel has noticed that today's Islamic militants (who among other things call themselves an "underground militia" but are called "terrorists" by their adversaries) view decapitation as a proper Islamic way of dealing with enemies, a practice that has the double advantage of making these Muslims feel closer to their glorious past while making their present-day adversaries tremble with terror, this last one being a practical effect that was doubtlessly one of the purposes also of the widespread decapitations in al-Andalus. The twenty-first-century *jihad* leader Abu Musab al-Zarqawi affirmed that beheading is a "most Islamic" form of execution; in a communication dating from May 11, 2004, after the decapitation of the American Nicholas Berg, Zarqawi said: "The Prophet...ordered the beheading of some of the prisoners of Badr who had their hands tied up.... He is our example and a good role model." Among early *ulama* who confirm this episode in the life of the Prophet are al-Waqidi (d. 822) and al-Baladhuri (d. ca. 892). See Gilles Kepel, "Escenificación de la muerte," *El Pais*, September 24, 2004.

50 Thus in the late twentieth and early twenty-first centuries, the massive government terror employed in the Middle East by Saddam Hussein, who like many rulers of al-Andalus was also a great builder of palaces and a celebrated protector of artists and poets, did keep Iraq united and in relative peace during his rule. Terror helped consolidate revolutionary rule after the execution of the king during the French Revolution, where the mass killings of peasants in La Vendée were particularly brutal. After the deposition and murder of the Russian czar and his family, mass terror of until then unheard-of proportions contributed to cementing the rule of Marxist-Leninists in the 1920s and 1930s, when in the Ukraine alone more than six million peasants were starved to break the political opposition, and some people engaged in cannibalism. For the horrors of the French Revolution, see, among others, Jean Dumont, *Pourquoi nous ne célébrons pas 1789* (Paris: ARGE, 1987); for the horrors of Marxism-Leninism in Russia, China, and other places, see *The Black Book of Communism: Crimes, Terror, Repression*, ed. Stéphane Courtois (Cambridge, MA: Harvard University Press, 2004).

51 At least for a time. With the absorption of many Muslims after the end of the *Reconquista* and the consequent presence of masses of suspected *conversos* from Islam and Judaism, Catholic rulers would resort to measures that included the expulsion of Jews and *Moriscos* and the use of the Inquisition to fish out and if necessarily kill heretics and apostates. Members of Jewish *converso* families, however, often continued to occupy high positions within the Church and the government, such as Bishop Pablo de Santa María, priest Hernando de Talavera (confessor of queen Isabel "La Católica" of Castile), Gabriel Sánchez (treasurer of King Ferdinand of Aragon), and Luis de Santángel (finance minister of King Fernando).

CHAPTER 5: WOMEN IN ISLAMIC SPAIN

1   As does the Arabist Manuela Marín, *Mujeres en al-Ándalus* (Madrid: Consejo Superior de
     Investigaciones Científicas, 2000), 157–61. Marín makes the subject part of a long general
     discussion on the status of young women, and she goes back and forth on the subject without
     ever committing to saying outright that yes, female circumcision was not only legal but also
     recommended by the authorities in al-Andalus. Female circumcision is nowhere mentioned
     in a widely circulated book in which Marín was the "chief consultant": *The Legacy of Muslim
     Spain*, ed. Salma Khadra Jayyusi; chief consultant Manuela Marín (Leiden: Brill, 1992, pub-
     lished under the auspices of the Project of Translation from Arabic [PROTA]). Soha Abboud-
     Haggar, professor of Islamic studies at the Complutense University of Madrid, omits men-
     tioning female circumcision in her otherwise excellent study of the religious roots of Islam's
     violence against women: "Las raíces de la violencia en los textos religiosos. Los textos religio-
     sos islámicos: El Corán y Al-Hadiz," *Raíces Profundas: La violencia contra las mujeres (Anti-
     güedad y Edad Media*, ed. María Jesús Fuente y Remedios Morán (Madrid: Polifemo), 2011,
     45–66. Janina Safran's excellent *Defining Boundaries in al-Andalus: Muslims, Christians, and
     Jews in Islamic Iberia* (Ithaca, NY: Cornell University Press, 2013) does not to mention it either
     (nor does it mention stonings, crucifixions, etc.).
2   Trans. 'A'isha 'Abdarahman at-Tarjumana and Ya'qub Johnson, Center for Jewish-Muslim
     Engagement, University of Southern California Center for Religion and Civic Culture, accessed
     May 14, 2015, http://www.usc.edu/org/cmje/religious-texts/hadith/muwatta/002-mmt.php and
     http://www.usc.edu/org/cmje/religious-texts/hadith/muwatta/020-mmt.php. The non-Maliki
     Sahih Muslim collection also takes female circumcision for granted: bk. 3, no. 684.
3   The Arabist Manuela Marín is either disingenuous or not thinking clearly when she gives a
     testimony from a Muslim man complaining about some of his "women" refusing circumci-
     sion as proof that some women in al-Andalus refused it: by definition, these "women" would
     not be Muslims but likely women from Christian lands, because female circumcision was
     done not on a Muslim adult *woman* but on *a little girl* on the verge of puberty; *women* cir-
     cumcised as adults would be uncircumcised sexual slaves, whose circumcision the *Muwatta*
     recommends if the master is not going to sell them. The Office on Women's Health of the
     U.S. Department of Health and Human Services explains the age range at which female cir-
     cumcision (or female genital mutilation, or female genital cutting [FGC]) is performed in the
     twenty-first century in Islamic countries: "FGC is performed on infants, girls, and women
     of all ages. The age at which girls are cut can vary widely from country to country, and even
     within countries. *Most often, FGC happens before a girl reaches puberty.... In Egypt, about 90
     percent of girls are cut between 5 and 14 years old* [emphasis added]. However, in Yemen, more
     than 75 percent of girls are cut before they are 2 weeks old. The average age at which a girl
     undergoes FGC is decreasing in some countries (Burkina Faso, Côte d'Ivoire, Egypt, Kenya,
     and Mali). Researchers think it's possible that the average age of FGC is getting lower so that it
     can be more easily hidden from authorities in countries where there may be laws against it. It
     is also possible that FGC is performed on younger girls because they are less able to resist." See
     the fact sheet on female genital cutting produced by the Office on Women's Health, accessed
     October 6, 2015, http://womenshealth.gov/publications/our-publications/fact-sheet/female-
     genital-cutting.html.
4   *Al-Tafri*, 585.
5   Ibid., 28 (565v). From *hatenar*, "to circumcise" (44b:1).
6   *The Risala of 'Abdullah ibn Abi Zayd al-Qayrawani (310/922–386/996). A Treatise on Maliki
     Fiqh*, trans. Aisha Bewley, with the translator's inclusion of clarifying comments by Mus-
     lim scholar al-Azhari in brackets, Aisha Bewley's Islamic Home Page, http://www.muwatta.
     com/ebooks/english/risala_ibn_abi_zayd_salutations.pdf (accessed June 5, 2010), 29.9b. The
     Spanish translation is blunter: the "recommended" circumcision consists of "the removal
     [excisión] of the clitoris." See *Compendio de derecho islámico [Risala fi-l-fiqh] Ibn Abi Zayd*

al-Qayrawani, trans. Jesús Rosalido Gambotti (Madrid: Editorial Trotta, S.A., 1950), chap. 29. The translation by Alhaj Bello Mohammad Daura, *The Risala: A Treatise on Maliki Fiqh*, at the Islamic Law Base, http://www.iium.edu.my/deed/lawbase/risalah_maliki/, does not differ from Bewley's.

7　*A Madinan View on the Sunnah, Courtesy, Wisdom, Battles, and History by Abu Muhammad Abdullah Ibn Abi Zayd al-Qayrawani*, trans. Abdassamad Clarke (London: Ta-Ha Publishers, 1999), 95.

8　In fact, the legal scholar Lyda Favali points out that a majority of early *fuqaha* agreed with Malik's teaching that female circumcision was a sunnah—a proper religious practice derived from the actions and sayings of Muhammad handed down through the traditions or the *ahadith*—though the extent of the circumcision would vary: "Differences among various schools of Islam exist on the nature of the obligation (mandatory, advisable), and on its purport (does it refer to all of the clitoris, or only the hood etc.).... It is a *sunna* according to the majority [of early *fuqaha*], and according to Malik. Moreover, according to al-Shafii, it will be compulsory for men and women. For women, circumcision will involve only the excision of the hood of the clitoris." See Lyda Favali, "What Is Missing? (Female Genital Surgeries—Infibulation, Excision, Clitoridectomy—in Eritrea)," *Global Jurists Frontiers* 1, no. 2 (2001): 42. As of 2002, female circumcision in Egypt was still widely practiced though forbidden by the legal code: see Baudouin Dupret, "Sexual Morality at the Egyptian Bar: Female Circumcision, Sex Change Operations, and Motives for Suing," *Islamic Law and Society* 9, no. 1 (2002): 42–69. In the twentieth and twenty-first centuries, conflicting *fatwas* have been issued on the subject: on May 28, 1949, Egyptian *fuqaha* decided that it is not a sin to reject female circumcision; on June 23, 1951, they stated that female circumcision is desirable because it curbs "nature" (i.e. sexual drive among women), and that medical concerns over the practice are irrelevant; on January 29, 1981, the Great Sheikh of Al-Azhar (probably the most famous university of the Islamic world) stated that parents must follow the lessons of Muhammad and not listen to medical authorities, because the latter often change their minds, and that parents must do their duty and have their daughters circumcised; on June 24, 2007, the Mufti of Egypt, Ali Gum, announced that the custom was now prohibited.

9　*Sahih Muslim*, bk. 3, no. 684.

10　*Sunnan Abu-Dawud*, bk. 41, no. 5251: "Narrated Umm Atiyyah al-Ansariyyah: A woman used to perform circumcision in Medina. The Prophet (peace-be-upon-him) said to her: 'Do not cut severely as that is better for a woman and more desirable for a husband.'"

11　Octave Pesle, *La Femme Musulmane dans le Droit, la Réligion et les Moeurs* (Rabat: Les éditions la porte, 1946), 104–5. These female experts on female circumcision may be the ones referred to as "doctors" in the twentieth- and twenty-first-century glowing accounts of the civilization of al-Andalus. Even in Egypt, as of 2012, a majority of women have undergone female circumcision (or female genital mutilation). See *BBC Newsnight* report on "female genital mutilation" in Egypt by Sue Lloyd at https://www.youtube.com/watch?v=bObvzSHRKT8.

12　Abdassamad Clarke in *A Madinan View on the Sunnah*, 96.

13　*Compendio del Tafsir del Coran de Al-Qurtubi*, vol. 1, trans. Zakanya Maza Abu Mubarak (Granada: Cdad. Musulmana e Spanola de la Mezquita del Temor de Allah, 2005), 337.

14　"Las *Leyes de Moros* son el libro de *Al-Tafri*," *Revistas científicas complutenses*, no. 4 (1997): 165. Again, she fails to mention the practice of female circumcision.

15　*Muwatta*, 49.3. For the forced circumcision of Catholics, see Eulogius, *Epistola ad Wiliesindum*, 330, cit. Reinhardt Dozy, *Histoire des musulmanes d'Espagne* (Leiden: Brill, 1861), 1.ii, 319.

16　For Carly Fiorina's long-standing enthusiasm about the Islamic Caliphate's tolerance, "protection" of its citizens, creativity, and superiority over any civilization before it, see her speech as CEO of Hewlett Packard in Minneapolis, Minnesota, titled "Technology, Business, and Our Way of Life: What's Next," September 26, 2001, at http://www.hp.com/hpinfo/execteam/speeches/fiorina/minnesota01.html.

17   *Brill Encylopaedia of Islam, Second Edition,* "muhsan."

18   For the stoning of the adulterous *muhsan,* see, among other Maliki legal treatises and manuals, *Muwatta,* 20, 28.28, and 41.41; *Al-Tafri* 2.561–66; *Risala,* 37.23; Ibn Rushd, *Bidayat,* vol. 2, 56.

19   *Muwatta,* 41.1.5.

20   Ibid., 41.1.11.

21   *Al-Tafri,* 562–64.

22   *Bidayat,* vol. 2, 56.6.2.

23   *Islamic Jurisprudence: Shafii's Risala,* trans. Majid Khadduri (Baltimore: Johns Hopkins Press, 1061), 138.

24   *Dos tratados de legislación musulmana. 1. Leyes de moros del siglo XIV 2. Suma de los principales mandamientos y devedamientos de la ley y çunna, por don Içe de Gebir, Alfaquí Mayor de la aljama de Segovia. Año de 1492,* ed. Pascual de Gayangos (Madrid: Academia de la Historia. Memorial histórico español, 1853), vol. 5, *Suma:* XLIV.

25   María Luisa Ávila, "Women in Andalusi Biographical Sources," in *Writing the Feminine: Women in Arab Sources,* ed. Manuela Marín and Randi Deguilhem (London: I.B., Tauris, 2002), 158.

26   Manuela Marín, "Mujeres veladas: religión y sociedad en al-Andalus," *Arenal: Revista de historia de las mujeres* 4 (1997): 36. Even male children could be married before puberty: see, for example, the widely used Maliki legal treatise *Mudawwana,* in André Colomer, *Droit Musulman: Les Personnes. La famille* (Rabat: La Porte, 1962), 121; or Ibn Asim al-Andalusi's Maliki legal manual *Tuhfat al-Hukkam,* trans. Bello Muhammad Daura (Zaria: Ahmadu Bello University, 1989), para. 546.

27   Soha Abboud-Haggar, *El Tratado Jurídico de Al-Tafri de Ibn Al-Gallab: Manuscrito Aljamiado De Almonacid De La Sierra (Zaragoza). Edición, Estudio, Glosario y Confrontación Con El Original Árabe* (Zaragoza: Institución "Fernando el Católico," 1999), 2:588.

28   Cristina de la Puente, "Juridical Sources for the Study of Women: Limitations of the Female's Capacity to Act according to Maliki Law," in Marín and Deguilhem, *Writing the Feminine,* 102. A legal source not mentioned by de la Puente is *Sahih Muslim,* bk. 026, no. 5395: "A'isha reported that Sauda (Allah be pleased with her) went out (in the fields) in order to answer the call of nature even after the time when veil had been prescribed for women. She had been a bulky lady, significant in height amongst the women, and she could not conceal herself from him who had known her. 'Umar b. Khattab saw her and said: Sauda, by Allah, you cannot conceal from us. Therefore, be careful when you go out. She ('A'isha) said: She turned back. Allah's Messenger (may peace be upon him) was at that time in my house having his evening meal and there was a bone in his hand. She (Sauda) came in and said: Allah's Messenger. I went out and 'Umar said to me so and so. She ('A'isha) reported: There came the revelation to him and then it was over; the bone was then in his hand and he had not thrown it and he said: 'Permission has been granted to you that you may go out for your needs.'" See *Sahih Muslim,* trans. Abdul Hamid Siddiqui, Center for Jewish-Muslim Engagement, University of Southern California, at http://www.cmje.org/religious-texts/hadith/muslim/.

29   Al-Zubaydi, *Tabaqat al-nahwiyin wa-l-lugawiyin,* ed. M.A. Ibrahim (Cairo: 1984), 286, cit. Marín, "Mujeres veladas," 34.

30   Rachel Arié, *Études sur la civlisation de l'Espagne musulmane* (Leiden: Brill, 1990), 85–86.

31   Leopoldo Torres Balbás, "Miniaturas medievales españolas de influjo islámico," *Al-Andalus* 15 (1950): 191–202; Manuela Marín, "Las mujeres en al-Andalus: fuentes e historiografía," in Celia del Moral, ed., *Arabes, judías y cristianas: Mujeres en la Europa medieval* (Granada: Universidad de Granada, 1993), 42.

32   Cf. Ibn Hazm, *Naqt-al-Arus,* trans. Luis Seco de Lucena (Valencia: Alemal y Vives, 1974), 127; *alim* Ibn Abdun in Emilio García Gómez and Evariste LéviProvençal, *Sevilla a comienzos del siglo XII. El Tratado de Ibn Abdun* (Seville: Servicio de Publicaciones del Ayuntamiento de Sevilla, 1981), 156–57; Marín, "Mujeres veladas," 23–38. According to Ibn Hazm, only two women in the history of Islam ever occupied a public position of authority, none of them in

Maliki-ruled al-Andalus: one as administrator of the public market and the other as "judge of injustices."

33   *A Madinan View on the Sunnah*, 98.

34   *Al-Tafri*, 34–35; *The Muwatta of Imam Malik Narrated by Yahya B. Yahya B. Kathir al-Laith Al-Andalusi*, trans. F. Amira Zrien Matrahi (Karachi: Darul Ishaat, 2005), 2.18.72.

35   There are several available translations: *The Risala: A Treatise of Maliki Fiqh*, trans. Alhaj Bello Mohammad Daura at the Islamic law base, http://www.iium.edu.my/deed/lawbase/risalah_maliki/; *The Risala of Abdullah ibn Abi Zayd al-Qayrawani*, trans. A. Bewley, http://bewley.virtualave.net/Risalatitl.html, which I use unless otherwise specified; *Risala: Traité Agregé de Droit Malekite et Morale Musulmane*, translated and annotated E. Fagnan (Paris: Paul Geuthner, 1914).

36   *Al-Tafri*, 589.

37   *Dos tratados de legislación musulmana*, vol. 5.

38   *Sahih Al-Bukhari*, trans. Dr. Muhammad Muhsin Khan of Medina Islamic University (Chicago: Kazi Publications, 1976), vol. 8, bk. 76, no. 572.

39   *A Madinan View on the Sunnah*, 99.

40   *Partial Translation of Sunna Abu Dawud*, trans. Ahmad Hasan, Center for Muslim-Jewish Engagment, University of Southern California, bk. 31, no. 4000, accessed July 29, 2012, http://www.cmje.org/religious-texts/hadith/abudawud/.

41   De la Puente, "Juridical Sources for the Study of Women," 103–4. Local *fuqaha* such as those of Almeria might allow women to go to the baths, but this does not indicate that their trip was for anything other than religious ablutions, including ablutions prior to marriage. This seems to be overlooked in Rachid El Hour, "La indumentaria de las mujeres andalusíes a través de *Zagrat ak-Rawwd Fi Taljis Taqdir al-Fard* de Ibn Baq," in *Tejer y vestir: De la antigüedad al islam*, ed. Manuela Marín (Madrid: Consejo Superior de Investigaciones Científicas, 2001), 106–97. According to Malik's *Muwaddana*, the husband had the last word on whether or not the wife could leave the house: "where the husband forbids his wife from going out, the final decision is determined by the husband's will (*irada*) and the wife has no right to choose": see de la Puente, "Juridical Sources for the Study of Women," 95. Any actual "bathing" activity would take place among slave girls.

42   *The History of the Mohammedan Dynasties in Spain by Ahmed Ibn Mohammed al-Makkari*, trans. Pascual de Gayangos (1840; rpt. New York: Johnson Reprint, 1964) vol. 2, app. B, no. xx.

43   Marín, "Mujeres veladas," 34; Marín and Deguilhem, *Writing the Feminine*, xvi. But the situation would also depend on the degree of fundamentalism or traditionalism of the husband's faith: the more traditional the husband, no matter what his economic condition, the less public activity would his wife or wives have. The formula continues to operate in Maliki Morocco: see Abderrazak Moulay Rachid, *La condition de la femme au Maroc* (Rabat: Editions de la faculté des Sciences Juridiques, Economiques et Sociales de Rabat, 1985), 311–12.

44   Among many examples, see the long braided hair in the early-sixth-century ivory panel of the Empress Ariadne and the flocks of hair in the enameled and silver-gilt medallion of the Empress Zoe (1028–1050) and in the enameled and silver Khakhuli Triptych of Empress Maria of Alania (1071–1078) in John Beckwith, *The Art of Constantinople* (London: Phaedon, 1961), 37, 107, 110. A few empresses, notably Irene, ruled the empire on their own. None of this was conceivable in Islamic society.

45   Ioli Kalavrezou, *Byzantine Women and Their World* (New Haven: Yale University Press, 2003), 70.

46   There are paintings showing Greek women without veils in public. See the "Presentation of the Virgin in the Temple" (a fresco circa thirteenth to fourteenth century), where four women figures have beautiful hair held back with white hair bands only, another woman has hair held back with white band and a head mantle, and three other women have their heads covered in white scarves with colored stripes: http://www.macedonianheritage.gr/Hellenic-Macedonia/en/img_C2A11b.html; see more paintings at http://www.macedonianheritage.

gr/HellenicMacedonia/en/img_D27a.html and http://www.macedonianheritage.gr/Athos/ General/AthosArt.html. See also Herbert Norris, *Ancient European Costume and Fashion* (London: J.M. Dent and Sons, 1938).

47   "Marriage of Theophobos to the sister of the emperor Theophilos, crowned by the patriarch," in Helen C. Evans, ed., *Byzantium: Faith and Power* (New York: Metropolitan Museum of Art, 2004), 217.

48   Judith Herrin, *Byzantium: The Surprising Life of a Medieval Empire* (Princeton, NJ: Princeton University Press, 2008), 179. No veil required.

49   Kalavrezou, *Byzantine Women and Their World*, 30.

50   So much so that there is a homily that does not forbid women to go to the baths but urges women not to bathe when men are there: Kalavrezou, *Byzantine Women and Their World*, 146.

51   Albrecht Berger, *Das Bad in der byzantinischen Zeit* (Munich: Institut für Byzantinistik und neugriechische Philologie der Universität, 1982). The "problem" of modesty was solved by having separate days for women to use the public baths.

52   Kalavrezou, *Byzantine Women and Their World*, 140.

53   For the influence of the *Iliad* in the *Alexiad*, see Anastasia Drandaki, Demetra Papanikola-Bakirtzi, and Anastasia Tourta, eds., *Heaven and Earth: Art of Byzantium from Greek Collections* (Athens: Hellenic Ministry of Culture, 2014), 192.

54   On the educated women of the Greek Roman Empire, see Herrin, *Byzantium: The Surprising Life of a Medieval Empire*, 238, 330–31; on the education of nuns, see 122.

55   *Muwatta*, 51.1.3. Perhaps motivated by a Western reluctance to think positively of what they consider an onerous imposition on women, many Western scholars today find it difficult accepting that veiling and indeed veiling the face is an Islamic teaching rather than a copycat thing. But the practice is perfectly justified to separate the sexes in order to avoid fornication and to foster marriage, a family, and general social stability as per divine law. Straining to find other sources for veiling not only diminishes Islam's originality (already damaged by the impact of the more advanced culture and scientific and philosophical texts of the Greek Roman Empire over Bedouins coming out of the desert) but also violates Ockham's razor.

56   *Mudawwana*, tome 1, vol. 1, bk. 1 (Of Ritual Purity), 85. The *Mudawwana* has been summarized by tome, book, and number by G.H. Bousquet in "La *Moudawwana*," *Annales de l'Institut d'Études Orientales* 16 (1958), 17 (1959), and 20 (1962), and *Revue algérienne, tunisienne et marocaine de législation et de jurisprudence* 74 (1958), 75 (1959), and 77 (1961). All my references to the *Mudawwana* are taken from this work, unless otherwise noted. But prayer must be conducted with the face and the hands uncovered before Allah.

57   *A Madinan View on the Sunnah*, 99.

58   Nayer Honarvar describes the pre-Islamic Bedouin custom of abducting women from one another's tribes: "Behind the Veil: Women's Rights in Islamic Societies," *Journal of Law and Religion*, 6, no. 2 (1988): 359. See quotations in my text.

59   See *Behind the Veil, produced and directed by Eve Arnold* from Impact Films, reviewed by Lois Grant Beck, "Behind the Veil by Eve Arnold," *American Anthropologist*, New Series, 79, no. 1 (March 1977): 195–96. See also Unni Wikan, *Behind the Veil in Arabia: Women in Oman* (Baltimore: Johns Hopkins University Press, 1982).

60   As late as the sixteenth century, this was still stipulated in the *Leyes de Moros*, CLXXXVII, and in the *Suma de lso principales devedamientos y mandamientos de la ley* (XLVI), used by Muslims living in Christian lands.

61   For this and the following, see María Luisa Ávila, "Las mujeres 'sabias' en al-Andalus," *La mujer en al-Andalus: Reflejos históricos de su actividad y categorías sociales*, ed. María Jesús Viguera (Madrid: Universidad Autónoma, 1989), 146–49. Ávila continues: "[In al-Andalus Muslim] women find themselves in an unsurmountable plane of inferiority.... This is important because one of the battle grounds between those who argue for the 'Western' character of al-Andalus and those who argue that it was no different from other Muslim lands is that of the freedom of the Hispano-Arabic woman in relation to women in the rest of the Islamic world.

The work of Henri Pérès on Andalusian poetry of the eleventh century provided arguments to the defenders of the idea that Hispano-Arabic society was radically different from Muslim society and one of those arguments was the supposed freedom of women. In a long review, García Gómez demonstrated that many of the phrases on which Pérès based his research to build his arguments did not reflect the ways and customs particular to al-Andalus, and very likely were not even from the Iberian peninsula. It seems that this call to attention fell on deaf ears because the defenders of Andalusian westernness, headed by Sánchez Albornoz, continued to hold on to the theories of Pérès."

62   María Luisa Ávila, "The Structure of the Family in Al-Andalus," in Manuela Marín and Julio Samsó, eds., *The Formation of al-Andalus* (Aldershot: Ashgate, 1998), 1:476.

63   Thus David Nirenberg, *Communities of Violence: Persecution of Minorities in the Middle Ages* (Princeton, NJ: Princeton University Press, 1996), 136, states that Jewish men often had intercourse with Gentile women, usually Muslim ones. He does not make the necessary distinction between Muslim-controlled territory and Christian-controlled territory, or between a slave Muslim woman and a *muhsan*. Therefore Nirenberg overlooks that, had a Jewish man had intercourse with a *muhsan* Muslim woman in Islamic territory, it would have cost the Jewish man his life. The intercourse he refers to could have taken place only under Christian rule.

64   These women were "traditionists," who through memorization helped pass on ahadith, or narratives on the life of Muhammad and his early followers. See Ignaz Goldziher, *Muslim Studies*, trans. C. R. Barber and S. M. Stern (New York: SUNY, 1977) 2:366–68. The examples in the various ahadith collections sometimes are transmitted within the narrative by women who are part of the chain of transmission listed in the narrative itself, beginning with Muhammad's wives, most often Aisha.

65   Goldziher, *Muslim Studies*, 367. Another was Abida al-Madaniyyah, who was instrumental in helping transmit Maliki tradition as the wife of *alim* Habib Dahhun. She had been a female slave given to him as a present (Goldziher, *Muslim Studies*, 366).

66   Ávila, "The Structure of the Family in Al-Andalus," 476. All of this, of course, is very different from the case of a Catholic nun such as Saint Teresa of Ávila, who moved about freely, who was named a Doctor of the Church, and whose writings became authoritative.

67   Teresa Garulo, *Diwan de las poetisas de al-Andalus* (Madrid: Hiperion, 1986), 35.

68   Of the thirty-four women poets mentioned in the most rigorous scholarly anthology of female poetry in al-Andalus, seven were sexual slaves, A number of the free Muslim women belonged to well-off or noble families. Several came from *ulama* families. One was the daughter of a fruit vendor. See Garulo, *Diwan*, 25 and 27.

69   Such as being part of a delegation to approach the caliph, or while petitioning a ruler: see Garulo, *Diwan*, 32.

70   Admiringly cited by Hillenbrand, "Medieval Córdoba as a Cultural Centre," 121.

71   Averroes, *Antología*, ed. Miguel Cruz Hernández (Seville: Fundación El Monte, 1998), 236.

72   Octave Pesle, *Le Mariage et la Répudiation Chez les Malékites* (Rabat: Félix Moncho, 1936), 95.

73   *Bukhari*, vol. 7, bk. 62, no. 64.

74   Prepubescent women were still being married in Maliki North Africa in the twentieth century despite efforts by the colonial French administration to curtail the practice: L. P. Fauque, "Le mariage des musulmanes algériens," *Revue algérienne, tunisienne et marocaine de législation et de jurisprudence* 44 (1961): 65. Even in the early twenty-first century, some Maliki clerics in North Africa have approved marriage of the woman at nine years of age: "Un teólogo marroquí promueve las bodas con niñas. La fatua afirma que chicas de 9 años 'dan mejor resultado' que las de 20," *El Pais* (Madrid), August 12, 2008. See also "Morocco Cleric Says Girls Can Marry at 9," AFP, September 23, 2008: "Morocco's top body of Islamic scholars has condemned a Muslim theologian for issuing a religious decree that girls as young as nine years old can marry. Morocco's high council of Ulemas 'denounces the utilisation of religion to legitimise the marriage of nine-year-old girls,' it said in a statement on Sunday. Sheikh Mohamed Ben Abderrahman Al-Maghraoui earlier this month said the marriage of nine-

year-old girls was allowed by Islam as the Prophet Mohammed consummated the marriage to one of his wives when she was that age."

75   *Muwatta*, 40.1; Ibn Rushd, *Bidayat*, The Book of Tadbir, 54.2.2–54.2.3. See also Cristina de la Puente, "Límites legales del concubinato: normas y tabúes en la exclavitud sexual según la bidya de Ibn Rushd," *Al-Qantara* 28, no. 2 (Julio–Diciembre 2007): 409–33. The female slave had to belong to the owner without restrictions to become a sexual slave. Marriage contracts in Islamic lands could include clauses whereby the wife could request a divorce if the husband took a sexual slave or new wife that the first wife did not approve of. The sexual slave's fornication with anyone but her master was punishable, although less severely than in the case of a wife, who lost her life by stoning. For this and the following, see also Joaquín Vallvé Bermejo, *Al-Andalus: sociedad a instituciones* (Madrid: Real Academia de la Historia, 1999), 51.

76   Or the poet at the Umayyad court, Yazid Ibn Rabiah Ibn Mufarrig (d. 688), who had a slave boy, Burd, as his homosexual lover: *Maqamat Al-luzumiyah by al-Saraqusti*, trans. James T. Monroe (Leiden: Brill, 2001), 256n18.

77   For this and the following, see Joaquín Prats et al., *Geografía e historia de España* (Madrid: Anaya, 1998), 75; and Pedro Chalmeta Gendrón, "El *Kitab fi adab al-hisba* (Libro de buen gobierno del zoco) de al-Saqati," *Al-Ándalus* 33 (1968): 369–81: Some unscrupulous merchants sold at a very high price very beautiful female sexual slaves who spoke *Romance* (one of the Spanish dialects derived from Latin) and looked like *rumies* (inhabitants of the Spanish Christian kingdoms who were highly desired by the Muslim males) but were not (383). The merchants also had an older woman, an accomplice, who would certify, sometimes fraudulently, that the sexual slave had completed her *istibra* (the religiously mandated time after menstruation), so that the merchant could sell the girl at a premium to a buyer inflamed with desire who wanted to have sex with the slave as soon as he bought her (369). The merchants sometimes also prostituted the female slaves that they were supposed to sell (373–74). Berber sexual slaves were considered obedient and hard-working; black ones from Nubia were also obedient, "as if they had been created to obey, but they are also thieves and untrustworthy"; the ones from India "cannot stand humiliation, they commit the most horrendous crimes, and they die easily"; Armenian ones were "beautiful, thrifty and not at all docile to men" (375).

78   Of course no respectable Muslim woman could inspire such "love poetry" since she was covered from head to toe. Writing to a friend of his, Abu Bakr al-Bardai recounts: "One day I went to the slave market to appease my contrite heart and I saw there a golden girl, who had been made to veil her face, who had an undulating figure, upright breasts…a mouth red like a bleeding wound, and inside a string of pearls…her neck so svelte that young tree branches would envy it, a waist that a hand could grasp, hips that reminded one of the dunes of the desert…two feet made for kissing rather than walking. People at the market were offering for her large sums of money…and her price kept going up…until a young man arrived, sincere in his love, who did not hesitate to put his fortune on the line to save his heart…and nobody could offer more than he did. When the slave girl escaped me, it was as if the desires of all the people there had gathered inside me. So my friend, buy a slave girl for this your friend before you regret having let him die." Cit. Fernando de la Granja Santamaría, "La venta de la esclava en el Mercado," in his *Estudios de historia de al-Andalus* (Madrid: Real Academia de la Historia, 1999), 57–58.

79   *Al-Maqamat al-luzumiyah by Abu l-Tahir Muhammad Ibn Yusuf al-Tamimi al-Saraqusti Ibn al-Astarkuwi*, trans. James T. Monroe (Leiden: Brill, 2001): "[He] began to sing and recite love poetry…saying: 'What a plight did God Almighty ordain for men because of beautiful women, when He tempted men by means of them…. Today I entered the slave market with a yearning soul and a tender heart, where a slave-girl—and what a slave-girl!—was put up for sale; one whose beauty penetrated and flowed into men's souls; one who played with men's passions and fantasies as *maysir* players do with gambling arrows…. She left a flame in my heart.'" (274); "[The] friendship and attachment of a slave-girl bright as the sun was turned against me, a slave-girl who would deserve to be ransomed both today and tomorrow,

who spoke with the eloquence of Sahban; who used pleasant expressions while eschewing idle talk or trivial speech; who possessed a beauty beyond compare or measure." (259) "Today I chanced upon a slave-girl so amazing that she enters and dominates men's minds; one wondrously beautiful, dazzingly perfect, whom a vendor sold only yesterday, while regret over losing her is already distressing him today, so that he has complained to me of his passion and disclosed his fortune and wealth. I agreed with him so that we should conceal his prosperity let it be divulged hereabouts and lest the girl's new owner should become reluctant to part with her at a low price. But a man who is doomed will inevitably be undone!" (193–94). It turns out that the narrator, blinded by "love" for the slave girl, is tricked out of his money in this *maqamah*, a literary form which is often satirical. The homosexual poetry of al-Andalus, which has delighted so many modern scholars, was of course about slave-boys of the wealthy or well-positioned courtier-poets, as in the case of the Umayyad poet Ibn Mufarrig and his lovely verses to his slave-boy Burd: *Ibn Khallikan''s Biographical Dictionary translated from the Arabic by B. Mac Guckin de Slane* (Paris: Oriental Translation Fund of Great Britain and Ireland, 1871), 236. All this is obviously very romantic and charming.

80 As shown conclusively by Anne Walthall, *Servants of the Dynasty: Palace Women in World History* (Berkeley: University of California Press, 2008), 65–66.

81 Fatima Mernissi, *Forgotten Queens of Islam* (Minneapolis: University of Minnesota Press, 1997), 58. The "queens" presented in this book were harem sexual slaves.

82 Cit. Camilla Adang, "Women's Access to Public Space according to al-Muhalla bi-l-Athbar," in Marín and Deguilhem, *Writing the Feminine*, 75.

83 Khalil Athamina, "How Did Islam Contribute to Change the Legal Status of Women: The Case of the *Jawari*, or the *Female Slaves*," *Al-Qantara* 28, no. 2 (July–December 2007): 383–408.

84 Bertrice Small, "Concubines Confidential," *New York Times*, June 11, 1989.

85 The Mamluk empire relied for the continuation of the Mamluk corps on a constant supply of slaves bought in the slave markets, or taken as prisoners in wars and raids on foreign lands. If becoming a Mamluk or a slave of the Mamluks had been as wonderful as the Western academic specialists proclaim, Egypt would have had no shortage of people enthusiastically volunteering for slavery from the poorer classes of the local population and no need to buy slaves or raid foreign lands for captives.

86 David Nicolle, *Acre 1291: Bloody Sunset of the Crusader States* (Botley: Osprey Publishing, 2005), 33.

87 Bernard Lewis, *Race and Slavery in the Middle East* (Oxford: Oxford University Press, 1994), chap. 1. For the consequences of the social inferiority of even the slave soldiers (regularly used as an example of the wonderful nature of slavery in Islam), see Daniel Pipes, *Slave Soldiers and Islam: The Genesis of a Military System* (New Haven: Yale University Press, 1981), 14, 28.

88 Hilary Kilpatrick, "Women as Poets and Chattels: *Abu l-Faraj al-Isbahani's al-ima al-sawair*," *Quaderni di Studi Arabi* 9 (1991): 161–76; Jonathan Brockop, *Early Maliki Law: Abd al-Hakam and His Major Compendium of Jurisprudence* (Leiden: Brill, 2000), 116–17. For male slaves as soldiers of Islam, see, among others, Pipes, *Slave Soldiers and Islam*. Of course female and male slavery predates Islam. It was under Islam, however, that the use of slaves reached its greatest refinement. In particular the transformation of Christian children, kidnapped or bought, into Muslim warriors is an extraordinary achievement.

89 A good short introduction to the question of slavery in the *umma* is L. O. Sanneh, "Slavery, Islam, and the Jakhanke People of West Africa," *Africa: Journal of the International African Institute*, 16, no. 1 (1976): 80–97; on race and slavery in the Islamic Middle East, see Lewis, *Race and Slavery in the Middle East*; for the question of the emancipation of slaves in Islam, see William Gervase Clarence-Smith, *Islam and the Abolition of Slavery* (Oxford: Oxford University Press, 2006); for a condensed look at al-Andalus, see Darío Fernández-Morera, "Islam's Christian Captives," *Modern Age* 50, no. 1 (Winter 2008): 63–66. For the detailed religious strictures on freed slaves, see Malik, *Muwatta*, bk. 38. In those Muslim societies that, after the nineteenth century and Western influence, eventually went against a literal interpretation of Islamic law in order to

grant emancipation, slaves achieved integration more effectively than they had in, say, the United States. Because it continued to rely on a close reading of Islamic texts that justify slavery, Qatar did not abolish slavery until 1952; for the same reasons, Yemen and Saudi Arabia did not abolish it until 1962 and Mauritania until 1980. Slavery condoned by local interpreters of Muslim law continues to exist in some Muslim countries in the twenty-first century.

90   Ibn Hazm, *Naqt -al-Arus*, ed., C. F. Seybold, trans., L. Seco de Lucena (Valencia: 1974), 130. Ibn Hazm points out that before the Abbasids took power in Islam, no caliph had a slave mother. The change brought about by the Abbasids in the Middle East was continued by the Umayyads in al-Andalus.

91   *Abenalcotía el Cordobés: Historia de la conquista de España*, ed. and trans. Julián Ribera (Madrid: Real Academia de la Historia, 1929), xxxi, 4.

92   Moral, *Arabes, judías y cristianas*, 146.

93   According to Ibn Idhari al-Marrakushi in his *Kitab al-bayan al-mughrib fi akhbar muluk al-andalus wal-maghrib* (*Book of the Amazing Story of the History of the Kings of Spain and Morocco*), trans. Edmond Fagnan (as *Al-Bayano'l-Mogrib* (*Histoire de l'Afrique et de l'Espagne*) (Alger: Imprimerie Orientale: P. Fontana, 1904)], 2:74–75, 97, 153, 198, 259, 385, 418–19. This thirteenth-century work cites very early sources going back to al-Razi in the ninth century.

94   Amelina Ramón Guerrero, "Abd al-Rahman V al-Mustazhir," *Homenaje al Prof. Jacinto Bosch Vilá* (Granada: Universidad de Grnada, 1991), 1:317.

95   Joaquín Vallvé Bermejo, *Al-Andalus: sociedad e instituciones* (Madrid: Real Academia de la Historia, 1999), 41.

96   Abd al-Wahid al-Marrakushi, *Kitab al-muyib fi taljis ajbar al-Magrib* [the book of what is admirable in the summary of the news of the Maghrib], trans. Ambrosio Huici Miranda (Tetuán: Editora Marroqui, 1955), 215.

97   Ibn al-Khatib, 159.

98   Cit. Pierre Guichard, *Structures Sociales 'Orientales' et 'Occidentales' dans l'Espagne Musulmane* (Paris: Mouton, 1977), 124.

99   *Ibn al-Jatib. Historia delos Reyes de la alhambra (Al-Lamha al-badriyya). Resplandor de la luna llena acerca de la dinastía nazarí*, trans. José María Casciaro Ramírez (Granada: University of Granada, 2010), 126.

100 Felipe Maíllo Salgado, *De la desaparición de al-Andalus* (Madrid: Abada, 2011), 39 and n27.

101 C. E. Bosworth, "Kiz," *Brill Encyclopaedia of Islam, Second Edition*, ed. P. Bearman et al. (Leiden: Brill, 2011), Brill Online, Northwestern University Library, accessed August 28, 2011, http://www.encislam.brill.nl.turing.library.northwestern.edu/subscriber/uid=1705/entry?result_number=7&entry=islam_SIM4414&search_text=concubine&refine_editions=islam_islam#hit.

102 *Brill Encyclopedia of Islam, Second Edition*, "Al-Sakaliba," accessed March 5, 2015, Brill Online, Northwestern University. See also Daniel Pipes, *Slave Soldiers and Islam*; Patricia Crone, *Slaves on Horses: The Evolution of the Islamic Polity* (Cambrdige: Cambridge University Press, 2003).

103 E. Lévi-Provençal, "Sakaliba," *Brill's First Encyclopedia of Islam (1913–1936)* (Leiden: Brill, 1993), 77.

104 Mohammed Meouak, "Les marges de l'administration hispano-umayyade (milieu IIe/VIIIe-debut Ve–XIe siècles," *Estudios onomástico-biográficos de Al-Andalus* 6 (1994): 305–36.

105 See *Brill Encyclopaedia of Islam, Second Edition*, "Mamluk."

106 Bernard Lewis, *Race and Color in Islam* (New York: Harper & Row, 1971), 38, 64. For the Circassian hegemony, see *Brill Encyclopaedia of Islam*, "Mamluk."

107 *The History of al-Tabari: The Revolt of the Zanj*, trans. David Waines (New York: State University of New York Press, 1992), vol. 36. A twentieth-century Muslim historian has attempted a revisionist account of the revolt in "The Zanj Revolt Reconsidered," *International Journal of African Historial Studies* 10, no. 3 (1977): 443–81.

108 Lewis, *Race and Color in Islam*, illustrations on 59–60.

109 Jacques Heers, *Les Négriers en terres d'Islam: La Première traite des Noirs, VIIe–XVIe siècle*

(Paris: Perrin, 2003); J. Alexander, "Islam, Archaeology, and Slavery in Africa," *World Archaeology* 33, no. 1 (June 2001): 44–60.

110 Thus Ibn Khaldun, in his *History of the Berbers*, tells of the kings of the "black nations," namely those of Sudan, etc. (see Ibn Khaldoun, *Histoire des berberes et des dynasties musulmanes de la'afrique septentrionale*, trans. Le Baron de Slane [Paris: Librairie Orientaliste, 1927], 2:105–15). So does al- Maqqari when explaining the musical instruments characteristic of "blacks," and those of "Berbers" (see *The History of the Mohammedan Dynasties in Spain*, 1:59). Ibn Battuta writes that the flesh of the women of the Tuareg is very white (see Ibn Battuta, *A través del islam*, trans. Serafín Fanjul and Federico Arbós [Madrid: Alianza, 2005], 826). Many Tuareg in fact have green eyes, and many Berbers from the Kabilia have white complexions (such as soccer players Benzema [Karim Ibn Zema] and Zinedine Zidane) and green eyes (Zidane), which might betray the centuries of Roman and Greek presence in North Africa, as well as that of the Germanic Vandals. In his *Proverbs*, al-Maydani wrote, "The African black, when hungry, steals; and when sated, he fornicates" (see *Arabum proverbia viclibus intruxit, latine vertit, commentario illustravit et sumtibus suit: Amtal al-Arab*, ed. Georg Wilhelm Freytag [Bonn: 1839], 2:404). Traveling through Africa, Ibn Battuta cited both the presumed qualities of the black nations (ruthless application of the law, beating their children if they disobey, their Muslim piety) and the faults of those without proper Islamic learning (the nakedness of women, the people's clothes, their disgusting food, their cannibalism, etc.), all of which leaves the impression that they are infantile, cowardly, and stupid (see *A través del Islam*, 820–21, 823). In the *Arabian Nights*, the worst thing about the adultery of the wives of King Sahzman and his brother Shariyar is that their infidelity was with blacks; and in *Nights* 468, a black slave is rewarded for his goodness by being transformed into a white man. The Andalusian *qadi* Said al-Andalusi (1029–1070) wrote a book classifying the races of the world: in it he accounted the inhabitants of the extreme North and South as barbarians, describing northern Europeans as mentally deficient because of undercooking by the sun, and blacks as fickle, foolish, violent, and stupid because of overcooking; in contrast, Arabs were done just right (see Lewis, *Race and Color in Islam*, 35–36). Ibn Khaldun wrote that blacks accept slavery because of their "low degree of humanity and their proximity to the animal stage" (Lewis, *Race and Color in Islam*, 38). Lewis cites numerous other Arab texts from many centuries illustrating the Arabs' and Persians' self-awareness of their difference from and superiority over African blacks as well as the blacks' awe of the Arabs (Lewis, *Race and Color in Islam*, 31–38). As late as the eighteenth century, there were racial civil wars between "blacks and whites" in Morocco, with the whites being the Moors (Lewis, *Race and Color in Islam*, 76–77).

111 Sanneh, "Slavery, Islam, and the Jakhanke People of West Afric," 80–97. See also Ronald Segal, *Islam's Black Slaves* (New York: Farrar, 2001).

112 *Al-Bayano'l-Mogrib*, 1:38.

113 Lewis, *Race and Slavery in the Middle East*, 47–48. It must be pointed out that some of the personages of early Islam had black slave women among their ancestors and that one of these personages, Bilal Ibn Rabah, had been born a black slave (25).

114 *Islam from the Prophet Muhammad to the Capture of Constantiniple*, ed. and trans. Bernard Lewis (New York: Oxford University Press, 1987), 2:209.

115 "Ut Aethiops, qui famelicus furatur, satiatus stuprum facit." Proverb 326 in *Arabum Proverbia*, trans. with commentary by G. W. Freytag (Bonn: A. Marcus, 1839), 2:404. The word *stuprum* has a wider connotation than "rape" in English; it also means any unlawful sexual intercourse or "fornication." Rhetorical parallelism, however, suggests that the meaning here should be "rape," a violent act akin to stealing.

116 "[The younger of the two brother kings] found the Queen, his wife, asleep on his own carpet bed embracing with both arms a black cook of loathsome aspect and foul with kitchen grease and grime. When he saw this the world waxed black before his sight and he said: 'If such case happen while I am yet within sight of the city, what will be the doings of this damned whore during my long absence at my brother's court?' So he drew his scimitar, and cutting the two in four pieces

with a single blow, left them on the carpet and returned presently to his camp without letting anyone know what had happened." The narrative continues when the younger brother spies his brother's wife, accompanied by the female sexual slaves of the harem, also having sex with a monstrous black slave, who, quite pointedly, is described as coming down from a tree and later climbing back on it: "a postern of the palace, which was carefully kept private, swung open, and out of it came twenty slave girls surrounding his brother's wife, who was wondrous fair, a model of beauty and comeliness and symmetry and perfect loveliness, and who paced with the grace of a gazelle which panteth for the cooling stream. Thereupon Shah Zaman drew back from the window, but he kept the bevy in sight, espying them from a place whence he could not be espied. They walked under the very lattice and advanced a little way into the garden till they came to a jetting fountain a-middlemost a great basin of water. Then they stripped off their clothes, and behold, ten of them were women, concubines of the King, and the other ten were white slaves. Then they all paired off, cach with cach. But the Queen, who was left alone, presently cried out in a loud voice, 'Here to me, O my lord Saeed!' And then sprang with a drop leap from one of the trees a big slobbering blackamoor with rolling eyes which showed the whites, a truly hideous sight. He walked boldly up to her and threw his arms round her neck while she embraced him as warmly. Then he bussed her and winding his legs round hers, as a button loop clasps a button, he threw her and enjoyed her. On like wise did the other slaves with the girls till all had satisfied their passions, and they ceased not from kissing and clipping, coupling and carousing, till day began to wane, when the Mamelukes [here synonym for 'white slaves' rather than slave warriors] rose from the damsels' bosoms and the blackamoor slave dismounted from the Queen's breast. The men resumed their disguises and all except the Negro, who swarmed up the tree, entered the palace and closed the postern door as before." *The Arabian Nights*, Sir Richard Burton, translator, 1850. Burton's is the unexpurgated translation: all others omit some of the more "offensive" elements of the *Arabian Nights*.

117   Robert C. Davis, *Christian Slaves, Muslim Masters: White Slavery in the Mediterranean, the Barbary Coast, and Italy 1500–1800* (New York: Palgrave Macmillan, 2004). I thank Seymour Drescher for this information. Some scholars have pointed to the part played by Jewish merchants (Islamic sources refer to them as *al-Radhaniyya*) in the medieval traffic of European slaves to Islamic lands: "Al-Radhaniyya," *Brill Encyclopaedia of Islam, Second Edition*, Brill Online, Northwestern University Library, accessed August 28, 2011, http://www.encislam.brill.nl.turing.library.northwestern.edu/subscriber/uid=1705/entry?result_number=20&entry=islam_SIM6168&search_text=jawari&refine_editions=islam_islam#hit. But they were not the only ones who engaged in the traffic of slaves, in which merchants from all groups participated.

118   Ibn Hawqal, *Configuration de la terre (Kitab surat al-Ard)*, trans. J.H. Kramers and G. Wiet (Paris: Maisonneuve, 1964), 1:109. By the tenth century, the name "Slav" was applied to any fair-haired and fair-skinned slave from Europe or the Balkans, and not just from the Slavic lands. Jewish slave merchants were said to be part of the trade in Christian slaves, often sold to them by other Christians. Visigoth laws from the seventh to the eighth centuries reiterate prohibitions for Jews to own or sell Christian slaves and for Christians to sell Christian slaves to Jews. In eighth-century France, church councils repeatedly forbade the sale of Christian slaves; in the tenth century, King Louis the Pious granted special permission to a Jewish merchant from Zaragoza to trade in foreign slaves but to sell them only in the kingdom of France (see Norman Roth, *Jews, Visigoths, and Muslims in Medieval Spain: Cooperation and Conflict* [Leiden: Brill, 1994], 154).

119   Michelle Hamilton, *Representing Others in Medieval Iberian Literature* (New York: Palgrave Macmillan, 2007), 28–29.

120   See Ramón Peralta, professor of constitutional law at the Universidad Complutense of Madrid, *Teoría de Castilla* (Madrid: Actas: 2006).

121   Cf. Hillenbrand, "Medieval Córdoba as a Cultural Centre," 121.

122   Marín, *Mujeres en al-Andalus*, 310.

123 Joaquín Vallvé Bermejo, *Al-Andalus: Sociedad a instituciones* (Madrid: Real Academia de la Historia, 1999), 52.

124 The separation of the sexes even within the house or the tent was paramount in the case of adults who had not suckled together (see Pesle, *Le Mariage et la Répudiation*, 114–15).

125 *Faqih* Ibn Abdun in *Islam from the Prophet Muhammad to the Capture of Constantinople, Vol. II: Religion and Society*, ed. and trans. Bernard Lewis (Oxford: Oxford University Press, 1987), 161–65, where Muslim law regulated even cemeteries: "No seller should be allowed to sell his merchandise in cemeteries for they do nothing but look at the faces of mourning women nor should young men, during holidays, be allowed to loiter along the paths that connect tombs, lurking until women pass by. The market inspector (muhtasib) must prevent this from happening with stern resolve, aided by the local judge (qadi). The authorities must also ban people from remaining in empty spaces that separate tombs as they may be intent on seducing women. To prevent this, an inspection should be carried out twice a day; this duty is assigned to the muhtasib. Police are required to search the round enclosures that surround some graves for they sometimes turn into dens of iniquity, especially during the summer when pathways are empty during the nap hour.... The windows of military barracks must remain shut as well as those of rooms on the upper floors and doors facing towards cemeteries so that women cannot be seen. The Quran reciter who prays for the deceased should neither be a young nor a single man (even if he is blind) for many evils stem from this."

126 Such as in the Nazari kingdom, where Almeria seems to have been more relaxed in allowing women to go to the baths. For the generalized admiration toward the *taifa* kingdoms, compare this rhapsodic entry on "Spain" from the *Encyclopedia of Homosexuality*: "During the caliphate and taifas periods (tenth and eleventh centuries), cosmopolitan, literate, prosperous Andalus was the leading civilization anywhere around the Mediterranean. It has also been described as the homeland of Arabic philosophy and poetry" (*Encyclopedia of Homosexuality*, ed. Wayne Dynes [New York: Garland, 1990]).

127 The most thorough such effort is Mernissi, *Forgotten Queens of Islam*. The failure of such presumably "feminist" endeavors is basically recognized by Nada Mourtada-Sabbah and Adrian Gully, "'I Am, by God, Fit for High Positions': On the Political Role of Women in al-Andalus," *British Journal of Middle Eastern Studies* 30, no. 2 (November 2003): 183–209.

128 Cf. al-Marrakushi, 144. "Treatise writers such as al-Ghazali warn against 'feminine intrigues,'" according to María Jesús Viguera Molíns, "A Borrowed Space: Andalusi and Maghribi Women in Chronicles," in Marín and Deguilhem, *Writing the Feminine*, 171.

129 Henry Kamen, "Review of *Queenship and Political Power in Medieval and Early Modern Spain*, ed. Theresa Earenfight," *English Historical Review* 122, no. 493 (2006): 1174–75.

130 Amancio Isla Frez, "Reinas de los godos," *Hispania* 64/2, no. 217 (2004): 410. Islamic nations did not have "Califhas."

131 Theresa Earenfight, ed., *Queenship and Political Power in Medieval and Early Modern Spain* (Aldershot: Ashgate, 2005), xvi.

132 For this and the following, see Vicenta Márquez de la Plata and Luis Valero de Bernabel, *Reinas medievales españolas* (Madrid: Alderabán Ediciones, 2000); Nuria Silleras-Fernández, *Power, Piety, and Patronage in Late Medieval Queenship* (New York: Palgrave Macmillan 2008); Earenfight, *Queenship and Political Power in Medieval and Early Modern Spain*.

133 The closest thing we may have is the alleged presence of courageous Muslim women behind the early Muslim armies, taking care of the wounded and rejecting the love of those men who fled from battle. See Dozy, *Histoire des musulmanes d'Espagne*, 1.i, 11.

134 Indispensable for understanding the evolution of this system is Ramón Peralta, *Teoría de Castilla* (Madrid: ACTAS, 2006), which builds on the work of earlier scholars such as J. Pérez de Urbel, *El condado de Castilla* (Madrid: Editorial Siglo Ilustrado, 1969). See also Maíllo Salgado, *De la desaparición de al-Andalus*, 61, which shows that Christian peasant soldiers could become caballeros-villanos (villagers-knights).

135 This and the following according to Heath Dillard, *Daughters of the Reconquest: Women in Castilian Town Society, 1100–1300* (Cambridge: Cambridge University Press, 1984).

136 Ibid., 148

137 Ibid., 151.

138 Ibid.

139 Ibid., 159.

140 Ibid., 159–60.

141 Ibid., 163–64.

142 Ibid., 164–66.

143 Ibid., 149.

144 Ibid., 150.

145 Ibid., 154.

146 Ibid., 152.

147 Samuel G. Armistead, "Kharjas and Villancicos," *Journal of Arabic Literature* 34, no. 2 (2003): 3–19; Richard Hitchcock, "The 'Kharjas' as Early Romance Lyrics: A Review," *Modern Language Review* 75, no. 3 (July 1980): 481–91; Richard Hitchcock, "The Fate of the Kharjas: A Survey of Recent Publications," *Bulletin of the British Society for Middle Eastern Studies* 12, no. 2 (1985): 172–90.

148 Federico Corriente, "Las *xarajat* en árabe andalusí," *Al-Qantara* 8, nos. 1–2 (1987): 203–64.

149 According to Ibn Said, following Ibn Khaldun, in Manuel Gómez Moreno, "El Kitab al-Muqtataf Min Azahir al-turaf de Ibn Said," *Al-Andalus* 13, no. 1 (1948): 28–31 and in Emilio García Gómez, "La ley de Mussafia se aplica a la poesía estrófica arábigoandaluza," *Al-Andalus* 21 (1962): 1–20; Alan Jones, "Romance Scansion and the 'Muwaššahat': An Emperor's New Clothes?" *Journal of Arabic Literature* 11 (1980): 36–55.

150 Maria Milagros Rivera Garretas, ed., *Libres para ser: Mujeres creadoras de cultura en la Europa medieval* (Madrid: Narcea, 2001).

151 In the thirteenth century, abbesses in Burgos and Palencia had to be restrained by the pope from exceeding their powers. See Thomas Oestereich, "Abbess," *The Catholic Encyclopedia* (New York: Robert Appleton Company, 1907), vol. 1, accessed March 2, 2009, http://www.newadvent.org/cathen/01007e.htm. The Catholic tradition of powerful women abbesses would continue well into the sixteenth century: see the extraordinary life of Saint Teresa of Ávila.

152 Theresa Earenfight, "Without the Persona of the Prince: Kings, Queens, and the Idea of Monarchy in Late Medieval Europe," *Gender and History* 19, no. 1 (April 2007): 3.

153 Joseph F. O'Callaghan, "The Many Roles of the Medieval Queen: Some Examples from Castile," in Earenfight, *Queenship and Political Power in Medieval and Early Modern Spain*, 20–32.

154 Frez, "Reinas de los godos," 410.

155 For the public role of women in general and queens in particular among the Visigoths, see Jurate Rosales, *Los Godos* (Barcelona: Ariel, 2004), trans. as *Goths and Balts: The Missing Link of European History*, trans. Danute Rosales (Lemont: Vydunas Youth Fund, 2004), and Frez, "Reinas de los godos." For the public role of empresses in the Christian Greek Roman Empire, see Judith Herren, *Women in Purple: Rulers of Medieval Byzantium* (London: Weidenfeld and Nicolson, 2001). It was women, of course, who first testified to what may be the central event in Christianity, Christ's resurrection. And the role of the Virgin Mary as the mother of God and since then as supreme intercessor is by definition greater than that of any woman or man in either Islam or Judaism, regardless of Islam's veneration of the Virgin Mary. Islam sees the Virgin Mary as the admired mother of a prophet but not of God Himself. For a good treatment of the Muslim veneration of the Virgin Mary, see Barbara Freyer Stowasser, *Women in the Qur'an, Traditions, and Interpretation* (Oxford: Oxford University Press, 1994), 66–82.

CHAPTER 6: THE TRUTH ABOUT THE JEWISH COMMUNITY'S "GOLDEN AGE"

1   A shorter version of this chapter appeared as "Some Overlooked Realities of Jewish Life under Islamic Rule in Medieval Spain," *Comparative Civilizations Review* 68 (Spring 2013): 21–34.

2   Bernard Lewis, "The Pre-Islamic Jews," *Judaism* (Fall 1968): 101. As pointed out by Tudor Parfitt, Martin Kramer, and Bernard Lewis, many Jewish scholars have contributed to this idealization by overlooking daily oppression and playing up Jewish prosperity under Islam in contrast to the situation under Christianity. For a critique of this phenomenon, see Tudor Parfitt, ed., *Israel and Ishmael: Studies in Muslim-Jewish Relations* (Richmond, England: Curzon, 2000), 207–25; Martin Kramer, ed., *The Jewish Discovery of Islam* (Tel Aviv: Moshe Dayan Center for Middle Eastern and African Studies, 1999); Bernard Lewis, *The Jews of Islam* (Princeton, NJ: Princeton University Press, 1984). David J. Wasserstein, professor of Jewish studies at Vanderbilt University, is a good representative of the scholarly tendency criticized by Parfitt, Kramer, and Lewis. See his otherwise excellent "The Muslims and the Golden Age of the Jews in Al-Andalus," in Uri Rubi and David J. Wasserstein, eds., *Dhimmis and Others: Jews and Christians and the World of Classical Islam* (Tel Aviv: Eisenbrauns, 1997), 179–96, where he correctly points out that Jewish life improved after the Islamic conquest, compared to the way it was in the Visigoth kingdom. Literary scholar Américo Castro, responsible for the popularity of the term *convivencia*, is the foremost representative of this tendency in the twentieth century. I thank the historian of Islam Richard Pipes, publisher of *Middle East Quarterly*, for calling my attention to this phenomenon.

3   See chapter 7, "The Christian Condition," for more on this subject. As a result of these discriminatory laws, many Jews converted, some doubtlessly sincerely, but others only to remain in Catholic Spain rather than live elsewhere; they continued practicing Judaism in secret. The reiteration of these laws in each successive church council, and the councils' complaints about their lack of success in converting the Jews, suggest that they were not effective. The Muslim invasion took place in A.D. 711, and it found a Jewish community still strong enough to be of help in the conquest. Benzion Netanyahu's *The Origins of the Inquisition in Fifteenth-Century Spain* (New York: New York Review Books, 2001) traces back to the sixth and seventh centuries in Spain the origins of the European anti-Jewish ethos, and argues that many Jews sincerely converted to Christianity, that unconverted Jews looked on the converts to Christianity with great animosity, and that it was mostly the lower classes that felt economically threatened by Jews and demonstrated the greatest enmity against them. See also the best study of the Spanish Inquisition: Henry Kamen, *The Spanish Inquisition: A Historical Revision* (New Haven, CT: Yale University Press, 1999).

4   Several Muslim historians confirm what appears to have been a customary procedure: *Ajbar Machmua*, trans. Emilio Lafuente y Alcántara (Madrid, 1867; rpt. Madrid: El Bibliófilo, 1984), 25, 27, 29; al-Maqqari in *The History of the Mohammedan Dynasties in Spain*, trans. Pascual de Gayangos (London: 1840; rpt. London: Johnson Reprint Company, 1964), 1:280–82; Ibn Idari al-Marrakusi, *Historia de al-Andalus*, trans. Francisco Fernández González (1860; rpt. Malaga: Aljaima, 1999), 17–42; Ibn al-Qutiya, *Historia de la conquista de España de Abenalcotía el cordobés*, trans. Julián Ribera (Madrid: Revista de Archivos, 1926), 8. Gayangos and other historians argue that Jews invited Muslims to invade the Visigothic realm and afterward "everywhere made common cause with them" (*The History of the Mohammedan Dynasties in Spain*, 1:531n18). Francisco Cantera Burgos states that Jews constituted a "fifth column" before the invasion: see his "Christian Spain," in Cecil Roth, *The Dark Ages: Jews in Christian Europe, 711–1096* (Tel Aviv: Jewish History Publications, 1966), 357, 450n1. According to Salo Baron, Spanish mistrust of Jews and *conversos* in the Middle Ages and beyond was perhaps based on Jews' having been a "fifth column" for the Muslim invasion of Spain: see *A Social and Religious History of the Jews* (New York: Columbia University Press, 1958), 5:135–36. According to Alan Harris Cutler, "the Christians of Franco-Germany also saw the Jews as a potential Islamic 'fifth column' and at times persecuted the Jews very severely for this precise reason": see *The Jew as Ally of the Muslim:*

Medieval Roots of Anti-Semitism (Notre Dame: University of Notre Dame Press, 1986), 395n17. Norman Roth gives no importance to the Jewish part in the Islamic invasion of Spain: "The Jews and the Muslim Conquest of Spain," *Jewish Social Studies* 38 (1976): 145–58. Elyahu Ashtor points out that Jews supported Muslims against Christian rebels (such as Umar ibn Hafsun, Saint Eulogius, et al.) and against Christians in the North (such as King Alfonso III of Asturias, reigned ca. 866–910) who attacked Muslims in the South, and sat with Muslims in the Christian Council of Córdoba (863) to make sure the council did not encourage Christian rebelliousness: *The Jews of Moslem Spain* (Philadelphia: Jewish Publication Society, 1973; trans. Jenny Maklowitz Klein of *Korot ha-Yehudim bi-Sefarad ha-Muslemit*), 1:68–69, 92–93, 98–99. According to Arthur J. Zuckerman, there was a Judeo-Islamic conspiracy to seize Catholic Barcelona in 852: see his *Jewish Princedom in Feudal France, 768–900 (Study in Jewish History)* (New York: Columbia University Press, 1972), 316–18. A contingent of Jewish troops from Africa under the command of Kaula-al-Yehudi was part of the Muslim army that defeated the Visigoths at Guadalete (Jerez), and the Muslim conquerors favored Jewish immigration from many lands as part of their political design against the Spanish Catholics: Amador de los Ríos, *Historia social, política y religiosa de los judíos de España y Portugal* (Madrid: Fontanet, 1875), 1:116–17n1–2, 118–19. None of this endeared the Jewish community to the Catholics in the North and to the Catholic *dhimmis* under Muslim rule ("Mozarabs").

5   Sidney David Markman, *Jewish Remnants in Spain: Wanderings in a Lost World* (Mesa: Scribe Publishers, 2003), 7. In North Africa and the Middle East, Muslims soon realized that they could use the Jewish community, unhappy with its treatment in the Christian Greek Roman Empire, to help keep the Christians under control. A. S. Tritton cites several Muslim sources on the matter: *The Caliphs and Their Non-Muslim Subjects: A Critical Study of the Covenant of Umar* (London: Frank Cass, 1930; rpt. 1970), 94–95. Alan Harris Cutler and Helen Elmquist cite Christian primary sources that attribute the persecutions of Jews in Europe in 1010 and the 1060s to the widespread belief in the collusion of Jews with Islam and argue that the "association of Jew with Muslim was the crucial factor in the persecution of 1096" as well: *The Jew as Ally of the Muslim*, 400–402. News of the alleged joint attack by Jews and Muslims against the Church of the Holy Sepulchre in 966, and of the Muslim Fatimids' actual destruction of the same church in 1010, had reached Europe and fostered animosity against Jews; it was doubtlessly a motivation for the eventual massacre of Jews during the conquest of Jerusalem in 1099 during the First Crusade (*The Jew as Ally of the Muslim*, 403–5). The Christian Greeks had long accused Jews of being in collusion with Muslims, and when Jerusalem capitulated to Islam in 638, the Orthodox patriarch of Jerusalem, Sophronios, requested and obtained Muslim protection against Jews to avoid a repetition of the massacres of Greek Christians that had taken place in the city in 614: see my next note and Joshua Starr, *Jews in the Byzantine Empire (Research and Source Works Series, No. 386)* (Farnborough: Gregg, 1969), 109.

6   Like Muslims later, Persians took advantage of Jewish-Christian enmity: Elliott Horowitz, "'The Vengeance of the Jews Was Stronger Than Their Avarice': Modern Historians and the Persian Conquest of Jerusalem in 614," *Jewish Social Studies* 4, no. 2 (1998): 1–25; *Reckless Rites: Purim and the Legacy of Jewish Violence* (Princeton, NJ: Princeton University Press, 2004), 229. A number of primary sources blame Jewish retaliatory killings of Christians upon the Persian conquest of Jerusalem in 614: Theophanes the Confessor (d. 818) in *The Chronicle of Theophanes Confessor: Byzantine and Near Eastern History A.D. 284–813*, ed. Cyril Mango and Roger Scott with the assistance of Geoffrey Greatrex (Oxford: Clarendon Press, 1997), 431, who claims ninety thousand Christians killed upon the conquest of Jerusalem; Antiochus Strategos of Mar Saba in "Antiochus Strategos, The Capture of Jerusalem by the Persians in 614 A.D.," trans. F. C. Coneybeare, *English Historical Review* 25 (1910): 502–17; an Arabic version of Strategos's account confirms the charges: G. Garitte, ed. *Expugnationis Hierosolymae A.D. 614: Recensiones Arabicae, I–II*, CSCO 340–41, 347–48, Arab. 26–29 (Louvain: Peeters, 1973–74); the Armenian bishop Sebeos, in *The Armenian History Attributed to Sebeos*, trans. R. W. Thomson (Liverpool: Liverpool University Press, 1999), pt. 1, pp. 68–69. See also Hein-

rich Graetz, *History of the Jews* (Philadelphia: Jewish Publication Society of America, 1894), 3:18–22. The *Jewish Encyclopedia* states that the story of Jews' buying Christians and then massacring them at the Mamilla Pool in Jerusalem is fiction (see "Chosroes (Khosru) II. Parwiz," www.jewishencyclopedia.com). Recent Israeli archaeological excavations in Jerusalem have discovered thousands of remains of men, women, and children, with a majority of them of women, in the site of the Mamilla Pool, dating back to the times of the Persian conquest of the city. See Yossi Nagar (who attributes the massacre to the Persians), "Human Skeletal Remains from the Mamilla Cave, Jerusalem," Israeli Antiquities Authority website, www.antiquities.org.il/article_Item_eng.asp?sec_id=17&sub_subj_id=179. Israeli archaeologist Ronny Reich estimates the total dead at sixty thousand before the Persians stopped the carnage: see Gil Zohar, "Massacre at Mamilla," *Jerusalem Post*, March 2, 2006, www.jpost.com/LocalIsrael/InJerusalem/Article.aspx?id=14894.

7   Peter Scholliers, *Food, Drink, and Identity: Cooking, Eating, and Drinking in Europe since the Middle Ages* (Brussels: Berg, 2001), 207–8. Historian Luis A. García Moreno observes that the news of the alliance between Jews and Persians against the Christians of the Greek Roman Empire in the early seventh century may have played a factor in the Visigoth laws, beginning with King Sisebut (612–621), that tried to force the Jews to convert to Christianity, in order to eliminate them as potential helpers of the enemies of the Visigoth kingdom: *Los judíos de la España antigua* (Madrid: RIALP, 2005), 129–30.

8   As does, for example, even Bernard Lewis, "The Judeo-Islamic Heritage," *Pe'amim* 20 (1984): 3–13. For a critique of Lewis's more recent views, see Andrew G. Bostom, "What Went Wrong with Bernard Lewis," *American Thinker*, March 17, 2013. A more balanced account that, nonetheless, does not consider the political explanation that we have outlined, can be found in Mark R. Cohen's excellent "The Convivencia of Jews and Muslims in the High Middle Ages," *The Meeting of Civilizations: Muslim, Christian, and Jewish*, ed. Moshe Maoz (Brighton, England: Sussex Academic Press, 2009), 54–65.

9   Rabbi Moses ben Jacob Ibn Ezra (b. Granada ca. 1055, d. after 1138)—writing in Arabic— described the change in the fortunes of Spanish Jewry: "And when the Arabs conquered the Peninsula of al-Andalus…from the Goths, who had been victorious over the Romans…, after a long time our diaspora captured its own personality, [and] laboriously learned its language and became outstanding in its use, penetrating the subtlety of its intentions, training in the true inflection of its words, tasting the sweetness of its verses, until God revealed to it the secrets of the Hebrew language and its grammar…. All this was speedily learned by our minds, understanding what they had earlier ignored" (*Mose Ibn Ezra: Kitab al-muhadara wal-mudakara*, ed. and trans. Montserrat Abumalham [Madrid: Consejo Superior de Investigaciones Científicas, 1985], 2:61–62). Much has been written on the subject of Jewish culture in Islamic Spain. See, for example, Menahem Mansoor, *Jewish History and Thought* (Hoboken, NJ: Ktav Publishing House, 1991); Angela Navarro Petro, *Literatura hispanohebrea* (s. x–xiii) (Córdoba: El Almendro, 1988); Angel Sainz-Badillos, *Literatura hebrea en la España medieval* (Madrid: Fundación Amigos de Sefarad, 1991).

10   Fernando Díaz Esteban, "Los *dimmies* a nueva luz," *Anaquel de estudios árabes* 9 (1998): 30.

11   Lewis, *The Jews of Islam*, 67.

12   Malik, *al-Muwatta*, 21; *Qur'an* 9:27. For the quotations from Quran, I use *The Qur'an: Text, Translation, and Commentary* by Abdullah Yusuf Ali (Elmhurst, NY: Tahrike Tarsile Qur'an, 2001) unless otherwise stated. For the following limitations, see also Maliki treatises listed in chapter 3 on the Muslim condition, as well as the "Pact" or "Covenant" of Umar I, and historian al-Maqqari, cited below. This covenant, attributed to the Caliph Umar I (ruled 634–644), is extant in several forms; it may not date from the time of Umar, but it nevertheless indicates an actual cultural practice in medieval Islamic lands. It was bestowed on the defeated Greek Christians of the Greek Roman Empire upon the Muslim conquest of Jerusalem and applied to Jews as well. One version can be read online at www.fordham.edu/halsall/pgc.asp?page=jewish/jewsumar.html. The best study is probably Tritton, *The Caliphs*

and Their Non-Muslim Subjects. Among other references to the yellow sign forced on Jews in Spain, see *The History of the Mohammedan Dynasties in Spain*, 1:116. This had been standard Islamic practice toward Jews in the Middle East, and Christians eventually imitated it. As late as the sixteenth century, a North African anti-Jewish treatise considered the Sephardim's association with Muslim rulers a violation of the *dhimma* agreement, which by means of the *jizya* indicates the debasement and contempt in which the "protected ones" must be held: G. Vajda, "Un traité maghrebin 'adversos Judaeos': 'Ahkam al-dimma' du Sayh Muhammad b. Abd al Karim al-Magili," in *Études d'orientalisme dédiées a la mémoire de Lévi-Provençal*, ed. R. Brunschvig et al. (Paris: Maisonneuve, 1962), 2:806.

13   Al-Makkari, 1:103.

14   The best account of this brilliant man seems to be Norman Roth, *Jews, Visigoths, and Muslims in Medieval Spain: Cooperation and Conflict* (Leiden: Brill, 1994), 79ff. Roth cites a Muslim source showing that Hasdai was a specialist in "Jewish law."

15   Even in the Visigoth kingdom, the harsh laws against Jews were not always enforced or successful, perhaps were too "flexible," to judge by the repeated admonishments in the Visigoth Code regarding the need to enforce the previous laws, the creation of new laws to reinforce the previous laws, the punishments listed against Christians who violated the laws by helping Jews, and the existence of a Jewish community still strong enough to have been a factor in the Muslim invasion. See *Lex Visigothorum (Forum judicum)*, bk. 12, title 3. In the Christian kingdoms, several Jews attained positions of great influence in the royal courts, and many exemptions were granted to the Jewish communities at various times.

16   Alejandro García Sanjuán, "Violencia contra los judíos," in *De muerte violenta: Política, religión, y violencia en al-Andalus*, ed. Maribel Fierro (Madrid: Consejo Superior de Investigaciones Científicas, 2004), 170 and n7. Felipe Maíllo Salgado has noticed the implausibility of seeing Ibn Naghrela as leading Muslim armies into battle, as is repeated by scholarly admirers of this "Golden Age" of Judaism (he calls this unfounded belief of well-known scholars who promote the "Golden Age of Judaism," such as David J. Wasserstein, simply "unreal" and unsubstantiated by any Muslim or Christian source): Felipe Maíllo Salgado, "Los judíos en las fuentes andalucíes y magrebíes," in *Del pasado judío en los reinos medievales hispánicos*, ed. Yolanda Moreno Koch and Ricardo Izquierdo Benito (Cuenca: Universidad de Castilla-La Mancha, 2005), 169–204.

17   "Islamic law protected [Christians' and Jews'] life, property, and freedom and, with certain restrictions, granted them also the right to exercise their religion. On the other hand, it demanded from them segregation and subservience, conditions that under a weak or wicked government could and did lead to situations bordering on lawlessness and even to outright persecutions." S. D. Goitein, *A Mediterranean Society: The Jewish Communities of the Arab World as Portrayed in the Documents of the Cairo Geniza* (Berkeley: University of California Press, 1971), 2:289.

18   Ibn al-Jatib, *Historia de los Reyes de la Alhambra*, trans. José María Casciaro Ramírez (Granada: University of Granada, 2010), 187–88.

19   De los Ríos, *Historia social, política, y religiosa de los judíos de España y Portugal*, 1:208–9.

20   Ibid., 1:226.

21   Reinhart Dozy, *Histoire des Musulmanes d'Espagne* (Leiden: Brill, 1932), 3:73.

22   Sanjuán, "Violencia contra los judíos," 167n3.

23   Maíllo Salgado, "Los judíos en las fuentes andalucíes y magrebíes," 181–82.

24   This embarrassing situation actually confirmed the greatness of the rabbi because of the marvelous way he handled the problem. Ibn Naghrela did not use his influence on the ruler of Granada to punish the merchant. Instead, upon learning that the man was in some financial difficulties, he sent him a large sum of money. Afterward, every time Ibn Naghrela rode by, the Muslim merchant praised him effusively: de los Ríos, *Historia social, política, y religiosa de los judíos de España y Portugal*, 1:215n2.

25   Ibid., 1:215n3.

26 Translation by Bernard Lewis in his *Islam in History: Ideas, Men, and Events in the Middle East* (La Salle, IL: Open Court, 1973), 159–61.

27 Cf. Gabriel Martínez Gros, "Ibn Hazm contre les Juifs: Un bouc emissaire jusqu'au jugement dernier," *Atalaya* 5 (1994): 123–34. Jewish thinkers reacted against Ibn Hazm's attacks: Camilla Adang, "A Jewish Reply to Ibn Hazm: Solomon b. Adret's Polemic against Islam," *Judíos en tierras de Islam: Judíos y musulmanes en al-Andalus y el Magreb* (Madrid: Casa de Velázquez, 2002), 179–209.

28 Emilio García Gómez, "Polémica religiosa entre Ibn Hazm e Ibn al-Nagrila," *Al-Andalus* 4 (1932): 1–28; Ignaz Goldziher, "Proben muhammedanischer Polemik gegen den Talmud," *Jeschurun: Zeitschrift fur die Wissenschaft des Judentums* 8 (1872): 76–104.

29 Dozy, *Histoire des Musulmanes d'Espagne*, 3:23.

30 De los Ríos, *Historia social, política, y religiosa de los judíos de España y Portugal*, 1:229n1.

31 Emilio Garcia Gomez, *El siglo XI en primera persona: Las memorias de Abd Allah, el último rey Ziri de Granada, destronado por los almoravides* (Madrid: Alianza, 2005). Abd Allah also complained that ruler Badis Ibn Habbus "did not listen to any other views than those of 'the Jew,' because of the trust he had in him" (see Sanjuán, "Violencia contra los judíos," 175.)

32 Sanjuán, "Violencia contra los judíos," 177.

33 Goitein, *A Mediterranean Society*, 2:278.

34 Abd al-Hasan Ali ibn al-Husayn Masudi, *Les Prairies d'Or*, trans. Barbier de Meynard and Pavet de Courteille, revised and corrected by Charles Pellat (Paris: Societé Asiatique, Collection d'Ouvrages Orientaux, 1971), 3:592. For traditional Islamic anti-Judaism in general, see Hava Lazarus-Yafeh, ed., *Muslim Authors on Jews and Judaism: The Jews among Their Muslim Neighbours* (Jerusalem: Zalman Shazar Center for Jewish History, 1996); Rose G. Lewis, "Christians and Jews," *Midstream* 32, no. 3 (March 1986): 25–28; Norman Arthur Stillman, "Traditional Islamic Attitudes toward Jews and Judaism," in *The Solomon Goldman Lectures: Perspectives in Jewish Learning*, ed. Nathaniel Stampfer (Chicago: Spertus College of Judaica Press, 1985), 4:75–84.

35 Heinrich Graetz, *Geschichte der Juden* (Leipzig: Oskar Leiner, 1871), 6:66.

36 Sanjuán, "Violencia contra los judíos," 172–73.

37 Camilla Adang, *Muslim Writers on Judaism and the Hebrew Bible from Ibn Rabban to Ibn Hazm* (Leiden: Brill, 1996), 63.

38 Reinhart Dozy, *Scriptorum arabum loci de Abbadidis* (Hildesheim/New York: Georg Olms, 1992, rpt. of 1863 ed.), 2:16.

39 Sanjuán, "Violencia contra los judíos," 174.

40 For a general description of the prosperity achieved by the Jewish community and the power of Jewish leaders during the *taifa* period, and how this prosperity and power fueled anti-Jewish sentiment, see Lewis, *The Jews of Islam*. See also Sanjuán, "Violencia contra los judíos," 169–70.

41 Sanjuán, "Violencia contra los judíos," 170; de los Ríos, *Historia social, política, y religiosa de los judíos de España y Portugal*, 1:235.

42 Serafín Fanjul, *Al-Andalus contra España* (Madrid: Siglo XXI, 2002), 248.

43 As does Norman Kohn: "As I see it, the deadliest kind of antisemitism... has little to do with real conflicts of interest between living people, or even with racial prejudice as such. At its heart lies the belief that Jews—all Jews everywhere—form a conspiratorial body set on ruining and then dominating the rest of mankind. And this belief is simply a modernized secularized version of the popular medieval view": Norman Kohn, *Warrant for Genocide: The Myth of the Jewish World-Conspiracy and the "Protocols of the Elders of Zion"* (New York: Harper & Row, 1967), 16.

44 This is the standard interpretation. Vincent Lagardère, however, argues that *al-murabitun* meant "those who are like fortresses" (against the polytheists): see his *Les almoravides* (Paris: L'Harmattan, 1989), 16.

45 Yitzhak Baer, *A History of the Jews in Christian Spain* (Philadelphia: Jewish Publication Society of America, 1961), 1:65. In the Kingdom of Aragon, royal enactments between 1257 and

1340 show that Jews were exempted from a number of regulations. See Joseph Jacobs, *An Inquiry into the Sources of the History of the Jews in Spain* (London: D. Nutt, 1894): they could be exempted from wearing the "badge" that marked them as Jews (xxi); they were exempt from local taxation and from lodging the king (xxii); they could hold landed property, castles, and manors (xxii); they could be bailiffs and clerks of towns (xxiii); and they could continue their practice of polygamy through the purchase of a "license" that would allow them to marry a second wife (xxv). These lists of royal enactments are more likely to reflect actual practice than the statutes of the *fueros*, which could be passed without being always observed. Rabbi Isaac Abravanel served as treasurer to Alfonso V, King of Portugal, and later to King Ferdinand of Aragon. Jews who had converted to Christianity (*conversos*) likewise enjoyed the favor of monarchs and the nobility, and some members of formerly Jewish families reached important positions within government, such as the wealthy Luis de Santangel, tax collector and financial officer to Ferdinand and Isabella, and Gabriel Sánchez, treasurer and counselor to the kingdom of Aragon. Jewish converts to Christianity could also rise within the ranks of the Catholic church, such as Bishop Pablo de Santa María, formerly known as Solomon Halevi, and also, to a lesser extent, Abner of Burgos, who became Abner of Valladolid, and Joshua Ha-Lorki, who adopted the name Jeronimo de Santa Fe upon being converted by the influence of Saint Vincent Ferrer. Under the Visigoths, Archbishop Julian of Toledo became primate of the whole of Spain. None of this, however, stopped members of the largely peasant Catholic masses from looking with suspicion and envy upon both Jews and conversos.

46 Graetz, *Geschichte der Juden*, 6:77–82.

47 De los Ríos, *Historia social, política, y religiosa de los judíos de España y Portugal*, 1:293, 298ff. It was Yacub who ordered the deportation of the entire Christian population of Granada to North Africa.

48 See Francisco Javier Simonet, *Historia de los mozárabes de España* (Madrid: Turner, 1983), vol. 4; Vincent Lagardère, "Communautés mozarabes et pouvoir almoravide en 519 H/1125," *Andalus Studia Islamica* 67 (1988): 99–119; Delfina Serrano Ruano, "Dos fetvas sobre la expulsión de los mozárabes al Magreb en 1126," *Anaquel de estudios árabes* 2 (1991): 163–82; de los Ríos, *Historia social, política, y religiosa de los judíos de España y Portugal*, 1:298. See also online the classic article by Ramon Menendez Pidal at www.vallenajerilla.com/glosas/irradiacionlinguistica.htm.

49 Moises Orfali Levi, "Maimónides ante el problema de las conversiones simuladas: Tolerancia y 'Halaja,'" in *Sobre la vida y la obra de Maimónides: I Congreso Internacional* (Córdoba, 1985), ed. Jesus Pelaez del Rosal (Córdoba: El Almendro, 1991), 375–93. For the accusation of apostasy from Islam against Maimonides, see document 59 in *Islam: From the Prophet Muhammad to the Capture of Constantinople*, ed. and trans. Bernard Lewis (Oxford: Oxford University Press, 1987), 2:191–92.

50 *Al-Makkari*, 2:520n18, lv, n23.

51 Herbert Alan Davidson, *Moses Maimonides: The Man and His Works* (New York: Oxford University Press, 2004), 27–28, claims that most scholars have exaggerated Almohad persecution and that many Christians and Jews remained in al-Andalus practicing their religion, though under harassment.

52 "The fear of Jewish assimilation into Christian society has often led Orthodox leaders to discourage the possibility of close contact between members of the two faiths, while it has also acted as a significant brake on developing interfaith relations even amongst Progressive rabbis": *A Dictionary of Jewish-Christian Relations*, ed. Edward Kessler and Neil Wenborn (Cambridge: Cambridge University Press, 2005), 39. "The implications of the [genetic] research to this point seem to be that once a Jewish community was founded, its genetic integrity remained remarkably consistent. Marriage partners were chosen from a fairly closed gene pool. Relatively few 'outside' women or men married or converted in": Yaakov Kleiman, *DNA and Tradition: The Genetic Link to the Ancient Hebrews* (Jerusalem and New York: Devora Publishing, 2004), 41.

53 The idea was to follow the right path in order to walk through life always in the company of God, even in everyday, seemingly insignificant situations (*halakh* means literally "to walk," hence the word *halakhah*, or "the law"—that is, "the path"). By adhering to the law, *every individual* behaved as a Jewish priest used to behave at the ancient Jerusalem Temple, where he had to follow numerous elaborate ritual procedures. In the treatise *Shulchan Aruch*, the rules on what to do on getting up in the morning are a marvelous example of this rigorous self-discipline. See Rabbi Solomon Ganzfried, *Code of Jewish Law (Kitzur Shulchan Aruch)*, trans. Hayman E. Goldin (New York: Hebrew Publishing Co., 1927), vol. 1, chaps. 1–5. This is the abridged (*kitzur*) version, which also takes into account the Ashkenazi additions by the Polish rabbi Moïse ben Israël Isserlès (ca. 1520–1572) of the sixteenth-century Spanish Sephardic rabbi Joseph Ephraim Caro's monumental *Shulchan Aruch* (Venice, 1565). Unless otherwise specified, my *Shulchan Aruch* references are to this abridged version. For the deep spiritual relevance of the ubiquitous Jewish legal apparatus of Orthodox Judaism, see Isador Twersky, "The *Shulhan Arukh*: Enduring Code of Jewish Law," in Jacob Neusner, *An Introduction to Judaism: A Textbook and Reader* (Louisville, KY: Westminster/John Knox Press, 1991), 336–38.

54 Cf. the medieval documents of the Cairo Geniza in Goitein, *A Mediterranean Society*, 2:276.

55 E. Mary Smallwood, *The Jews under Roman Rule: From Pompey to Diocletian (Studies in Judaism in Late Antiquity)* (Leiden: Brill, 1976), 127. The legal status of Jews in the Roman Empire was complex and included not only controls but also various forms of autonomy. "In Judea itself, it appears as if the patriarch of the Jews had the authority to act as a judge in civil actions that pitted Jews against each other, or in matters of religious law. Roman governors could, and did, act to support the decisions of these courts": David Stone Potter, *The Roman Empire at Bay, A.D. 180–395* (New York: Routledge, 2004), 424. The best-known example is of course the case of Roman governor Pontius Pilate as told in the Christian New Testament.

56 Potter, *The Roman Empire at Bay*, 425. Potter argues that a close reading of Constantine's legislation shows a pattern not of anti-Jewish persecution but of making things harder for all non-Christians in order to make things easier for Christians, for whom legislation prior to Constantine had worked precisely in the opposite direction. In present-day Israel, the government has traditionally exempted religion students from army service, and recent attempts to end this policy have faced strong resistance from a number of religious authorities.

57 Thus the *Shulchan Aruch*, the treatise on Jewish law written by widely respected sixteenth-century Spanish rabbi Joseph Caro, wisely recommended that Jews be generally guarded in dealings with non-Jews. In one example, it explains that a non-Jew who raised geese might try to make a goose look fat before selling it to a Jew by sticking a needle under the wing of the goose, so the flesh swelled and the animal looked fat (1:29).

58 The lack of communitarian cohesiveness among the three cultures, which may indicate a basic structural weakness in al-Andalus, and the contrasting presence of communitarian cohesiveness within each of the three cultures, were to a certain extent analogous to the problems of the weakening of community feelings in truly mixed "diverse" communities that Harvard social scientist Robert Putnam has found in his studies on diversity in the United States in the twenty-first century. For Putnam's findings, see his "E Pluribus Unum: Diversity and Community in the Twenty-First Century: The 2006 Johan Skytte Prize Lecture," *Scandinavian Political Studies* 30, no. 2 (2007): 137–74, online at www.utoronto.ca/ethnicstudies/Putnam.pdf.

59 For this and the previous examples, see María Jesús Viguera Molins, "Cristianos, judíos, y musulmanes en al-Andalus," in *Cristianos, musulmanes, y judíos en la España medieval: de la aceptación al rechazo* (Valladolid: Ambito, 2004), 52, 62–63.

60 H. I. Idris, *La Berbérie orientale sous les Zirides* (Paris: 1962), 2:766n437. Curiously, a scholar today cites this case as an example of Jewish-Muslim *convivencia* since, after all, the Muslims and the Jew were sharing a well: Christine Mazzoli-Guintard, *Vivre à Cordue au Moyen Age: Solidarité citadines en terre d'Islam aux Xe–Xie siècles* (Rennes: Presses Universitaires de Rennes, 2003), 89.

61   Basilio Pavón, *Ciudades Hispano-Musulmanas* (Madrid: MAPFRE, 1992), 72–77; Leopoldo
      Torres Balbás, *Ciudades hispanomusulmanas* (Madrid: Ministerio de asuntos exteriores, 1977),
      1:197, 209–15; 2:650. An unusual example of this exclusiveness was the city of Lucena, where
      Jews were a majority and lived in the inner city. Twelfth-century Muslim historian Abu Abd
      Allah Abdullah Muhammed ibn Muhammed al-Idrisi writes that "Jews would not allow Mus-
      lims to enter the Jewish inner city. They are wealthier than any of the countries under Muslim
      domination, and they keep on their guard against the enterprises of their rivals": *Description de
      l'Afrique et de l'Espagne par Edrisi*, ed. and trans. R. Dozy and M. J. de Goeje (Leiden: Brill, 1968),
      252–53. Some scholars believe that, *initially*, Jews began congregating in exclusively Jewish
      neighborhoods, not because they were forced to do so but because Jewish dwellings developed
      around and near the synagogue, which was the center of Jewish life: Israel Abrahams, *Jewish Life
      in the Middle Ages* (London: E. Goldston, 1932; rpt. 2009), 1. In case of necessity, Jews would live
      adjacent to Muslim or Christian quarters, or even share with them a particular building, but each
      family would live in one part of the building, as shown in some medieval documents from the
      Cairo Geniza: see Goitein, *A Mediterranean Society*, 2:262–63, 5:310.
62   Goitein, *A Mediterranean Society*, 2:88–290.
63   S. D. Goitein wrote, "In view of this far-reaching segregation it is not astonishing that the
      Geniza letters contain practically no reference to the spiritual life of non-Jewish commu-
      nities" (see Goitein, *A Mediterranean Society*, 2:277). This, however, did not stop the most
      learned rabbis from writing polemical works against the other religions.
64   Maimonides made clear that God had commanded Jews to obey the instructions of the rab-
      binical sages not only of the past but also of the future. See *Mishneh Torah. Sefer Ahavah
      (The Book of Love). Hilchot Berachot (The Laws of Blessings)*, trans. with commentaries and
      notes by Rabbi Eliyahu Touger (New York and Jerusalem: Moznaim Publishing, 1997), 11:13.
      Unless otherwise indicted, all my citations from *Mishneh Torah* are taken from Rabbi Touger's
      edition, which uses the uncensored text of the *Mishneh Torah*. Writing in the first century,
      Joseph ben Mattathyahu (who took the Roman name Flavius Josephus) praised the hierocratic
      nature of Jewish governance: "And what could be a better or more righteous policy than ours
      which makes us esteem God the head of the universe, which commits to the priests generally
      the administration of the principal affairs, and entrusts the rule over the other priests to the
      supreme high priest?" See Flavius Josephus, "Against Apion" (*Contra Apionem*), in *The Judaic
      Tradition: Jewish Writings from Antiquity to the Modern Age*, ed. and trans. Nahum N. Glatzer
      (London/Northvale, NJ: Jason Aronson, 1961), 143. In Christian Spain, the Jewish commu-
      nity's effort to keep away the non-Jewish world extended to the point of not pooling Jewish
      fiscal contributions to the rulers with that of the non-Jewish inhabitants of the city. This iso-
      lation was to the liking of monarchs, since it reinforced their unique jurisdiction over Jews.
      See, among many secondary works, Abraham A. Neuman, *The Jews in Spain: Their Social,
      Political, and Cultural Life during the Middle Ages* (Philadelphia: Jewish Publication Society
      of America, 1942), 1:14–15, 34, 112; and Jon Irving Bloomberg, *The Jewish World in the Middle
      Ages* (Hoboken, NJ: Ktav, 2000), 164.
65   Baer, *A History of the Jews in Christian Spain*, 2:34
66   Abravanel is said to have offered Ferdinand very large sums of money to stop the expulsion.
      Working in the synagogue itself was another group of rabbis concerned with the actual func-
      tioning of the synagogue and the reading and exegesis of the religious texts. As Yitzhak Baer
      observed, there could be friction between these two groups—the more pious synagogue rabbis
      and the more "cosmopolitan" rabbinical leader or leaders. But García Moreno points out that
      frequently the two groups would be connected: thus in the Jewish community of Mahon in
      the fifth century, the leader of the Jewish community, Theodor, was also the head of the syna-
      gogue. García Moreno points out that already under the Visigoths the Jewish community had
      abandoned the Jewish custom of annual elections (coinciding with the beginning of the Jewish
      year in September) of the leaders of the community and of the synagogue. For García Moreno's
      observtions, see his *Los judíos de la España antigua* (Madrid: RIALP, 2005), 91–92, 121.

67 Stern, *Jewish Identity in Early Rabbinic Writings*, 109.

68 Simha Assaf, *Haonshin ahare hatimat haTalmud: Omer letoldot hamishpa haivri* (Jerusalem: Legal Library, 1922), 62. I thank Rifka Cook for translating this material.

69 Daniel Jeremy Silver, *Maimonidean Criticism and the Maimonidean Controversy 1180–1240* (Leiden: Brill, 1965), 72–73.

70 Baer, *A History of the Jews in Christian Spain*, 1:65.

71 Abrahams, *Jewish Life in the Middle Ages*, 49.

72 Gerald J. Blidstein, "The 'Other' in Maimonidean Law," *Jewish History* 18 (2004): 184, 190n16.

73 *Mishneh Torah. Sefer Zemanim (The Book of Seasons). Hilchot Eruvin (The Laws of Eruvin)* 6:21.

74 For this and the following examples, see Baer, *A History of the Jews in Christian Spain*, 1:284–94 and 315–24, 2:452. See also Daniel Richter, ed., *Die Responsen des Rabbi Ascher ben Jechiel (Rosch)* (Zürich: Schulthess Polygraphischer Verlag, 1992), 106–8 and n235; and Simha Assaf, *Haonshin ahare hatimat haTalmud*, 62, 63, 67, 69, 72, 74, 76–79, 86–87.

75 Silver, *Maimonidean Criticism and the Maimonidean Controversy 1180–1240*, 153.

76 Enrique Cantera Montenegro, "La justicia en las aljamas castellanas a fines del siglo XV: La frontera oriental del reino de Castilla," *Sefarad* 52, no. 2 (1992): 338.

77 Avraham Grossman, *Pious and Rebellious: Jewish Women in Medieval Europe* (Lebanon, NH: Brandeis University Press, 2004), 218ff. Grossman acknowledges that this might be literary hyperbole but argues that the repetition of the motif indicates conviction; and he considers the possibility that "The Prince" might have been influenced on wife beating by his Muslim surroundings.

78 Abrahams, *Jewish Life in the Middle Ages*, 49–51, 94; Montenegro, "La justicia en las aljamas castellanas a fines del siglo XV," 339. After 1380, Jewish authorities had to request royal permission to execute other Jews. See also de los Ríos, *Historia social, política, y religiosa de los judíos de España y Portugal*, 1:289.

79 For the decree in the early *Lex romana visigothorum* (506) forbidding Jews from persecuting Jewish apostates to Catholicism and for the irregular enforcement of these laws, see *Lex romana visigothorum*, ed. Gustavus Haenel (Leipzig: Teubner, 1848), 250 ("*Codicis Theodosiani. Liber xvi. Titulus ii–iv*"): "Eum, qui ex Iudaeo christianus factus est, inquietari a Iudaeis non liceat vel aliqua pulsare iniuria"; Baer, *A History of the Jews in Christian Spain*, 1:18; for Constantine's legislation forbidding the Jewish stoning of apostates, see Amnon Linder, *The Jews in Roman Imperial Legislation* (Detroit and Jerusalem: Wayne State University Press and the Israel Academy of Sciences and Humanities, 1999), 121.

80 Rabbi Emanuel B. Quint, *Jewish Jurisprudence* (London: Routledge, 1980), 170–71; Basil Herring, *Jewish Ethics and Halakhah for Our Time* (New York: Ktav Publications of Yeshiva University Press, 1984), 162.

81 Rabbi Emanuel Quint, *A Restatement of Rabbinic Civil Law* (Jerusalem: Gefen, 2004), 10:258–60.

82 *Mishneh Torah. Sefer HaMada (The Book of Knowledge). Hilchot Avodat Kochavim (The Laws of the Worship of Stars and Their Statutes*, 2:9.

83 *Hilchot Avodat Kochavim* 3:1–2.

84 Ibid., 3:10.

85 *Mishneh Torah. Sefer Shofetim (The Book of Judges). Hilchot Melachim U'Milchamoteichem (The Laws of Kings and Their Wars)*, 11:4.

86 *Hilchot Melachim U'Milchamoteichem (The Laws of Kings and Their Wars)*, 11:4; *Hilchot Avodat Kochavim* 10:1; *Sefer HaMada. Hilchot Avodat Kochavim Umazalot VChukkot HaAkum*, 9:4.

87 Touger in his edition of *Hilchot Avodat Kochavim*, 171n8.

88 Roth, *Jews, Visigoths, and Muslims in Medieval Spain*, 217–18.

89 David Novak's contention, for which he cites medieval Ashkenazi authority Rabbi Tam, that medieval Judaism did not consider Christians idolaters is difficult to sustain, at least for Islamic Spain. See David Novak, *The Jewish Social Contract* (Princeton, NJ: Princeton

University Press, 2005), 207–8. That Christians were not idolaters was not the view of Caro's *Shulchan Aruch* either.

90   Blidstein, "The 'Other' in Maimonidean Law," 190n19.

91   *Hilchot Avodat Kochavim*, 10:1. Heretics and apostates must be killed: "It is a mitzvah [an obligation] to eradicate *minnim* and *apikorsim*, and to cause them to descend to the pit of destruction since they cause difficulty to the Jews and sway the people away from God." "Therefore a person who worships false gods is to be hanged, just as one who blasphemes against God is hanged. Both are executed by being stoned to death" (*Hilchot Avodat Kochavim V'Chukkoteihem—The Laws of the Worship of Stars and Their Statutes*, 2:6; Rabbi Touger explains: "They are not executed by hanging. Rather, after the condemned is stoned to death, his corpse is hanged for a fleeting second.")

92   *Sefer Shofetim (The Book of Judges), Hilchot Melachim U'Milchamoteichem (The Laws of Kings and Their Wars)*, 11:4.

93   Touger, *Hilchot Melachim U'Milchamoteichem*, 235–36. Maimonides's text continues: "Can there be a greater stumbling block than [Christianity]?... Christianity caused the Jews to be slain by the sword, their remnants to be scattered and humbled, the Torah to be altered, and the majority of the world to err and serve a god other than the Lord" (11:4).

94   Norman Roth, *Medieval Jewish Civilization: An Encyclopedia* (London: Routledge, 2002), 532. Roth points out that, since not many Jews lived in Christian Spain, these largely anti-Christian writings reflected not a personal experience of oppression at the hands of Spanish Christians but a more general or "theoretical" animosity. The number of Jewish "polemical" works written by learned rabbis in medieval Spain is even larger than the number of contemporary Christian polemical works. For a detailed study of this largely anti-Christian polemical literature, see Daniel J. Lasker, "The Jewish Critique of Christianity under Islam in the Middle Ages," *Proceedings of the American Academy for Jewish Research* 57 (1990–91): 121–53. For a study of anti-Christian Jewish polemical and satirical literature in *Catholic* Spain, see Daniel J. Lasker, "Teaching Christianity to Jews: The Case of Medieval Jewish Anti-Christian Polemics," *Judaism and Education: Essays in Honor of Walter I. Ackerman*, ed. Haim Marantz (Beer Sheva: Ben-Gurion University of the Negev Press, 1998), 73–86. One possible explanation is that Christianity was the heretical religion (all first Christians, including Jesus, were Jews), while Islam was not.

95   *Hilchot Melachim U'Milchamoteihem—The Laws of Kings and Their Wars*, 11.4.

96   *Epistles of Maimonides: Crisis and Leadership*, ed. David Hartman and trans. Abraham S. Halkin (Philadelphia: Jewish Publication Society, 1985), 126. Maimonides's views might have been influenced by his experience under the Berber Almohads, but in this passage he refers to *Arabs*, not to Berbers, so this explanation is not quite sufficient.

97   The *Mishneh Torah* does miss the complexity of the *Mishna* and the dialectical, sometimes contradictory nuances of rabbinical discussions in the *Mishna*'s massive later commentary, the *Gemara*. Maimonides may have intended to diminish the accessibility of the work by writing it not in Arabic, as he did in his other books, but in Hebrew, a language then known mostly to learned Jews. Maimonides makes an analogous point in his *Guide for the Perplexed* regarding the need to disguise higher and esoteric knowledge to keep it away from the ignorant masses. See the cleverly ironic comments by Harry A. Wolfson (1926), who compared the criticisms against the *Jewish Encyclopedia* with earlier critiques against other attempts to summarize Jewish knowledge, including the attacks against Maimonides: cited by Martin Ritter, "Scholarship as a Priestly Craft: Harry A. Wolfson on Tradition in a Secular Age," in *Jewish Studies between the Disciplines/Judaistik zwischen den Disziplinen: Papers in Honor of Peter Schäfer on the Occasion of His Sixtieth Birthday*, ed. Peter Schäfer, Klaus Herrmann, Margarete Schlüter, and Giuseppe Veltri (Leiden: Brill, 2003), 445. For Maimonides's own elitist views on knowledge, see his *Guide for the Perplexed*, 3:51. From Maimonides, Leo Strauss may have learned this idea of a higher knowledge to be hidden from the average reader, and he then generalized it to his study of many other philosophers.

98 Elka Klein, *Jews, Christian Society, and Royal Power in Medieval Barcelona* (Ann Arbor: University of Michigan, 2006), 118.

99 The burning of Maimonides's work was soon extended to the burning of the Talmud by the Christian authorities. However, in what is probably the best treatment of the controversy, professor of Jewish history Daniel Jeremy Silver has argued convincingly that the anti-Maimonidean rabbis were innocent of denouncing the book to the Christian authorities, and the likely culprit would have been a Jewish convert to Christianity: *Maimonidean Criticism and the Maimonidean Controversy 1180–1240*, 148–97. Silver's book is also excellent in describing the cultural differences between the medieval Sephardic Jewish community of Spain and other medieval Jewish communities (Ashkenazic, especially Rhenish; Sarfatic or French; and Provençal). Interestingly, later in the century Pope Nicholas III certified to the Jewish community of Rome that the *Moreh* was perfectly acceptable and that the pope was "particularly happy with Maimonides's arguments against the Aristotelian doctrine of the eternity of matter" (Silver, *Maimonidean Criticism and the Maimonidean Controversy 1180–1240*, 14).

100 See, among many authorities, Rabbi Dr. Moshe Zemer, *Evolving Halakhah: A Progressive Approach to Traditional Jewish Law* (Woodstock, VT: Jewish Lights Publishing, 1999), who points out the unhistorical use that anti-Semites have made of such texts; Jacob Katz, *Exclusiveness and Tolerance: Studies in Jewish-Gentile Relations in Medieval and Modern Times* (Scripta Judaica, 3) (Westport, CT: Greenwood Press, 1980).

101 Maimonides was also very influential in the medieval Sephardic world in general, in the Mediterranean basin and the Middle East. He had less influence among the Ashkenazi Jews of central and eastern Europe. See Goitein, *A Mediterranean Society*, 1:95.

102 See one of Maimonides's references to the "Sages of Spain," in *Sefer Kinyan (The Book of Acquisition). Hilchot Mechirah (The Laws of Selling)*, 11:18. See also the excellent introduction to *Mishneh Torah* by Rabbi Eliyahu Touger: *Maimonides: Mishneh Torah. Sefer Nezikin (The Book of Damages). Hilchot Nizkei Mammon (The Laws of Damage to Property). Hilchot Geneivah (The Laws of Theft). Hilchot Gezelah Va'Avedah (The Laws of Robbery and Lost Property). Hilchot Chovel Umazik (The Laws of Personal Injury). Hilchot Rotze'ach Ush'mirat Nefesh (The Laws of Murder and of the Protection of Human Life)*, trans. with commentaries and notes by Rabbi Eliyahu Touger (New York/Jerusalem: Moznaim Publishing Corporation, 1997), "Introduction," 9.

103 *Mishneh Torah. Sefer Kedushah (The Book of Holiness). Hilchot Maachalot Asurot (The Laws of Forbidden Foods)*, 17:9.

104 *Sefer Kedushah. Hilchot Maachalot Asurot*, 3:12–13. In medieval Spain nonpracticing Jews would not be numerous, for as Maimonides admonished in *Mishneh Torah*, one who does not follow the law will not share in the afterlife (*Sefer HaMada. Hilchot Teshuvah* 3:11). See also Stern, *Jewish Identity in Early Rabbinic Writings*.

105 Blidstein, "The 'Other' in Maimonidean Law," 181.

106 Stern, *Jewish Identity in Earlier Rabbinic Writings*, 145.

107 Ibid., 148–49.

108 "Whenever a commodity was ordered from overseas or out of town with no business friend available for supervising its transport, the letter would state whether it should be carried by Jews only, or by trustworthy gentiles as well. 'I am not quiet when I send it with a Muslim; perhaps I shall find a Jew,' writes a man...apologizing that he had not yet dispatched a piece of fabric.... 'I made four copies of this letter, in order to give them to coreligionists traveling in different boats, but the third copy I gave to the proprietor of the Ibn al-Qaqddar, for no Jew traveled in that ship.'" Goitein, *A Mediterranean Society*, 2:276.

109 Cf. Stern, *Jewish Identity in Early Rabbinic Writings*, 35, 60, 94, 103, and 151; Davidson, *Moses Maimonides*, 214.

110 *Mishneh Torah. Sefer Kedushah: Hilchot Issurei Biah*, 24. Rabbi Touger points out that this prohibition, as well as the prohibition against establishing a covenant with Gentiles, applied to all Gentile nations (Touger, in his ed. and trans. of *Mishneh Torah. Hilchot Avodat Kochavim*,

184, Commentary, Halachah 1). The anxiety about purity of lineage operated also among the rabbis in medieval Catholic Spain, as shown in some of their extant *responsa*. Thus Rabbi Jacob Issachar wrote toward the end of the thirteenth century: "I certify over my signature to all whom this document may reach that witnesses appeared before my teacher, Rabbi Isaac, son of Rabbi Eliakim, who was presiding at the court session, and that he received proper and legal testimony from aged and venerable men of the country concerning the family of the brothers David and Azriel, to the effect that they were of pure descent, without any family taint, and that they could intermarry with the most honored families in Israel; for there had been no admixture of impure blood in the paternal or maternal antecedents and their collateral relatives": Neuman, *The Jews in Spain*, 2:5–6.

111 *Hilchot Maachalot Asurot*, 17, 9; *Hilchot Issurei Biah (The Laws of Forbidden Sexual Relations)*, 24 and 25.

112 Goitein, *A Mediterranean Society*, 2:277.

113 Cf. *Mishneh Torah. Sefer Nashim (The Book of Women), Hilchot Ishut (The Laws of Marriage)*, and *Sefer Kedushah (The Book of Holiness). Hilchot Issurei Biah (The Laws of Forbidden Sexual Relations)*. The *Mishneh Torah* abounds in injunctions towards the "gentiles" most of which could not have been put in practice because Jews did not live in a kingdom of their own, but which nevertheless indicate the difficulties that medieval Jewish culture, at least as reflected in medieval Jewish law, created for *convivencia*. Among many: "A gentile who studies Torah is liable to the death penalty. They should be involved in the study of their Seven Mitzvot only" (*Hilchot Melachim U'Milchamoteiheim—The Laws of Kings and Their Wars*, 10.9); "[A] gentile who sleeps with a Jewish maiden who has been betrothed to a Jew is stoned to death.... A gentile who converts after cursing God's name, worshipping false gods, sleeping with his fellow gentile's wife, or killing his fellow gentile is exempt from punishment" (ibid., 9.7; 10.4); "To lend to a gentile at interest as Deuteronomy 23:21 states: 'Take interest from a gentile.' Based on the oral tradition, we have learned that this is a positive commandment" (*Hilchot Hesodei HaTorah—The Laws Which Are the Foundations of the Torah*, no. 198); "Not to lend at interest to a Jew, as Leviticus 25:37 states 'Do not lend him your money at interest'" (ibid., 235); "Not to show favor to the worshippers of false gods" (ibid., 50); "With regard to a gentile idolater with whom we are not at war...we should not try to cause their deaths. It is however forbidden to save their lives if their lives are threatened. For example, if such a person fell into the sea, one should not rescue him. Leviticus 19: 16 states 'Do not stand idly by while your brother's blood is at stake.' This does not apply with regard to such individuals because they are not 'your brother'" (*Hilchot Roze'ach Ushmirat Nefesh—The Laws of Murder and the Protection of Human Life*, 4.11); "One should not take medication from a gentile for any affliction for which one may desecrate the Sabbath" (ibid., 12.9); "Just as it is forbidden to sell weaponry to a gentile, so too, is it forbidden to sell it to a Jew who will sell it to a gentile. It is permitted to sell weapons to the soldiers of the country in which one lives because they defend the Jewish inhabitants of the land" (ibid., 12.13); "The following rules apply when an animal that has fallen is owned by a gentile but the burden it is carrying is owned by a Jew. If the gentile is the one driving his donkey, one is not obligated toward him. If not, one is obligated to unload and reload it because of the distress suffered by the Jew. Similarly if the animal that has fallen is owned by a Jews, but the burden it is carrying is owned by a gentile, one is obligated to unload and reload it because of the distress suffered by the Jew. When, however, both the animal and the burden are owned by a gentile, a passerby is not obligated to concern himself with the animal unless there is the possibility that animosity will be aroused" (ibid., 13.9); Rabbi Touger comments on this law: "In contrast to the last clause of this halachah, the Rambam does not mention the possibility of animosity arising in the instance at hand, because since the burden being carried belongs to a Jew, the gentile owner will not suspect that it was a difference of religion that motivated the passerby's indifference (*Bayit Chadash*, Choshen Mishpat 272)" (ibid., n24).

114 Stern, *Jewish Identity in Ancient Rabbinical Writings*, 92, 104, 117. That intermarriage or con-

cubinage happened, even if rarely, *before* the Muslim invasion and under Catholic rule, and at least in the case of Jewish men and Christian women, is shown by the sixteenth Canon of the Council of Elovia (304), the sixty-fourth Canon of the Council of Toledo (589), and the sixty-third Canon of the Fourth Council of Toledo (633), which stipulate that the daughters of Catholics must not marry or be mistresses of unrepentant heretics, Jews, or schismatics.

115 Goitein, *A Mediterranean Society*, 5:314–16. The end of the document is missing. The couple was first denounced by members of a Muslim group that went around following the Quran's injunction "to order people to do what is proper and to restrain them from what is improper" (Quran 3:104 and passim).

116 Stern, *Jewish Identity in Ancient Rabbinical Writings*, 24. In Catholic Spain, the famous theological polemics between Jews and Catholics sometimes degenerated to the level of mutual accusations as to who were more inclined to sexual debauchery, rabbis or priests. See Roth, *Medieval Jewish Civilization: An Encyclopedia*, 529. Commenting on these debates, Roth dismisses any presumed reference to Jesus, insulting or not, in the Talmudic literature. Building on earlier scholarship, a recent work by Peter Schafer reaches a different conclusion: Peter Schafer, *Jesus in the Talmud* (Princeton, NJ: Princeton University Press, 2007).

117 Yehuda ben Asher, *Zikhron Yehuda* (Berlin, 1846), nos. 91 and 93, cit. Yom Tov Assis, "Sexual Behavior in Medieval Hispano-Jewish Society," in *Jewish History: Essays in Honor of Chimen Abramsky*, ed. Ada Rapoport Albert and Steven J. Zipperstein (London: P. Halban, 1988), 25–60. Asher was reacting to lewd poetry by Todros Abulafia, who barely escaped excommunication by the rabbis.

118 Assis, "Sexual Behavior in Medieval Hispano-Jewish Society," 45. In practice, of course, a Jewish male might get away with having sex with a non-Jewish woman, but a Jewish woman would be severely punished or killed if she had sex with a non-Jewish man: see David Nirenberg, *Communities of Violence: Persecution of Minorities in the Middle Ages* (Princeton, NJ: Princeton University Press, 1996), 136, which argues that Jewish men often had intercourse with Gentile women, usually Muslim ones. But Nirenberg overlooks that these Muslim women were likely slaves, not *hurras* or *muhsanas*, sleeping with whom would have cost the Jewish man his life. Medieval Jewish exclusionary practices led literary scholar Américo Castro to see in them the inspiration for the later Spanish concern with "purity of blood," which was among the Spanish Inquisition's preoccupations: *The Spaniards: An Introduction to Their History* (Berkeley: University of California Press, 1971). Castro's idea has been criticized by many, among them Netanyahu, *The Origins of the Inquisition in Fifteenth-Century Spain*, and Henry Kamen, *The Spanish Inquisition: A Historical Revision* (New Haven, CT: Yale University Press, 1999), probably the best study of the Spanish Inquisition.

119 Davidson, *Moses Maimonides*, 254.

120 The non-Jews' presumed lower morals included a proclivity to engage in homosexuality and bestiality (Stern, *Jewish Identity in Ancient Rabbinical Writings*, 24–25). The *Cairo Geniza* documents such statements by Sephardic businessmen as "He is a Christian and I am a Jew—he is not my companion," and "The Bible has said: never trust gentiles," the last one referring to Psalm 144:8, "Whose mouth speaks lies and whose handshake is falsehood": Goitein, *A Mediterranean Society*, 2:275.

121 *Shulchan Aruch*, 1:xlvi. See also *Shulchan Aruch* (2000 Project Genesis), www.torah.org/advanced/shulchanaruch/archives.html, chap. 10b of the section *Yoreh Deah* and in chap. 11 of the same section: 139:15; 146:15; 147:1–5; 151:1–4, 11–14; 267:3–5, 11, 14–18. My references to the *Yoreh Deah* section are taken from this online edition.

122 *Shulchan Aruch*, 4:clxviii, clxvii, clxvii, and clxvii; 2:lxv; cf. Maimonides, *Mishneh Torah. Sefer Mishpatim. Hilchot Malveh Vloveh* 5:1, 9, and 11. For the unsuccessful efforts of some Spanish rabbis in the thirteenth and fourteenth centuries to treat Gentiles in the same way as Jews with regard to usury, see Neuman, *The Jews in Spain*, 1:197.

123 *Shulchan Aruch*, 4:clxvii. Sephardic Jews living in Islamic lands may have kept some of these practices even in modern times: according to Peter Scholliers, in twentieth-century Algiers "Jews

often employed Muslim maids, but would not want them to handle their food because they considered them impure. Moreover, they maintained an even stricter religious/moral prohibition on intermarriage than the Christians." See Scholliers, *Food, Drink, and Identity*, 208.

124 Baer, *A History of the Jews in Christian Spain*, 2:34. Baer is referring here to Jews in Catholic lands, but his observation would be applicable to Jews in Islamic Spain as well.

125 Unlike Karaism in the Middle East and Egypt, the importance of Karaism in medieval Spain and its ultimate fate are rarely mentioned in standard works on the Jewish religion. In general, Karaism is dismissed as a heretical dead end. See, for example, Neusner, *An Introduction to Judaism*, 279–84, 286. But even specialized works sometimes omit it or mention it only in passing. The reason may be that the history of Karaism has been written by the victors, the Orthodox. Practically all scholarly works on Karaism are written by non-Karaites. Thus Nathan Schur's *History of the Karaites* (Frankfurt am Main: Peter Lang, 1992), which dismisses Karaism as a sect and heresy of Judaism, dedicates six lines to the actual physical conflict in Spain (68–69), which he summarizes as an "expulsion." A Karaite online resource, but one that does not seem to include Karaite anti-Orthodox writings, can be found at kjuonline. com/Suggested%20Reading%20List.htm. A good specialized examination of the purely religious conflict, but leaving out the historical events of the destruction of Karaism in Spain, is Daniel J. Lasker, "Rabbinism and Karaism: The Contest for Supremacy," in R. Jospe and S. M. Wagner, *Great Schisms in Jewish History* (New York: Ktav Publishing House, 1981), 47–72.

126 Martin A. Cohen, "Anan Ben David and Karaite Origins," *Jewish Quarterly Review*, 68, no. 3 (January 1978): 129–45. This is an unusually sympathetic study by a non-Karaite.

127 Maimonides wrote: "The mitzvot given to Moses at Mount Sinai were all given together with their explanations.... 'The Torah' refers to the written law; 'the mitzvah,' to its explanation. [God] commanded us to fulfill 'the Torah' according to [the instructions of] 'the mitzvah.' 'The mitzvah' is called the Oral Law. Moses, our teacher, personally transcribed the entire Torah before he died. He gave a Torah scroll to each tribe and placed another scroll in the ark as a testimonial.... 'The mitzva'—the explanation of the Torah—he did not transcribe. Instead, he commanded it [verbally] to the elders": see the Rambam's Introduction to the Mishneh Torah. *Hilchot Yesodei HaTorah (The Laws [Which Are] the Foundations of the Torah)]*. Also according to Maimonides, there are three kinds of individuals who deny the Torah: One of them is a person "who says Torah, even one verse or one word, is not from God. If he says: 'Moses made these statements independently,' he is denying Torah." Another is one "who denies the Torah's interpretation, the oral law, or disputes [the authority of] its spokesmen [the rabbis] as did Tzadok, and Beitus." The third kind of denier is "one who says that though the Torah came from God, the Creator has replaced one mitzvah with another one and nullified the Torah, for example, the Christians and the Arabs." See *Hilchot Teshuvah* 3:8. Rabbi Touger notes that the word *Christians* appears in the original manuscript of the *Mishneh Torah* but was deleted by censorship in most publications of the text (Touger, *Hilchot Teshuvah*, 78). Jacob Neusner explains that *Torah* means "Law," "Teaching," "Learning," or "Instruction" and technically refers only to the five books of the Pentateuch. *Tanakh* is an acronym of three components, namely the "*Torah*" proper, consisting of the five books of the Pentateuch, plus "*Neviim*" or Prophets, plus "*Ketuvim*" or Writings, which include Psalms, Proverbs, and other books. After the Oral Law was received, it was handed down orally by generations of rabbinical sages until it was written down around the third century in a text known as the *Mishna* (which means "repetition," as in "study and review"). The *Mishna* was discussed and interpreted orally for centuries by learned rabbis until their discussions and interpretations were written down in the sixth century to make up what is known as the *Gemara* (which means "learning by tradition," or "studying"). The *Gemara* and the *Mishna* constitute the formidable text known as the *Talmud* (which means "instruction," or "learning"), although it is the *Gemara* itself that sometimes is referred to as "the *Talmud*" proper. But rabbinical statements on Jewish law also make use of a vast collection of narratives and discussions of narratives and legal issues known as the *Midrash*. For a good modern attempt to explain this complicated process, see

Neusner, *An Introduction to Judaism*, 157–254. Neusner argues that the *Mishna* by itself cannot be considered "the Oral Law."

128 Schur, *History of the Karaites*, 64–65. Schur is a non-Karaite scholar. Anan, the reputed founder of Karaism, also considered Jesus a saintly man. In this, Karaism agreed with Islam's view of Jesus (Isa). Karaism, however, rejected both Islam and Christianity as valid religions.

129 Goitein, *A Mediterranean Society*, 5:313.

130 Schur, *History of the Karaites*, 68. For this and the following, see also Baer, *A History of the Jews in Christian Spain*. None of these historians was a Karaite.

131 Daniel J. Lasker, "Karaism in Twelfth-Century Spain," *Journal of Jewish Thought and Philosophy* 1 (1992): 179. The *Jewish Encyclopedia* allocates only one paragraph to Spanish Karaism in its entry on Judaism in Spain, though still more than any other encyclopedia.

132 Michael Walzer, *The Jewish Political Tradition* (New Haven, CT: Yale University Press, 2003), 2:345–46. Since Karaites did not keep the same Jewish calendar and did not celebrate main Jewish holidays, and since Maimonides said that one should not treat them as non-Jews as long as they did not "desecrate" Jewish holidays, Maimonides's celebrated "openness" turns out to be impracticable. In fact, Maimonides called for the physical elimination of the Karaites, whose heresy might lead good Jews into "complete heresy" (very likely Christianity): see Blidstein, "The 'Other' in Maimonidean Law," 184, 189. But other scholars cite Maimonides's contradictory views on whether the Karaites were heretics or not: Yaakov Y. Teppler, *Birkat HaMinim: Jews and Christians in Conflict in the Ancient World*, trans. Susan Weingarten (Tubingen: Mohr Siebeck, 2007), 42–43. Perhaps for him Karaism was certainly a dangerous heresy but not a "complete" one like Christianity. Maimonides was "aware of Karaite views on the Oral Law, prophecy, and Halakhah": Lasker, "Karaism in Twelfth-Century Spain," 180.

133 Lasker, "Karaism in Twelfth-Century Spain," 181.

134 Judah M. Rosenthal, "The Talmud on Trial: The Disputation at Paris in the Year 1240," *Jewish Quarterly Review* 47, no. 1 (July 1956): 65; Baer, *A History of the Jews in Christian Spain*, 1:50–51, 390n45. There may be some confusion between the identity of Cidellius and Joseph Farissol.

135 Rosenthal, "The Talmud on Trial," 65.

136 Baer, *A History of the Jews in Christian Spain*, 1:390n45.

137 Rosenthal, "The Talmud on Trial," 66.

138 Judah Alharizi, "Rabbanite versus Karaite," in *The Book of Tahkemoni: Jewish Tales from Medieval Spain*, ed. David Simha Segal (Portland: Littman Library of Jewish Civilization, 2001), 167–74.

139 Rosenthal, "The Talmud on Trial," 66.

140 William Harris Rule, *History of the Karaite Jews* (London: Longmans, Green, and Company, 1870), 153.

141 Lasker, "Karaism in Twelfth-Century Spain," 179, 195. Orthodox polemicists have pointed to the lack of extant writings from Spanish Karaites as proof of their lack of creativity, overlooking that such paucity may indicate instead the thoroughness of the destruction of Karaite culture.

142 Baer, *A History of the Jews in Christian Spain*, 2:456.

143 Michael L. Brown, *Answering Jewish Objections to Jesus: Traditional Jewish Objections* (San Francisco: Purple Pomegranate Productions, 2009), vol. 5.

CHAPTER 7: THE CHRISTIAN CONDITION

1 For this, see Eva Lapiedra Gutiérrez, *Cómo los musulmanes llamaban a los cristianos hispánicos* (Alicante: Generalitat Valenciana-Instituto de Cultura "Juan Gil Albert," 1997); Manuel Rincón Álvarez, *Mozárabes y mozarabías* (Salamanca: University of Salamanca, 2006), 15–16; Francisco Bueno García, *Los mozárabes* (Malaga: Buentos, 2012); Dominique Urvoy,

"Les aspects symboliques du vocable 'mozarabe': Essai de réinterpretation," *Studia Islamica* 78 (1993): 117–53. For the designation *al-hamra*, see Ignaz Goldziher, *Muslim Studies* (New Brunswick, NJ: Transaction Publishers, 2006), 243. For the other names given to the Catholic *dhimmis*, see José Amador de los Ríos, *Historia crítica de la literatura española* (Madrid: Rodríguez, 1865), 2:17. "Redness" was associated not only with Spaniards but also with other Indo-European populations that had rosy cheeks, such as Greeks and Persians. See Bernard Lewis, *Race and Color in Islam* (New York: Harper & Row, 1970), 8 and n7.

2   *Histoire des Almohades d'Abd el-Wahid al-Merrakechi*, trans. Edmond Fagnan (Algiers: Adolphe Jourdan, 1893), 113, 114. In the course of a humorous discussion of a doubtful *hadith*, Ibn Qutaybah mentions the name *pigs* given to Christians in Muslim popular lore. See *Le traité des divergences du hadit d'Ibn Qutaybah: Traduction annotée du Kitab Tawil Muhtalif al-Hadit*, trans. Gérard Lecomte (Damascus: Institut Français de Damas, 1962), 80. Ibn Qutaybah's amusing discussion of this *hadith* also mentions the name *monkeys* applied to Jews; the discussion involves monkeys fornicating and stoning other monkeys. In the secondary sources I have examined, no Islamic studies scholar has pointed out the use of the name *pigs* to refer to Christians in al-Andalus. Much better known is that Christians called *marranos* (pigs) those Jews who had converted to Christianity but practiced Judaism in secret. On the use of the word *pig* by Muslims to refer to Christians in an insulting manner—a use possibly derived from the Quran—see Hans Jansen, scholar of Islamic thought at the University of Utrecht, *Islam voor varkens, apen, ezels en andere beesten* (Amsterdam: Van Praag, 2008). Jansen's argument that the use of this insulting term and of *monkeys* and *asses* to refer to "People of the Book" originates in the Quran has not found ready acceptance among other Islamic studies scholars. Eyewitness accounts show that in Egypt during the nineteenth and twentieth centuries, Muslims sometimes shouted "pig!" (*khanzir*) at Christian missionaries and threw stones at them, as Eulogius in the ninth century narrates happened to priests in Muslim Córdoba: Heather J. Sharkey, *American Evangelicals in Egypt: Missionary Encounters in an Age of Empire* (Princeton, NJ: Princeton University Press, 2008), 224. (Indeed, the great Mallorcan philosopher and missionary Ramon Lull was stoned to death in North Africa, probably in Tunis, in 1315 while preaching to Muslims.) A nineteenth-century account points out that the insult *khanzir* is matched only in offensiveness by *Ibn al-Yahudi* (son of a Jew): Eugène Gellion-Danglar, *Lettres sur L'Egypte Contemporaine 1815–1875* (1876; rpt. Forgotten Books.com, 2013), 89. Another traveler explains: "[The Muslim] utmost note of execration [against Christians] is not 'dog of a Christian' as most writers put it, but 'swine of a Christian.' *Khanzir* is the word and with a hoggish guttural": John T. Durward, *Holy Land and Holy Writ* (Baraboo, WI: Pilgrim Publishing Company, 1913), 642.

3   As Cyrille Aillet points out in his formidable and most up-to-date study of the Mozarabs, "it is improbable that the Muslims of al-Andalus used [the term *Mozarabs*] to designate the native Christians": Cyrille Aillet, *Les mozarabes: christianisme, islamisation, et arabisation en péninsule ibérique (IXe–XIIe siècle)* (Madrid: Casa de Velázquez, 2010), 3.

4   Miguel Ángel Ladero Quesada, *La formación medieval de España: Territorios; Regiones; Reinos* (Madrid: Alianza, 2004), 16. Ladero Quesada also points out that "until the twelfth century, Christians, especially those in the Pyrenean area, frequently called the lands of 'al-Andalus' Hispania, and so did the 'gothicists' from the kingdom of Leon, since they considered it unliberated territory."

5   Manuel Gómez Moreno used the term *Mozarab* to refer to churches built in the North by these refugees from the South; see his landmark book *Iglesias mozárabes* (Madrid: Centro de Estudios Históricos, 1919). This conflation, among other things, has prompted art historians such as Isidro Bango Torviso to reject the term *Mozarab* to designate the art of these refugees in Catholic lands in favor of "art of the Reconquest."

6   *Chronica mozarabica de 754*, ed. and trans. José Eduardo López Pereira (Zaragoza: University of Zaragoza, 1980), 26.

7   See P. Chalmeta, *Brill Encyclopaedia of Islam, Second Edition*, "muwalad": "[*Muwallad* is] a

word belonging to the vocabulary of stock-breeders and designating the product of a crossing (*tawlīd*) of two different animal breeds, thus a hybrid, of mixed blood. It is hardly surprising that it was extended to humans from the time when the feeling arose that the purity of the Arab race had been altered following the conquests, the influx of elements of other stocks and mixed marriages. In a more limited sense, *muwallad* designates a cross-breed, half-caste or even, as Dozy states (*Suppl.*, s.v.) 'one who, without being of Arab origin, has been born among the Arabs and received an Arabic education.'...In al-Andalus, the *muwalladūn* constituted a particular category of the population.... *Muwallad* has given rise to Spanish *muladí* and, according to Eguilaz (an opinion rejected by Dozy), to *mulato*. The mediaeval Latin transcription was *mollites*...[*muwalladun*] designated the descendants of non-Arab neo-Muslims, brought up in the Islamic religion by their recently-converted parents. Thus they are the members of the second generation (the sons) and, by extension, those of the third generation (the grandsons). A convert or neo-Muslim was called *musālima* or *asālima*. More precisely still, *aslamī* was used to designate the ex-Christian convert, whereas the term *islāmī* was reserved for the former Jew."

8   The Islamic law scholar Felipe Maíllo Salgado elaborates: "Initially it meant anyone who was a 'neo-convert' to Islam since in principle non-Arabs could only enter Islam as 'clients' of an Arab. Thus *mawla* came to be synonymous with 'non-Arab Muslim.' Also freed slaves would become, as well as their descendants, 'clients' of the former owner.... Though in theory they were not to be considered socially inferior, in practice the *mawali* were early on considered lowly people, and the life of a client was worth less than that of an Arab." Felipe Maíllo Salgado, *Diccionario de derecho islámico* (Gijón: TREA, 2005), 225–26. The system had some similarities to the vassalage of European feudalism.

9   See, among others, Luis García de Valdeavellano, *Historia de España I: De los orígenes a la Baja Edad Media* (Madrid: Revista de Occidente, 1968), pt. 4, pp. 421–22. How Christians gradually disappear under Muslim rule has been examined in the case of the Holy Land, formerly a Christian land, by Islamic and Asian studies scholar Raphael Israeli, *Green Crescent Over Nazareth: The Displacement of Christians by Muslims in the Holy Land* (Oxford: Routledge, 2014).

10   *The Muwatta of Imam Malik Narrated by Yahya B. Yahya B. Kathir al-Laith Al-Andalusi*, trans. F. Amira Zrien Matrahi (Karachi: Darul Ishaat, 2005), 17.24.46; Malik follows Quran 9:29. I use the version of the *Muwatta* compiled by Malik's student from Córdoba, Yahya al-Laithi.

11   Arabist Francisco Javier Simonet, *Historia de los mozárabes de España* (1897–1908; rpt. Madrid: Turner, 1983), 1:92. Simonet explains: "The *jizya* could be imposed two ways: individually and collectively. If individual, the obligation was inherent to the individual and ended with his conversion to Islam or his death. If collective, that is, if it had been imposed on the community of a town or region, the total value of the *jizya* could not diminish or increase regardless of the reduction or increase of the population subject to the collective *jizya*; the entire community was responsible for continuing to pay the *jizya*" (ibid.).

12   *Islam from the Prophet Muhammad to the Capture of Constantinople*, ed. and trans. Bernard Lewis (Oxford: Oxford University Press, 1987), 2:224. The Islamic State has made use of Umar's words to justify its exploitation of non-Muslims. See Ibn Rajab al-Hanbali, "My provision was placed for me in the shade of my spear," in Islamic State publication *Dabiq* 4 Issue (1435 Dhul-Hijjah), 10–13.

13   *Brill Encyclopaedia of Islam, Second Edition*, "dhimmi."

14   Among other manuals cited throughout this book, see Soha Abboud-Haggar, *El Tratado Jurídico de Al-Tafri de Ibn Al-Gallab: Manuscrito Aljamiado De Almonacid De La Sierra (Zaragoza): Edición, Estudio, Glosario y Confrontación Con El Original Árabe* (Zaragoza: Institución Fernando el Católico, 1999), 2:564–65; al-Qayrawani, *Risala*, 37.27; Muhammad b. Iyad, *Kitab Ibn al-Mawwaz*, cit. Delfina Serrano, "Legal Practice in an Andalusi-Magrhibi Source from the Twelfth Century," *Islamic Law and Society* 7, no. 2 (2000): 199–200.

15   *Al-Tafri*, 566.

16 *Muwatta*, 43.15.8b; *Risala*, 37.04.

17 *Muwatta*, 36.18; *Al-Tafri*, 572.

18 *Al-Tafri*, 557; *Risala*, 37.20.

19 María Arcas Campoy, "El testimonio de las mujeres en el derecho malikí," in *Homenaje al Prof. Jacinto Bosch Vilá*, 76–77. For al-Qayrawani: "A hundred women are not worth more than two and these two equal one man" (474).

20 Bernard Lewis, *Race and Slavery in the Middle East: An Historical Enquiry* (Oxford: Oxford University Press, 1992), chap. 1.

21 *Al-Tafri*, 44–45; *Mudawwana*, bk. 1.2, in "La *Moudawwana* (Recension de Sahnoun). Analyse par G. H. Bousquet," *Annales de l'Institut d'Études Orientales*, (1958), 16:182; Maliki *faqih* Ibn Habib according to Janina M. Safran, "Identity and Differentiation in Ninth-Century al-Andalus," *Speculum* 76, no. 3 (July 2001): 582.

22 *Mudawwana*, tome 5, vol. 3, no. 695.

23 *Muwatta*, 53.2.3; *Risala*, 43.01; *Al-Tafri*, 585; *Leyes de moros* CCCVI.

24 *Mudawwana*, tome 3, vol. 2, no. 1898.

25 *Muwatta*, 38.7.12; *Risala*, 31.3a1.

26 *Muwatta*, 38.7.

27 *Mudawwana*, tome 4, vol. 2, no. 652; al-Shafii, *Kitab al-Umm*, iv, 118–19, in *Islam from the Prophet Muhammad to the Capture of Constantinople*, 2:220. The prohibition persisted even in the twentieth-century Maliki culture of Morocco in the more enlightened official version of the Maliki *Mudawwana*: see André Colomer, *Droit Musulman: Les Personnes. La famille* (Rabat: La Porte, 1962), 100. For the decline of Christianity under Islam in the East, see Bat Ye'or, *The Decline of Eastern Christianity under Islam: From Jihad to Dhimmitude* (Madison: Fairleigh Dickinson University Press, 1996). Christianity has lost ground to Islam everywhere Muslims have conquered Christian territory.

28 *Mudawwana*, tome 4, vol. 2, no. 657.

29 *Muwatta*, 28.16; *Mudawwana*, tome 4, vol. 3, no. 652.

30 A document from tenth-century Umayyad Córdoba forbids *dhimmis* from building temples (*kanais*): Christine Mazzoli-Guintard, *Vivre à Cordue au Moyen Age: Solidarité citadines en terre d'Islam aux Xe–Xie siècles* (Rennes: Presses Universitaires de Rennes, 2003), 57. "After the Muslim conquest, the Christians were prohibited from building any new churches; all they could do was repair and restore existing buildings, which in theory they were permitted to keep. In fact, however, over the centuries numerous churches were confiscated and converted into mosques, or even destroyed (cf. A. Fattal, *Le statut legal des non musulmanes en pays d'Islam*, Beirut, 1958, 174–203)": "Kanisa," *Encyclopaedia of Islam, Second Edition*. On the prohibition to walk through cemeteries in Umayyad Córdoba, see Mazzoli-Guintard, *Vivre à Cordue au Moyen Age*, 207. On the Pact of Umar, of which there are a few extant copies with minor variations, including a copy found in Spain, see A. S. Tritton, *The Caliphs and Their Non-Muslim Subjects: A Critical Study of the Covenant of Umar* (London: Frank Cass and Company, 1930; rpt. 1970). That the original document may date not from the time of Umar I, the second caliph, but possibly from the Umayyad eighth century is irrelevant for its effects, since medieval Muslims, including Malik, accepted it as normative and it guided their policy toward the *dhimmis* throughout the Islamic empire. Eva Lapiedra Gutiérrez offers a good study of the connection between persecutions in the Middle East and persecutions in Islamic Spain in "Los mártires de Córdoba y la política anticristiana contemporánea en oriente," *Al-Qantara* 15, no. 2 (1994): 453–62. Some versions of the Pact of Umar can be accessed online; see, e.g., www.fordham.edu/halsall/source/pactumar. html. For more on these rules, see the *Muwatta*, the *Mudawwana*, *al-Tafri*, and various historical accounts of the Umayyad caliphate, including *al-Maqqari*.

31 *Dos tratados de legislación musulmana. 1. Leyes de moros del siglo XIV 2. Suma de los principales mandamientos y devedamientos de la ley y çunna, por don Içe de Gebir, Alfaquí Mayor de la aljama de Segovia. Año de 1492*, ed. Pascual de Gayangos (Madrid: Academia de la Historia. Memorial histórico español, 1853), vol. 5, chapters I and VI of the *Suma*.

32   C. M. Woodhouse, *Modern Greece: A Short History* (London: Faber & Faber, 1998), 101. I thank τήν γυναίκα μου, Ιωάννα for this information.

33   *A Madinan View on the Sunnah, Courtesy, Wisdom, Battles, and History by Abu Muhammad Abdullah Ibn Abi Zayd al-Qayrawani*, trans. Abdassamad Clarke (London: Ta-Ha Publishers, 1999), 113.

34   Circumcision is one of the obligations for keeping *fitra* (the proper nature of the human body): *Muwatta*, 49.3.3. For the forced circumcision of Catholics under the Umayyads, see Eulogius, *Epistola ad Wiliesindum*, 330, cit. R. Dozy, *Histoire des musulmanes d'Espagne* (Leiden: Brill, 1932), 1.ii, 319.

35   Charles-Emanuel Doufourcq, *La vie cotidienne dans l'Europe mediévale sous domination arabe* (Paris: Hachette, 1978), 213–14.

36   Maribel Fierro, "Christian Success and Muslim Fear in Andalusi Writings during the Almoravid and Almohad Periods," *Israel Oriental Studies XVII. Dhimmis and Others: Jews and Christians and the World of Classical Islam*, ed. Uri Rubin and David J. Wasserstein (Winona Lake, IN: Eisenbrauns, 1997), 157.

37   The same pattern had been evident in lands that Islam had previously conquered and colonized: see Ye'or, *The Decline of Eastern Chrsitianity under Islam*. Recent efforts by pro-Islamic Arabists to deny that Muslim cities were de facto divided into Muslim, Jewish, and Christian neighborhoods does not withstand scrutiny: see chapter 3 of this book.

38   John S. Koliopoulos and Thanos M. Veremis, *Greece: The Modern Sequel, from 1831 to the Present* (New York: New York University Press, 2002), 266.

39   Susana Calvo Capilla, "Las primeras mezquitas de al-Andalus a través de las fuentes árabes (92/711–170/785)," *Al-Qantara* 27, no. 1 (Enero–Julio 2007): 143–79.

40   Joaquín Vallvé Bermejo, *La división territorial de la España musulmana* (Madrid: Consejo Superior de Investigaciones Científicas, 1986). Other origins of the name al-Andalus have been proposed, but this one seems to me the most probable.

41   The presumably Catholic *morisco* Núñez Muley in his *Memorial*, according to Luis del Mármol Carvajal, *Historia de la rebelión y castigo de los moriscos de Granada* (Madrid: BAE, 1946), bk. 2, pp. x, 165, cit. Serafín Fanjul, *Al-Andalus contra España* (Madrid: Siglo XXI, 2002), 19.

42   Archaeological evidence in the North African region of Cyrenaica indicates the destruction of churches by the Islamic conquerors: W. M. Widrig and R. Goodchild, "The West Church at Apollonia in Cyrenaica," *Papers of the British School at Rome* (1960): 71n. This fact contrasts with the relative leniency reported by the Nestorian Christians, who were considered heretical by Orthodox Christianity. But according to the late *Chronicle of Siird*, the Arabs camping at Hira before the Battle of Qadisiyya profaned churches, monasteries, and convents: Addai Scher, *Histoire nestorienne: cronique de Séert* (Paris: Firmin-Didot, 1950, in the *Patrologia orientalis* series, *Seconde Partie*, t. 13 fasc. 4), 627. For Islam's destruction of churches, see also Khuri Hitti, *History of Syria* (New York: Macmillan, 1951), 511; Ali Wigdan, *The Arab Contribution to Islamic Art* (Cairo: Cairo American University in Cairo Press, 1999), 21; *Atlas of World Art*, ed. John Onians (London: Laurence King, 2004), 128. Upon the Muslim defeat of the Crusader kingdom in Palestine, the procedure was repeated: Daniella Talman-Heller, *Islamic Piety in Medieval Syria: Mosques, Cemeteries, and Sermons under the Zangis and Ayyubids (1146–1260)* (Leiden: Brill, 2007), 36.

43   Huseyin Abiva and Noura Durkee, *A History of Muslim Civilization* (Skokie, IL: IQRA International Foundation, 2003), 66; Robert Hillenbrand, *Islamic Architecture: Form, Function, and Meaning* (New York: Columbia University Press, 1994), 136; *The Iconographic Encyclopaedia of the Arts and Sciences: Architecture*, ed. W. N. Lockington (Philadelphia: Iconographic Publishing, 1888), 4:126.

44   *The Iconographic Encyclopaedia of the Arts and Sciences: Architecture*, 4:125; Eugène-Emmanuel Viollet-le-Duc, *Discourses on Architecture* (Boston: James R. Osgood, 1875), 452; John Moschus (d. 619 or 634), cit. Robert G. Hoyland, *Seeing Islam as Others Saw It* (Princeton, NJ: Darwin Press, 1997), 63; Theophilus of Edessa, cit. Hoyland, *Seeing Islam as Others Saw It*, 651 ("Walid

demolished the great church of Damascus and built a mosque in its place. He also ordered the public records to be written no longer in Greek, but in Arabic"); Theophanes Confessor (d. 818) in *The Chronicle of Theophanes Confessor*, trans. Cyril Mango and Roger Scott (Oxford: Clarendon Press, 197), 524.

45 According to Eutichyus of Alexandria, cit. Rafi Grasman and Myriam Rosen-Ayalon, "The Two Great Syrian Umayyad Mosques: Jerusalem and Damascus," *Muqarnas: An Annual of the Visual Culture of the Islamic World* 16 (1999): 11.

46 Capilla, "Las primeras mezquitas de al-Andalus a través de las fuentes árabes," 164n63.

47 J. Vallvé, "Sobre algunos problemas de la invasión musulmana," *Anuario de Estudios Medievales* 4 (1967): 367.

48 Ibn Idari, cit. Juan Signes Cordoñer, "Bizancio y al-Ándalus en los siglos IX y X," *Bizancio y la península ibérica: De la antigüedad tardía a la edad moderna*, ed. Inmaculada Pérez Martín and Pedro Bádenas de la Peña (Madrid: Consejo Superior de Investigaciones Científicas, 2004), 234–35; Antonio Almagro Cárdenas, *Museo granadino de antigüedades árabes* (Granada: Imprenta de la Lealtad, 1886), 31. The best recent studies of the mosque of Córdoba are by Pedro Marfil: "Arqueología. La Basílica de San Vicente: En la Catedral de Córdoba," *Arte, Arqueología e Historia*, no. 14 (2007): 185–96; and "Arqueología en la Mezquita de Córdoba," *Arte, Arqueología e Historia*, no. 6 (1999): 94–100. A more specialized synthesis is "Córdoba de Teodosio a Abd al-Rahman III," *Anejos del Archivo Español de Arqueología* 23 (2000): 117–41. See a list of Marfil's works at dialnet.unirioja.es/servlet/autor?codigo=281455. See also Isidro Bango Torviso, Manuel Bendala Galán, and Gonzalo Máximo Borrás Guales, *Manual de arte español* (Madrid: Silex, 2003), 211, 219. The later amplification of the mosque under al-Hakam II was directed by a former white slave, Abd al-Rahman "The Slav" (*Manual de arte español*, 219).

49 Capilla, "Las primeras mezquitas de al-Andalus a través de las fuentes árabes," 143–79.

50 Eulogius Toletanus, *Memorialis Santorum. Liber Tertius*, iii, in J. P. Migne, ed. *Patrologia latina* (Paris: 1852), vol. 115, online at artflx.uchicago.edu.turing.library.northwestern.edu/cgibin/philologic/getobject.pl?c.4615:1:5:3.pld.

51 *The History of the Mohammedan Dynasties in Spain by Ahmed Ibn Mohammed al-Makkari*, trans. Pascual de Gayangos (1840; rpt. New York: Johnson Reprint, 1964), 1:41.

52 For example, the church of Calatrava was converted to a mosque in 1195: *Kitab al-muyib fi talljis ajbar al-magrib by Abu Muhammad Abd Al-Wahid Al-Marrakusi*, trans. Ambrosio Huici Miranda (Tetuán: Instituto General Franco de Estudios e Investigación Hispano-Arabe, 1955), 236.

53 Capilla, "Las primeras mezquitas de al-Andalus a través de las fuentes árabes," 143–79. Cf. *Muwatta*, 17.17.24.46: "The people of *dhimma* and the magians [Zoroastrian Persians] do not have to pay any *zakat* on their palms or their vines or their crops or their livestock. This is because *zakat* is imposed on the Muslims to purify them and to be given back to their poor, whereas *jizya* is imposed on the people of the Book to humble them."

54 Capilla, "Las primeras mezquitas de al-Andalus a través de las fuentes árabes," 153.

55 Ibn Hayyan, *Muqtabis*, 5:322–23.

56 See chapter 6 of this book for a detailed discussion of medieval Spain's Jewish community, where a "culture of tolerance" certainly was not evident. Jewish authorities endeavored to keep the behavior of the population within the boundaries of religious law and were generally successful in their efforts.

57 Gabriel García Voltá, *El reino perdido de los visigodos* (Barcelona: Bruguera, 1977), 30; Pablo C. Díaz, "Monasticism and Liturgy," in *The Visigoths: Studies in Culture and Society*, ed. Alberto Ferreiro (Leiden: Brill, 1999), 192; Roger Collins, *Visigothic Spain, 409–711* (London: Blackwell, 2004), 67–69. For a succinct account of the heresy of Arianism, see *Catholic Encyclopaedia*, www.newadvent.org/cathen/01707c.htm. A comprehensive study is Richard Patrick Croslar, *The Search for the Christian Doctrine of God: The Arian Controversy, 318–381* (London: T&T Clark, 1988). Under Muslim domination, some Catholics fell back into heresy, and the weakened Catholic bishops had no way to control it.

58 Raúl González Salinero, "Catholic Anti-Judaism in Visigoth Spain," in Ferreiro, *The Visigoths*, 123–50.

59 One example among many: canon 7 of the Tenth Council of Toledo, under King Recceswinth in 656, laments that some Christians are still selling Christian slaves to Jews, something forbidden under canon 66 of the Ninth Council of Toledo (633) and canon 14 of the Third Council of Toledo (589). One possible reason these laws weren't applied was that those who applied the law applied it "flexibly," or that bribery proved effective: in 599 Pope Gregory I praised King Recared for his efforts in spite of the Jews' attempts to bribe him to prevent enacting the laws. See Solomon Katz, "Pope Gregory the Great and the Jews," *Jewish Quarterly Review* 24 (1933–34): 111–36. But it should be noted that the Jewish community in Rome, under the direct protection of the popes, never suffered persecutions until Mussolini's era.

60 Thus undermining the thesis according to which the Catholic Church is to blame for the laws: *Los judíos en la España antigua*: del primer encuentro al primer repudio (Madrid: RIALP, 2015), 125, 149.

61 One of Pope Gregory the Great's letters makes reference to the efforts of wealthy Jews to bribe the functionaries of Recared's government: L. A. García Moreno, *Los judíos de la España antigua: Del primer encuentro al primer repudio* (Madrid: RIALP, 2005), 72.

62 Marie-Thérèse Urvoy, ed., *Le psautier mozarabe de Hafs le Goth* (Toulouse: Presses universitaires du Mirail, 1994).

63 The *Fuero juzgo* (*Forum judicum* or *Lex visigothorum*) can be consulted online at the Cervantes Virtual site, www.cervantesvirtual.com/obra/fuero-juzgo-en-latin-y-castellano-0/. The extant texts of Visigoth laws through the centuries have been gathered in *Leges Visigothorum*, ed. Karl Zeumer (Hannover: Hahniani, 1902).

64 The literature on the subject is ample. See, for the following, among many: Raúl González Salinero, *Las conversiones forzozas de los judíos en el reino visigodo* (Roma: CSIC, 2000); B. S. Bachrach, *Early Medieval Jewish Policy in Western Europe* (Minneapolis: University of Minnesota, 1977), 6; José Amador de los Ríos, *Historia social, política y religiosa de Los Judíos de España* (Madrid: T. Fortanet, 1875), 1:77–116; *Estudios históricos, políticos y literarios sobre Los Judíos de España* (Buenos Aires: Solar, 1942), 3–19; García Moreno, *Los judíos de la España antigua*, 143–46; D. Borobio, "Iniciación cristiana en la Iglesia hispana de los siglos VI al X," *Salmanticensis* 42 (1995): 31; José Orlandis, "Hacia una mejor comprensión del problema judío en el reino visigodo-católico de España," *Gli Ebrei nell'Alto Medioevo: Settimane di Studio del Centro Italiano di Studi sull'Alto Medioevo, XXVI (1978)* (Spoleto: Centro Italiano di Studi sull'Alto Medioevo, 1980), 156; A. M. Rabello, "La conversione di Recaredo al cattolicesimo (587) e le sue ripercussioni sulla condizione giuridica degli Ebrei," *Index* 12 (1983–84): 382; Solomon Katz, *The Jews in the Visigothic and Frankish Kingdoms of Spain and Gaul* (Cambridge, MA: Medieval Academy of America, 1937), 12; Bernard S. Jackson, ed., *Jewish Law Association Studies IV: The Boston Conference* (Atlanta: Scholars Press, 1990), 91–93. A power-based or "political" explanation is given by Sidney David Markman: "By the time of the arrival of the Germanic barbarian hordes from northern and eastern Europe in the fifth century C.E., Jewish communities and the Jewish population were already numerous and influential. The growing strength of the Jews encouraged the Visigoths, who replaced the Romans as the rulers of Spain, to enact social legislation curbing the growing influence of Judaism among both Christians and pagans." See Sidney David Markman, *Jewish Remnants in Spain: Wanderings in a Lost World* (Mesa: Scribe Publishers, 2003), 6. Presumably, the growing strength of the Jewish community and the consequent resentment of the Catholic population could have been reinforced by the arrival of many Jews whom Merovingian king Dagobert (reigned 623–639) had expelled from France: see Jose Orlandis, *La vida en España en tiempo de los Godos* (Madrid: Ediciones Rialp, S.A., 1991), 129. Another possible factor could have been the lasting animosity against Jews that resulted from persecutions of Jewish Christians (such as Saints Stephen, James, and Paul), and especially from the killing of Jesus, in which Jewish authorities were supposed to have been involved—a rather un-Christian animosity that the Church did not counter, or did not counter enough.

65   Also pointed out by García Moreno, *Los judíos de la España antigua*, 129–30.
66   The earliest reference to Julian's Jewish ancestry is the *Chronica mozarabica* of 754. García Moreno (*Los judíos en la España antigua*, 112) observes that all of Julian's writings contain attacks against the dangers posed by Jews and by crypto-Judaism. García Moreno notes that in an early work (*Historia Wambae*) "Jews from [the French city of] Narbonne are described as perfidious and as principal collaborators in the rebellion of the treacherous [Visigoth] duke Paulo in his effort to destroy the Christian kingdom of the Visigoths in Spain."
67   "Qui autem audent aut disponere aliam fidem aut proferre aut tradere alium symbolum volentibus converti ad scientiam veritatis vel ex gentibus vel Iudaeis vel hereticis quibuscumque, si quidem aut episcopi aut clerici fuerint, alienos se esse episcopos ab episcopatu et clericos a clero, si vero monachi aut laici fuerint, anathemate feriri" V1341, f. 66rb in 3, *Konzil von Toledo*, Project pseudoisidor at http://www.pseudoisidor.mgh.de/html/107.htm.
68   For this and the following, see García Moreno, *Los judíos de la España antigua*, 145–46.
69   García Moreno makes reference to a medieval "tradition" that starts with Christian historian Lucas de Tuy (d. 1249) and according to which Egica's son and successor, King Witiza (d. 710, succeeded by King Rodrigo, the last Visigoth king), rescinded Egica's decree, and he allowed back those Jews who had fled and wanted to return. García Moreno (147) dismisses this narrative and criticizes the following historians for accepting it: Bernard S. Bachrach, *Early Medieval Jewish Policy in Western Europe* (Minneapolis: University of Minnesota, 1977), 23ff; José Orlandis, *Konziliengeschichte. Die Synoden auf der Iberischen Halbinsel bis zum Einbruch des Islam* (Paderborn: F. Schöning, 1981), 321.
70   *Chronica mozarabica*, 44.4–7.
71   Ernesto Livacic Gazzano, *Las siete partidas* (Santiago de Chile: Andrés Bello, 1982), 21; Roger Collins, *La España visigoda: 409–711* (Barcelona: Crítica, 2004), 239.
72   See, among others, Marie-Thérèse Urvoy, *Essai de critique littéraire dans le nouveau monde arabo-islamique* (Paris: Cerf, 2011). For an example of the preservation of Visigoth spirituality in the midst of an Islamic world, see Marie-Thérèse Urvoy, ed. *Le psautier mozarabe de Hafs le Goth* (Toulouse: Presses universitaires du Mirail, 1994).
73   Isidro Bango Torviso, *Alta Edad Media: De la tradición hispanogoda al románico* (Madrid: Silex, 1989), 62, 89–90.
74   For a summary of this contribution, see Gonzalo Menéndez Pidal, "Le Rayonnement de la culture isidorienne: Les mozarabes," *Cahiers d'Histoire Mondiale* 6, no. 4 (1961): 714–31; H. Terrasse, "L'Espagne musulmane et l'héritage Wisigothique," in *Études d'Orientalisme dédiées a la mémoire de Lévi-Provençal* (Paris: Masonneuve, 1962), 2:757–66; Jacques Fontaine and Christine Pellistrandi, eds. *L'Europe Héritière de l'Espagne Wisigothique* (Madrid: Rencontres de la Casa de Velázquez, 1992). See also chapter 2 of this book. For the Umayyads' intermarriage with white slaves from the Balkans and other European lands, see Ibn Hazm, *Naqt al-Arus*, trans. Luis Seco de Lucena (Valencia: Cronista Almela y Vives, 1974), 129–30. See also chapter 5 of this book. In Spain, the intermarriage of rulers with women from the northern Catholic kingdoms continued unabated. The list of "Arabic" intellectuals who in fact descended from Christians is impressive. Historian Ibn al-Qutiya was the son of a Goth woman, and Ibn Hazm's grandfather was a Christian convert to Islam. See also chapter 1 of this book.
75   Joaquín Vallvé Bermejo, *Al-Andalus: Sociedad e instituciones* (Madrid: Real Academia de la Historia, 1999), 16.
76   Richard Eugene Chandler and Kessel Schwartz, *A New History of Spanish Literature* (Baton Rouge: Louisiana State University Press, 1991), 200; N. de la R., "Sobre el nombre y la patria del autor de la muwassaha," *Al-Andalus* 2, no. 1 (1934): 215–22; "Kabra," *Encyclopaedia of Islam, Second Edition*, ed. P. Bearman et al. (Brill, 2011), *Brill Online*, accessed at Northwestern University Library, September 6, 2011.
77   This corroborates Simonet's intuition, offered long before the discovery of the *jarchas*, regarding the survival of Romance among the *dhimmis*. Of course, some Islamic studies experts are unhappy with this and claim that the *jarchas* are not in Romance but in another form of

Arabic characteristic of al-Andalus. For this fantastic option and a summary of the various views on the linguistic nature of the *jarchas*, see Aillet, *Les mozarabes*, 13–15.

78   See chapter 5 of this book for a discussion of Muslim women and sexual slavery. According to Ibn Idhari, Umayyad ruler Abd al-Rahman I was blond; Hisham I had fair complexion and reddish hair; Muhammad had "rosy skin"; Abd Allah had a rosy face, blue eyes, and blond hair; Abd al-Rahman III had fair skin and blue eyes, and he tinted his blond hair black to seem more Arabic; al-Hakam II had a "reddish-blond complexion"; Hisham II was blond and blue-eyed, and had a reddish beard; Abd al-Rahman V al-Mustazhir (who was assassinated in Córdoba in 1024) was blond, the son of a sexual slave; and according to Ibn al-Kardabus, the last Umayyad caliph, Marwan II, was "white, had rosy skin, and blue eyes." See *Al-Bayano 'l-Mogrib*, trans. E. Fagnan (Algiers: Imprimérie orientale, 1904), 2:74, 97, 198, 259, 385, 419; Ibn al-Kardabus, *Historia de al-Andalus (Kitab al-Iktifa)*, trans. Felipe Maíllo Delgado (Madrid: Akal, 1986), 75; Amelina Ramón Guerrero, "Abd al-Rahman V al-*Mustazhir*," in *Homenaje al Prof. Jacinto Bosch Vilá* (Granada: Universidad de Granada, 1991), 1:317. Ibn Hazm tells us that already in the Middle East the Umayyads were practically all the sons of non-Muslim slave women.

79   The heresy of Muhammad Ibn Masarra: Manuel Asín Palacios, *El islam cristianizado: Estudio del sufismo a través de las obras de Abenarabí de Murcia* (Madrid: Plutarco, 1931).

80   See chapter 1 of this book. See also Robert M. Haddad, *Syrian Christians in Muslim Society: An Interpretation* (Princeton, NJ: Princeton University Press, 1970), 11–22. For the role of both Persian Zoroastrians and Christians, see Aptin Khanbaghi, *The Fire, the Star, and the Cross: Minority Religions in Medieval and Early Modern Iran* (London: I. B. Tauris, 2006), 47–51: Muslim chronicler Ibn al-Nadim testified that, in tenth-century Iran, the majority of philosophers were still Christian (49). The Greek Roman Empire may have influenced even some aspects of the legal thought of Islam: see Louis Milliot, *Introduction á l'Etude du Droit Musulman* (Paris: Recueil Sirey, 1953), 772.

81   Reluctantly, the Catholic Church allowed the Mozarabic rite to resume in a few parishes in Toledo after the reconquest of the city by Catholic forces in the twelfth century. Unfortunately, the Visigoth musical script has not been deciphered, and so the music of the Mozarabic rite heard today is an imperfect reconstruction of a rite that dates back to Visigoth Spain and perhaps even before. A listener can still perceive, however, that its sounds are redolent of those of the Greek Orthodox Church, which has preserved more of the sounds of the Christian rituals of the early centuries than has the Roman Catholic Church. The Roman Catholic Church adopted Gregorian ritual reforms in the twelfth century.

82   Aillet, *Les mozarabes: christianisme, islamisation, et arabisation en péninsule ibérique (IXe–XIIe siècle)* (Madrid: Casa de Velázquez, 2010), 83–84. Al-Maqqari writes that Elvira was "close to the site of today's Granada": *Al-Makkari*, 1:44.

83   María Jesús Viguera Molins, "Cristianos, judíos y musulmanes en al-Andalus," in *Cristianos, musulmanes y judíos en la España Medieval: De la aceptación al rechazo*, ed. Julio Valdeón Baruque, ed. (Valladolid: Ambito, 2004), 56–57.

84   Norman Roth, *Jews, Visigoths, and Muslims in Medieval Spain: Cooperation and Conflict* (Leiden: Brill, 1994), 60.

85   See, for instance, *Catholic Encyclopedia*, "Spalato Macarsca," which shows that the reform was not implemented in Dalmatia (today's Croatia) until 1111, http://www.newadvent.org/cathen/14207a.htm. One can imagine its difficulties in the lands of the Islamic empire.

86   Aillet, *Les mozarabes*. Many scholars condemn the Catholic *dhimmis* for putting up resistance, something that scholars would praise in any other subaltern group.

87   See the most detailed treatments of social unrest in Islamic Spain: Roberto Marín Guzmán, *Sociedad, política y protesta popular en la España musulmana* (San José de Costa Rica: Universidad de Costa Rica, 2006); Charles-Emanuel Dufourcq, *La vie quotidienne dans l'Europe mediévale sous la domination arabe* (Paris: Hachette, 1978). The writings of Ibn Garcia best represent this self-conciousness movement (*shuubiya*). For the name "al-adhal" (vile rabble)

that "original" Muslims (conquerors and descendants of the conquerors) applied to the Muladis, see "Muwallad," *Encyclopaedia of Islam, Second Edition*.

88 Roberto Marín-Guzmán, "The Causes of the Revolt of Umar Ibn Hafsun in al-Andalus (880–928): A Study in Medieval Islamic Social History," *Arabica*, t. 42, fasc. 2 (June 1995): 219.

89 For the example of Iran, see Khanbaghi, *The Fire, the Star, and the Cross*, 3, and Maíllo Salgado.

90 For this and the following, see Ibn Hayyan's *al-Muqtabis*, 2:1, in J. Vallvé and F. Ruiz Girela, *La primera década del reinado de Al-Hakam I, según el Muqtabis II, 1 de Ben Hayyan de Córdoba (m. 469 h./1076 J.C.)* (Madrid: Real Academia de la Historia, 2003), 33, 334, 112ff.

91 Al-Hakam's personal guard included Catholic mercenaries. The use of soldiers belonging to a religion different from that of the despot they serve is not uncommon: in twentieth-century Spain, Francisco Franco's *guardia mora*, or Moorish Guard, served him well.

92 See Libyan ruler Muammar Gaddafi's reported use of black mercenaries to quell the insurrection of 2011: "Has Gaddafi Unleashed a Mercenary Force on Libya?" *The Guardian*, February 22, 2011. Al-Qutiyya tells of Muladi revolts and alliances with the "polytheists" (Catholics in the North of Spain) against Muhammad in *Historia de la conquista de España de Abenalcotía el cordobés*, trans. Julián Ribera (Madrid: Revista de Archivos, 1926), 74–75.

93 Dufourcq, *La vie quotidienne dans l'Europe médiévale sous la domination arabe*, 210–11.

94 Reinhart Dozy considered her the daughter of Ibn Hafsun; she could also have been his granddaughter. See Francisco Ortiz Lozano, *Bobastro*, 532–33; for the tenth-century act of beatification, see 569–70.

95 For this and the following, see Ibn Idhari, *Al-Bayano 'l-Mogrib*, 2:173–323, which constantly references the problems Ibn Hafsun posed for the three Umayyad rulers; Ibn Hayyan of Córdoba, *Crónica del Califa Abdarrahman IIII an-Nasir Entre los Años 912 y 942 (al-Muqtabis V)*, trans. María Jesús Viguera and Federico Corriente (Zaragoza: Anubar, 1981), 76. Secondary sources: Francisco Ortiz Lozano, *Bobastro: La ciudad de la perdición* (Ardales, 2010), 531–33, 570, 571ff.; Manuel Acién Almansa, *Entre el feudalismo y el Islam: Umar Ibn Hafsun en los historiadores, en las fuentes, y en la historia* (1994; revised ed. Jaén: Universidad de Jaén, 1997); Roberto Marín-Guzmán, "The Causes of the Revolt of Umar Ibn Hafsun in al-Andalus (880–928): A Study in Medieval Islamic Social History," *Arabica*, t. 42. fasc. 2 (June 1995): 180–221; Maribel Fierro, "Cuatro preguntas en torno a Ibn Hafsun," *Al-Qantara* 16 (1995): 221–57, rpt. and trans. in Manuela Marín, *The Formation of Al-Andalus* (Aldershot: Ashgate, 1998), pt. 1, pp. 291–328; David J. Wasserstein, "Inventing Tradition and Constructing Identity: The Genealogy of Umar Ibn Hafsun Between Christianity and Islam," *Al-Qantara* 23 (2002): 269–97; Simonet, *Historia de los mozárabes de España*, vol. 3, chap. 23.

96 Such as Fierro, "Cuatro preguntas en torno a Ibn Hafsun."

97 *Al-Bayano 'l-Mogrib*, 2:57.

98 *Al-Muqtabis*, 148ff.

99 *Al-Bayan Al-Mugrib: Nuevos fragmentos almóravides y almohades*, translated and annotated by Ambrosio Huici Miranda (Valencia: Bautista, 1963), 85.

100 *Al-Muqtabis*, 117.

101 Manuel Gómez Moreno, *Iglesias mozárabes*, 10–11. Most of the revolts seem to have originated in *muladi* and Berber discontent against Umayyad rule.

102 For the following, see Saint Eulogius's account in Juan Gil, ed., *Corpus scriptorum muzarabicorum* (Madrid: Instituto Antonio de Nebrija, 1973), 2:305–474; J. M. Sáez, *El movimiento martirial de Córdoba: Notas sobre la bibliografía* (Alicante: Universidad de Alicante, 2008); Dufourcq, *La vie quotidienne dans l'Europe médiévale sous la domination arabe*, chs. 11–12.; Francisco Javier Simonet, *Historia de los mozárabes de España* (1897–1908; rpt. Madrid: Turner, 1983), 4 vols., especially 2:357–472.

103 See, among many, the cases in Pakistan of Asia Bibi, a forty-five-year-old Christian woman, and Agnes Nuggo, accused separately by neighbors and condemned to death for blasphemy in 2010 and 2011: "Christian Woman Sentenced to Death in Pakistan for 'Blasphemy,'" *The Telegraph*, November 9, 2010.

104 Eulogius wrote that the Muslim authorities placed *ulama* and rabbis in the seats of those bishops and priests who had refused to participate in the church council: Simonet, *Historia de los mozárabes de España*, 2:360. Israeli historian Elyahu Ashtor observes that Jews supported Muslims against Christian rebels (such as Umar ibn Hafsun and Eulogius) and against Christians in the North (such as King Alfonso III of Asturias ca. 866–910, who attacked Muslims in the South) and that Jews sat with Muslims in the Christian Council of Córdoba (863) to make sure the council did not encourage Christian rebelliousness: *The Jews of Moslem Spain* (Philadelphia: Jewish Publication Society, 1973; trans. Jenny Maklowitz Klein of *Korot ha-Yehudim bi-Sefarad ha-Muslemit*), 1:68–69, 92–93, 98–99.

105 Manuel Cecilio Díaz y Díaz, "Los mozárabes. Una minoría combativa," in *Existe una identidad mozárabe?*, ed. Cyrille Aillet, Mayte Penclas, and Philippe Roisse (Madrid: Casa de Velázquez, 2008), 7. In English scholarship, among many other examples of the unsympathetic treatment of the Catholic martyrs are Ann Christys, *Christians in al-Andalus (711–1000)* (Richmond: Curzon Press, 2002), 28–51; Jessica Coope, *The Martyrs of Córdoba* (London: University of Nebraska Press, 1995); Kenneth Baxter Wolf, *Christian Martyrs in Muslim Spain* (Cambridge: Cambridge University Press, 1988). The most sympathetic scholarly treatment is in Spanish and dates back to the end of the nineteenth century, but it could not be published until later because of its pro-Catholic stance: Simonet, *Historia de los mozárabes de España*, especially 2:357–472.

106 Simonet, *Historia de los mozárabes de España*, 2:364, 408. Eulogius reports that Muslims kept their distance from Christian priests for fear of contamination and avoided talking to Christians for the same reason and that stones and rotten food were thrown at priests during Christian funeral processions.

107 Whereas the expulsion of the *moriscos* by the Spanish authorities is well known, these expulsions of Christians are known only to specialists, thanks to the deafening media and academic silence on the fate of Christian *dhimmis*. For an account of some of these expulsions, see Vincent Lagardère, "Communautés mozarabes et pouvoir almoravide en 519 H/1125 en al-Andalus," *Studia Islamica* 67 (1988): 99–119; Delfina Serrano Ruano, "Dos fetuas sobre la expulsión de mozárabes al Magreb en 1126," *Anaquel de Estudios Árabes* 2 (1991): 163–82. Note that earlier, the Umayyad ruler al-Hakam I had expelled Muladis to Africa.

108 Roth, *Jews, Visigoths, and Muslims in Medieval Spain*, 38. Professor Roth's sarcasm against the Visigoths deserves full quotation: "For all the glorification of the 'Great Christian monarchy' of legendary Visigothic Spain that one encounters in chronicles, etc., the fact is that the Visigoths had fled Spain and abandoned it to the invading Muslims. The Christians of the Reconquest…learned well the lesson…of *convivencia*. That was only one of the many things that made Spain great, and which the rest of Europe could have learned from it to its profit."

EPILOGUE

1 For Ibn Hazm's view of Islam as fundamentally anti-Christian, see Miguel Asín Palacios, *Abenházam de Córdoba y su historia crítica de las ideas religiosas* (Madrid: Archivos, bibliotecas y Museos, 1928), 2:77.

2 Edward Said, *Culture and Imperialism* (New York: Vintage, 1994), 195.

3 Hardly any Zoroastrians can be found in Iran today. For the astonishment of the Arabs upon their conquest of Zoroastrian Persia (Iran), see Mohsen Azizi, *La domination arabe et l'épanouissement du sentiment national en Iran* (Paris: Les Presses Modernes, 1938). For the havoc caused in India, from which medieval Islam took so much, including "Arabic" numerals, see K. S. Lal, *Growth of Muslim Population in Medieval India (A.D. 1000–1800)* (Delhi: Research Publications in Social Sciences, 1973). For the destruction of Hindu-Buddhist Sind, see Nobel Prize in Literature winner V. S. Naipaul's most readable *Among the Believers* (New York: Vintage, 1982).

4 *Muqaddimah*, trans. Franz Rosenthal, abr. ed. (Princeton, NJ: Princeton University Press, 1967), 2:39, 429–30.

5   Ibn Khaldun, *The Muqaddimah: An Introduction to History*, trans. Franz Rosenthal (New York: Pantheon, 1958), 2:267, 269. Arabs used poor construction materials, such as wood, plaster, and brick. These materials can still be seen today in Andalusian palaces, delicately beautiful on the surface, such as the Alhambra. This is an architectural approach based largely on "smoke and mirrors." Even the *Grove Encyclopedia of Islamic Art and Architecture,* very partial to Islamic culture, tells us that "[in Nasrid architecture] palaces and civic buildings were...decorated with simulated arches of colored plaster to give the illusion of dynamism and ethereality. Gravity is apparently absent from Nasrid architecture, but in reality structures are static and primitive in composition, for thick walls counterbalance the thrust of the light wooden roofs, below which hang decorative ceilings of wood or occasionally plaster." *Grove Encyclopedia of Islamic Art and Architecture*, ed. Jonathan M. Bloom and Sheila S. Blair (Oxford: Oxford University Press, 2009), 157.

6   Dominique Urvoy, *Histoire de la pensée arabe e islamique* (Paris: Seuil, 2006), 13. The impact of Greek thought on Arabic linguistic writings in C. II. M. Versteegh, *Greek Elements in Arabic Linguistic Thinking* (Leiden: Brill, 1977).

7   Oleg Grabar, "Islamic Art and Byzantium," *Dumbarton Oaks Papers* 18 (1964): 87–88.

8   Robert M. Haddad, *Syrian Christians in Muslim Society: An Interpretation* (Princeton, NJ: Princeton University Press, 1970), 11–22. For the role of both Persian Zoroastrians and Christians, see Aptin Khanbaghi, *The Fire, the Star, and the Cross: Minority Religions in Medieval and Early Modern Iran* (London: I. B. Tauris, 2006), 47–51. The Greek Roman Empire may have influenced even some aspects of the legal thought of Islam: see Louis Milliot, *Introduction à l'Etude du Droit Musulman* (Paris: Recueil Sirey, 1953), 772. For Ibn al-Nadim, see Khanbaghi, *The Fire, the Star, and the Cross*, 49.

9   Norman Roth, *Jews, Visigoths, and Muslims in Medieval Spain: Cooperation and Conflict* (Leiden: Brill, 1994), 42.

10   In contrast with their kind views on Muslim rule over Christians, many academics were outraged when economist Robert W. Fogel, later a Nobel Prize winner, demonstrated that the average black slave in the American South was generally treated well and in fact lived longer and had a higher caloric intake than the average northern white city dweller. It was also disturbing that Fogel, who was not Christian, had concluded that Christianity (the various Protestant and especially Puritan churches) had been a key factor in the antislavery movement and the War Between the States. See Robert W. Fogel and Stanley L. Engermann, *Time on the Cross: The Economics of American Slavery* (1974; rpt. New York: W. W. Norton, 2013).

11   Cyrille Aillet, *Les mozarabes* (Madrid: Casa de Velázquez, 2010), 112–13. John O. Hunwick describes the condition of the *dhimmis* well, except that he upgrades them to second-class citizenship because he does not distinguish among the several other classes: "they were, and were intended to be, second-class citizens—a minority preferably not to be seen and certainly not to be heard" (John O. Hunwick, "The Rights of *Dhimmis* to Maintain a Place of Worship: A 15th-Century *Fatwa* from Tlemcen," *Al-Qantara* 12, no. 1 (1991): 133.

12   Haddad, *Syrian Christians in Muslim Society*, 5. In medieval times, Muslim chronicles paid even less attention to the Christian *dhimmis* of Spain than today's Western historians do. These days there are research centers and websites, sponsored by prestigious universities, dedicated to the Spanish *moriscos* (Muslim converts to Catholicism), the Spanish *conversos* (or *anusim*, or *marranos*: false or suspect Jewish converts to Catholicism), and their descendants. But there are no analogous centers, sponsored by prestigious universities, on the long-vanished Christian *dhimmis* of Spain.

13   Quoted by historian Francisco García Fitz, "Las Navas de Tolosa, ¿un punto de inflexión en las dinámicas históricas peninsulares?" *1212–1214: El trienio que hizo a Europa* (Pamplona: Fondo de publicacones del gobierno de Navarra, 2011), 57.

14   See *Toledo y Bizancio*, ed. Miguel Cortés Arrese (Cuenca: Universidad de Castilla–La Mancha, 2002).

Select Bibliography

Full bibliographical information on all works cited in this book, including archaeological and numismatic sources, can be found in the notes to the chapters.

PRIMARY SOURCES

Christian sources have been all too often neglected by Arabists in their studies of Islamic Spain. Yet they are valuable not only by themselves (some of them provide the earliest extant accounts of and reactions to the Muslim conquest and, in the case of the *Chronica mozarabica* of 754, the most reliable account) but also because they help to corroborate, dispute, or complete the assertions in the Muslim chronicles and biographies, which are at times chauvinistically propagandistic about al-Andalus and Islam—as acknowledged by the Spanish Arabist Jorge Aguadé in his edition of the *Kitab al-Tarij*, 78 ("in general, history in the medieval Islamic world has been but a specialty at the service of religious sciences and tradition"), and F. Rosenthal, *A History of Muslim Historiography* (Leiden: Brill, 1968), 42ff. To facilitate finding and consultation, titles and names in the titles are usually alphabetized according to their spelling in the particular edition and language where they appear.

Abd al-Malik B. Habib (m.238/853): *Kitab al-Tarij (La Historia)*. Edition and study by Jorge Aguadé. Madrid: Consejo Superior de Investigaciones Científicas, 1991.
Abd al-Wahid al-Marrakushi. *Histoire des almohades*. Translated by Edmond Fagnan. Algiers: Adolphe Jourdan, 1893.
———. *Abu Muhammad Abd al-Wahid al-Marrakusi: Lo admirable en el resumen de las noticias del Magrib (Kitab al-Muyib Fi Taljis Ajbar al-Magrib)*. Translated by Ambrosio Huici Miranda. Tetuán: Editora Marroquí (Instituto General Franco de Estudios e Investigación Hispano-Árabe), 1955.
Abu Abd Allah Abdullah Muhammed ibn Muhammed al-Idrisi. *Description de l'Afrique et de l'Espagne par Edrisi*. Edited and translated by R. Dozy and M.J. de Goeje. Leiden: Brill, 1968.
Abu Muhammad Abd Allah Ibn Abi Zayd al-Qayrawani. *Risala ou traité agrégé de droit Malékite et moral musulmane*. Translated by Edmond Fagnan. Paris: Geuthner, 1914, http://gallica.bnf. fr/ark:/12148/bpt6k5813421p.
———. *Compendio de derecho islámico [Risala fi-l-fiqh] Ibn Abi Zayd al Qayrawani*. Translated by Jesús Rosalido Gambotti. Madrid: Editorial Trotta, S.A., 1950.
———. *The Risala of 'Abdullah ibn Abi Zayd al-Qayrawani (310/922–386/996): A Treatise on Maliki*

Fiqh. Translated by Aisha Bewley, http://www.muwatta.com/ebooks/english/risala_ibn_abi_ zayd_salutations.pdf.

———. *The Risala: A Treatise on Maliki Fiqh*. Translated by Alhaj Bello Mohammad Daura at the Islamic Law Base, http://www.iium.edu.my/deed/lawbase/risalah_maliki/.

Abu Ubayd al-Qasim Ibn Salam. *The Book of Revenue (Kitab al-Anwal)*. Translated by Imran Ahsan Khan Nyazee. London: Center for Muslim Contributions to Civilization, 2005.

Ajbar Machmuá. Edited and translated by Emilio Lafuente y Alcántara. Madrid: Bibliófilo, 1984.

Alfonso X. *Las siete partidas*. Edited by Real Academia de la Historia. Madrid: Imprenta Real, 1807. 3 vols.

———. *Primera crónica general de España que mandó componer Alfonso el Sabio y se continuaba bajo Sancho IV en 1289*. Edited and study by Ramón Menéndez Pidal with the collaboration of Antonio G. Solalinde, Manuel Muñoz Cortés, and José Gómez Pérez. Madrid: Gredos, 1955, 2 vols.

Antiochus Strategos of Mar Saba. "Antiochus Strategos: The Capture of Jerusalem by the Persians in 614 A.D." Translated by F. C. Coneybeare, *English Historical Review* 25 (1910): 502–17.

Ascher ben Jechiel (Rosch). *Die Responsen des Rabbi Ascher ben Jechiel (Rosch)*. Edited and study by Daniel Richter. Zürich: Schulthess Polygraphischer Verlag, 1992.

al-Bukhari. *Sahih Al-Bukhari*. Translated by Dr. Muhammad Muhsin Khan of Medina Islamic University. Chicago: Kazi Publications, 1976, 3 vols.

Chronica Byzantia-Arabica (743 A.D.). In *Corpus scriptorum muzarabicorum*, edited by Juan Gil, 1:7–14. Madrid: Instituto Antonio de Nebrija, 1973.

Chronica mozarabica (754 A.D.). Edited by Juan Gil. *Corpus scriptorum muzarabicorum*. Madrid: Instituto Antonio de Nebrija, 1973, 1:15–54.

Chronique de Michel le Syrien, Patriarche Jacobite d'Antioche (1166–1199). Edited and translated by J. B. Chabot. Brussels: Culture et Civilisation, 1963, 2 vols.

"Covenant of Umar." In *The Caliphs and Their Non-Muslim Subjects: A Critical Study of the Covenant of Umar*, written by A. S. Tritton. First published London: Frank Cass and Company, 1930. Reprint, 1970.

Crónica Albeldense (883 A.D.), *Crónica Rotense* (888 A.D.), and *Crónica Profética* (883 A.D.). In "Las primeras crónicas de la Reconquista: El ciclo de Alfonso III," edited by Manuel Gómez Moreno. *Boletín de la Academia de la Historia* (Madrid: Archivos) Tomo C. (1932): 600–62.

Crónicas anónimas de Sahagún. Edited by Antonio Ubieto Arteta. Zaragoza: Pedro Garcés de Cariñena, 1987.

Die Chronik Alfons' III: Untersuchung und kritische Edition der vier Redaktionen. Edited and study by Jan Prelog. Frankfurt: Peter Lang, 1980.

Dos tratados de legislación musulmana. 1. Leyes de moros del siglo XIV 2. Suma de los principales mandamientos y devedamientos de la ley y çunna, por don Içe de Gebir, Alfaquí Mayor de la aljama de Segovia. Año de 1492. Edited by Pascual de Gayangos. Madrid: Academia de la Historia. Memorial histórico español, 1853, vol. 5.

al-Ghazali on Malik's opposition to music. Duncan B. Macdonald. "Emotional Religion in Islam as Affected by Music and Singing: Being a Translation of a Book of the Ihya Ulum al-Din of al-Ghazzali with Analysis, Annotation, and Appendices." *Journal of the Royal Asiatic Society* (1901): 201 and n2.

Hymnodia Gothica (Analecta Hymnica Medii Aevi, XXVII). Edited by Clemens Blume. First published Leipzig: Fues's 1897. Reprint, Augsburg: Rauner, 2004.

Ibn Abd al-Hakam. *Conquista de África del Norte y de España*. Translated by Eliseo Vidal Beltrán. Valencia: Anubar, 1966.

Ibn al-Athir. *Annales du Maghreb et de l'Espagne*. Translated by Edmond Fagnan. Algiers: Adolphe Jourdan, 1898.

Ibn al-Gallab. *El tratado jurídico de al-Tafri de Ibn Gallab. Manuscrito aljamiado de Almonacid de la Sierra (Zaragoza): Edición, glosario y confrontación con el original árabe por Soha Abboud Haggar*. Zaragoza: Institución Fernando el Católico, 1999.

Ibn Hawqal. *Configuration de la Terre (Kitab Surat al-Ard)*. Translated by J.H. Kramers and G. Wiet. Paris: Maisonneuve, 1964, 1:107–16.

Ibn Hayyan. *Al-Muqtabis* 2:1. In J. Vallvé and F. Ruiz Girela, *La primera década del reinado de Al-Hakam I, según el Muqtabis II, 1 de Ben Hayyan de Córdoba (m. 469 h./1076 J.C.)*. Madrid: Real Academia de la Historia, 2003.

———. *Crónica del Califa Abdarrhman III an-Nasir entre los años 912 y 942 (al-Muqtabis V)*. Translated by M. Jesús Viguera and Federico Corriente. Zaragoza, 1981.

Ibn Hazm. *Naqt -al-Arus*. Translated by Luis Seco de Lucena. Valencia: Alemal y Vives, 1974.

———. *Fisal*. In *Abenházam de Córdoba y su historia crítica de las ideas religiosas*, translated by Miguel Asín Palacios, vols. 3–5. Madrid: Turner, 1984.

Ibn Idhari al-Marrakushi. *Histoire de l'Afrique et de l'Espagne: Intitulée Al-Bayano 'l-Mogrib*. Translated by Edmond Fagnan. Algiers: Imprimérie orientale, 1904, 2 vols.

———. *Historia de al-Andalus*. Translated by Francisco Fernández González. Malaga: Aljaima, 1999.

Ibn Idris al-Shafii. *Islamic jurisprudence: Shafii's Risala*. Translated by Majid Khadduri. Baltimore: Johns Hopkins University Press, 1961.

Ibn al-Kardabus. *Historia de al-Andalus (Kitab al-Iktifa)*. Translated by Felipe Maíllo Salgado. Madrid: Akal, 1986.

Ibn Khaldoun. *Les Prolégomènes d'Ibn Khaldoun*. Translated by M. de Slane. Paris: Librairie orientaliste Paul Geuthner, 1934, 3 vols.

Ibn Khaldun. *The Muqaddimah: An Introduction to History*. Translated by Franz Rosenthal. First published 1969. Reprint, Princeton, NJ: Princeton University Press, 2004.

Ibn Khaldūn. *Histoire des Berbères*. Translated by M. de Slane. Paris: Librairie Orientaliste, 1925, vol. 1.

Ibn Mohammed al-Maqqari. *The History of the Mohammedan Dynasties in Spain by Ahmed Ibn Mohammed al-Makkari*. Translated by Pascual de Gayangos. First published Madrid, 1840. Reprint, New York: Johnson, 1964, 2 vols.

Ibn al-Qutiyya, *Historia de la conquista de España de Abenalcotía el cordobés*. Translated by Julián Ribera. Madrid: Revista de Archivos, 1926, 2 vols.

Ibn Rushd. *Bidayat al-Mujtahid: Distinguished Jurist's Primer*. Translated by Imran Azhan Khan Nyazee. Reading: Garnet, 1996, 2 vols.

———. *Averroes: El libro del Yihad*. Translated by Carlos Quirós. Oviedo: Pentalfa Ediciones, 2009.

Ibn al-Tabari. *The History of al-Tabari*. Translated by R. Stephen Humphreys et al. New York: State University of New York Press, 1990, 39 vols.

———. *Al-Tabari's Book of Jihad: A Translation from the Original Arabic with an Introduction, Commentary and Notes by Yasir S. Ibrahim*. Lewiston, NY: Edwin Mellen Press, 2007.

Isidore of Seville, Saint. *Isidore of Seville's History of the Kings of the Goths, Vandals, and Suevi*. Translated by Guido Donini and Gordon B. Ford. Leiden: Brill, 1966.

John, Bishop of Nikiû. *Chronicle*. Translated by R.H. Charles. Oxford: Oxford University Press, 1916.

al-Khushani. *Historia de los jueces de Córdoba por Alxojaní*. Translated by Julián Ribera. First published 1914. Reprint, Madrid: Renacimiento, 2005.

Leges visigothorum. In *Monumenta Germaniae Historica* LL nat. Germ. 1:1, edited by Karl Zeumer. Hannover/Leipzig, 1902.

Liudprand, Bishop of Cremona. *The Complete Works of Liudprand of Cremona*. Translated by Paolo Squatriti. Washington, DC: The Catholic University of America Press, 2007.

Maimonides. *Mishneh Torah*. Translated with commentaries and notes by Rabbi Eliyahu Touger. New York/Jerusalem: Moznaim Publishing Corporation, 1997, 20 vols.

———. *Epistles of Maimonides: Crisis and Leadership*. Edited by David Hartman. Translated by Abraham S. Halkin. Philadelphia: Jewish Publication Society, 1985.

Malik Ibn Anas. *Muwatta of Imam Malik narrated by Yahya B. Yahya B. Kathir al-Laith al-Andalusi*. Translated by F. Amira Zrien Matraji. Corrected and revised by Dr. Mahmood Matraji. Karachi: Darul Ishaat, 2005.

Masudi (mort en 345/956): Les Prairies d'Or. Translated by C. Barbier de Meynard, Abel Pavet de Courteille, Charles Pellat. Paris: Société asiatique, 1962, 9 vols.

Materialien zur malikitischen Rechtsliteratur. Edition and study by Miklos Muranyi. Wiesbaden: Otto Harrassowitz, 1984.

"Polemic between a Saracen and a Christian," attributed to John Damascene (A.D. 676–749). In Adel Theodor Khoury, *Les théologiens byzantins et l'Islam: Textes et auteurs (VIIIe–XIIIe s.).* Louvain: Nauwlaerts, 1969, 68–82.

Rabbinical Medieval *Responsa (Teshuvot).* See Maimonides's *Epistles*; Ascher ben Jeschiel; Simha Assaf; Yizhak Baer; Yom Tov Assis.

al-Razi. *Crónica del moro Rasis.* Edited by Diego Catalán. Translated by María Soledad de Andrés. Madrid: Gredos, 1975.

Rodrigo Jiménez de Rada: Historia de los hechos de España. Translated by Juan Fernández Valverde. Madrid: Alianza, 1989.

Sahnun Ibn Said. *La Moudawwana.* In the following volumes dedicated entirely to the work: *Annales de l'Institut d'Études Orientales* 16 (1958), 17 (1959), and 20 (1962), and *Revue algérienne, tunisienne et marocaine de législation et de jurisprudence* 74 (1958), 75 (1959), and 77 (1961), complete summary translated by G. H. Bousquet.

Said al-Andalusi. *Kitab Tabakat al-Umam (Livre des Catégories des Nations).* Translated by Régis Blachère. Paris: La Rose, 1935.

Sebeos. *The Armenian History Attributed to Sebeos.* Translated by R. W. Thomson. Liverpool: Liverpool University Press, 1999, pt. I.

Les théologiens byzantins et l'Islam: textes et auteurs (VIIIe–XIIIe s). Edited by Adel Theodor Khoury. Louvain: Nauwlaerts, 1969, 68–82.

Theophanes the Confessor. *The Chronicle of Theophanes Confessor: Byzantine and Near Eastern History A.D. 284–813.* Translated by Cyril Mango and Roger Scott, with the assistance of Geoffrey Greatrex. Oxford: Clarendon Press, 1997.

Secondary Sources

Abboud-Haggar, Soha. "Las raíces de la violencia en los textos religiosos islámicos: El Corán y al-Hadiz." *Raíces profundas: La violencia contra las mujeres (Antigüedad y Edad Media).* Edited by María Jesús Fuente and Remedios Morán. Madrid: Polifemo, 2011, 45–66.

———. "Al-Gihad según el manuscrito aljamiado de al-Tafri de Ibn al-Gallab." *Sharq al-Andalus* 12 (1995): 232–338.

Abrahams, Israel. *Jewish Life in the Middle Ages.* London: E. Goldston, 1932. Reprinted in 2009.

Aguilera Pleguezuelo, José. "El derecho malikí aplicado en al-Andalus: Teoría y práctica jurídicas," *Actas de las II Jornadas de Cultura Arabe e Islámica.* Madrid: Instituto Hispano-Arabe de Cultura, 1980, 16–27.

Aharoni, Yohanan. *The Land of the Bible: A Historical Geography.* London: Burns and Oates, 1979.

Aillet, Cyrille. *Les mozarabes, christianisme, islamisation et arabisation en péninsule ibérique (IXe–XIIe siècle).* Madrid: Casa de Velazquez, 2010.

———. ¿Existe una identidad mozárabe? *Historia, lengua y cultura de los cristianos de al-Andalus (siglos IX–XII).* Edited by Cyrille Aillet, Mayte Penelas, and Philippe Roisse. Madrid: Casa de Velazquez, 2008).

Alvarez Palenzuela, Vicente A., and Luis Suárez Fernández. *Historia de España: La España musulmana y los inicios de los reinos cristianos (711–1157).* Madrid: Gredos, 1991.

Arnaldez, R. "La guerre sainte selon Ibn Hazm." *Études d'Orientalisme Dediées a la Mémoire de Lévi-Provençal.* Paris: Maisonneuve, 1962, vol. 2.

Ashtor, Elyahu. *The Jews of Moslem Spain.* Translated by Jenny Maklowitz Klein of *Korot ha-Yehudim bi-Sefarad ha-Muslemit.* Philadelphia: The Jewish Publication Society, 1973, vol. 1.

Asín Palacios, Miguel. *Abenházam de Córdoba y su historia crítica de las ideas religiosas*. Madrid: Turner, 1984, vols. 1–2.

Assaf, Simha. *HaOnshin aare atimat ha-Talmud: Omer le-toldot ha-mishpa ha-ivri*. Jerusalem: Defus, 1921.

Assis, Yom Tov. "Sexual Behavior in Medieval Hispano-Jewish Society." *Jewish History: Essays in Honor of Chimen Abramsky*. Edited by Ada Rapoport Albert and Steven J. Zipperstein. London: P. Halban, 1988, 25–60.

Ávila, María Luisa. "Women in Andalusi Biographical Sources." *Writing the Feminine: Women in Arab Sources*. Edited by Manuela Marín and Randi Deguilhem. London: I. B., Tauris, 2002, 149–63.

Azizi, Mohsen. *La domination arabe et l'épanouissement du sentiment national en Iran*. Paris: Les Presses Modernes, 1938.

Baer, Yitzhak. *A History of the Jews in Christian Spain*. Philadelphia: Jewish Publication Society of America, 1961, 2 vols.

Bango Torviso, Isidro G. *Alta Edad Media: De la tradición hispanogoda al románico*. Madrid: Silex, 1989.

———. "Un gravísimo error en la historiografía española: El empleo equivocado del término mozárabe." *Simposio internacional "El legado de al-Andalus."* Edited by Manuel Valdés Fernández. Madrid: Fundación del Patrimonio Histórico de Castilla y León, 2007, 73–88.

———. "711/842: Siglo y medio de la cultura material de la España cristiana desde la invasión; Musulmanes y cristianos determinantes de una mistificación 'históricocultural' que no cesa." *Anales de la Historia del Arte* 22, num. especial II (2012): 57–90.

Baron, Salo. *A Social and Religious History of the Jews*. New York: Columbia University Press, 1958, vol. 5.

Beltrán Torreira, Federico-Mario. "El concepto de barbarie en la Hispania visigoda." *Antigüedad y cristianismo* 3 (1986): 46–57.

Blidstein, Gerald J. "The 'Other' in Maimonidean Law." *Jewish History* 18 (2004): 173–95.

Bonner, Michael. "Some Observations concerning the Early Development of Jihad on the Arab-Byzantine Frontier." *Studia Islamica*, no. 75. (1992): 19.

Bousquet, G. H. "Some Critical and Sociological Remarks on the Arab Conquest and the Theories Proposed on This." In *The Expansion of the Early Islamic State*, edited by Fred M. Donner, 15–22. Burlington: Ashgate, 2008.

———. "Observations on the Nature and Causes of the Arab Conquest." In *The Expansion of the Early Islamic State,* edited by Fred M. Donner, 23–36.

Butler, Alfred J. *The Arab Conquest of Egypt and the Last Thirty Years of the Roman Dominion*. First published 1902. Reprint, Oxford: Oxford University Press, 1978.

Caballero, Zoreda, Luis and Pedro Mateos Cruz, eds. *Escultura decorativa tardorromana y altomedieval en la Península Ibérica*. Madrid: Consejo Superior de Investigaciones Científicas, 2007.

Caballero Zoreda, Luis, ed. *El siglo VII frente al siglo VII: Arquitectura*. Madrid: Consejo Superior de Investigaciones Científicas, 2009.

Calvo Capilla, Susana. "Las primeras mezquitas de al-Andalus a través de las fuentes árabes (92/711–170/785)." *Al-Qantara* xxvii 1 (Enero–Julio 2007): 143–79.

Cantera Montenegro, Enrique. "La justicia en las aljamas castellanas a fines del siglo XV: La frontera oriental del reino de Castilla." *Sefarad* 52, no. 2 (1992): 337–53.

Carmona, Alfonso. "Le Malékisme et les conditions requises pour l'exercise de la judicature." *Islamic Law and Society* 7, no. 2: 122–58.

Carrobles Santos, Jesús, Rafael Barroso Cabrera, Jorge Morín de Pablos, and Fernando Valdés Fernández. *Regia Sedes Toletana: La topografía de la ciudad de Toledo en la antigüedad tardía y alta edad media*. Toledo: Real Fundación de Toledo, 2007.

Cavarnos, Constantine. *Cultural and Educational Continuity of Greece from Antiquity to the Present*. Belmont: Institute for Byzantine and Modern Greek Studies, 1995.

Castellanos Gómez, Juan, Lieutenant General. *Geoestrategia en la España musulmana: Las campañas militares de Almanzor*. Madrid: Ministerio de Defensa, 2002.

Chalmeta Gendrón, Pedro. *Invasión e islamización: La sumisión de Hispania y la formación de al-Andalus.* Jaén: Universidad de Jaén, 2002.

Cobreros, Jaime. *Guía del prerrománico en España: Visigodo; Asturiano; Mozárabe.* Madrid: Anaya, 2005.

Constantelos, Demetrios. *Christian Hellenism: Essays and Studies in Continuity and Change.* New Rochelle, NY, and Athens: Aristide D. Caratzas, 1999.

Cortés Arrese, Miguel, ed. *Toledo y Bizancio.* Cuenca: Universidad de Castilla-La Mancha, 2002.

Crawford, Paul F. "Four Myths About the Crusades." *Intercollegiate Review* 46, no. 1 (Spring 2011): 13–22.

———. "Imagination and the Templars: The Development of the Order State in the Early Fourteenth Century." *Annual Review [Epeteris] of the Cyprus Research Center* 30 (2004): 113–21.

———, ed. *The Templar of Tyre: Part III of "The Deeds of the Cypriots."* Farnham: Ashgate, 2003.

Cressier, Patrice. "Les chapiteaux de la Grande Mosquée de Cordoue." *Madrider Mitteilungen* 25 (1994): 257–313.

Crone, P., and M. Hinds, *God's Caliph. Religious Authority in the First Centuries of Islam.* Cambridge: Cambridge University Press, 1986.

Cruz Hernández, Miguel. "La persecución anti-Masarri durante el reinado de Abd al-Rahman al-Nasir Li-din Allah, según Ibn Hayyan." *Al-Qantara* 2, nos. 1/2 (1981): 51–67.

Cutler, Alan Harris. *The Jew as Ally of the Muslim: Medieval Roots of Anti-Semitism.* Notre Dame: University of Notre Dame Press, 1986.

Davidson, Herbert Alan. *Moses Maimonides: The Man and His Works.* New York: Oxford University Press, 2004.

Davis, Robert C. *Christian Slaves, Muslim Masters: White Slavery in the Mediterranean, the Barbary Coast, and Italy 1500–1800.* New York: Palgrave McMillan, 2003.

Dawson, Christopher. *The Making of Europe: An Introduction to the History of European Unity.* First published 1932. Reprint, Washington, DC: The Catholic University of America Press, 2003.

———. *Religion and the Rise of Western Culture.* First published 1950. Reprint, New York: Image Books, 1991.

Decker, Michael. "Agriculture and Agricultural Technology." *The Oxford Handbook of Byzantine Studies.* Edited by Robin Cormack, John F. Haldon, and Elizabeth Jeffreys. Oxford: Oxford University Press, 2008, 397–405.

Delbrück, Hans. *The Barbarian Invasions.* Translated by Walter J. Renfroe Jr. Lincoln: University of Nebraska Press, 1980.

Dewald, Ernest T. "The Appearance of the Horseshoe Arch in Western Europe." *American Journal of Archaeology* 26, no. 3 (July–September 1922): 316–37.

Díaz y Díaz, Manuel C. "Les arts libéraux d'après les écrivains espagnols et insulaires au VIIe et VIIIe siécles." *Arts Libéraux et Philosophie au Moyen Âge. Actes du Quatrième Congrés International de Philosophie Médiévale.* Montreal: Institut D'Études Médiévales, 1969, 37–46.

———. "La *Lex Visigothorum* y sus manuscritos: un ensayo de interpretación." *Anuario de Historia del Derecho Español* 6 (1976): 163–223.

Domínguez Ortiz, Antonio. *España: Tres Milenios de Historia.* Madrid: Marcial Pons, 2007.

Dozy, Reinhart. *Histoire des musulmans d'Espagne jusqu'a la conquête de l'andalousie par les almoravides.* Edited and revised by E. Lévi-Provençal. Leiden: Brill, 1932, 3 vols.

Duchesne, Ricardo. *The Uniqueness of Western Civilization.* Leiden: Brill, 2011.

Fanjul, Serafín. "Mujer y sociedad en el *Tarij Al-Mustabsir* de Ibn al-Muyawir." *Al-Qantara* 8, nos. 1/2 (1987): 165–90.

———. *Al-Andalus contra España: La forja del mito.* Madrid: Siglo XXI, 2005.

———. *La quimera de al-Andalus.* Madrid: Siglo XXI, 2005.

Farhat-Holzman, Laina. *Strange Birds from Zoroaster's Nest: An Overview of Revealed Religions.* Kansas City: Nonetheless Press, 2003.

Fattal, Antoine. *Le statut légal des non-musulmans en pays d'Islam.* Beirut: Imprimérie Catholique, 1958; 1995.

Félix, Ana Fernández. *Cuestiones jurídicas del Islam temprano: La Utbiyya y el proceso de formación de la sociedad islámica andalusí*. Madrid: Consejo Superior de Investigaciones Científicas, 2003.

Fernández-Morera, Darío. "Cervantes and Islam: A Contemporary Analogy." *Cervantes y su mundo III*. Edited by Kurt Reichenberger and Robert Lauer. Kassel: Reichenberger, 2005, 123–66.

———. "Some Overlooked Realities of Jewish Life under Islamic Rule in Medieval Spain." *Comparative Civilizations Review*, no. 68 (Spring 2013): 21–35.

Fierro, Maribel. "Religious dissension in Al-Andalus: Ways of Exclusion and Inclusion." *Al-Qantara* 22, no. 2 (2001): 463–87.

———. *Abd al-Rahman III of Cordoba*. London: OneWorld Publications, 2005.

———. *The Almohad Revolution: Politics and Religion in the Islamic West during the Twelfth-Thirteenth Centuries (Variorum Collected Studies)*. Hampshire: Ashgate, 2012.

Fierro, Maribel, and Francisco García Fitz, eds. *El cuerpo derrotado: Cómo trataban musulmanes y cristianos a los enemigos vencidos* (Península Ibérica, ss. VIII-XIII). Madrid: Consejo Superior de Investigaciones Científicas, 2008.

Fogel, Robert W., and Stanley L. Engermann. *Time on the Cross: The Economics of American Slavery*. First published 1974. Reprint, New York: W. W. Norton, 2013.

Fontaine, Jacques, and Christine Pellistrandi, eds. *L'Europe Héritière de l'Espagne Wisigothique*. Madrid: Rencontres de la Casa de Velázquez, 1992.

Forneas, J. M. "Datos para un estudio de la *mudawwana* de Sahnun en al-Andalus." *Actas del IV Coloquio Hispano-Tunecino*. Madrid: Instituto Hispano-Arabe de Cultura, 1983, 93–118.

Franke, F. R. "Die freiwilligen Märtyrer von Cordova und das Verhältnis der Mozaraber zun Islam." *Spanische Forschungen des Görresgesellschaft* 13 (1953): 1–170 [far superior to later English books by K. B. Wolf and J. A. Coope].

Gangutia Elicegui, Elvira. "Teodoro Pródromo y Ben Quzmán." *Erytheia* 4 (1984): 56–61.

García Fitz, Francisco. *Las Navas de Tolosa*. Madrid: Ariel, 2008.

———. "La Reconquista: Un estado de la cuestión." *Clio y Crimen*, no. 6 (2009): 142–215.

García Moreno, Luis A. "Fuentes protobizantinas de la España tardoantigua (ss. V-VIII)." *Erytheia* 9, no. 1 (1988): 11–22.

———. "The Creation of Byzantium's Spanish Province." *Byzantion* 66 (1996): 101–19.

———. "Literatura antimusulmana de tradición bizantina entre los mozárabes." *Hispania Sacra* 57 (2005): 7–45.

———. "Spanish Gothic Consciousness." *The Visigoths: Studies in Culture and Society*. Edited by Alberto Ferreiro: London: Brill, 1999, 303–23.

———. "Patria Española y etnia goda (siglos VI-VIII)." *De Hispania a España. El nombre y el concepto a través de los siglos*. Edited by V. Palacio Atard. Madrid: Temas de Hoy, 2005, 41–53.

———. *España 702-719: La conquista musulmana*. Seville: Universidad de Sevilla, 2013.

García Sanjuán, Alejandro. "Violencia contra los judíos." *De muerte violenta: Política, religión y violencia en al-Andalus*. Edited by Maribel Fierro. Madrid: Consejo Superior de Investigaciones Científicas, 2004, 167–206.

Goitein, S. D. *A Mediterranean Society: The Jewish Communities of the Arab World as Portrayed in the Documents of the Cairo Geniza*. Berkeley: University of California Press, 1971, 5 vols.

Gómez Moreno, Manuel. *Iglesias mozárabes: Arte español de los siglos IX a XI*. Madrid: Junta para ampliación de estudios, centro de estudios históricos, 1919.

Gouguenheim, Sylvain. *Aristote au mont SaintMichel : Les racines grecques de l'Europe chrétienne*. Paris: Seuil, 2008.

Graber, Oleg. "Islamic Art and Byzantium." *Dumbarton Oaks Papers* 18 (1964): 67–88.

Graetz, Heinrich. *History of the Jews*. Philadelphia: The Jewish Publication Society of America, 1894, vol. 3.

Guichard, Pierre. *Al-Andalus frente a la conquista cristiana: los musulmanes de Valencia, siglos XI al XIII*. Valencia: Universidad de Valencia, 2001.

Gutas, Dimitri . *Greek Thought, Arabic Culture: The Graeco-Arabic Translation Movement in Baghdad and Early Abbasid Society (Second–Fourth/Eighth–Tenth centuries)*. London: Routledge, 1998.

Haddad, Robert M. *Syrian Christians in Muslim Society: An Interpretation*. Princeton, NJ: Princeton University Press, 1970.

Hannam, James. *The Genesis of Science: How the Christian Middle Ages Launched the Scientific Revolution*. Washington, DC: Regnery Publishing, 2011.

Harris, Michael H. *History of Libraries in the Western World*. Metuchen and London: Scarecrow Press, 1995.

Horowitz, Elliot. " 'The Vengeance of the Jews Was Stronger than Their Avarice': Modern Historians and the Persian Conquest of Jerusalem in 614." *Jewish Social Studies* 4, no. 2: 1–25.

———. *Reckless Rites: Purim and the Legacy of Jewish Violence*. Princeton, NJ: Princeton University Press, 2004.

Irvine, Judith T. "Who Was Akilaos? A Problem in Medical Historiography." *Bulletin of the History of Medicine* 77, no. 1 (Spring 2003): 12–24.

Israeli, Raphael. *Green Crescent over Nazareth: The Displacement of Christians by Muslims in the Holy Land*. London: Frank Cass, 2002.

———. *War, Peace, and Terror in the Middle East*. London: Routledge, 2003.

———. *Hatred, Lies, and Violence in the Islamic World*. New Brunswick, NJ: Transaction Publishers, 2014.

Jansen, Hans. *The Dual Nature of Islamic Fundamentalism*. Ithaca: Cornell University Press, 1997.

———. *De historische Mohammed: De verhalen uit Medina*. Amsterdam: Arbeiderspers, 2007.

———. *Islam voor varkens, apen, ezels en andere beesten: 250 vragen over de Islam*. Amsterdam: Van Praag, 2008.

Jiménez Pedrajas, Rafael. *Historia de los mozárabes en al Ándalus*. Córdoba: Almuzara, 2013.

Kaldellis, Anthony. *The Christian Parthenon: Classicism and Pilgrimage in Byzantine Athens*. Cambridge: Cambridge University Press, 2009.

———. "Classical Scholarship in Twelfth-Century Byzantium." In *Medieval Greek Commentary on the Nicomachean Ethics*, edited by C. Barber and D. Jenkins. Leiden and Boston: Brill, 2008.

———. *Hellenism in Byzantium: The Transformation of Greek Identity and the Reception of the Classical Tradition*. Cambridge: Cambridge University Press, 2007.

———. *The Byzantine Republic: People and Power in New Rome*. Cambridge: Harvard University Press, 2015.

Kamen, Henry. *The Spanish Inquisition: A Historical Revision*. New Haven: Yale University Press, 1999.

———. *The Myth of the Spanish Inquisition* (BBC Documentary, 1994), https://www.youtube.com/watch?v=CY-pS6iLFuc.

Karsh, Efraim. *Islamic Imperialism: A History*. New Haven: Yale University Press, 2007.

Khanbaghi, Aptin. *The Fire, the Star, and the Cross: Minority Religions in Medieval and Early Modern Iran*. London: I. B. Tauris, 2006.

Khoury, Adel Theodor. *Toleranz im Islam*. Munich: Kaiser, 1980.

Kramer, Martin, ed. *The Jewish Discovery of Islam*. Tel Aviv: Moshe Dayan Center for Middle Eastern and African Studies, 1999.

———. *Ivory Towers of Sand: The Failure of Middle Eastern Studies in America*. Washington, DC: Washington Institute for Middle East Policy, 2001.

Ladero Quesada, Miguel Ángel. *La formación medieval de España: Territorios; Regiones; Reinos*. Madrid: Alianza, 2004.

Lagardère, Vincent. "Communautés mozarabes et pouvoir almoravide en 519 H/1125 en Andalus." *Studia Islamica*, no. 67 (1988): 99–119.

———. *Les Almoravides: Le djihâd andalou (1106–1143)*. Paris: L'Harmattan, 1998.

Lapiedra Gutiérrez, Eva. *Cómo los musulmanes llamaban a los cristianos hispánicos*. Alicante: Generalitat Valenciana-Instituto de Cultura "Juan Gil Albert," 1997.

Lasker, Daniel J. "Karaism in Twelfth-Century Spain." *Journal of Jewish Thought and Philosophy* 1 (1992): 179–95.

———. "The Jewish Critique of Christianity under Islam in the Middle Ages." *Proceedings of the American Academy for Jewish Research* 57 (1990–91): 121–53.

———. "Rabbanism and Karaism: The Contest for Supremacy." *Great Schisms in Jewish History.* Edited by Raphael Jospe and Stanley M. Wagner. Denver: Center for Judaic Studies, University of Denver, 1981, 47–72.

Lewis, Bernard. *The Jews of Islam.* Princeton, NJ: Princeton University Press, 1984.

———. *Islam from the Prophet Muhammad to the Capture of Constantinople.* Edited and translated by Bernard Lewis. Oxford: Oxford University Press, 1987, 2 vols.

López, R. S. "Mohammed and Charlemagne: A Revision." *Speculum* 18 (1943): 14–38.

Maíllo Salgado, Felipe. "La guerra santa según el derecho maliki." *Studia Historica* 1, no. 2 (1983): 29–65.

———. *Diccionario de derecho islámico.* Gijón: TREA, 2006.

———. *Acerca de la conquista árabe de Hispania: imprecisiones, equívocos y patrañas.* Guijón: TREA (Biblioteca Arabo-Románica e Islámica), 2011.

———. *De la desaparición de al-Andalus.* Madrid: Abada, 2011.

Maravall, José Antonio. *El concepto de España en la Edad Media.* Madrid: Instituto de Estudios Políticos, 1964.

Makdisi, George. *The Rise of Colleges: Institutions of Learning in Islam and the West.* Edinburgh: Edinburgh University Press, 1981, 224–25.

Marfil, Pedro. "La basílica de San Vicente: En la Catedral de Córdoba." *Arte, arqueología e historia* (2007), 185–96.

———. "Los baños del Alcázar califal de Córdoba." *El agua a través de la historia.* Edited by Soledad Gómez Navarro. Córdoba: Asociación "Arte, arqueología e historia," 2004, 49–76.

———. "Córdoba de Teodosio a Abd al-Rahman III." *Anejos de la Asociación Española de Arqueología XXIII* (2000): 117–41.

———. "La sede episcopal de San Vicente en la Santa Iglesia Catedral de Córdoba." *Al-Mulk: Anuario de estudios arabistas* (2006): n6, 35–58.

———. "La iglesia de Santa Catalina del antiguo convento de Santa Clara (Córdoba): Aspectos arqueológicos." *Jornadas europeas de patrimonio.* Seville: Junta de Andalucía, 1996, 52–54.

———. "Arqueología en la Mezquita de Córdoba." *Arte, Arqueología e Historia,* no. 6 (1999): 94 100.

———. "La visión romántica de la Córdoba Omeya." *Ruta del Califato: Un recorrido histórico-monumental de Córdoba a Granada.* Edited by Julia Saiz-Pardo de Benito. Granada: Fundación El Legado Andalusí, 2005, 205–12.

Marlin, George. *Christian Persecutions in the Middle East: A 21st Century Tragedy.* South Bend, IN: St. Augustine's Press, 2015.

Marín, Manuela, Julio Samsó, and Ma. Isabel Fierro, eds. *The Formation of al-Andalus.* Hampshire: Ashgate, 1998. 2 vols.

Marín, Manuela. *Mujeres en al-Andalus.* Madrid: Consejo Superior de Investigaciones Científicas, 2000.

———. "Inqibad an al-sultan: Ulama and Political Power in al-Andalus." *Saber religioso y poder político en el Islam: Actas del simposio internacional (Granada 15–18 octubre 1991).* Madrid: Agencia Española de Cooperación Internacional, 127–140.

———. "Dos textos andalucíes sobre Bizancio." *Erytheia* 13 (1992): 45–52.

———. "Rûm in the Works of Three Spanish Muslim Geographers." *Graeco-Arabica* 3 (1983): 109–17.

———. "Constantinopla en los geógrafos árabes," *Erytheia* 9, no. 1 (1988): 49–60.

Márquez de la Plata, Vicenta, and Luis Valen de Bernabé. *Reinas medievales españolas.* Madrid: Alderabán, 2000.

Mattei, Roberto de. *Guerra santa, guerra giusta: Islam e cristianesimo in guerra.* Milan: Piemme, 2002. Translated as *Holy War, Just War: Islam and Christendom at War.* Rockford: Rockford Institute, 2007.

Millar, Fergus. *A Greek Roman Empire*. Berkeley: University of California Press, 2007.

Miller, Kathryn A. "Muslim Minorities and the Obligation to Emigrate to Islamic Territory: Two Fatwas from Fifteenth-Century Granada." *Islamic Law and Society* 7, no. 2 (2000): 256–87.

Miranda Calvo, José, Commander. *Consideraciones militares sobre la conquista arábiga: Del Guadalete a Toledo*. Madrid: Patronato José María Quadrado del Consejo Superior de Investigaciones Científicas, 1973.

Morabia, Alfred. *Le jihad dans l'Islam médiéval: Le 'combat sacré' des origines au XIIe siècle*. Préface by Roger Arnaldez. Paris: Albin Michel, 1993.

Moutsopoulos, Evanghélos. "Arts libéraux et philosophie à byzance." *Arts Libéraux et Philosophie au Moyen Âge: Actes du Quatrième Congrés International de Philosophie Médievale*. Montreal: Institut D'Études Médiévales, 1969, 79–88.

Mueller, Christian. *Gerichtspraxis im Stadtstaat Cordoba: Zum Recht der Gesellschaft in einer malikitisch-islamischen Rechtstradition des 5./11 Jahrhunderts*. Leiden: Brill, 1999.

Mundell Mango, Marlia, ed. *Byzantine Trade, 4th–12th Centuries: The Archaeology of Local, Regional, and International Exchange—Papers of the Thirty-Eighth Spring Symposium of Byzantine . . . for the Promotion of Byzantine Studies*. Farnham: Ashgate, 2009.

Muranyi, Miklos. *Die Rechtsbuecher des Qairawaners Sahnun b. Sa'id: Entstehungsgeschichte und Werkueberlieferung*. Stuttgart: Steiner, 1999.

Netanyahu, Benzion. *The Origins of the Inquisition in Fifteenth-Century Spain*. New York: New York Review of Books, 2001.

Nicolle, David, and Angus McBride. *Armies of the Muslim Conquest*. London: Osprey, 1993.

Norwich, John Julius. *A Short History of Byzantium*. New York: Vintage, 1999.

O'Leary, De Lacy. *How Greek Science Passed to the Arabs*. First published London: Broadway House, 1948. Reprint, 2001.

Orfali, Moises. "Maimonides ante el problema de las conversiones simuladas: Tolerancia y 'Halaja.'" *Sobre la vida y la obra de Maimonides: I Congreso Internacional* (Córdoba, 1985). Edited by Jesús Peláez del Rosal. Córdoba: El Almendro, 1991, 375–93.

Orlandis, José. *La vida en España en tiempo de los godos*. Madrid: Rialp, 1991.

———. *Historia del reino visigodo español*. Madrid: Rialp, 2003.

Ortiz Lozano, Francisco. *Bobastro: La ciudad de la perdición: Gloria y refugio de la cristiandad*. Ardales: Francisco Ortiz Lozano, 2010.

Osaba, Esperanza. "Influenza delle leggi constantiniane nella *lex visigothorum*." *Diritto e storia*, no. 2 (2003).

Pavón Benito, Julia, ed. *Reinas de Navarra en la Edad Media*. Madrid: Silex; Gobierno de Navarra, 2014.

———. "Muladíes. Lectura política de una conversión: los Banu-Qa-si (714–924)." *Anaquel de estudios árabes*, no. 17 (2006): 189–202.

Pavón Maldonado, Basilio. *Ciudades Hispano-Musulmanas*. Madrid: MAPFRE, 1992.

———. "Influjos occidentales en el califato de Córdoba." *Al-Andalus* 33, no. 1 (1968): 206.

———. *Tratado de arquitectura hispanomusulmana*. Madrid: Consejo Superior de Investigaciones Científicas, 2009, 3 vols.

Peña, J. I. Ruiz de la. "La monarquía asturiana (718–918)." *El reino de León en la Alta Edad Media. III: La monarquía asturleonesa. De Pelayo a Alfonso VI. 718–1109*. León: Centro de Estudios e Investigación, San Isidoro, 1995, 120–27.

Perea, Alicia. *El tesoro Visigodo de Guarrazar*. Madrid: Consejo Superior de Investigaciones Cientificas, 2001.

———. *El tesoro Visigodo de Torredonjimeno*. Madrid: Consejo Superior de Investigaciones Cientificas, 2009.

Pipes, Daniel. *Slave Soldiers and Islam: The Genesis of a Military System*. New Haven: Yale University Press, 1981.

———. "Mawlas: Freed Slaves and Converts in Early Islam." *Muslims and Others in Early Islamic Society*. Ed. Robert Hoyland. Farnham: Ashgate, 2004, 277–322.

———. *Greater Syria: The History of an Ambition*. Oxford: Oxford University Press, 1990.

———. *Miniatures: Views of Islamic and Middle Eastern Politics.* New Brunswick, NJ: Transaction Publishers, 2003.

———. *Nothing Abides: Perspectives on the Middle East and Islam.* New Brunswick, NJ: Transaction Publishers, 2015.

Pirenne, Henri. *Mohammed and Charlemagne.* First published, 1935. Reprint, New York: Barnes and Noble, 1956.

Prado-Vilar, Francisco. "Circular Visions of Fertility and Punishment: Caliphal Ivory Caskets from al-Andalus." *Muqarnas* 14 (1997): 19–41.

La Puente, Cristina de. "Juridical Sources for the Study of Women: Limitations of the Female's Capacity to Act According to Maliki Law." *Writing the Feminine: Women in Arab Sources,* edited by Manuela Marín and Randi Deguilhem, 95–110. London: I. B. Tauris, 2002.

Ratzinger, Joseph Cardinal. "Perspectivas y tareas del catolicismo en la actualidad y de cara al futuro." In *El Concilio III de Toledo: XIV Centenario 589–1989,* edited by Alfred F. Havighurst, 107. Toledo: Arzobispado de Toledo, 1991.

Rincón Álvarez, Manuel. *Mozárabes y mozarabías.* Salamanca: Universidad de Salamanca, 2003.

Riising, Anne. "The Fate of Henri Pirenne's Theses on the Consequence of the Islamic Invasion." In *Problems in European Civilization: The Pirenne Thesis; Analysis, Criticism, and Revision,* edited by Alfred F. Havighurst, 102–6. Boston: D. C. Heath and Company, 1958.

Ríos, Amador de los. *Historia social, política y religiosa de los judíos de España y Portugal.* Madrid: Fontanet, 1875, vol. 1.

Ripoll, Gisela, and Eduardo Carrera. "Art wisigoth en *Hispania*: en quête d'une révision nécessaire." *Perspective,* no. 2 (June 2009): 256–67.

Rodríguez Magda, Rosa María. *Inexistente al-andalus: de cómo los intelectuales reinventan el Islam.* Oviedo: Nobel, 2008.

Rosales, Jurate. *Los Godos.* Barcelona: Ariel, 2004. Translated as *Goths and Balts.* Chicago: Vydino Fondas, 2004.

———. "Las cuatro mentiras sobre los godos." Preprint of Universidad de Los Andes, Facultad de Letras y Educación, Mérida, Venezuela (July 2, 2008): 1–26.

———. "El idioma que hablaron los godos." *La Torre del Virrey* (Valencia, Spain), n3, Serie 6 (February 2010): 1–12.

Rosenthal, Franz. *The Classical Heritage in Islam.* Translated by Emile and Jenny Marmorstein Berkeley: University of California Press, 1965.

Rucquoi, Adeline. "Les Wisigoths: fondement de la nation Espagne." In *L'Europe Héritière de l'Espagne Wisigothique,* edited by Jacques Fontaine and Christine Pellistrandi, 341–52. Madrid: Rencontres de la Casa de Velázquez, 1992.

Ruiz de la Peña, J. I. "La monarquía asturiana (718–918)." In *El reino de León en la Alta Edad Media: III: La monarquía asturleonesa; De Pelayo a Alfonso VI, 718–1109,* edited by Centro de estudios e investigación, 120–27. León: Centro de Estudios e Investigación, San Isidoro, 1995.

Schacht, Joseph. *Esquisse d'une histoire du droit musulman.* Paris: Librairie orientale et americaine, 1953.

Scott, Emmet. *Muhammad and Charlemagne Revisited: The History of a Controversy.* London: New English Review Press, 2012.

Serrano, Ana, María Jesús Viguera, et al. *Ibn Khaldun: The Mediterranean in the 14th century: Rise and Fall of Empires.* Seville: Legado Andalusí, 2006.

Starr, Joshua. *Jews in the Byzantine Empire.* Research and Source Works Series, No. 386. Farnborough: Gregg, 1969.

Stern, Sacha. *Jewish Identity in Early Rabbinic Writings.* Leiden: Brill, 1994.

Stouraitis, Ioannis. "Roman Identity in Byzantium: A Critical Approach." *Byzantinische Zeitschrift* 107, no. 1 (2014): 175–220.

Strantoine, Helène. *Imperator Hispaniae: Les idéologies impériales dans le royaume de Léon (IXe–XII siècles).* Madrid: Casa de Velázquez, 2012.

Teppler, Yaakov Y. *Birkat ha minim: Jews and Christians in Conflict in the Ancient World*. Tübingen: Mohr Siebeck, 2007.

Tété, Godwin. *La traite et l'esclavage négriers*. Paris: L'Harmattan, 1997.

Torres Balbás, Leopoldo. *Ciudades hispanomusulmanas*. Madrid: Ministerio de asuntos exteriores, 1977.

Toubert, Pierre. "Byzantium and the Mediterranean Agrarian Civilization." In *The Economic History of Byzantium: From the Seventh through the Fifteenth Century*, edited by Angeliki E. Laiou, 377–91. Washington, DC: Dumbarton Oaks, 2002.

Turki, Abdel Magid. "La vénération pour Malik et la physionomie du malikisme andalou." *Studia Islamica*, no. 33 (1971): 41–66.

Udovitch, Abraham L. "Theory and Practice of Islamic Law: Some Evidence from the Geniza." *Studia Islamica*, no. 32 (1970): 19–29.

Urbano, Arthur P. *The Philosophical Life. Biography and the Crafting of Intellectual Identity in Late Antiquity*. Washington, DC: The Catholic University of America Press, 2013.

Urvoy, Dominique. "Sur l'évolution de la notion de Gihad dans l'Espagne musulmane." *Mélanges de la Casa de Velázquez* 9 (1973): 335–71.

———. *Histoire de la pensée árabe et islamique*. Paris: Seuil, 2006.

———. *La mésentente: Un dictionnaire des difficultés doctrinales du dialogue islamo-chrétien*. Paris: Broché, 2014.

Urvoy, Marie-Thérése. "Que nous apprend la poésie arabe des chrétiens d'al Andalus?" In *¿Existe una identidad mozárabe? Historia, lengua y cultura de los cristianos de al-Andalus (siglos IX-XII)*, edited by Cyrille Aillet, Mayte Penelas, and Philippe Roisse, 159–166. Madrid: Casa de Velazquez, 2008.

———. *Le psautier mozarabe de Hafs le Goth*. Edited and study by M.-T. Urvoy. Toulouse: PUM, 1994.

———. *Essai de critique littéraire dans le nouvau monde arabo-islamique*. Paris: Cerf, 2011.

Urvoy, Marie-Thérése, and Dominique Urvoy. *Abécédaire du christianisme et de l'Islam*. Paris: Editions de Paris, 2008.

Vallejo Girvés, Margarita. *Bizancio y la España tardo antigua (Ss. V-VIII): Un capítulo de historia mediterránea*. Alcalá de Henares: Universidad de Alcalá de Henares, 1993.

Vallvé Bermejo, Joaquín. "El nombre de al-Andalus," *Al-Qantara* 4, no. 2 (1983): 301–55.

———. "Libertad y esclavitud en el califato de Córdoba." *Actas de las II Jornadas de cultura árabe e islámica* (1980). Madrid: Instituto Hispano-Árabe de Cultura, 1985, 565–78.

———. *Al-Andalus. Sociedad e Instituciones*. Madrid: Real Academia de la Historia, 1999.

Valverde Castro, María R. *Ideología, simbolismo y ejercicio del poder real en la monarquía visigoda: Un proceso de cambio*. Salamanca: Universidad de Salamanca, 2000.

Versteegh, C. H. M. *Greek Elements in Arabic Linguistic Thinking*. Leiden: Brill, 1977.

Vico, Jesús, and María Cruz Cors. "La moneda visigoda." *Gaceta numismática*, no. 169 (June 2008): 25–26.

Vryonis, Speros. *Byzantium and Europe*. New York: Harcourt, Brace and World, 1967.

Wells, Peter S. *Barbarians to Angels*. New York: W. W. Norton, 2008.

Wiegers, Gerard. *Islamic Literature in Spanish and Aljamiado: Yva of Segovia (fl.1450), His Antecedents and Successors*. Leiden: Brill, 1994.

Wigdan, Ali. *The Arab Contribution to Islamic Art: From the Seventh to the Fifteenth Centuries*. Cairo: Cairo American University in Cairo Press, 1999.

Wilken, Robert Louis. "Christianity Face to Face with Islam." *First Things*, January 2009, 19–26.

Williams, Stephen, and Gerard Friell. *The Rome That Did Not Fall: The Survival of the East in the Fifth Century*. New York: Routledge, 1999.

Acknowledgments

THIS BOOK WOULD not have been possible without the research of dedicated scholars writing in different countries, languages, disciplines, and centuries. To all of them I offer my admiration and gratitude.

I thank Jed Donahue, vice president of publications and editor in chief of ISI Books, for his support and patience, and for his advice, which made this a better piece of writing. The final responsibility for the form and content of this book is of course mine. I thank Mark C. Henrie, former senior vice president of ISI, for his interest in the subject, which led to the eventual writing of this book. Thanks should also go to the former editor in chief of ISI Books, Jeremy Beer, who asked me to write it.

I am grateful to those who, one way or another, and sometimes without realizing it, made possible the writing of this book—among them Cherie Berzon, Joseph Barton, Laina Farhat-Holzman, Gary Saul Morson, Vera and Klaus Müller-Bergh, Margaret Schmidt, and Joanna Spilioti. Special thanks should go to the library staff at Northwestern University, its Acquisitions Department, and especially its efficient Interlibrary Loan Department.

Index

About the Author

DARÍO FERNÁNDEZ-MORERA is Associate Professor in the Department of Spanish and Portuguese at Northwestern University. A former member of the National Council on the Humanities, he holds a BA from Stanford University, an MA from the University of Pennsylvania, and a PhD from Harvard University. He has published several books and many articles on cultural, literary, historical, and methodological issues in Spain, Latin America, and the United States.

ISI Books is the publishing imprint of the **Intercollegiate Studies Institute**, whose mission is to inspire college students to discover, embrace, and advance the principles and virtues that make America free and prosperous.

Founded in 1953, ISI teaches future leaders the core ideas behind the free market, the American Founding, and Western civilization that are rarely taught in the classroom.

ISI is a nonprofit, nonpartisan, tax-exempt educational organization. The Institute relies on the financial support of the general public—individuals, foundations, and corporations—and receives no funding or any other aid from any level of the government.

www.isi.org